READ
Reason
Write

AN ARGUMENT TEXT AND READER

NINTH EDITION

Dorothy U. Seyler

 Higher Education

Boston   Burr Ridge, IL   Dubuque, IA   New York   San Francisco   St. Louis
Bangkok   Bogotá   Caracas   Kuala Lumpur   Lisbon   London   Madrid   Mexico City
Milan   Montreal   New Delhi   Santiago   Seoul   Singapore   Sydney   Taipei   Toronto

 **Higher Education**

Published by McGraw-Hill, an imprint of The McGraw-Hill Companies, Inc., 1221 Avenue of the Americas, New York, NY 10020. Copyright © 2010, 2008, 2005, 2002, 1999, 1995, 1991, 1987, 1984 by The McGraw-Hill Companies. All rights reserved. No part of this publication may be reproduced or distributed in any form or by any means, or stored in a database or retrieval system, without the prior written consent of The McGraw-Hill Companies, Inc., including, but not limited to, in any network or other electronic storage or transmission, or broadcast for distance learning.

This book is printed on acid-free paper.

1 2 3 4 5 6 7 8 9 0 DOC/DOC 0 9

ISBN: 978-0-07-338378-1
MHID: 0-07-337378-3

Editor in Chief: *Michael Ryan*
Editorial Director: *Beth Mejia*
Publisher: *David Patterson*
Sponsoring Editor: *Christopher Bennem*
Developmental Editor: *Phil Butcher*
Editorial Coordinator: *Jesse Hassenger*
Marketing Manager: *Allison Jones*
Media Project Manager: *Jennifer Barrick*
Text Permissions Editor: *Marty Moga*
Production Editor: *Leslie LaDow*
Manuscript Editor: *Jan Fehler*
Designers: *Margarite Reynolds* & *Linda Robertson*
Cover: *Margarite Reynolds*
Photo Research Coordinator: *Natalia Peschiera*
Photo Researcher: *Jennifer Blankenship*
Production Supervisor: *Louis Swaim*
Composition: *10/12 Palatino by Laserwords Private Limited*
Printing: *45# Publishers Thinbulk by R.R. Donnelley & Sons*

Cover (left to right): © BananaStock/JupiterImages (background); © Erin Siegal/Reuters/Landov; © Photodisc/Getty Images, © Damon Winter/The New York Times/Redux Pictures; © David R. Frazier Photolibrary, Inc./Alamy; © Erik Isakson/Getty Images.

The credits section for this book begins on page 637 and is considered an extension of the copyright page.

Library of Congress Cataloging-in-Publication Data
Seyler, Dorothy U.
　　Read, reason, write : an argument text and reader/Dorothy U. Seyler.—9th ed.
　　　　p. cm.
　　Includes bibliographical references and index.
　　ISBN-13: 978-0-07-338378-1 (alk. paper)
　　ISBN-10: 0-07-338378-3 (alk. paper)
1.　English language—Rhetoric. 2. Persuasion (Rhetoric) 3. College readers. 4. Report writing. I. Title.
　　PE1408.S464 2009
　　808'.0427—dc22

　　　　　　　　　　　　　　　　　　　　　　　　　　　　　　　2009017266

The Internet addresses listed in the text were accurate at the time of publication. The inclusion of a Web site does not indicate an endorsement by the authors or McGraw-Hill, and McGraw-Hill does not guarantee the accuracy of the information presented at these sites.

www.mhhe.com

About the Author

DOROTHY U. SEYLER has just retired as Professor of English at Northern Virginia Community College. A Phi Beta Kappa graduate of the College of William and Mary, Dr. Seyler holds advanced degrees from Columbia University and the State University of New York at Albany. She taught at Ohio State University, the University of Kentucky, and Nassau Community College before moving with her family to Northern Virginia.

She is the author of *Understanding Argument, Doing Research* (second edition), *The Reading Context* and *Steps to College Reading* (both in their third editions), and *Patterns of Reflection* (now in its seventh edition). In 2007 Dr. Seyler was elected to membership in the Cosmos Club in Washington, DC.

Professor Seyler has published articles in professional journals and popular magazines. She is currently working on a narrative nonfiction book on early nineteenth-century traveler William John Bankes. She enjoys tennis and golf, traveling, and writing about both sports and travel.

Contents

Preface   xv

SECTION 1   **CRITICAL READING AND ANALYSIS**   **1**

Chapter 1   **WRITERS AND THEIR SOURCES**   **2**

Reading, Writing, and the Contexts of Argument   4

Responding to Sources   4

Abraham Lincoln, "The Gettysburg Address"   **5**

The Response to Content   5

The Analytic Response   6

The Evaluation Response   7

The Research Response   7

Deborah Tannen, "Who Does the Talking Here?"   **8**

Active Reading: Use Your Mind!   11

Guidelines for Active Reading   11

Richard Morin, "Political Ads and the Voters They Attract"   **12**

Writing Summaries   14

Guidelines for Writing Summaries   14

Acknowledging Sources Informally   17

Referring to People and Sources   17

Joel Achenbach, "The Future Is Now"   **19**

Presenting Direct Quotations: A Guide to Form and Style   22

Reasons for Using Quotation Marks   22

A Brief Guide to Quoting   22

For Reading and Analysis   25

Howard Gardner, "The End of Literacy? Don't Stop Reading"   **25**

Azar Nafisi, "Words of War"   **29**

Suggestions for Discussion and Writing   31

Chapter 2   **RESPONDING CRITICALLY TO SOURCES**   **32**

Traits of the Critical Reader/Thinker   33

Examining the Rhetorical Context of a Source   33

Who Is the Author?   34

What Type—or Genre—of Source Is It?   34

What Kind of Audience Does the Author Anticipate?   34

What Is the Author's Primary Purpose?   35
What Are the Author's Sources of Information?   35
Analyzing the Style of a Source   36
Denotative and Connotative Word Choice   37
Tone   39
Level of Diction   40
Sentence Structure   40
Metaphors   42
Organization and Examples   43
Repetition   43
Hyperbole, Understatement, and Irony   44
Quotation Marks, Italics, and Capital Letters   44
Dave Barry, "In a Battle of Wits with Kitchen Appliances, I'm Toast"   45
Writing About Style   47
Understanding Purpose and Audience   48
Planning the Essay   48
Drafting the Style Analysis   49
A Checklist for Revision   49
Ellen Goodman, "In Praise of a Snail's Pace"   50
Student Essay: James Goode, "A Convincing Style"   53
Analyzing Two or More Sources   54
Guidelines for Preparing a Contrast Essay   55
Kent Garber, "Eyeing the Oil Under the Gulf"   56
Bob Keefe, "National Debate: Weighing Advances vs. Fears"   58
For Reading and Analysis   60
Andrew Vachss, "Watch Your Language"   61
George Orwell, "A Hanging"   64
Suggestions for Discussion and Writing   69

SECTION 2   THE WORLD OF ARGUMENT   71

Chapter 3   UNDERSTANDING THE BASICS OF ARGUMENT   72
Characteristics of Argument   73
Argument Is Conversation with a Goal   73
Argument Takes a Stand on an Arguable Issue   73
Argument Uses Reasons and Evidence   73
Argument Incorporates Values   74
Argument Recognizes the Topic's Complexity   74
The Shape of Argument: What We Can Learn from Aristotle   74
Ethos (About the Writer/Speaker)   74
Logos (About the Logic of the Argument)   75
Pathos (About Appeals to the Audience)   75

Karios (About the Occasion or Situation)   76

The Language of Argument   77

Facts   77

Inferences   78

Judgments   78

Sam Wang and Sandra Aamodt, "Your Brain Lies to You"   80

The Shape of Argument: What We Can Learn from Toulmin   83

Claims   84

Grounds (or Data or Evidence)   86

Warrants   86

Backing   87

Qualifiers   88

Rebuttals   88

Using Toulmin's Terms to Analyze Arguments   88

Les Schobert, "Let the Zoo's Elephants Go"   89

For Debate and Analysis   91

T. R. Reid, "Let My Teenager Drink"   91

Joseph A. Califano, Jr., "Don't Make Teen Drinking Easier"   93

Suggestions for Discussion and Writing   97

Chapter 4   WRITING EFFECTIVE ARGUMENTS   98

Know Your Audience   99

Who Is My Audience?   99

What Will My Audience Know about My Topic?   99

Where Does My Audience Stand on the Issue?   100

How Should I Speak to My Audience?   100

Understand Your Writing Purpose   101

What Type (Genre) of Argument Am I Preparing?   102

What Is My Goal?   102

Will the Rogerian or Conciliatory Approach Work for Me?   103

Move from Topic to Claim to Possible Support   103

Selecting a Topic   104

Drafting a Claim   104

Listing Possible Grounds   105

Listing Grounds for the Other Side or Another Perspective   105

Planning Your Approach   106

Draft Your Argument   107

Guidelines for Drafting   108

Revise Your Draft   108

Rewriting   108

Editing   109

A Few Words about Words and Tone   110

Proofreading   111
A Checklist for Revision   111
For Analysis and Debate   112
Tunku Varadarajan, "That Feeling of Being Under Suspicion"   *112*
Colbert I. King, "You Can't Fight Terrorism with Racism"   *115*
Suggestions for Discussion and Writing   118

Chapter 5   LEARNING MORE ABOUT ARGUMENT: INDUCTION, DEDUCTION, ANALOGY, AND LOGICAL FALLACIES   119
Induction   120
Mark A. Norell and Xu Xing, "The Varieties of Tyrannosaurs"   *121*
Deduction   122
"The Declaration of Independence"   *126*
Analogy   130
Zbigniew Brzezinski, "War and Football"   *132*
Logical Fallacies   134
Causes of Illogic   134
Fallacies That Result from Oversimplifying   135
Fallacies That Result from Ignoring the Issue   139
For Reading and Analysis   144
Elizabeth Cady Stanton, "Declaration of Sentiments"   *144*
Gregory Rodriguez, "Mongrel America"   *146*

Chapter 6   READING, ANALYZING, AND USING VISUALS AND STATISTICS IN ARGUMENT   152
Responding to Visual Arguments   153
Guidelines for Reading Photographs   154
Guidelines for Reading Political Cartoons   154
Guidelines for Reading Advertisements   154
Reading Graphics   159
Understanding How Graphics Differ   159
Guidelines for Reading Graphics   160
The Uses of Authority and Statistics   163
Judging Authorities   163
Understanding and Evaluating Statistics   165
Guidelines for Evaluating Statistics   165
Writing the Investigative Argument   166
Gathering and Analyzing Evidence   167
Planning and Drafting the Essay   169
Guidelines for Writing an Investigative Argument   169
Analyzing Evidence: The Key to an Effective Argument   169
Preparing Graphics   170
A Checklist for Revision   170

Student Essay: Garrett Berger, "Buying Time"   171
For Reading and Analysis   176
Joe Navarro, "Every Body's Talking"   *176*
Suggestions for Discussion and Writing   181

SECTION 3   **STUDYING SOME ARGUMENTS BY GENRE**   **183**

Chapter 7   **DEFINITION ARGUMENTS**   **184**
Defining as Part of an Argument   185
When Defining *Is* the Argument   186
Strategies for Developing an Extended Definition   186
   Guidelines for Evaluating Definition Arguments   188
Preparing a Definition Argument   189
A Checklist for Revision   190
Student Essay: Laura Mullins, "Paragon or Parasite?"   190
For Analysis and Debate   193
Susan Jacoby, "Best Is the New Worst"   *193*
Robin Givhan, "Glamour, That Certain Something"   *195*
Suggestions for Discussion and Writing   198

Chapter 8   **EVALUATION ARGUMENTS**   **199**
Characteristics of Evaluation Arguments   200
Types of Evaluation Arguments   201
   Guidelines for Analyzing an Evaluation Argument   202
Preparing an Evaluation Argument   203
   A Checklist for Revision   204
Student Review: Ian Habel, "Winchester's Alchemy: Two Men and a Book"   205
Evaluating an Argument: The Rebuttal or Refutation Essay   207
   Guidelines for Preparing a Refutation or Rebuttal Argument   207
David Sadker, "Gender Games"   *208*
For Analysis and Debate   210
Robert H. Bork, "Addicted to Health"   *210*
Suggestions for Discussion and Writing   215

Chapter 9   **THE POSITION PAPER: CLAIMS OF VALUE**   **216**
Characteristics of the Position Paper   217
   Guidelines for Analyzing a Claim of Value   218
Preparing a Position Paper   218
   A Checklist for Revision   220
Student Essay: Chris Brown, "Examining the Issue of Gun Control"   220

For Analysis and Debate   223

Joseph Bernstein, "Animal Rights v. Animal Research: A Modest Proposal"   223

Timothy Sprigge, "A Reply to Joseph Bernstein"   226

Suggestions for Discussion and Writing   230

Chapter 10   ARGUMENTS ABOUT CAUSE   231

Characteristics of Causal Arguments   232

Mill's Methods for Investigating Causes   234

Guidelines for Analyzing Causal Arguments   235

Preparing a Causal Argument   236

A Checklist for Revision   238

For Analysis and Debate   238

Lester C. Thurow, "Why Women Are Paid Less Than Men"   238

Gloria Steinem, "Supremacy Crimes"   241

Suggestions for Discussion and Writing   246

Chapter 11   PRESENTING PROPOSALS: THE PROBLEM/SOLUTION ARGUMENT   247

Characteristics of Problem/Solution Arguments   248

Guidelines for Analyzing Problem/Solution Arguments   249

James Q. Wilson, "A New Strategy for the War on Drugs"   250

Preparing a Problem/Solution Argument   254

A Checklist for Revision   255

For Analysis and Debate   256

Irshad Manji, "When Denial Can Kill"   256

Jonathan Swift, "A Modest Proposal"   258

Suggestions for Discussion and Writing   266

SECTION 4   THE RESEARCHED AND FORMALLY DOCUMENTED ARGUMENT   267

Chapter 12   LOCATING, EVALUATING, AND PREPARING TO USE SOURCES   268

Selecting a Good Topic   269

What Type of Paper Am I Preparing?   269

Who Is My Audience?   269

How Can I Select a Good Topic?   270

What Kinds of Topics Should I Avoid?   271

Writing a Tentative Claim or Research Proposal   271

Preparing a Working Bibliography   272

Basic Form for Books   273

Basic Form for Articles   274

Locating Sources   276
   The Book Catalog   276
   The Reference Collection   276
   Electronic Databases   277
   Guidelines for Using Online Databases   278
   The Internet   279
   Guidelines for Searching the Web   280
   Field Research   280
Evaluating Sources, Maintaining Credibility   283
   Guidelines for Evaluating Sources   284

Chapter 13   WRITING THE RESEARCHED ESSAY   286
   Guidelines for Studying Sources   287
Avoiding Plagiarism   287
   What Is Common Knowledge?   289
Using Signal Phrases to Avoid Misleading Readers   289
   Guidelines for Appropriately Using Sources   290
Organizing the Paper   293
Drafting the Essay   294
Revising the Paper: A Checklist   304
The Completed Paper   306
Sample Student Essay in MLA Style   306

Chapter 14   FORMAL DOCUMENTATION: MLA STYLE, APA STYLE   313
   Guidelines for Using Parenthetical Documentation   314
The Simplest Patterns of Parenthetical Documentation   315
Placement of Parenthetical Documentation   316
Parenthetical Citations of Complex Sources   316
Preparing MLA Citations for a "Works Cited" List   319
   Forms for Books: Citing the Complete Book   320
   Forms for Books: Citing Part of a Book   322
   Forms for Periodicals: Articles in Journals and Magazines Accessed in Print   323
   Forms for Periodicals: Articles in Newspapers Accessed in Print   325
   Forms for Web Sources   326
   Forms for Other Print and Non-print Sources   327
Author/Year or APA Style   330
   APA Style: In-Text Citations   330
APA Style: Preparing a List of References   333
   Form for Books   333
   Form for Articles   334
   Electronic Sources   335
Sample Student Essay in APA Style   336

SECTION 5   A COLLECTION OF READINGS   341

Chapter 15   THE MEDIA: IMAGE AND REALITY   343

Derrick Speight, "Of Losers and Moles: You Think Reality TV Just Writes Itself?"   344

Shelby Steele, "Notes from the Hip-Hop Underground"   347

Peggy Noonan, "The Blogs Must Be Crazy"   351

Stephen Hunter, "Leading Men: Looking at Presidential Contenders Through a Hollywood Lens"   354

Katherine Ellison, "What's Up, Doc? A Bloody Outrage, That's What"   359

Jean Kilbourne, "In Your Face . . . All Over the Place!"   363

Michelle Cottle, "Turning Goys into Girls"   373

Chapter 16   THE ENVIRONMENT: HOW GREEN DO WE GO?   380

Michael Novacek, "The Sixth Extinction: It Happened to Him. It's Happening to You"   382

James Howard Kunstler, "Wake Up, America. We're Driving Toward Disaster."   386

NRDC, "Snake Oil" Ad   389

Charles Krauthammer, "Carbon Chastity"   390

Wired Magazine, Editorial, "Inconvenient Truths: Get Ready to Rethink What It Means to Be Green"   393

Alex Steffen, "Counterpoint: Dangers of Focusing Solely on Climate Change"   395

wecansolveit.org Ad   397

Anna Quindlen, "Don't Mess with Mother"   398

Chapter 17   SPORTS TALK—SPORTS BATTLES   401

David Oliver Relin, "Who's Killing Kids' Sports?"   402

Gordon Gee, "My Plan to Put the College Back in College Sports"   406

Sally Jenkins, "Education, Athletics: The Odd Couple"   409

William Saletan, "The Beam in Your Eye: If Steroids Are Cheating, Why Isn't LASIK?"   412

Michael Sokolove, "To the Victor, the Drug Test"   417

Nature, Editorial, "A Sporting Chance"   421

Rosanna Tomiuk, "Bridging the Human Divide"   423

Chapter 18   EDUCATION: WHAT'S HAPPENING ON CAMPUS?   426

Ted Gup, "So Much for the Information Age"   427

Barbara Ehrenreich, "Guys Just Want to Have Fun"   431

David Cole, "Laptops vs. Learning"   433

Fred von Lohmann, "Copyright Silliness on Campus"   435

Katha Pollitt, "Sweatin' to the Koran?"   437

Harry Lewis, "A Separate and Unequal Exercise"   440

Clive Thompson, "I'm So Totally, Digitally Close to You"   442

Chapter 19   CENSORSHIP AND FREE SPEECH DEBATES   451

Rich Thomaselli and T. L. Stanley, "Phillip Morris: No Smoking in Movies"   452

SmokeFreeMovies. ucsf.edu Ad   455

Evan R. Goldstein, "Smoking in the Movies"   456

Mark Mathabane, "If You Assign My Book, Don't Censor It"   458

Ken Dautrich and John Bare, "Why the First Amendment (and Journalism) Might Be in Trouble"   462

Andrew J. McClurg, "Online Lessons on Unprotected Sex"   466

Anne Applebaum, "Let a Thousand Filters Bloom"   468

David McHardy Reid, "Business Is Business"   470

Chapter 20   ETHICS AND THE LAW—CURRENT AND ENDURING DEBATES   472

Michael Hoxie, Letters to the Editor: "The Court's Handgun Common Sense"   474

Arthur Kellerman, "Guns for Safety? Dream on, Scalia"   475

Linda J. Collier, "Adult Crime, Adult Time"   477

Richard Cohen, "Kids Who Kill Are Still Kids"   481

Michael Loud, "Tying Our Hands"   483

Richard E. Mezo, "Why It Was Called 'Water Torture'"   487

Darius Rejali, "Five Myths About Torture and Truth"   489

Chapter 21   MARRIAGE AND GENDER ISSUES: THE DEBATES CONTINUE   493

Linda J. Waite, "Social Science Finds: 'Marriage Matters'"   494

Stuart Taylor, Jr., "Gay Marriage by Judicial Decree"   503

Richard Just, "Justice Delivered"   506

Michael Kinsley, "Abolish Marriage"   510

Chong-Suk Han, "Gay Asian-American Male Seeks Home"   513

Judith D. Auerbach, "The Overlooked Victims of AIDS"   517

Leonard Sax, "Why Gender Matters"   519

Chapter 22   GLOBALISM: HOW DO WE FIT IN?   531

Thomas L. Friedman, "Understanding Globalization"   533

David Brooks, "The Cognitive Age"   541

David Rothkopf, "The Superclass: They're Global Citizens. They're Hugely Rich. And They Pull the Strings."   543

Pranab Bardhan, "Inequality in India and China: Is Globalization to Blame?"   547

Robert J. Samuelson, "Rx for Global Poverty"   551

Fareed Zakaria, "The Post-American World"   553

Chapter 23   **THE AMERICAN DREAM: REALITY, MYTH, GOAL?**   **562**

Eugene Robinson, "Tattered Dream"   564

Firoozeh Dumas, "The 'F Word'"   566

E. J. Dionne, Jr., "The Engaged Generation"   570

A Look at the Immigration Debate:

   Mae M. Ngai, "No Human Being Is Illegal"   573

   Marcela Sanchez, "Our Sad Neglect of Mexico"   577

   Amy Chua, "Immigrate, Assimilate"   580

   Martin Luther King, Jr., "I Have a Dream"   585

Appendix: Understanding Literature   589

Getting the Facts: Active Reading, Summary, and Paraphrase 590

Paul Lawrence Dunbar, "Promise" 590

Langston Hughes, "Early Autumn" 591

   Summary of "Early Autumn" 592

William Shakespeare, "Sonnet 116" 593

   Paraphrase of "Sonnet 116" 593

   Seeing Connections: Analysis 595

   Analysis of Narrative Structure 595

   Analysis of Character 596

   Analysis of Elements of Style and Tone 597

Drawing Conclusions: Interpretation 597

Writing About Literature 598

Andrew Marvell, "To His Coy Mistress" 599

Christopher Marlowe, "The Passionate Shepherd to His Love" 560

Sir Walter Raleigh, "The Nymph's Reply to the Shepherd" 601

A. E. Housman, "Is My Team Ploughing" 602

Amy Lowell, "Taxi" 604

Kate Chopin, "The Story of an Hour" 604

Ursula K. Le Guin, "The Ones Who Walk Away From Omelas" 607

Susan Glaspell, Trifles 612

Sample Student Literary Analysis 630

Suggestions for Discussion and Writing 635

Credits   637

Index   643

Preface

I have written in previous prefaces to *Read, Reason, Write* that being asked to prepare a new edition is much like being asked back to a friend's home. Although you count on it, you are still delighted when the invitation comes. I am happy that the eighth edition kept old friends and made new ones as well and that once again I am writing a preface, this time to the ninth edition. With this ninth edition, *Read, Reason, Write* becomes 25 years old! Over all of these years, the text has grown in size—most books have—but also in stature within the teaching community and in its value to students. Of course, even though I have just retired from full-time teaching, neither this text nor I am getting older—only better.

Although some important new material strengthens the ninth edition, the essential character of *Read, Reason, Write* remains the same. This text still unites instruction in critical reading and analysis, argument, and research strategies with a rich collection of readings that provide both practice for these skills and new ideas and insights for readers. A key purpose of *Read, Reason, Write* remains the same: to help students develop into better writers of the kinds of papers they are most often required to write, both in college and in the workplace, that is, summaries, analyses, reports, arguments, and documented essays. To fulfill this key purpose, the text must do more than offer instruction and opportunities for practice; it must also show students how these skills connect in important ways. Through all of its years, this text has been committed to showing students how reading, analytic, argumentative, and research skills are interrelated and how these skills combine to develop each student's critical thinking ability.

FEATURES OF *READ, REASON, WRITE*

- An emphasis on good reading skills for effective arguing and writing.
- Instruction, models, and practice in understanding reading context and analyzing elements of style.
- Instruction, models, and practice in writing summaries and book reviews.
- Focus on argument as contextual: written (or spoken) to a specific audience with the expectation of counterarguments.
- Explanations and models of various types of arguments that bridge the gap between an understanding of logical structures and the ways we actually write arguments.

- Presentation of Aristotelian, Toulmin, and Rogerian models of argument as useful guides to analyzing the arguments of others and organizing one's own arguments.
- In-depth coverage of induction, deduction, analogy, and logical fallacies.
- Guidelines and revision boxes throughout the text that provide an easy reference for students.
- Instruction, models, and practice in finding and evaluating sources and in composing and documenting researched papers.
- A rich collection of readings, both timely and classic, that provides examples of the varied uses of language and strategies for argument.
- A brief but comprehensive introduction to reading and analyzing literature, found in the Appendix.

NEW FEATURES IN THE NINTH EDITION

This new edition maintains the key features of previous editions while adding new material that will make the ninth edition even more helpful to both students and instructors. Significant changes include:

- An even greater emphasis on visual argument throughout the text. The two color inserts and each chapter's opening visual remain, but now each chapter has additional visuals throughout.
- A more user-friendly organization of the argument material. Now divided into two sections, with Section 2 covering the same basic four chapters on argument as before and a new Section 3 bringing together, in individual chapters, discussion of five genres of argument.
- A slimmer book! We have put this text on a bit of a diet, eliminating the chapter on classic arguments and tightening the coverage of research.
- MLA documentation has been updated to correspond to the third edition of the *MLA Style Manual* and the seventh edition of the *MLA Handbook*.
- With 35 readings in the instructional chapters and 61 readings in the anthology chapters, the text has a total of 96 readings in addition to 6 student essays. Fifty-three of the readings are new, and some of those from the eighth edition are in new places, paired with new pieces, providing a fresh outlook.
- Of the nine chapters in the anthology section, four are entirely new. The other five all have some new readings to refresh and update those chapters.
- The four new chapters include a completely new chapter on education that focuses entirely on college issues, a chapter on the environment that presents various views on climate change and its impact, a chapter on globalization, and a final chapter on the American dream. New pieces in existing chapters include a debate over the Supreme Court's recent handgun decision, three articles debating the uses of interrogation techniques, restrictions or new

ratings of films that show characters smoking, essays debating the restrictions on enhancement strategies used by athletes, a look at court decisions on gay marriage, and a study of gender differences influencing teen sexual choices.

- New chapters and old, new works and reused favorites together offer a rich blend of types of argument and a wide range of important issues for our time.

ACKNOWLEDGMENTS

No book of value is written alone. I am pleased to acknowledge the contributions of others in shaping this text. My thanks are due—as always—to the library staff at the Annandale Campus of Northern Virginia Community College who have helped me find needed information. I would also like to thank all of the students whose essays grace this text. They should be proud of the skill and effort they put into their writing.

I appreciate as well the many good suggestions of the following reviewers of the ninth edition:

Diann L. Baecker, *Virginia State University*
Joy Bodenmiller, *Jamestown Community College*
Linda Brender, *Macomb Community College*
Joyce Camper, *Howard University*
Ronald Clark Brooks, *Oklahoma State University*
Rebecca Cargile, *Freed-Hardeman University*
Ben Desure, *Pittsburgh Technical Institute*
Carol Dillon, *University of Nebraska at Omaha*
Kamela Edwards, *Montgomery College*
Nancy Feather, *Pittsburgh Technical Institue*
Emily Forand, *Paradise Valley Community College*
Michael Fukuchi, *Barton College*
Carolyn Harrison, *Oakland Community College*
Lisa Hine, *Oakland University*
Raymond Lacina, *Delta College*
Heather Milton, *University of Florida*
Bryan Moore, *Arkansas State University*
Mary Anne Nagler, *Oakland Community College*
Rebecca Neagle, *Wake Technical Community College*
Margaret Payne, *Freed-Hardeman University*
Kristi Strother, *Community College of Denver*
P. Rachael Wilson, *Montgomery College*

My former editor Steve Pensinger needs to be remembered for steering me through four editions. I am also grateful to Tim Julet and Alexis Walker for guidance through the fifth edition and to Chris Narozny, developmental editor of the sixth edition. My hat's off to Lisa Moore, executive editor for the sixth and seventh editions; to Christopher Bennem, sponsoring editor for the eighth and ninth editions; and to Joshua Feldman, my hardworking developmental editor of both the seventh and eighth editions. Finally, I must thank Phil Butcher, my dedicated developmental editor of this edition. I have been blessed with a chorus of voices enriching this text throughout its twenty-five-year life: May you all live long and prosper!

I'll close by once again dedicating *Read, Reason, Write* to my daughter Ruth who, in spite of her own career and interests, continues to give generously of her time, reading possible essays for each new edition and listening patiently to my endless debates about changes. And for all students who use my text: May you understand that it is the liberal education that makes continued growth of the human spirit both possible and pleasurable.

Dorothy U. Seyler

Northern Virginia Community College

Critical Reading and Analysis

CHAPTER 1

Writers and Their Sources

READ: What is the situation in the photo—who are the two figures, where are they, how do they differ?

REASON: What ideas are suggested by the photo?

REFLECT/WRITE: Why might this visual have been chosen for Chapter 1?

"Are you happy with your new car?" Oscar asks.

"Oh, yes, I love my new car," Rachel responds.

"Why?" queries Oscar.

"Oh, it's just great—and dad paid for most of it," Rachel exclaims.

"So you like it because it was cheap," Oscar says. "But, wasn't your father going to pay for whatever car you chose?"

"Well, yes—within reason."

"Then why did you choose the Corolla? Why is it so great?"

Rachel ponders a moment and then replies: "It's small enough for me to feel comfortable driving it, but not so small that I would be frightened by trucks. It gets good mileage, and Toyota cars have a good reputation."

"Hmm. Maybe I should think about a Corolla. Then again, I wouldn't part with my Miata!" Oscar proclaims.

A simple conversation, right? In fact, this dialogue represents an **argument.** You may not recognize it as a "typical" argument. After all, there is no real dispute between Oscar and Rachel—no yelling, no hurt feelings. But in its most basic form, an argument is a *claim* (Rachel's car is great) supported by *reasons* (the car's size, mileage, and brand). Similar arguments could be made in favor of this car in other contexts. For instance, Rachel might have seen (and been persuaded by) a television or online Toyota advertisement, or she might have read an article making similar claims in a magazine such as *Consumer Reports.* In turn, she might decide to develop her argument into an essay or speech for one of her courses.

READING, WRITING, AND THE CONTEXTS OF ARGUMENT

Arguments, it seems, are everywhere. Well, what about this textbook, you counter. Its purpose is to inform, not to present an argument. True—to a degree. But textbook authors also make choices about what is important to include and how students should learn the material. Even writing primarily designed to inform says to readers: Do it my way! Well, what about novels, you "argue." Surely they are not arguments. A good point—to a degree. The ideas about human life and experience we find in novels are more subtle, more indirect, than the points we meet head-on in many arguments. Still, expressive writing presents ideas, ways of seeing the world. It seems that arguments can be simple or profound, clearly stated or implied. And we can find them in much—if not most—of our uses of language.

You can accept this larger scope of argument and still expect that in your course on argument and critical thinking you probably will not be asked to write a textbook or a novel. You might, though, be asked to write a summary or a style analysis, so you should think about how those tasks might connect to the world of argument. Count on this: You will be asked to write! Why work on your writing skills? Here are good answers to this question:

- Communication skills are the single most important skill sought by employers.
- The better writer you become, the better reader you will be.
- The more confident a writer you become, the more efficiently you will handle written assignments in all your courses.
- The more you write, the more you learn about who you are and what really matters to you.

You are about to face a variety of writing assignments. Always think about what role each assignment asks of you. Are you a student demonstrating knowledge? A citizen arguing for tougher drunk-driving laws? A scholar presenting the results of research? A friend having a conversation about a new car? Any writer—including you—will take on different roles, writing for different audiences, using different strategies to reach each audience. There are many kinds of argument and many ways to be successful—or unsuccessful—in preparing them. Your argument course will be challenging. This text will help you meet that challenge.

RESPONDING TO SOURCES

If this is a text about *writing* arguments, why does it contain so many readings? (You noticed!) There are good reasons for the readings you find here:

- College and the workplace demand that you learn complex information through reading. This text will give you lots of practice.

- You need to read to develop your critical thinking skills.
- Your reading will often serve as a basis for writing. In a course on argument, the focus of attention shifts from you to your subject, a subject others have debated before you. You will need to understand the issue, think carefully about the views of others, and only then join in the conversation.

To understand how critical thinkers may respond to sources, let's examine "The Gettysburg Address," Abraham Lincoln's famous speech dedicating the Gettysburg Civil War battlefield. We can use this document to see the various ways writers respond—in writing—to the writing of others.

THE GETTYSBURG ADDRESS | ABRAHAM LINCOLN

Fourscore and seven years ago our fathers brought forth on this continent a new nation, conceived in liberty and dedicated to the proposition that all men are created equal. Now we are engaged in a great civil war, testing whether that nation, or any nation so conceived and so dedicated, can long endure. We are met on a great battlefield of that war. We have come to dedicate a portion of that field as a final resting place for those who here gave their lives that that nation might live. It is altogether fitting and proper that we should do this. But, in a larger sense, we cannot dedicate—we cannot consecrate—we cannot hallow—this ground. The brave men, living and dead, who struggled here have consecrated it far above our poor power to add or to detract. The world will little note nor long remember what we say here, but it can never forget what they did here. It is for us, the living, rather to be dedicated here to the unfinished work which they who fought here have thus far so nobly advanced. It is rather for us to be here dedicated to the great task remaining before us—that from these honored dead we take increased devotion to that cause for which they gave the last full measure of devotion; that we here highly resolve that these dead shall not have died in vain; that this nation, under God, shall have a new birth of freedom; and that government of the people, by the people, for the people shall not perish from the earth.

What Does It Say?   THE RESPONSE TO CONTENT

Instructors often ask students to *summarize* their reading of a complex chapter, a supplementary text, or a series of journal articles on library reserve. Frequently, book report assignments specify that summary and evaluation be combined. Your purpose in writing a summary is to show your understanding of the work's main ideas and of the relationships among those ideas. If you can put what you have read into your own words and focus on the text's chief points, then you have command of that material. Here is a sample restatement of Lincoln's "Address":

> Our nation was initially built on a belief in liberty and equality, but its future is now being tested by civil war. It is appropriate for us to dedicate this battlefield, but those who fought here have dedicated it better than we. We should dedicate ourselves to continue the fight to maintain this nation and its principles of government.

Sometimes it is easier to recite or quote famous or difficult works than to state, more simply and in your own words, what has been written. The ability to summarize reflects strong writing skills. For more coverage of writing summaries, see pages 14–17. (For coverage of paraphrasing, a task similar to summary, see also pp. 14–17.)

How Is It Written?
How Does It Compare
with Another Work?   THE ANALYTIC RESPONSE

Summary requirements are often combined with analysis or evaluation, as in a book report. Most of the time you will be expected to *do something* with what you have read, and to summarize will be insufficient. Frequently you will be asked to analyze a work—that is, to explain the writer's choice of style (or the work's larger rhetorical context). You will want to examine sentence patterns, organization, metaphors, and other techniques selected by the writer to convey attitude and give force to ideas. Developing your skills in analysis will make you both a better reader and a better writer.

Many writers have examined Lincoln's word choice, sentence structure, and choice of metaphors to make clear the sources of power in this speech.* Analyzing Lincoln's style, you might examine, among other elements, his effective use of *tricolon:* the threefold repetition of a grammatical structure, with the three points placed in ascending order of significance.

> Lincoln uses two effective tricolons in his brief address. The first focuses on the occasion for his speech, the dedication of the battlefield: "we cannot dedicate—we cannot consecrate—we cannot hallow. . . ." The best that the living can do is formally dedicate; only those who died there for the principle of liberty are capable of making the battlefield "hallow." The second tricolon presents Lincoln's concept of democratic government, a government "of the people, by the people, for the people." The purpose of government—"for the people"—resides in the position of greatest significance.

A second type of analysis, a comparison of styles of two writers, is a frequent variation of the analytic assignment. By focusing on similarities and differences in writing styles, you can see more clearly the role of choice in writing

---

* See, for example, Gilbert Highet's essay, "The Gettysburg Address," in *The Clerk of Oxenford: Essays on Literature and Life* (New York: Oxford UP, 1954), to which I am indebted in the following analysis.

and may also examine the issue of the degree to which differences in purpose affect style. One student, for example, produced a thoughtful and interesting study of Lincoln's style in contrast to that of Martin Luther King, Jr., as revealed in his "I Have a Dream" speech (see pp. 585–588):

> Although Lincoln's sentence structure is tighter than King's and King likes the rhythms created by repetition, both men reflect their familiarity with the King James Bible in their use of its cadences and expressions. Instead of saying eighty-seven years ago, Lincoln, seeking solemnity, selects the biblical expression "Fourscore and seven years ago." Similarly, King borrows from the Bible and echoes Lincoln when he writes "Five score years ago."

Is It Logical?
Is It Adequately Developed?
Does It Achieve Its Purpose?   THE EVALUATION RESPONSE

Even when the stated purpose of an essay is "pure" analysis, the analysis implies a judgment. We analyze Lincoln's style because we recognize that "The Gettysburg Address" is a great piece of writing and we want to see how it achieves its power. On other occasions, evaluation is the stated purpose for close reading and analysis. The columnist who challenges a previously published editorial has analyzed the editorial and found it flawed. The columnist may fault the editor's logic or lack of adequate or relevant support for the editorial's main idea. In each case the columnist makes a negative evaluation of the editorial, but that judgment is an informed one based on the columnist's knowledge of language and the principles of good argument.

Part of the ability to judge wisely lies in recognizing each writer's (or speaker's) purpose, audience, and occasion. It would be inappropriate to assert that Lincoln's address is weakened by its lack of facts about the battle. The historian's purpose is to record the number killed or to analyze the generals' military tactics. Lincoln's purpose was different.

> As Lincoln reflected upon this young country's being torn apart by civil strife, he saw the dedication of the Gettysburg battlefield as an opportunity to challenge the country to fight for its survival and the principles upon which it was founded. The result was a brief but moving speech that appropriately examines the connection between the life and death of soldiers and the birth and survival of a nation.

These sentences establish a basis for an analysis of Lincoln's train of thought and use of metaphors, an analysis grounded in an understanding of Lincoln's purpose and the context in which he spoke.

How Does It Help Me to Understand
Other Works, Ideas, Events?   THE RESEARCH RESPONSE

Frequently you will read not to analyze or evaluate but rather to use the source as part of learning about a particular subject. Lincoln's address is significant for the Civil War historian both as an event of that war and as an influence on our thinking about that war. "The Gettysburg Address" is also vital to the biographer's study of Lincoln's life or to the literary critic's study either of famous speeches or of the Bible's influence on English writing styles. Thus Lincoln's brief speech is a valuable source for students in a variety of disciplines. It becomes part of their research process. Able researchers study it carefully, analyze it thoroughly, place it in its proper historical, literary, and personal contexts, and use it to develop their own arguments.

To practice reading and responding to sources, study the following article by Deborah Tannen. The exercises that follow will check your reading skills and your understanding of the various responses to reading just discussed. Use the prereading questions to become engaged with Tannen's essay.

WHO DOES THE TALKING HERE? | DEBORAH TANNEN

Professor of linguistics at Georgetown University, Deborah Tannen writes popular books on the uses of language by "ordinary" people. Among her many books are *Talking from 9 to 5* (1994) and *I Only Say This Because I Love You* (2004). Her response to the debate over who talks more, men or women, was published in the *Washington Post* on July 15, 2007.

PREREADING QUESTIONS What is the occasion for Tannen's article—what is she responding to? Who does most of the talking in your family—and are you okay with the answer?

1   It's no surprise that a one-page article published this month in the journal *Science* inspired innumerable newspaper columns and articles. The study, by Matthias Mehl and four colleagues, claims to lay to rest, once and for all, the stereotype that women talk more than men, by proving—scientifically—that women and men talk equally.

2   The notion that women talk more was reinforced last year when Louann Brizendine's "The Female Brain" cited the finding that women utter, on average, 20,000 words a day, men 7,000. (Brizendine later disavowed the statistic, as there was no study to back it up.) Mehl and his colleagues outfitted 396 college students with devices that recorded their speech. The female subjects spoke an average of 16,215 words a day, the men 15,669. The difference is insignificant. Case closed.

3   Or is it? Can we learn who talks more by counting words? No, according to a forthcoming article surveying 70 studies of gender differences in talkativeness. (Imagine—70 studies published in scientific journals, and we're still asking the question.) In their survey, Campbell Leaper and Melanie Ayres found that counting words yielded no consistent differences, though number of words per speaking turn did (Men, on average, used more).

This doesn't surprise me. In my own research on gender and language, I **4** quickly surmised that to understand who talks more, you have to ask: What's the situation? What are the speakers using words for?

The following experience conveys the importance of situation. I was **5** addressing a small group in a suburban Virginia living room. One man stood out because he talked a lot, while his wife, who was sitting beside him, said nothing at all. I described to the group a complaint common among women about men they live with: At the end of a day she tells him what happened, what she thought and how she felt about it. Then she asks, "How was your day?"—and is disappointed when he replies, "Fine," "Nothing much" or "Same old rat race."

The loquacious man spoke up. "You're right," he said. Pointing to his wife, **6** he added, "She's the talker in our family." Everyone laughed. But he explained, "It's true. When we come home, she does all the talking. If she didn't, we'd spend the evening in silence."

The "how was your day?" conversation typifies the kind of talk women **7** tend to do more of: spoken to intimates and focusing on personal experience, your own or others'. I call this "rapport-talk." It contrasts with "report-talk"— giving or exchanging information about impersonal topics, which men tend to do more.

Studies that find men talk- **8** ing more are usually carried out in formal experiments or public contexts such as meetings. For example, Marjorie Swacker observed an academic conference where women presented 40 percent of the papers and were 42 percent of the audience but asked only 27 percent of the questions; their questions were, on average, also shorter by half than the men's questions. And David and Myra Sadker showed that boys talk more in mixed-sex classrooms—a context common among college students, a factor skewing the results of Mehl's new study.

Many men's comfort with **9** "public talking" explains why a man who tells his wife he has nothing to report about his day might later find a funny story to tell at dinner with two other couples (leaving his wife wondering, "Why didn't he tell me first?").

10   In addition to situation, you have to consider what speakers are doing with words. Campbell and Ayres note that many studies find women doing more "affiliative speech" such as showing support, agreeing or acknowledging others' comments. Drawing on studies of children at play as well as my own research of adults talking, I often put it this way: For women and girls, talk is the glue that holds a relationship together. Their best friend is the one they tell everything to. Spending an evening at home with a spouse is when this kind of talk comes into its own. Since this situation is uncommon among college students, it's another factor skewing the new study's results.

11   Women's rapport-talk probably explains why many people think women talk more. A man wants to read the paper, his wife wants to talk; his girlfriend or sister spends hours on the phone with her friend or her mother. He concludes: Women talk more.

12   Yet Leaper and Ayres observed an overall pattern of men speaking more. That's a conclusion women often come to when men hold forth at meetings, in social groups or when delivering one-on-one lectures. All of us—women and men—tend to notice others talking more in situations where we talk less.

13   Counting may be a start—or a stop along the way—to understanding gender differences. But it's understanding when we tend to talk and what we're doing with words that yields insights we can count on.

QUESTIONS FOR READING AND REASONING

1.   What was the conclusion of the researchers who presented their study in *Science?*

2.   Why are their results not telling the whole story, according to Tannen? Instead of counting words, what should we study?

3.   What two kinds of talk does Tannen label? Which gender does the most of each type of talking?

4.   What is Tannen's main idea or thesis?

QUESTIONS FOR REFLECTING AND WRITING

1.   How do the details—and the style—in the opening and concluding paragraphs contribute to the author's point? Write a paragraph answer to this question. Then consider: Which one of the different responses to reading does your paragraph illustrate?

2. Do you agree with Tannen that understanding how words are used must be part of any study of men and women talking? If so, why? If not, how would you respond to her argument?

3. "The Gettysburg Address" is a valuable document for several kinds of research projects. For what kinds of research would Tannen's essay be useful? List several possibilities and be prepared to discuss your list with classmates.

ACTIVE READING: USE YOUR MIND!

Reading is not about looking at black marks on a page—or turning the pages as quickly as we can. Reading means constructing meaning, getting a message. We read with our brains, not our eyes and hands! This concept is often underscored by the term *active reading*. To help you always achieve active reading, not passive page turning, follow these guidelines.

GUIDELINES for Active Reading

- **Understand your purpose in reading.** Do not just start turning pages to complete an assignment. Think first about your purpose. Are you reading for knowledge on which you will be tested? Focus on your purpose as you read, asking yourself, "What do I need to learn from this work?"

- **Reflect on the title before reading further.** Titles are the first words writers give us. Take time to look for clues in a title that may reveal the work's subject and perhaps the writer's approach or attitude as well. Henry Fairlie's title "The Idiocy of Urban Life," for example, tells you both Fairlie's subject (urban or city living) and his position (urban living is idiotic).

- **Become part of the writer's audience.** Not all writers have you and me in mind when they write. As an active reader, you need to "join" a writer's audience by learning about the writer, about the time in which the piece was written, and about the writer's expected audience. For readings in this text you are aided by introductory notes; be sure to study them.

- **Predict what is coming.** Look for a writer's main idea or purpose statement. Study the work's organization. Then use this information to anticipate what is coming. When you read "There are three good reasons for requiring a dress code in schools," you know the writer will list *three* reasons.

- **Concentrate.** Slow down and give your full attention to reading. Watch for transition and connecting words that show you how the parts of a text connect. Read an entire article or chapter at one time—or you will need to start over to make sense of the piece.

- **Annotate as you read.** The more senses you use, the more active your involvement. That means marking the text as you read (or taking notes if the material is not yours). Underline key sentences, such as the writer's thesis. Then, in the margin, indicate that it is the thesis. With a series of examples (or reasons), label them and number them. When you look up a word's definition, write the definition in the margin next to the word. Draw diagrams to illustrate concepts; draw arrows to connect example to idea. Studies have shown that students who annotate their texts get higher grades. Do what successful students do.

- **Keep a reading journal.** In addition to annotating what you read, you may want to develop the habit of writing regularly in a journal. A reading journal gives you a place to note impressions and reflections on your reading, your initial reactions to assignments, and ideas you may use in your next writing.

EXERCISE: Active Reading

Read the following selection, noting the annotations that have been started for you. As you read, add your own annotations. Then write a journal entry—four to five sentences at least—to capture your reactions to the following column.

POLITICAL ADS AND THE VOTERS THEY ATTRACT | RICHARD MORIN

A former journalist with the *Washington Post*, Richard Morin wrote a regular Sunday column titled "Unconventional Wisdom" that presented interesting new information from the social sciences. The following column appeared November 23, 2003.

Topic.

Note: Both types of ads work—why?

1   Even though it pains me to report it, those negative political advertisements designed to scare the pants off us appear to work quite well. But here's a surprise—so do those positive ads filled with happy children and cascading violins.

2   What's the connection? Both depend on manipulating the emotions of viewers.

3   What's more, emotion-drenched political ads are most effective among sophisticated voters, who probably would be the most chagrined to learn that they're suckers for political mudslinging and cheerleading, claims Ted Brader, a political science professor and researcher at the Institute for Social Research at the University of Michigan.

4   "Emotions are so central to what makes us tick," Brader said. "Political scientists for years have basically ignored them. But if you think about what causes us to do anything in life, political or otherwise, there are always strong emotions involved."

His study, which he is expanding into a book, began as research for his 5
PhD at Harvard University. Brader recruited 286 voting-age men and women
in 11 Massachusetts communities during the weeks leading up to the 1998
Democratic gubernatorial primary. The race pitted incumbent Attorney General Scott Harshbarger against former state senator Patricia McGovern.

Test subjects were randomly assigned to one of four groups. Each group 6
watched a half-hour local news broadcast that featured one of four seemingly genuine 30-second campaign ads that Brader had prepared. Two ads
were positive in tone and two were negative. The names of the candidates
were alternated so that each one was featured an equal number of times in
the ads.

The scripts for the two positive ads were identical. What was different were 7
the accompanying sounds and images. One ad featured uplifting "cues"—
symphonic music and warm, colorful images of children intended to inspire an
even more enthusiastic reaction to the upbeat message—while the other used
bland visual and audio enhancements.

The scripts for the two negative ads also were the same. But one featured 8
tense, discordant music and grainy pictures of crime scenes to create a sense
of fear. The other ad lacked the scary special effects.

The test subjects answered a survey before and after the experiment that 9
measured, among other things, interest in the campaign and candidate preference. And yes, after the study the participants were let in on the secret.
"They were 'debriefed' after their participation and given a written explanation that the political ads they saw were completely fictitious, made by me for
the study and not by the candidates, and there was not necessarily any connection between what is said in the ads and the candidates' actual positions,"
Brader said.

It's good that he did eventually 'fess up, because the enhanced ads worked 10
better than Brader or his faculty advisers suspected they would. When enthusiasm cues were added to a positive script, the test subjects' self-reported likelihood to vote on Election Day was a whopping 29 percentage points higher
than those of subjects who saw the positive ad without the emotion-enhancing
cues.

The negative ad with fear-inducing cues was particularly effective in per- 11
suading viewers to vote for the candidate promoted in the ad. Nearly 10 percent of those who saw the "fear" ad switched allegiance, and 20 to 25 percent
were less certain of their choice after seeing their favored candidate dragged
through the mud.

Those exposed to fear cues also could remember more details of related 12
news stories shown in the broadcast. It also made them more likely to want
to obtain more information about the candidates, suggesting one benefit
to negative ads: "They may scare people into thinking" about political campaigns, Brader said.

Brader also found that better-informed, better-educated voters were 13
more susceptible to fear-inducing and enthusiasm-enhancing ads than

less-knowledgeable voters. "That really contradicts the traditional claim that emotional appeals work primarily on the ignorant masses," or those who are otherwise easily led, he said.

14   Why are smarties so susceptible to emotional ads? Brader doesn't know. It could be, he said, that such ads "resonate with people who are already emotional about politics to begin with because they have a vested interest."

15   For political consultants, this is news they can use. "Candidates should aim positive ads at their base of support and fear ads at undecided and opposing voters," Brader advised. "Front-runners, incumbents in times of peace and prosperity, and members of the majority party in a district should rely principally on enthusiasm. Their opponents—trailing candidates, challengers, members of the minority party—should be drawn to the use of fear."

WRITING SUMMARIES

Preparing a good summary is not always as easy as it looks. *A summary briefly restates, in your own words, the main points of a work in a way that does not misrepresent or distort the original.* A good summary shows your grasp of main ideas and your ability to express them clearly. You need to condense the original while giving all key ideas appropriate attention. As a student you may be assigned a summary to:

- Show that you have read and understood assigned works.
- Complete a test question.
- Have a record of what you have read for future study or to prepare for class discussion.
- Explain the main ideas in a work that you will also examine in some other way, such as in a book review.

When assigned a summary, pay careful attention to word choice. Avoid judgment words, such as: "Brown then proceeds to develop the *silly* idea that. . . ." Follow these guidelines for writing good summaries.

GUIDELINES for Writing Summaries

1. **Write in a direct, objective style, using your own words.** Use few, if any, direct quotations, probably none in a one-paragraph summary.

2. **Begin with a reference to the writer (full name) and the title of the work and then state the writer's thesis.** (You may also want to include where and when the work was published.)

3. **Complete the summary by providing other key ideas.** Show the reader how the main ideas connect and relate to one another.

4. **Do not include specific examples, illustrations, or background sections.**

5. **Combine main ideas into fewer sentences than were used in the original.**

6. **Keep the parts of your summary in the same balance as you find in the original.** If the author devotes about 30 percent of the essay to one idea, that idea should get about 30 percent of the space in your summary.

7. **Select precise, accurate verbs to show the author's relationship to ideas.** Write Jones *argues*, Jones *asserts*, Jones *believes*. Do not use vague verbs that provide only a list of disconnected ideas. Do *not* write Jones *talks about,* Jones *goes on to say.*

8. **Do not make any judgments about the writer's style or ideas.** Do *not* include your personal reaction to the work.

EXERCISE: Summary

With these guidelines in mind, read the following two summaries of Deborah Tannen's "Who Does the Talking Here" (see pp. 8–10). Then answer the question: What is flawed or weak about each summary? To aid your analysis, (1) underline or highlight all words or phrases that are inappropriate in each summary, and (2) put the number of the guideline next to any passage that does not adhere to that guideline.

SUMMARY 1

I really thought that Deborah Tannen's essay contained some interesting ideas about how men and women talk. Tannen mentioned a study in which men and women used almost the same number of words. She goes on to talk about a man who talked a lot at a meeting in Virginia. Tannen also says that women talk more to make others feel good. I'm a man, and I don't like to make small talk.

SUMMARY 2

In Deborah Tannen's "Who Does the Talking Here?" (published July 15, 2007), she talks about studies to test who talks more—men or women. Some people think the case is closed—they both talk about the same number of words. Tannen goes on to say that she thinks people use words differently. Men talk a lot at events; they use "report-talk." Women use "rapport-talk" to strengthen relationships; their language is a glue to maintain relationships. So just counting words does not work. You have to know why someone is speaking.

Although we can agree that the writers of these summaries have read Tannen's essay, we can also find weaknesses in each summary. Certainly the second summary is more helpful than the first, but it can be strengthened by eliminating some details, combining some ideas, and putting more focus on Tannen's main idea. Here is a much-improved version.

REVISED SUMMARY

In Deborah Tannen's essay "Who Does the Talking Here?" (published July 15, 2007), Tannen asserts that recent studies to determine if men or women do the most talking are not helpful in answering that question. These studies focus on just counting the words that men and women use. Tannen argues that the only useful study of this issue is one that examines how each gender uses words and in which situations each gender does the most talking. She explains that men tend to use "report-talk" whereas women tend to use "rapport-talk." That is, men will do much of the talking in meetings when they have something to report. Women, on the other hand, will do more of the talking when they are seeking to connect in a relationship, to make people feel good. So, if we want to really understand the differences, we need to stop counting words and listen to what each gender is actually doing with the words that are spoken.

At times you may need to write a summary of a page or two rather than one paragraph. Frequently, long reports are preceded by a one-page summary. A longer summary may become part of an article-length review of an important book. Or instructors may want a longer summary of a lengthy or complicated article or text chapter. The following is an example of a summary of a lengthy article on cardiovascular health.

SAMPLE LONGER SUMMARY

In her article "The Good Heart," Anne Underwood (*Newsweek,* October 3, 2005) explores recent studies regarding heart disease that, in various ways, reveal the important role that one's attitudes have on physical health, especially the health of the heart. She begins with the results of a study published in the *New England Journal of Medicine* that examined the dramatic increase in cardiovascular deaths after an earthquake in Los Angeles in 1994. People who were not hurt by the quake died as a result of the fear and stress brought on by the event. As Underwood explains in detail, however, studies continue to show that psychological and social factors affect coronaries even more than sudden shocks such as earthquakes. For example, according to Dr. Michael Frenneaux, depression "at least doubles an otherwise healthy person's heart-attack risk." A Duke University study showed that high levels of hostility also raised the risk of death by heart disease. Another study showed that childhood traumas can increase heart disease risks by 30 to 70 percent. Adults currently living under work and family stress also increase their risks significantly.

How do attitudes make a difference? A number of studies demonstrate that negative attitudes, anger, and hostile feelings directly affect the chemistry of the body in ways that damage blood vessels. They also can raise blood pressure. Less directly, people with these attitudes and under stress often eat more, exercise less, and are more likely to smoke. These behaviors add to one's risk. Some physicians are seeking to use this information to increase the longevity of heart patients. They are advising weight loss and exercise, yoga and therapy, recognizing, as Underwood concludes, that "the heart does not beat in isolation, nor does the mind brood alone."

Observe the differences between the longer summary of Anne Underwood's article and the paragraph summary of Deborah Tannen's essay:

- Some key ideas or terms may be presented in direct quotation.
- Results of studies may be given in some detail.
- Appropriate transitional and connecting words are used to show how the parts of the summary connect.
- The author's name is often repeated to keep the reader's attention on the article summarized, not on the author of the summary.

ACKNOWLEDGING SOURCES INFORMALLY

You must always identify sources you are using and make clear to readers how you are using them. Even when you are not writing a formally documented paper, you must identify each source by author. What follows are some of the conventions of writing to use when writing about sources.

Referring to People and Sources

Readers in academic, professional, and business contexts expect writers to follow specific conventions of style when referring to authors and to various kinds of sources. Study the following guidelines and examples and then mark the next few pages for easy reference—perhaps by turning down a corner of the first and last pages.

References to People

- In a first reference, give the person's full name (both the given name and the surname): *Ellen Goodman, Robert J. Samuelson.* In second and subsequent references, use only the last name (surname): *Goodman, Samuelson.*
- Do not use Mr., Mrs., or Ms. Special titles such as President, Chief Justice, or Doctor may be used in the first reference with the person's full name.
- Never refer to an author by her or his first name. Write *Dickinson*, not *Emily*; *Whitman*, not *Walt*.

References to Titles of Works

Titles of works must *always* be written as titles. Titles are indicated by capitalization and by either quotation marks or italics.

Guidelines for Capitalizing Titles

- The first and last words are capitalized.
- The first word of a subtitle is capitalized.
- All other words in titles are capitalized except
  — Articles (*a, an, the*).
  — Coordinating conjunctions (*and, or, but, for, nor, yet, so*).
  — Prepositions (*in, for, about*).

Titles Requiring Quotation Marks

Titles of works published within other works—within a book, magazine, or newspaper—are indicated by quotation marks.

ESSAYS	"The Real Pregnancy Problem"
SHORT STORIES	"The Story of an Hour"
POEMS	"To Daffodils"
ARTICLES	"Choose Your Utopia"
CHAPTERS	"Writers and Their Sources"
LECTURES	"Crazy Mixed-Up Families"
TV EPISODES	"Resolved: Drug Prohibition Has Failed" (one debate on the television show *Firing Line*)

Titles Requiring Italics

Titles of works that are separate publications and, by extension, titles of items such as works of art and Web sites are in italics.

PLAYS	*A Raisin in the Sun*
NOVELS	*War and Peace*
NONFICTION BOOKS	*Read, Reason, Write*
BOOK-LENGTH POEMS	*The Odyssey*
MAGAZINES AND JOURNALS	*Wired*
NEWSPAPERS	*Wall Street Journal*
FILMS	*The Wizard of Oz*
PAINTINGS	*The Birth of Venus*
TELEVISION PROGRAMS	*Star Trek*
WEB SITES	*worldwildlife.org*
DATABASES	*Proquest*

Read the following article (published April 13, 2008, in the *Washington Post*) and respond by answering the questions that follow. Observe, as you read, how the author refers to the various sources he uses to develop his article and how he presents material from those sources. We will use this article as a guide to handling quotations.

THE FUTURE IS NOW: IT'S HEADING RIGHT AT US, BUT WE NEVER SEE IT COMING | JOEL ACHENBACH

A former humor columnist and currently a staff writer for the *Washington Post*, Joel Achenbach also has a regular blog on **washingtonpost.com.** His books include anthologies of his columns and *Captured by Aliens: The Search for Life and Truth in a Very Large Universe* (2003). The following article was published April 13, 2008.

PREREADING QUESTIONS What is nanotechnology? What do you think will be the next big change—and what field will it come from?

The most important things happening in the world today won't make tomorrow's front page. They won't get mentioned by presidential candidates or Chris Matthews[1] or Bill O'Reilly[2] or any of the other folks yammering and snorting on cable television. 1

They'll be happening in laboratories—out of sight, inscrutable and unhyped until the very moment when they change life as we know it. 2

Science and technology form a two-headed, unstoppable change agent. Problem is, most of us are mystified and intimidated by such things as biotechnology, or nanotechnology, or the various other -ologies that seem to be threatening to merge into a single unspeakable and incomprehensible thing called biotechnonanogenomicology. We vaguely understand that this stuff is changing our lives, but we feel as though it's all out of our control. We're just hanging on tight, like Kirk and Spock when the Enterprise starts vibrating at Warp 8. 3

What's unnerving is the velocity at which the future sometimes arrives. Consider the Internet. This powerful but highly disruptive technology crept out of the lab (a Pentagon think tank, actually) and all but devoured modern civilization—with almost no advance warning. The first use of the word "internet" to refer to a computer network seems to have appeared in this newspaper on Sept. 26, 1988, in the Financial section, on page F30—about as deep into the paper as you can go without hitting the bedrock of the classified ads. 4

The entire reference: "SMS Data Products Group Inc. in McLean won a $1,005,048 contract from the Air Force to supply a defense data network internet protocol router." Perhaps the unmellifluous compound noun "data network internet protocol router" is one reason more of us didn't pay attention. A couple of months later, "Internet"—still lacking the "the" before its name—finally elbowed its way to the front page when a virus shut down thousands of computers. The story referred to "a research network called Internet," which "links as many as 50,000 computers, allowing users to send a variety of information to each other." The scientists knew that computer networks could be powerful. But how many knew that this Internet thing would change the way we communicate, publish, sell, shop, conduct research, find old friends, do homework, plan trips and on and on? 5

---

[1] Political talk-show host on MSNBC.—Ed.

[2] Radio and television talk-show host on the FOX News Channel.—Ed.

6   Joe Lykken, a theoretical physicist at the Fermilab research center in Illinois, tells a story about something that happened in 1990. A Fermilab visitor, an English fellow by the name of Tim Berners-Lee, had a new trick he wanted to demonstrate to the physicists. He typed some code into a little blank box on the computer screen. Up popped a page of data.

7   Lykken's reaction: *Eh.*

8   He could already see someone else's data on a computer. He could have the colleague e-mail it to him and open it as a document. Why view it on a separate page on some computer network?

9   But of course, this unimpressive piece of software was the precursor to what is known today as the World Wide Web. "We had no idea that we were seeing not only a revolution, but a trillion-dollar idea," Lykken says.

10   Now let us pause to reflect upon the fact that Joe Lykken is a very smart guy—you don't get to be a theoretical physicist unless you have the kind of brain that can practically bend silverware at a distance—and even he, with that giant cerebral cortex and the billions of neurons flashing and winking, saw the proto-Web and harrumphed. It's not just us mortals, even scientists don't always grasp the significance of innovations. Tomorrow's revolutionary technology may be in plain sight, but everyone's eyes, clouded by conventional thinking, just can't detect it. "Even smart people are really pretty incapable of envisioning a situation that's substantially different from what they're in," says Christine Peterson, vice president of Foresight Nanotech Institute in Menlo Park, Calif.

11   So where does that leave the rest of us?

12   In technological Palookaville.

13   Science is becoming ever more specialized; technology is increasingly a series of black boxes, impenetrable to but a few. Americans' poor science literacy means that science and technology exist in a walled garden, a geek ghetto. We are a technocracy in which most of us don't really understand what's happening around us. We stagger through a world of technological and medical miracles. We're zombified by progress.

14   Peterson has one recommendation: Read science fiction, especially "hard science fiction" that sticks rigorously to the scientifically possible. "If you look out into the long-term future and what you see looks like science fiction, it might be wrong," she says. "But if it doesn't look like science fiction, it's definitely wrong."

15   That's exciting—and a little scary. We want the blessings of science (say, cheaper energy sources) but not the terrors (monsters spawned by atomic radiation that destroy entire cities with their fiery breath).

16   Eric Horvitz, one of the sharpest minds at Microsoft, spends a lot of time thinking about the Next Big Thing. Among his other duties, he's president of the Association for the Advancement of Artificial Intelligence. He thinks that, sometime in the decades ahead, artificial systems will be modeled on living things. In the Horvitz view, life is marked by robustness, flexibility, adaptability. That's where computers need to go. Life, he says, shows scientists "what we can do as engineers—better, potentially."

Our ability to monkey around with life itself is a reminder that ethics, **17** religion and old-fashioned common sense will be needed in abundance in decades to come. . . . How smart and flexible and rambunctious do we want our computers to be? Let's not mess around with that Matrix business.

Every forward-thinking person almost ritually brings up the mortality issue. **18** What'll happen to society if one day people can stop the aging process? Or if only rich people can stop getting old?

It's interesting that politicians rarely address such matters. The future in **19** general is something of a suspect topic . . . a little goofy. Right now we're all focused on the next primary, the summer conventions, the Olympics and their political implications, the fall election. The political cycle enforces an emphasis on the immediate rather than the important.

And in fact, any prediction of what the world will be like more than, say, **20** a year from now is a matter of hubris. The professional visionaries don't even talk about predictions or forecasts but prefer the word "scenarios." When Sen. John McCain, for example, declares that radical Islam is the transcendent challenge of the 21st century, he's being sincere, but he's also being a bit of a soothsayer. Environmental problems and resource scarcity could easily be the dominant global dilemma. Or a virus with which we've yet to make our acquaintance. Or some other "wild card."

Says Lykken, "Our ability to predict is incredibly poor. What we all thought **21** when I was a kid was that by now we'd all be flying around in anti-gravity cars on Mars."

Futurists didn't completely miss on space travel—it's just that the things **22** flying around Mars are robotic and take neat pictures and sometimes land and sniff the soil.

Some predictions are bang-on, such as sci-fi writer Arthur C. Clarke's **23** declaration in 1945 that there would someday be communications satellites orbiting the Earth. But Clarke's satellites had to be occupied by repairmen who would maintain the huge computers required for space communications. Even in the late 1960s, when Clarke collaborated with Stanley Kubrick on the screenplay to "2001: A Space Odyssey," he assumed that computers would, over time, get bigger. "The HAL 9000 computer fills half the spaceship," Lykken notes.

Says science-fiction writer Ben Bova, "We have built into us an idea that **24** tomorrow is going to be pretty much like today, which is very wrong."

The future is often viewed as an endless resource of innovation that will **25** make problems go away—even though, if the past is any judge, innovations create their own set of new problems. Climate change is at least in part a consequence of the invention of the steam engine in the early 1700s and all the industrial advances that followed.

Look again at the Internet. It's a fantastic tool, but it also threatens to dis- **26** perse information we'd rather keep under wraps, such as our personal medical data, or even the instructions for making a fission bomb.

27   We need to keep our eyes open. The future is going to be here sooner than we think. It'll surprise us. We'll try to figure out why we missed so many clues. And we'll go back and search the archives, and see that thing we should have noticed on page F30.

QUESTIONS FOR READING AND REASONING

1.   What is Achenbach's subject? What is his thesis? Where does he state it?

2.   What two agents together are likely to produce the next big change?

3.   Summarize the evidence Achenbach provides to support the idea that we don't recognize the next big change until it is here.

4.   If we want to try to anticipate the next big change, what should we do?

5.   What prediction did Arthur C. Clarke get right? In what way was his imagination incorrect? What can readers infer from this example?

6.   Are big changes always good? Explain.

7.   How does Achenbach identify most of his sources? He does not identify Chris Matthews or Bill O'Reilly in paragraph 1. What does this tell you about his expected audience?

PRESENTING DIRECT QUOTATIONS: A GUIDE TO FORM AND STYLE

Although most of your papers will be written in your own words and style, you will sometimes use direct quotations. Just as there is a correct form for references to people and to works, there is a correct form for presenting borrowed material in direct quotations. Study the guidelines and examples and then mark these pages, as you did the others, for easy reference.

Reasons for Using Quotation Marks

We use quotation marks in four ways:

- To indicate dialogue in works of fiction and drama.
- To indicate the titles of some kinds of works.
- To indicate the words that others have spoken or written.
- To separate ourselves from or call into question particular uses of words.

The following guidelines apply to all four uses of quotation marks, but the focus will be on the third use.

A Brief Guide to Quoting

1. *Quote accurately.* Do not misrepresent what someone else has written. Take time to compare what you have written with the original.

2. *Put all words taken from a source within quotation marks.* (To take words from a source without using quotation marks is to plagiarize, a form of stealing punished in academic and professional communities.)

3. *Never change any of the words within your quotation marks.* Indicate any deleted words with ellipses [spaced periods (. . .)]. If you need to add words to make the meaning clear, place the added words in [square brackets], not (parentheses).

4. *Always make the source of the quoted words clear.* If you do not provide the author of the quoted material, readers will have to assume that you are calling those words into question—the fourth reason for quoting. Observe that Achenbach introduces Joe Lykken in paragraph 6 and then uses his last name or "he" through the next three paragraphs so that readers always know to whom he is referring and quoting.

5. *When quoting an author who is quoted by the author of the source you are using, you must make clear that you are getting that author's words from your source, not directly from that author.*

   For example:

ORIGINAL:	"We had no idea that we were seeing not only a revolution, but a trillion-dollar idea."
INCORRECT:	Referring to his first experience with the World Wide Web, Lykken observed: "We had no idea that we were seeing . . . a revolution."
CORRECT:	To make his point about our failure to recognize big changes when they first appear, Achenbach quotes theoretical physicist Joe Lykken's response to first seeing the World Wide Web: "We had no idea that we were seeing . . . a revolution."

6. *Place commas and periods inside the closing quotation mark—even when only one word is quoted:*

   Unable to anticipate big changes coming from modern science, we are, Achenbach observes, in "technological Palookaville."

7. *Place colons and semicolons outside the closing quotation mark:*

   Achenbach jokingly explains our reaction to the complexities of modern technologies in his essay "The Future Is Now": "We're zombified by progress."

8. *Do not quote unnecessary punctuation.* When you place quoted material at the end of a sentence you have written, use only the punctuation needed to complete your sentence.

ORIGINAL:	The next big change will be "happening in laboratories—out of sight, inscrutable, and unhyped."

INCORRECT:	Achenbach explains that we will be surprised by the next big change because it will, initially, be hidden, "happening in laboratories—."
CORRECT:	Achenbach explains that we will be surprised by the next big change because it will, initially, be hidden, "happening in laboratories."

9. *When the words you quote are only a part of your sentence, do not capitalize the first quoted word, even if it was capitalized in the source.* **Exception:** You introduce the quoted material with a colon.

INCORRECT:	Achenbach observes that "The future is often viewed as an endless resource of innovation."
CORRECT:	Achenbach observes that "the future is often viewed as an endless resource of innovation."
ALSO CORRECT:	Achenbach argues that we count too much on modern science to solve problems: "The future is often viewed as an endless resource of innovation."

10. *Use single quotation marks (the apostrophe key on your keyboard) to identify quoted material within quoted material:*

    Achenbach explains that futurists "prefer the word 'scenarios.'"

11. *Depending on the structure of your sentence, use a colon, a comma, or no punctuation before a quoted passage.* A colon provides a formal introduction to a quoted passage. (See the example in item 9.) Use a comma only when your sentence requires it. Quoted words presented in a "that" clause are not preceded by a comma.

ORIGINAL:	"What's unnerving is the velocity at which the future sometimes arrives."
CORRECT:	"What's unnerving," Achenbach notes, "is the velocity at which the future sometimes arrives."
ALSO CORRECT:	Achenbach observes that we are often unnerved by "the velocity at which the future sometimes arrives."

12. *To keep quotations brief, omit irrelevant portions. Indicate missing words with ellipses.* For example: Achenbach explains that "we want the blessings of science . . . but not the terrors." Some instructors want the ellipses placed in square brackets—[. . .]—to show that you have added them to the original. Modern Language Association (MLA) style does not require the square brackets unless you are quoting a passage that already has ellipses as part of that passage. The better choice would be not to quote that passage.

13. *Consider the poor reader.*
    - Always give enough context to make the quoted material clear.
    - Do not put so many bits and pieces of quoted passages into one sentence that your reader struggles to follow the ideas.

- Make sure that your sentences are complete and correctly constructed. Quoting is never an excuse for a sentence fragment or distorted construction.

> **NOTE:** All examples of quoting given above are in the present tense. We write that "Achenbach notes," "Achenbach believes," "Achenbach asserts." Even though his article was written in the past, we use the present tense to describe his ongoing ideas.

FOR READING AND ANALYSIS

As you read the following articles, practice active reading, including annotating each essay. Concentrate first on what each author has to say but also observe the organization of the essay and each author's use of quotations and references to other authors and works.

THE END OF LITERACY? DON'T STOP READING | HOWARD GARDNER

A professor in the Harvard Graduate School of Education, Dr. Gardner teaches cognitive psychology and is the author of more than 20 books, including *Multiple Intelligences* (2006). Current interests of his include responsible behavior at work and the ethics of the digital media. The following essay was published February 17, 2008.

PREREADING QUESTIONS Why might an author wonder about the end of literacy? How many books do you read each year? Do you think your book reading is typical?

What will happen to reading and writing in our time? 1

Could the doomsayers be right? Computers, they maintain, are destroy- 2 ing literacy. The signs—students' declining reading scores, the drop in leisure reading to just minutes a week, the fact that half the adult population reads no books in a year—are all pointing to the day when a literate American culture becomes a distant memory. By contrast, optimists foresee the Internet ushering in a new, vibrant participatory culture of words. Will they carry the day?

Maybe neither. Let me suggest a third possibility: Literacy—or an ensem- 3 ble of literacies—will continue to thrive, but in forms and formats we can't yet envision.

That's what has always happened as writing and reading have evolved over 4 the ages. It was less than 100,000 years ago that our human predecessors first made meaningful marks on surfaces, noting the phases of the moon or drawing animals on cave walls. Within the past 5,000 years, societies across the

Near East's Fertile Crescent began to use systems of marks to record important trade exchanges as well as pivotal events in the present and the past. These marks gradually became less pictorial, and a decisive leap occurred when they began to capture certain sounds reliably: U kn red ths sntnz cuz Inglsh feechurs "graphic-phoneme correspondences."

5   A master of written Greek, Plato feared that written language would undermine human memory capacities (much in the same way that we now worry about similar side effects of "Googling"). But libraries made the world's knowledge available to anyone who could read. The 15th-century printing press disturbed those who wanted to protect and interpret the word of God, but the availability of Bibles in the vernacular allowed laypeople to take control of their spiritual lives and, if historians are correct, encouraged entrepreneurship in commerce and innovation in science.

6   In the past 150 years, each new medium of communication—telegraph, telephone, movies, radio, television, the digital computer, the World Wide Web—has introduced its own peculiar mix of written, spoken and graphic languages and evoked a chaotic chorus of criticism and celebration.

7   But of the changes in the media landscape over the past few centuries, those featuring digital media are potentially the most far-reaching. Those of us who grew up in the 1950s, at a time when there were just a few computers in the world, could never have anticipated the ubiquity of personal computers (back then, IBM's Thomas Watson famously declared that there'd be a market for perhaps five computers in the world!). A mere half-century later, more than a billion people can communicate via e-mail, chat rooms and instant messaging; post their views on a blog; play games with millions of others worldwide; create their own works of art or theater and post them on YouTube; join political movements; and even inhabit, buy, sell and organize

in a virtual reality called Second Life. No wonder the chattering classes can't agree about what this all means.

Here's my take.   8

Once we ensured our basic survival, humans were freed to pursue other 9 needs and desires, including the pleasures of communicating, forming friendships, convincing others of our point of view, exercising our imagination, enjoying a measure of privacy. Initially, we pursued these needs with our senses, our hands and our individual minds. Human and mechanical technologies to help us were at a premium. It's easy to see how the emergence of written languages represented a boon. The invention of the printing press and the emergence of readily available books, magazines and newspapers allowed untold millions to extend their circle, expand their minds and expound their pet ideas.

For those of us of a 19th- or 20th-century frame of mind, books play a spe- 10 cial, perhaps even spiritual, role. Works of fiction—the writings of Jane Austen, Leo Tolstoy, Toni Morrison, William Faulkner—allow us to inhabit fascinating worlds we couldn't have envisioned. Works of scholarship—the economic analyses of Karl Marx and John Maynard Keynes, the histories of Thucydides and Edward Gibbon—provide frameworks for making sense of the past and the present.

But now, at the start of the 21st century, there's a dizzying set of literacies 11 available—written languages, graphic displays and notations. And there's an even broader array of media—analog, digital, electronic, hand-held, tangible and virtual—from which to pick and choose. There will inevitably be a sorting-out process. Few media are likely to disappear completely; rather, the idiosyncratic genius and peculiar limitations of each medium will become increasingly clear. Fewer people will write notes or letters by hand, but the elegant hand-written note to mark a special occasion will endure.

I don't worry for a nanosecond that reading and writing will disappear. 12 Even in the new digital media, it's essential to be able to read and write fluently and, if you want to capture people's attention, to write well. Of course, what it means to "write well" changes: Virginia Woolf didn't write the same way that Jane Austen did, and Arianna Huffington's blog won't be confused with Walter Lippmann's columns. But the imaginative spheres and real-world needs that all those written words address remain.

I also question the predicted disappearance of the material book. When 13 they wanted to influence opinions, both the computer giant Bill Gates and the media visionary Nicholas Negroponte wrote books (the latter in spite of his assertion that the material book was becoming anachronistic). The convenience and portability of the book aren't easily replaced, though under certain circumstances—a month-long business trip, say—the advantages of Amazon's hand-held electronic Kindle reading device trumps a suitcase full of dog-eared paperbacks.

Two aspects of the traditional book may be in jeopardy, however. One is 14 the author's capacity to lay out a complex argument, which requires the reader to study and reread, following a circuitous course of reasoning. The Web's speedy browsing may make it difficult for digital natives to master Kant's "Critique of Pure Reason" (not that it was ever easy).

15   The other is the book's special genius for allowing readers to enter a private world for hours or even days at a time. Many of us enjoyed long summer days or solitary train rides when we first discovered an author who spoke directly to us. Nowadays, as clinical psychologist Sherry Turkle has pointed out, young people seem to have a compulsion to stay in touch with one another all the time; periods of lonely silence or privacy seem toxic. If this lust for 24/7 online networking continues, one of the dividends of book reading may fade away. The wealth of different literacies and the ease of moving among them—on an iPhone, for example—may undermine the once-hallowed status of books.

16   But whatever our digital future brings, we need to overcome the perils of dualistic thinking, the notion that what lies ahead is either a utopia or a dystopia. If we're going to make sense of what's happening with literacy in our culture, we need to be able to triangulate: to bear in mind our needs and desires, the media as they once were and currently are, and the media as they're continually transforming.

17   It's not easy to do. But maybe there's a technology, just waiting to be invented, that will help us acquire this invaluable cognitive power.

QUESTIONS FOR READING

1. What is Gardner's subject?
2. Why is it controversial? State the "sides" of the issue in your own words.
3. Briefly summarize Gardner's history of language development. Why do the new digital media seem to be the most powerful change?

QUESTIONS FOR REASONING AND ANALYSIS

1. What is the author's thesis, the claim of his argument?
2. What is Gardner's attitude toward books? How does he defend the future of books? What are the threats to the traditional book?
3. Gardner refers to a number of important writers. Find a short biography of any with whom you are unfamiliar.
4. In paragraph 16, the author uses three key terms: *utopia, dystopia,* and *triangulate.* Explain his point in paragraph 16, after checking definitions of these terms as necessary.

QUESTIONS FOR REFLECTING AND WRITING

1. Why is it important to Gardner to observe that Bill Gates, to influence others, wrote a book? How does this fact advance his argument?
2. Do you agree with the author that, for today's young people, solitary time seems "toxic"? Is it toxic for you? Why or why not?

3. Many would argue that complex ideas need lengthy development in complex sentences. Will people used to Internet and PowerPoint "reading" be prepared to understand and present complex ideas? If not, how will the United States continue to lead the world in research and development? Ponder these questions and be prepared to discuss them.

WORDS OF WAR | AZAR NAFISI

Dr. Nafisi is Visiting Professor at the Foreign Policy Institute of Johns Hopkins University's School of Advanced International Studies. She taught at the University of Tehran before her expulsion for refusing to wear the traditional veil. She is best known for her widely published and highly acclaimed book *Reading Lolita in Tehran* (2004). The following *New York Times* article appeared March 27, 2003.

PREREADING QUESTIONS What does the title suggest that this essay will be about? From what you know of the author, what does the title refer to?

These days I am often asked what I did in Tehran as bombs fell during the 1 Iran-Iraq war. My interlocutors are invariably surprised, if not shocked, when I tell them that I read James, Elliot, Plath and great Persian poets like Rumi and Hafez. Yet it is precisely during such times, when our lives are transformed by violence, that we need works of imagination to confirm our faith in humanity, to find hope amid the rubble of a hopeless world. Memoirs from concentration camps and the gulag attest to this. I keep returning to the words of Leon Staff, a Polish poet who lived in the Warsaw ghetto: "Even more than bread we now need poetry, in a time when it seems that it is not needed at all."

I think back to the eight-year war with Iraq, a time when days and nights 2 seemed indistinguishable, and were reduced to the sound of the siren, warning us of the next air attack. I often reminded my students at Allameh Tabatabai University that while guns roared and the Winter Palace was stormed, Nabokov sat at his desk writing poetry.

My Tehran classroom at times overflowed with students who ignored the 3 warnings about Iraq's chemical bombs so they could reckon with Tolstoy's ability to defamiliarize (a term coined by the Russian Formalist critics) everyday reality and offer it to us through new eyes. The excitement that came from discovering a hidden truth about *Anna Karenina* told me that Iraqi missiles had not succeeded in their mission. Indeed, the more Saddam Hussein wanted us to be defined by terror, the more we craved beauty.

If I felt compelled to keep rereading the classics, it was in order to see 4 the light in the eyes of my students. I remember two young women, clad from head to toe in black chadors, looking as if nothing in the world mattered more than the idea that *Pride and Prejudice* was subversive because it taught us about our right to make our own choices.

Among my scribbled notes from those days, I found a quote from Saul 5 Bellow about writers in the Soviet work camps. To my friends in the United

States who are skeptical about the importance of imagination in times of war, let me share his words: "Perhaps to remain a poet in such circumstances is also to reach the heart of politics. The human feelings, human experiences, the human form and face, recover their proper place—the foreground."

6   And so a new war has begun, though this time it is my adopted country and not the country of my birth that is fighting Iraq. Nothing will replace the lives lost. Still, I will take some comfort now as I did then by opening a book.

QUESTIONS FOR READING

1. What is the first war referred to by the author? What current (2003) war does she refer to?
2. What did Russian writer Nabokov do during World War II?
3. What did Nafisi's chador-clad students in Tehran learn from *Pride and Prejudice*?

QUESTIONS FOR REASONING AND ANALYSIS

1. What book is Nabokov probably most famous for? Why are you not surprised by a reference to him by Nafisi? (Be sure that you can identify all authors and titles referred to by Nafisi. Google will help.)
2. Why do we need poetry and great works of fiction during times of war?
3. State Nafisi's thesis in your own words.

QUESTIONS FOR REFLECTING AND WRITING

1. Do you agree that we crave beauty? That we need imaginative literature to keep us connected to our humanity? Nafisi believes these pleasures are essential to what it means to be human. If you disagree, how would you challenge her assertions?
2. In what ways is war dehumanizing—for both soldiers and civilians? Be prepared to discuss this topic in class.

1. Bill Gates has argued that e-books will replace paper books in the not-too-distant future. What are the advantages of e-books? What are the advantages of paper books? Are there any disadvantages to either type of book? Which would you prefer? How would you argue for your preference?

2. Write a one-paragraph summary of either Howard Gardner's or Azar Nafisi's essay. Be sure that your summary clearly states the author's main idea, the claim of his or her argument. Take your time and polish your word choice.

3. Read actively and then prepare a one-and-a-half-page summary of Linda J. Waite's "Social Science Finds: 'Marriage Matters'" (pp. 494–502). Your readers want an accurate and balanced but much shorter version of the original because they will not be reading the original article. Explain not only what the writer's main ideas are but also how the writer develops her essay. That is, what kind of research supports the article's thesis? Pay close attention to your word choice.

GOING ONLINE

Azar Nafisi refers to a number of writers in her essay. Select one unfamiliar to you and see what you can learn online. Prepare a page of information to share with your class.

Responding Critically to Sources

READ: What is the situation? Who is hiding under the bed?

REASON: Whom do we expect to be under the bed? What strategy has been used?

REFLECT/WRITE: What makes this cartoon clever?

In some contexts, the word *critical* carries the idea of harsh judgment: "The manager was critical of her secretary's long phone conversations." In other contexts, though, the term means to evaluate carefully. When we speak of the critical reader or critical thinker, we have in mind someone who reads actively, who thinks about issues, and who makes informed judgments. Here is a profile of the critical reader or thinker:

TRAITS OF THE CRITICAL READER/THINKER

- **Focused on the facts.**
  Give me the facts and show me that they are relevant to the issue.
- **Analytic.**
  What strategies has the writer/speaker used to develop the argument?
- **Open-minded.**
  Prepared to listen to different points of view, to learn from others.
- **Questioning/skeptical.**
  What other conclusions could be supported by the evidence presented?
  How thorough has the writer/speaker been?
  What persuasive strategies are used?
- **Creative.**
  What are some entirely different ways of looking at the issue or problem?
- **Intellectually active, not passive.**
  Willing to analyze logic and evidence.
  Willing to consider many possibilities.
  Willing, after careful evaluation, to reach a judgment, to take a stand on issues.

EXAMINING THE RHETORICAL CONTEXT OF A SOURCE

Reading critically requires preparation. Instead of "jumping into reading," begin by asking questions about the work's rhetorical context. Rhetoric is about the *art of writing* (or *speaking*). Someone has chosen to shape a text in a particular way at this time for an imagined audience to accomplish a specific goal. The better you understand all of the decisions shaping a particular text, the better you will understand that work. And, then, the better you will be able to judge the significance of that work. So, you need, as much as possible, to answer the following five questions before reading. Then complete your answers while you read—or by doing research and thinking critically after you finish reading.

Who Is the Author?

Key questions to answer include:

- *Does the author have a reputation for honesty, thoroughness, and fairness?* Read the biographical note, if there is one. Ask your instructor about the author or learn about the author in a biographical dictionary or online. Try *Book Review Digest* (in your library or online) for reviews of the author's books.
- *Is the author writing within his or her area of expertise?* People can voice opinions on any subject, but they cannot transfer expertise from one subject area to another. A football player endorsing a political candidate is a citizen with an opinion, not an expert on politics.
- *Is the author identified with a particular group or set of beliefs? Does the biography place the writer or speaker in a particular institution or organization?* For example, a member of a Republican administration may be expected to favor a Republican president's policies. A Roman Catholic priest may be expected to take a stand against abortion. These kinds of details provide hints, but you should not decide, absolutely, what a writer's position is until you have read the work with care. Be alert to reasonable expectations but avoid stereotyping.

What Type—or Genre—of Source Is It?

Are you reading a researched and documented essay by a specialist—or the text of a speech delivered the previous week to a specific audience? Is the work an editorial—or a letter to the editor? Does the syndicated columnist (such as Dave Barry who appears later in this chapter) write humorous columns? Is the cartoon a comic strip or a political cartoon from the editorial page of a newspaper? (You will see both kinds of cartoons in this text.) Know what kind of text you are reading before you start. That's the only way to give yourself the context you need to be a good critical reader.

What Kind of Audience Does the Author Anticipate?

Understanding the intended audience helps you answer questions about the depth and sophistication of the work and a possible bias or slant.

- *Does the author expect a popular audience, a general but educated audience, or a specialist audience of shared expertise? Does the author anticipate an audience that shares cultural, political, or religious values?* Often you can judge the expected audience by noting the kind of publication in which the article appears, the publisher of the book, or the venue for the speech. For example, *Reader's Digest* is written for a mass audience, and *Psychology Today* for a general but more knowledgeable reader. By contrast, articles in the *Journal of the American Medical Association* are written by physicians and research scientists for a specialized reader. (It would be inappropriate, then, for a general reader to complain that an article in *JAMA* is not well written because it is too difficult.)

- *Does the author expect an audience favorable to his or her views? Or with a "wait and see" attitude? Or even hostile?* Some newspapers and television news organizations are consistently liberal whereas others are noticeably conservative. (Do you know the political leanings of your local paper? Of the TV news that you watch? Of the blogs you choose?) Remember: All arguments are "slanted" or "biased"—that is, they take a stand. That's as it should be. Just be sure to read or listen with an awareness of the author's particular background, interests, and possible stands on issues.

What Is the Author's Primary Purpose?

Is the work primarily informative or persuasive in intent? Designed to entertain or be inspiring? Think about the title. Read a book's preface to learn of the author's goals. Pay attention to tone as you read.

What Are the Author's Sources of Information?

Much of our judgment of an author and a work is based on the quality of the author's choice of sources. So always ask yourself: Where was the information obtained? Are sources clearly identified? Be suspicious of those who want us to believe that their unnamed "sources" are "reliable." Pay close attention to dates. A biography of King George III published in 1940 may still be the best source. An article urging more development based on county population statistics from the 1990s is no longer reliable.

> **NOTE:** None of the readings in this textbook were written for publication in this textbook. They have all come from some other context. To read them with understanding you must identify the original context and think about how that should guide your reading.

EXERCISES: Examining the Context

1. For each of the following works, comment on what you might expect to find. Consider author, occasion, audience, and reliability.
   a. An article on the Republican administration, written by a former campaign worker for a Democratic presidential candidate.
   b. A discussion, published in the Boston *Globe,* of the New England Patriots' hope for the next Super Bowl.
   c. A letter to the editor about conservation, written by a member of the Sierra Club. (What is the Sierra Club? Check out its Web site.)
   d. A column in *Newsweek* on economics. (Look at the business section of this magazine. Your library has it.)
   e. A 1988 article in *Nutrition Today* on the best diets.

    f.   A biography of Benjamin Franklin published by Oxford University Press.

    g.   A *Family Circle* article about a special vegetarian diet written by a physician. (Who is the audience for this magazine? Where is it sold?)

    h.   A *New York Times* editorial written after the Supreme Court's striking down of Washington DC's handgun restrictions.

    i.   A speech on new handgun technology delivered at a convention of the National Rifle Association.

    j.   An editorial in your local newspaper titled "Stop the Highway Killing."

2.   Analyze an issue of your favorite magazine. Look first at the editorial pages and the articles written by staff, then at articles contributed by other writers. Answer these questions for both staff writers and contributors:

    a.   Who is the audience?

    b.   What is the purpose of the articles and of the entire magazine?

    c.   What type of article dominates the issue?

3.   Select one environmental Web site and study what is offered. The EnviroLink Network (**www.envirolink.org**) will lead you to many sites. Write down the name of the site you chose and its address (URL). Then answer these questions:

    a.   Who is the intended audience?

    b.   What seems to be the primary purpose or goal of the site?

    c.   What type of material dominates the site?

    d.   For what kinds of writing assignments might you use material from the site?

ANALYZING THE STYLE OF A SOURCE

Critical readers read for implication and are alert to tone or nuance. When you read, think not only about *what* is said but also about *how* it is said. Consider the following passage:

> Bush's stupid "war"—so much for the Congress declaring war—drags on, costing unhappy taxpayers billions, while the "greatest army in the world" cannot find the real villain hiding somewhere in a cave.

This passage observes that the Iraq war continues, costing much money, while the United States still has not found the perpetrator of 9/11. But, it actually says more than that, doesn't it? Note the writer's attitude toward Bush, the war, and the U.S. military.

How can we rewrite this passage to make it more favorable? Here is one version produced by students in a group exercise:

> President Bush continues to defend the war in Iraq—which Congress never declared but continues to fund—in spite of the considerable cost to stabilize that country and the region. Meanwhile more troops will be needed to finally capture bin Laden and bring him to justice.

The writers have not changed their view that the Iraq war is costing a lot and that so far we have failed to capture bin Laden. But, in this version neither Bush nor the military is ridiculed. What is the difference in the two passages? Only the word choice.

Denotative and Connotative Word Choice

The students' ability to rewrite the passage on the war in Iraq to give it a positive attitude tells us that, although some words may have similar meanings, they cannot always be substituted for one another without changing the message. Words with similar meanings have similar *denotations.* Often, though, words with similar denotations do not have the same connotations. A word's *connotation* is what the word suggests, what we associate the word with. The words *house* and *home,* for example, both refer to a building in which people live, but the word *home* suggests ideas—and feelings—of family and security. Thus the word *home* has a strong positive connotation. *House* by contrast brings to mind a picture of a physical structure only because the word doesn't carry any "emotional baggage."

We learn the connotations of words the same way we learn their denotations—in context. Most of us, living in the same culture, share the same connotative associations of words. At times, the context in which a word is used will affect the word's connotation. For example, the word *buddy* usually has positive connotations. We may think of an old or trusted friend. But when an unfriendly person who thinks a man may have pushed in front of him says, "Better watch it, *buddy,*" the word has a negative connotation. Social, physical, and language contexts control the connotative significance of words. Become more alert to the connotative power of words by asking what words the writers could have used instead.

NOTE: Writers make choices; their choices reflect and convey their attitudes. *Studying the context in which a writer uses emotionally charged words is the only way to be sure that we understand the writer's attitude.*

EXERCISES: Connotation

1. For each of the following words or phrases, list at least two synonyms that have a more negative connotation than the given word:
   a. child
   b. persistent
   c. thin
   d. a large group
   e. scholarly
   f. trusting
   g. underachiever
   h. quiet
2. For each of the following words, list at least two synonyms that have a more positive connotation than the given word:
   a. notorious
   b. fat
   c. politician
   d. old (people)
   e. fanatic
   f. reckless
   g. sot
   h. cheap

3. Read the following paragraph and decide how the writer feels about the activity described. Note the choice of details and the connotative language that make you aware of the writer's attitude.

    Needing to complete a missed assignment for my physical education class, I dragged myself down to the tennis courts on a gloomy afternoon. My task was to serve five balls in a row into the service box. Although I thought I had learned the correct service movements, I couldn't seem to translate that knowledge into a decent serve. I tossed up the first ball, jerked back my racket, swung up on the ball—clunk—I hit the ball on the frame. I threw up the second ball, brought back my racket, swung up on the ball—ping—I made contact with the strings, but the ball dribbled down on my side of the net. I trudged around the court, collecting my tennis balls; I had only two of them.

4. Write a paragraph describing an activity that you liked or disliked without saying how you felt. From your choice of details and use of connotative language, convey your attitude toward the activity. (The paragraph in exercise 3 is your model.)

5. Select one of the words listed below and explain, in a paragraph, what the word connotes to you personally. Be precise; illustrate your thoughts with details and examples.

    a. nature   d. geek
    b. mother   e. playboy
    c. romantic   f. artist

COLLABORATIVE EXERCISES: On Connotation

1. List all of the words you know for *human female* and for *human male*. Then classify them by connotation (positive, negative, neutral) and by level of usage (formal, informal, slang). Is there any connection between type of connotation and level of usage? Why are some words more appropriate in some social contexts than in others? Can you easily list more negative words used for one sex than for the other? Why?

2. Some words can be given a different connotation in different contexts. First, for each of the following words, label its connotation as positive, negative, or neutral. Then, for each word with a positive connotation, write a sentence in which the word would convey a more negative connotation. For each word with a negative connotation, write a sentence in which the word would suggest a more positive connotation.

    a. natural   d. free
    b. old   e. chemical
    c. committed   f. lazy

3. Each of the following groups of words might appear together in a thesaurus, but the words actually vary in connotation. After looking up any words whose connotation you are unsure of, write a sentence in which each word is used

correctly. Briefly explain why one of the other words in the group should not be substituted.

a. brittle, hard, fragile
b. quiet, withdrawn, glum
c. shrewd, clever, cunning
d. strange, remarkable, bizarre
e. thrifty, miserly, economical

Tone

We can describe a writer's attitude toward the subject as positive, negative, or (rarely) neutral. Attitude is the writer's position on, or feelings about, his or her subject. The way that attitude is expressed—the voice we hear and the feelings conveyed through that voice—is the writer's *tone*. Writers can choose to express attitude through a wide variety of tones. We may reinforce a negative attitude through an angry, somber, sad, mocking, peevish, sarcastic, or scornful tone. A positive attitude may be revealed through an enthusiastic, serious, sympathetic, jovial, light, or admiring tone. We cannot be sure that just because a writer selects a light tone, for example, the attitude must be positive. Humor columnists such as Dave Barry often choose a light tone to examine serious social and political issues. Given their subjects, we recognize that the light and amusing tone actually conveys a negative attitude toward the topic.

COLLABORATIVE EXERCISES: On Tone

With your class partner or in small groups, examine the following three paragraphs, which are different responses to the same event. First, decide on each writer's attitude. Then describe, as precisely as possible, the tone of each paragraph.

1. It is tragically inexcusable that this young athlete was not examined fully before he was allowed to join the varsity team. The physical examinations given were unbelievably sloppy. What were the coach and trainer thinking of not to insist that each youngster be examined while undergoing physical stress? Apparently they were not thinking about our boys at all. We can no longer trust our sons and our daughters to this inhumane system so bent on victory that it ignores the health—indeed the very lives—of our children.

2. It was learned last night, following the death of varsity fullback Jim Bresnick, that none of the players was given a stress test as part of his physical examination. The oversight was attributed to laxness by the coach and trainer, who are described today as being "distraught." It is the judgment of many that the entire physical education program must be reexamined with an eye to the safety and health of all students.

3. How can I express the loss I feel over the death of my son? I want to blame someone, but who is to blame? The coaches, for not administering more rigorous physical checkups? Why should they have done more than other coaches have done before or than other coaches are doing at other schools? My son, for not telling me that he felt funny after practice? His teammates, for not telling

the coaches that my son said he did not feel well? Myself, for not knowing that something was wrong with my only child? Who is to blame? All of us and none of us. But placing blame will not return my son to me; I can only pray that other parents will not have to suffer so. Jimmy, we loved you.

Level of Diction

In addition to responding to a writer's choice of connotative language, observe the *level of diction* used. Are the writer's words primarily typical of conversational language or of a more formal style? Does the writer use slang words or technical words? Is the word choice concrete and vivid or abstract and intellectual? These differences help to shape tone and affect our response to what we read. Lincoln's word choice in "The Gettysburg Address" (see p. 5) is formal and abstract. Lincoln writes: "on this continent" rather than "in this land," "we take increased devotion" rather than "we become more committed." Another style, the technical, will be found in some articles in this text. The social scientist may write that "the child . . . is subjected to extremely punitive discipline," whereas a nonspecialist, more informally, might write that "the child is controlled by beatings or other forms of punishment."

One way to create an informal style is to choose simple words: *land* instead of *continent*. To create greater informality, a writer can use contractions: *we'll* for *we will.* There are no contractions in "The Gettysburg Address."

> **NOTE:** In your academic and professional writing, you should aim for a style informal enough to be inviting to readers but one that, in most cases, avoids contractions or slang words.

Sentence Structure

Attitude is conveyed and tone created primarily through word choice, but sentence structure and other rhetorical strategies are also important. Studying a writer's sentence patterns will reveal how they affect style and tone. When analyzing these features, consider the following questions:

1.   *Are the sentences generally long or short, or varied in length?*
Are the structures primarily:

- *Simple* (one independent clause)
  In 1900 empires dotted the world.
- *Compound* (two or more independent clauses)
  Women make up only 37 percent of television characters, yet women make up more than half of the population.
- *Complex* (at least one independent and one dependent clause)
  As nations grew wealthier, traditional freedom wasn't enough.

Sentences that are both long and complex create a more formal style. Compound sentences joined by *and* do not increase formality much because such sentences are really only two or more short, simple patterns hooked together. On the other hand, a long "simple" sentence with many modifiers will create a more formal style. The following example, from an essay on leadership by Michael Korda, is more complicated than the sample compound sentence above:

- *Expanded simple sentence*

  [A] leader is like a mirror, reflecting back to us our own sense of purpose, putting into words our own dreams and hopes, transforming our needs and fears into coherent policies and programs.

In "The Gettysburg Address" three sentences range from 10 to 16 words, six sentences from 21 to 29 words, and the final sentence is an incredible 82 words. All but two of Lincoln's sentences are either complex or compound-complex sentences. By contrast, in "Watch Your Language," Andrew Vachss includes a paragraph (9) with five sentences. These five sentences are composed of 6, 6, 14, 8, and 14 words. The third and fifth sentences are complex in structure—note the greater number of words as well—but the other three are all simple sentences.

2. *Does the writer use sentence fragments (incomplete sentences)?*

Although many instructors struggle to rid student writing of fragments, professional writers know that the occasional fragment can be used effectively for emphasis. Science fiction writer Bruce Sterling, thinking about the "melancholic beauty" of a gadget no longer serving any purpose, writes:

- Like Duchamp's bottle-rack, it becomes a found objet d'art. A metallic fossil of some lost human desire. A kind of involuntary poem.

The second and third sentences are, technically, fragments, but because they build on the structure of the first sentence, readers can add the missing words *It becomes* to complete each sentence. The brevity, repetition of structure, and involvement of the reader to "complete" the fragments all contribute to a strong conclusion to Sterling's paragraph.

3. *Does the writer seem to be using an overly simplistic style? If so, why?*

Overly simplistic sentence patterns, just like an overly simplistic choice of words, can be used to show that the writer thinks the subject is silly or childish or insulting. In one of her columns, Ellen Goodman objects to society's oversimplifying of addictions and its need to believe in quick and lasting cures. She makes her point with reference to two well-known examples—but notice her technique:

- Hi, my name is Jane and I was once bulimic but now I am an exercise guru . . .
- Hi, my name is Oprah and I was a food addict but now I am a size 10.

4.   *Does the writer use parallelism (coordination) or antithesis (contrast)?*

When two phrases or clauses are parallel in structure, the message is that they are equally important. Look back at Korda's expanded simple sentence. He coordinates three phrases, asserting that a leader is like a mirror in these three ways:

- Reflects back our purpose
- Puts into words our dreams
- Transforms our needs and fears

Antithesis creates tension. A sentence using this structure says "not this" but "that." Lincoln uses both parallelism and antithesis in one striking sentence:

- The world will little note nor long remember
     <u>what</u> we say here,
  but it [the world] can never forget
     <u>what</u> they did here.

Metaphors

When Korda writes that a leader is like a mirror, he is using a *simile.* When Lincoln writes that the world will not remember, he is using a *metaphor*— actually *personification.* Metaphors, whatever their form, all make a comparison between two items that are not really alike. The writer is making a *figurative comparison,* not a literal one. The writer wants us to think about some ways in which the items are similar. Metaphors state directly or imply the comparison; similes express the comparison using a connecting word; personification always compares a nonhuman item to humans. The exact label for a metaphor is not as important as:

- Recognizing the use of a figure of speech
- Identifying the two items being compared
- Understanding the point of the comparison
- Grasping the emotional impact of the figurative comparison.

REMEMBER: We need to pay attention to writers' choices of metaphors. They reveal much about their feelings and perceptions of life. And, like connotative words, they affect us emotionally even if we are not aware of their use. Become aware. Be able to "open up"—explain—metaphors you find in your reading.

EXERCISE: Opening Up Metaphors

During World War II, E. B. White, the essayist and writer of children's books, defined the word *democracy* in one of his *New Yorker* columns. His definition contains a series of metaphors. One is: Democracy "is the hole in the stuffed shirt through which the sawdust slowly trickles." We can open up or explain the metaphor this way:

> Just as one can punch a hole in a scarecrow's shirt and discover that there is only sawdust inside, nothing to be impressed by, so the idea of equality in a democracy "punches" a hole in the notion of an aristocratic ruling class and reveals that aristocrats, underneath, are ordinary people, just like you and me.

Here are two more of White's metaphors on democracy. Open up each one in a few sentences.

> Democracy is "the dent in the high hat."
> Democracy is "the score at the beginning of the ninth."

Organization and Examples

Two other elements of writing, organization and choice of examples, also reveal attitude and help to shape the reader's response. When you study a work's organization, ask yourself questions about both placement and volume. Where are these ideas placed? At the beginning or end—the places of greatest emphasis—or in the middle, suggesting that they are less important? With regard to volume, ask yourself, "What parts of the discussion are developed at length? What points are treated only briefly?" *Note:* Sometimes simply counting the number of paragraphs devoted to the different parts of the writer's subject will give you a good understanding of the writer's main idea and purpose in writing.

Repetition

Well-written, unified essays will contain some repetition of key words and phrases. Some writers go beyond this basic strategy and use repetition to produce an effective cadence, like a drum beating in the background, keeping time to the speaker's fist pounding the lectern. In his repetition of the now-famous phrase "I have a dream," Martin Luther King, Jr., gives emphasis to his vision of an ideal America (see pp. 585–588). In the following paragraph a student tried her hand at repetition to give emphasis to her definition of liberty:

> Liberty is having the right to vote and not having other laws which restrict that right; it is having the right to apply to the university of your choice without being rejected because of race. Liberty exists when a gay man has the right to a teaching position and is not released from the position when the news of his orientation is disclosed. Liberty exists when a woman who has been

offered a job does not have to decline for lack of access to day care for her children, or when a 16-year-old boy from a ghetto can get an education and is not instead compelled to go to work to support his needy family.

These examples suggest that repetition generally gives weight and seriousness to writing and thus is appropriate when serious issues are being discussed in a forceful style.

Hyperbole, Understatement, and Irony

These three strategies create some form of tension to gain emphasis. Hyperbole overstates:

- "I will love you through all eternity!"

Understatement says less than is meant:

- Coming in soaking wet, you say, "It's a bit damp outside."

Irony creates tension by stating the opposite of what is meant:

- To a teen dressed in torn jeans and a baggy sweatshirt, the parent says, "Dressed for dinner, I see."

Quotation Marks, Italics, and Capital Letters

Several visual techniques can also be used to give special attention to certain words. A writer can place a word or phrase within quotation marks to question its validity or meaning in that context. Ellen Goodman writes, for example:

- I wonder about this when I hear the word "family" added to some politician's speech.

Goodman does not agree with the politician's meaning of the word *family.* The expression *so-called* has the same effect:

- There have been restrictions on the Tibetans' so-called liberty.

Italicizing a key word or phrase or using all caps also gives additional emphasis. Dave Barry, in his essay beginning on page 45, uses all caps for emphasis:

- Do you want appliances that are smarter than you? Of course not. Your appliances should be *DUMBER* than you, just like your furniture, your pets and your representative in Congress.

Capitalizing words not normally capitalized has the same effect of giving emphasis. As with exclamation points, writers need to use these strategies sparingly, or the emphasis sought will be lost.

EXERCISES: Recognizing Elements of Style

1. Name the technique or techniques used in each of the following passages. Then briefly explain the idea of each passage.
   a. We are becoming the tools of our tools. (Henry David Thoreau)
   b. The bias and therefore the business of television is to *move* information, not collect it. (Neil Postman)
   c. If guns are outlawed, only the government will have guns. Only the police, the secret police, the military. The hired servants of our rulers. Only the government—and a few outlaws. (Edward Abbey)
   d. Having read all the advice on how to live 900 years, what I think is that eating a tasty meal once again will surely doom me long before I reach 900 while not eating that same meal could very well kill me. It's enough to make you reach for a cigarette! (Russell Baker)
   e. If you are desperate for a quick fix, either legalize drugs or repress the user. If you want a civilized approach, mount a propaganda campaign against drugs. (Charles Krauthammer)
   f. Oddly enough, the greatest scoffers at the traditions of American etiquette, who scorn the rituals of their own society as stupid and stultifying, voice respect for the customs and folklore of Native Americans, less industrialized people, and other societies they find more "authentic" than their own. (Judith Martin)
   g. Text is story. Text is event, performance, special effect. Subtext is ideas. It's motive, suggestions, visual implications, subtle comparisons. (Stephen Hunter)
   h. This flashy vehicle [the school bus] was as punctual as death: seeing us waiting at the cold curb, it would sweep to a halt, open its mouth, suck the boy in, and spring away with an angry growl. (E. B. White)
2. Read the following essay by Dave Barry. Use the questions that precede and follow the essay to help you determine Barry's attitude toward his subject and to characterize his style.

IN A BATTLE OF WITS WITH KITCHEN APPLIANCES, I'M TOAST | DAVE BARRY

A humor columnist for the *Miami Herald* since 1983, Dave Barry is now syndicated in more than 150 newspapers. A Pulitzer Prize winner in 1988, Barry has written several books, including *Dave Barry Slept Here* (1989). The following column appeared in March 2000.

PREREADING QUESTIONS What is Barry's purpose in writing? What does he want to accomplish in this column—besides being funny?

1　　Recently the *Washington Post* printed an article explaining how the appliance manufacturers plan to drive consumers insane.

2　　Of course they don't *say* they want to drive us insane. What they SAY they want to do is have us live in homes where "all appliances are on the Internet, sharing information" and appliances will be "smarter than most of their owners." For example, the article states, you could have a home where the dishwasher "can be turned on from the office" and the refrigerator "knows when it's out of milk" and the bathroom scale "transmits your weight to the gym."

3　　I frankly wonder whether the appliance manufacturers, with all due respect, have been smoking crack. I mean, did they ever stop to ask themselves WHY a consumer, after loading a dishwasher, would go to the office to start it? Would there be some kind of career benefit?

4　　YOUR BOSS: What are you doing?

5　　YOU (tapping computer keyboard): I'm starting my dishwasher!

6　　YOUR BOSS: That's the kind of productivity we need around here!

7　　YOU: Now I'm flushing the upstairs toilet!

8　　Listen, appliance manufacturers: We don't NEED a dishwasher that we can communicate with from afar. If you want to improve our dishwashers, give us one that senses when people leave dirty dishes on the kitchen counter, and shouts at them: "PUT THOSE DISHES IN THE DISHWASHER RIGHT NOW OR I'LL LEAK ALL OVER YOUR SHOES!"

9　　Likewise, we don't need a refrigerator that knows when it's out of milk. We already have a foolproof system for determining if we're out of milk: We ask our wives. What we could use is a refrigerator that refuses to let us open its door when it senses that we are about to consume our fourth Jell-O Pudding Snack in two hours.

10　　As for a scale that transmits our weight to the gym: Are they NUTS? We don't want our weight transmitted to our own EYEBALLS! What if the gym decided to transmit our weight to all these other appliances on the Internet? What if, God forbid, our refrigerator found out what our weight was? We'd never get the door open again!

11　　But here is what really concerns me about these new "smart" appliances: Even if we like the features, we won't be able to use them. We can't use the appliance features we have NOW. I have a feature-packed telephone with 43 buttons, at least 20 of which I am afraid to touch. This phone probably can communicate with the dead, but I don't know how to operate it, just as I don't know how to operate my TV, which has features out the wazooty and requires THREE remote controls. One control (44 buttons) came with the TV; a second (39 buttons) came with the VCR; the third (37 buttons) was brought here by the cable man, who apparently felt that I did not have enough buttons.

12　　So when I want to watch TV, I'm confronted with a total of 120 buttons, identified by such helpful labels as PIP, MTS, DBS, F2, JUMP and BLANK. There are three buttons labeled POWER but there are times—especially if my son and his friends, who are not afraid of features, have changed the settings—when I honestly cannot figure out how to turn the TV on. I stand there, holding three remote controls, pressing buttons at random, until eventually I give up and go turn on the dishwasher. It has been, literally, years since I have successfully recorded a TV show. That is how "smart" my appliances have become.

And now the appliance manufacturers want to give us even MORE fea- 13 tures. Do you know what this means? It means that some night you'll open the door of your "smart" refrigerator, looking for a beer, and you'll hear a pleasant, cheerful voice—recorded by the same woman who informs you that Your Call Is Important when you call a business that does not wish to speak with you personally—telling you: "Your celery is limp." You will not know how your refrigerator knows this, and, what is worse, you will not know who else your refrigerator is telling about it ("Hey, Bob! I hear your celery is limp!"). And if you want to try to make the refrigerator STOP, you'll have to decipher Owner's Manual instructions written by and for nuclear physicists ("To disable the Produce Crispness Monitoring feature, enter the Command Mode, then select the Edit function, then select Change Vegetable Defaults, then assume that Train A leaves Chicago traveling westbound at 47 mph, while Train B . . .").

Is this the kind of future you want, consumers? Do you want appliances 14 that are smarter than you? Of course not. Your appliances should be DUMBER than you, just like your furniture, your pets and your representatives in Congress. So I am urging you to let the appliance industry know, by phone, letter, fax and e-mail, that when it comes to "smart" appliances, you vote NO. You need to act quickly. Because while you're reading this, your microwave oven is voting YES.

QUESTIONS FOR READING AND REASONING

1. After thinking about Barry's subject and purpose, what do you conclude to be his thesis? Does he have more than one main idea?

2. How would you describe the essay's tone? Serious? Humorous? Ironic? Angry? Something else? Does a nonserious tone exclude the possibility of a degree of serious purpose? Explain your answer.

QUESTIONS FOR REFLECTING AND WRITING

1. What passages in the article do you find funniest? Why?

2. What strategies does Barry use to create tone and convey attitude? List, with examples, as many as you can.

WRITING ABOUT STYLE

What does it mean to "do a style analysis"? A style analysis answers the question "How is it written?" Let's think through the steps in preparing a study of a writer's choice and arrangement of language.

Understanding Purpose and Audience

A style analysis is not the place for challenging the ideas of the writer. A style analysis requires the discipline to see how a work has been put together *even if you disagree with the writer's views.* You do not have to agree with a writer to appreciate his or her skill in writing.

If you think about audience in the context of your purpose, you should conclude that a summary of content does not belong in a style analysis. Why? Because we write style analyses for people who have already read the work. Remember, though, that your reader may not know the work in detail, so you will need to give examples to illustrate the points of your analysis.

Planning the Essay

First, organize your analysis according to elements of style, not according to the organization of the work. Scrap any thoughts of "hacking" your way through the essay, commenting on the work paragraph by paragraph. This approach invites summary and means that you have not selected an organization that supports your purpose in writing. Think of an essay as like the pie in Figure 2.1. We could divide the pie according to key ideas—if we were summarizing. But we can also carve the pie according to elements of style, the techniques we have discussed in this chapter. This is the general plan you want to follow for your essay.

Choose those techniques you think are most important in creating the writer's attitude and discuss them one at a time. Do not try to include the entire pie; instead, select three or four elements to examine in some detail. If you were asked to write an analysis of the Dave Barry column, for example, you might select his use of quotation marks, hyperbole, and irony. These are three techniques that stand out in Barry's writing.

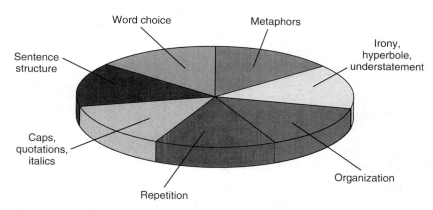

FIGURE 2.1 Analyzing Style

Drafting the Style Analysis

If you were to select three elements of style, as in the Dave Barry example above, your essay might look something like this:

Paragraph 1: Introduction	1. Attention-getter 2. Author, title, publication information of article/book 3. Brief explanation of author's subject 4. Your thesis—that you will be looking at style
Paragraph 2: First body paragraph	Analysis of quotation marks. (See below for more details on body paragraphs.)
Paragraph 3: Second body paragraph	1. Topic sentence that introduces analysis of hyperbole 2. Three or more examples of hyperbole 3. Explanation of how each example connects to the author's thesis—that is, how the example of hyperbole works to convey attitude. This is your analysis; don't forget it!
Paragraph 4: Third body paragraph	Analysis of irony—with same three parts as listed above.
Paragraph 5: Conclusion	Restate your thesis: We can understand Barry's point through a study of these three elements of his style.

A CHECKLIST FOR REVISION ■·■

When revising and polishing your draft, use these questions to complete your essay.

☐ Have I handled all titles correctly?

☐ Have I correctly referred to the author?

☐ Have I used quotation marks correctly when presenting examples of style? (Use the guidelines in Chapter 1 for these first three questions.)

☐ Do I have an accurate, clear presentation of the author's subject and thesis?

☐ Do I have enough examples of each element of style to show my readers that these elements are important?

☐ Have I connected examples to the author's thesis? That is, have I shown my readers how these techniques work to develop the author's attitude?

To reinforce your understanding of style analysis, read the following essay by Ellen Goodman, answer the questions that follow, and then study the student essay that analyzes Goodman's style.

IN PRAISE OF A SNAIL'S PACE | ELLEN GOODMAN

Author of *Close to Home* (1979), *At Large* (1981), and *Keeping Touch* (1985), collections of her essays, Ellen Goodman has been a feature writer for the Boston *Globe* since 1967 and a syndicated columnist since 1976. The following column was published August 13, 2005.

PREREADING QUESTIONS Why might someone write in praise of snail mail? What does Goodman mean by "hyperactive technology"?

1   CASCO BAY, Maine—I arrive at the island post office carrying an artifact from another age. It's a square envelope, handwritten, with a return address that can be found on a map. Inside is a condolence note, a few words of memory and sympathy to a wife who has become a widow. I could have sent these words far more efficiently through e-mail than through this "snail mail." But I am among those who still believe that sympathy is diluted by two-thirds when it arrives over the Internet transom.

2   I would no more send an e-condolence than an e-thank you or an e-wedding invitation. There are rituals you cannot speed up without destroying them. It would be like serving Thanksgiving dinner at a fast-food restaurant.

3   My note goes into the old blue mailbox and I walk home wondering if slowness isn't the only way we pay attention now in a world of hyperactive technology.

4   Weeks ago, a friend lamented the trouble she had communicating with her grown son. It wasn't that her son was out of touch. Hardly. They were connected across miles through e-mail and cell phone, instant-messaging and text-messaging. But she had something serious to say and feared that an e-mail would elicit a reply that said: I M GR8. Was there no way to get undivided attention in the full in-box of his life? She finally chose a letter, a pen on paper, a stamp on envelope.

5   How do you describe the times we live in, so connected and yet fractured? Linda Stone, a former Microsoft techie, characterizes ours as an era of "continuous partial attention." At the extreme end are teenagers instant-messaging while they are talking on the cell phone, downloading music and doing

homework. But adults too live with all systems go, interrupted and distracted, scanning everything, multi-technological-tasking everywhere.

We suffer from the illusion, Stone says, that we can expand our personal 6 bandwidth, connecting to more and more. Instead, we end up overstimulated, overwhelmed and, she adds, unfulfilled. Continuous partial attention inevitably feels like a lack of full attention.

But there are signs of people searching for ways to slow down and listen 7 up. We are told that experienced e-mail users are taking longer to answer, freeing themselves from the tyranny of the reply button. Caller ID is used to find out who we don't have to talk to. And the next "killer ap," they say, will be e-mail software that can triage the important from the trivial.

Meanwhile, at companies where technology interrupts creativity and 8 online contact prevents face-to-face contact, there are no e-mail-free Fridays. At others, there are bosses who require that you check your BlackBerry at the meeting door.

If a ringing cell phone once signaled your importance to a client, now that 9 client is impressed when you turn off the cell phone. People who stayed connected 10 ways, 24-7, now pride themselves on "going dark."

10   "People hunger for more attention," says Stone, whose message has been welcomed even at a conference of bloggers. "Full attention will be the aphrodisiac of the future."

11   Indeed, at the height of our romance with e-mail, "You've Got Mail" was the cinematic love story. Now e-mail brings less thrill—"who will be there?" And more dread—"how many are out there?" Today's romantics are couples who leave their laptops behind on the honeymoon.

12   As for text-message flirtation, a young woman ended hers with a man who wrote, "C U L8R." He didn't have enough time to spell out Y-O-U?

13   Slowness guru Carl Honore began "In Praise of Slowness" after he found himself seduced by a book of condensed classic fairy tales to read to his son. One-minute bedtime stories? We are relearning that paying attention briefly is as impossible as painting a landscape from a speeding car.

14   It is not just my trip to the mailbox that has brought this to mind. I come here each summer to stop hurrying. My island is no Brigadoon: WiFi is on the way, and some people roam the island with their cell phones, looking for a hot spot. But I exchange the Internet for the country road.

15   Georgia O'Keeffe once said that it takes a long time to see a flower. No technology can rush the growth of the leeks in the garden. All the speed in the Internet cannot hurry the healing of a friend's loss. Paying attention is the coin of this realm.

16   Sometimes, a letter becomes the icon of an old-fashioned new fashion. And sometimes, in this technological whirlwind, it takes a piece of snail mail to carry the stamp of authenticity.

QUESTIONS FOR READING AND REASONING

1. What has Goodman just done? How does this action serve the author as a lead-in to her subject?

2. What is Goodman's main idea or thesis?

3. What examples illustrate the problem the author sees in our times? What evidence does Goodman present to suggest that people want to change the times?

4. What general solutions does Goodman suggest?

QUESTIONS FOR REFLECTING AND WRITING

1. How do the details at the beginning and end of the essay contribute to Goodman's point? Write a paragraph answer to this question. Then consider: Which one of the different responses to reading does your paragraph illustrate?

2. The author describes our time as one of "continuous partial attention." Does this phrase sum up our era? Why or why not? If you agree, do you think this is a problem? Why or why not?

3. For what kinds of research projects would this essay be useful? List several possibilities to discuss with classmates.

STUDENT ESSAY

A Convincing Style

James Goode

Ellen Goodman's essay, "In Praise of a Snail's Pace," is not, of course, about snails. It is about a way of communicating that our society has largely lost or ignored: the capability to pay full attention in communications and relationships. Her prime example of this is the "snail mail" letter, used for cards, invitations, and condolences. Anything really worth saying, she argues, must be written fully and sent by mail to make us pay attention. Goodman's easy, winning style of word choice and metaphor persuades us to agree with her point, a point also backed up by the logic of her examples.

"In Praise of a Snail's Pace" starts innocently. The author is merely taking a walk to the post office with a letter, surely nothing unusual. But as Goodman describes her letter, she reveals her belief that "snail mail" is a much more authentic way of sharing serious tidings than a message that "arrives over the Internet transom." The letter, with its "square" envelope and "handwritten" address, immediately sounds more personal than the ultramodern electronic message. The words have guided the reader's thinking. Goodman also describes our times as "connected yet fractured" and us as living in a world of "continuous partial attention." "Being connected" becomes synonymous by the end of the essay with "not paying attention." Word choice is crucial here. The author creates in the reader's mind a dichotomy: be fast and false, or slow down and mean it.

Goodman's metaphors make a point, too. "A picture is worth a thousand words" and the pictures created by the words here further the fast/slow debate. The idea that sending an e-condolence would be "like serving Thanksgiving dinner at a fast food restaurant" gives an instant image of the worthlessness of an email condolence note. The mother trying to get attention in the "full in-box" of her son's life shows us that a divided and distracted brain answering five hundred e-mails cannot be expected to concentrate on any of them. Again, trying to pay attention briefly is just as impossible as "painting a landscape from a speeding car." The "tyranny" of the reply button must be overcome by our "going dark." Getting away from our electronic world, Goodman reasons, helps us restore meaning to what we do.

But while the reader listens to clever words and paints memorable mind pictures, any resistance is worn away with a steady stream of examples. From the author mailing an envelope to Georgia O'Keefe's remark that it takes a long time to see a flower, example after example supports her view. The mother wishing for the total attention of her son and the office workers' turning off cell phones and computers have already been mentioned. Linda Stone, a former Microsoft techie and a credible authority on modern communications and their effects on users, is quoted several times. Goodman notes with excellent effect that Stone's message has been received even at a conference of bloggers—if the most connected group out there supports this, why shouldn't everyone else? The author herself comes to an island every year to escape the mad hurry of the business world by wandering country roads. These examples build until the reader is convinced that snail mail is the mark of authenticity and connectedness.

"In Praise of a Snail's Pace" is a thoughtful essay that takes aim at the notion that one person can do it all and still find meaning. The "connected" person is in so much of a hurry that he or she must not be really interested in much of anything. By showing "interrupted and distracted" readers that "no technology can rush the growth of leeks in the garden," the author makes a convincing case for the real effectiveness of written mail. Whether through word choice, metaphor, or example, Ellen Goodman's message comes through: Slow down and send some "snail mail" and be really connected for once.

ANALYZING TWO OR MORE SOURCES

Scientists examining the same set of facts do not always draw the same conclusions; neither do historians and biographers agree on the significance of the same documents. How do we recognize and cope with these disparities? As critical readers we analyze what we read, pose questions, and refuse to believe everything we find in print or online. To develop these skills in recognizing differences, instructors frequently ask students to contrast the views of two or more writers. In psychology class, for example, you may be asked to contrast the views of Sigmund Freud and John B. Watson on child development. In a communications course, you may be asked to contrast the moderator styles of two talk-show hosts. We can examine differences in content or presentation, or both. Here are guidelines for preparing a contrast of sources.

GUIDELINES for Preparing a Contrast Essay

- **Work with sources that have something in common.** Think about the context for each, that is, each source's subject and purpose. (It would not make much sense to contrast a textbook chapter, for example, with a TV talk show because their contexts are so different.)

- **Read actively to understand the content of the two sources.** Tape films, radio, or TV shows so that you can listen/view them several times, just as you would read a written source more than once.

- **Analyze for differences, focusing on your purpose in contrasting.** If you are contrasting the ideas of two writers, for example, then your analysis will focus on ideas, not on writing style. To explore differences in two news accounts, you may want to consider all of the following: the impact of placement in the newspaper/magazine, accompanying photographs or graphics, length of each article, what is covered in each article, and writing styles. Prepare a list of specific differences.

- **Organize your contrast.** It is usually best to organize by points of difference. If you write first about one source and then about the other, the ways that the sources differ may not be clear for readers. Take the time to plan an organization that clearly reveals your contrast purpose in writing. To illustrate, a paper contrasting the writing styles of two authors can be organized according to the following pattern:

  Introduction: Introduce your topic and establish your purpose to contrast styles of writer A and writer B.

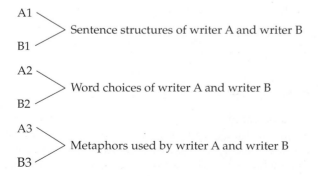

  Conclusion: Explain the effect of the differences in style of the writers.

- **Illustrate and discuss each of the points of difference for each of the sources.** Provide examples and explain the impact of the differences.
- **Always write for an audience who may be familiar with your general topic but not with the specific sources you are discussing.** Be sure to provide adequate context (names, titles of works, etc.).

EXERCISE: Analyzing Two Sources

Whenever two people choose to write on the same topic, there are bound to be differences in choice of specifics and emphasis—and that's before there are differences in philosophy and political or social perspective. Therefore, when we are seeking information and analysis of a subject, we are wise to read widely—not to settle for only one source for our information. And when reading newspapers, newsmagazines, and journals of opinion (and blogs online), we need to be aware of the "leaning" of each source and alert to clues to the writer's (or the periodical's) political perspective.

Read the following two articles on the subject of offshore oil drilling, an issue heavily debated in 2008 as a result of higher gasoline prices. Analyze each article on the following points of possible difference: length of treatment, differences in key points about the drilling, differences in how the issue is framed—in the context provided—and differences in style and tone. Then answer the questions: Is one author/periodical more favorable to drilling than the other? If so, how do you know?

Bring detailed notes to class for discussion of the two sources, or write an analysis that contrasts the two articles on three or four points of difference.

EYEING THE OIL UNDER THE GULF; AMID THE DEBATE OVER OFFSHORE DRILLING, A REALITY CHECK

KENT GARBER

This article appeared on August 18, 2008, in *U.S. News & World Report*.

1   At the Royal Sonesta Hotel in downtown New Orleans later this month, the U.S. government is offering for lease, as part of a regularly scheduled sale, 18 million acres in the Gulf of Mexico that are open for oil and natural gas drilling. The tracts could potentially yield as much as 400 million barrels of oil. The lease auction is just one example of how much oil exploration is currently occurring in the Gulf of Mexico. But the sale also reveals the limits of new drilling, as 400 million barrels is barely enough to meet the nation's oil needs for 19 days.

2   Listening to the debate swirling in Washington over offshore oil, however, it would be easy to conclude that nothing much is happening in the Gulf of Mexico today. GOP lawmakers, engaging in some old-fashioned political theater during the first part of Congress's August recess, occupied the dimmed Capitol to call for an end to the congressional moratorium on opening up new coastal areas to drilling and to decry Democratic opposition to the idea.

Republican presidential candidate John McCain has been trumpeting the cause almost daily on the campaign trail. And even presumptive Democratic nominee Barack Obama, as part of his new energy plan, has modified his earlier opposition to expanded drilling.

Their motivation is simple. Two thirds of Americans say they favor more 3 drilling, mainly out of hope that gas prices will fall as a result.

But in reality, the country's oil situation is far more complex and dynamic 4 than the Washington debate lets on. New drilling activities, either planned or already underway, are being largely overlooked. At the same time, there are major obstacles to boosting production in a timely and sizable manner, particularly shortages of complex drilling equipment. Perhaps most important, the Department of Energy estimates that, even if Congress removed all restrictions on offshore drilling, the impact on global oil prices would be "insignificant."

Bidding war. Today, the Gulf of Mexico, which produces more than a quar- 5 ter of the country's domestic crude oil, is actually in the midst of a resurgence. New technology is allowing companies to push farther into deeper water, and oil production there is up.

A bidding war for rights to millions of acres in the Gulf is quietly building. 6 In 2007, the number of leases issued to oil companies there jumped by about 25 percent, and the average bid price for a single tract has soared this year by 50 percent to nearly $6 million, according to GOMExplorer, which gathers data on the Gulf's oil and gas industry.

This is partly a matter of timing. Earlier this decade, many oil companies let 7 leases idle because the price of oil was too low to make a profit or they were pursuing other projects. Some unused leases terminate after 10 years, and in the past two years, many expired leases became available again. Another factor is the expansion of deep-water drilling, which has become more profitable with new technology and rising oil prices. A government report, released in May, found that 72 percent of oil production in the Gulf of Mexico in 2007 came from deep-water drilling, and the number of deep-water projects has doubled since 2002.

Despite all this activity, oil experts say the fruits of these projects won't 8 come close to reversing the downward spiral in U.S. oil production. Fields have aged, and many reserves have been depleted. These trends have prompted oil executives to push for opening up more land. "What you have is a scarcity of resources," says Dory Stiles, investor relations manager for Murphy Oil Corp., an oil and gas exploration firm. "Companies are looking for more opportunities to explore."

Yet even if Congress opens up the 574 million acres now off limits along 9 the outer continental shelf, tight supplies of equipment and labor will severely constrain exploration in the next decade. Only a limited number of shipyards are capable of building the necessary $700 million drilling rig, and many of the rigs being built today are going to Brazil, West Africa, and Southeast Asia, where the oil business is also booming. Even then, it usually takes at least seven to 10 years for the oil to start flowing.

NATIONAL DEBATE: WEIGHING ADVANCES VS. FEARS

BOB KEEFE

This article on offshore oil drilling was published on August 2, 2008, in the Atlanta Journal-Constitution.

1   Santa Barbara, Calif.—What sticks in Charlie Eckberg's mind about that horrible January of 1969 was how the mighty Pacific went silent.

2   Oil from a blowout under a drilling platform six miles offshore made the water so thick and heavy that the crashing surf Eckberg was used to hearing at his beachfront home was eerily quieted, like a fallen giant.

3   "And then you started to see the animals," he recalled.

4   First were birds, too many to count, Eckberg said. Then came the oil-coated seals and otters and other sea life.

5   "It changed my life," he said of the sight.

6   Today, Eckberg can't look at the oil platforms still dotting the sea off Santa Barbara without disdain. Now 60, he has become an environmental activist, an eco-friendly real estate developer and director of a group called Get Oil Out.

7   But government and oil industry officials say the fears that drive Eckberg and others to oppose offshore drilling are misplaced. Almost 40 years after the blowout at Union Oil Co.'s Platform A resulted in the nation's most environmentally damaging drilling accident, they say new offshore technologies and techniques make it almost impossible for a similar disaster to occur.

8   That's a point President Bush has pushed repeatedly as he lifted an executive order banning new offshore oil exploration. He is asking Congress to lift its ban.

9   This week, the Interior Department took steps to jump-start new offshore oil exploration, announcing plans for a lease program that could open up new areas off the coasts of several states, including Georgia, to drilling if Congress lifts the ban. On Friday, the department will begin taking public and industry comment on the plan.

10   "The technology has improved, the safety systems we now require have greatly improved, and the [industry] has a good record," said Randall Luthi, director of the department's Minerals Management Service, which handles offshore oil field regulations and leases.

11   Luthi and others said new tools that make offshore drilling safer include:

- Seismic technology and directional drilling techniques that let oil companies drill 100 exploratory wells from a single offshore platform. That reduces the number of derricks and therefore the potential for problems, they say.

- Automatic shutoff valves underneath the seabed that can cut the flow of oil immediately if there's a problem or a storm coming. Blowout prevention equipment can automatically seal off pipes in the case of an unexpected pressure buildup.

- Undersea pipelines and wellheads that can be monitored with special equipment such as unmanned, camera-equipped underwater vehicles and sensor-equipped devices called "smart pigs." The devices move through pipelines and can detect weak spots and blockages.

- Advances in metallurgy and construction techniques that have made platforms stronger and more likely to withstand hurricanes and other calamities.

"Any human endeavor has some level of risk," said Dave Mica, director 12 of the Florida Petroleum Council, which is pushing for drilling off the Florida coast. "We can't eliminate all of it, but we're trying."

Interior Secretary Dirk Kempthorne said hurricanes Katrina and Rita pro- 13 vided the ultimate test of modern-day drilling operations. About 3,000 of the 4,000 oil platforms currently in the Gulf of Mexico were in the direct path of the two hurricanes in 2005, yet there were no major spills, he said.

"The shutoff valves below the ocean floor, all of them worked," Kemp- 14 thorne said. "There was no significant loss of oil."

With polls showing most Americans back new offshore drilling, many poli- 15 ticians are on board.

In Florida, longtime drilling opponent Gov. Charlie Crist last month abruptly 16 changed his position, saying offshore drilling is safe and that Floridians need relief from high-energy prices—even though any new drilling wouldn't result in oil for years, if not decades. Crist is a potential running mate for presidential candidate John McCain, who also favors increased offshore drilling.

Georgia Gov. Sonny Perdue also has said he backs offshore drilling, as 17 have 12 of Georgia's 15 representatives and senators.

"This is exactly what our nation needs right now," Rep. Jack Kingston, a 18 Savannah Republican, said in a statement following Bush's lifting of the executive ban. "Domestic exploration is step one."

Still, spills occur. Last year alone, according to the Interior Department's 19 Minerals Management Service, about 2,225 barrels of oil were spilled in coastal waters because of mishaps involving offshore rigs. Even though the Interior Department and others did not deem them major spills, more than 16,280 barrels of oil were spilled in 2005, the year Hurricanes Katrina and Rita hit.

Just last week near New Orleans, a spill occurred in the Mississippi River 20 after a tanker ship hit a barge carrying 419,000 gallons of oil.

Given that many existing oil platforms and other equipment are decades 21 old, it's surprising there haven't been more spills, said Bruce Bullock, director of the Maguire Energy Institute at Southern Methodist University in Dallas.

Bullock, who worked for an offshore oil services company for 25 years 22 before joining academia, also cautioned that offshore drilling and well management operations are only part of the equation. The nation's worst oil spill involved a tanker—the Exxon Valdez—not an offshore platform.

"Let's say you're talking about offshore Florida," Bullock said. "In reality, 23 there's probably more risk of an incident from a tanker going down the coast to get into the Gulf or vice versa than there is putting a well in 1,000 feet of water."

24   And improvements in technology or not, offshore drilling is still plenty risky, opponents say.

25   "Even if they aren't spewing out of their rigs, the entire process is incredibly dirty," said Jennette Gayer, policy advocate for the group Environment Georgia. "There's no way you can tell me it won't have an impact on our coast—and our coast in Georgia is incredibly valuable."

26   In Santa Barbara, Eckberg said technological improvements in drilling aren't what matters in a world struggling with global warming, high-energy prices, hostile foreign suppliers and other oil-related problems.

27   "It's not about whether it's safe to drill again or not," Eckberg said. "It's about whether it's safe for mankind to use this product or not."

MAKING OFFSHORE DRILLING SAFER

Government and oil industry officials point to several innovations they say make offshore oil drilling a much less risky proposition than it once was. Among them:

"Smart pigs"

The sensor-equipped devices can travel through pipelines and identify weak spots and blockages before they result in blowouts.

Blowout preventers

Large valves atop oil wells, often computer-controlled, that can be quickly closed when well pressure surpasses a safe level.

Ocean engineering rovers

Remote-controlled, camera-equipped small submarines that can be used to inspect drilling equipment deep beneath the ocean's surface.

Double-hulled tankers

Now the industry standard, double hulls provide an extra layer of protection against hull piercings caused by groundings and collisions.

FOR READING AND ANALYSIS

Now read and analyze the following two essays to prepare yourself for discussion.

WATCH YOUR LANGUAGE | ANDREW VACHSS

Andrew Vachss is an attorney whose only clients are children. He also writes mystery novels and maintains a dramatic and useful Web site. The following article, with the subtitle lead: "If you want to fight against the abuse of children," originally appeared in *Parade* magazine, June 5, 2005.

PREREADING QUESTIONS Based on the title and subtitle lead-in and what you know about the author, what do you expect this essay to be about? How important is the language we use to label or "name" an action?

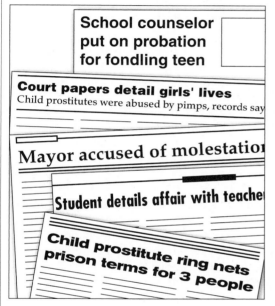

School counselor put on probation for fondling teen

Court papers detail girls' lives
Child prostitutes were abused by pimps, records say

Mayor accused of molestatio

Student details affair with teache

Child prostitute ring nets prison terms for 3 people

Years ago, I participated in the rescue of a child from bondage. Destiny (not her real name) was 13. She had been repeatedly raped by a pair of predators to "educate" her. Then, along with several other young girls, she was forced to sell herself to strangers. Each day, she woke to the threat of disfiguring brutality if she failed to bring in sufficient money that night. Later, it was reported that "pimps" had been arrested, and "a number of child prostitutes were taken into custody." 1

What was wrong with calling Destiny a "child prostitute"? After all, she was a child, and she was engaged in prostitution. 2
First, the word itself implies a judgment of character. Don't we call people who sell out their moral convictions in exchange for personal gain "whores"? More important, prostitution implies a *willing* exchange. Ultimately, the term "child prostitution" implies that little children are "seductive," that they "volunteer" to have sex with adults in exchange for cash (which, of course, the children never see).

The difference between calling Destiny a "child prostitute" and a "prostituted child" is not purely semantic. It is more than the difference between a hard truth and a pernicious lie. It not only injures the victims; it actively gives aid and comfort to the enemy. By allowing the term "child prostitution" to gain a foothold in our language, we lose ground that can never be recovered. Look at the following examples: 3

- A judge spares a predatory pedophile a long prison sentence on the grounds that "it takes two to tango." Another grants work-release to a sex offender, declaring that the 5-year-old victim was "unusually promiscuous."

- A teacher is arrested for sexual intercourse with a minor student in her class. The newspapers describe the conduct as "a forbidden love affair."
- A young actor, in an interview given before his drug-overdose death, describes how he "lost his virginity" when he was 3 or 4 years old.

4   How have such grotesque distortions taken control of our language? To answer that question, we must first ask another: Who profits? Who benefits from pervasive cultural language that trivializes violence against children?

5   Pedophiles are very familiar with the power of language. They would have us believe that child pornography is a free-speech issue. They know that if they succeed in placing "child prostitution" anywhere on the continuum of voluntary sexual activity, they will have established a beachhead from which to launch future assaults.

6   We must understand that such language is no accident—it is the deliberate product of cultural lobbyists. There is a carefully orchestrated campaign to warp public perception, a perception that affects everything from newspaper coverage to legislation and even jury verdicts.

7   If they can get us to accept that children consent to sex for money, it will be easier to sell the idea that they can consent to sex for "love." But an adult male who sexually abuses little boys is no more "homosexual" than one who victimizes little girls is "heterosexual." They are both predatory pedophiles. There is no such thing as a child prostitute; there are only prostituted children.

8   When we use terms such as "lose one's virginity" in referring to adult sex acts with children instead of calling it "rape," or when we say that teachers "have affairs" with their pupils instead of saying that the teachers sexually exploit them, the only beneficiaries are the predators who target children.

9   This is not about political correctness. It is about telling the truth. In any culture, language is the undercurrent that drives the river of public perception. That undercurrent has been polluted for too long. If we really want to protect our children, it's time to watch our language.

WHAT WORDS REALLY SAY

When it comes to child abuse, the language we use can distort the reality of the crime and create a roadblock to justice. The next time you hear a news report, keep in mind what the following terms actually mean . . . and the consequences of the conduct described.

PEDOPHILE

An individual with intense, recurrent sexually arousing fantasies and urges toward prepubescent children. Those who decide to act on such feelings can be termed "predatory pedophiles." The predatory pedophile is as dangerous as cancer and as camouflaged in approach. His presence becomes known only by the horrendous damage left in his wake. Predatory pedophiles most often operate inside a child's "circle of trust." He (or she) may be a teacher, a doctor, a scout leader, a police officer, an athletic coach, a religious counselor, or a child-care professional. They are protected not only by our ignorance of their presence but also by our unwillingness to confront the truth.

FONDLING

Nonpenetrative sexual misconduct with a child, often resulting in severe emotional damage to the victim.

MOLESTATION

Sexual assault of a child, often resulting in both physical and emotional damage.

NONVIOLENT INCEST

The rape by extortion of a child by a family member, creating a climate of oppression and fear in the child's daily life that inevitably results in profound long-term damage.

INTERGENERATIONAL LOVE

The sexual exploitation of a child under the guise of a consensual relationship. This pedophiles' perversion of the word "love" is routinely promoted in all their literature as "harmless" or even "beneficial" to the victim.

CHILD PROSTITUTE

A child, often held captive against his or her will, who is physically and/or emotionally coerced into performing sex acts with adults for the profit of others.

QUESTIONS FOR READING

1. What is Vachss's topic? (Be more precise than "language use.")
2. Explain the author's definition of "child prostitute." Why is this label inappropriate for Destiny, in the author's view?
3. What does Vachss mean by the label "predatory pedophiles"?
4. Who gains from the distorted language shown in the box? What do they gain?

QUESTIONS FOR REASONING AND ANALYSIS

1. What is Vachss's thesis? Where does he state it?
2. Analyze the author's word choice, examples, and metaphors. How do these strategies contribute to Vachss's argument?
3. How would you characterize the essay's tone? How is the tone created?

QUESTIONS FOR REFLECTING AND WRITING

1. How did you answer the second prereading question? After reading Vachss's essay, do you think that you should answer the question differently? Why or why not?
2. Do you agree with the author that our language does distort the truth, putting children at risk? Why or why not?
3. What, if anything, do you want the courts to do with predatory pedophiles? With online child pornography? Why?

A HANGING | GEORGE ORWELL

George Orwell (1903–1950), the pseudonym of Eric Arthur Blair, was a British essayist and novelist best known for his political satires *Animal Farm* (1945) and *1984* (1949). He is also well known for his essay "Politics and the English Language," the essay that set the standard for the analysis of doublespeak in political language. In the following essay, published in *Shooting an Elephant and Other Essays* (1950), Orwell captures the telling details of a brief scene he witnessed.

PREREADING QUESTIONS Why might a writer choose to tell the story of a hanging? What kinds of issues might emerge from such a story?

1   It was in Burma, a sodden morning of the rains. A sickly light, like yellow tinfoil, was slanting over the high walls into the jail yard. We were waiting outside the condemned cells, a row of sheds fronted with double bars, like small animal cages. Each cell measured about ten feet by ten and was quite bare within except for a plank bed and a pot of drinking water. In some of them brown silent men were squatting at the inner bars, with their blankets draped round them. These were the condemned men, due to be hanged within the next week or two.

2   One prisoner had been brought out of his cell. He was a Hindu, a puny wisp of a man, with a shaven head and vague liquid eyes. He had a thick, sprouting moustache, absurdly too big for his body, rather like a moustache of a comic man on the films. Six tall Indian warders were guarding him and getting him ready for the gallows. Two of them stood by with rifles and fixed bayonets, while the others handcuffed him, passed a chain through his handcuffs and fixed it to their belts, and lashed his arms tight to his sides. They crowded very close about him, with their hands always on him in a careful, caressing grip, as though all the while feeling him to make sure he was there. It was like

men handling a fish which is still alive and may jump back into the water. But he stood quite unresisting, yielding his arms limply to the ropes, as though he hardly noticed what was happening.

Eight o'clock struck and a bugle call, desolately thin in the wet air, floated 3 from the distant barracks. The superintendent of the jail, who was standing apart from the rest of us, moodily prodding the gravel with his stick, raised his head at the sound. He was an army doctor, with a grey toothbrush moustache and a gruff voice. "For God's sake hurry up, Francis," he said irritably. "The man ought to have been dead by this time. Aren't you ready yet?"

Francis, the head jailer, a fat Dravidian in a white drill suit and gold specta- 4 cles, waved his black hand. "Yes sir, yes sir," he bubbled. "All iss satisfactorily prepared. The hangman iss waiting. We shall proceed."

"Well, quick march, then. The prisoners can't get their breakfast till this 5 job's over."

We set out for the gallows. Two warders marched on either side of the 6 prisoner, with their rifles at the slope; two others marched close against him, gripping him by arm and shoulder, as though at once pushing and support-ing him. The rest of us, magistrates and the like, followed behind. Suddenly, when we had gone ten yards, the procession stopped short without any order or warning. A dreadful thing had happened—a dog, come goodness knows whence, had appeared in the yard. It came bounding among us with a loud volley of barks, and leapt round us wagging its whole body, wild with glee at finding so many human beings together. It was a large woolly dog, half Aire-dale, half pariah. For a moment it pranced round us, and then, before anyone could stop it, it had made a dash for the prisoner, and jumping up tried to lick his face. Everyone stood aghast, too taken aback even to grab at the dog.

"Who let that bloody brute in here?" said the superintendent angrily. 7 "Catch it, someone!"

A warder, detached from the escort, charged clumsily after the dog, but 8 it danced and gambolled just out of his reach, taking everything as part of the game. A young Eurasian jailer picked up a handful of gravel and tried to stone the dog away, but it dodged the stones and came after us again. Its yaps echoed from the jail walls. The prisoner, in the grasp of the two warders looked on incuriously, as though this was another formality of the hanging. It was several minutes before someone managed to catch the dog. Then we put my handkerchief through its collar and moved off once more, with the dog still straining and whimpering.

It was about forty yards to the gallows. I watched the bare brown back of 9 the prisoner marching in front of me. He walked clumsily with his bound arms, but quite steadily, with that bobbing gait of the Indian who never straightens his knees. At each step his muscles slid neatly into place, the lock of hair on his scalp danced up and down, his feet printed themselves on the wet gravel. And once, in spite of the men who gripped him by each shoulder, he stepped slightly aside to avoid a puddle on the path.

It is curious, but till that moment I had never realised what it means to 10 destroy a healthy, conscious man. When I saw the prisoner step aside to avoid the puddle, I saw the mystery, the unspeakable wrongness, of cutting a life short when it is in full tide. This man was not dying, he was alive just as we were alive. All the organs of his body were working—bowels digesting food, skin renewing itself, nails growing, tissues forming—all toiling away in solemn foolery. His nails would still be growing when he stood on the drop, when he was falling through the air with a tenth of a second to live. His eyes saw the yellow gravel and the grey walls, and his brain still remembered, foresaw, reasoned—reasoned even about puddles. He and we were a party of men walking together, seeing, hearing, feeling, understanding the same world; and in two minutes, with a sudden snap, one of us would be gone—one mind less, one world less.

11   The gallows stood in a small yard, separate from the main grounds of the prison, and overgrown with tall prickly weeds. It was a brick erection like three sides of a shed, with planking on top, and above that two beams and a cross-bar with the rope dangling. The hangman, a grey-haired convict in the white uniform of the prison, was waiting beside his machine. He greeted us with a servile crouch as we entered. At a word from Francis the two warders, gripping the prisoner more closely than ever, half led, half pushed him to the gallows and helped him clumsily up the ladder. Then the hangman climbed up and fixed the rope round the prisoner's neck.

12   We stood waiting, five yards away. The warders had formed in a rough circle round the gallows. And then, when the noose was fixed, the prisoner began crying out on his god. It was a high, reiterated cry of "Ram! Ram! Ram! Ram!," not urgent and fearful like a prayer or a cry for help, but steady, rhythmical, almost like the tolling of a bell. The dog answered the sound with a whine. The hangman, still standing on the gallows, produced a small cotton bag like a flour bag and drew it down over the prisoner's face. But the sound, muffled by the cloth, still persisted, over and over again: "Ram! Ram! Ram! Ram! Ram!"

13   The hangman climbed down and stood ready, holding the lever. Minutes seemed to pass. The steady, muffled crying from the prisoner went on and on, "Ram! Ram! Ram!" never faltering for an instant. The superintendent, his head on his chest, was slowly poking the ground with his stick; perhaps he was counting the cries, allowing the prisoner a fixed number—fifty, perhaps, or a hundred. Everyone had changed colour. The Indians had gone grey like bad coffee, and one or two of the bayonets were wavering. We looked at the lashed, hooded man on the drop, and listened to his cries—each cry another second of life; the same thought was in all our minds: oh, kill him quickly, get it over, stop that abominable noise!

14   Suddenly the superintendent made up his mind. Throwing up his head he made a swift motion with his stick. "Chalo!" he shouted almost fiercely.

15   There was a clanking noise, and then dead silence. The prisoner had vanished, and the rope was twisting on itself. I let go of the dog, and it galloped immediately to the back of the gallows; but when it got there it stopped short, barked, and then retreated into a corner of the yard, where it stood among the weeds, looking timorously out at us. We went round the gallows to inspect

the prisoner's body. He was dangling with his toes pointed straight down-wards, very slowly revolving, as dead as a stone.

The superintendent reached out with his stick and poked the bare body; 16 it oscillated, slightly. "*He's* all right," said the superintendent. He backed out from under the gallows, and blew out a deep breath. The moody look had gone out of his face quite suddenly. He glanced at his wrist-watch. "Eight min-utes past eight. Well, that's all for this morning, thank God."

The warders unfixed bayonets and marched away. The dog, sobered and 17 conscious of having misbehaved itself, slipped after them. We walked out of the gallows yard, past the condemned cells with their waiting prisoners, into the big central yard of the prison. The convicts, under the commend of ward-ers armed with lathis, were already receiving their breakfast. They squatted in long rows, each man holding a tin pannikin, while two warders with buckets marched round ladling out rice; it seemed quite a homely, jolly scene, after the hanging. An enormous relief had come upon us now that the job was done. One felt an impulse to sing, to break into a run, to snigger. All at once every-one began chattering gaily.

The Eurasian boy walking beside me nodded towards the way we had 18 come, with a knowing smile: "Do you know, sir, our friend (he meant the dead man), when he heard his appeal had been dismissed, he pissed on the floor of his cell. From fright.—Kindly take one of my cigarettes, sir. Do you not admire my new silver case, sir? From the boxwallah, two rupees eight annas. Classy European style."

Several people laughed—at what, nobody seemed certain.   19

Francis was walking by the superintendent, talking garrulously: "Well, sir, 20 all hass passed off with the utmost satisfactoriness. It wass all finished—flick! like that. It iss not always so—oah, no! I have known cases where the doctor wass obliged to go beneath the gallows and pull the prisoner's legs to ensure decease. Most disagreeable!"

"Wriggling about, eh? That's bad," said the superintendent.   21

"Ach, sir, it iss worse when they become refractory! One man, I recall, 22 clung to the bars of hiss cage when we went to take him out. You will scarcely credit, sir, that it took six warders to dislodge him, three pulling at each leg. We reasoned with him. 'My dear fellow,' we said, 'think of all the pain and trouble you are causing to me!' But no, he would not listen! Ach, he wass very troublesome!"

I found that I was laughing quite loudly. Everyone was laughing. Even the 23 superintendent grinned in a tolerant way. "You'd better all come out and have a drink," he said quite genially. "I've got a bottle of whisky in the car. We could do with it."

We went through the big double gates of the prison, into the road. "Pull- 24 ing at his legs!" exclaimed a Burmese magistrate suddenly, and burst into a loud chuckling. We all began laughing again. At this moment Francis's anec-dote seemed extraordinarily funny. We all had a drink together, native and European alike, quite amicably. The dead man was a hundred yards away.

QUESTIONS FOR READING

1. How did Orwell come to witness this hanging? What was his connection?
2. What action by the prisoner made Orwell reflect on what the group was doing?
3. What is the reaction of those watching to the prisoner's cries when he is standing on the gallows?
4. What is the most common reaction as the witnesses leave the gallows and walk back through the main prison yard?

QUESTIONS FOR REASONING AND ANALYSIS

1. What does Orwell accomplish by opening with a description of the row of condemned cells?
2. Study the description of the prisoner and his guards in paragraph 2. What seems ironic about the picture Orwell draws? How does this help to suggest his attitude toward the hanging?
3. What is the significance of the dog? Why does Orwell describe this incident as a "dreadful thing" that happened? How is this scene ironic?
4. Orwell has only one brief passage of general comments; almost all of the essay is narration. What inferences are we encouraged to draw from the details of the event? How would you state Orwell's subject? His thesis? What details from the essay support your assertion of Orwell's thesis?

QUESTIONS FOR REFLECTING AND WRITING

1. What is your emotional reaction to the essay? Has Orwell moved you in any way? Why or why not?
2. Is this essay just about capital punishment? What is Orwell suggesting about being human—and inhuman?
3. Have you had occasion to be distressed or embarrassed by a particular event? If so, what was your reaction? Did you laugh? Or want a drink? Or try to stop what was happening that was upsetting to you? Can you explain why we react to distress by laughter?

SUGGESTIONS FOR DISCUSSION AND WRITING

1. Analyze the style of one of the essays from Section 5 of this text. Do not comment on every element of style; select several elements that seem to characterize the writer's style and examine them in detail. Remember that style analyses are written for an audience familiar with the work, so summary is not necessary.

2. Many of the authors included in this text have written books that you will find in your library. Select one that interests you, read it, and prepare a review of it that synthesizes summary, analysis, and evaluation. Prepare a review of about 300 words; assume that the book has just been published.

3. Choose two newspaper and/or magazine articles that differ in their discussion of the same person, event, or product. You may select two different articles on a person in the news, two different accounts of a news event, an advertisement and a *Consumer Reports* analysis of the same product, or two reviews of a book or movie. Analyze differences in both content and presentation and then consider why the two accounts differ. Organize by points of difference and write to an audience not necessarily familiar with the articles.

4. Choose a recently scheduled public event (the Super Bowl, the Olympics, a presidential election, the Academy Award presentations, the premiere of a new television series) and find several articles written before and several after the event. First compare articles written after the event to see if they agree factually. If not, decide which article appears to be more accurate and why. Then examine the earlier material and decide which was the most and which the least accurate. Write an essay in which you explain the differences in speculation before the event and why you think these differences exist. Your audience will be aware of the event but not necessarily aware of the articles you are studying.

The World of Argument

CHAPTER 3

Understanding the Basics of Argument

CUL DE SAC   **BY RICHARD THOMPSON**

READ: What is the situation? What is the reaction of the younger children? What does the older boy try to do?

REASON: Why is the older boy frustrated?

REFLECT/WRITE: What can happen to those who lack scientific knowledge?

In this section we will explore the processes of thinking logically and analyzing issues to reach informed judgments. Remember: Mature people do not need to agree on all issues to respect one another's good sense, but they do have little patience with uninformed or illogical statements masquerading as argument.

CHARACTERISTICS OF ARGUMENT

Argument Is Conversation with a Goal

When you enter into an argument (as speaker, writer, or reader), you become a participant in an ongoing debate about an issue. Since you are probably not the first to address the issue, you need to be aware of the ways that the issue has been debated by others and then seek to advance the conversation, just as you would if you were having a more casual conversation with friends. If the time of the movie is set, the discussion now turns to whose car to take or where to meet. If you were to just repeat the time of the movie, you would add nothing useful to the conversation. Also, if you were to change the subject to a movie you saw last week, you would annoy your friends by not offering useful information or showing that you valued the current conversation. Just as with your conversation about the movie, you want your argument to stay focused on the issue, to respect what others have already contributed, and to make a useful addition to our understanding of the topic.

Argument Takes a Stand on an Arguable Issue

A meaningful argument focuses on a debatable issue. We usually do not argue about facts. "Professor Jones's American literature class meets at 10:00 on Mondays" is not arguable. It is either true or false. We can check the schedule of classes to find out. (Sometimes the facts change; new facts replace old ones.) We also do not debate personal preferences for the simple reason that they are just that—personal. If the debate is about the appropriateness of boxing as a sport, for you to declare that you would rather play tennis is to fail to advance the conversation. You have expressed a personal preference, interesting perhaps, but not relevant to the debate.

Argument Uses Reasons and Evidence

Some arguments merely "look right." That is, conclusions are drawn from facts, but the facts are not those that actually support the assertion, or the conclusion is not the only or the best explanation of those facts. To shape convincing arguments, we need more than an array of facts. We need to think critically, to analyze the issue, to see relationships, to weigh evidence. We need to avoid the temptation to "argue" from emotion only, or to believe that just stating our opinion is the same thing as building a sound argument.

Argument Incorporates Values

Arguments are based not just on reason and evidence but also on the beliefs and values we hold and think that our audience may hold as well. In a reasoned debate, you want to make clear the values that you consider relevant to the argument. In an editorial defending the sport of boxing, one editor wrote that boxing "is a sport because the world has not yet become a place in which the qualities that go into excellence in boxing [endurance, agility, courage] have no value" (*Washington Post,* February 5, 1983). But James J. Kilpatrick also appeals to values when he argues, in an editorial critical of boxing, that we should not want to live in a society "in which deliberate brutality is legally authorized and publicly applauded" (*Washington Post,* December 7, 1982). Observe, however, the high level of seriousness in the appeal to values. Neither writer settles for a simplistic personal preference: "Boxing is exciting," or "Boxing is too violent."

Argument Recognizes the Topic's Complexity

Much false reasoning (the logical fallacies discussed in Chapter 5) results from a writer's oversimplifying an issue. A sound argument begins with an understanding that most issues are terribly complicated. The wise person approaches such ethical concerns as abortion or euthanasia or such public policy issues as tax cuts or trade agreements with the understanding that there are many philosophical, moral, and political issues that complicate discussions of these topics. Recognizing an argument's complexity may also lead us to an understanding that there can be more than one "right" position. The thoughtful arguer respects the views of others, seeks common ground when possible, and often chooses a conciliatory approach.

THE SHAPE OF ARGUMENT: WHAT WE CAN LEARN FROM ARISTOTLE

Still one of the best ways to understand the basics of argument is to reflect on what the Greek philosopher Aristotle describes as the three "players" in any argument: the *writer* (or *speaker*), the *argument itself,* and the *reader* (or *audience*). Aristotle also reminds us that the occasion or "situation" (*karios*) is important in understanding and evaluating an argument. Let's examine each part of this model of argument.

Ethos (About the Writer/Speaker)

It seems logical to begin with *ethos* because without this player we have no argument. We could, though, end with the writer because Aristotle asserts that this player in any argument is the most important. No argument, no matter how logical, no matter how appealing to one's audience, can succeed if the audience rejects the arguer's credibility, his or her *ethical* qualities.

Think how often in political contests those running attack their opponent's character rather than the candidate's programs. Remember the smear campaign against Obama—he is (or was) a Muslim and therefore unfit to be president, the first point an error of fact, the second point an emotional appeal to voters' fears. Candidates try these smear tactics, even without evidence, because they understand that every voter they can convince of an opponent's failure of *ethos* is a citizen who will vote for them. Many American voters want to be assured that a candidate is patriotic, religious (but of course not fanatic!), a loyal spouse, and a loving parent. At times, unfortunately, we even lose sight of important differences in positions as we focus on the person instead. But, this tells us how much an audience values their sense of the arguer's credibility. During his campaign for reelection, after the Watergate break-in, Nixon was attacked with the line: "Would you buy a used car from this guy?" (In defense of used-car salespeople, not all are untrustworthy!)

Logos (About the Logic of the Argument)

Logos refers to the argument itself—to the assertion and the support for it. Aristotle maintains that part of an arguer's appeal to his or her audience lies in the logic of the argument and the quality of the support provided. Even the most credible of writers will not move thoughtful audiences with inadequate evidence or sloppy reasoning. Yes, "arguments" that appeal to emotions, to our needs and fantasies, will work for some audiences—look at the success of advertising, for example. But, if you want to present a serious claim to critical readers, then you must pay attention to your argument. Paying attention means not only having good reasons but also organizing them clearly. Your audience needs to see *how* your evidence supports your point. Consider the following argument in opposition to the war on Iraq.

> War can be justified only as a form of self-defense. To initiate a war, we need to be able to show that our first strike was necessary as a form of self-defense. The Bush administration argued that Iraq had weapons of mass destruction and intended to use them against us. Responding to someone's "intent" to do harm is always a difficult judgment call. But, in this case, there were no weapons of mass destruction so there could not have been any intent to harm the United States, or at least none that was obvious and immediate. Thus we must conclude that this war was not the right course of action for the United States.

You may disagree (many will) with this argument's assertion, but you can respect the writer's logic, the clear connecting of one reason to the next. One good way to strengthen your credibility is to get respect for clear reasoning.

Pathos (About Appeals to the Audience)

Argument implies an audience, those whose views we want to influence in some way. Aristotle labels this player *pathos*, the Greek word for both passion and suffering (hence *pathology*, the study of disease). Arguers need to be aware of their audience's feelings on the issue, the attitudes and values that will affect their response to the argument. There are really two questions arguers must answer: "How can I engage my audience's interest?" and "How can I engage their sympathy for my position?"

Some educators and health experts believe that childhood obesity is a major problem in the United States. Other Americans are much more focused on the economy—or their own careers. Al Gore is passionately concerned about the harmful effects of global warming; others, though increasingly fewer, think he lacks sufficient evidence of environmental degradation. How does a physician raise reader interest in childhood obesity? How does Gore convince doubters that we need to reduce carbon emissions? To prepare an effective argument, we need always to plan our approach with a clear vision of how best to connect to a specific audience—one which may or may not agree with our interests or our position.

Karios (About the Occasion or Situation)

While *Ethos, Logos,* and *Pathos* create the traditional three-part communication model, Aristotle adds another term to enhance our understanding of any argument "moment." The term *karios* refers to the occasion for the argument, the situation that we are in. What does this moment call for from us? Is the lunch table the appropriate time and place for an argument with your coworker over her failure to meet a deadline that is part of a joint project? You have just received a 65 on your history test; is this the best time to e-mail your professor to protest the grade? Would the professor's office be the better place for your discussion than an e-mail sent from your BlackBerry minutes after you have left class?

The concept of *karios* asks us to consider what is most appropriate for the occasion, to think through the best time, place, and genre (type of argument) to make a successful argument. This concept has special meaning for students in

Personal confrontation at a business meeting: Not cool.

a writing class who sometimes have difficulty thinking about audience at all. When practicing writing for the academic community, you may need to modify the language or tone that you more typically use in other situations.

We argue in a specific context of three interrelated parts, as illustrated in Figure 3.1.

We present support for an assertion to a specific audience whose expectations and character we have given thought to when shaping our argument. And we present ourselves as informed, competent, and reliable so that our audience will give us their attention.

THE LANGUAGE OF ARGUMENT

We could title this section the *languages* of argument because arguments come in visual language as well as in words. But visual arguments—cartoons, photos, ads—are almost always accompanied by some words: figures speaking in bubbles, a caption, a slogan (Nike's "Just Do It!"). So we need to think about the kinds of statements that make up arguments, whether those arguments are legal briefs or cartoons, casual conversations or scholarly essays. To build an argument we need some statements that support other statements that present the main idea or claim of the argument.

- Claims: usually either inferences or judgments, for these are debatable assertions.
- Support: facts, opinions based on facts (inferences), or opinions based on values, beliefs, or ideas (judgments) or some combination of the three.

Let's consider what kinds of statements each of these terms describes.

Facts

Facts are statements that are verifiable. Factual statements refer to what can be counted or measured or confirmed by reasonable observers or trusted experts.

There are twenty-six desks in Room 110.

In the United States about 400,000 people die each year as a result of smoking.

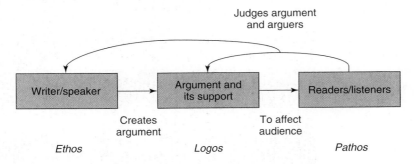

FIGURE 3.1 Aristotelian Structure of Argument

These are factual statements. We can verify the first by observation—by counting. The second fact comes from medical records. We rely on trusted record-keeping sources and medical experts for verification. By definition, we do not argue about the facts. Usually. Sometimes "facts" change, as we learn more about our world. For example, only in the last 30 years has convincing evidence been gathered to demonstrate the relationship between smoking and various illnesses of the heart and lungs. And sometimes "facts" are false facts. These are statements that sound like facts but are incorrect. For example: Nadel has won more Wimbledon titles than Federer. Not so.

Inferences

Inferences are opinions based on facts. Inferences are the conclusions we draw from an analysis of facts.

> There will not be enough desks in Room 110 for upcoming fall-semester classes.
>
> Smoking is a serious health hazard.

Predictions of an increase in student enrollment for the coming fall semester lead to the inference that most English classes scheduled in Room 110 will run with several more students per class than last year. The dean should order new desks. Similarly, we infer from the number of deaths that smoking is a health problem; statistics show more people dying from tobacco than from AIDS, or murder, or car accidents, causes of death that get media coverage but do not produce nearly as many deaths.

Inferences vary in their closeness to the facts supporting them. That the sun will "rise" tomorrow is an inference, but we count on its happening, acting as if it is a fact. However, the first inference stated above is based not just on the fact of twenty-six desks but on another inference—a projected increase in student enrollment—and two assumptions. The argument looks like this:

FACT:	There are twenty-six desks in Room 110.
INFERENCE:	There will be more first-year students next year.
ASSUMPTIONS:	1. English will remain a required course.
	2. No additional classrooms are available for English classes.
CLAIM:	There will not be enough desks in Room 110 for upcoming fall-semester classes.

This inference could be challenged by a different analysis of the facts supporting enrollment projections. Or, if additional rooms can be found, the dean will not need to order new desks. Inferences can be part of the support of an argument, or they can be the claim of an argument.

Judgments

Judgments are opinions based on values, beliefs, or philosophical concepts. (Judgments also include opinions based on personal preferences, but we have already

> **NOTE:** Placing such qualifiers as "I believe," "I think," or "I feel" in an assertion does not free you from the need to support that claim. The statement "I believe that President Bush was a great president" calls for an argument based on evidence and reasons.

excluded these from argument.) Judgments concern right and wrong, good and bad, better or worse, should and should not:

> No more than twenty-six students should be enrolled in any English class.
>
> Cigarette advertising should be eliminated, and the federal government should develop an antismoking campaign.

To support the first judgment, we need to explain what constitutes overcrowding, or what constitutes the best class size for effective teaching. If we can support our views on effective teaching, we may be able to convince the college president that ordering more desks for Room 110 is not the best solution to an increasing enrollment in English classes. The second judgment also offers a solution to a problem, in this case a national health problem. To reduce the number of deaths, we need to reduce the number of smokers, either by encouraging smokers to quit or not to start. The underlying assumption: Advertising does affect behavior.

EXERCISE: Facts, Inferences, and Judgments

Compile a list of three statements of fact, three inferences, and three judgments. Try to organize them into three related sets, as illustrated here:

- Smoking is prohibited in some restaurants.
- Secondhand smoke is a health hazard.
- Smoking should be prohibited in all restaurants.

We can classify judgments to see better what kind of assertion we are making and, therefore, what kind of support we need to argue effectively.

FUNCTIONAL JUDGMENTS (guidelines for judging how something or someone works or could work)

Tiger Woods is the best golfer to play the game.

Antismoking advertising will reduce the number of smokers.

AESTHETIC JUDGMENTS (guidelines for judging art, literature, music, or natural scenes)

The sunrise was beautiful.

The Great Gatsby's structure, characters, and symbols are perfectly wedded to create the novel's vision of the American dream.

ETHICAL JUDGMENTS (guidelines for group or social behavior)

Lawyers should not advertise.

It is discourteous to talk during a film or lecture.

MORAL JUDGMENTS (guidelines of right and wrong for judging individuals and for establishing legal principles)

Taking another person's life is wrong.

Equal rights under the law should not be denied on the basis of race or gender.

Functional and aesthetic judgments generally require defining key terms and establishing criteria for the judging or ranking made by the assertion. How, for example, do we compare golfers? On the amount of money won? The number of tournaments won? Or the consistency of winning throughout one's career? What about the golfer's quality and range of shots? Ethical and moral judgments may be more difficult to support because they depend not just on how terms are defined and criteria established but on values and beliefs as well. If taking another person's life is wrong, why isn't it wrong in war? Or is it? These are difficult questions that require thoughtful debate.

EXERCISES: Understanding Assumptions, Facts, False Facts, Inferences, and Judgments

1. Categorize the judgments you wrote for the previous exercise (p. 79) as either aesthetic, moral, ethical, or functional. Alternatively, compile a list of three judgments that you then categorize.
2. For each judgment listed for exercise 1, generate one statement of support, either a fact or an inference or another judgment. Then state any underlying assumptions that are part of each argument.
3. Read the following article and then complete the exercise that follows. This exercise tests both careful reading and your understanding of the differences among facts, inferences, and judgments.

YOUR BRAIN LIES TO YOU | SAM WANG and SANDRA AAMODT

Dr. Samuel S.H. Wang is a professor of molecular biology and neuroscience at Princeton, where he manages a research lab. Dr. Sandra Aamodt, former editor of *Nature Neuroscience,* is a freelance science writer. Drs. Wang and Aamodt are the authors of *Welcome to Your Brain: Why You Lose Your Car Keys but Never Forget How to Drive and Other Puzzles of Everyday Life* (2008). The following article appeared on June 27, 2008, in the *New York Times.*

FALSE beliefs are everywhere. Eighteen percent of Americans think the   1
sun revolves around the earth, one poll has found. Thus it seems slightly less egregious that, according to another poll, 10 percent of us think that Senator Barack Obama, a Christian, is instead a Muslim. The Obama campaign has created a Web site to dispel misinformation. But this effort may be more

difficult than it seems, thanks to the quirky way in which our brains store memories—and mislead us along the way.

The brain does not simply gather and stockpile information as a comput- 2 er's hard drive does. Current research suggests that facts may be stored first in the hippocampus, a structure deep in the brain about the size and shape of a fat man's curled pinkie finger. But the information does not rest there. Every time we recall it, our brain writes it down again, and during this re-storage, it is also reprocessed. In time, the fact is gradually transferred to the cerebral cortex and is separated from the context in which it was originally learned. For example, you know that the capital of California is Sacramento, but you probably don't remember how you learned it.

This phenomenon, known as source amnesia, can also lead people to for- 3 get whether a statement is true. Even when a lie is presented with a disclaimer, people often later remember it as true.

With time, this misremembering only gets worse. A false statement from a 4 non-credible source that is at first not believed can gain credibility during the months it takes to reprocess memories from short-term hippocampal storage to longer-term cortical storage. As the source is forgotten, the message and its implications gain strength. This could explain why, during the 2004 presidential campaign, it took some weeks for the Swift Boat Veterans for Truth campaign against Senator John Kerry to have an effect on his standing in the polls.

Even if they do not understand the neuroscience behind source amnesia, 5 campaign strategists can exploit it to spread misinformation. They know that if their message is initially memorable, its impression will persist long after it is debunked. In repeating a falsehood, someone may back it up with an opening line like "I think I read somewhere" or even with a reference to a specific source.

In one study, a group of Stanford students was exposed repeatedly to 6 an unsubstantiated claim taken from a Web site that Coca-Cola is an effective paint thinner. Students who read the statement five times were nearly one-third more likely than those who read it only twice to attribute it to *Consumer Reports* (rather than *The National Enquirer,* their other choice), giving it a gloss of credibility.

Adding to this innate tendency to mold information we recall is the way our 7 brains fit facts into established mental frameworks. We tend to remember news that accords with our worldview, and discount statements that contradict it.

In another Stanford study, 48 students, half of whom said they favored 8 capital punishment and half of whom said they opposed it, were presented with two pieces of evidence, one supporting and one contradicting the claim that capital punishment deters crime. Both groups were more convinced by the evidence that supported their initial position.

Psychologists have suggested that legends propagate by striking an emo- 9 tional chord. In the same way, ideas can spread by emotional selection, rather than by their factual merits, encouraging the persistence of falsehoods about Coke—or about a presidential candidate.

Journalists and campaign workers may think they are acting to counter 10 misinformation by pointing out that it is not true. But by repeating a false rumor, they may inadvertently make it stronger. In its concerted effort to "stop the smears," the Obama campaign may want to keep this in mind. Rather than emphasize that Mr. Obama is not a Muslim, for instance, it may be more effective to stress that he embraced Christianity as a young man.

11   Consumers of news, for their part, are prone to selectively accept and remember statements that reinforce beliefs they already hold. In a replication of the study of students' impressions of evidence about the death penalty, researchers found that even when subjects were given a specific instruction to be objective, they were still inclined to reject evidence that disagreed with their beliefs.

12   In the same study, however, when subjects were asked to imagine their reaction if the evidence had pointed to the opposite conclusion, they were more open-minded to information that contradicted their beliefs. Apparently, it pays for consumers of controversial news to take a moment and consider that the opposite interpretation may be true.

13   In 1919, Justice Oliver Wendell Holmes of the Supreme Court wrote that "the best test of truth is the power of the thought to get itself accepted in the competition of the market." Holmes erroneously assumed that ideas are more likely to spread if they are honest. Our brains do not naturally obey this admirable dictum, but by better understanding the mechanisms of memory perhaps we can move closer to Holmes's ideal.

Label each of the following sentences as F (fact), FF (false fact), I (inference), or J (judgment).

_____ 1. Campaigns have trouble getting rid of misinformation about their candidate.

_____ 2. When we reprocess information we may get the information wrong, but we always remember the source.

_____ 3. The Obama campaign should stress that he became a Christian as a young man.

_____ 4. Most of us remember information that matches our view of the world.

_____ 5. When students were told to be objective in evaluating evidence, they continued to reject evidence they disagreed with.

_____ 6. Coke is an effective paint thinner.

_____ 7. True statements should be accepted and false statements rejected.

_____ 8. Justice Holmes was wrong about the power of truth to spread more widely than falsehood.

_____ 9. The more we understand about the way the world works, the better our chances of separating truth from falsehood.

_____ 10. Americans do not seem to understand basic science.

THE SHAPE OF ARGUMENT: WHAT WE CAN LEARN FROM TOULMIN

British philosopher Stephen Toulmin adds to what we have learned from Aristotle by focusing our attention on the basics of the argument itself. First, consider this definition of argument: *An argument consists of evidence and/or reasons presented in support of an assertion or claim that is either stated or implied.* For example:

CLAIM:	We should not go skiing today
EVIDENCE:	because it is too cold.
EVIDENCE:	Because some laws are unjust,
CLAIM:	civil disobedience is sometimes justified.
EVIDENCE:	It's only fair and right for academic institutions to
CLAIM:	accept students only on academic merit.

The parts of an argument, Toulmin asserts, are actually a bit more complex than these examples suggest. Each argument has a third part that is not stated in the preceding examples. This third part is the "glue" that connects the support—the evidence and reasons—to the argument's claim and thus fulfills the logic of the argument. Toulmin calls this glue an argument's *warrants*. These are the principles or assumptions that allow us to assert that our evidence or reasons—what Toulmin calls the *grounds*—do indeed support our claim. (Figure 3.2 illustrates these basics of the Toulmin model of argument.)

Look again at the sample arguments to see what warrants must be accepted to make each argument work:

CLAIM:	We should not go skiing today.
EVIDENCE:	It is too cold.
ASSUMPTIONS (WARRANTS):	When it is too cold, skiing is not fun; the activity is not sufficient to keep one from becoming uncomfortable. AND: Too cold is what is too cold for me.
CLAIM:	Civil disobedience is sometimes justified.
EVIDENCE:	Some laws are unjust.
ASSUMPTIONS (WARRANTS):	To get unjust laws changed, people need to be made aware of the injustice. Acts of civil disobedience will get people's attention and make them aware that the laws need changing.
CLAIM:	Academic institutions should accept students only on academic merit.
EVIDENCE:	It is fair and right.
ASSUMPTIONS (WARRANTS):	Fair and right are important values. AND: Academic institutions are only about academics.

CLAIM:	Academic institutions should accept students only on academic merit.
EVIDENCE:	It is only fair and right.
WARRANT:	(1) Fair and right are important values. (2) Academic institutions are only about academics.

FIGURE 3.2 The Toulmin Structure of Argument

Assumptions play an important role in any argument, so we need to be sure to understand what they are. Note, for instance, the second assumption operating in the first argument: The temperature considered uncomfortable for the speaker will also be uncomfortable for her companions—an uncertain assumption. In the second argument, the warrant is less debatable, for acts of civil disobedience usually get media coverage and thus dramatize the issue. The underlying assumptions in the third example stress the need to know one's warrants. Both warrants will need to be defended in the debate over selection by academic merit only.

COLLABORATIVE EXERCISE: Building Arguments

With your class partner or in small groups, examine each of the following claims. Select two, think of one statement that could serve as evidence for each claim, and then think of the underlying assumption(s) that complete each of the arguments.

1. Professor X is not a good instructor.
2. Americans need to reduce the fat in their diets.
3. Tiger Woods is a great golfer.
4. Military women should be allowed to serve in combat zones.
5. College newspapers should be free of supervision by faculty or administrators.

Toulmin was particularly interested in the great range in the strength or probability of various arguments. Some kinds of arguments are stronger than others because of the language or logic they use. Other arguments must, necessarily, be heavily qualified for the claim to be supportable. Toulmin developed his language to provide a strategy for analyzing the degree of probability in a given argument and to remind us of the need to qualify some kinds of claims. You have already seen how the idea of warrants, or assumptions, helps us think about the "glue" that presumably makes a given argument work. Taken together, Toulmin terms and concepts help us analyze the arguments of others and prepare more convincing arguments of our own.

Claims

A claim is what the argument asserts or seeks to prove. It answers the question "What is your point?" In an argumentative speech or essay, the claim is the speaker or writer's main idea or thesis. Although an argument's claim "follows" from reasons and evidence, we often present an argument—whether written or spoken—with the claim stated near the beginning of the presentation. We can better understand an argument's claim by recognizing that we can have claims of fact, claims of value, and claims of policy.

Claims of Fact

Although facts usually support claims, we do argue over some facts. Historians and biographers may argue over what happened in the past, although they are more likely to argue over the significance of what happened. Scientists also argue over the facts, over how to classify an unearthed fossil, for example, or whether the fossil indicates that the animal had feathers. For example:

CLAIM: The small, predatory dinosaur *Deinonychus* hunted its
                prey in packs.

This claim is supported by the discovery of several fossils of *Deinonychus* close together and with the fossil bones of a much larger dinosaur. Their teeth have also been found in or near the bones of dinosaurs that have died in a struggle.

Assertions about what will happen are sometimes classified as claims of fact, but they can also be labeled as inferences supported by facts. Predictions about a future event may be classified as claims of fact:

CLAIM: The United States will win the most gold medals at the 2008
                Olympics.

CLAIM: I will get an A on tomorrow's psychology test.

What evidence would you use today to support each of these claims? (And, did the first one turn out to be correct?)

Claims of Value

These include moral, ethical, and aesthetic judgments. Assertions that use such words as *good* or *bad, better* or *worse,* and *right* or *wrong* will be claims of value. The following are all claims of value:

CLAIM: Roger Federer is a better tennis player than Andy Roddick.

CLAIM: *Adventures of Huckleberry Finn* is one of the most significant
                American novels.

CLAIM: Cheating hurts others and the cheater too.

CLAIM: Abortion is wrong.

Arguments in support of judgments demand relevant evidence, careful reasoning, and an awareness of the assumptions one is making. Support for claims of value often include other value statements. For example, to support the claim that censorship is bad, arguers often assert that the free exchange of ideas is good and necessary in a democracy. The support is itself a value statement. The arguer may believe, probably correctly, that most people will more readily agree to the support (the free exchange of ideas is good) than to the claim (censorship is bad).

Claims of Policy

Finally, claims of policy are assertions about what should or should not happen, what the government ought or ought not to do, how to best solve social problems. Claims of policy debate, for example, college rules, state gun laws, or federal aid to Africans suffering from AIDS. The following are claims of policy:

CLAIM:	College newspapers should not be controlled in any way by college authorities.
CLAIM:	States should not have laws allowing people to carry concealed weapons.
CLAIM:	The United States must provide more aid to African countries where 25 percent or more of the citizens have tested positive for HIV.

Claims of policy are often closely tied to judgments of morality or political philosophy, but they also need to be grounded in feasibility. That is, your claim needs to be doable, to be based on a thoughtful consideration of the real world and the complexities of public policy issues.

Grounds (or Data or Evidence)

The term *grounds* refers to the reasons and evidence provided in support of a claim. Although the words *data* and *evidence* can also be used, note that *grounds* is the more general term because it includes reasons or logic as well as examples or statistics. We determine the grounds of an argument by asking the question "Why do you think that?" or "How do you know that?" When writing your own arguments, you can ask yourself these questions and answer by using a *because* clause:

CLAIM:	Smoking should be banned in restaurants because
GROUNDS:	secondhand smoke is a serious health hazard.
CLAIM:	Federer is a better tennis player than Roddick because
GROUNDS:	1. he has been ranked number one longer than Roddick,
	2. he has won more tournaments than Roddick, and
	3. he has won more major tournaments than Roddick.

Warrants

Why should we believe that your grounds do indeed support your claim? Your argument's warrants answer this question. They explain why your evidence really is evidence. Sometimes warrants reside in language itself, in the meanings of the words we are using. If I am *younger* than my brother, then my brother must be *older* than I am. In a court case attempting to prove that Jones murdered Smith, the relation of evidence to claim is less assured. If the police investigation has been properly managed and the physical evidence is substantial, then Smith may be Jones's murderer. The prosecution has—presumably beyond a reasonable doubt—established motive, means, and opportunity for Smith to commit the murder. In many arguments based on statistical data, the argument's warrant rests on complex analyses of the statistics—and on the conviction that the statistics have been developed without error. In some philosophical arguments, the warrants are the logical structures (often shown mathematically) connecting a sequence of reasons. Still, without taking courses in statistics and logic, you can develop an alertness to the "good sense" of some arguments and the "dubious sense" of others. You know, for example, that good SAT scores are a predictor of success in college. Can you argue that you will do well in college because you have good SATs? No. We can determine only a statistical probability. We cannot turn probabilities about a group of people into a warrant about one person in the group. (In addition, SAT scores are only one predictor. Another key variable is motivation.)

What is the warrant for the Federer claim?

CLAIM:	Federer is a better tennis player than Roddick.
GROUNDS:	The three facts listed above.
WARRANT:	It is appropriate to judge and rank tennis players on these kinds of statistics. That is, the better player is one who has held the number one ranking for the longest time, has won the most tournaments, and also has won the most major tournaments.

Backing

Standing behind an argument's warrant may be additional *backing*. Backing answers the question "How do we know that your evidence is good evidence?" You may answer this question by providing authoritative sources for the data used (for example, the Census Bureau or the U.S. Tennis Association). Or, you may explain in detail the methodology of the experiments performed or the surveys taken. When scientists and social scientists present the results of their research, they anticipate the question of backing and automatically provide a detailed explanation of the process by which they acquired their evidence. In criminal trials, defense attorneys challenge the backing of the prosecution's argument. They question the handling of blood samples sent to labs for DNA testing, for instance. The defense attorneys want jury members to doubt the *quality* of the evidence, perhaps even to doubt the reliability of DNA testing altogether.

This discussion of backing returns us to the point that one part of any argument is the audience. To create an effective argument, you need to assess the potential for acceptance of your warrants and backing. Is your audience likely to share your values, your religious beliefs, or your scientific approach to issues? If you are speaking to a group at your church, then backing based on the religious beliefs of that church may be effective. If you are preparing an argument for a general audience, then using specific religious assertions as warrants or backing probably will not result in an effective argument.

Qualifiers

Some arguments are absolute; they can be stated without qualification. *If I am younger than my brother, then he must be older than I am.* Most arguments need some qualification; many need precise limitations. If, when playing bridge, I am dealt eight spades, then my opponents and partner together must have five spade cards—because there are thirteen cards of each suit in a deck. My partner *probably* has one spade but *could be* void of spades. My partner *possibly* has two or more spades, but I would be foolish to count on it. When bidding my hand, I must be controlled by the laws of probability. Look again at the smoking ban claim. Observe the absolute nature of both the claim and its support. If second-hand smoke is indeed a health hazard, it will be that in *all* restaurants, not just in some. With each argument we need to assess the need of qualification that is appropriate to a successful argument.

Sweeping generalizations often come to us in the heat of a debate or when we first start to think about an issue. For example: *Gun control is wrong because it restricts individual rights.* But on reflection surely you would not want to argue against all forms of gun control. (Remember: An unqualified assertion is understood by your audience to be absolute.) Would you sell guns to felons in jail or to children on the way to school? Obviously not. So, let's try the claim again, this time with two important qualifiers:

QUALIFIED   Adults without a criminal record should not be restricted in the
CLAIM: purchase of guns.

Others may want this claim further qualified to eliminate particular types of guns or to control the number purchased or the process for purchasing. The gun-control debate is not about absolutes; it is all about which qualified claim is best.

Rebuttals

Arguments can be challenged. Smart debaters assume that there are people who will disagree with them. They anticipate the ways that opponents can challenge their arguments. When you are planning an argument, you need to think about how you can counter or rebut the challenges you anticipate. Think of yourself as an attorney in a court case preparing your argument *and* a defense of the other attorney's challenges to your argument. If you ignore the important role of rebuttals, you may not win the jury to your side.

USING TOULMIN'S TERMS TO ANALYZE ARGUMENTS

Terms are never an end in themselves; we learn them when we recognize that they help us to organize our thinking about a subject. Toulmin's terms can aid your reading of the arguments of others. You can "see what's going on" in an argument if you analyze it, applying Toulmin's language to its parts. Not all terms will be useful for every analysis because, for example, some arguments will not have qualifiers or rebuttals. But to recognize that an argument is *without qualifiers* is to learn something important about that argument.

First, here is a simple argument broken down into its parts using Toulmin's terms:

GROUNDS:	Because Dr. Bradshaw has an attendance policy,
CLAIM:	students who miss more than seven classes will
QUALIFIER:	most likely (last year, Dr. Bradshaw did allow one student, in unusual circumstances, to continue in the class) be dropped from the course.
WARRANT:	Dr. Bradshaw's syllabus explains her attendance policy, a
BACKING:	policy consistent with the concept of a discussion class that depends on student participation and consistent with the attendance policies of most of her colleagues.
REBUTTAL:	Although some students complain about an attendance policy of any kind, Dr. Bradshaw does explain her policy and her reasons for it the first day of class. She then reminds students that the syllabus is a contract between them; if they choose to stay, they agree to abide by the guidelines explained on the syllabus.

This argument is brief and fairly simple. Let's see how Toulmin's terms can help us analyze a longer, more complex argument. Read actively and annotate the following essay while at the same time noting the existing annotations using Toulmin's terms. Then answer the questions that follow the article.

LET THE ZOO'S ELEPHANTS GO | LES SCHOBERT

The author has spent more than thirty years working in zoos, primarily in care of elephants. He has been a curator of both the Los Angeles and North Carolina zoos. His argument was published October 16, 2005, in the *Washington Post*.

PREREADING QUESTIONS What are some good reasons to have zoos? What are some problems associated with them?

The Smithsonian Institution is a national treasure, but when it comes to   1   Toulmin's terms.
elephants, its National Zoo is a national embarrassment.

In 2000 the zoo euthanized Nancy, an African elephant that was suffering   2
from foot problems so painful that standing had become difficult for her. Five years later the zoo has announced that Toni, an Asian elephant, is suffering from arthritis so severe that she, too, may be euthanized.

The elephants' debilitating ailments are probably a result of the inade-   3 ⌐   Grounds.
quate conditions in which they have been held. The same story is repeated in   ⌐
zoos across the country.

Backing.

4   When I began my zoo career 35 years ago, much less was known about elephants than is known today. We now understand that keeping elephants in tiny enclosures with unnatural surfaces destroys their legs and feet. We have learned that to breed naturally and rear their young, elephants must live in herds that meet their social requirements. And we have come to realize that controlling elephants through domination and the use of ankuses (sharply pointed devices used to inflict pain) can no longer be justified.

Claim.

5   Zoos must change the concept of how elephants are kept in captivity, starting with how much space we allot them. Wild elephants may walk 30 miles a day. A typical home range of a wild elephant is 1,000 square miles. At the National Zoo, Toni has access to a yard of less than an acre. Zoo industry standards allow the keeping of elephants in as little as 2,200 square feet, or about 5 percent of an acre.

Grounds.

6   Some zoos have begun to reevaluate their ability to house elephants. After the death of two elephants in 2004, the San Francisco Zoo sent its surviving elephants to a sanctuary in California. This year the Detroit Zoo closed its elephant exhibit on ethical grounds, and its two surviving elephants now thrive at the California sanctuary as well.

Rebuttal to counterargument.

7   But attitudes at other zoos remain entrenched. To justify their outdated exhibits, some zoos have redefined elephant longevity and natural behavior. For example, National Zoo officials blame Toni's arthritis on old age. But elephants in the wild reproduce into their fifties, and female elephants live long after their reproductive cycles cease. Had she not been captured in Thailand at the age of 7 months, Toni, at age 39, could have had decades more of life as a mother and a grandmother. Instead, she faces an early death before her 40th birthday, is painfully thin and is crippled by arthritis.

Claim, qualified (options explained). Grounds.

8   The National Zoo's other elephants face the same bleak future if changes are not made. A preserve of at least 2 square miles—1,280 acres, or almost eight times the size of the National Zoo—would be necessary to meet an elephant's physical and social needs. Since this is not feasible, the zoo should send its pachyderms to a sanctuary. One such facility, the Elephant Sanctuary in Tennessee, offers 2,700 acres of natural habitat over which elephants can roam and heal from the damage caused by zoo life. The sanctuary's soft soil,

Grounds.

varied terrain, freedom of choice and freedom of movement have restored life to elephants that were suffering foot and joint diseases after decades in zoos and circuses.

Claim restated. Warrant (states values).

9   The National Zoo has the opportunity to overcome its troubled animal-care history by joining progressive zoos in reevaluating its elephant program. The zoo should do right by its elephants, and the public should demand nothing less.

QUESTIONS FOR READING

1.   What is the occasion that led to the writing of this article?

2.   What is Schobert's subject?

3.   State his claim in a way that shows that it is a solution to a problem.

QUESTIONS FOR REASONING AND ANALYSIS

1.   What type of evidence (grounds) does the author provide?
2.   What are the nature and source of his backing?
3.   What makes his opening effective?
4.   What values does Schobert express? What assumption does he make about his readers?

QUESTIONS FOR REFLECTING AND WRITING

1.   Are you surprised by any of the facts about elephants presented by Schobert? Do they make sense to you, upon reflection?
2.   Should zoos close down their elephant houses? Why or why not?
3.   Are there any alternatives to city zoos with small elephant houses besides elephant sanctuaries?

You have seen how Toulmin's terms can help you to see what writers are actually "doing" in their arguments. You have also observed from both the short and the longer argument that writers do not usually follow the terms in precise order. Indeed, you can find both grounds and backing in the same sentence, or claim and qualifiers in the same paragraph, and so on. Still, the terms can help you to sort out your thinking about a claim you want to support. Now use your knowledge of argument as you read and analyze the following arguments.

FOR DEBATE AND ANALYSIS

LET MY TEENAGER DRINK | T. R. REID

A former Tokyo correspondent and London Bureau Chief for the *Washington Post*, T.R. Reid is now the *Post's* Rocky Mountain correspondent. He is also the author of several books on Japan, including *Ski Japan* (1994) and *Confucius Lives Next Door: What Living in the East Teaches Us about Living in the West* (2000). His argument for teen drinking was published May 4, 2003.

PREREADING QUESTIONS Do you or did you drink "underage"? If so, did this lead to any problems? Do you think the drinking age should be lowered in the United States?

My 16-year-old called me from a bar. She said my 17-year-old was there, too, along with the rest of the gang from high school: "Everything's fine, Dad. We'll be home after last call."   1

I breathed a quiet sigh of relief. Like many other parents, I knew my teenagers were out drinking that Saturday night. Unlike most American kids, though, my daughters were drinking safely, legally and under close adult supervision—in the friendly neighborhood pub two blocks from our London home.   2

3   My kids could do that because Britain, like almost every other developed nation, has decided that teenagers are going to drink whether it's legal or not—and that attempts at prohibition inevitably make things worse.

4   Some countries have no minimum drinking age—a conservative approach that leaves the issue up to families rather than government bureaucrats. In most Western democracies, drinking becomes legal in the late teens. In Britain, a 16-year-old can have a beer in a pub if the drink accompanies a meal. Most publicans we knew were willing to call a single bag of potato chips—sorry, "crisps"—a full meal for purposes of that law.

5   And yet teen drinking tends to be a far more dangerous problem in the prohibitionist United States than in those more tolerant countries. The reason lies in the law itself. Because of our nationwide ban on drinking before the age of 21, American teenagers tend to do their drinking secretly, in the worst possible places—in a dark corner of the park, at the one house in the neighborhood where the adults have left for the weekend, or, most commonly, in the car.

6   Amid a national outcry over an epidemic of "binge drinking," the politicians don't like to admit that this problem is largely a product of the liquor laws. Kids know they have to do all their drinking before they get to the dance or the concert, where adults will be present.

7   On campus, this binge of fast and furious drinking is known as "pregaming." Any college student will tell you that the pre-game goal is to get good and drunk—in the dorm room or in the car—before the social event begins. It would be smarter, and more pleasant for all concerned, to stretch out whatever alcohol there is over the course of an evening. But Congress in its wisdom has made this safer approach illegal.

8   Our family currently has kids at three U.S. universities. The deans of all three schools have sent us firm letters promising zero tolerance for underage drinking. In conversation, though, the same deans concede readily that their teenage students drink every weekend—as undergraduates always have.

9   The situation would be vastly easier to manage, these educators say, if they could allow the kids to drink in public—thus obviating the "pre-game" binge—and provide some kind of adult presence at the parties.

10   But those obvious steps would make a school complicit in violating the prohibition laws—and potentially liable for civil lawsuits.

11   The deans lament that there is no political will to change the national drinking age—or even to hand the issue back to the states. Politicians, after all, garner support and contributions from the interest groups by promising to "stop teen drinking."

But, of course, the law doesn't stop teens from drinking. "Most college 12 students drink . . . regardless of the legal drinking age, without harming themselves or anyone else," writes Richard Keeling, editor of the *Journal of American College Health.*

As a wandering *Post* correspondent, I have raised teenagers in three 13 places: Tokyo, London and Colorado. No parent will be surprised to read that high school and college students had easy access to alcohol in all three places. In all three countries, kids sometimes got drunk. But overseas, they did their drinking at a bar, a concert or a party. There were adults—and, often, police—around to supervise. As a result, most teenagers learned to use alcohol socially and responsibly. And they didn't have to hide it from their parents.

In the United States, our kids learn that drinking is something to be done 14 in the dark, and quickly. Is that the lesson we want to teach them about alcohol use? It makes me glad my teenagers had the legal right to go down the street to that pub.

QUESTIONS FOR READING

1.   What is Reid's claim?
2.   Explain the term "pre-gaming."
3.   What do college administrators say is their position on underage drinking on campus? What do they say actually happens on their campuses?

QUESTIONS FOR REASONING AND ANALYSIS

1.   Analyze Reid's argument, using Toulmin's terms. What passages contain his evidence (grounds)? Does he qualify his claim? (Study his word choice throughout.)
2.   Evaluate Reid's argument. What kind of evidence does he use? Is it convincing? With what audience(s) might his argument be most successful?

QUESTIONS FOR REFLECTING AND WRITING

1.   Do you agree with Reid? If so, is that because you want to drink legally or because you think he has a convincing argument?
2.   If you disagree, what are your counterarguments? Organize a rebuttal for class debate or for an essay.

DON'T MAKE TEEN DRINKING EASIER | JOSEPH A. CALIFANO, JR.

Joseph Califano is a lawyer and former secretary of Health, Education, and Welfare (1977–1979). The author of nine books, he is founder and currently president of the National Center on Addiction and Substance Abuse at Columbia University. His rebuttal to T. R. Reid's article was published in the *Washington Post* on May 11, 2003.

PREREADING QUESTIONS Given what you know about Joseph Califano, what do you expect his position to be?

1   T. R. Reid's May 4 [2003] op-ed piece, "Let My Teenager Drink," is a dangerous example of what happens if we let anecdote trump facts. Reid jumps from the comfort he derives from his 16- and 17-year-old daughters "out drinking Saturday night" at a neighborhood pub in London, where it is legal, to the conclusion that the English and Europeans have far fewer problems with teen drinking than we do in the United States, where the age to legally buy alcohol is 21.

2   Let's start with the facts. In 2001 the Justice Department released an analysis comparing drinking rates in Europe and the United States. The conclusion: American 10th-graders are less likely to use and abuse alcohol than people of the same age in almost all European countries, including Britain. British 15- and 16-year-olds were more than twice as likely as Americans to binge drink (50 percent vs. 24 percent) and to have been intoxicated within the past 30 days (48 percent vs. 21 percent). Of Western European nations, only Portugal had a lower proportion of young people binge drinking, which is defined as having five or more drinks in a row.

3   That same year, in a study of 29 nations, including Eastern and Western Europe, the World Health Organization found that American 15-year-olds were less likely than those in 18 other nations to have been intoxicated twice or more. British girls and boys were far likelier than their U.S. counterparts to have been drunk that often (52 and 51 percent vs. 28 and 34 percent).

4   Then there are the consequences of teen drinking. This month a Rand study that followed 3,400 people from seventh grade through age 23 reported that those who had three or more drinks within the past year, or any drink in the past month, were likelier to use nicotine and illegal drugs, to have stolen items within the past year and to have problems in school. In a report issued last December, the American Medical Association found that teen drinking—not bingeing, just drinking—can seriously damage growth processes of the brain and that such damage "can be long term and irreversible." The AMA warned that "short term or moderate drinking impairs learning and memory far more in youth than in adults" and that "adolescents need only drink half as much to suffer the same negative effects." This exhaustive study concluded that teen drinkers "perform worse in school, are more likely to fall behind and have an increased risk of social problems, depression, suicidal thoughts and violence."

5   Alcohol is a major contributing factor in the three leading causes of teen death—accidents, homicide and suicide—and increases the chances of juvenile delinquency and crime. Studies at the National Center on Addiction and Substance Abuse at Columbia University have found that teenagers who drink are more likely than those who do not to have sex and have it at an earlier age and with multiple partners.

6   There are many reasons why teens drink, but I doubt that states setting the drinking age at 21 is one of them. Focus groups of young women suggest

that the increase in their binge drinking is related to their wanting to "be one of the boys" and to reduce inhibition, particularly because of the pressure many feel to have sex. Few understand that, on average, one drink has the impact on a woman that it takes two drinks to have on a man. Adolescents of both sexes who have low self-esteem or learning disabilities, or who suffer eating disorders, are at higher risk of drinking.

As for the alcohol industry's role: The Center on Alcohol Marketing and 7 Youth at Georgetown University recently revealed that during the past two years, those under 21 heard more beer and liquor commercials on the radio than did adults. The Kaiser Family Foundation Teen Media Monitor, released in February, identified Coors Light and Budweiser beers as two of the five largest advertisers on the most popular television shows for teen boys. For the alcohol industry, it's a good long-term investment, because underage drinkers are likelier to become heavy adult drinkers and grow up to become that 9 percent of adult drinkers who consume 46.3 percent of the alcohol sold in the United States. If Mr. Reid thinks that politicians are hanging tough on the drinking age of 21 in order to "garner support and contributions from interest groups," I suggest he take a look at the political contributions from the alcohol industry to keep the price down by killing tax increases (and in this Congress to roll taxes back) and to prevent content and caloric labeling of its products.

Fortunately, overwhelming majorities of teens in the United States (84 8 percent) and adults (83 percent) favor keeping the legal drinking age of 21. Rather than paint rosy but unrealistic pictures of life in countries where teens can legally buy alcohol, we need to get serious about preventing underage drinking. We need to address the many factors that influence teens to drink: genetics, family situation, peer pressure, schools, access to alcohol, alcohol advertising targeting teens. The best place to start is to help parents understand the consequences of their teen's drinking.

QUESTIONS FOR READING

1. What is Califano's initial purpose in writing?
2. How do American teens compare with European teens in terms of alcohol consumption, binge drinking, and intoxication?
3. What are the consequences of teen drinking?
4. What are some of the causes of teen drinking?
5. How do American adults and teens feel about this country's drinking age?

QUESTIONS FOR REASONING AND ANALYSIS

1. Analyze Califano's argument using Toulmin's terms.
2. Analyze the author's organization. What does he do first? Second? And so on? How does his organization help his rebuttal?

3.   Evaluate Califano's argument. What kind of evidence (grounds) does he use? Is it effective?

QUESTIONS FOR REFLECTING AND WRITING

1.   Do you agree with Califano? If so, then presumably you accept the legal drinking age of 21—right? If you disagree with Califano, what are your counterarguments?
2.   Usually, what kind of argument works best with you, one based on personal experience and anecdote or one based on statistics?

1. What are some problems caused by college students' drinking? You may be able to offer some answers to this questions based on your knowledge and experience. You may also want to go online for some statistics about college drinking and health and safety risks. Drawing on both experience and data, what claim can you support?

2. Compare the style and tone in Reid's and Califano's essays. Has each one written in a way that works for the author's approach to this issue? Be prepared to explain your views or develop them into a comparative analysis of style.

3. Explore further into the strongly debated issue of zoos. Check your library's electronic database for recent articles. If you are near a zoo, take a look at the animals and the zoo's programs and schedule an interview with one of the curators. Where does your new information lead you? Can you defend a position on zoos?

GOING ONLINE

A good starting place for online research about college drinking and health and safety risks is at **www.collegedrinkingprevention.gov**, or conduct your own search.

CHAPTER 4

Writing Effective Arguments

READ: Who are the figures in the drawing? What are they doing?

REASON: What details in the drawing help you to date the scene? The central figure is probably what historical person?

REFLECT/WRITE: What is significant about the moment captured in this drawing?

The basics of good writing remain much the same for works as seemingly different as the personal essay, the argument, and the researched essay. Good writing is focused, organized, and concrete. Effective essays are written in a style and tone that are suited to both the audience and the writer's purpose. These are sound principles, all well known to you. But how, exactly, do you achieve them when writing argument? This chapter will help you answer that question.

KNOW YOUR AUDIENCE

Too often students plunge into writing without thinking much about audience, for, after all, their "audience" is only the instructor who has given the assignment, just as their purpose in writing is to complete the assignment and get a grade. These views of audience and purpose are likely to lead to badly written arguments. First, if you are not thinking about readers who may disagree with you, you may not develop the best defense of your claim—which may need a rebuttal to possible counterarguments. Second, you may ignore your essay's needed introductory material on the assumption that the instructor, knowing the assignment, has a context for understanding your writing. To avoid these pitfalls, use the following questions to sharpen your understanding of audience.

Who Is My Audience?

If you are writing an essay for the student newspaper, your audience consists—primarily—of students, but do not forget that faculty and administrators also read the student newspaper. If you are preparing a letter-to-the-editor refutation of a recent column in your town's newspaper, your audience will be the readers of that newspaper—that is, adults in your town. Some instructors give assignments that create an audience such as those just described so that you will practice writing with a specific audience in mind.

If you are not assigned a specific audience, imagine your classmates, as well as your instructor, as part of your audience. In other words, you are writing to readers in the academic community. These readers are intelligent and thoughtful, expecting sound reasoning and convincing evidence. These readers also represent varied values and beliefs, as they are from diverse cultures and experiences. Do not confuse the shared expectations of writing conventions with shared beliefs.

What Will My Audience Know About My Topic?

What can you expect a diverse group of readers to know? Whether you are writing on a current issue or a centuries-old debate, you must expect most readers to have some knowledge of the issues. Their knowledge does not free you from the responsibility of developing your support fully, though. In fact, their knowledge creates further demands. For example, most readers know the main arguments on both sides of the abortion issue. For you to write as if they do not—and thus to ignore the arguments of the opposition—is to produce an argument that probably adds little to the debate on the subject.

On the other hand, what some readers "know" may be little more than an overview of the issues from TV news—or the emotional outbursts of a family member. Some readers may be misinformed or prejudiced, but they embrace their views enthusiastically nonetheless. So, as you think about the ways to develop and support your argument, you will have to assess your readers' knowledge and sophistication. This assessment will help you decide how much background information to provide or what false facts need to be revealed and dismissed.

Where Does My Audience Stand on the Issue?

Expect readers to hold a range of views, even if you are writing to students on your campus or to an organization of which you are a member. It is not true, for instance, that all students want coed dorms or pass/fail grading. And, if everyone already agrees with you, you have no reason to write. An argument needs to be about a topic that is open to debate. So:

- Assume that some of your audience will probably never agree with you but may offer you grudging respect if you compose an effective argument.
- Assume that some readers do not hold strong views on your topic and may be open to convincing, if you present a good case.
- Assume that those who share your views will still be looking for a strong argument in support of their position.
- Assume that if you hold an unpopular position your best strategy will be a conciliatory approach. (See p. 103 for a discussion of the conciliatory argument.)

How Should I Speak to My Audience?

Your audience will form an opinion of you based on how you write and how you reason. The image of argument—and the arguer—that we have been creating in this text's discussion is of thoughtful claims defended with logic and evidence. However, the heated debate at yesterday's lunch does not resemble this image of argument. Sometimes the word *persuasion* is used to separate the emotionally charged debate from the calm, intellectual tone of the academic argument. Unfortunately, this neat division between argument and persuasion does not describe the real world of debate. The thoughtful arguer also wants to be persuasive, to win over the audience. And highly emotional presentations can contain relevant facts in support of a sound idea. Instead of thinking of two separate categories—argument and persuasion—think instead of a continuum from the most rigorous logic at one end to extreme flights of fantasy on the other. Figure 4.1 suggests this continuum with some kinds of arguments placed along it.

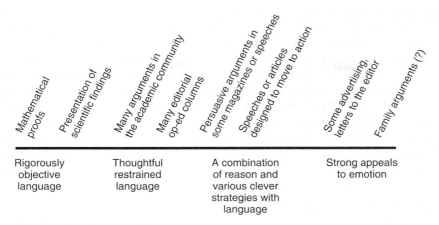

FIGURE 4.1 A Continuum of Argumentative Language

Where should you place yourself along the continuum in the language you choose and the tone you create? You will have to answer this question with each specific writing context. Much of the time you will choose "thoughtful, restrained language" as expected by the academic community, but there may be times that you will use various persuasive strategies. Probably you will not select "strong appeals to emotion" for your college or workplace writing. Remember that you have different roles in your life, and you use different *voices* as appropriate to each role. Most of the time, for most of your arguments, you will want to use the serious voice you normally select for serious conversations with other adults. This is the voice that will help you establish your credibility, your *ethos.*

As you learned in Chapter 2, irony is a useful rhetorical strategy for giving one's words greater emphasis by actually writing the opposite of what you mean. Many writers use irony effectively to give punch to their arguments. Irony catches our attention, makes us think, and engages us with the text. Sarcasm is not quite the same as irony. Irony can cleverly focus reader attention on life's complexities. Sarcasm is more often vicious than insightful, relying on harsh, negative word choice. Probably in most of your academic work, you will want to avoid sarcasm and think carefully about using any strongly worded appeal to your readers' emotions. Better to persuade your audience with the force of your reasons and evidence than to lose them because of the static of nasty language. But the key, always, is to know your audience and understand how best to present a convincing argument to that specific group.

UNDERSTAND YOUR WRITING PURPOSE

There are many types or genres of argument and different reasons for writing—beyond wanting to write convincingly in defense of your views. Different types of arguments require different approaches, or different kinds of evidence. It helps to be able to recognize the kind of argument you are contemplating.

What Type (Genre) of Argument Am I Preparing?

Here are some useful ways to classify arguments and think about their support.

- **Investigative paper similar to those in the social sciences.** If you are asked to collect evidence in an organized way to support a claim about advertising strategies or violence in children's TV programming, then you will be writing an investigative essay. You will present evidence that you have gathered and analyzed to support your claim.

- **Evaluation.** If your assignment is to explain why others should read a particular book or take a particular professor's class, then you will be preparing an evaluation argument. Be sure to think about your criteria: What makes a book or a professor good? Why do you dislike Amy Winehouse? Is it really her music—or her lifestyle?

- **Definition.** If you are asked to explain the meaning of a general or controversial term, you will be writing a definition argument. What do we mean by *wisdom?* What are the characteristics of *cool?* A definition argument usually requires both specific details to illustrate the term and general ideas to express its meaning.

- **Claim of values.** If you are given the assignment to argue for your position on euthanasia, trying juveniles as adults, or the use of national identification cards, recognize that your assignment calls for a position paper, a claim based heavily on values. Pay close attention to your warrants or assumptions in any philosophical debate.

- **Claim of policy.** If you are given a broad topic: "What should we do about _____?" and you have to fill in the blank, your task is to offer solutions to a current problem. What should we do about childhood obesity? About home foreclosures? These kinds of questions are less philosophical and more practical. Your solutions must be workable.

- **A Refutation or Rebuttal.** If you are given the assignment to find a letter to the editor, a newspaper editorial, or an essay in this text with which you disagree, your job is to write a refutation essay, a specific challenge to a specific argument. You know, then, that you will repeatedly refer to the work you are rebutting, so you will need to know it thoroughly.

What Is My Goal?

It is also helpful to consider your goal in writing—beyond completing an assignment. Does your topic—or the assignment—call for a strong statement of views (i.e., "These are the steps we must take to reduce childhood obesity")? Or, is your goal an exploratory one, a thinking through of possible answers to a more philosophical question ("Why is it often difficult to separate performance from personality when we evaluate a star?")? Thinking about your goal as well as the argument's genre will help you decide on the kinds of evidence needed and on the approach you take and tone you select.

Will the Rogerian or Conciliatory Approach Work for Me?

Psychologist Carl Rogers asserts that the most successful arguments take a conciliatory approach. The characteristics of this approach include:

- Showing respect for the opposition in the language and tone of the argument.
- Seeking common ground by indicating specific facts and values that both sides share.
- Qualifying the claim to bring opposing sides more closely together.

In their essay "Euthanasia—A Critique," authors Peter A. Singer and Mark Siegler provide a good example of a conciliatory approach. They begin their essay by explaining and then rebutting the two main arguments in favor of euthanasia. After stating the two arguments in clear and neutral language, they write this in response to the first argument:

> We agree that the relief of pain and suffering is a crucial goal of medicine. We question, however, whether the care of dying patients cannot be improved without resorting to the drastic measure of euthanasia. Most physical pain can be relieved with the appropriate use of analgesic agents. Unfortunately, despite widespread agreement that dying patients must be provided with necessary analgesia, physicians continue to underuse analgesia in the care of dying patients because of the concern about depressing respiratory drive or creating addiction. Such situations demand better management of pain, not euthanasia.

In this paragraph the authors accept the value of pain management for dying patients. They go even further and offer a solution to the problem of suffering among the terminally ill—better pain management by doctors. They remain thoughtful in their approach and tone throughout, while sticking to their position that legalizing euthanasia is not the solution.

Consider how you can use the conciliatory approach to write more effective arguments. It will help you avoid "overheated" language and maintain your focus on what is doable in a world of differing points of view. There is the expression that "you can catch more flies with honey than with vinegar." Using "honey" instead of "vinegar" might also make you feel better about yourself.

MOVE FROM TOPIC TO CLAIM TO POSSIBLE SUPPORT

When you write a letter to the editor of a newspaper, you have chosen to respond to someone else's argument that has bothered you. In this writing context, you already know your topic and, probably, your claim as well. You also know that your purpose will be to refute the article you have read. In composition classes, the context is not always so clearly established, but you will usually be given some guidelines with which to get started.

Selecting a Topic

Suppose that you are asked to write an argument that is in some way connected to First Amendment rights. Your instructor has limited and focused your topic choice and purpose. Start thinking about possible topics that relate to freedom of speech and censorship issues. To aid your topic search and selection, use one or more invention strategies:

- Brainstorm (make a list).
- Freewrite (write without stopping for 10 minutes).
- Map or cluster (connect ideas to the general topic in various spokes, a kind of visual brainstorming).
- Read through this text for ideas.

Your invention strategies lead, let us suppose, to the following list of possible topics:

Administrative restrictions on the college newspaper
Hate speech restrictions or codes
Deleting certain books from high school reading lists
Controls and limits on alcohol and cigarette advertising
Restrictions on violent TV programming
Dress codes/uniforms

Looking over your list, you realize that the last item, dress codes/uniforms, may be about freedom but not freedom of speech, so you drop it from consideration. All of the other topics have promise. Which one do you select? Two considerations should guide you: interest and knowledge. First, your argument is likely to be more thoughtful and lively if you choose an issue that matters to you. But, unless you have time for study, you are wise to choose a topic about which you already have some information and ideas. To continue the example, let's suppose that you decide to write about television violence because you are concerned about violence in American society, and you have given this issue some thought. It is time to phrase your topic as a tentative thesis or claim.

Drafting a Claim

Good claim statements will keep you focused in your writing—in addition to establishing your main idea for readers. Give thought, then, both to your position on the issue and to the wording of your claim. *Claim statements to avoid:*

- Claims using vague words such as *good* or *bad*.

    VAGUE: TV violence is bad for us.

    BETTER: We need more restrictions on violent TV programming.

- Claims in loosely worded "two-part" sentences.

    UNFOCUSED: Campus rape is a serious problem, and we need to do
    something about it.

> **BETTER:**   College administrators and students need to work together to reduce both the number of campus rapes and the fear of rape.

- Claims that are not appropriately qualified.

> **OVERSTATED:**   Violence on television is making us a violent society.
>
> **BETTER:**   TV violence is contributing to viewers' increased fear of violence and insensitivity to violence.

- Claims that do not help you focus on your purpose in writing.

> **UNCLEAR PURPOSE:**   Not everyone agrees on what is meant by violent TV programming.

(Perhaps this is true, but more important, this claim suggests that you will define violent programming. Such an approach would not keep you focused on a First Amendment issue.)

> **BETTER:**   Restrictions on violent TV programs can be justified.

(Now your claim directs you to the debate over restrictions of content.)

Listing Possible Grounds

As you learned in Chapter 3, you can generate grounds to support a claim by adding a "because" clause after a claim statement. We can start a list of grounds for the topic on violent TV programming in this way:

We need more restrictions on violent television programming *because*

- Many people, including children and teens, watch many hours of TV (get stats).
- People are affected by the dominant activities/experiences in their lives.
- There is a connection between violent programming and desensitizing and fear of violence and possibly more aggressive behavior in heavy viewers (get detail of studies).
- Society needs to protect young people.

You have four good points to work on, a combination of reasons and inferences drawn from evidence.

Listing Grounds for the Other Side or Another Perspective

Remember that arguments generate counterarguments. Continue your exploration of this topic by considering possible rebuttals to your proposed grounds. How might someone who does not want to see restrictions placed on television programming respond to each of your points? Let's think about them one at a time:

We need more restrictions on violent television programming because

1. *Many people, including children and teens, watch many hours of TV.*

Your opposition cannot really challenge your first point on the facts, only its relevance to restricting programming. The opposition might argue that if parents think their children are watching too much TV, they should turn it off. The restriction needs to be a family decision.

2.   *People are affected by the dominant activities/experiences in their lives.*

It seems common sense to expect people to be influenced by dominant forces in their lives. Your opposition might argue, though, that many people have the TV on for many hours but often are not watching it intently for all of that time. The more dominant forces in our lives are parents and teachers and peers, not the TV. The opposition might also argue that people seem to be influenced to such different degrees by television that it is not fair or logical to restrict everyone when perhaps only a few are truly influenced by their TV viewing to a harmful degree.

3.   *There is a connection between violent programming and desensitizing and fear of violence and possibly more aggressive behavior in heavy viewers.*

Some people are entirely convinced by studies showing these negative effects of violent TV programming, but others point to the less convincing studies or make the argument that if violence on TV were really so powerful an influence, most people would be violent or fearful or desensitized.

4.   *Society needs to protect young people.*

Your opposition might choose to agree with you in theory on this point—and then turn again to the argument that parents should be doing the protecting. Government controls on programming restrict adults, as well as children, whereas it may only be some children who should watch fewer hours of TV and not watch adult "cop" shows at all.

Working through this process of considering opposing views can help you see

- Where you may want to do some research for facts to provide backing for your grounds.
- How you can best develop your reasons to take account of typical counter arguments.
- If you should qualify your claim in some ways.

Planning Your Approach

Now that you have thought about arguments on the other side, you decide that you want to argue for a qualified claim that is also more precise:

> To protect young viewers, we need restrictions on violence in children's programs and ratings for prime-time adult shows that clearly establish the degree of violence in those shows.

This qualified claim responds to two points of the rebuttals. Our student hasn't given in to the other side but has chosen to narrow the argument to emphasize the protection of children, an area of common ground.

Next, it's time to check some of the articles in this text or go online to get some data to develop points 1 and 3. You need to know that 99 percent of homes have at least one TV; you need to know that by the time young people graduate from high school they have spent more time in front of the TV than in the classroom. Also, you can find the average number of violent acts by hour of TV in children's programs. Then, too, there are the various studies of fearfulness and aggressive behavior that will give you some statistics to use to develop the third point. Be sure to select reliable sources and then cite the sources you use. *Citing sources is not only required and right; it is also part of the process of establishing your credibility and thus strengthening your argument.*

Finally, how are you going to answer the point about parents controlling their children? You might counter that in theory this is the way it should be—but in fact not all parents are at home watching what their children are watching, and not all parents care enough to pay attention. However, all of us suffer from the consequences of those children who are influenced by their TV watching to become more aggressive or fearful or desensitized. These children grow up to become the adults the rest of us have to interact with, so the problem becomes one for the society as a whole to solve, not individual parents. If you had not disciplined yourself to go through the process of listing possible rebuttals, you may not have thought through this part of the debate.

DRAFT YOUR ARGUMENT

Many of us can benefit from a step-by-step process of invention—such as we have been exploring in the last few pages. In addition, the more notes you have from working through the Toulmin structure, the easier it will be to get started on your draft. Many students report that they can control their writing anxiety when they generate detailed notes. A page or two of notes that also suggest an organizational strategy can remove that awful feeling of staring at a blank computer screen.

In the following chapters on argument, you will find specific suggestions for organizing the various kinds of arguments. But you can always rely on one of the following two basic organizations for argument, regardless of the specific genre:

PLAN 1: ORGANIZING AN ARGUMENT

Attention-getting opening (why the issue is important, or current, etc.)

Claim statement

Reasons and evidence in order from least important to most important

Challenge to potential rebuttals or counterarguments

Conclusion that reemphasizes claim

PLAN 2: ORGANIZING AN ARGUMENT

Attention-getting opening

Claim statement (or possibly leave to the conclusion)

Order by arguments of opposing position, with your challenge to each

Conclusion that reemphasizes (or states for the first time) your claim

GUIDELINES for Drafting

- **Try to get a complete draft of an essay in one sitting, so that you can "see" the whole piece.**
- **If you can't think of a clever opening, state your claim and move on to the body of your essay.** After you draft your reasons and evidence, a good opening may occur to you.
- **If you find that you need something more in some parts of your essay, leave space there as a reminder that you will need to return to that paragraph later.**
- **Try to avoid using either a dictionary or thesaurus while drafting.** Your goal is to get the ideas down. You will polish later.
- **Learn to draft at your computer.** Revising is so much easier that you will be more willing to make significant changes if you work at your PC. If you are handwriting your draft, leave plenty of margin space for additions or for directions to shift parts around.

REVISE YOUR DRAFT

If you have drafted at the computer, begin revising by printing a copy of your draft. Most of us cannot do an adequate job of revision by looking at a computer screen. Then remind yourself that revision is a three-step process: rewriting, editing, and proofreading.

Rewriting

You are not ready to polish the writing until you are satisfied with the argument. Look first at the total piece. Do you have all the necessary parts: a claim, support, some response to possible counterarguments? Examine the order of your reasons and evidence. Do some of your points belong, logically, in a different place? Does the order make the most powerful defense of your claim? Be willing to move whole paragraphs around to test the best organization. Also reflect on the argument itself. Have you avoided logical fallacies? Have you qualified statements when appropriate? Do you have enough support? The best support?

Consider development: Is your essay long enough to meet assignment requirements? Are points fully developed to satisfy the demands of readers? One key to development is the length of your paragraphs. If most of your paragraphs are only two or three sentences, you have not developed the point of each paragraph satisfactorily. It is possible that some paragraphs need to be combined because they are really on the same topic. More typically, short paragraphs need further explanation of ideas or examples to illustrate ideas. Compare the following paragraphs for effectiveness:

First Draft of a Paragraph from an Essay on Gun Control

One popular argument used against the regulation of gun ownership is the need of citizens, especially in urban areas where the crime rate is higher, to possess a handgun for personal protection, either carried or kept in the home. Some citizens may not be aware of the dangers to themselves or their families when they purchase a gun. Others, more aware, may embrace the myth that "bad things only happen to other people."

Revised Version of the Paragraph with Statistics Added

One popular argument used against the regulation of gun ownership is the need of citizens, especially in urban areas where the crime rate is higher, to possess a handgun for personal protection, whether it is carried or kept in the home. Although some citizens may not be aware of the dangers to themselves or their families when they purchase a gun, they should be. According to the Center to Prevent Handgun Violence, from their Web page "Firearm Facts," "guns that are kept in the home for self-protection are 22 times more likely to kill a family member or friend than to kill in self-defense." The Center also reports that guns in the home make homicide three times more likely and suicide five times more likely. We are not thinking straight if we believe that these dangers apply only to others.

A quick trip to the Internet has provided this student with some facts to support his argument. Observe how he has referred informally but fully to the source of his information. (If your instructor requires formal MLA documentation in all essays, then you will need to add a Works Cited page and give a full reference to the Web site. See pp. 326–28.)

Editing

Make your changes, print another copy, and begin the second phase of revision: editing. As you read through this time, pay close attention to unity and coherence, to sentence patterns, and to word choice. Read each paragraph as a separate unit to be certain that everything is on the same subtopic. Then look at your use of transition and connecting words, both within and between paragraphs. Ask yourself: Have you guided the reader through the argument using appropriate connectors such as *therefore, in addition, as a consequence, also,* and so forth?

Read again, focusing on each sentence, checking to see that you have varied sentence patterns and length. Read sentences aloud to let your ear help you find awkward constructions or unfinished thoughts. Strive as well for word choice that is concrete and specific, avoiding wordiness, clichés, trite expressions, or incorrect use of specialized terms. Observe how Samantha edited one paragraph in her essay "Balancing Work and Family":

Draft Version of Paragraph

Women have come a long way in equalizing themselves, but inequality within marriages do exist. One reason for this can be found in the media. Just last week America turned on their televisions to watch a grotesque dramatization of skewed priorities. On *Who Wants to Marry a Millionaire,* a panel of women

Vague reference.

Wordy.

vied for the affections of a millionaire who would choose one of them to be his wife. This show said that women can be purchased. Also that men must provide and that money is worth the sacrifice of one's individuality. The show also suggests that physical attraction is more important than the building of a complete relationship. Finally, the show says that women's true value lies

in their appearance. This is a dangerous message to send to both men and women viewers.

Edited Version of Paragraph

Although women have come a long way toward equality in the workplace, inequality within marriages can still be found. The media may be partly to blame for this continued inequality. Just last week Americans watched a grotesque dramatization of skewed priorities. On *Who Wants to Marry a Millionaire,* a panel of women vied for the affections of a millionaire who would choose one of them to be his wife. Such displays teach us that women can be purchased, that men must be the providers, that the desire for money is worth the sacrifice of one's individuality, that physical attraction is more important than a complete relationship, and that women's true value lies in their appearance. These messages discourage marriages based on equality and mutual support.

Samantha's editing has eliminated wordiness and vague references and has combined ideas into one forceful sentence. Support your good argument by taking the time to polish your writing.

A Few Words About Words and Tone

You have just been advised to check your word choice to eliminate wordiness, vagueness, clichés, and so on. Here is a specific checklist of problems often found in student papers with some ways to fix the problems.

- *Eliminate clichés.* Do not write about "the fast-paced world we live in today" or the "rat race." First, do you know for sure that the pace of life for someone who has a demanding job is any faster than it was in the past? Using time effectively has always mattered. Also, clichés suggest that you are too lazy to find your own words.

- *Avoid jargon.* In the negative sense of this word, "jargon" refers to nonspecialists who fill their writing with "heavy-sounding terms" to give the appearance of significance. Watch for any overuse of "scientific" terms such as *factor* or *aspect,* or other vague, awkward language.

- *Avoid language that is too informal for most of your writing contexts.* What do you mean when you write: "*Kids* today watch too much TV"? Alternatives include *children, teens, adolescents.* These words are less slangy and more precise.

- *Avoid nasty attacks on the opposition.* Change "those jerks who are foolish enough to believe that TV violence has no impact on children" to language that explains your counterargument without attacking those who may disagree with you. After all, you want to change the thinking of your audience, not make them resent you for name-calling.

- *Avoid all discriminatory language.* In the academic community and the adult workplace, most people are bothered by language that belittles any one group. This includes language that is racist or sexist or reflects negatively on older or disabled persons or those who do not share your sexual orientation or religious beliefs. Just don't do it!

Proofreading

You also do not want to lose the respect of readers because you submit a paper filled with "little" errors—errors in punctuation, mechanics, and incorrect word choice. Most readers will forgive one or two little errors but will become annoyed if they begin to pile up. So, after you are finished rewriting and editing, print a copy of your paper and read it slowly, looking specifically at punctuation, at the handling of quotations and references to writers and to titles, and at those pesky words that come in two or more "versions": *to, too,* and *two; here* and *hear; their, there,* and *they're;* and so forth. If instructors have found any of these kinds of errors in your papers over the years, then focus your attention on the kinds of errors you have been known to make.

Refer to Chapter 1 for handling references to authors and titles and for handling direct quotations. Use a glossary of usage in a handbook for homonyms (words that sound alike but have different meanings), and check a handbook for punctuation rules. Take pride in your work and present a paper that will be treated with respect. What follows is a checklist of the key points for writing good arguments that we have just examined.

A CHECKLIST FOR REVISION ■·■·■·■·■·■·■·■·■·■·■·■·■·■·■·■·■·■·■

- ☐ Have I selected an issue and purpose consistent with assignment guidelines?
- ☐ Have I stated a claim that is focused, appropriately qualified, and precise?
- ☐ Have I developed sound reasons and evidence in support of my claim?
- ☐ Have I used Toulmin terms to help me study the parts of my argument, including rebuttals to counterarguments?
- ☐ Have I taken advantage of a conciliatory approach and emphasized common ground with opponents?
- ☐ Have I found a clear and effective organization for presenting my argument?
- ☐ Have I edited my draft thoughtfully, concentrating on producing unified and coherent paragraphs and polished sentences?
- ☐ Have I eliminated wordiness, clichés, jargon?
- ☐ Have I selected an appropriate tone for my purpose and audience?
- ☐ Have I used my word processor's spell check and proofread a printed copy with great care?

FOR ANALYSIS AND DEBATE

THAT FEELING OF BEING UNDER SUSPICION | TUNKU VARADARAJAN

Although he holds a law degree from Oxford University, Tunku Varadarajan has chosen journalism for his career. He has been an editorial writer for the London *Times,* a freelance writer for newspapers and magazines, and a media critic and columnist for the *Wall Street Journal.* Currently he is the *WSJ*'s editorial features editor. The following column appeared at WSJ.com, July 29, 2005.

PREREADING QUESTIONS Have you experienced profiling because either you are, or someone thinks that you look like, a Muslim? If so, how did this make you feel? Are you willing to tolerate profiling to advance the war against terrorism?

1   After the terrorist bombings in London, and the revelations that many of the perpetrators were of Pakistani origin, I find that I am—for the first time in my life—part of a "group" that is under broad but emphatic visual suspicion. In other words, I fit a visual "profile," and the fit is most disconcerting.

2   The fact that I am neither Muslim nor Pakistani is irrelevant: Who except the most absurdly expert physiognomist or anthropologist could tell from my face that I am not an Ali, or a Mohammed, or a Hassan; that my ancestors are all from the deepest South India; and that my line has worshipped not Allah but Lord Shiva—mightiest deity of the Hindu pantheon—for 2,000 years? I *will* be mistaken for Muslim at some point—just as earlier this week in Manhattan five young men were pulled off a sightseeing bus and handcuffed by police on suspicion that they might have been Islamist terrorists. Their names, published in the papers, revealed that they were in fact all Sikhs and Hindus—something few could have established by simply looking at them. (The Sikhs here were short-haired and unturbanned.)

3   What we had in this incident—what we must get used to—is a not irrational sequence: alarm, provoked by a belief that someone in the vicinity could do everyone around him great harm, followed instinctively by actions in which the niceties of social intercourse, the judgmental taboos that have been drilled into us, are set aside in the interest of self-preservation.

4   Terrorism has had many effects on society, and the foremost among them are philosophical, or spiritual. We are now called upon to adjust the way we live and think, and to do so we must also adjust the bandwidth of our tolerance. By this I don't mean that we must be less tolerant of others but that some among us must learn to tolerate—or put up with—hardships, inconvenience or a new set of presumptions, given the all-consuming nature of the threat we face, in which "the profiled" and "the profilers" alike are targets.

5   In evaluating the moral fitness of "profiling," I should stress that we are identifying people for *scrutiny,* not punishment. Recall the fate of Cinna the poet, in the Bard's *Julius Caesar,* who is killed by a mob that believes him,

because of his name, to be Cinna the conspirator. When scrutiny becomes stigma, and stigma leads to victimization, a clear jump to evil has occurred. This has not happened in America, and must not.

But what of "profiling" as a forensic tool? Here, one must be satisfied 6 either that profiling *ought* to be done or at least—per Bentham—that it isn't something that "ought *not* to be done." I am satisfied on the second count. The practice cannot be rejected with the old moral clarity. The profiling process is not precisely racial but broadly physical according to "Muslim type." (Does that make it worse or better?) The process under way now does not constitute racial profiling in the classic sense—Muslims, after all, come in flavors other than Pakistani, including white Chechens and black Somalis.

But there is no getting around profiling, surely, because of the life-or-death, 7 instant decisions involved. So we have to ask one section of society to bear up under heightened scrutiny, asking them also to work extra hard—visibly so—to expunge the threat. Meanwhile, and just as important, we must ask the rest of society not to stigmatize those who conform to the broad physical category while also not allowing feelings of racial and moral guilt to slow our society's response to danger.

If I'm sounding overly nuanced on a subject that should, in the view of 8 some, have bright moral outlines, it's because the devil resides in this predicament. We are all facing the quandary of the policeman chasing a suspect who might be armed. Does he shoot or hesitate, shout a warning and possibly get shot? In that situation, society asks that he take the risk of self-harm. In our current situation, large swaths of society might be eradicated. Suddenly we all feel like the cop, and some of us like the suspect.

9   I am just as concerned about catching terrorists (who may look like me) as anyone else who looks different. I can ask that the searches and scrutiny be done in a professional manner, with no insults and nothing that offends my dignity. I, too, see the absurdity of subjecting Chinese grandmothers to the same level of scrutiny as people from the Indian subcontinent at the airport check-in counter.

10   Do I *like* being profiled? Of course not. But my displeasure is yet another manifestation of the extraordinary power of terrorism. I am not being profiled because of racism but rather because Islamist fanatics have declared war on my society. They are the dark power that leads me to an experience in which my individuality is corroded. This is tragic; but it strengthens my resolve to support the war that seeks to destroy terrorism.

QUESTIONS FOR READING

1.   What event has led to Varadarajan's column?
2.   What are some effects of terrorism? What must people learn to tolerate?
3.   When is profiling morally acceptable? When does it become evil?
4.   Why is the current profiling not exactly racial? Why is it acceptable to Varadarajan? (Who is Bentham? If you do not know, look him up.)
5.   What, in the author's view, seems absurd about some airport scrutiny?

QUESTIONS FOR REASONING AND ANALYSIS

1.   What is Varadarajan's claim? What type of argument is this—that is, what is the author's approach to the issue?
2.   Why, in the author's view, is the debate lacking in "bright moral outlines"? Explain his analogy in paragraph 8.
3.   Who, for Varadarajan, is the real enemy, if it is not the profiler?
4.   Varadarajan's approach to a highly emotional issue is worth your reflection. What is the essay's tone? What voice do we hear "speaking" to us? How does his approach influence his argument?

QUESTIONS FOR REFLECTING AND WRITING

1.   Do you agree with the author that profiling is a complex philosophical issue? Why or why not?
2.   If profiling is acceptable, under what circumstances is it acceptable? Are there circumstances in which it is unacceptable, in your view? Explain and defend.

YOU CAN'T FIGHT TERRORISM WITH RACISM | COLBERT I. KING

A native Washingtonian, Colby King has held a number of positions in the government, including special agent for the State Department, and in banking, including at the World Bank. King joined the *Washington Post's* editorial board in 1990, began writing a weekly column in 1995, and became deputy editor of the editorial page in 2000. In 2003 he won a Pulitzer Prize for commentary. His column on fighting terrorism was published July 30, 2005.

PREREADING QUESTIONS Should police and airport security personnel use profiling to protect against terrorism? If profiling were used, would you be a suspect? Does how you answer the second question affect how you answer the first one?

During my day job I work under the title of deputy editorial page editor. 1 That entails paying more than passing attention to articles that appear on the op-ed page. Opinion writers, in my view, should have a wide range in which to roam, especially when it comes to edgy, thought-provoking pieces. Still, I wasn't quite ready for what appeared on the op-ed pages of Thursday's *New York Times* or Friday's *Post.*

A *New York Times* op-ed piece by Paul Sperry, a Hoover Institution media 2 fellow ["It's the Age of Terror: What Would You Do?"], and a *Post* column by Charles Krauthammer ["Give Grandma a Pass; Politically Correct Screening Won't Catch Jihadists"] endorsed the practice of using ethnicity, national origin and religion as primary factors in deciding whom police should regard as possible terrorists—in other words, racial profiling. A second *Times* column, on Thursday, by Haim Watzman ["When You Have to Shoot First"] argued that the London police officer who chased down and put seven bullets into the head of a Brazilian electrician without asking him any questions or giving him any warning "did the right thing."

The three articles blessed behavior that makes a mockery of the rights to 3 which people in this country are entitled.

Krauthammer blasted the random-bag-checks program adopted in the 4 New York subway in response to the London bombings, calling it absurd and a waste of effort and resources. His answer: Security officials should concentrate on "young Muslim men of North African, Middle Eastern and South Asian origin." Krauthammer doesn't say how authorities should go about identifying "Muslim men" or how to distinguish non-Muslim men from Muslim men entering a subway station. Probably just a small detail easily overlooked.

All you need to know is that the culprit who is going to blow you to bits, 5 Krauthammer wrote, "traces his origins to the Islamic belt stretching from Mauritania to Indonesia." For the geographically challenged, Krauthammer's birthplace of the suicide bomber starts with countries in black Africa and stops somewhere in the Pacific Ocean. By his reckoning, the rights and freedoms enjoyed by all should be limited to a select group. Krauthammer argued that authorities should work backward and "eliminate classes of people who are obviously not suspects." In the category of the innocent, Krauthammer would place children younger than 13, people older than 60 and "whole ethnic populations" starting with "Hispanics, Scandinavians and East Asians . . . and women," except "perhaps the most fidgety, sweaty, suspicious-looking, overcoat-wearing, knapsack-bearing young women."

6   Of course, by eliminating Scandinavians from his list of obvious terror suspects, Krauthammer would have authorities give a pass to all white people, since subway cops don't check passengers' passports for country of origin. As for sweaty, fidgety, knapsack-bearing, overcoat-wearing young women who happen to be black, brown or yellow? Tough nuggies, in Krauthammer's book. The age-60 cutoff is meaningless, too, since subway cops aren't especially noted for accuracy in pinning down stages of life. In Krauthammer's worldview, it's all quite simple: Ignore him and his son; suspect me and mine.

7   Sperry also has his own proxy for suspicious characters. He warned security and subway commuters to be on the lookout for "young men praying to Allah and smelling of flower water." Keep your eyes open, he said, for a "shaved head or short haircut" or a recently shaved beard or moustache. Men who look like that, in his book, are "the most suspicious train passengers."

8   It appears to matter not to Sperry that his description also includes huge numbers of men of color, including my younger son, a brown-skinned occasional New York subway rider who shaves his head and moustache. He also happens to be a former federal prosecutor and until a few years ago was a homeland security official in Washington. Sperry's profile also ensnares my older brown-skinned son, who wears a very short haircut, may wear cologne at times, and has the complexion of many men I have seen in Africa and the Middle East. He happens to be a television executive. But what the hell, according to Sperry, "young Muslim men of Arab or South Asian origin" fit the terrorist profile. How, just by looking, can security personnel identify a Muslim male of Arab or South Asian origin goes unexplained.

9   Reportedly, after Sept. 11, 2001, some good citizens of California took out after members of the Sikh community, mistaking them for Arabs. Oh, well, what's a little political incorrectness in the name of national security. Bang, bang—oops, he was Brazilian. Two young black guys were London bombers: one Jamaican, the other Somalian. Muslim, too. Ergo: Watch your back when around black men—they could be, ta-dum, Muslims.

10   So while advocates of racial profiling would have authorities subject men and women of black and brown hues to close scrutiny for criminal suspicions, they would look right past:

- White male Oklahoma bomber Timothy McVeigh, who killed 168 people, including 19 children, and damaged 220 buildings.

- White male Eric Rudolph, whose remote-controlled bomb killed a woman and an off-duty police officer at a clinic, whose Olympic Park pipe bomb killed a woman and injured more than 100, and whose bombs hit a gay club and woman's clinic.

- White male Dennis Rader, the "bind, torture, kill" (BTK) serial killer who terrorized Wichita for 31 years.

- D.C.-born and Silver Spring–raised white male John Walker Lindh, who converted to Islam and was captured in Afghanistan fighting for the Taliban.
- The IRA bombers who killed and wounded hundreds; the neo-fascist bombers who killed 80 people and injured nearly 300 in Bologna, Italy; and the truck bombings in Colombia by Pedro Escobar's gang.

But let's get really current. What about those non-Arab, non-South Asians **11** without black or brown skins who are bombing apartment buildings, train stations and theaters in Russia. They've taken down passenger jets, hijacked schools and used female suicide bombers to a fare-thee-well, killing hundreds and wounding thousands. They are Muslims from Chechnya, and would pass the Krauthammer/Sperry eyeball test for terrorists with ease. After all, these folks hail from the Caucasus; you can't get any more Caucasian than that.

What the racial profilers are proposing is insulting, offensive and—by **12** thought, word and deed, whether intentional or not—racist. You want estrangement? Start down that road of using ethnicity, national origin and religion as a basis for police action and there's going to be a push-back unlike any seen in this country in many years.

QUESTIONS FOR READING

1. What kind of argument is this? How do the opening paragraphs make the type of argument clear?
2. What are Krauthammer's views on random searches? Who should be targeted? Who ignored?
3. What are Sperry's views? Who would he profile?

QUESTIONS FOR REASONING AND ANALYSIS

1. What is King's claim? Where does he state it?
2. How does the author refute the arguments of Krauthammer and Sperry? List his points of rebuttal, both practical and value-based.
3. In paragraphs 10 and 11, King lists those who would not be stopped based on profiling. What is effective about the list? How might Krauthammer and Sperry respond to King's list?
4. Woven into the careful quoting and specific examples are lines that create a hard-edged tone to King's refutation. Find these lines and explain their effect.

QUESTIONS FOR REFLECTING AND WRITING

1. Has King effectively refuted Krauthammer and Sperry? Why or why not?
2. How does King's view differ from Varadarajan's? Can you offer any explanation for their differing positions on profiling?

1. Varadarajan argues that we lack "moral clarity" on the issue of profiling, that terrorism has created a situation of moral uncertainty. Do you agree? Develop an argument either to support or to refute this claim.

2. The two articles on profiling make for interesting comparisons beyond their differing positions on the issue. Do a comparative analysis of the style, format, and choice of evidence in the two essays.

3. Where do you stand on the issue of profiling? Be prepared to defend your position.

GOING ONLINE

You may want to go online to learn more about FBI profiling, about the U.S. government's position on profiling, and, certainly, about various bloggers' views on this topic.

Learning More About Argument: Induction, Deduction, Analogy, and Logical Fallacies

READ: What is the situation? What is Petey's reaction to the snowman? What is the reaction of the two children in the last frame?

REASON: What is surprising about the responses in the last frame? Is there any basis for their conclusions?

REFLECT/WRITE: What makes the cartoon amusing? What is its more serious message?

Y ou can build on your knowledge of the basics of argument, examined in Chapter 3, by understanding some traditional forms of argument: induction, deduction, and analogy. It is also important to recognize arguments that do not meet the standards of good logic.

INDUCTION

Induction is the process by which we reach inferences—opinions based on facts, or on a combination of facts and less debatable inferences. The inductive process moves from particular to general, from support to assertion. We base our inferences on the facts we have gathered and studied. In general, the more evidence, the more convincing the argument. No one wants to debate tomorrow's sunrise; the evidence for counting on it is too convincing. Most inferences, though, are drawn from less evidence, so we need to examine these arguments closely to judge their reasonableness.

The pattern of induction looks like this:

EVIDENCE: There is the dead body of Smith. Smith was shot in his bedroom between the hours of 11:00 P.M. and 2:00 A.M., according to the coroner. Smith was shot by a .32-caliber pistol. The pistol left in the bedroom contains Jones's fingerprints. Jones was seen, by a neighbor, entering the Smith home at around 11:00 the night of Smith's death. A coworker heard Smith and Jones arguing in Smith's office the morning of the day Smith died.

CLAIM: Jones killed Smith.

The facts are presented. The jury infers that Jones is a murderer. Unless there is a confession or a trustworthy eyewitness, the conclusion is an inference, not a fact. This is the most logical explanation; that is, the conclusion meets the standards of simplicity and frequency while accounting for all of the known evidence.

The following paragraph illustrates the process of induction. In their book *Discovering Dinosaurs,* authors Mark Norell, Eugene Gaffney, and Lowell Dingus answer the question "Did dinosaurs really rule the world?"

> For almost 170 million years, from the Late Triassic to the end of the Cretaceous, there existed dinosaurs of almost every body form imaginable: small carnivores, such as *Compsognathus* and *Ornitholestes,* ecologically equivalent to today's foxes and coyotes; medium-sized carnivores, such as *Velociraptor* and the troodontids, analogous to lions and tigers; and the monstrous carnivores with no living analogs, such as *Tyrannosaurus* and *Allosaurus.* Included among the ornithischians and the elephantine sauropods are terrestrial herbivores of diverse body form. By the end of the Jurassic, dinosaurs had even taken to the skies. The only habitats that dinosaurs did not dominate during the Mesozoic were aquatic. Yet, there were marine representatives, such as the primitive toothed bird *Hesperornis.* Like penguins, these birds were flightless, specialized for diving, and probably had to return to land to reproduce. In light of this broad morphologic diversity [number of body forms], dinosaurs did "rule

CLAIM:	Dinosaurs were the dominant life form during the Mesozoic Era.
GROUNDS:	The facts presented in the paragraph.
ASSUMPTION (WARRANT):	The facts are representative, revealing dinosaur diversity.

FIGURE 5.1 The Shape of an Inductive Argument

the planet" as the dominant life form on Earth during most of the Mesozoic [era that includes the Triassic, Jurassic, and Cretaceous periods, 248 to 65 million years ago].

Observe that the writers organize evidence by type of dinosaur to demonstrate the range and diversity of these animals. A good inductive argument is based on a sufficient volume of *relevant* evidence. The basic shape of this inductive argument is illustrated in Figure 5.1.

Observe the inductive process in the following section from Mark A. Norell and Xu Xing's "The Varieties of Tyrannosaurs."

THE VARIETIES OF TYRANNOSAURS | MARK A. NORELL and XU XING

Popular images often portray tyrannosaurs as solitary animals, or speedy, or both. Arguably the best evidence for such behavior is trackways, which are essentially snapshots of individual events. Trackways have indicated herding in sauropods, preserved the moment of a kill, and even suggested that some theropod dinosaurs hunted in packs. Unfortunately, only a couple of tyrannosaur trackways have been recovered, and some are not particularly informative. 1

Other evidence, though, suggests tyrannosaurs were gregarious. For example, some tyrannosaur excavations have yielded multiple individuals. One of those is a quarry that Barnum Brown excavated in the Red Deer River area of what is now Dinosaur Provincial Park in Alberta, Canada. The quarry was re-excavated by Philip J. Currie of the Royal Tyrrell Museum of Paleontology in Drumheller, Alberta. Currie's analysis of collections both old and new showed that several *Albertosaurus* individuals of various ages and sizes were preserved together. Because no other dinosaur species were preserved with those animals, Currie surmised that they died at the same time, perhaps while crossing a dangerous river. Although the find is not definitive evidence for pack behavior, it and other similar depositions of multiple tyrannosaurs are at least highly suggestive that such behavior took place. 2

As for the speed of tyrannosaurs, some fantastic claims have suggested the huge animals could reach sprinterlike speeds. But those claims fail to take account of some basic issues in the physics of movement of large animals. John R. Hutchinson, now at the University of London's Royal Veterinary College, and his colleagues digitally modeled the hind limb and hips of a *T. rex* 3 [see "A Weighty Matter," by Adam Summers, June 2002]. By varying the controllable factors in the model such as posture and the total weight of the animal, Hutchinson was able to calculate how big the muscles of the hind limb must have been for the animal to move at various speeds.

4   His simulations clearly showed that *T. rex* adults could never have run much faster than twenty-five miles an hour. Going faster would have tied up such a high percentage of the total body mass in the hindlimb muscles that the rest of the animal would have been emaciated.

5   In fact, the fastest runners were probably juvenile *T. rex's* and other smaller tyrannosaurs. That suggests the various tyrannosaur species would have exploited different prey in areas where they lived together—just as cheetahs, leopards, and lions do in Africa today. The speed analysis also suggests that *T. rex* and other big species would have gone from speedy youth to lumbering adulthood.

QUESTIONS FOR ANALYSIS

1.   What, specifically, are the authors' two topics?
2.   Underline all statements that are inferences, number them, and then identify the evidence given for each inference.
3.   What general inference about our understanding of dinosaurs do the authors imply?

COLLABORATIVE EXERCISE: Induction

With your class partner or in small groups, make a list of facts that could be used to support each of the following inferences:

1.   Whole-wheat bread is nutritious.
2.   Fido must have escaped under the fence during the night.
3.   Sue must be planning to go away for the weekend.
4.   Students who do not hand in all essay assignments fail Dr. Bradshaw's English class.
5.   The price of Florida oranges will go up in grocery stores next year.

DEDUCTION

Although induction can be described as an argument that moves from particular to general, from facts to inference, deduction cannot accurately be described as the reverse. Deductive arguments are more complex. *Deduction is the reasoning process that draws a conclusion from the logical relationship of two assertions, usually one broad judgment or definition and one more specific assertion, often an inference.* Suppose, on the way out of American history class, you say, "Abraham Lincoln certainly was a great leader." Someone responds with the expected question "Why do you think so?" You explain: "He was great because he performed

CLAIM:	Lincoln was a great leader.
GROUNDS:	1. People who perform with courage and clear purpose in a crisis are great leaders.
	2. Lincoln was a person who performed with courage and a clear purpose in a crisis.
ASSUMPTION (WARRANT):	The relationship of the two reasons leads, logically, to the conclusion.

FIGURE 5.2 The Shape of a Deductive Argument

with courage and a clear purpose in a time of crisis." Your explanation contains a conclusion and an assertion about Lincoln (an inference) in support. But behind your explanation rests an idea about leadership, in the terms of deduction, *a premise.* The argument's basic shape is illustrated in Figure 5.2.

Traditionally, the deductive argument is arranged somewhat differently from these sentences about Lincoln. The two reasons are called *premises;* the broader one, called the *major premise,* is written first and the more specific one, the *minor premise,* comes next. The premises and conclusion are expressed to make clear that assertions are being made about categories or classes. To illustrate:

MAJOR PREMISE: All people who perform with courage and a clear purpose in a crisis are great leaders.

MINOR PREMISE: Lincoln was a person who performed with courage and a clear purpose in a crisis.

CONCLUSION: Lincoln was a great leader.

If these two premises are correctly, that is, logically, constructed, then the conclusion follows logically, and the deductive argument is *valid.* This does not mean that the conclusion is necessarily *true.* It does mean that if you accept the truth of the premises, then you must accept the truth of the conclusion, because in a valid argument the conclusion follows logically, necessarily. How do we know that the conclusion must follow if the argument is logically constructed? Let's think about what each premise is saying and then diagram each one to represent each assertion visually. The first premise says that all people who act a particular way are people who fit into the category called "great leaders":

The second premise says that Lincoln, a category of one, belongs in the category of people who act in the same particular way that the first premise describes:

If we put the two diagrams together, we have the following set of circles, demonstrating that the conclusion follows from the premises:

We can also make negative and qualified assertions in a deductive argument. For example:

PREMISE: No cowards can be great leaders.

PREMISE: Falstaff was a coward.

CONCLUSION: Falstaff was not a great leader.

Or, to reword the conclusion to make the deductive pattern clearer: No Falstaff (no member of this class) is a great leader. Diagramming to test for validity, we find that the first premise says no A's are B's:

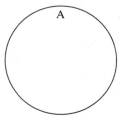 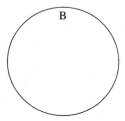

The second premise asserts all C's are A's:

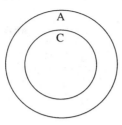

Put together, we see that the conclusion follows necessarily from the premises: No C's can possibly be members of class B.

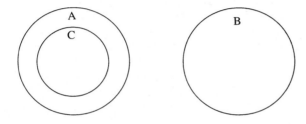

Some deductive arguments merely look right, but the two premises do not lead logically to the conclusion that is asserted. We must read each argument carefully or diagram each one to make certain that the conclusion follows from the premises. Consider the following argument: *Unions must be communistic because they want to control wages.* The sentence contains a conclusion and one reason, or premise. From these two parts of a deductive argument we can also determine the unstated premise, just as we could with the Lincoln argument: *Communists want to control wages.* If we use circles to represent the three categories of people in the argument and diagram the argument, we see a different result from the previous diagrams:

Diagramming the argument reveals that it is invalid; that is, it is not logically constructed because the statements do not require that the union circle be placed inside the communist circle. We cannot draw the conclusion we want from any two premises, only from those that provide a logical basis from which a conclusion can be reached.

We must first make certain that deductive arguments are properly constructed or valid. But suppose the logic works and yet you do not agree with the claim? Your complaint, then, must be with one of the premises, a judgment or inference that you do not accept as true. Consider, as an example, the following argument:

MAJOR PREMISE:	(All) dogs make good pets.
MINOR PREMISE:	Fido is a dog.
CONCLUSION:	Fido will make a good pet.

This argument is valid. (Diagram it; your circles will fit into one another just as with the Lincoln argument.) However, you are not prepared to agree, necessarily, that Fido will make a good pet. The problem is with the major premise. For the argument to work, the assertion must be about *all* dogs, but we know that not all dogs will be good pets.

When composing a deductive argument, your task will be to defend the truth of your premises. Then, if your argument is valid (logically constructed), readers will have no alternative but to agree with your conclusion. If you disagree with someone else's logically constructed argument, then you must show why one of the premises is not true. Your counterargument will seek to discredit one (or both) of the premises. The Fido argument can be discredited by your producing examples of dogs that have not made good pets.

A deductive argument can serve as the core of an essay, an essay that supports the argument's claim by developing support for each of the premises. Since the major premise is either a broad judgment or a definition, it will need to be defended on the basis of an appeal to values or beliefs that the writer expects readers to share. The minor premise, usually an inference about a particular situation (or person), would be supported by relevant evidence, as with any inductive argument. You can see this process at work in the Declaration of Independence. Questions follow the Declaration to guide your analysis of this famous example of the deductive process.

THE DECLARATION OF INDEPENDENCE |

In Congress, July 4, 1776
The unanimous declaration of the thirteen
United States of America

1   When in the course of human events, it becomes necessary for one people to dissolve the political bands which have connected them with another, and to assume among the powers of the earth, the separate and equal station to

which the Laws of Nature and of Nature's God entitle them, a decent respect to the opinions of mankind requires that they should declare the causes which impel them to the separation.

We hold these truths to be self-evident, that all men are created equal, 2 that they are endowed by their Creator with certain unalienable rights, that among these are life, liberty and the pursuit of happiness. That to secure these rights, governments are instituted among men, deriving their just powers from the consent of the governed. That whenever any form of government becomes destructive of these ends, it is the right of the people to alter or to abolish it, and to institute new government, laying its foundation on such principles and organizing its powers in such form, as to them shall seem most likely to effect their safety and happiness. Prudence, indeed, will dictate that governments long established should not be changed for light and transient causes; and accordingly all experience hath shown, that mankind are more disposed to suffer, while evils are sufferable, than to right themselves by abolishing the forms to which they are accustomed. But when a long train of abuses and usurpations, pursuing invariably the same object evinces a design to reduce them under absolute despotism, it is their right, it is their duty, to throw off such government, and to provide new guards for their future security. Such has been the patient sufferance of these Colonies; and such is now the necessity which constrains them to alter their former systems of government. The history of the present King of Great Britain is a history of repeated injuries and usurpations, all having in direct object the establishment of an absolute tyranny over these States. To prove this, let facts be submitted to a candid world.

He has refused his assent to laws, the most wholesome and necessary for 3 the public good.

He has forbidden his Governors to pass laws of immediate and press- 4 ing importance, unless suspended in their operation till his assent should be obtained; and when so suspended, he has utterly neglected to attend to them.

He has refused to pass other laws for the accommodation of large districts 5 of people, unless those people would relinquish the right of representation in the Legislature, a right inestimable to them and formidable to tyrants only.

He has called together legislative bodies at places unusual, uncomfort- 6 able, and distant from the depository of their public records, for the sole purpose of fatiguing them into compliance with his measures.

He has dissolved representative houses repeatedly, for opposing with 7 manly firmness his invasions on the rights of the people.

He has refused for a long time, after such dissolutions, to cause others to 8 be elected; whereby the legislative powers, incapable of annihilation, have returned to the people at large for their exercise; the State remaining in the meantime exposed to all the dangers of invasion from without and convulsions within.

He has endeavoured to prevent the population of these States; for that 9 purpose obstructing the laws of naturalization of foreigners; refusing to pass others to encourage their migration hither, and raising the conditions of new appropriations of lands.

10   He has obstructed the administration of justice, by refusing his assent to laws for establishing judiciary powers.

11   He has made judges dependent on his will alone, for the tenure of their offices, and the amount and payment of their salaries.

12   He has erected a multitude of new offices, and sent hither swarms of officers to harass our people, and eat out their substance.

13   He has kept among us, in times of peace, standing armies without the consent of our legislatures.

14   He has affected to render the military independent of and superior to the civil power.

15   He has combined with others to subject us to a jurisdiction foreign to our constitution, and unacknowledged by our laws; giving his assent to their acts of pretended legislation:

16   For quartering large bodies of armed troops among us:

17   For protecting them, by a mock trial, from punishment for any murders which they should commit on the inhabitants of these States:

18   For cutting off our trade with all parts of the world:

19   For imposing taxes on us without our consent:

20   For depriving us, in many cases, of the benefits of trial by jury:

21   For transporting us beyond seas to be tried for pretended offences:

22   For abolishing the free system of English laws in a neighbouring Province, establishing therein an arbitrary government, and enlarging its boundaries so as to render it at once an example and fit instrument for introducing the same absolute rule into these Colonies:

23   For taking away our Charters, abolishing our most valuable laws, and altering fundamentally the forms of our governments:

24   For suspending our own Legislatures, and declaring themselves invested with power to legislate for us in all cases whatsoever.

25   He has abdicated government here, by declaring us out of his protection and waging war against us.

26   He has plundered our seas, ravaged our coasts, burnt our towns, and destroyed the lives of our people.

27   He is at this time transporting large armies of foreign mercenaries to complete the works of death, desolation and tyranny, already begun with circumstances of cruelty and perfidy scarcely paralleled in the most barbarous ages, and totally unworthy the head of a civilized nation.

28   He has constrained our fellow citizens taken captive on the high seas to bear arms against their country, to become the executioners of their friends and brethren, or to fall themselves by their hands.

29   He has excited domestic insurrections amongst us, and has endeavoured to bring on the inhabitants of our frontiers, the merciless Indian savages, whose known rule of warfare, is an undistinguished destruction of all ages, sexes, and conditions.

30   In every stage of these oppressions we have petitioned for redress in the most humble terms; our repeated petitions have been answered only by

repeated injury. A prince whose character is thus marked by every act which may define a tyrant is unfit to be the ruler of a free people.

Nor have we been wanting in attention to our British brethren. We have 31 warned them from time to time of attempts by their legislature to extend an unwarrantable jurisdiction over us. We have reminded them of the circumstances of our emigration and settlement here. We have appealed to their native justice and magnanimity, and we have conjured them by the ties of our common kindred to disavow these usurpations, which would inevitably interrupt our connections and correspondence. They too have been deaf to the voice of justice and of consanguinity. We must, therefore, acquiesce in the necessity, which denounces our separation, and hold them, as we hold the rest of mankind, enemies in war, in peace friends.

We, therefore, the Representatives of the United States of America, in 32 General Congress assembled, appealing to the Supreme Judge of the world for the rectitude of our intentions, do, in the name, and by the authority of the good people of these Colonies, solemnly publish and declare, That these United Colonies are, and of right ought to be Free and Independent States; that they are absolved from all allegiance to the British Crown, and that all political connection between them and the State of Great Britain, is and ought to be totally dissolved; and that as Free and Independent States, they have full power to levy war, conclude peace, contract alliances, establish commerce, and to do all other acts and things which Independent States may of right do. And for the support of this declaration, with a firm reliance on the protection of Divine Providence, we mutually pledge to each other our lives, our fortunes, and our sacred honor.

QUESTIONS FOR ANALYSIS

1. What is the Declaration's central deductive argument? State the argument in the shape illustrated above: major premise, minor premise, conclusion. Construct a valid argument. If necessary, draw circles representing each of the three terms in the argument to check for validity. (*Hint:* Start with the claim "George III's government should be overthrown.")

2. Which paragraphs are devoted to supporting the major premise? What kind of support has been given?

3. Which paragraphs are devoted to supporting the minor premise? What kind of support has been given?

4. Why has more support been given for one premise than the other?

EXERCISES: Completing and Evaluating Deductive Arguments

Turn each of the following statements into valid deductive arguments. (You have the conclusion and one premise, so you will have to determine the missing premise that would complete the argument. Draw circles if necessary to test for validity.) Then decide which arguments have premises that could be supported. Note the kind of support that might be provided. Explain why you think some arguments have insupportable premises. Here is an example:

PREMISE:	All Jesuits are priests.
PREMISE:	No women are priests.
CONCLUSION:	No women are Jesuits.

Since the circle for women must be placed outside the circle for priests, it must also be outside the circle for Jesuits. Hence the argument is valid. The first premise is true by definition; the term *Jesuit* refers to an order of Roman Catholic priests. The second premise is true for the Roman Catholic Church, so if the term *priest* is used only to refer to people with a religious vocation in the Roman Catholic Church, then the second premise is also true by definition.

1. Mrs. Ferguson is a good teacher because she can explain the subject matter clearly.
2. Segregated schools are unconstitutional because they are unequal.
3. Michael must be a good driver because he drives fast.
4. The media clearly have a liberal bias because they make fun of religious fundamentalists.

ANALOGY

The argument from analogy is an argument based on comparison. Analogies assert that since A and B are alike in several ways, they must be alike in another way as well. The argument from analogy concludes with an inference, an assertion of a significant similarity in the two items being compared. The other similarities serve as evidence in support of the inference. The shape of an argument by analogy is illustrated in Figure 5.3.

Although analogy is sometimes an effective approach to an issue because clever, imaginative comparisons are often moving, analogy is not as rigorously logical as either induction or deduction. Frequently an analogy is based on only two or three points of comparison, whereas a sound inductive argument presents many examples to support its conclusion. Further, to be convincing, the points of comparison must be fundamental to the two items being compared. An argument for a county leash law for cats developed by analogy with dogs may cite the following similarities:

GROUNDS:	A has characteristics 1, 2, 3, and 4.
	B has characteristics 1, 2, and 3.
CLAIM:	B has characteristic 4 (as well).
ASSUMPTION	If B has three characteristics in common with A, it must have
(WARRANT):	the key fourth characteristic as well.

FIGURE 5.3 The Shape of an Argument by Analogy

- Cats are pets, just like dogs.
- Cats live in residential communities, just like dogs.
- Cats can mess up other people's yards, just like dogs.
- Cats, if allowed to run free, can disturb the peace (fighting, howling at night), just like dogs.

Does it follow that cats should be required to walk on a leash, just like dogs? If such a county ordinance were passed, would it be enforceable? Have you ever tried to walk a cat on a leash? In spite of legitimate similarities brought out by the analogy, the conclusion does not logically follow because the arguer is overlooking a fundamental difference in the two animals' personalities. Dogs can be trained to a leash; most cats (Siamese are one exception) cannot be so trained. Such thinking will produce sulking cats and scratched owners. But the analogy, delivered passionately to the right audience, could lead community activists to lobby for a new law.

Observe that the problem with the cat-leash-law analogy is not in the similarities asserted about the items being compared but rather in the underlying assumption that the similarities logically support the argument's conclusion. A good analogy asserts many points of comparison and finds likenesses that are essential parts of the nature or purpose of the two items being compared. The best way to challenge another's analogy is to point out a fundamental difference in the nature or purpose of the compared items. For all of their similarities, when it comes to walking on a leash, cats are *not* like dogs.

EXERCISES: Analogy

1. Analyze the following analogies. List the stated and/or implied points of comparison and the conclusion in the pattern illustrated on page 130. Then judge each argument's logic and effectiveness as a persuasive technique. If the argument is not logical, state the fundamental difference in the two compared items. If the argument could be persuasive, describe the kind of audience that might be moved by it.

   a. College newspapers should not be under the supervision or control of a faculty sponsor. Fortunately, no governmental sponsor controls the *New York Times,* or we would no longer have a free press in this country. We need a free college press, too, one that can attack college policies when they are wrong.

   b. Let's recognize that college athletes are really professional and start paying them properly. College athletes get a free education, and spending money from boosters. They are required to attend practices and games, and—if they play football or basketball—they bring in huge revenues for their "organization." College coaches are also paid enormous salaries, just like professional coaches, and often college coaches are tapped to coach professional teams. The only difference: The poor college athletes don't get those big salaries and huge signing bonuses.

   c. Just like any business, the federal government must be made to balance its budget. No company could continue to operate in the red as the government does and expect to be successful. A constitutional amendment requiring a balanced federal budget is long overdue.

2. Read and analyze the following analogy by Zbigniew Brzezinski. The questions that follow his article will aid your analysis.

WAR AND FOOTBALL | ZBIGNIEW BRZEZINSKI

Former national security advisor to President Jimmy Carter, Dr. Brzezinski is an expert on politics and foreign affairs. He has published many books and articles, including *The Grand Chessboard: American Primacy and Its Geostrategic Imperative* (1997), and currently works at the Center for Strategic and International Studies. His article on football was published in the *Washington Post* on January 7, 2000.

1   I discovered American football late in life. Initially, I thought the game was a bore. When I saw my first football match after coming to America as a child reared on soccer, I was even appalled. Why are all these men, helmeted and wearing protective gear, bending over and then piling on top of one another? I was mystified by their conspiratorial huddling. And when I first heard the referee announce "penalty declined," I remember turning to my American guide and naively noting that it was chivalrous of the rewarded team to have done so.

2   After my appointment to the White House in the mid-'70s, I was favored by invitations to sit in the Redskins' owner's box—and the Washington thing to do, of course, was to go. Before long it dawned on me: The game is unique in the manner it translates into sport all the main ingredients of real warfare. Henceforth I was hooked.

Consider the following parallels: 3

- The owners of the teams are like heads of state. Some are nasty dictators, 4 some merely preside like monarchs. Some posture and are loudmouths, but all are treated with a deference worthy of kings. The senior Cooke— my occasional and very regal host—both reigned and ruled; his son merely reigned. The new, post-Cooke owner conveys an intelligent passion for football, reminiscent of President Nixon, that will probably benefit the team.

- The coaches are the CinCs, to use Washington jargon. They set the overall 5 strategy and supervise its tactical implementation in the course of combat. In constant wireless contact with their forces as well as with their scouting experts (a k a intelligence), examining instant play photos (a k a overhead imagery) and consulting their deputies for offensive and defensive operations, they are clearly the commanders in chief. Some are like Gen. Eisenhower; others remind you of Gen. MacArthur. The truly victorious ones (e.g., Gibbs or Parcells) reflect the needed ability to simultaneously inspire, intimidate and innovate.

- The quarterbacks, as is often noted, are the field commanders. They make 6 last-minute tactical decisions on the basis of direct observation of hostile deployments, and they're expected, when necessary, to improvise tactically, though in the context of their CinCs' overall strategy. Some hustle and take risks; some stay put and just grind away. Again, shades of Gen. Patton or of Gen. Westmoreland.

- The teams engage in offensive and defensive maneuvers, as in real war. 7 They rely either on a concentration of power (especially in ground attacks), on flanking attacks or on sudden deployment behind enemy lines (passing). Deception, speed and force are the required ingredients for success. Skill, precision and iron discipline are instilled by intense training.

- Good intelligence is also essential. Hence much effort is spent on the con- 8 stant monitoring of the enemy's tactics, with specialists (high in the stands, equipped with long-distance observation equipment) seeking to spot potential weaknesses while identifying also the special strengths of the opponent. Timely strategic as well as tactical adjustments (especially during halftime) are often a key to the successful completion of the campaign (a k a game).

- As in real combat, teams suffer casualties, and these can cripple even a 9 strong team. It is especially important to protect the field commander-quarterbacks; they are a key target of enemy action since their loss can be especially disruptive.

- Last but not least, the home front also plays a role. Systematic motivation 10 of the morale of civilians (the spectators) can play an important role in stirring the combatants into greater passion while demoralizing the enemy. The home-field advantage is thus the equivalent to fighting in the defense of your own homeland.

11   Once I understood the above, the mindless piles of bodies, the strange posturing of grown men and the armored uniforms all came to make sense to me. A great game. Like a war.

QUESTIONS FOR READING

1. What were Brzezinski's initial views of American football?
2. What are the points of comparison between football and war? State these in summary form in your own words.

QUESTIONS FOR REASONING AND ANALYSIS

1. The author's subject is clear, as is his use of analogy as a strategy. But, what is his purpose in writing? What does he want readers to conclude from his analogy? (Consider: How do you read the last two sentences? What are most people's attitudes toward war?)
2. What, then, is Brzezinski's thesis, the claim of his argument?
3. What elements of style add to the analogy's effectiveness? How would you describe the essay's tone?

QUESTIONS FOR REFLECTING AND WRITING

1. What kinds of readers are least likely to be moved by the author's analogy? Why?
2. If you do not accept Brzezinski's analogy, how would you counter it?

LOGICAL FALLACIES

A thorough study of argument needs to include a study of logical fallacies because so many "arguments" fail to meet standards of sound logic and good sense. Before examining specific types of arguments that do not work, let's consider briefly why people offer arguments that aren't sensible.

Causes of Illogic

Ignorance

One frequent cause for illogical debate is simply a lack of knowledge of the subject. Some people have more information than others. The younger you are, the less you can be expected to know about or understand complex issues. On the other hand, if you want to debate a complex or technical issue, then you cannot use ignorance as an excuse for producing a weak argument. Instead, read as much as you can, listen carefully to discussions, ask questions, and select topics about which you have knowledge or will research before writing.

Egos

Ego problems are another cause of weak arguments. Those with low self-esteem often have difficulty in debates because they attach themselves to their ideas and then feel personally attacked when someone disagrees with them. Remember: Self-esteem is enhanced when others applaud our knowledge and thoughtfulness, not our irrationality.

Prejudices

The prejudices and biases that we carry around, having absorbed them "ages ago" from family and community, are also sources of irrationality. Prejudices range from the worst ethnic, religious, or sexist stereotypes to political views we have adopted uncritically (Democrats are all bleeding hearts; Republicans are all rich snobs) to perhaps less serious but equally insupportable notions (if it's in print, it must be right). People who see the world through distorted lenses cannot possibly assess facts intelligently and reason logically from them.

A Need for Answers

Finally, many bad arguments stem from a human need for answers—any answers—to the questions that deeply concern us. We want to control our world because that makes us feel secure, and having answers makes us feel in control. This need can lead to illogic from oversimplifying issues.

Based on these causes of illogic, we can usefully divide fallacies into (1) oversimplifying the issue and (2) ignoring the issue by substituting emotion for reason.

Fallacies That Result from Oversimplifying

Errors in Generalizing

Errors in generalizing include overstatement and hasty or faulty generalization. All have in common an error in the inductive pattern of argument. The inference drawn from the evidence is unwarranted, either because too broad a generalization is made or because the generalization is drawn from incomplete or incorrect evidence.

Overstatement occurs when the argument's assertion is unqualified—referring to all members of a category. Overstatements often result from stereotyping, giving the same traits to everyone in a group. Overstatements are frequently signaled by words such as *all, every, always, never,* and *none.* But remember that assertions such as "children love clowns" are understood to refer to "all children," even though the word *all* does not appear in the sentence. It is the writer's task to qualify statements appropriately, using words such as *some, many,* or *frequently,* as appropriate.

Overstatements are discredited by finding only one exception to disprove the assertion. One frightened child who starts to cry when the clown approaches will destroy the argument. Here is another example:

- Lawyers are only interested in making money.

(What about lawyers who work to protect consumers, or public defenders who represent those unable to pay for a lawyer?)

Hasty or faulty generalizations may be qualified assertions, but they still over-simplify by arguing from insufficient evidence or by ignoring some relevant evidence. For example:

- Political life must lead many to excessive drinking. In the last six months the paper has written about five members of Congress who have either confessed to alcoholism or have been arrested on DUI charges.

  (Five is not a large enough sample from which to generalize about *many* politicians. Also, the five in the newspaper are not a representative sample; they have made the news because of their drinking.)

Forced Hypothesis

The *forced hypothesis* is also an error in inductive reasoning. The explanation (hypothesis) offered is "forced," or illogical, because either (1) sufficient evidence does not exist to draw any conclusion or (2) the evidence can be explained more simply or more sensibly by a different hypothesis. This fallacy often results from not considering other possible explanations. You discredit a forced hypothesis by providing alternative conclusions that are more sensible or just as sensible as the one offered. Consider the following example:

- Professor Redding's students received either A's or B's last semester. He must be an excellent teacher.

  (The grades alone cannot support this conclusion. Professor Redding could be an excellent teacher; he could have started with excellent students; he could be an easy grader.)

Non Sequitur

The term *non sequitur,* meaning literally "it does not follow," could apply to all illogical arguments, but the term is usually reserved for those in which the conclusions are not logically connected to the reasons. In a hasty generalization, for example, there is a connection between support (five politicians in the news) and conclusion (many politicians with drinking problems), just not a convincing connection. With the *non sequitur* there is no recognizable connection, either because (1) whatever connection the arguer sees is not made clear to others or because (2) the evidence or reasons offered are irrelevant to the conclusion. For example:

- Donna will surely get a good grade in physics; she earned an A in her biology class.

  (Doing well in one course, even one science course, does not support the conclusion that the student will get a good grade in another course. If Donna is not good at math, she definitely will not do well in physics.)

Slippery Slope

The *slippery slope* argument asserts that we should not proceed with or permit A because, if we do, the terrible consequences X, Y, and Z will occur. This type of argument oversimplifies by assuming, without evidence and usually by ignoring historical examples, existing laws, or any reasonableness in people, that X, Y, and Z will follow inevitably from A. This kind of argument rests on the belief that most people will not want the final, awful Z to occur. The belief, however accurate, does not provide a sufficiently good reason for avoiding A. One of the best-known examples of slippery slope reasoning can be found in the gun-control debate:

- If we allow the government to register handguns, next it will register hunting rifles; then it will prohibit all citizen ownership of guns, thereby creating a police state or a world in which only outlaws have guns.

  (Surely no one wants the final dire consequences predicted in this argument. However, handgun registration does not mean that these consequences will follow. The United States has never been a police state, and its system of free elections guards against such a future. Also, citizens have registered cars, boats, and planes for years without any threat of their confiscation.)

False Dilemma

The *false dilemma* oversimplifies by asserting only two alternatives when there are more than two. The either–or thinking of this kind of argument can be an effective tactic if undetected. If the arguer gives us only two choices and one of those is clearly unacceptable, then the arguer can push us toward the preferred choice. For example:

- The Federal Reserve System must lower interest rates, or we will never pull out of the recession.

  (Clearly, staying in a recession is not much of a choice, but the alternative may not be the only or the best course to achieve a healthy economy. If interest rates go too low, inflation can result. Other options include the government's creating new jobs and patiently letting market forces play themselves out.)

False Analogy

When examining the shape of analogy, we also considered the problems with this type of argument. (See p. 130.) Remember that you challenge a false analogy by noting many differences in the two items being compared or by noting a significant difference that has been ignored.

Post Hoc Fallacy

The term *post hoc*, from the Latin *post hoc, ergo propter hoc* (literally, "after this, therefore because of it") refers to a common error in arguments about cause.

One oversimplifies by confusing a time relationship with cause. Reveal the illogic of *post hoc* arguments by pointing to other possible causes:

- We should throw out the entire city council. Since the members were elected, the city has gone into deficit spending.

  (Assuming that deficit spending in this situation is bad, was it caused by the current city council? Or did the current council inherit debts? Or is the entire region suffering from a recession?)

EXERCISES: Fallacies That Result from Oversimplifying

1. Here is a list of the fallacies we have examined so far. Make up or collect from your reading at least one example of each fallacy.
   a. Overstatement
   b. Stereotyping
   c. Hasty generalization
   d. Forced hypothesis
   e. *Non sequitur*
   f. Slippery slope
   g. False dilemma
   h. False analogy
   i. *Post hoc* fallacy

2. Explain what is illogical about each of the following arguments. Then name the fallacy represented. (Sometimes an argument will fit into more than one category. In that case name all appropriate terms.)
   a. Everybody agrees that we need stronger drunk-driving laws.
   b. The upsurge in crime on Sundays is the result of the reduced rate of church attendance in recent years.
   c. The government must create new jobs. A factory in Illinois has laid off half its workers.
   d. Steve has joined the country club. Golf must be one of his favorite sports.
   e. Blondes have more fun.
   f. You'll enjoy your Volvo; foreign cars never break down.
   g. Gary loves jokes. He would make a great comedian.
   h. The economy is in bad shape because of the Federal Reserve Board. Ever since they expanded the money supply, the stock market has been declining.
   i. Either we improve the city's street lighting, or we will fail to reduce crime.
   j. DNA research today is just like the study of nuclear fission. It seems important, but it's just another bomb that will one day explode on us. When will we learn that government must control research?
   k. To prohibit prayer in public schools is to limit religious practice solely to internal belief. The result is that an American is religiously "free" only in his own mind.
   l. Professor Johnson teaches in the political science department. I'll bet she's another socialist.
   m. Coming to the aid of any country engaged in civil war is a bad idea. Next we'll be sending American troops, and soon we'll be involved in another Vietnam.
   n. We must reject affirmative action in hiring or we'll have to settle for incompetent employees.

3. Examine the logic in this famous passage from Lewis Carroll's *Alice in Wonderland*. What logical fallacy does the king commit?

The King turned pale, and shut his note-book hastily. "Consider your verdict," he said to the jury, in a low trembling voice.

"There's more evidence to come yet, please your Majesty," said the White Rabbit, jumping up in a great hurry: "this paper has just been picked up."

"What's in it?" said the Queen.

"I haven't opened it yet," said the White Rabbit; "but it seems to be a letter, written by the prisoner to—to somebody."

"It must have been that," said the King, "unless it was written to nobody, which isn't usual, you know."

"Who is it directed to?" said one of the jurymen.

"It isn't directed at all," said the White Rabbit; "in fact, there's nothing written on the *outside*." He unfolded the paper as he spoke, and added, "It isn't a letter, after all: it's a set of verses."

"Are they in the prisoner's handwriting?" asked another of the jurymen.

"No, they're not," said the White Rabbit, "and that's the queerest thing about it." (The jury all looked puzzled.)

"He must have imitated somebody else's hand," said the King. (The jury all brightened up again.)

"Please, your Majesty," said the Knave, "I didn't write it, and they can't prove that I did: there's no name signed at the end."

"If you didn't sign it," said the King, "that only makes the matter worse. You *must* have meant some mischief, or else you'd have signed your name like an honest man."

There was a general clapping of hands at this: it was the first really clever thing the King had said that day.

"That *proves* his guilt, of course," said the Queen, "so, off with—"

"It doesn't prove anything of the sort!" said Alice. "Why, you don't even know what they're about!"

Fallacies That Result from Ignoring the Issue

There are many ways to divert attention from the issue under debate. Of the six discussed here, the first three try to divert attention by introducing a separate issue or "sliding by" the actual issue. The following three divert by appealing to the audience's emotions or prejudices. In the first three the arguer tries to give the impression of good logic. In the last three the arguer charges forward on emotional manipulation alone.

Begging the Question

To assume that part of your argument is true without supporting it is to *beg the question*. Arguments seeking to pass off as proof statements that must themselves be supported are often introduced with such phrases as "the fact is" (to introduce opinion),"obviously," and "as we can see." For example:

- Clearly, lowering grading standards would be bad for students, so a pass/fail system should not be adopted.

  (Does a pass/fail system lower standards? No evidence has been given. If so, is that necessarily bad for students?)

Red Herring

The *red herring* is a foul-smelling argument indeed. The debater introduces a side issue, some point that is not relevant to the debate:

- The senator is an honest woman; she loves her children and gives to charities.

  (The children and charities are side issues; they do not demonstrate honesty.)

Straw Man

The *straw man* argument attributes to opponents incorrect and usually ridiculous views that they do not hold so that their position can be easily attacked. We can challenge this illogic by demonstrating that the arguer's opponents do not hold those views or by demanding that the arguer provide some evidence that they do:

- Those who favor gun control just want to take all guns away from responsible citizens and put them in the hands of criminals.

  (The position attributed to proponents of gun control is not only inaccurate but actually the opposite of what is sought by gun-control proponents.)

Ad Hominem

One of the most frequent of all appeals to emotion masquerading as argument is the *ad hominem* argument (literally, argument "to the man"). When someone says that "those crazy liberals at the ACLU just want all criminals to go free," or a pro-choice demonstrator screams at those "self-righteous fascists" on the other side, the best retort may be silence, or the calm assertion that such statements do not contribute to meaningful debate.

Common Practice or Bandwagon

To argue that an action should be taken or a position accepted because "everyone is doing it" is illogical. The majority is not always right. Frequently when someone is defending an action as ethical on the ground that everyone does it, the action isn't ethical and the defender knows it isn't. For example:

- There's nothing wrong with fudging a bit on your income taxes. After all, the superrich don't pay any taxes, and the government expects everyone to cheat a little.

  (First, not everyone cheats on taxes; many pay to have their taxes done correctly. And if it is wrong, it is wrong regardless of the number who do it.)

Ad Populum

Another technique for arousing an audience's emotions and ignoring the issue is to appeal *ad populum*, "to the people," to the audience's presumed shared values and beliefs. Every Fourth of July, politicians employ this tactic, appealing to God, mother, apple pie, and "traditional family values." Simply reject the argument as illogical.

- Good, law-abiding Americans must be sick of the violent crimes occurring in our once godly society. But we won't tolerate it anymore; put the criminals in jail and throw away the key.

(This does not contribute to a thoughtful debate on criminal justice issues.)

EXERCISES: Fallacies That Result from Ignoring the Issue

1. Here is a list of fallacies that result from ignoring the issue. Make up or collect from your reading at least one example of each fallacy.
    a. Begging the question
    b. Red herring
    c. Straw man
    d. *Ad hominem*
    e. Common practice or bandwagon
    f. *Ad populum*
2. Explain what is illogical about each of the following arguments. Then name the fallacy represented.
    a. Gold's book doesn't deserve a Pulitzer Prize. She had been married four times.
    b. I wouldn't vote for him; many of his programs are basically socialist.
    c. Eight out of ten headache sufferers use Bayer to relieve headache pain. It will work for you, too.
    d. We shouldn't listen to Colman McCarthy's argument against liquor ads in college newspapers because he obviously thinks young people are ignorant and need guidance in everything.
    e. My roommate Joe does the craziest things; he must be neurotic.
    f. Since so many people obviously cheat the welfare system, it should be abolished.
    g. She isn't pretty enough to win the contest, and besides she had her nose "fixed" two years ago.
    h. Professors should chill out; everybody cheats on exams from time to time.
    i. The fact is that bilingual education is a mistake because it encourages students to use only their native language and that gives them an advantage over other students.
    j. Don't join those crazy liberals in support of the American Civil Liberties Union. They want all criminals to go free.
    k. Real Americans understand that free trade agreements are evil. Let your representatives know that we want American goods protected.
3. Examine the following letter to the editor by Christian Brahmstedt that appeared in the *Washington Post* on January 2, 1989. If you think it contains logical fallacies, identify the passages and explain the fallacies.

HELP THOSE WHO HELP, NOT HURT, THEMSELVES

1 In the past year, and repeatedly throughout the holiday season, the *Post* has devoted an abnormally large share of newsprint to the "plight" of the vagrants who wander throughout the city in search of free handouts: i.e., the "homeless."

2 As certain as taxes, the poor shall remain with civilization forever. Yet these "homeless" are certainly not in the same category as the poor. The poor of civilization, of which we have all been a part at one time in our lives, are proud and work hard until a financial independence frees them from the category. The "homeless" do not seek work or pride. They are satisfied to beg and survive on others' generosity.

3 The best correlation to the "homeless" I have witnessed are the gray squirrels on Capitol Hill. After feeding several a heavy dose of nuts one afternoon, I returned the next day to see the same squirrels patiently waiting for a return feeding. In the same fashion, the "homeless" are trained by Washington's guilt-ridden society to continue begging a sustenance rather than learning independence.

4 The *Post* has preached that these vagrants be supported from the personal and federal coffers—in the same manner as the squirrels on Capitol Hill. This support is not helping the homeless; it is only teaching them to rely on it. All of our parents struggled through the depression as homeless of a sort, to arise and build financial independence through hard work.

5 The "homeless" problem will go away when, and only when, Washingtonians refuse to feed them. They will learn to support themselves and learn that society demands honest work for an honest dollar.

6 It would be better for Washington citizens to field their guilt donations to the poor, those folks who are holding down two or more jobs just to make ends meet, rather than throwing their tribute to the vagrants on the sewer grates. The phrase "help those who help themselves" has no more certain relevance than to the "homeless" issue.

EXERCISE: Analyzing Arguments

Analyze the following letter to the editor titled "Beer Commercials Do No Harm," published on January 28, 1989, and written by James C. Sanders, president of the Beer Institute. How effectively does Sanders make his case? How convincing is the evidence that he presents? Do you accept his warrant that his evidence is authoritative? If not, what do you think he should have included in the letter? Try to answer these questions in detail to be prepared for class discussion.

BEER COMMERCIALS DO NOT HARM

1   With respect to the letter to the editor of Jan. 13 concerning the banning of beer commercials, we believe it is appropriate to respond. While the tragedy of drunk driving and other abuses of alcohol beverages is of concern to us all, there are much broader problems and solutions that must be addressed.

2   First, we must consider the empirical evidence on the effect or lack of effect of alcohol beverage advertising and its impact on abuse. There exists a substantial body of evidence that suggests that the only impact of alcohol beverage advertising is that of brand preference, shifting those who choose to drink to a particular beverage or brand name.

3   There exists no sound evidence that alcohol beverage advertising has an adverse impact on abuse. Alcohol beverage advertising does not promote excessive consumption, influence nondrinkers to become drinkers or induce young people to drink.

4   In fact, studies show that parents and peers, respectively, are the major contributors to a young person's decision to consume or not to consume. Furthermore, studies have shown that "the best controlled studies show no overall effect of alcohol advertising on consumption."

5   Another related issue is the right to commercial free speech. The alcohol beverage industry—specifically, the beer and wine industries—advertises on television legal products whose responsible, moderate consumption is enjoyed by the majority of our population. This is not to disregard a certain percentage of citizens who should not consume our product—specifically, underage persons and alcoholics.

6   The alcohol beverage industry is concerned and involved in programs that educate, inform and support positive, realistic solutions to alcohol abuse. We are working with many organizations whose goals are to reduce the problems associated with the misuse of our products. Radical or empirically unsound approaches to alcohol problems serve only to divert us from sound, positive solutions.

FOR READING AND ANALYSIS

DECLARATION OF SENTIMENTS | ELIZABETH CADY STANTON

Elizabeth Cady Stanton (1815–1902) was one of the most important leaders of the women's rights movement. Educated at the Emma Willard Seminary in Troy, New York, Stanton studied law with her father before her marriage. At the Seneca Falls Convention in 1848 (the first women's rights convention), Stanton gave the opening speech and read her "Declaration of Sentiments." She founded and became president of the National Women's Suffrage Association in 1869.

PREREADING QUESTION As you read, think about the similarities and differences between this document and the "Declaration of Independence." What significant differences in wording and content do you find?

1   When, in the course of human events, it becomes necessary for one portion of the family of man to assume among the people of the earth a position different from that which they have hitherto occupied, but one to which the laws of nature and of nature's God entitle them, a decent respect to the opinions of mankind requires that they should declare the causes that impel them to such a course.

2   We hold these truths to be self-evident: that all men and women are created equal; that they are endowed by their Creator with certain inalienable rights; that among these are life, liberty, and the pursuit of happiness; that to secure these rights governments are instituted, deriving their just powers from the consent of the governed. Whenever any form of government becomes destructive of these ends, it is the right of those who suffer from it to refuse allegiance to it, and to insist upon the institution of a new government, laying its foundation on such principles, and organizing its powers in such form, as to them shall seem most likely to effect their safety and happiness. Prudence, indeed, will dictate that governments long established should not be changed for light and transient causes; and accordingly all experience hath shown that mankind are more disposed to suffer, while evils are sufferable, than to right themselves by abolishing the forms to which they were accustomed. But when a long train of abuses and usurpations, pursuing invariably the same object evinces a design to reduce them under absolute despotism, it is their duty to throw off such government, and to provide new guards for their future security. Such has been the patient sufferance of the women under this government, and such is now the necessity which constrains them to demand the equal station to which they are entitled.

3   The history of mankind is a history of repeated injuries and usurpations on the part of man toward woman, having in direct object the establishment of an absolute tyranny over her. To prove this, let facts be submitted to a candid world.

He has never permitted her to exercise her inalienable right to the elective 4 franchise.

He has compelled her to submit to laws, in the formation of which she had 5 no voice.

He has withheld from her rights which are given to the most ignorant and 6 degraded men—both natives and foreigners.

Having deprived her of this first right of a citizen, the elective franchise, 7 thereby leaving her without representation in the halls of legislation, he has oppressed her on all sides.

He has made her, if married, in the eye of the law, civilly dead. 8

He has taken from her all right in property, even to the wages she earns. 9

He has made her, morally, an irresponsible being, as she can commit many 10 crimes with impunity, provided they be done in the presence of her husband. In the covenant of marriage, she is compelled to promise obedience to her husband, he becoming, to all intents and purposes, her master—the law giving him power to deprive her of her liberty, and to administer chastisement.

He has so framed the laws of divorce, as to what shall be the proper 11 causes, and in case of separation, to whom the guardianship of the children shall be given, as to be wholly regardless of the happiness of women—the law, in all cases, going upon a false supposition of the supremacy of man, and giving all power into his hands.

After depriving her of all rights as a married woman, if single, and the 12 owner of property, he has taxed her to support a government which recognizes her only when her property can be made profitable to it.

He has monopolized nearly all the profitable employments, and from 13 those she is permitted to follow, she receives but a scanty remuneration. He closes against her all the avenues to wealth and distinction which he considers most honorable to himself. As a teacher of theology, medicine, or law, she is not known.

He has denied her the facilities for obtaining a thorough education, all colleges being closed against her. 14

He allows her in Church, as well as State, but a subordinate position, claiming Apostolic authority for her exclusion from the ministry, and, with some exceptions, from any public participation in the affairs of the Church. 15

He has created a false public sentiment by giving to the world a different code of morals for men and women, by which moral delinquencies which exclude women from society, are not only tolerated, but deemed of little account in man. 16

He has usurped the prerogative of Jehovah himself, claiming it as his right 17 to assign for her a sphere of action, when that belongs to her conscience and to her God.

He has endeavored, in every way that he could, to destroy her confidence 18 in her own powers, to lessen her self-respect, and to make her willing to lead a dependent and abject life.

Now in view of this entire disfranchisement of one-half the people of this 19 country, their social and religious degradation—in view of the unjust laws above mentioned, and because women do feel themselves aggrieved, oppressed, and fraudulently deprived of their most sacred rights, we insist that they have immediate admission to all the rights and privileges which belong to them as citizens of the United States.

20   In entering upon the great work before us, we anticipate no small amount of misconception, misrepresentation, and ridicule; but we shall use every instrumentality within our power to effect our object. We shall employ agents, circulate tracts, petition the State and National legislatures, and endeavor to enlist the pulpit and the press in our behalf. We hope this Convention will be followed by a series of Conventions embracing every part of the country.

QUESTIONS FOR READING

1. Summarize the ideas of paragraphs 1 and 2. Be sure to use your own words.
2. What are the first three facts given by Stanton? Why are they presented first?
3. How have women been restricted by law if married or owning property? How have they been restricted in education and work? How have they been restricted psychologically?
4. What, according to Stanton, do women demand? How will they seek their goals?

QUESTIONS FOR REASONING AND ANALYSIS

1. What is Stanton's claim? With what does she charge men?
2. Most—but not all—of Stanton's charges have been redressed, however slowly. Which continue to be legitimate complaints, in whole or in part?

QUESTIONS FOR REFLECTING AND WRITING

1. Do we need a new declaration of sentiments for women? If so, what specific charges would you list? If not, why not?
2. Do we need a declaration of sentiments for other groups—children, minorities, the elderly, animals? If so, what specific charges should be listed? Select one group (that concerns you) and prepare a declaration of sentiments for that group. If you do not think any group needs a declaration, explain why.

MONGREL AMERICA | GREGORY RODRIGUEZ

A senior fellow at New America Foundation, Gregory Rodriguez is currently working on a book on America's changing views on race as a result of Mexican immigration. His essay, published in the January/February 2003 issue of *Atlantic Monthly*, was one of several written by New America Foundation scholars examining "the state of the union."

PREREADING QUESTIONS What does Rodriguez mean by "mongrel" America? What are some of the ways in which immigrants of the last thirty years have changed this country?

Are racial categories still an important—or even a valid—tool of govern- 1 ment policy? In recent years the debate in America has been between those who think that race is paramount and those who think it is increasingly irrel- evant, and in the next election cycle this debate will surely intensify around a California ballot initiative that would all but prohibit the state from asking its citizens what their racial backgrounds are. But the ensuing polemics will only obscure the more fundamental question: What, when each generation is more racially and ethnically mixed than its predecessor, does race even mean anymore? If your mother is Asian and your father is African-American, what, racially speaking, are you? (And if your spouse is half Mexican and half Russian Jewish, what are your children?)

Five decades after the end of legal segregation, and only thirty-six years 2 after the Supreme Court struck down anti-miscegenation laws, young African- Americans are considerably more likely than their elders to claim mixed heritage. A study by the Population Research Center, in Portland, Oregon, projects that the black intermarriage rate will climb dramatically in this cen- tury, to a point at which 37 percent of African-Americans will claim mixed ancestry by 2100. By then more than 40 percent of Asian-Americans will be mixed. Most remarkable, however, by century's end the number of Latinos claiming mixed ancestry will be more than two times the number claiming a single background.

Not surprisingly, intermarriage rates for all groups are highest in the states 3 that serve as immigration gateways. By 1990 Los Angeles County had an inter- marriage rate five times the national average. Latinos and Asians, the groups that have made up three quarters of immigrants over the past forty years, have helped to create a climate in which ethnic or racial intermarriage is more accepted today than ever before. Nationally, whereas only eight percent of foreign-born Latinos marry non-Latinos, 32 percent of second-generation and 57 percent of third-generation Latinos marry outside their ethnic group. Similarly, whereas only 13 percent of foreign-born Asians marry non-Asians, 34 percent of second-generation and 54 percent of third-generation Asian- Americans do.

Meanwhile, as everyone knows, Latinos are now the largest minority group 4 in the nation. Two thirds of Latinos, in turn, are of Mexican heritage. This is sig- nificant in itself, because their sheer numbers have helped Mexican-Americans do more than any other group to alter the country's old racial thinking. For instance, Texas and California, where Mexican-Americans are the largest minority, were the first two states to abolish affirmative action: when the col- lective "minority" populations in those states began to outnumber whites, the racial balance that had made affirmative action politically viable was subverted.

Many Mexican-Americans now live in cities or regions where they are 5 a majority, changing the very idea of what it means to be a member of a

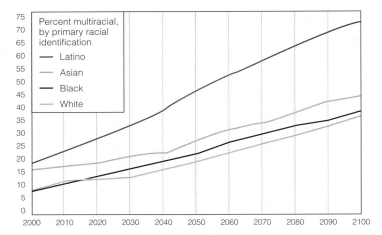

PROJECTED MULTIRACIAL POPULATION, 2000–2100 Led by Latinos, Americans are intermarrying and producing mixed-race children at a rapid rate.

"minority" group. Because of such demographic changes, a number of the policies designed to integrate nonwhites into the mainstream—affirmative action in college admissions, racial set-asides in government contracting—have been rendered more complicated or even counterproductive in recent years. In California cities where whites have become a minority, it is no longer clear what "diversity" means or what the goals of integration policies should be. The selective magnet-school program of the Los Angeles Unified School District, for example, was originally developed as an alternative to forced busing—a way to integrate ethnic-minority students by encouraging them to look beyond their neighborhoods. Today, however, the school district is 71 percent Latino, and Latinos' majority status actually puts them at a disadvantage when applying to magnet schools.

6   But it is not merely their growing numbers (they will soon be the majority in both California and Texas, and they are already the single largest contemporary immigrant group nationwide) that make Mexican-Americans a leading indicator of the country's racial future; rather, it's what they represent. They have always been a complicating element in the American racial system, which depends on an oversimplified classification scheme. Under the pre-civil-rights formulation, for example, if you had "one drop" of African blood, you were fully black. The scheme couldn't accommodate people who were part one thing and part another. Mexicans, who are a product of intermingling—both cultural and genetic—between the Spanish and the many indigenous peoples of North and Central America, have a history of tolerating and even reveling in such ambiguity. Since the conquest of Mexico, in the sixteenth century, they have practiced mestizaje—racial and cultural synthesis—both in their own country and as they came north. Unlike the English-speaking settlers of the western frontier, the Spaniards were willing everywhere they went to allow

racial and cultural mixing to blur the lines between themselves and the natives. The fact that Latin America is far more heavily populated by people of mixed ancestry than Anglo America is the clearest sign of the difference between the two outlooks on race.

Nativists once deplored the Mexican tendency toward hybridity. In the mid-nineteenth century, at the time of the conquest of the Southwest, Secretary of State James Buchanan feared granting citizenship to a "mongrel race." And in the late 1920s Representative John C. Box, of Texas, warned his colleagues on the House Immigration and Naturalization Committee that the continued influx of Mexican immigrants could lead to the "distressing process of mongrelization" in America. He argued that because Mexicans were the products of mixing, they harbored a relaxed attitude toward inter-racial unions and were likely to mingle freely with other races in the United States.   7

Box was right. The typical cultural isolation of immigrants notwithstanding, those immigrants' children and grandchildren are strongly oriented toward the American melting pot. Today two thirds of multiracial and multiethnic births in California involve a Latino parent. Mexicanidad, or "Mexicanness" is becoming the catalyst for a new American cultural synthesis.   8

In the same way that the rise in the number of multiracial Americans muddles U.S. racial statistics, the growth of the Mexican-American mestizo population has begun to challenge the Anglo-American binary view of race. In the 1920 census Mexicans were counted as whites. Ten years later they were reassigned to a separate Mexican "racial" category. In 1940 they were officially reclassified as white. Today almost half the Latinos in California, which is home to a third of the nation's Latinos (most of them of Mexican descent), check "other" as their race. In the first half of the twentieth century Mexican-American advocates fought hard for the privileges that came with being white in America. But since the 1960s activists have sought to reap the benefits of being nonwhite minorities. Having spent so long trying to fit into one side or the other of the binary system, Mexican-Americans have become numerous and confident enough to simply claim their brownness—their mixture. This is a harbinger of America's future.   9

The original melting-pot concept was incomplete: it applied only to white ethnics (Irish, Italians, Poles, and so forth), not to blacks and other nonwhites. Israel Zangwill, the playwright whose 1908 drama _The Melting Pot_ popularized the concept, even wrote that whites were justified in avoiding intermarriage with blacks. In fact, multiculturalism—the ideology that promotes the permanent coexistence of separate but equal, cultures in one place—can be seen as a by-product of America's exclusion of African-Americans from the melting pot; those whom assimilation rejected came to reject assimilation. Although the multicultural movement has always encompassed other groups, blacks gave it its moral impetus.   10

But the immigrants of recent decades are helping to forge a new American identity, something more complex than either a melting pot or a confederation   11 of separate but equal groups. And this identity is emerging not as a result of politics or any specific public policies but because of powerful underlying cultural forces. To be sure, the civil-rights movement was instrumental in the initial assault on racial barriers. And immigration policies since 1965 have tended to favor those immigrant groups—Asians and Latinos—who are most open to intermarriage. But in recent years the government's major contribution to the country's growing multiracialism has been—as it should continue to be—a retreat from dictating limits on interracial intimacy and from exalting (through such policies as racial set-asides and affirmative action) race as the most important American category of being. As a result, Americans cross racial lines more often than ever before in choosing whom to sleep with, marry, or raise children with.

12   Unlike the advances of the civil-rights movement, the future of racial identity in America is unlikely to be determined by politics or the courts or public policy. Indeed, at this point perhaps the best thing the government can do is to acknowledge changes in the meaning of race in America and then get out of the way. The Census Bureau's decision to allow Americans to check more than one box in the "race" section of the 2000 Census was an important step in this direction. No longer forced to choose a single racial identity, Americans are now free to identify themselves as mestizos—and with this newfound freedom we may begin to endow racial issues with the complexity and nuance they deserve.

QUESTIONS FOR READING

1. What are the projected numbers of mixed ancestry for African Americans, Asian Americans, and Latinos?

2. Where are intermarriage rates the highest currently?

3. What is America's largest minority?

4. Where will Mexican Americans soon be the majority group?

5. What kinds of programs have these demographic changes affected?

6. What has long been the attitude of Mexicans toward racial mixing?

7. What is the difference between the melting pot and multiculturalism?

8. What is the new racial identity, and what are emerging attitudes toward the identifying of race in America?

QUESTIONS FOR REASONING AND ANALYSIS

1. What is Rodriguez's subject? What is his claim—what is changing, what is causing the change, and what is Rodriguez's attitude toward the changes?

2. What *type* of argument is this? That is, what kind of evidence does Rodriguez use to support his claim?

3. Why should the changes in demographics that Rodriguez examines change government policies? How does the author support his view on these changes?

4. Evaluate Rodriguez's argument. Do his predictions seem credible? Are the changes he describes consistent with your experiences?

QUESTIONS FOR REFLECTING AND WRITING

1. What group is least likely to agree with the author's conclusions about policy change? Has Rodriguez convinced you of the appropriateness of eliminating such policies as affirmative action and racial set-asides? Why or why not?

2. Is the ongoing blending of cultures good for families? Good for the country? Why or why not? Be prepared to defend your position—with good evidence and good reasons, not with emotion and illogic.

CHAPTER 6

Reading, Analyzing, and Using Visuals and Statistics in Argument

READ: This famous photograph was frequently reprinted and referred to in congressional debates in 1964. What is its subject?

REASON: What details make it dramatic? What message does it send?

REFLECT/WRITE: How does the photo make you feel? What does it lead you to contemplate?

We live in a visual age. Many of us go to movies to appreciate and judge the film's visual effects. The Internet is awash in pictures and colorful icons. Perhaps the best symbol of our visual age is *USA Today*, a paper filled with color photos and many tables and other graphics as a primary way of presenting information. *USA Today* has forced the more traditional papers to add color to compete. We also live in a numerical age. We refer to the events of September 11, 2001, as 9/11—without any disrespect. This chapter brings together these markers of our times as they are used in argument—and as argument. Finding statistics and visuals used as part of argument, we also need to remember that cartoons and advertisements are arguments in and of themselves.

RESPONDING TO VISUAL ARGUMENTS

Many arguments bombard us today in visual forms. These include photos, political cartoons, and advertising. Most major newspapers have a political cartoonist whose drawings appear regularly on the editorial page. (Some comic strips are also political in nature, at least some of the time.) These cartoons are designed to make a political point in a visually clever and amusing way. (That is why they are both "cartoons" and "political" at the same time.) Their uses of irony and caricatures of known politicians make them among the most emotionally powerful, indeed stinging, of arguments.

Photographs accompany many newspaper and magazine articles, and they often tell a story. Indeed some photographers are famous for their ability to capture a personality or a newsworthy moment. So accustomed to these visuals today, we sometimes forget to study photographs. Be sure to examine each photo, remembering that authors and editors have selected each one for a reason.

Advertisements are among the most creative and powerful forms of argument today. Remember that ads are designed to take your time (for shopping) and your money. Their messages need to be powerful to motivate you to action. With some products (what most of us consider necessities), ads are designed to influence product choice, to get us to buy brand A instead of brand B. With other products, ones we really do not need or which may actually be harmful to us, ads need to be especially clever. Some ads do provide information (car X gets better gas mileage than car Y). Other ads (perfume ads, for example) take us into a fantasy land so that we will spend $50 on a small but pretty bottle. Another type of ad is the "image advertisement," an ad that assures us that a particular company is top-notch. If we admire the company, we will buy its goods or services.

Here are guidelines for reading visual arguments with insight. You can practice these steps with the exercises that follow.

GUIDELINES for Reading Photographs

- **Is a scene or situation depicted?** If so, study the details to identify the situation.
- **Identify each figure in the photo.**
- **What details of scene or person(s) carry significance?**
- **How does the photograph make you feel?**

GUIDELINES for Reading Political Cartoons

- **What scene is depicted?** Identify the situation.
- **Identify each of the figures in the cartoon.** Are they current politicians, figures from history or literature, the "person in the street," or symbolic representations?
- **Who speaks the lines in the cartoon?**
- **What is the cartoon's general subject?** What is the point of the cartoon, the claim of the cartoonist?

GUIDELINES for Reading Advertisements

- **What product or service is being advertised?**
- **Who seems to be the targeted audience?**
- **What is the ad's primary strategy?** To provide information? To reinforce the product's or company's image? To appeal to particular needs or desires? For example, if an ad shows a group of young people having fun and drinking a particular beer, to what needs/desires is the ad appealing?
- **Does the ad use specific rhetorical strategies such as humor, understatement, or irony?**
- **What is the relation between the visual part of the ad (photo, drawing, typeface, etc.) and the print part (the text, or copy)?** Does the ad use a slogan or catchy phrase? Is there a company logo? Is the slogan or logo clever? Is it well known as a marker of the company? What may be the effect of these strategies on readers?
- **What is the ad's overall visual impression?** Consider both images and colors used.

EXERCISES: Analyzing Photos, Cartoons, and Ads

1. Analyze the photo on page 155, using the guidelines previously listed.
2. Review the photos that open Chapters 1, 4, 6, 13, 14, 15, 18, and 24. Select the one you find most effective. Analyze it in detail to show why you think it is the best.
3. Analyze the cartoon on page 155 using the guidelines listed previously. You may want to jot down your answers to the questions to be well prepared for class discussion.

4. Review the cartoons that open Chapters 2, 3, 5, 9, 10, 12, 16, 17, 19, 21, 22, and 23. Select the one you find most effective. Analyze it in detail to show why you think it is the cleverest.

5. Analyze the ads on pages 156–58 and in the color insert, again using the guidelines listed above. After answering the guideline questions, consider these as well: Will each ad appeal effectively to its intended audience? If so, why? If not, why not?

Frank and Ernest

© 2005 Thaves. Reprinted with permission. Newspaper dist. by NEA, Inc.

the river of life

....

Retracing a historic journey to help fight malaria.

....

In 1858, Scottish missionary David Livingstone embarked on a historic journey along the Zambezi River in southern Africa. On that trip, malaria claimed the life of Livingstone's wife, Mary. Livingstone himself also later died from the disease.

Today, 150 years later, malaria remains a threat. Over one million people, mostly children and pregnant women, die from malaria each year. About 40 percent of the global population is vulnerable to the disease.

But an unprecedented global action—by governments and corporations, NGOs and health organizations—has been mobilized against malaria. And this combined effort is yielding results:

• Across Africa, people are receiving anti-malarial medications, as well as bed nets and insecticides that protect against the mosquitoes that transmit the disease.

Photo by Helge Bendl

• In Rwanda, malaria cases are down by 64 percent, and deaths by 66 percent. Similar results are seen in Ethiopia and Zambia. And in Mozambique, where 9 out of 10 children had been infected, that number is now 2 in 10.

• Scientists are expanding the pipeline of affordable, effective anti-malarial medicines, while also making progress on discovering a vaccine.

April 25 is World Malaria Day. As part of that event, a team of medical experts will retrace Livingstone's journey along the Zambezi, the "River of Life." As part of the Roll Back Malaria Zambezi Expedition, they will travel 1,500 miles in inflatable boats through Angola, Namibia, Botswana, Zambia, Zimbabwe and Mozambique.

By exposing the difficulties of delivering supplies to remote areas, the expedition will demonstrate that only a coordinated, cross-border action can beat back the disease, and turn the lifeline of southern Africa into a "River of Life" for those threatened by malaria.

ExxonMobil is the largest non-pharmaceutical private-sector contributor to the fight against malaria. But our support is more than financial. We are actively partnering with governments and agencies in affected countries, enabling them to combat malaria with the same disciplined, results-based business practices that ExxonMobil employs in its global operations.

Livingstone once said, "I am prepared to go anywhere, provided it be forward." The communities burdened by this disease cannot move forward until malaria is controlled and, someday, eradicated. We urge everyone to join in this global effort.

For more information, visit www.zambezi-expedition.org and www.rollbackmalaria.org.

ExxonMobil
Taking on the world's toughest energy challenges.

THEY'D RATHER BE IN COLORADO.

Taking the same dull vacation can start eating away at you after a while. So why not try Colorado? The mountains. The magic. The plains. The people. The history. The culture. The fun. The sheer exhilaration of something new. Something you can't experience anywhere else.

Call us or give our Web site a nibble.

COLORADO

1-800-COLORADO · WWW.COLORADO.COM

In the middle of this whole oil mess, ethanol is a bright spot.

America is spending more than $1 billion a day on imported oil—wreaking havoc on the economy and driving up the price of everything from gasoline to groceries. On the other hand, ethanol is saving Americans 15% or more at the pump.* At $4 per gallon, that's a $12 savings on 20 gallons—every time you fill up.

Ethanol adds billions of gallons of cleaner burning, renewable fuel to our nation's total fuel supply—putting downward pressure on prices. Reducing our dangerous and expensive addiction to imported oil. Keeping billions of dollars right here in America.

Ethanol is an important component in our nation's long-term energy strategy. It's working for us today—and will contribute even more tomorrow.

ethanol
fueling America's future

*Read the research and discover more about the benefits of ethanol for our economy, our environment and our nation's energy security at **DrivingEthanol.org**.

READING GRAPHICS

Graphics—photographs, diagrams, tables, charts, and graphs—present a good bit of information in a condensed but also visually engaging format. Graphics are everywhere: in textbooks, magazines, newspapers. It's a rare training session or board meeting that is conducted without the use of graphics to display information. So, you want to be able to read graphics and create them, when appropriate, in your own writing. First, study the chart below that illustrates the different uses of various visuals. Then general guidelines for reading graphics follow. The guidelines will use Figure 6.1 to illustrate points. Study the figure repeatedly as you read through the guidelines.

Understanding How Graphics Differ

Each type of visual serves specific purposes. You can't use a pie chart, for example, to explain a process; you need a diagram or a flowchart. So, when reading graphics, understand what each type can show you. When preparing your own visuals, select the graphic that will most clearly and effectively present the particular information you want to display.

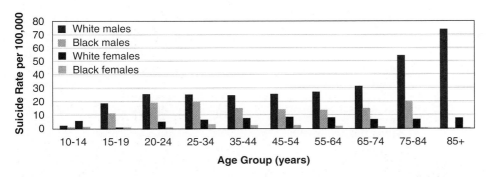

FIGURE 6.1 Differences in Suicide Rate According to Race, Gender, and Age
(Source: Data from the U.S. Bureau of the Census, 1994)

TYPE	PURPOSE	EXAMPLE
Diagram	show details demonstrate process	drawing of knee tendons photosynthesis
Table	list numerical information	income of U.S. households
Bar chart	comparative amounts of related numbers	differences in suicide rates by age and race
Pie chart	relative portions of a whole	percentages of Americans by educational level
Flowchart	steps in a process	purification of water
Graph	relationship of two items	income increases over time
Map	information relative to a geographical area	locations of world's rain forests

GUIDELINES for Reading Graphics

1. **Locate the particular graphic referred to in the text and study it at that point in your reading.** Graphics may not always be placed on the same page as the text reference. Stop your reading to find and study the graphic; that's what the writer wants you to do. Find Figure 6.1 on the previous page.

2. **Read the title or heading of the graphic.** Every graphic is given a title. What is the subject of the graphic? What kind of information is provided? Figure 6.1 shows differences in suicide rates by race, gender, and age.

3. **Read any notes, description, and the source information at the bottom of the graphic.** Figure 6.1 came from the U.S. Bureau of the Census for 1994. Critical questions: What is this figure showing me? Is the information coming from a reliable source? Is it current enough to still be meaningful?

4. **Study the labels—and other words—that appear as part of the graphic.** You cannot draw useful conclusions unless you understand exactly what is being shown. Observe in Figure 6.1 that the four bars for each age group (shown along the horizontal axis) represent white males, black males, white females, and black females, in that order, for each age category.

5. **Study the information, making certain that you understand what the numbers represent.** Are the numerals whole numbers, numbers in hundreds or thousands, or percentages? In Figure 6.1 we are looking at suicide *rates per 100,000 people* for four identified groups of people at different ages. So, to know exactly how many white males between 15 and 19 commit suicide, we need to know how many white males between 15 and 19 there are (or were in 1994) in the United States population. The chart does not give us this information. It gives us *comparative rates* per 100,000 people in each category and tells us that almost 20 in every 100,000 of white males between 15 and 19 commit suicide.

6. **Draw conclusions.** Think about the information in different ways. Critical questions: What does the author want to accomplish by including these

figures? How are they significant? What conclusions can you draw from Figure 6.1? Answer the following questions to guide your thinking.

a. Which of the four compared groups faces the greatest risk from suicide over his or her lifetime? Would you have guessed this group? Why or why not? What might be some of the causes for the greatest risk to this group?

b. What is the greatest risk factor for increased suicide rate—race, gender, age, or a combination? Does this surprise you? Would you have guessed a different factor? Why?

c. Which group, as young teens, is at greatest risk? Are you surprised? Why or why not? What might be some of the causes for this?

Graphics provide information, raise questions, explain processes, engage us emotionally, make us think. Study the various graphics in the exercises that follow to become more expert in reading and responding critically to visuals.

EXERCISES: Reading and Analyzing Graphics

1. Study the pie charts in Figure 6.2 and then answer the following questions.
   a. What is the subject of the charts?
   b. In addition to the information within the pie charts, what other information is provided?
   c. Which group increases by the greatest relative amount? How would you account for that increase?
   d. Which figure surprises you the most? Why?
2. Study the line graph in Figure 6.3 and then answer the following questions.
   a. What two subjects are treated by the graph?
   b. In 2000 what percentage of men's income did women earn?
   c. During which five-year period did men's incomes increase by the greatest amount?

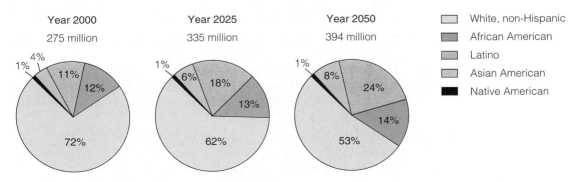

FIGURE 6.2 The Shifting of U.S. Racial-Ethnic Mix (Sources: U.S. Bureau of the Census. *Current Population Reports* P25:1130, 1996; James Henslin, *Sociology: A Down-to-Earth Approach*, 5th ed.)

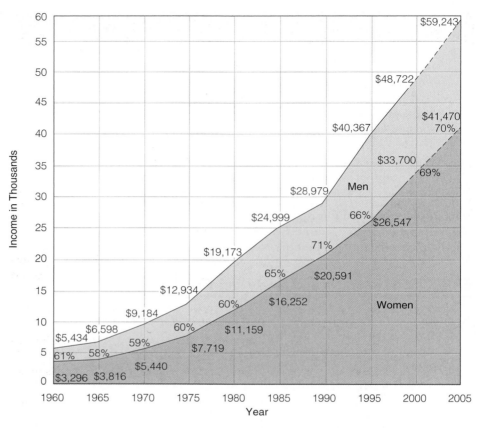

Note: The income jump from 1990 to 1995 is probably due to a statistical procedure. The 1995 source (for 1990 income) uses "median income," while the 1997 source (for 1995 income) merely says "average earnings." How the "average" is computed is not stated. Broken lines indicate the author's estimates.

FIGURE 6.3 What Percentage of Men's Income Do Women Earn? The Gender Gap Over Time (Source: James M. Henslin, *Sociology,* 5th ed.)

  d. Does the author's prediction for the year 2005 suggest that income equality for women will have taken place?

  e. Are you bothered by the facts on this graph? Why or why not?

3. Study the table in Figure 6.4 and then answer the following questions.

  a. What is being presented and compared in this table?

  b. What, exactly, do the numerals in the second line represent? What, exactly, do the numerals in the third line represent? (Be sure that you understand what these numbers mean.)

  c. For the information given in lines 2, 3, 4, and 5, in which category have women made the greatest gains on men?

  d. See if you can complete the missing information in the last line. Where will you look to find out how many men and women were single parents in 2000?

  e. Which figure surprises you the most? Why?

	1970		2000	
	MEN	**WOMEN**	**MEN**	**WOMEN**
Estimated life expectancy	67.1	74.1	74.24	79.9
% high school graduates	53	52	87	88
% of BAs awarded	57	43	45	55
% of MAs awarded	60	40	45	55
% of PhDs awarded	87	13	61	39
% in legal profession	95	5	70	30
Median earnings	$26,760	$14,232	$35,345	$25,862
Single parents	1.2 million	5.6 million	n/a	n/a

FIGURE 6.4 Men and Women in a Changing Society (Sources: for 1970: *1996 Statistical Abstract,* U.S. Dept. of Commerce, Economics and Statistics Administration, Bureau of the Census. 2000 data: National Center for Education Statistics http://nces.ed.gov/fastfacts)

4. Maps, as you can see from color plate 3, can be used to show all kinds of infor-
    mation, not just the locations of cities, rivers, or mountains. Study the map and
    then answer the questions that follow.
    a. What, exactly, does the map show? Why does it not "look right"?
    b. How many electoral votes did each candidate win?
    c. How are the winning states for each candidate clustered? What conclusions
        can you draw from observing this clustering?
    d. What advice would you have given to each party to ensure that party's presi-
        dential win in 2012?
    e. How would the map look if it were drawn to show population by state? Would
        the red states look bigger or smaller?

THE USES OF AUTHORITY AND STATISTICS

Most of the visuals you have just studied provide a way of presenting statistics—
data that many today consider essential to defending a claim. One reason you
check the source information accompanying graphics is that you need to know—
and evaluate—the authority of that source. When a graphic's numbers have
come from the Census Bureau, you know you have a reliable source. When the
author writes that "studies have shown . . .," you want immediately to become
suspicious of the authority of the data. All elements of the arguments we read—
and write—need to be evaluated. They all contribute to the writer's credibility,
or lack thereof.

Judging Authorities

We know that movie stars and sports figures are not authorities on soft drinks
and watches. But what about *real* authorities? When writers present the opinions or research findings of authorities as support for a claim, they are saying to readers that the authority is trustworthy and the opinions valuable. But

what they are asserting is actually an assumption or warrant, part of the glue connecting evidence to claim. Remember: Warrants can be challenged. If the "authority" can be shown to lack authority, then the logic of the argument is destroyed. Use this checklist of questions to aid your evaluation of authorities.

☐ *Is the authority actually an authority on the topic under discussion?* When a famous scientist supports a candidate for office, he or she speaks as a citizen, not as an authority.

☐ *Is the work of the authority still current?* Times change; expertise does not always endure. Galileo would be lost in the universe of today's astrophysicists. Be particularly alert to the dates of information in the sciences in general, in genetics and the entire biomedical field, in health and nutrition. It is almost impossible to keep up with the latest findings in these areas of research.

☐ *Does the authority actually have legitimate credentials?* Are the person's publications in respected journals? Is he or she respected by others in the same field? *Just because it's in print does not mean it's a reliable source!*

☐ *Do experts in the field generally agree on the issue?* If there is widespread disagreement, then referring to one authority does not do much to support a claim. This is why you need to understand the many sides of a controversial topic before you write on it, and you need to bring knowledge of controversies and critical thinking skills to your reading of argument. This is also why writers often provide a source's credentials, not just a name, unless the authority is quite famous.

☐ *Is the authority's evidence reliable, so far as you can judge, but the interpretation of that evidence seems odd, or seems to be used to support strongly held beliefs?* Does the evidence actually connect to the claim? A respected authority's work can be stretched or manipulated in an attempt to support a claim that the authority's work simply does not support.

EXERCISES: Judging Authorities

1. Jane Goodall has received worldwide fame for her studies of chimpanzees in Gombe and for her books on those field studies. Goodall is a vegetarian. Should she be used as an authority in support of a claim for a vegetarian diet? Why or why not? Consider:
   a. Why might Goodall have chosen to become a vegetarian?
   b. For what arguments might Goodall be used as an authority?
   c. For what arguments might she be used effectively for emotional appeal?
2. Suppose a respected zoologist prepares a five-year study of U.S. zoos, compiling a complete list of all animals at each zoo. He then updates the list for each of the five years, adding births and deaths. When he examines his data, he finds that deaths are one and one-half times the number of births. He considers this loss alarming and writes a paper arguing for the abolishing of zoos on the grounds that too many animals are dying. Because of his reputation, his

article is published in a popular science magazine. How would you evaluate his authority and his study?

a. Should you trust the data? Why or why not?

b. Should you accept his conclusions? Why or why not?

c. Consider: What might be possible explanations for the birth/death ratio?

Understanding and Evaluating Statistics

There are two useful clichés to keep in mind: "Statistics don't lie, but people lie with statistics" and "There are lies, damned lies, and statistics." The second cliché is perhaps a bit cynical. We don't want to be naïve in our faith in numbers, but neither do we want to become so cynical that we refuse to believe any statistical evidence. What we do need to keep in mind is that when statistics are presented in an argument they are being used by someone interested in winning that argument.

Some writers use numbers without being aware that the numbers are incomplete or not representative. Some present only part of the relevant information. Some may not mean to distort, but they do choose to present the information in language that helps their cause. There are many ways, some more innocent than others, to distort reality with statistics. Use the following guidelines to evaluate the presentation of statistical information.

GUIDELINES for Evaluating Statistics

Study these questions to be alert to the ways data can be misleading in both the arguments you read and those you write.

- **Is the information current and therefore still relevant?** Crime rates in your city based on 1990 census data probably are no longer relevant, certainly not current enough to support an argument for increased (or decreased) police department spending.

- **If a sample was used, was it randomly selected and large enough to be significant?** Sometimes in medical research, the results of a small study are publicized to guide researchers to important new areas of study. When these results are reported in the press or on TV, however, the small size of the study is not always made clear. Thus one week we learn that coffee is bad for us, the next week that it is okay.

- **What information, exactly, has been provided?** When you read "Two out of three chose the Merit combination of low tar and good taste," you must ask yourself "Two-thirds of how many altogether?"

- **How have the numbers been presented?** And what is the effect of that presentation? Numbers can be presented as fractions, whole numbers, or percentages. Writers who want to emphasize budget increases will use whole numbers—billions of dollars. Writers who want to de-emphasize those increases select percentages. Writers who want their readers to respond to the numbers in a specific way add words to direct their thinking: "a *mere* 3 percent increase" or "the *enormous* $5 billion increase."

EXERCISES: Reading Tables and Charts and Using Statistics

1. Figure 6.5, a table from the *Statistical Abstract of the United States, 2008,* shows U.S. family income data from 1980 to 2005. Percentages and median income are given for all families and then, in turn, for white, black, Asian, and Hispanic families. Study the data and then complete the exercises that follow.
   a. In a paper assessing the advantages of a growing economy, you want to include a paragraph on family income growth to show that a booming economy helps everyone, that "a rising tide lifts all boats." Select data from the table that best support your claim. Write a paragraph beginning with a topic sentence and including your data as support. Think about how to present the numbers in the most persuasive form.
   b. Write a second paragraph with the following topic sentence: "Not all Americans have benefited from the boom years" or "a rising tide does not lift all boats." Select data from the table that best support this topic sentence and present the numbers in the most persuasive form.
   c. Exchange paragraphs with a classmate and evaluate each other's selection and presentation of evidence.
2. Go back to Figure 6.1 (p. 159) and reflect again on the information that it depicts. Then consider what conclusions can be drawn from the evidence and what the implications of those conclusions are. Working in small groups or with a class partner, decide how you want to use the data to support a point.
3. Figure 6.6 (p. 168), another table from the *Statistical Abstract,* presents mean earnings by degree earned. First, be sure that you know the difference between mean and median (which is the number used in Figure 6.5). Study the data and reflect on the conclusions you can draw from the statistics. Consider: Of the various groups represented, which group most benefits from obtaining a college degree—as opposed to having only a high school diploma?

WRITING THE INVESTIGATIVE ARGUMENT

The first step in writing an investigative argument is to select a topic to study. Composition students can write successful investigative essays on the media, on campus issues, and on various local concerns. Although you begin with a topic—not a claim—since you have to gather evidence before you can see what it means, you should select a topic that holds your interest and that you may have given some thought to before choosing to write. For example, you may have noticed some clever ads for jeans or beer, or perhaps you are bothered by plans for another shopping area along a major street near your home. Either one of these topics can lead to an effective investigative, or inductive, argument.

[Constant dollars based on CPI-U-RS deflator. Families as of March of the following year (60,309 represents 60,309,000). Based on Current Population Survey, Annual Social and Economic Supplement (ASEC): see text, Sections 1 and 13, and Appendix III. For data collection changes over time, see <http://www.census.gov/hhes/www/income/histinc/hstchg.html>. For definition of median, see Guide to Tabular Presentation]

| Year | Number of families (1,000) | Percent distribution | | | | | | | Median income (dollars) |
		Under $15,000	$15,000–$24,999	$25,000–$34,999	$35,000–$49,999	$50,000–$74,999	$75,000–$99,999	$100,000 and over	
ALL FAMILIES [1]									
1980	60,309	10.3	12.1	12.6	18.9	24.5	12.0	9.6	47,173
1990	66,322	10.2	10.6	11.3	16.8	22.6	13.4	15.2	51,202
2000 [2]	73,778	8.1	9.7	10.7	15.0	20.7	14.3	21.5	57,508
2004 [3]	76,866	9.2	10.3	10.6	14.5	20.4	13.6	21.4	55,869
2005	77,418	8.9	10.0	10.7	14.6	20.3	13.5	21.8	56,194
WHITE									
1980	52,710	8.4	11.3	12.5	19.2	25.6	12.7	10.3	49,150
1990	56,803	7.8	10.0	11.2	17.2	23.4	14.2	16.2	53,464
2000 [2]	61,330	6.7	9.0	10.3	15.0	21.2	14.9	22.8	60,112
2004 [3,4,5]	63,084	7.6	9.7	10.3	14.3	20.9	14.3	22.9	58,620
2005 [4,5]	63,414	7.2	9.3	10.5	14.7	21.0	14.1	23.2	59,317
BLACK									
1980	6,317	26.1	19.0	13.6	16.7	15.5	6.1	3.0	28,439
1990	7,471	27.0	15.1	13.1	14.4	16.9	7.0	6.4	31,027
2000 [2]	8,731	17.6	15.4	13.6	15.9	18.0	9.4	10.1	38,174
2004 [3,4,6]	8,906	20.8	14.9	13.1	15.4	17.1	9.3	9.4	36,323
2005 [4,6]	9,051	20.5	15.6	13.3	14.7	16.4	9.2	10.2	35,464
ASIAN AND PACIFIC ISLANDER									
1990	1,536	8.7	9.0	8.0	12.8	23.4	15.2	22.7	61,185
2000 [2]	2,982	6.9	6.9	8.1	12.6	18.9	16.0	30.6	70,981
2004 [3,4,7]	3,142	6.2	7.5	8.3	13.1	20.4	13.7	30.8	67,608
2005 [4,7]	3,208	7.8	7.7	7.0	11.8	19.7	14.4	31.6	68,957
HISPANIC ORIGIN [8]									
1980	3,235	18.5	18.9	16.1	18.6	18.3	6.2	3.6	33,021
1990	4,981	19.9	17.0	14.8	17.3	17.4	7.3	6.2	33,935
2000 [2]	8,017	14.5	16.1	14.3	17.8	18.8	9.5	8.9	39,043
2004 [3]	9,521	15.4	17.6	15.0	16.7	17.5	8.3	9.5	36,625
2005	9,868	14.7	16.3	15.2	17.4	18.2	8.9	9.3	37,867

[1] Includes other races not shown separately.   [2] Data reflect implementation of Census 2000-based population controls and a 28,000 household sample expansion to 78,000 households.   [3] Data have been revised to reflect a correction to the weights in the 2005 ASEC.   [4] Beginning with the 2003 Current Population Survey (CPS), the questionnaire allowed respondents to choose more than one race. For 2002 and later, data represent persons who selected this race group only and excludes persons reporting more than one race. The CPS in prior years allowed respondents to report only one race group. See also comments on race in the text for Section 1.   [5] Data represent White alone, which refers to people who reported White and did not report any other race category.   [6] Data represent Black alone, which refers to people who reported Black and did not report any other race category.   [7] Data represent Asian alone, which refers to people who reported Asian and did not report any other race category.   [8] People of Hispanic origin may be of any race.

Source: U.S. Census Bureau, *Current Population Reports*, P60-231; and Internet sites <http://www.census.gov/prod/2006pubs/p60-231.pdf> (released August 2006) and <http://www.census.gov/hhes/www/income/histinc/f23.html>.

FIGURE 6.5 Money Income of Families—Percent Distribution by Income Level in Constant (2005) Dollars: 1980 to 2005

Gathering and Analyzing Evidence

Let's reflect on strategies you will need to use to gather evidence for a study of magazine ads for a particular kind of product (the topic of the sample student paper that follows).

• Select a time frame and a number of representative magazines.

[In dollars. For persons 18 years old and over with earnings. Persons as of March the following year. Based on Current Population Survey; see text, Section 1, and Appendix III. For definition of mean, see Guide to Tabular Presentation]

Characteristic	Total persons	Mean earnings by level of highest degree (dol.)							
		Not a high school graduate	High school graduate only	Some college, no degree	Asso-ciate's	Bache-lor's	Master's	Profes-sional	Doctorate
All persons [1] . . .	**39,579**	**19,915**	**29,448**	**31,421**	**37,990**	**54,689**	**67,898**	**119,009**	**92,863**
Age:									
25 to 34 years old. . . .	34,004	20,355	26,820	30,473	33,011	44,960	48,185	75,600	62,268
35 to 44 years old. . . .	45,373	22,516	32,637	39,124	41,110	60,297	72,098	126,520	97,109
45 to 54 years old. . . .	49,486	24,416	35,209	41,068	42,936	66,776	79,555	137,115	117,324
55 to 64 years old. . . .	46,561	25,071	33,424	41,005	42,532	56,142	69,981	129,956	87,125
65 years old and over . .	35,879	16,995	24,847	26,672	34,303	49,050	62,322	100,847	85,854
Sex:									
Male.	48,034	23,222	35,248	38,768	46,201	67,980	86,667	139,773	105,163
Female	26,897	14,294	22,208	24,086	30,912	40,684	49,573	82,268	66,411
White [2].	40,717	20,264	30,569	32,191	38,788	55,785	69,112	122,975	93,412
Male.	49,611	23,556	36,753	39,849	47,534	69,852	89,207	142,879	105,657
Female	30,125	14,086	22,590	24,248	31,005	40,344	49,281	84,125	66,728
Black [2].	30,472	17,216	23,904	27,291	33,198	47,101	56,057	100,030	79,087
Male.	34,165	19,890	27,360	31,919	38,441	52,070	64,000	(B)	(B)
Female	27,314	14,300	20,449	23,798	29,722	43,516	50,831	76,298	(B)
Hispanic [3].	27,760	19,294	25,659	28,539	33,053	45,933	62,449	83,239	99,774
Male.	31,008	21,632	29,471	33,288	38,764	54,700	74,365	91,546	(B)
Female	22,887	14,365	19,864	23,073	27,673	37,003	50,314	(B)	(B)

B Base figure too small to meet statistical standards for reliability of a derived figure.   [1] Includes other races, not shown separately.   [2] For persons who selected this race group only. See footnote 2, Table 217.   [3] Persons of Hispanic origin may be of any race.

Source: U.S Census Bureau, Current Population Survey. See Internet site <http://www.census.gov/population/www/socdemo/educ-attn.html>.

FIGURE 6.6 Mean Earnings by Highest Degree Earned: 2005

- Have enough magazines to render at least twenty-five ads on the product you are studying.
- Once you decide on the magazines and issues to be used, pull *all* ads for your product. Your task is to draw useful conclusions based on adequate data objectively collected. You can't leave some ads out and have a valid study.
- Study the ads, reflecting on the inferences they allow you to draw. The inferences become the claim of your argument. You may want to take the approach of classifying the ads, that is, grouping them into categories by the various appeals used to sell the product.

More briefly, consider your hunch that your area does not need another shopping mall. What evidence can you gather to support a claim to that effect? You could locate all existing strip or enclosed malls within a 10-mile radius of the proposed new mall site, visit each one, and count the number and types of stores already available. You may discover that there are plenty of malls but that the area really needs a grocery store or a bookstore. So instead of reading to find evidence to support a claim, you are creating the statistics and doing the analysis to guide you to a claim. Just remember to devise objective procedures for collecting evidence so that you do not bias your results.

Planning and Drafting the Essay

You've done your research and studied the data you've collected; how do you put this kind of argument together? Here are some guidelines to help you draft your essay.

GUIDELINES for Writing an Investigative Argument

- **Begin with an opening paragraph that introduces your topic in an interesting way.** Possibilities include beginning with a startling statistic or explaining what impact the essay's facts will have on readers.

- **Devote space early in your paper to explaining your methods or procedures, probably in your second or third paragraph.** For example, if you have obtained information through questionnaires or interviews, recount the process: the questions asked, the number of people involved, the basis for selecting the people, and so on.

- **Classify the evidence that you present.** Finding a meaningful organization is part of the originality of your study and will make your argument more forceful. It is the way you see the topic and want readers to see it. If you are studying existing malls, you might begin by listing all of the malls and their locations. But then do not go store by store through each mall. Rather, group the stores by type and provide totals.

- **Consider presenting evidence in several ways, including in charts and tables as well as within paragraphs.** Readers are used to visuals, especially in essays containing statistics.

- **Analyze evidence to build your argument.** Do not ask your reader to do the thinking. No data dumps! Explain how your evidence *is* evidence by discussing the connection between facts and the inferences they support.

Analyzing Evidence: The Key to an Effective Argument

This is the thinking part of the process. Anyone can count stores or collect ads. What is your point? How does the evidence you have collected actually support your claim? You must guide readers through the evidence. Consider this example:

In a study of selling techniques used in computer ads in business magazines, a student, Brian, found four major selling techniques, one of which he classifies as "corporate emphasis." Brian begins his paragraph on corporate emphasis thus:

> In the technique of corporate emphasis, the advertiser discusses the whole range of products and services that the corporation offers, instead of specific elements. This method relies on the public's positive perception of the company, the company's accomplishments, and its reputation.

Brian then provides several examples of ads in this category, including an IBM ad:

> In one of its eight ads in the study, IBM points to the scientists on its staff who have recently won the Nobel Prize in physics.

But Brian does not stop there. He explains the point of this ad, connecting the ad to the assertion that this technique emphasizes the company's accomplishments:

> The inference we are to draw is that IBM scientists are hard at work right now in their laboratories developing tomorrow's technology to make the world a better place in which to live.

Preparing Graphics

Tables, bar charts, and pie charts are particularly helpful ways to present statistical evidence you have collected for an inductive argument. One possibility is to create a pie chart showing your classification of ads (or stores or questions on a questionnaire) and the relative amount of each item. For example, suppose you find four selling strategies. You can show in a pie chart the percentage of ads using each of the four strategies.

Computers help even the technically unsophisticated prepare simple charts. You can also do a simple table. When preparing graphics, keep these points in mind:

- Every graphic must be referred to in the text at the appropriate place—where you are discussing the information in the visual. Graphics are not disconnected attachments to an argument. They give a complete set of data in an easy-to-digest form, but some of that data must be discussed in the essay.
- Every graphic (except photographs) needs a label. Use Figure 1, Figure 2, and so forth. Then refer to each graphic by its label.
- Every graphic needs a title. Always place a title after Figure 1 (and so forth), on the same line, at the top of your visual.
- In a technically sophisticated world, hand-drawn graphics are not acceptable. Underline the graphic's title line, or place the visual within a box. (Check the tool bar at the top of your screen.) Type elements within tables. Use a ruler or compass to prepare graphics, or learn to use the graphics programs in your computer.

A CHECKLIST FOR REVISION ■▪■▪■▪■▪■▪■▪■▪■▪■▪■▪■▪■▪■▪■

☐ Have I stated a claim that is precise and appropriate to the data I have collected?

☐ Have I fully explained the methodology I used in collecting my data?

☐ Have I selected a clear and useful organization?

☐ Have I presented and discussed enough specifics to show readers how my data support my conclusions?

☐ Have I used graphics to present the data in an effective summary form?

☐ Have I revised, edited, and proofread my paper?

STUDENT ESSAY

BUYING TIME

Garrett Berger

Chances are you own at least one wristwatch. Watches allow us immediate access to the correct time. They are indispensable items in our modern world, where, as the saying is, time is money. Today the primary function of a wristwatch does not necessarily guide its design; like clothes, houses, and cars, watches have become fashion statements and a way to flaunt one's wealth.

Introduction connects to reader.

To learn how watches are being sold, I surveyed all of the full-page ads from the November issues of four magazines. The first two, *GQ* and *Vogue,* are well-known fashion magazines. *The Robb Report* is a rather new magazine that caters to the overclass. *Forbes* is of course a well-known financial magazine. I was rather surprised at the number of advertisements I found. After surveying 86 ads, marketing 59 brands, I have concluded that today watches are being sold through five main strategies: DESIGN/BRAND appeal, CRAFTSMANSHIP, ASSOCIATION, FASHION appeal, and EMOTIONAL appeal. The percentage of ads using each of these strategies is shown in Figure 1.

Student explains his methodology of collecting ads. Paragraph concludes with his thesis.

In most DESIGN/BRAND appeal ads, only a picture and the brand name are used. A subset of this category uses the same basic strategy with a slogan or phrases to emphasize something about the brand or product. A Mont Blanc ad shows a watch profile with a contorted metal link band, asking the question, "Is that you?" The reputation of the name and the appeal of the design sell the watch. Rolex, perhaps the best-known name in high-end watches, advertises, in *Vogue,* its "Oyster Perpetual Lady-Datejust Pearlmaster." A close-up of the

Discussion of first category.

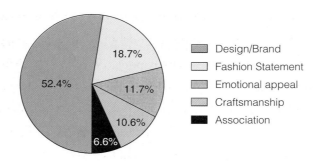

FIGURE 1 Percentage of Total Ads Using Each Strategy

watch face showcases the white, mother-of-pearl dial, sapphire bezel, and diamond-set band. A smaller, more complete picture crouches underneath, showing the watch on its side. The model name is displayed along a gray band that runs near the bottom. The Rolex crest anchors the bottom of the page. Forty-five ads marketing 29 brands use the DESIGN/BRAND strategy. A large picture of the product centered on a solid background is the norm.

Discussion of second category. 　CRAFTSMANSHIP, the second strategy, focuses on the maker, the horologer, and the technical sides of form and function. Brand heritage and a unique, hand-crafted design are major selling points. All of these ads are targeted at men, appearing in every magazine except *Vogue*. Collector pieces and limited editions were commonly sold using this strategy. The focus is on accuracy and technical excellence. Pictures of the inner works and cutaways, technical information, and explanations of movements and features are popular. Quality and exclusivity are all-important.

Detailed examples to illustrate second category. 　A Cronoswiss ad from *The Robb Report* is a good example. The top third pictures a horologer, identified as "Gerd-R Lange, master watchmaker and founder of Cronoswiss in Munich," directly below. The middle third of the ad shows a watch, white-faced with a black leather band. The logo and slogan appear next to the watch. The bottom third contains copy beginning with the words: "My watches are a hundred years behind the times." The rest explains what that statement means. Mr. Lange apparently believes that technical perfection in horology has already been attained. He also offers his book,

The Fascination of Mechanics, free of charge along with the "sole distributor for North America" at the bottom. A "Daniel Roth" ad from the same magazine displays the name across the top of a white page; towards the top, left-hand corner a gold buckle and black band lead your eye to the center, where a gold watch with a transparent face displays its inner works exquisitely. Above and to the right, copy explains the exclusive and unique design accomplished by inverting the movement, allowing it to be viewed from above.

The third strategy is to sell the watch by establishing an ASSOCIATION with an object, experience, or person, implying that its value and quality are beyond question. In the six ads I found using this approach, watches are associated with violins, pilots, astronauts, hot air balloons, and a hero of the free world. This is similar to the first strategy, but relies on a reputation other than that of the maker. The watch is presented as being desirable for the connections created in the ad.

Parmigiani ran an ad in *The Robb Report* featuring a gold watch with a black face and band illuminated by some unseen source. A blue-tinted violin rises in the background; the rest of the page is black. The brief copy reads: "For those who think a Stradivarius is only a violin. The Parmigiani Toric Chronograph is only a wristwatch." "The Moon Watch" proclaims an Omega ad from *GQ*. Inset on a white background is a picture of an astronaut on the moon saluting the American flag. The silver watch with a black face lies across the lower part of the page. The caption reads: "Speedmaster Professional. The first and only watch worn on the moon." Omega's logo appears at the bottom. Figure 2 shows another Omega use of this strategy.

The fourth strategy is to present the watch simply as a FASHION statement. In this line of attack, the ads appeal to our need to be current, accepted, to fit in and be like everyone else, or to make a statement, setting us apart from others as hip and cool. The product is presented as a necessary part of our wardrobes. The watch is fashionable and will send the "right" message. Design and style are the foremost concerns; "the look" sells the watch.

Discussion of third category.

Discussion of fourth category.

FIGURE 2 Example of Association Advertising

Environmentally friendly plastic bags are a beautiful thing. Ecoflex, one of the latest breakthroughs from BASF, is a biodegradable plastic that can be used in bags and packaging. It's shelf stable for one full year, then completely decomposes in compost within a few weeks. Innovation is popping up everywhere. Learn more at basf.com/stories

Helping Make Products Better

BASF
The Chemical Company

got milk?

Lean machine.

When it comes
to winning titles,
perfect form helps.
So I serve up milk.
Studies suggest
people pursuing a
healthy weight could
lose more weight
and burn more fat by
including 24 ounces
a day of lowfat or
fat free milk in their
reduced-calorie
diet, instead of
8 ounces or less.
That's what I call
a nice return.

milk
your diet. Lose
weight!
24 oz. / 24 hours

Search for:

| flights | hotels | cars | vacation packages | cruises | deals | maps |

Whatever it is you're looking for in a hotel, find it at Expedia. From the everyday to the out of this world, Expedia offers you great low rates, photos, amenity lists and more. So you can find the hotel that's right for you.

Expedia.com
Don't just travel. Travel Right.

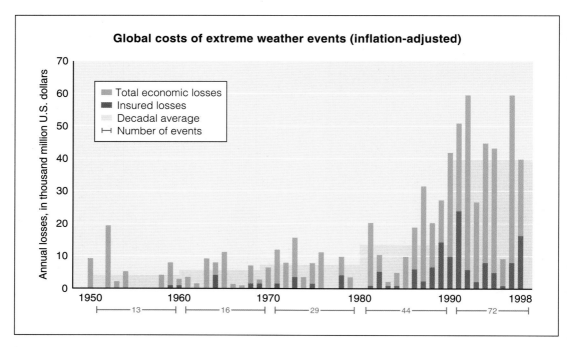

DATA SOURCE: Intergovernmental Panel on Climate Changes

Estimated Number of Adults and Children Living with HIV/AIDS, by Country.

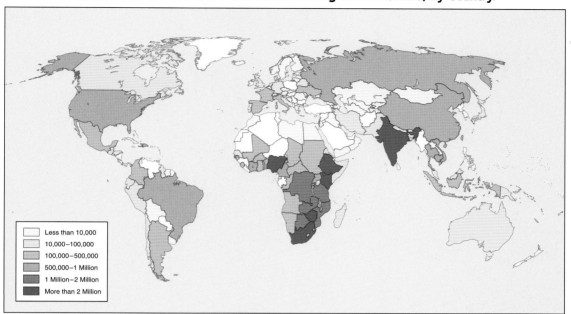

Less than 10,000
10,000−100,000
100,000−500,000
500,000−1 Million
1 Million−2 Million
More than 2 Million

DATA SOURCE: World Health Organization

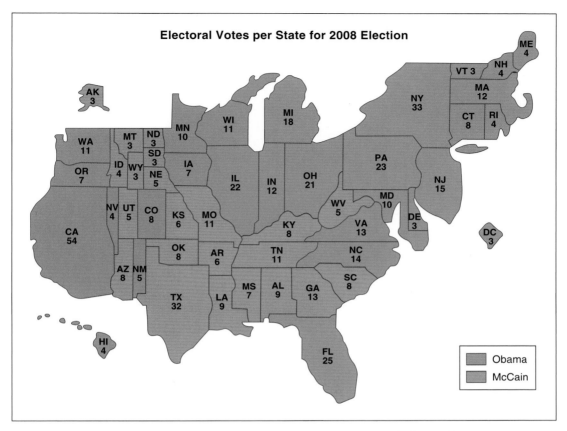

Electoral Votes per State for 2008 Election

ME 4
VT 3
NH 4
NY 33
MA 12
CT 8
RI 4
AK 3
MT 3
ND 3
MN 10
WI 11
MI 18
PA 23
NJ 15
WA 11
SD 3
ID 4
WY 3
NE 5
IA 7
IL 22
IN 12
OH 21
MD 10
DE 3
OR 7
NV 4
UT 5
CO 8
KS 6
MO 11
KY 8
WV 5
VA 13
DC 3
CA 54
OK 8
AR 6
TN 11
NC 14
AZ 8
NM 5
TX 32
LA 9
MS 7
AL 9
GA 13
SC 8
FL 25
HI 4

Obama
McCain

Note: States drawn in proportion to number of electoral votes. Total electoral votes: 538

(Source: Based on a map that originally appeared in New York Times. November 5, 2002. Reprinted by permission of NYT Graphics. From O'Connor and Sabato, American Government © 2002; published by Allyn and Bacon, Boston, MA Copyright © 2002 by Pearson Education. Updated for the 2008 election by the author.)

Techno Marine has an ad in *GQ* which shows a large close-up of a watch running down the entire length of the left side of the page. Two alternate color schemes are pictured on the right, separating small bits of copy. At the bottom on the right are the name and logo. The first words at the top read: "Keeping time—you keep your closet up to the minute, why not your wrist? The latest addition to your watch wardrobe should be the AlphaSport." Longines uses a similar strategy in *Vogue*. Its ad is divided in half lengthwise. On the left is a black-and-white picture of Audrey Hepburn. The right side is white with the Longines' logo at the top and two ladies' watches in the center. Near the bottom is the phrase "Elegance is an Attitude." Retailers appear at the bottom. The same ad ran in *GQ*, but with a man's watch and a picture of Humphrey Bogart. A kind of association is made, but quality and value aren't the overriding concerns. The point is to have an elegant attitude like these fashionable stars did, one that these watches can provide and enhance.

The fifth and final strategy is that of EMOTIONAL appeal. The ads using this approach strive to influence our emotional responses and allege to influence the emotions of others towards us. Their power and appeal are exerted through the feelings they evoke in us. Nine out of ten ads rely on a picture as the main device to trigger an emotional link between the product and the viewer. Copy is scant; words are used mainly to guide the viewer to the advertiser's desired conclusions.

A Frederique Constant ad pictures a man, wearing a watch, mulling over a chess game. Above his head are the words "Inner Passion." The man's gaze is odd; he is looking at something on the right side of the page, but a large picture of a watch superimposed over the picture hides whatever it is that he is looking at. So we are led to the watch. The bottom third is white and contains the maker's logo and the slogan "Live your Passion." An ad in *GQ* shows a man holding a woman. He leans against a rock; she reclines in his arms. Their eyes are closed, and both have peaceful, smiling expressions. He is wearing a

Discussion of fifth category.

Tommy Hilfiger watch. The ad spans two pages; a close-up of the watch is presented on the right half of the second page. The only words are the ones in the logo. This is perhaps one of those pictures that are worth a thousand words. The message is he got the girl because he's got the watch.

Strong conclusion; the effect of watch ads.

Even more than selling a particular watch, all of these ads focus on building the brand's image. I found many of the ads extremely effective at conveying their messages. Many of the better-known brands favor the comparatively simple DESIGN/BRAND appeal strategy, to reach a broader audience. Lesser-known, high-end makers contribute many of the more specialized strategies. We all count and mark the passing hours and minutes. And society places great importance on time, valuing punctuality. But these ads strive to convince us that having "the right time" means so much more than "the time."

FOR READING AND ANALYSIS

EVERY BODY'S TALKING | JOE NAVARRO

Joe Navarro spent more than twenty-five years in the FBI, specializing in counter-intelligence and profiling. He is recognized as an authority on nonverbal messages, especially given off by those who are lying, and he continues to consult to government and industry. He has also turned his expertise to poker and has published, with Marvin Karlines, *Read 'Em and Reap* (2006), a guide to reading the nonverbal messages from poker opponents. The following essay appeared in the *Washington Post* on June 24, 2008.

PREREADING QUESTIONS What does the term "counterintelligence" mean? How much attention do you give to body language messages from others?

1   Picture this: I was sailing the Caribbean for three days with a group of friends and their spouses, and everything seemed perfect. The weather was beautiful, the ocean diaphanous blue, the food exquisite; our evenings together were full of laughter and good conversation.

2   Things were going so well that one friend said to the group, "Let's do this again next year." I happened to be across from him and his wife as he spoke those words. In the cacophony of resounding replies of "Yes!" and "Absolutely!" I noticed that my friend's wife made a fist under her chin as she grasped her necklace. This behavior stood out to me as powerfully as if someone had shouted, "Danger!"

I watched the words and gestures of the other couples at the table, and 3 everyone seemed ecstatic—everyone but one, that is. She continued to smile, but her smile was tense.

Her husband has treated me as a brother for more than 15 years, and I con- 4 sider him the dearest of friends. At that moment I knew that things between him and his wife were turning for the worse. I did not pat myself on the back for making these observations. I was saddened.

For 25 years I worked as a paid observer. I was a special agent for the 5 FBI specializing in counterintelligence—specifically, catching spies. For me, observing human behavior is like having software running in the background, doing its job—no conscious effort needed. And so on that wonderful cruise, I made a "thin-slice assessment" (that's what we call it) based on just a few sig- nificant behaviors. Unfortunately, it turned out to be right: Within six months of our return, my friend's wife filed for divorce, and her husband discovered painfully that she had been seeing someone else for quite a while.

When I am asked what is the most reliable means of determining the health 6 of a relationship, I always say that words don't matter. It's all in the language of the body. The nonverbal behaviors we all transmit tell others, in real time, what we think, what we feel, what we yearn for or what we intend.

Now I am embarking on another cruise, wondering what insights I will 7 have about my travel companions and their relationships. No matter what, this promises to be a fascinating trip, a journey for the mind and the soul. I am with a handful of dear friends and 3,800 strangers, all headed for Alaska; for an observer it does not get any better than this.

While lining up to board on our first day, I notice just ahead of me a cou- 8 ple who appear to be in their early 30s. They are obviously Americans (voice, weight and demeanor).

Not so obvious is their dysfunctional relationship. He is standing stoically, 9 shoulders wide, looking straight ahead. She keeps whispering loudly to him, but she is not facing forward. She violates his space as she leans into him. Her face is tense and her lips are narrow slivers each time she engages him with what clearly appears to be a diatribe. He occasionally nods his head but avoids contact with her. He won't let his hips near her as they start to walk side by side. He reminds me of Bill and Hillary Clinton walking toward the Marine One helicopter immediately after the Monica Lewinsky affair: looking straight ahead, as much distance between them as possible.

I think everyone can decipher this one from afar because we have all seen 10 situations like this. What most people will miss is something I have seen this young man do twice now, which portends poorly for both of them. Every time she looks away, he "disses" her. He smirks and rolls his eyes, even as she stands beside him. He performs his duties, pulling their luggage along; I sus- pect he likes to have her luggage nearby as a barrier between them. I won't witness the dissolution of their marriage, but I know it will happen, for the research behind this is fairly robust. When two people in a relationship have contempt for each other, the marriage will not last.

When it comes to relationships and courtship behaviors, the list of useful 11 cues is long. Most of these behaviors we learned early when interacting with

TORSO	ARMS	HANDS AND FINGERS	FEET AND LEGS
LEANING AWAY FROM SOMEONE: Means we dislike or disagree with them. LEANING TOWARD SOMEONE: Means we like or agree with them.	FINGERTIPS SPREAD APART ON A SURFACE: A display of confidence and authority.	THUMBS UP: A good indication of positive thoughts.	JIGGLING/KICKING FOOT: Indicates discomfort.
SPLAYING OUT: A sign of comfort becomes a territorial or dominance display when there are serious issues being discussed.	ARMS AKIMBO: Establishes dominance or communicates there are 'issues.'	STEEPLING: (FINGERTIP TO FINGERTIP) A powerful display of confidence.	CROSSING LEGS: Indicates we are comfortable.
CROSSED ARMS: Suddenly crossing arms tightly is a sign of discomfort.	ARMS BEHIND THE BACK: Says "don't draw near"—keeps people at bay.	NECK TOUCHING: Indicates emotional discomfort, doubt or insecurity.	TOE POINTS UPWARD: Signals a good mood.

Illustrations by Peter Arkle. Reprinted by permission.

our mothers. When we look at loving eyes, our own eyes get larger, our pupils dilate, our facial muscles relax, our lips become full and warm, our skin becomes more pliable, our heads tilt. These behaviors stay with us all of our lives.

12   I watched two lovers this morning in the dining room. Two young people, perhaps in their late 20s, mirror each other, staring intently into each other's eyes, chin on hand, head slightly tilted, nose flaring with each breath. They are trying to absorb each other visually and tactilely as they hold hands across the table.

13   Over time, those who remain truly in love will show even more indicators of mirroring. They may dress the same or even begin to look alike as they

adopt each other's nonverbal expressions as a sign of synchrony and empathy. They will touch each other with kind hands that touch fully, not with the fingertips of the less caring.

They will mirror each other in ways that are almost imperceptible; they will 14 have similar blink rates and breathing rates, and they will sit almost identically. They will look at the same scenery and not speak, merely look at each other and take a deep breath to reset their breathing synchrony. They don't have to talk. They are in harmony physically, mentally and emotionally, just as a baby is in exquisite synchrony with its mother who is tracing his every expression and smile.

As I walk through the ship on the first night, I can see the nonverbals of 15 courtship. There is a beautiful woman, tall, slender, smoking a cigarette outside. Two men are talking to her, both muscular, handsome, interested. She has crossed her legs as she talks to them, an expression of her comfort. As she holds her cigarette, the inside of her wrist turns toward her newfound friends. Her interest and comfort with them resounds, but she is favoring one of them. As he speaks to her, she preens herself by playing with her hair. I am not sure he is getting the message that she prefers him; in the end, I am sure it will all get sorted out.

At the upscale lounge, a man is sitting at the bar talking animatedly to the 16 woman next to him and looking at everyone who walks by. The woman has begun the process of ignoring him, but he does not get it. After he speaks to her a few times, she gathers her purse and places it on her lap. She has turned slightly away from him and now avoids eye contact. He has no clue; he thinks he is cool by commenting on the women who pass by. She is verbally and nonverbally indifferent.

The next night it is more of the same. This time, I see two people who just 17 met talking gingerly. Gradually they lean more and more into each other. She is now dangling her sandal from her toes. I am not sure he knows it. Perhaps he sees it all in her face, because she is smiling, laughing and relaxed. Communication is fluid, and neither wants the conversation to end. She is extremely interested.

All of these individuals are carrying on a dialogue in nonverbals. The 18 socially adept will learn to read and interpret the signs accurately. Others will make false steps or pay a high price for not being observant. They may end up like my friend on the Caribbean cruise, who missed the clues of deceit and indifference.

This brings me back to my friend and his new wife, who are on this won- 19 derful voyage. They have been on board for four days, and they are a delight individually and together. He lovingly looks at her; she stares at him with love and admiration. When she holds his hand at dinner, she massages it ever so gently. Theirs is a strong marriage. They don't have to tell me. I can sense it and observe it. I am happy for them and for myself. I can see cues of happiness, and they are unmistakable. You can't ask for more.

QUESTIONS FOR READING

1. What is Navarro's subject? (Do not answer "taking cruises"!)
2. What clues are offered to support the conclusion that the two cruise couples' relationships are about to dissolve?
3. What are the nonverbal messages that reveal loving relationships?
4. What nonverbal messages should the man in the lounge be observing?

QUESTIONS FOR REASONING AND ANALYSIS

1. What is Navarro's claim?
2. What kind of evidence does he provide?
3. How do the illustrations contribute to the argument? What is effective about the author's opening?

QUESTIONS FOR REFLECTING AND WRITING

1. Has the author convinced you that nonverbal language reveals our thoughts and feelings? Why or why not?
2. Can you "read" the nonverbal language of your instructors? Take some time to analyze each of your instructors. What have you learned? (You might also reflect on what messages you may be sending in class.)

SUGGESTIONS FOR DISCUSSION AND WRITING

For all investigative essays—inductive arguments—follow the guidelines in this chapter and use the student essay as your model. Remember that you will need to explain your methods for collecting data, to classify evidence and present it in several formats, and also to explain its significance for readers. Just collecting data does not create an argument. Here are some possible topics to explore:

1. Study print ads for one type of product (e.g., cars, cosmetics, cigarettes) to draw inferences about the dominant techniques used to sell that product. Remember that the more ads you study, the more support you have for your inferences. You should study at least twenty-five ads.

2. Study print ads for one type of product as advertised in different types of magazines clearly directed to different audiences to see how (or if) selling techniques change with a change in audience. (Remember: To demonstrate no change in techniques can be just as interesting a conclusion as finding changes.) Study at least twenty-five ads, in a balanced number from the different magazines.

3. Select a major figure currently in the news and conduct a study of bias in one of the news magazines (e.g., *Time, U.S. News & World Report,* or *Newsweek*) or a newspaper. Use at least eight issues of the magazine or newspaper from the last six months and study all articles on your figure in each of those issues. To determine bias, look at the amount of coverage, the location (front pages or back pages), the use of photos (flattering or unflattering), and the language of the articles.

4. Conduct a study of amounts of violence on TV by analyzing, for one week, all prime-time programs that may contain violence. (That is, eliminate sitcoms and decide whether you want to include or exclude news programs.) Devise some classification system for types of violence based on your prior TV viewing experience before beginning your study—but be prepared to alter or add to your categories based on your viewing of shows. Note the number of times each violent act occurs. You may want to consider the total length of time (per program, per night, per type of violent act) of violence during the week you study. Give credit to any authors in this text or other publications for any ideas you borrow from their articles.

5. As an alternative to topic 4, study the number and types of violent acts in children's programs on Saturday mornings. (This and topic 4 are best handled if you can record and then replay the programs several times.)

6. Conduct a survey and analyze the results on some campus issue or current public policy issue. Prepare questions that are without bias and include questions to get information about the participants so that you can correlate

answers with the demographics of your participants (e.g., age, gender, race, religion, proposed major in college, political affiliation, or whatever else you think is important to the topic studied). Decide whether you want to survey students only or both students and faculty. Plan how you are going to reach each group.

Studying Some Arguments by Genre

CHAPTER 7

Definition Arguments

Get Fuzzy: © Darby Conley/Dist. by United Feature Syndicate, Inc.

READ: How does the little dog respond to the big dog's questions?

REASON: Does the big dog expect the responses he gets to his questions? How do you know?

REFLECT/WRITE: What is a rhetorical question? What is the risk of using one?

"Define your terms!" someone yells in the middle of a heated debate. Although yelling may not be the best strategy, the advice is sound for writers of argument. People do disagree over the meaning of words. We cannot let words mean whatever we want and still communicate, but we do need to understand that many words have more than one meaning. In addition, some words carry strong connotations, the emotional associations we attach to them. For this reason, realtors never sell *houses;* they always sell *homes.* They want you to believe that the house they are showing will become the home in which you will feel happy and secure.

Many important arguments turn on the definition of key terms. If you can convince others that you have the correct definition, then you are well on your way to winning your argument. The Civil Rights movement, for example, really turned on a definition of terms. Leaders argued that some laws are unjust, that because it is the law does not necessarily mean it is right. Laws requiring separate schools and separate drinking fountains and seats at the back of the bus for blacks were, in the view of civil rights activists, unjust laws, unjust because they are immoral and as such diminish us as humans. If obeying unjust laws is immoral, then it follows that we should not obey such laws. And when we recognize that obeying such laws hurts us, then we have an obligation to act to remove unjust laws. Civil disobedience—illegal behavior to some—becomes, by definition, the best moral behavior.

Andrew Vachss, in his essay "Watch Your Language" (see pp. 61–63), argues that there are no child prostitutes, only prostituted children. Yes, there are children who engage in sex for money. But, Vachss argues, that is not the complete definition of a prostitute. A prostitute chooses to exchange sex for money; a prostitute chooses this line of work. Children do not choose; they are exploited by adults, beaten and in other ways abused if they do not work for the adult in control of them. If we agree with his definition, Vachss expects that we will also agree that the adults must be sought, charged, and punished for their abuse of those prostituted children.

DEFINING AS PART OF AN ARGUMENT

There are two occasions for defining words as a part of your argument.

- You need to define any technical terms that may not be familiar to readers— or that readers may not understand as fully as they think they do. David Norman, early in his book on dinosaurs, writes:

  Nearly everyone knows what some dinosaurs look like, such as *Tyrannosaurus, Triceratops,* and *Stegosaurus.* But they may be much more vague about the lesser known ones, and may have difficulty in distinguishing between dinosaurs and other types of prehistoric creatures. It is not at all unusual to overhear an adult, taking a group of children around a museum display, being reprimanded sharply by the youngsters for failing to realize that a woolly mammoth was not a dinosaur, or—more forgivably—that a giant flying reptile such as *Pteranodon,* which lived at the time of the dinosaurs, was not a dinosaur either.

So what exactly is a dinosaur? And how do paleontologists decide on the groups they belong to?

Norman answers his questions by explaining the four characteristics that all dinosaurs have. That is, he provides what is often referred to as a *formal definition*. He places the dinosaur in a class, established by four criteria, and then distinguishes this animal from other animals that lived a long time ago. His definition is not open to debate. He is presenting the definition and classification system that paleontologists, the specialists, have established.

- You need to define any word you are using in a special way. If you were to write: "We need to teach discrimination at an early age," you should add: "by *discrimination* I do not mean prejudice. I mean discernment, the ability to see differences." (*Sesame Street* has been teaching children this good kind of discrimination for many years.) The word *discrimination* used to have only a positive connotation; it referred to an important critical thinking skill. Today, however, the word has been linked to prejudice; to discriminate is to act on one's prejudice against some group. Writing today, you need to clarify if you are using the word in its original, positive meaning.

WHEN DEFINING *IS* THE ARGUMENT

We also turn to definition because we believe that a word is being used incorrectly or is not fully understood. Columnist George Will once argued that we should forget *values* and use instead the word *virtues*—that we should seek and admire virtues, not values. His point was that the term *values*, given to us by today's social scientists, is associated with situational ethics, or with an "if it feels good do it" approach to action. He wants people to return to the more old-fashioned word *virtues* so that we are reminded that some behavior is right and some is wrong, and that neither the situation nor how we might "feel" about it alters those truths. In discussions such as Will's the purpose shifts. Instead of using definition as one step in an argument, definition becomes the central purpose of the argument. Will rejects the idea that *values* means the same thing as *virtues* and asserts that it is virtue—as he defines it—that must guide our behavior. An extended definition *is* the argument.

STRATEGIES FOR DEVELOPING AN EXTENDED DEFINITION

Arguing for your meaning of a word provides your purpose in writing. But, it may not immediately suggest ways to develop such an argument. Let's think in terms of what definitions essentially do: They establish criteria for a class or category and then exclude other items from that category. (A pen is a writing instrument that uses ink.) Do you see your definition as drawing a line or as setting up two entirely separate categories? For example:

When does interrogation   become   torture?

One might argue that some strategies for making the person questioned uncomfortable are appropriate to interrogation (reduced sleep or comforts, loud noise). But, at some point (stretching on a rack or waterboarding) one crosses a line to torture. To define torture, you have to explain where that line is—and how the actions on one side of the line are different from those on the other side.

What are the characteristics of wisdom as opposed to knowledge?

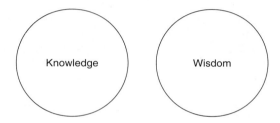

Do we cross a line from knowledge to become wise? Not many would agree with this, more likely arguing that wisdom requires traits or skills that are not to be found by increasing one's knowledge. The categories are separate.

Envisioning these two approaches supports the more abstract thinking that defining requires. Then what? Use some of the basic strategies of good writing:

- *Descriptive details.* Illustrate with specifics. List the traits of a leader or a courageous person. Explain the behaviors that we find in a wise person, or the behaviors that should be called torture. Describe the situations in which liberty can flourish, or the situations that result from unjust laws. Remember to use negative traits as well as positive ones. That is, show what is *not* covered by the word you are defining.

- *Examples.* Develop your definition with actual or hypothetical examples. Churchill, Lincoln, and FDR can all be used as examples of leaders. Solomon is generally acknowledged as a good example of a wise person. You can also create a hypothetical wise or courteous person, or a person whose behavior you would consider virtuous.

- *Comparison and/or contrast.* Clarify and limit your definition by contrasting it with words of similar—but not exactly the same—meanings. For example, what are the differences between knowledge and wisdom or interrogation and torture? The goal of your essay is to establish subtle but important differences so that your readers understand precisely what you want a given word to mean. In an essay at the end of this chapter, Robin Givhan distinguishes among *glamour, charisma,* and *cool* as a way to develop her definition of *glamour.*

- *History of usage or word origin.* The word's original meanings can be instructive. If the word has changed meaning over time, explore these changes as clues to how the word can (or should) be used. If you want readers to reclaim *discrimination* as a positive trait, then show them how that was part of the word's original meaning before the word became tied to prejudice. Word origin—etymology—can also give us insight into a word's meaning. Many words in English come from another language, or they are a combination of two words. The words *liberty* and *freedom* can usefully be discussed by examining etymology. Most dictionaries provide some word origin information, but the best source is, always, the *Oxford English Dictionary.*

- *Use or function.* A frequent strategy for defining is explaining an item's use or function: A pencil is a writing instrument. A similar approach can give insight into more general or abstract words as well. For example, what do we have—or gain—by emphasizing virtues instead of values? Or, what does a wise person *do* that a non-wise person does not do?

- *Metaphors.* Consider using figurative comparisons. When fresh, not clichés, they add vividness to your writing while offering insight into your understanding of the word.

GUIDELINES for Evaluating Definition Arguments

When reading definition arguments, what should you look for? The basics of good argument apply to all arguments: a clear statement of claim, qualified if appropriate, a clear explanation of reasons and evidence, and enough relevant evidence to support the claim. How do we recognize these qualities in a definition argument? Use the following points as guides to evaluating:

- **Why is the word being defined?** Has the writer convinced you of the need to understand the word's meaning or change the way the word is commonly used?

- **How is the word defined?** Has the writer established his or her definition, clearly distinguishing it from what the writer perceives to be objectionable definitions? It is hard to judge the usefulness of the writer's position if the differences in meaning remain fuzzy. If George Will is going to argue for using *virtues* instead of *values,* he needs to be sure that readers understand the differences he sees in the two words.

- **What strategies are used to develop the definition?** Can you recognize the different types of evidence presented and see what the writer is doing in his or her argument? This kind of analysis can aid your evaluation of a definition argument.

- **What are the implications of accepting the author's definition?** Why does George Will want readers to embrace *virtues* rather than *values*?

Will's argument is not just about subtle points of language. His argument is about attitudes that affect public policy issues. Part of any evaluation of a definition argument must include our assessment of the author's definition.

• **Is the definition argument convincing?** Do the reasons and evidence lead you to agree with the author, to accept the idea of the definition and its implications as well?

PREPARING A DEFINITION ARGUMENT

In addition to the guidelines for writing arguments presented in Chapter 4, you can use the following advice specific to writing definition arguments.

Planning

1. *Think:* Why do you want to define your term? To add to our understanding of a complex term? To challenge the use of the word by others? If you don't have a good reason to write, find a different word to examine.
2. *Think:* How are you defining the word? What are the elements/parts/steps in your definition? Some brainstorming notes are probably helpful to keep your definition concrete and focused.
3. *Think:* What strategies will you use to develop and support your definition? Consider using several of these possible strategies for development:
   • *Word origin or history of usage.*
   • *Descriptive details.*
   • *Comparison and/or contrast.*
   • *Examples.*
   • *Function or use.*
   • *Metaphors.*

Drafting

1. Begin with an opening paragraph or two that introduces your subject in an interesting way. Possibilities include the occasion that has led to your writing—explain for instance, a misunderstanding about your term's meaning that you want to correct.
2. Do *not* begin by quoting or paraphrasing a dictionary definition of the term. "According to Webster . . ." is a tired approach lacking reader interest. If the dictionary definition were sufficient, you would have no reason to write an entire essay to define the term.
3. State your claim—your definition of the term—early in your essay, if you can do so in a sentence or two. If you do not state a brief claim, then establish your purpose in writing early in your essay. (You may find that there are too many parts to your definition to combine into one or two sentences.)

4. Use several specific strategies for developing your definition. Select several strategies from the list above and organize your approach around these strategies. That is, you can develop one paragraph of descriptive details, another of examples, another of contrast with words that are not exactly the same in meaning.

5. Consider specifically refuting the error in word use that led to your decision to write your own definition. If you are motivated to write based on what you have read, then make a rebuttal part of your definition argument.

6. Consider discussing the implications of your definition. You can give weight and value to your argument by defending the larger significance of readers' embracing your definition.

A CHECKLIST FOR REVISION ■·

☐ Do I have a good understanding of my purpose? Have I made this clear to readers?

☐ Have I clearly stated my definition? Or clearly established the various parts of the definition that I discuss in separate paragraphs?

☐ Have I organized my argument, building the parts of my definition into a logical, coherent structure?

☐ Have I used specifics to clarify and support my definition?

☐ Have I used the basic checklist for revision in Chapter 4 (see p. 111)?

STUDENT ESSAY

PARAGON OR PARASITE?

Laura Mullins

Attention-getting introduction.

Do you recognize this creature? He is low maintenance and often unnoticeable, a favorite companion of many. Requiring no special attention, he grows from the soil of pride and rejection, feeding regularly on a diet of ignorance and insecurity, scavenging for hurt feelings and defensiveness, gobbling up dainty morsels of lust and scandal. Like a cult leader clothed in a gay veneer,

Clever extended metaphor.

disguising himself as blameless, he wields power. Bewitching unsuspecting but devoted groupies, distracting them from honest self-examination, deceiving them into believing illusions of grandeur or, on the other extreme, unredeemable

Subject introduced.

worthlessness, he breeds jealousy, hate, and fear; thus, he thrives. He is Gossip.

One of my dearest friends is a gossip. She is an educated, honorable, compassionate, loving woman whose character and judgment I deeply admire and respect. After sacrificially raising six children, she went on to study medicine and become a doctor who graciously volunteers her expertise. How, you may be wondering, could a gossip deserve such praise? Then you do not understand the word. My friend is my daughter's godmother; she is my gossip, or *god-sib,* meaning sister-in-god. Derived from Middle English words *god,* meaning spiritual, and *sip/sib/syp,* meaning kinsman, this term was used to refer to a familiar acquaintance, close family friend, or intimate relation, according to the *Oxford English Dictionary.* As a male, he would have joined in fellowship and celebration with the father of the newly born; if a female, she would have been a trusted friend, a birth-attendant or midwife to the mother of the baby. The term grew to include references to the type of easy, unrestrained conversation shared by these folks.

Etymology of gossip *and early meanings.*

As is often the case with words, the term's meaning has certainly evolved, maybe eroded from its original idea. Is it harmless, idle chat, innocuous sharing of others' personal news, or back-biting, rumor-spreading, and manipulation? Is it a beneficial activity worthy of pursuit, or a deplorable danger to be avoided?

Current meanings.

In her article "Evolution, Alienation, and Gossip" (for the Social Issues Research Centre in Oxford, England), Kate Fox writes that "gossip is not a trivial pastime; it is essential to human social, psychological, and even physical well-being." Many echo her view that gossip is a worthy activity, claiming that engaging in gossip produces endorphins, reduces stress, and aids in building intimate relationships. Gossip, seen at worst as a harmless outlet, is encouraged in the workplace. Since much of its content is not inherently critical or malicious, it is viewed as a positive activity. However, this view does nothing to encourage those speaking or listening to evaluate or examine motive or purpose; instead, it seems to reflect the "anything goes" thinking so prevalent today.

Good use of sources to develop definition.

Conversely, writer and high school English and geography teacher Lennox V. Farrell of Toronto, Canada, in his essay titled "Gossip: An Urban Form of Sorcery," presents gossip as a kind of "witchcraft . . . based on using unsubstantiated accusations by those who make them, and on uncritically accepting these by those enticed into listening." Farrell uses gossip in its more widely understood definition, encompassing the breaking of confidences, inappropriate sharing of indiscretions, destructive tale-bearing, and malicious slander.

What, then, is gossip? We no longer use the term to refer to our children's godparents. Its current definition usually comes with derogatory implications. Imagine a backyard garden: you see a variety of greenery, recognizing at a glance that you are looking at different kinds of plants. Taking a closer look, you will find the gossip vine; inconspicuously blending in, it doesn't appear threatening, but ultimately it destroys. If left in the garden it will choke and then suck out life from its host. Zoom in on the garden scene and follow the creeping vine up trees and along a fence where two neighbors visit. You can overhear one woman saying to the other, "I know I should be the last to tell you, but your husband is being unfaithful to me." (Caption from a cartoon by Alan De la Nougerede.)

The current popular movement to legitimize gossip seems an excuse to condone the human tendency to puff-up oneself. Compared in legal terms, gossip is to conversation as hearsay is to eyewitness testimony; it's not credible. Various religious doctrines abhor the idea and practice of gossip. An old Turkish proverb says, "He who gossips to you will gossip of you." From the Babylonian Talmud, which calls gossip the three-pronged tongue, destroying the one talking, the one listening, and the one being spoken of, to the Upanishads, to the Bible, we can conclude that no good fruit is born from gossip. Let's tend our gardens and check our motives when we have the urge to gossip. Surely we can find more noble pursuits than the self-aggrandizement we have come to know as gossip.

Good use of metaphor to depict gossip as negative.

Conclusion states view that gossip is to be avoided—the writer's thesis.

FOR ANALYSIS AND DEBATE

BEST IS THE NEW WORST | SUSAN JACOBY

A graduate of Michigan State University, Susan Jacoby is the author of nine books and numerous articles in newspapers and magazines. Her most recent book, a best seller, is *The Age of American Unreason* (2008). Currently she is director of the New York branch of the Center for Inquiry. Her essay on the word *elite* was published on May 30, 2008, in the *New York Times*.

PREREADING QUESTIONS What do you think the word *elite* means? Are *elite* and *elitist* synonyms?

PITY the poor word "elite," which simply means "the best" as an adjective 1 and "the best of a group" as a noun. What was once an accolade has turned poisonous in American public life over the past 40 years, as both the left and the right have twisted it into a code word meaning "not one of us." But the newest and most ominous wrinkle in the denigration of all things elite is that the slur is being applied to knowledge itself.

Senator Hillary Clinton's use of the phrase "elite opinion" to dismiss the 2 near unanimous opposition of economists to her proposal for a gas tax holiday was a landmark in the use of elite to attack expertise supposedly beyond the comprehension of average Americans. One might as well say that there is no point in consulting musicians about music or ichthyologists about fish.

The assault on "elite" did not begin with politicians, although it does 3 have political antecedents in sneers directed at "eggheads" during the anti-Communist crusades of the 1950s. The broader cultural perversion of its meaning dates from the late 1960s, when the academic left pinned the label on faculty members who resisted the establishment of separate departments for what were then called "minority studies." In this case, two distinct faculty groups were tarred with elitism—those who wanted to incorporate black and women's studies into the core curriculum, and those who thought that blacks and women had produced nothing worthy of study. Instead of elitist, the former group should have been described as "inclusionary" and the latter as "bigoted."

The second stage of elite-bashing was conceived by the cultural and 4 political right. Conservative intellectuals who rose to prominence during the Reagan administration managed the neat trick of reversing the '60s usage of "elite" by applying it as a slur to the left alone. "Elite," often rendered in the plural, became synonymous with "limousine liberals" who opposed supposedly normative American values. That the right-wing intellectual establishment also constituted a powerful elite was somehow obscured.

"Elite" and "elitist" do not, in a dictionary sense, mean the same thing. An 5 elitist is someone who does believe in government by an elite few—an anti-democratic philosophy that has nothing to do with elite achievement. But the terms have become so conflated that Americans have come to consider both elite and elitist synonyms for snobbish.

6   All the older forms of elite-bashing have now devolved into a kind of aggressive denial of the threat to American democracy posed by public ignorance.

7   During the past few months, I have received hundreds of e-mail messages calling me an elitist for drawing attention to America's knowledge deficit. One of the most memorable came from a man who objected to my citation of a statistic, from a 2006 National Geographic-Roper survey, indicating that nearly two-thirds of Americans age 18 to 24 cannot find Iraq on a map. "Why should I care whether my mechanic knows where Iraq is, as long as he knows how to fix my car?" the man asked.

8   But what could be more elitist than the idea that a mechanic cannot be expected to know the location of a country where thousands of Americans of his own generation are fighting and dying?

9   Another peculiar new use of "elitist" (often coupled with "Luddite") is its application to any caveats about the Internet as a source of knowledge. After listening to one of my lectures, a college student told me that it was elitist to express alarm that one in four Americans, according to the National Constitution Center, cannot name any First Amendment rights or that 62 percent cannot name the three branches of government. "You don't need to have that in your head," the student said, "because you can just look it up on the Web."

10   True, but how can an information-seeker know what to look for if he or she does not know that the Bill of Rights exists? There is no point-and-click formula for accumulating a body of knowledge needed to make sense of isolated facts.

11   It is past time to retire the sliming of elite knowledge and education from public discourse. Do we want mediocre schools or the best education for our children? If we need an operation, do we want an ordinary surgeon or the best, most elite surgeon available?

12   America was never imagined as a democracy of dumbness. The Declaration of Independence and the Constitution were written by an elite group of leaders, and although their dream was limited to white men, it held the seeds of a future in which anyone might aspire to the highest—let us say it out loud, elite—level of achievement.

QUESTIONS FOR READING

1. What does the word *elite* mean?
2. What has it come to mean in American politics?
3. How was the word first distorted in the 1960s? What group has created the second stage of elite-bashing? What was clever about their distortion?
4. In what context is the word often used today?

QUESTIONS FOR REASONING AND ANALYSIS

1. What is Jacoby's claim? What does she want readers to understand about the word *elite*?

2.   Jacoby observes that when we need a surgeon we want an elite one, not an ordinary one. What makes this an effective analogy?

3.   The author also offers another rhetorical question in paragraph 11. How are we to answer it? Is this a good strategy?

QUESTIONS FOR REFLECTION AND WRITING

1.   Jacoby presents some statistics in paragraphs 7, 9, and 10 to show America's "democracy of dumbness." Do these numbers surprise you? Do they upset you? Explain.

2.   The author argues that we need to have information in order to use the Internet effectively. Does this assertion make sense to you? Why or why not?

3.   Do you want leaders with elite educations? Why or why not?

GLAMOUR, THAT CERTAIN SOMETHING | ROBIN GIVHAN

Robin Givhan is a graduate of Princeton and holds a master's degree in journalism from the University of Michigan. She is fashion editor for the *Washington Post* and has won a Pulitzer Prize (2006) for criticism, the first time the prize has been awarded to a fashion writer. Givhan's coverage of the world of fashion frequently becomes a study of culture, as we see in the following column, published February 17, 2008, shortly before the 2008 Academy Awards show.

PREREADING QUESTIONS **What is the difference between glamour and good looks? What famous people do you consider glamorous?**

Glamour isn't a cultural necessity, but its usefulness can't be denied.   1

It makes us feel good about ourselves by making us believe that life can 2 sparkle. Glamorous people make difficult tasks seems effortless. They appear to cruise through life shaking off defeat with a wry comment. No matter how hard they work for what they have, the exertion never seems to show. Yet the cool confidence they project doesn't ever drift into lassitude.

Hollywood attracts people of glamour—as well as the misguided souls who 3 confuse it with mere good looks—because that is where it is richly rewarded. And the Academy Awards are the epicenter of it all. We'll watch the Oscars next Sunday to delight in the stars who glide down the red carpet like graceful swans or who swagger onto the stage looking dashing.

Of course, we'll watch for other reasons, too. There's always the possibil- 4 ity of a supremely absurd fashion moment or an acceptance speech during which the winner becomes righteously indignant—Michael Moore-style—or practically hyperventilates like Halle Berry. While Moore, a nominee, is not glamorous, he is compelling for the sheer possibility of an impolitic eruption. Berry isn't glamorous either, mostly because nothing ever looks effortless with her. (She has even expressed anguish over her beauty.) Mostly, though, we will watch in search of "old Hollywood" glamour. But really, is there any other kind?

5   Among the actors who consistently manage to evoke memories of Cary Grant or Grace Kelly are George Clooney and Cate Blanchett. There's something about the way they present themselves that speaks to discretion, sex appeal and glossy perfection. As an audience, we think we know these actors but we really don't. We know their image, the carefully crafted personality they display to the public. If they have been to rehab, they went quietly and without a crowd of paparazzi.

6   Their lives appear to be an endless stream of lovely adventures, minor mishaps that turn into cocktail party banter, charming romances and just enough gravitas to keep them from floating away on a cloud of frivolity.

7   These actors take pretty pictures because they seem supremely comfortable with themselves. It's not simply their beauty we're seeing; it's also an unapologetic pleasure in being who they are.

8   Oscar nominee Tilda Swinton has the kind of striking, handsome looks of Anjelica Huston or Lauren Bacall. But Swinton doesn't register as glamorous as much as cool. She looks a bit androgynous and favors the eccentric Dutch design team of Viktor & Rolf, which once populated an entire runway show with Swinton doppelgangers. Coolness suggests that the person knows something or understands something that average folks haven't yet figured out. Cool people are a step ahead. Glamour is firmly situated in the now.

9   There's nothing particularly intimate about glamour, which is why it plays so well on the big screen and why film actors who embody it can sometimes be disappointing in real life. Glamour isn't like charisma, which is typically described as the ability to make others feel important or special.

10   Neither quality has much to do with a person's inner life. Glamour is no measure of soulfulness or integrity. It isn't about truth, but perception. *Redbook* traffics in truth. *Vogue* promotes glamour.

Although Hollywood is the natural habitat for the glitterati, they exist every- 11 where: politics, government, sports, business. Tiger Woods brought glamour to golf with his easy confidence and his ability to make the professional game look as simple as putt-putt. Donald Trump aspires to glamour with his flashy properties and their gold-drenched decor. But his efforts are apparent, his yearning obvious. The designer Tom Ford is glamorous. The man never rumples.

In the political world, Barack Obama has glamour. Bill Clinton has charisma. 12 And Hillary Clinton has an admirable work ethic. Bill Clinton could convince voters that he felt their pain. Hillary Clinton reminds them detail by detail of how she would alleviate it. Glamour has a way of temporarily making you forget about the pain and just think the world is a beautiful place of endless possibilities.

Ronald Reagan evoked glamour. His white-tie inaugural balls and morning- 13 coat swearing-in were purposefully organized to bring a twinkle back to the American psyche. George W. Bush has charisma, a.k.a. the likability factor, although it does not appear to be helping his approval rating now. Still, he remains a back-slapper and bestower of nicknames.

Charisma is personal. Glamour taps into a universal fairy tale. It's uncon- 14 cerned with the nitty-gritty. Instead, it celebrates the surface gloss. And sometimes, a little shimmer can be hard to resist.

QUESTIONS FOR READING

1. How does glamour make us feel?
2. Where do we usually find glamour? Why?
3. Which celebrities today best capture Hollywood's glamour of the past?
4. What traits do the glamorous have?
5. Explain the differences among glamour, charisma, and cool.

QUESTIONS FOR REASONING AND ANALYSIS

1. Examine the opening three sentences in paragraph 12. What makes them effective?
2. What are the specific strategies Givhan uses to develop her definition?
3. What is Givhan's claim?

QUESTIONS FOR REFLECTION AND WRITING

1. Givhan asserts that glamour is in the present but "cool people are a step ahead." Does this contrast make sense to you? Why or why not?
2. Do we ever really know the glamorous, charismatic, and cool celebrities? Explain.
3. Some young people aspire to be cool. How would you advise them? What should one do, how should one behave, to be cool? Is "cool" a trait that we can "put on" if we wish? Why or why not?

SUGGESTIONS FOR DISCUSSION AND WRITING

1. In the student essay, Laura Mullins defines the term *gossip*. Select one of the following words to define and prepare your own extended definition argument, using at least three of the strategies for defining described in this chapter. For each word in the list, you see a companion word in parentheses. Use that companion word as a word that you contrast with the word you are defining. (For example, how does gossip differ from conversation?) The idea of an extended definition argument is to make fine distinctions among words similar in meaning.

courtesy (manners)	hero (star)
wisdom (knowledge)	community (subdivision)
patriotism (chauvinism)	freedom (liberty)

2. Select a word you believe is currently misused. It can be misused because it has taken on a negative (or positive) connotation that it did not originally have, or because it has changed meaning and lost something in the process. A few suggestions include: *awful, fabulous, exceptional* (in education), *propaganda.*

3. Define a term that is currently used to label people with particular traits or values. Possibilities include *nerd, yuppie, freak, jock, redneck, bimbo, wimp.* Reflect, before selecting this topic, on why you want to explain the meaning of the word you have chosen. One purpose might be to explain the word to someone from another culture. Another might be to defend people who are labeled negatively by a term; that is, you want to show why the term should not have a negative connotation.

Evaluation Arguments

"*Great PowerPoint, Kevin, but the answer is no.*"

READ: What is the situation? Who speaks the words in quotations?

REASON: What do you infer to be on the laptop screen?

REFLECT/WRITE: What is the cartoonist's attitude toward PowerPoint presentations? Toward modern society?

" I really love Ben's Camaro; it's so much more fun to go out with him than to go with Gregory in his Volvo wagon," you confide to a friend. "On the other hand, Ben always wants to see the latest horror movie—and boy are they horrid! I'd much rather watch one of our teams play—whatever the season; sports events are so much more fun than horror movies!"

"Well, at least you and Ben agree not to listen to Amy Winehouse CDs. Her life is so messed up; why would anyone admire her music?" your friend responds.

CHARACTERISTICS OF EVALUATION ARGUMENTS

Evaluations. How easy they are to make. We do it all the time. So, surely an evaluation argument should be easy to prepare. Not so fast. Remember at the beginning of the discussion of argument in Chapter 3, we observed that we do not argue about personal preferences because there is no basis for building an argument. If you don't like horror movies, then don't go to them—even with Ben! However, once you assert that sporting events are more fun than horror movies, you have shifted from personal preference to the world of argument, the world in which others will judge the effectiveness of your logic and evidence. On what basis can you argue that one activity is more fun than the other? And, always more fun? And, more fun for everyone? You probably need to qualify this claim and then you will need to establish the criteria by which you have made your evaluation. Although you might find it easier to defend your preference for a car for dates, you, at least in theory, can build a convincing argument for a qualified claim in support of sporting events. Your friend, though, will have great difficulty justifying her evaluation of Winehouse based on Winehouse's lifestyle. An evaluation of her music needs to be defended based on criteria about music—unless she wants to try to argue that any music made by people with unconventional or immoral lifestyles will be bad music, a tough claim to defend.

In a column for *Time* magazine, Charles Krauthammer argues that Tiger Woods is the greatest golfer ever to play the game. He writes:

> How do we know? You could try Method 1: Compare him directly with the former greatest golfer, Jack Nicklaus. . . . But that is not the right way to compare. You cannot compare greatness directly across the ages. There are so many intervening variables: changes in technology, training, terrain, equipment, often rules and customs.
>
> How then do we determine who is greatest? Method 2: The Gap. Situate each among his contemporaries. Who towers? . . . Nicklaus was great, but he ran with peers: Palmer, Player, Watson. Tiger has none.

Krauthammer continues with statistics to demonstrate that there is no one playing now with Tiger who comes close in number of tournaments won, number of majors won, and number of strokes better in these events than the next player. He then applies the Gap Method to Babe Ruth in baseball, Wayne Gretzky in hockey, and Bobby Fischer in chess to demonstrate that it works to reveal true greatness in competition among the world's best.

Krauthammer clearly explains his method, his basic criterion for judging greatness. Then he provides the data to support his conclusions about who are or were the greatest in various fields. His is a convincing evaluation argument.

These examples suggest some key points about evaluation arguments:

- **Evaluation arguments are arguments, not statements of personal preferences.** As such, they need a precise, qualified claim and reasons and evidence for support, just like any argument.
- **Evaluation arguments are about "good" and "bad," "best" and "worst."** These arguments are not about what we should or should not do or why a situation is the way it is. The debate is not whether one should select a boyfriend based on the kind of car he drives or why horror movies have so much appeal for many viewers. The argument is that sports events are great entertainment, or better entertainment than horror movies.
- **Evaluation arguments need to be developed based on a clear statement of the criteria for evaluating.** Winehouse has won Grammys for her music— why? By what standards of excellence do we judge a singer? A voice with great musicality and nuance? The selection of songs with meaningful lyrics? The ability to engage listeners—the way the singer can "sell" a song? The number of recordings sold and awards won? All of these criteria? Something else?
- **Evaluation arguments, to be successful, may need to defend the criteria, not just to list them and show that the subject of the argument meets those criteria.** Suppose you want to argue that sporting events are great entertainment because it is exciting to cheer with others, you get to see thrilling action, and it is good, clean fun. Are sports always "good, clean fun"? Some of the fighting in hockey matches is quite vicious. Some football players get away with dirty hits. Krauthammer argues that his Method 2 provides the better criterion for judging greatness and then shows why it is the better method. Do not underestimate the challenge of writing an effective evaluation argument.

TYPES OF EVALUATION ARGUMENTS

The examples we have examined above are about people or items or experiences in our lives. Tiger Woods is the greatest golfer ever, based on the Gap Method criterion. Sports events are more fun to attend than horror movies. We can (and do!) evaluate just about everything we know or do or buy. This is one type of evaluation argument. In this category we would place the review—of a book, movie, concert, or something similar.

A second type of evaluation is a response to another person's argument. We are not explaining why the car or college, sitcom or singer, that we especially value is good or great or the best, based on stated criteria. Instead, we are responding to one specific argument we have read (or listened to) that we think is flawed, flawed in many ways or in one significant way that essentially destroys the argument. This type of evaluation argument is called a rebuttal or refutation argument.

Sometimes our response to what we consider a really bad argument is to go beyond the rebuttal and write a counterargument. Rather than writing about the limitations and flaws in our friend's evaluation of Winehouse as a singer not to be listened to, we decide to write our own argument evaluating Winehouse's strengths as a contemporary singer. This counterargument is best described as an evaluation argument, not a refutation. Similarly, we can disagree with someone's argument defending restrictions placed by colleges on student file sharing. But, if we decide to write a counterargument defending students' rights to share music files, we have moved from rebuttal to our own position paper, our own argument based on values. Counterarguments are best seen as belonging to one of the other genres of argument discussed in this section of the text.

GUIDELINES for Analyzing an Evaluation Argument

The basics of good argument apply to all arguments: a clear statement of claim, qualified as appropriate, a clear explanation of reasons and evidence, and enough relevant evidence to support the claim. When reading evaluation arguments, use the following points as additional guides:

- **What is the writer's claim?** Is it clear, qualified if necessary, and focused on the task of evaluating?

- **Has the writer considered audience as a basis for both claim and criteria?** Your college may be a good choice for you, given your criteria for choosing, but is it a good choice for your audience? Qualifications need to be based on audience: College A is a great school for young people in need of B and with X amount of funds. Or: *The Da Vinci Code* is an entertaining read for those with some understanding of art history and knowledge of the Roman Catholic Church.

- **What criteria are presented as the basis for evaluation?** Are they clearly stated? Do they seem reasonable for the topic of evaluation? Are they defended if necessary?

- **What evidence and/or reasons are presented to show that the item under evaluation passes the criteria test?** Specifics are important in any evaluation argument.

- **What are the implications of the claim?** If we accept the Gap Method for determining greatness, does that mean that we can never compare stars from different generations? If we agree with the rebuttal argument, does that mean that there are no good arguments for the claim in the essay being refuted?

- **Is the argument convincing?** Does the evidence lead you to agree with the author? Do you want to buy that car, listen to that CD, read that book, see that film as a result of reading the argument?

PREPARING AN EVALUATION ARGUMENT

In addition to the guidelines for writing arguments presented in Chapter 4, you can use the following advice specific to writing evaluation arguments.

Planning

1. *Think:* Why do you want to write this evaluation? Does it matter, or are you just sharing your personal preferences? Select a topic that requires you to think deeply about how we judge that item (college, book, CD, etc.).

2. *Think about audience:* Try to imagine writing your evaluation for your classmates, not just your instructor. Instead of thinking about an assignment to be graded, think about why we turn to reviews, for example. What do readers want to learn? They want to know if they should see that film. Your job is to help them make that decision.

3. *Think:* What are my criteria for evaluation? And, how will I measure my topic against them to show that my evaluation is justified? You really must know how you would determine a great singer or a great tennis player before you write, or you risk writing only about personal preferences.

4. *Establish a general plan:* If you are writing a review, be sure to study the work carefully. Can you write a complete and accurate summary? (It is easier to review a CD than a live concert because you can replay the CD to get all the details straight.) You will need to balance summary, analysis, and evaluation in a review—and be sure that you do not mostly write summary or reveal the ending of a novel or film! If you are evaluating a college or a car, think about how you would order your criteria. Do you want to list all criteria first and then show how your item connects to them, point by point? Or, do you want the criteria to unfold as you make specific points about your item? To analyze a film, consider the plot, the characters, the actors who play the lead characters, any special effects used, and the author's (and director's) "take" on the story. If the "idea" of the film is insignificant, then it is hard to argue that it is a great film. Analysis of style in a book needs to be connected to that book's intended audience; style and presentation will vary depending on the knowledge and sophistication of the intended reader. If, for example, you have difficulty understanding a book aimed at a general audience, then it is fair to say that the author has not successfully reached his or her audience. But if you are reviewing a book intended for specialists, then your difficulties in reading are not relevant to a fair evaluation of that book. You can point out, though, that the book is tough going for a nonspecialist—just as you could point out that a movie sequel is hard to follow for those who did not see the original film.

Drafting

1. Begin with an opening paragraph or two that engages your reader while introducing your subject and purpose in writing. Is there a specific occasion that has led to your writing? And what, exactly, are you evaluating?

2. Either introduce your criteria next and then show how your item for evaluation meets the criteria, point by point, through the rest of the essay; or, decide on an order for introducing your criteria and use that order as your structure. Put the most important criterion either first or last. It can be effective to put the most controversial point last.

3. If you are writing a review, then the basic criteria are already established. You will need some combination of summary, analysis, and evaluation. Begin with an attention-getter that includes a broad statement of the work's subject or subject category: This is a *biography* of Benjamin Franklin; this is a *female action-hero film.* An evaluation in general terms can complete the opening paragraph. For example:

    Dr. Cynthia Pemberton's new book, *More Than a Game: One Woman's Fight for Gender Equity in Sport,* is destined to become a classic in sport sociology, sport history, and women's studies.

4. The rest of the review will then combine summary details, analysis of presentation, and a final assessment of the work in the concluding paragraph. From the same review, after learning specifics of content, we read:

    The target audience for this book includes educators, coaches, athletes, and administrators at any level. Additionally, anyone interested in studying women's sports or pursuing a Title IX case will love this book.

5. Consider discussing the implications of your evaluation. Why is this important? Obviously for a book or film or art show, for example, we want to know if this is a "must read" or "must see." For other evaluation arguments, let us know why we should care about your subject and your perspective. Charles Krauthammer does not just argue that Tiger Woods is the greatest golfer ever; he also argues that his Gap Method is the best strategy for evaluation. That's why he shows that it works not just to put Woods ahead of Nicklaus but also to put other greats in their exalted place in other sports.

A CHECKLIST FOR REVISION ■■■■■■■■■■■■■■■■■■■■■■■■■■■■■■■■■■

- ☐ Do I have a good understanding of my purpose? Have I made my evaluation purpose clear to readers?
- ☐ Have I clearly stated my claim?
- ☐ Have I clearly stated my criteria for evaluation—or selected the appropriate elements of content, style, presentation, and theme for a review?
- ☐ Have I organized my argument into a coherent structure by some pattern that readers can recognize and follow?
- ☐ Have I provided good evidence and logic to support my evaluation?
- ☐ Have I used the basic checklist for revision in Chapter 4? (See p. 111.)

STUDENT REVIEW

WINCHESTER'S ALCHEMY: TWO MEN AND A BOOK

Ian Habel

One can hardly imagine a tale promising less excitement for a general audience than that of the making of the *Oxford English Dictionary* (*OED*). The sensationalism of murder and insanity would have to labor intensely against the burden of lexicography in crafting a genuine page-turner on the subject. Much to my surprise, Simon Winchester, in writing *The Professor and the Madman: A Tale of Murder, Insanity, and the Making of the Oxford English Dictionary,* has succeeded in producing so compelling a story that I was forced to devour it completely in a single afternoon, an unprecedented personal feat.

The Professor and the Madman is the story of the lives of two apparently very different men and the work that brought them together. Winchester begins by recounting the circumstances that led to the incarceration of Dr. W. C. Minor, a well-born, well-educated, and quite insane American ex-Army surgeon. Minor, in a fit of delusion, had murdered a man whom he believed to have crept into his Lambeth hotel room to torment him in his sleep. The doctor is tried and whisked off to the Asylum for the Criminally Insane, Broadmoor.

The author then introduces readers to the other two main characters: the *OED* itself and its editor James Murray, a low-born, self-educated Scottish philologist. The shift in narrative focus is used to dramatic effect. The natural assumption on the part of the reader that these two seemingly unrelated plots must eventually meet urges us to read on in anticipation of that connection. As each chapter switches focus from one man to the other, it is introduced by a citation from the *OED,* reminding us that the story is ultimately about the dictionary. The citations also serve to foreshadow and provide a theme for the chapter. For example, the *OED* definition of *murder* heads the first chapter, relating to the details of Minor's crime.

Winchester acquaints us with the shortcomings of seventeenth- and eighteenth-century attempts at compiling a comprehensive dictionary of the English language. He takes us inside the meetings of the Philological Society, whose members proposed the compilation of the dictionary to end all dictionaries. The *OED* was to include examples of usage illustrating every shade of meaning for every word in the English language. Such a mammoth feat would require enlisting thousands of volunteer readers to comb the corpus of English literature in search of illustrative quotations to be submitted on myriad slips of paper. These slips of paper on each word would in turn be studied by a small army of editors preparing the definitions.

It is not surprising that our Dr. Minor, comfortably tucked away at Broadmoor, possessing both a large library and seemingly infinite free time, should become one of those volunteer readers. After all, we are still rightfully assuming some connection of the book's two plot lines. Yet what sets Dr. Minor apart from his fellow volunteers (aside from the details of his incarceration) is the remarkable efficiency with which he approached his task. Not content merely to fill out slips of paper for submission, Minor methodically indexed every possibly useful mention of any word appearing in his personal library. He then asked to be kept informed of the progress of the work, submitting quotations that would be immediately useful to editors. In this way he managed to "escape" his cell and plunge himself into the work of contemporaries, to become a part of a major event of his time.

Minor's work proved invaluable to the *OED*'s staff of editors, led by James Murray. With the two plot lines now intertwined, readers face such questions as "Will they find out that Minor is insane?" "Will Minor and Murray ever meet?" and "How long will they take to complete the dictionary?" The author builds suspense regarding a meeting of Minor and Murray by providing a false account of their first encounter, as reported by the American press, only to shatter us with the fact that this romantic version did not happen. I'll let Winchester give you the answers to these questions, while working his magic on you, drawing you into this fascinating tale of the making of the world's most famous dictionary.

EVALUATING AN ARGUMENT: THE REBUTTAL OR REFUTATION ESSAY

When your primary purpose in writing is to challenge someone's argument rather than to present your own argument, you are writing a *rebuttal* or *refutation*. A good refutation demonstrates, in an orderly and logical way, the weaknesses of logic or evidence in the argument. Study the following guidelines to prepare a good refutation essay and then study the sample refutation that follows. It has been annotated to show you how the author has structured his rebuttal.

GUIDELINES for Preparing a Refutation or Rebuttal Argument

1. **Read accurately.** Make certain that you have understood your opponent's argument. If you assume views not expressed by the writer and accuse the writer of holding those illogical views, you are guilty of the straw man fallacy, of attributing and then attacking a position that the person does not hold. Look up terms and references you do not know and examine the logic and evidence thoroughly.

2. **Pinpoint the weaknesses in the original argument.** Analyze the argument to determine, specifically, what flaws the argument contains. If the argument contains logical fallacies, make a list of the ones you plan to discredit. Examine the evidence presented. Is it insufficient, unreliable, or irrelevant? Decide, before drafting your refutation, exactly what elements of the argument you intend to challenge.

3. **Write your claim.** After analyzing the argument and deciding on the weaknesses to be challenged, write a claim that establishes that your disagreement is with the writer's logic, assumptions, or evidence, or a combination of these.

4. **Draft your essay, using the following three-part organization:**

   a. *The opponent's argument.* Usually you should not assume that your reader has read or remembered the argument you are refuting. Thus at the beginning of your essay, you need to state, accurately and fairly, the main points of the argument to be refuted.

   b. *Your claim.* Next make clear the nature of your disagreement with the argument you are rebutting.

   c. *Your refutation.* The specifics of your rebuttal will depend upon the nature of your disagreement. If you are challenging the writer's evidence, then you must present the more recent evidence to explain why the evidence used is unreliable or misleading. If you are challenging assumptions, then you must explain why they do not hold up. If your claim is that the piece is filled with logical fallacies, then you must present and explain each fallacy.

GENDER GAMES | DAVID SADKER

A professor of education at American University, David Sadker has written extensively on educational issues, especially on the treatment of girls in the classroom. He is the author of *Failing at Fairness: How Our Schools Cheat Girls* (1995). "Gender Games" appeared in the *Washington Post* on July 31, 2000. Read, study the annotations, and then answer the questions that follow.

(annotation: Attention-getting opening.)

1   Remember when your elementary school teacher would announce the teams for the weekly spelling bee? "Boys against the girls!" There was nothing like a gender showdown to liven things up. Apparently, some writers never left this elementary level of intrigue. A spate of recent books and articles takes us back to the "boys versus girls" fray but this time, with much higher stakes.

(annotation: Claim to be refuted.)

2   May's *Atlantic Monthly* cover story, "Girls Rule," is a case in point. The magazine published an excerpt from *The War Against Boys* by Christina Hoff Sommers, a book advancing the notion that boys are the real victims of gender bias while girls are soaring in school.

(annotation: What's right about the opponent's argument.)

3   Sommers and her supporters are correct in saying that girls and women have made significant educational progress in the past two decades. Females today make up more than 40 percent of medical and law school students, and more than half of college students. Girls continue to read sooner and write better than boys. And for as long as anyone can remember, girls have received higher grades than boys.

(annotation: 1st point of refutation.)

4   But there is more to these selected statistics than meets the eye. Although girls continue to receive higher report card grades than boys, their grades do not translate into higher test scores. The same girls who beat boys in the spelling bees score below boys on the tests that matter: the PSATs crucial for scholarships, the SATs and the ACTs needed for college acceptances, the GREs for graduate school and even the admission tests for law, business and medical schools.

(annotation: 2nd point of refutation.)

5   Many believe that girls' higher grades may be more a reflection of their manageable classroom behavior than their intellectual accomplishment. Test scores are not influenced by quieter classroom behavior. Girls may in fact be trading their initiative and independence for peer approval and good grades, a trade-off that can have costly personal and economic consequences.

(annotation: 3rd point of refutation.)

6   The increase in female college enrollment catches headlines because it heralds the first time that females have outnumbered males on college campuses. But even these enrollment figures are misleading. The female presence increases as the status of the college decreases. Female students are more likely to dominate two-year schools than the Ivy League. And wherever they are, they find themselves segregated and channeled into the least prestigious and least costly majors.

7   In today's world of e-success, more than 60 percent of computer science and business majors are male, about 70 percent of physics majors are males, and more than 80 percent of engineering students are male. But peek into language, psychology, nursing and humanities classrooms, and you will find a sea of female faces.

Higher female enrollment figures mask the "glass walls" that separate the 8 sexes and channel females and males into very different careers, with very different paychecks. Today, despite all the progress, the five leading occupations of employed women are secretary, receptionist, bookkeeper, registered nurse and hairdresser/cosmetologist.

Add this to the "glass ceiling" (about 3 percent of Fortune 500 top man- 9 agers are women) and the persistence of a gender wage gap (women with advanced degrees still lag well behind their less-educated male counterparts) and the crippling impact of workplace and college stereotyping becomes evident.

Even within schools, where female teachers greatly outnumber male teach- 10 ers, school management figures remind us that if there is a war on boys, women are not the generals. More than 85 percent of junior and senior high school principals are male, while 88 percent of school superintendents are male.

Despite sparkling advances of females on the athletic fields, two-thirds of 11 athletic scholarships still go to males. In some areas, women have actually lost ground. When Title IX was enacted in 1972, women coached more than 90 percent of intercollegiate women's teams. Today women coach only 48 percent of women's teams and only 1 percent of men's teams.

> 4th point of refutation.

If some adults are persuaded by the rhetoric in such books as *The War* 12 *Against Boys,* be assured that children know the score. When more than 1,000 Michigan elementary school students were asked to describe what life would be like if they were born a member of the opposite sex, more than 40 percent of the girls saw positive advantages to being a boy: better jobs, more money and definitely more respect. Ninety-five percent of the boys saw no advantage to being a female.

> 5th point of refutation.

The War Against Boys attempts to persuade the public to abandon sup- 13 port for educational initiatives designed to help girls and boys avoid crippling stereotypes. I hope the public and Congress will not be taken in by the book's misrepresentations. We have no time to wage a war on either our boys or our girls.

> Author concludes by stating his claim.

QUESTIONS FOR READING

1. What work, specifically, is Sadker refuting? What is the claim presented by this work?
2. What facts about girls does Sadker grant to Sommers?
3. What facts about girls create a different story, according to Sadker?

QUESTIONS FOR REASONING AND ANALYSIS

1. What is Sadker's claim? What is he asserting about girls?
2. What does Sadker think about the whole idea of books such as Sommers's?

QUESTIONS FOR REFLECTING AND WRITING

1. What statistic is most startling to you? Why?
2. Do you agree that Sadker's statistics are more significant in telling us how women are doing in school, sports, and work? If you disagree with Sadker, how would you counter his argument?
3. Think about your high school experiences. Do you think that teachers are waging a war against boys? What evidence do you have to support your views?

FOR ANALYSIS AND DEBATE

ADDICTED TO HEALTH | ROBERT H. BORK

A conservative legal scholar currently at the American Enterprise Institute for Policy Research, Robert Bork has been acting attorney general and solicitor general of the U.S. Court of Appeals. His appointment to the Supreme Court, rejected by the Congress, has led to a book by Bork on the whole affair and to other books and articles on legal and public policy issues. The following appeared in the *National Review* on July 28, 1997.

1   Government efforts to deal with tobacco companies betray an ultimate ambition to control Americans' lives.

2   When moral self-righteousness, greed for money, and political ambition work hand in hand they produce irrational, but almost irresistible, policies. The latest example is the war on cigarettes and cigarette smokers. A proposed settlement has been negotiated among politicians, plaintiffs' lawyers, and the tobacco industry. The only interests left out of the negotiations were smokers, who will be ordered to pay enormous sums with no return other than the deprivation of their own choices and pleasures.

3   It is a myth that today's Americans are a sturdy, self-reliant folk who will fight any officious interference with their liberties. That has not been true at least since the New Deal. If you doubt that, walk the streets of any American city and see the forlorn men and women cupping their hands against the wind to light cigarettes so that they can get through a few more smokeless hours in their offices. Twenty-five percent of Americans smoke. Why can't they demand and get a compromise rather than accepting docilely the exile that employers and building managers impose upon them?

4   The answer is that they have been made to feel guilty by self-righteous non-smokers. A few years back, hardly anyone claimed to be seriously troubled by tobacco smoke. Now, an entire class of the morally superior claim to be able to detect, and be offended by, tobacco smoke several offices away from their own. These people must possess the sense of smell of a deer or an Indian guide. Yet they will happily walk through suffocating exhaust smoke from buses rather than wait a minute or two to cross the street.

5   No one should assume that peace will be restored when the last cigarette smoker has been banished to the Alaskan tundra. Other products will be

pressed into service as morally reprehensible. If you would know the future, look at California—the national leader in health fanaticism. After a long day in Los Angeles flogging a book I had written, my wife and I sought relaxation with a drink at our hotel's outdoor bar. Our anticipation of pleasure was considerably diminished by a sign: "Warning! Toxic Substances Served Here." They were talking about my martini!

And martinis are a toxic substance, taken in any quantity sufficient to 6 induce a sense of well-being. Why not, then, ban alcohol or at least require a death's head on every martini glass? Well, we did once outlaw alcohol; it was called Prohibition. The myth is that Prohibition increased the amount of drinking in this country; the truth is that it reduced it. There were, of course, some unfortunate side effects, like Al Capone and Dutch Schultz. But by and large the mobsters inflicted rigor mortis upon one another.

Why is it, then, that the end of Prohibition was welcomed joyously by the 7 population? Not because alcohol is not dangerous. Not because the consumption of alcohol was not lessened. And not in order to save the lives of people with names like Big Jim and Ice Pick Phil. Prohibition came to an end because most Americans wanted to have a drink when and where they felt like it. If you insist on sounding like a law-and-economics professor, it ended because we thought the benefits of alcohol outweighed the costs.

That is the sort of calculation by which we lead our lives. Automobiles kill 8 tens of thousands of people every year and disable perhaps that many again. We could easily stop the slaughter. Cars could be made with a top speed of ten miles an hour and with exteriors the consistency of marshmallows. Nobody would die, nobody would be disabled, and nobody would bother with cars very much.

There are, of course, less draconian measures available. On most high- 9 ways, it is almost impossible to find anyone who observes the speed limits. On the theory of the tobacco precedent, car manufacturers should be liable for deaths caused by speeding; after all, they could build automobiles incapable of exceeding legal speed limits.

The reason we are willing to offer up lives and limbs to automobiles is, 10 quite simply, that they make life more pleasant (for those who remain intact)— among other things, by speeding commuting to work, by making possible family vacations a thousand miles from home, and by lowering the costs of products shipped from a distance. The case for regulating automobiles far more severely than we do is not essentially different from the case for heavy regulation of cigarettes or, soon, alcohol.

But choices concerning driving, smoking, and drinking are the sort of 11 things that ought to be left to the individual unless there are clear, serious harms to others.

The opening salvo in the drive to make smoking a criminal act is the pro- 12 posed settlement among the cigarette companies, plaintiffs' lawyers, and the states' attorneys general. We are told that the object is to protect teenagers and children (children being the last refuge of the sanctimonious). But many restrictions will necessarily affect adults, and the tobacco pact contains provisions that can only be explained as punishment for selling to adults.

13   The terms of the settlement plainly reveal an intense hatred of smoking. Opposition to the pact comes primarily from those who think it is not severe enough. For example, critics say the settlement is defective in not restricting the marketing of cigarettes overseas by American tobacco companies. Connecticut's attorney general, Richard Blumenthal, defended the absence of such a provision: "Given our druthers we would have brought them to their knees all over the world, but there is a limit to our leverage." So much for the sovereignty of nations.

14   What the settlement does contain is bad enough. The pact would require the companies to pony up $60 billion; $25 billion of this would be used for public-health issues to be identified by a presidential panel and the rest for children's health insurance. Though the purpose of the entire agreement is punitive, this slice is most obviously so.

15   The industry is also required to pay $308 billion over 25 years, in part to repay states for the cost of treating sick smokers. There are no grounds for this provision. The tobacco companies have regularly won litigation against plaintiffs claiming injury on the grounds that everybody has known for the past forty years that smoking can cause health problems. This $308 billion, which takes from the companies what they have won in litigation, says, in effect, that no one assumed the risk of his own behavior.

16   The provision is groundless for additional reasons. The notion that the states have lost money because of cigarettes ignores the federal and state taxes smokers have paid, which cover any amount the states could claim to have lost. Furthermore, a percentage of the population dies early from smoking. Had these people lived longer, the drain on Medicare and Medicaid would have been greater. When lowered pension and Social Security costs are figured in, it seems certain that government is better off financially with smoking than without it. If we must reduce the issue to one of dollars, as the attorneys general have done, states have profited financially from smoking. If this seems a gruesome and heartless calculation, it is. But don't blame me. The state governments advanced the financial argument and ought to live with its consequences, however distasteful.

17   Other provisions of the settlement fare no better under the application of common sense. The industry is to reduce smoking by teenagers by 30 percent in five years, 50 percent in seven years, and 60 percent in ten years. No one knows how the industry is to perform this trick. But if those goals are not met, the industry will be amerced $80 million a year for each percentage point it falls short.

18   The settlement assumes teenage smoking can be reduced dramatically by requiring the industry to conduct an expensive anti-smoking advertising campaign, banning the use of people and cartoon characters to promote cigarettes, and similar tactics. It is entirely predictable that this will not work. Other countries have banned cigarette advertising, only to watch smoking increase.

Apparently the young, feeling themselves invulnerable, relish the risk of smoking. Studies have shown, moreover, that teenagers are drawn to smoking not because of advertising but because their parents smoke or because of peer pressure. Companies advertise to gain or maintain market share among those who already smoke.

To lessen the heat on politicians, the pact increases the powers of the 19 Food and Drug Administration to regulate tobacco as an addictive drug, with the caveat that it may not prohibit cigarette smoking altogether before the year 2009. The implicit promise is that the complete prohibition of cigarettes will be seriously contemplated at that time. In the meantime, the FDA will subject cigarettes to stricter and stricter controls on the theory that tobacco is a drug.

Another rationale for prohibiting or sharply limiting smoking is the sup- 20 posed need to protect non-smokers from secondhand smoke. The difficulty is that evidence of causation is weak. What we see is a possible small increase in an already small risk which, as some researchers have pointed out, may well be caused by other variables such as misclassification of former smokers as non-smokers or such lifestyle factors as diet.

But the tobacco companies should take little or no comfort from that. 21 Given today's product-liability craze, scientific support, much less probability, is unnecessary to successful lawsuits against large corporations.

The pact is of dubious constitutionality as well. It outlaws the advertising 22 of a product it is legal to sell, which raises the problem of commercial speech protected by the First Amendment. The settlement also requires the industry to disband its lobbying organization, the Tobacco Institute. Lobbying has traditionally been thought to fall within the First Amendment's guarantee of the right to petition the government for the redress of grievances.

And who is to pay for making smoking more difficult? Smokers will have 23 the price of cigarettes raised by new taxes and by the tobacco companies' costs of complying with the settlement. It is a brilliant strategy: Smokers will pay billions to have their pleasure taken away. But if the tobacco settlement makes little sense as public policy, what can be driving it to completion? The motivations are diverse. Members of the plaintiff's bar, who have signally failed in litigation against tobacco to date, are to be guaranteed billions of dollars annually. The states' attorneys general have a different set of incentives. They are members of the National Association of Attorneys General, NAAG, which is commonly, and accurately, rendered as the National Association of Aspiring Governors.

So far they have got what they wanted. There they are, on the front pages 24 of newspapers all over the country, looking out at us, jaws firm, conveying images of sobriety, courage, and righteousness. They have, after all, done battle with the forces of evil, and won—at least temporarily.

Tobacco executives and their lawyers are said to be wily folk, however. 25 They may find ways of defeating the strictures laid upon them. It may be too soon to tell, therefore, whether the tobacco settlement is a major defeat or a victory for the industry. In any case, we can live with it. But whenever individual responsibility is denied, government control of our behavior follows. After cigarettes it will be something else, and so on *ad infinitum.* One would think we would have learned that lesson many times over and that we would have had enough of it.

QUESTIONS FOR READING

1. What is Bork's subject? (Do not answer smoking dangers, or secondhand smoke; be more precise.)
2. What people or organizations are his primary target? What is his attitude toward smokers' acceptance of their "exile"?
3. What are the specifics of the settlement with tobacco companies?
4. What assumption, in Bork's view, stands behind the requirement of anti-smoking ads? Does he agree with the assumption?

QUESTIONS FOR REASONING AND ANALYSIS

1. What is Bork's claim?
2. What kinds of grounds or evidence does he present in support of his claim?
3. What is the tone of his argument? (Do you think that he expects his readers to agree with him?)

QUESTIONS FOR REFLECTION AND WRITING

1. Has Bork supported his claim to your satisfaction? Why or why not?
2. Do you find any logical fallacies in his argument? If so, how would you challenge them?
3. Does Bork's essay warrant a rebuttal? Why or why not?

1. Think about sports stars you know. Write an argument defending one player as the best in his or her field of play. Think about whether you want to use Krauthammer's "Method 1" or "Method 2" or your own method for your criteria. (Remember that you can qualify your argument; you could write about the best college football player this year, for example.)

2. If you like music, think about what you might evaluate from this field. Who is the best rock band? Hip hop artist? Country-western singer? And so forth. Be sure to make your criteria for evaluation clear.

3. You have had many instructors—and much instruction—in the last 12+ years. Is there one teacher who is/was the best? Why? Is there a teaching method that stands out in your memory for the excellence of its approach? Find an evaluation topic from your educational experiences.

4. Select an editorial, op-ed column, letter to the editor, or one of the essays in this text as an argument with which you disagree. Prepare a refutation of the work's logic or evidence or both. Follow the guidelines for writing a refutation or rebuttal in this chapter.

5. What is your favorite book? Movie? Television show? Why is it your favorite? Does it warrant an argument that it is really good, maybe even the best, in some way or in some category (sitcoms, for example)? Write a review, following the guidelines for this type of evaluation argument given in this chapter.

The Position Paper: Claims of Values

READ: Who are the speakers? What is the situation?

REASON: What is the point of the cartoon? What does Dana Summers, the cartoonist, want readers to think about?

REFLECT/WRITE: Why does this cartoon make a good opening for a chapter on arguments based on values?

As we established in Chapter 4, all arguments involve values. Evaluation arguments require judgment—thoughtful judgment, one hopes, based on criteria—but judgment nonetheless. If you believe that no one should spend more than $25,000 for a car, then you will not appreciate the qualities that attract some people to Mercedes. When one argues that government tax rates should go up as income goes up, it is because one believes that it is *right* for government to redistribute income to some degree: The rich pay more in taxes, the poor get more in services. When countries ban the importing of ivory, they do so because they believe it is *wrong* to destroy the magnificent elephant just so humans can use their ivory tusks for decorative items. (Observe that the word *magnificent* expresses a value.)

Some arguments, though, are less about judging what is good or best, or less about how to solve specific problems, than they are about stating a position on an issue. An argument that defends a more general position (segregated schools are wrong) may imply action that should result (schools should be integrated), but the focus of the argument is first to state and defend the position. It is helpful to view these arguments, based heavily on values and a logical sequencing of ideas with less emphasis on specifics, as a separate type—genre—of argument. These claims of values are often called position papers.

CHARACTERISTICS OF THE POSITION PAPER

The position paper or claim of values may be the most difficult of arguments simply because it is often perceived to be the easiest. Let's think about this kind of argument:

- A claim based on values and argued more with logic than specifics is usually more general or abstract or philosophical than other types of argument. Greenpeace objects to commercial fishing that uses large nets that ensnare dolphins along with commercial fish such as tuna. Why? Because we ought not to destroy such beautiful and highly developed animals. Because we ought not to destroy more than we need, to waste part of nature because we are careless or in a hurry. The issue is about values for Greenpeace—though it may be about money for the commercial fishermen.

- The position paper makes a claim about what is right or wrong, good or bad, for us as individuals or as a society. Topics can range from capital punishment to pornography to endangered species.

- A claim based on values is often developed in large part by a logical sequencing of reasons. But a support of principles also depends on relevant facts. Remember the long list of specific abuses listed in the Declaration of Independence (see pp. 126–29). If Greenpeace can show that commercial fisheries can be successful using a different kind of net or staying away from areas heavily populated by dolphins, it can probably get more support for its general principles.

217

- A successful position paper requires more than a forceful statement of personal beliefs. If we can reason logically from principles widely shared by our audience, we are more likely to be successful. If we are going to challenge their beliefs or values, then we need to consider the conciliatory approach as a strategy for getting them to at least listen to our argument.

GUIDELINES for Analyzing a Claim of Value

When reading position papers, what should you look for? Again, the basics of good argument apply here as well as with definition arguments. To analyze claims of values specifically, use the following questions as guides:

- **What is the writer's claim?** Is it clear?
- **Is the claim qualified if necessary?** Some claims of value are broad philosophical assertions ("Capital punishment is immoral and bad public policy"). Others are qualified ("Capital punishment is acceptable only in crimes of treason").
- **What facts are presented?** Are they credible? Are they relevant to the claim's support?
- **What reasons are given in support of the claim?** What assumptions are necessary to tie reasons to claim? Make a list of reasons and assumptions and analyze the writer's logic. Do you find any fallacies?
- **What are the implications of the claim?** For example, if you argue for the legalization of all recreational drugs, you eliminate all "drug problems" by definition. But what new problems may be created by this approach? Consider more car accidents and reduced productivity for openers.
- **Is the argument convincing?** Does the evidence provide strong support for the claim? Are you prepared to agree with the writer, in whole or in part?

PREPARING A POSITION PAPER

In addition to the guidelines for writing arguments presented in Chapter 4, you can use the following advice specific to writing position papers or claims of value.

Planning

1. *Think:* What claim, exactly, do you want to support? Should you qualify your first attempt at a claim statement?
2. *Think:* What grounds (evidence) do you have to support your claim? You may want to make a list of the reasons and facts you would consider using to defend your claim.

3. *Think:* Study your list of possible grounds and identify the assumptions (warrants) and backing for your grounds.

4. *Think:* Now make a list of the grounds most often used by those holding views that oppose your claim. This second list will help you prepare counterarguments to possible rebuttals, but first it will help you test your commitment to your position. If you find the opposition's arguments persuasive and cannot think how you would rebut them, you may need to rethink your position. Ideally, your two lists will confirm your views but also increase your respect for opposing views.

5. *Consider:* How can I use a conciliatory approach? With an emotion-laden or highly controversial issue, the conciliatory approach can be an effective strategy. Conciliatory arguments include:
   - The use of nonthreatening language
   - The fair expression of opposing views
   - A statement of the common ground shared by opposing sides.

You may want to use a conciliatory approach when: (1) you know your views will be unpopular with at least some members of your audience; (2) the issue is highly emotional and has sides that are "entrenched" so that you are seeking some accommodations rather than dramatic changes of position; (3) you need to interact with members of your audience and want to keep a respectful relationship going. The sample student essay on gun control (at the end of this chapter) illustrates a conciliatory approach.

Drafting

1. Begin with an opening paragraph or two that introduces your topic in an interesting way. Possibilities include a statement of the issue's seriousness or reasons why the issue is currently being debated—or why we should go back to reexamine it. Some writers are spurred by a recent event that receives media coverage; recounting such an event can produce an effective opening. You can also briefly summarize points of the opposition that you will challenge in supporting your claim. Many counterarguments are position papers.

2. Decide where to place your claim statement. Your best choices are either early in your essay or at the end of your essay, after you have made your case. The second approach can be an effective alternative to the more common pattern of stating one's claim early.

3. Organize evidence in an effective way. One plan is to move from the least important to the most important reasons, followed by rebuttals to potential counterarguments. Another possibility is to organize by the arguments of the opposition, explaining why each of their reasons fails to hold up. A third approach is to organize logically. That is, if some reasons build on the accepting of other reasons, you want to begin with the necessary underpinnings and then move forward from those.

4. Provide a logical defense of or specifics in support of each reason. You have not finished your task by simply asserting several reasons for your claim. You also need to present facts or examples for or a logical explanation of each reason. For example, you have not defended your views on capital punishment by asserting that it is right or just to take the life of a murderer. Why is it right or just? Executing the murderer will not bring the victim back to life. Do two wrongs make a right? These are some of the thoughts your skeptical reader may have unless you explain and justify your reasoning. *Remember:* Quoting another writer's opinion on your topic does not provide proof for your reasons. It merely shows that someone else agrees with you.

5. Maintain an appropriate level of seriousness for an argument of principle. Of course, word choice must be appropriate to a serious discussion, but in addition be sure to present reasons that are also appropriately serious. For example, if you are defending the claim that music CDs should not be subject to content labeling because such censorship is inconsistent with First Amendment rights, do not trivialize your argument by including the point that young people are tired of adults controlling their lives. (This is another issue for another paper.)

A CHECKLIST FOR REVISION ∎▪∎▪∎▪∎▪∎▪∎▪∎▪∎▪∎▪∎▪∎▪∎▪∎▪∎▪∎

- ☐ Do I have a clear statement of my claim? Is it qualified, if appropriate?
- ☐ Have I organized my argument, building the parts of my support into a clear and logical structure that readers can follow?
- ☐ Have I avoided logical fallacies?
- ☐ Have I found relevant facts and examples to support and develop my reasons?
- ☐ Have I paid attention to appropriate word choice, including using a conciliatory approach if that is a wise strategy?
- ☐ Have I used the basic checklist for revision in Chapter 4 (see p. 111)?

STUDENT ESSAY

EXAMINING THE ISSUE OF GUN CONTROL

Chris Brown

The United States has a long history of compromise. Issues such as

representation in government have been resolved because of compromise,

forming some of the bases of American life. Americans, however, like to feel

Introduction connects ambivalence in American character to conflict over gun control.

that they are uncompromising, never willing to surrender an argument. This attitude has led to a number of issues in modern America that are unresolved, including the issue of gun control. Bickering over the issue has slowed progress toward legislation that will solve the serious problem of gun violence in America, while keeping recreational use of firearms available to responsible people. To resolve the conflict over guns, the arguments of both sides must be examined, with an eye to finding the flaws in both. Then perhaps we can reach some meaningful compromises.

Gun advocates have used many arguments for the continued availability of firearms to the public. The strongest of these defenses points to the many legitimate uses for guns. One use is protection against violence, a concern of some people in today's society. There are many problems with the use of guns for protection, however, and these problems make the continued use of firearms for protection dangerous. One such problem is that gun owners are not always able to use guns responsibly. When placed in a situation in which personal injury or loss is imminent, people often do not think intelligently. Adrenaline surges through the body, and fear takes over much of the thinking process. This causes gun owners to use their weapons, firing at whatever threatens them. Injuries and deaths of innocent people, including family members of the gun owner, result. Removing guns from the house seems to be the only solution to these sad consequences.

Responding to this argument, gun advocates ask how they are to defend themselves without guns. But guns are needed for protection from other guns. If there are no guns, people need only to protect themselves from criminals using knives, baseball bats, and other weapons. Obviously the odds of surviving a knife attack are greater than the odds of surviving a gun attack. One reason is that a gun is an impersonal weapon. Firing at someone from 50 feet away requires much less commitment than charging someone with a knife and stabbing repeatedly. Also, bullet wounds are, generally, more severe than knife wounds. Guns are also more likely to be misused when a dark figure is in one's house. To kill with the gun requires only to point and shoot; no recognition of

Student organizes by arguments for no gun control.

1. Guns for protection.

the figure is needed. To kill with a knife, by contrast, requires getting within arm's reach of the figure.

2. Recreational uses.
There are other uses of guns, including recreation. Hunting and target shooting are valid, responsible uses of guns. How do we keep guns available for recreation? The answer is in the form of gun clubs and hunting clubs. Many are already established; more can be constructed. These clubs can provide recreational use of guns for responsible people while keeping guns off the streets and out of the house.

3. Second Amendment rights.
The last argument widely used by gun advocates is the constitutional right to bear arms. The fallacies in this argument are that the Constitution was written in a vastly different time. This different time had different uses for guns, and a different type of gun. Firearms were defended in the Constitution because of their many valid uses and fewer problems. Guns were mostly muskets, guns that were not very accurate beyond close range. Also, guns took more than 30 seconds to load in the eighteenth century and could fire only one shot before reloading. These differences with today's guns affect the relative safety of guns then and now. In addition, those who did not live in the city at the time used hunting for food as well as for recreation; hunting was a necessary component of life. That is not true today. Another use of guns in the eighteenth century was as protection from animals. Wild animals such as bears and cougars were much more common. Settlers, explorers, and hunters needed protection from these animals in ways not comparable with modern life.

Finally, Revolutionary America had no standing army. Defense of the nation and of one's home from other nations relied on local militia. The right to bear arms granted in the Constitution was inspired by the need for national protection as well as by the other outdated needs previously discussed. Today America has a standing army with enough weaponry to adequately defend itself from outside aggressors. There is no need for every citizen to carry a musket, or an AK-47, for the protection of the nation. It would seem, then, that the Second Amendment does not apply to modern society.

To reach a compromise, we also have to examine the other side of the issue. Some gun-control advocates argue that all guns are unnecessary and should be outlawed. The problem with this argument is that guns will still be available to those who do not mind breaking the law. Until an economically sound and feasible way of controlling illegal guns in America is found, guns cannot be totally removed, no matter how much legislation is passed. This means that if guns are to be outlawed for uses other than recreational uses, a way must be found to combat the illegal gun trade that will evolve. Tough criminal laws and a large security force are all that can be offered to stop illegal uses of guns until better technology is available. This means that, perhaps, a good resolution would involve gradual restrictions on guns, until eventually guns were restricted only to recreational uses in a controlled setting for citizens not in the police or military.

Student establishes a compromise position.

Both sides on this issue have valid points. Any middle ground needs to offer something to each side. It must address the reasons people feel that they need guns for protection, allow for valid recreational use, and keep guns out of the hands of the public, except for properly trained police officers. Time and money will be needed to move toward the removal of America's huge handgun arsenal. But, sooner or later a compromise on the issue of gun control must be made to make America a safer, better place to live.

Conclusion restates student's claim.

FOR ANALYSIS AND DEBATE

ANIMAL RIGHTS V. ANIMAL RESEARCH: A MODEST PROPOSAL | JOSEPH BERNSTEIN

Dr. Joseph Bernstein is an assistant professor of orthopedics at the University of Pennsylvania's hospital and a senior fellow at the Leonard Davis Institute of Health Economics, also at the University of Pennsylvania. Bernstein's "modest proposal" for animal research appeared in the *Journal of Medical Ethics* in 1996 along with Timothy Sprigge's response.

PREREADING QUESTIONS What is the source of Bernstein's title? (*Hint:* Check Chapter 11.) Does the demand for advances in medicine justify the use of animals in research? Is the use of animals ethical so long as they are not abused? What constitutes abuse?

1   Many people love animals. Some animal lovers, though, in the name of their love, oppose the use of any animals in any medical research, regardless of the care given, regardless of the cause. Of course, many other animal lovers acknowledge the need for animal subjects in some medical studies, as long as no alternatives exist, and provided that care, respect and dignity are applied at all times. Unhappily, between the opponents of animal research and the researchers themselves lies no common ground, no place for an agreement to disagree: the opponents are not satisfied merely to abstain from animal experimentation themselves—they want everyone else to stop too.

2   Despite that, I would argue that in this case (to a far greater extent than, say, in the case of abortion) the animal rights question can be answered by exactly that tactic: the abstention of the opposition. Of course, I do not advocate abstention from debate; and, of course, abstention from performing research by those who are not researchers is not meaningful. Rather, I propose that the protesters—and every citizen they can enlist—abstain from the benefits of animal research. I say let the proponents of animal rights boycott the products of animal research. Let them place fair market-place pressure on ending activities they find reprehensible. Let them mobilise the tacit support they claim. Let the market for therapies derived from animal research evaporate, and with it much of the funding for such work. Let the animal lovers attain their desired goal without clamour, and without violence.

3   To assist them, I offer a modest proposal.

4   I suggest that we adopt a legal release form, readily available to all patients, which will enable them to indicate precisely which benefits of animal research they oppose—and from which, accordingly, they refuse to benefit. This form could be sent to all hospitals and physicians, and would be included in the patient's chart, much like operative consent forms, or Do Not Resuscitate instructions. It should resolve the issue once and for all.

5   This "Animal Research Advance Directive" would look something like this:

6   Dear Doctor:
Animals deserve the basic freedom from serving as experiment subjects against their will. Today, we who are committed to seeing the world's scientific laboratories free from unwilling and innocent animals, hereby refuse to benefit from research performed on these victims.

7   Accordingly, I ask that you care for me to the best of your abilities, but request that:

(CHECK ALL THAT APPLY)

8   ☐ You do not perform on me a coronary bypass operation, or fix any heart defect my child may be born with, as these operations and the heart lung

machine used during the procedures were developed using dogs. In fact, since the entire field of cardiology has been polluted by animal research for nearly a century, I cannot in good conscience accept any cardiological care.

☐ You treat my child for any disease she may develop, but do not give her 9 a vaccine that was tried first on a blameless animal. As I am not aware of any vaccines that were not animal-tested, please skip them all.

☐ You avoid offering any suggestions regarding my diet and habits, 10 when that information was derived from animal studies. This includes salt and fat intake, tobacco smoke, and various cancer-causing food additives. Do not bother to test my cholesterol levels, as the association between high cholesterol and heart disease is knowledge stolen from the suffering of the innocent.

☐ Should I develop a malignancy, you do not give me chemotherapy, as 11 those drugs were administered first to animals. I must also decline surgical treatment as well, since modern surgical technique and equipment owes its existence to sinful animal research. Finally, do not treat my disease with radia-tion, since that field, too, was contaminated by dog studies.

☐ You amputate my leg or arm should I break it in such fashion that it 12 requires surgery. Fracture fixation devices were designed through the suf-fering of dogs, so I must refuse repair of the bone. That probably will hurt a lot, but since I must refuse all pain medicine studied on rats (and that includes just about all of them), it is best if you just remove the damaged limb.

Needless to say, I will not accept an AIDS vaccine should one be devel- 13 oped, as unwilling Rhesus monkeys have been used in AIDS research.

Thank you for considering my wishes. Only through the concerted avoid- 14 ance of these ill-gotten technologies can we halt the barbaric practice of ani-mal research. Of course, I have no objection to studying disease on humans. To that end, I pledge my body to science upon my death. It probably will occur a lot sooner than I'd like.

QUESTIONS FOR READING

1. What is Bernstein "proposing"?
2. Why does he include such a long checklist? What does he want to make clear to readers?

QUESTIONS FOR REASONING AND ANALYSIS

1. Does Bernstein seriously expect to see the use of an "Animal Research Advance Directive"? How do you know the answer to this question?
2. What is the tone of this essay? What language and strategies help to create the tone?

QUESTIONS FOR REFLECTING AND WRITING

1.   Has Bernstein presented a convincing argument? Are his persuasive strategies effective? Explain your response.

2.   If you wanted to refute Bernstein's argument, how would you proceed?

A REPLY TO JOSEPH BERNSTEIN | TIMOTHY SPRIGGE

Endowment fellow in philosophy at the University of Edinburgh, Timothy Sprigge has contributed articles to scholarly journals of philosophy and published several books of philosophy, including *Theories of Existence* (1985) and *Rational Foundations of Ethics* (1990). His argument on the animal rights debate, a response to Joseph Bernstein's argument, also appeared in the *Journal of Medical Ethics* in 1996.

PREREADING QUESTIONS Does the demand for advances in medicine justify the use of animals in research? Is the use of animals ethical so long as they are not abused? What constitutes abuse?

1   Dr Bernstein's "A modest proposal" lays down a witty challenge to opponents of animal experimentation. However, matters are rather less clear cut than he evidently realises and there are various reasons, which I list below, why an anti-vivisectionist may feel no obligation to sign such directives under present conditions. Things would be different if (1) adequately funded facilities on the National Health Service were introduced which would make no use of further medical advances based on painful animal experimentation; (2) public funding for (painful) animal research and "alternative" research henceforth reflected the proportion of those who would not, and those who would, opt for these facilities.

2   (1) A first point is that Dr Bernstein does not distinguish between the use of animals in research which does, and that which does not, involve serious suffering for them (including that imposed by their housing, such as the extremes of boredom, but obviously not including being painlessly killed). The original anti-vivisection societies were, as their names imply, opposed to the cutting up of conscious live animals rather than to human use of animals in general (as may be the case with many animal rightists nowadays) and it seems to me reasonable to use "vivisection" today in a broader sense to cover all research which involves serious animal suffering (something worse, for example, than we feel when we receive an injection). Opponents of this are not necessarily opponents of all use of animals in medical research and it is not clear how many of the medical procedures Dr Bernstein lists were developed through work involving such serious suffering (as opposed, for example, to painless killing). It would facilitate rational debate if both defenders and critics of animal research were clearer on this point than they usually are.

3   (2) Even if, in practice, most of these procedures have been developed in ways which did involve serious animal suffering, it is another question whether they could have been developed without this. The anti-vivisectionist who

believes that they could have been, or even probably could have been, developed (by now) by other means has no reason to avoid them because of their unfortunate and, as he thinks, (probably) unnecessary history. In fact, I suggest, no one really knows how far medicine could have advanced had work of a kind which most anti-vivisectionists would condemn, been avoided.[1] If this is so, there is no bad faith in the anti-vivisectionist making use of advances in medicine which he/she guesses would probably have been gained in other ways had the ethics of the past been more like theirs now.

The autobahnen in Germany were originally developed for their utility in 4 transporting troops for aggressive war. Should those against aggressive war therefore not use those built in the Hitler period? Likewise Volkswagen cars were developed as cars for the people in the Third Reich as part of a plan to encourage love of that regime. Is one wrong to drive or travel in one today?

Many nations established their present borders in wars which involved all 5 manner of what we would now regard as atrocities. Should its decent citizens refuse loyalty to any country with such a past?

Few people would answer these questions affirmatively, doubtless believ- 6 ing that, since we cannot change past history, refusing to benefit from its evils, especially where similar benefits could probably have been won otherwise, would be a pointless sacrifice.

In short, one may avail oneself of knowledge and techniques which exist 7 now, however first acquired, with a clear conscience even if they were developed in ways which fall below what one would like to be the moral standards of today. Where procedures rely on very recent research he/she should perhaps avoid benefiting from it, if he/she can, because this is likely to be part of a current research programme which he/she should be attempting to discourage. But even here if one believes that similarly useful developments in medicine could have occurred without such pain for animals it is not unreasonable or inconsistent to avail oneself of it, in the absence of alternatives (either of procedures or research) which might have been developed instead in a society less ready to base itself on animal suffering.

(3) If our society had long been based on a culture which outlawed the 8 causing of serious pain to animals for human benefit it would have been so different through and through that no one can tell whether humans would have been better off or worse off now than they are. After all, we are the product of a history which, in innumerable ways, depended on behaviour which we would now dub immoral, and we just have to accept that for better or for worse. The moral question now is whether these practices can be justified in the light of the moral ideals to which we now aspire and the knowledge we now possess. So there is no more call on those of us who argue for the cessation of such animal experimentation as involves serious suffering to reject what was acquired in the past by means of it than there is for us to distance ourselves from most of our institutions with their morally mixed past.

(4) Judgments about whether people in the past are to be morally con- 9 demned for what they did are highly problematic. People act in a historical

context and cannot be expected to live by standards which have been developed since. The anti-vivisectionist thinks that we are now ready for higher standards, in our relations with animals. For one thing the technologies of discovery are more sophisticated and need not be so physically intrusive or painful as perhaps they were bound to be in the past. For another thing, surgery was so dreadful for everyone until the development of anaesthetics, that perhaps people could not be expected to be too sensitive about animals amidst so much inevitable pain for themselves. But, with medical advances meaning so much less pain for us humans of today (when the groups to which we belong behave themselves, as admittedly too few do), it is surely time to be more sensitive about the suffering of animals for our advantage.

10   It would clarify the whole debate enormously if the following were sharply distinguished: animal-based research which 1) must involve serious animal suffering; 2) does involve it but which could be replaced by research (whether using animals or not) which does not; 3) does not involve it. All sides might then agree that 2) is wrong (inasmuch as the suffering would be uncontentiously unnecessary) and attention could then be paid to how much falls into the first category and whether the benefits it may bring justify the harm both to animals and those who must render themselves callous to their suffering. As for category 3) that divides into various types the morality of which is, indeed, important but much less urgent. At any rate, I see no reason why an anti-vivisectionist should feel the need to avoid the benefits of research other than what he/she is sure is of the first type.

REFERENCE

1 Balls M. Recent progress towards reducing the use of animal experimentation in biomedical research. In: Garratini S, van Bekkum DW, eds. *The importance of animal experimentation for safety and biomedical research.* Dordrecht: Kluwer Academic Publishers, 1990: 228–9.

QUESTIONS FOR READING

1.   In replying to Bernstein's argument, Sprigge makes several distinctions. What distinctions does he make regarding use of animals in research? What distinction does he make with regard to the past and the present?

2.   What does the author assert regarding the behavior of people in the past? Have we opposed the use of animals for human advantages in the past?

3.   What distinctions does he recommend for the present use of animals in medical research? How will these distinctions clarify the debate?

QUESTIONS FOR REASONING AND ANALYSIS

1.   What is Sprigge's position with regard to the use of medical science based on animal research in the past?

2. To support his argument, Sprigge makes several analogies. Do they provide effective reasoning in support of his argument?

QUESTIONS FOR REFLECTING AND WRITING

1. Does Sprigge make a convincing argument for animal rights activists benefiting from medical science based on animal experiments in the past? Do you agree with him on this point? Why or why not?

2. Is Sprigge effective in establishing some common ground for both sides? If so, what is that common ground? If you think that he has failed to do this, explain why.

1. Chris Brown, in the student essay, writes a conciliatory argument seeking common ground on the volatile issue of gun control. Write your own conciliatory argument on this issue, offering a different approach than Brown, but citing Brown for any ideas you borrow from his essay. Alternatively, write a counterargument of his essay.

2. There are other "hot issues," issues that leave people entrenched on one side or the other, giving expression to the same arguments again and again without budging many, if any, readers. Do not try to write on any one of these about which you get strongly emotional. Select one that you can be calm enough over to write a conciliatory argument, seeking to find common ground. Some of these issues include same-sex marriage, legalizing recreational drugs, capital punishment, mainstreaming students with disabilities, the use of torture to interrogate terrorists. Exclude abortion rights from the list—it is too controversial for most writers to handle successfully.

3. Other issues that call for positions based on values stem from First Amendment rights. Consider a possible topic from this general area. Possibilities include:

   Hate speech should (or should not) be a crime.
   Obscenity and pornography on the Internet should (or should not) be restricted.
   Hollywood films should (or should not) show characters smoking.

4. Consider issues related to college life. Should all colleges have an honor code—or should existing codes be eliminated? Should students be automatically expelled for plagiarism? Should college administrators have any control over what is published in the college newspaper?

Arguments About Cause

READ: What is the scene? Who do the two figures in the front look like? Who speaks the words at the top?

REASON: What causes are suggested by the words? What causes are implied visually?

REFLECT/WRITE: What conclusion are we to draw from the cartoon?

Because we want to know *why* things happen, arguments about cause are both numerous and important to us. We begin asking why at a young age, pestering adults with questions such as "Why is the sky blue?" and "Why is the grass green?" And, to make sense of our world, we try our hand at explanations as youngsters, deciding that the first-grade bully is "a bad boy." The bully's teacher, however, will seek a more complex explanation because an understanding of the causes is the place to start to guide the bully to more socially acceptable behavior.

As adults we continue the search for answers. We want to understand past events: Why was President Kennedy assassinated? We want to explain current situations: Why do so many college students binge drink? And of course we also want to predict the future: Will the economy improve if there is a tax cut? All three questions seek a causal explanation, including the last one. If you answer the last question with a yes, you are claiming that a tax cut is a cause of economic improvement.

CHARACTERISTICS OF CAUSAL ARGUMENTS

Causal arguments vary not only in subject matter but in structure. Here are the four most typical patterns.

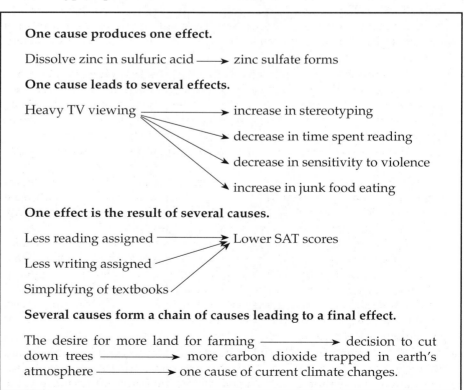

One cause produces one effect.

Dissolve zinc in sulfuric acid ⟶ zinc sulfate forms

One cause leads to several effects.

Heavy TV viewing ⟶ increase in stereotyping
⟶ decrease in time spent reading
⟶ decrease in sensitivity to violence
⟶ increase in junk food eating

One effect is the result of several causes.

Less reading assigned ⟶ Lower SAT scores
Less writing assigned
Simplifying of textbooks

Several causes form a chain of causes leading to a final effect.

The desire for more land for farming ⟶ decision to cut down trees ⟶ more carbon dioxide trapped in earth's atmosphere ⟶ one cause of current climate changes.

These models lead to several key points about causal arguments:

- **Most causal arguments are highly complex.** Except for some simple chemical reactions, most arguments about cause are difficult, can involve many steps, and are often open to challenge. Even arguments based in science lead to shrill exchanges. While scientists seek genetic markers for obesity, others argue that obesity is a result of a lack of willpower. Think, then, how much more open to debate are arguments about the worldwide economic downturn or arguments about human behavior. Many people think that "it's obvious" that violent TV and video games lead to more aggressive behavior as well as a loss of horror in the face of violence. And yet, psychologists, in study after study, have not demonstrated conclusively that there is a clear causal connection. One way to challenge this causal argument is to point to the majority of people who do not perform violent acts even though they have watched television and played video games while growing up.

- **Because of the multiple and intertwined patterns of causation in many complex situations, the best causal arguments keep focused on their purpose.** For example, you are concerned with global warming. Cows contribute to global warming. Are we going to stop cattle farming? Not likely. Factories contribute to global warming. Are we going to tear down factories? Not likely—but we can demand that smokestacks have filters to reduce harmful emissions. Focus your argument on the causes that readers are most likely to accept because they are most likely to accept the action that the causes imply.

- **Learn and use the specific terms and concepts that provide useful guides to thinking about cause.** First, when looking for the cause of an event, we look for an *agent*—a person, situation, another event that led to the effect. For example, a lit cigarette dropped in a bed caused the house fire—the lit cigarette is the agent. But why, we ask, did someone drop a lit cigarette on a bed? The person, old and ill, took a sleeping pill and dropped the cigarette when he fell asleep. Where do we stop in the chain of causes?

  Second, most events do not occur in a vacuum with a single cause. There are *conditions* surrounding the event. The man's age and health were conditions. Third, we can also look for *influences*. The sleeping pill certainly influenced the man to drop the cigarette. Some conditions and influences may qualify as *remote causes*. *Proximate causes* are more immediate, usually closer in time to the event or situation. The man's dozing off is a proximate cause of the fire. Finally, we come to the *precipitating cause,* the triggering event—in our example, the cigarette's igniting the combustible mattress fabric. Sometimes we are interested primarily in the precipitating cause; in other situations, we need to go further back to find the remote causes or conditions that are responsible for what has occurred.

- **Be alert to the difference between cause and correlation.** First, be certain that you can defend your pattern of cause and effect as genuine causation, not as correlation only. Married people are better off financially, are healthier, and report happier sex lives than singles or cohabiting couples. Is this a correlation only? Or, does marriage itself produce these effects? Linda Waite is one sociologist who argues that marriage is the cause. Another example: Girls who participate in after-school activities are much less likely to get pregnant. Are the activities a cause? Probably not. But there are surely conditions and influences that have led to both the decision to participate in activities and the decision not to become pregnant.

Mill's Methods for Investigating Causes

John Stuart Mill, a nineteenth-century British philosopher, explained in detail some important ways of investigating and demonstrating causal relationships: commonality, difference, and process of elimination. We can benefit in our study of cause by understanding and using his methods.

1. *Commonality.* One way to isolate cause is to demonstrate that one agent is *common* to similar outcomes. For instance, twenty-five employees attend a company luncheon. Late in the day, ten report to area hospitals, and another four complain the next day of having experienced vomiting the night before. Public health officials will soon want to know what these people ate for lunch. Different people during the same 12-hour period had similar physical symptoms of food poisoning. The common factor may well have been the tuna salad they ate for lunch.

2. *Difference.* Another way to isolate cause is to recognize one key *difference.* If two situations are alike in every way but one, and the situations result in different outcomes, then the one way they differ must have caused the different outcome. Studies in the social sciences are often based on the single-difference method. To test for the best teaching methods for math, an educator could set up an experiment with two classrooms similar in every way except that one class devotes 15 minutes three days a week to instruction by drill. If the class receiving the drill scores much higher on a standard test given to both groups of students, the educator could argue that math drills make a measurable difference in learning math. But the educator should be prepared for skeptics to challenge the assertion of only one difference between the two classes. Could the teacher's attitude toward the drills also make a difference in student learning? If the differences in student scores are significant, the educator probably has a good argument, even though a teacher's attitude cannot be controlled in the experiment.

3. *Process of elimination.* One can develop a causal argument around a technique we all use for problem solving: *the process of elimination.* When something happens, we examine all possible causes and eliminate them, one by one, until we are satisfied that we have isolated the actual cause (or causes). When the Federal Aviation Administration has to investigate a plane crash, it uses this process, exploring possible causes such as mechanical failure, weather, human error, or terrorism. Sometimes the process isolates more

than one cause or points to a likely cause without providing absolute proof. You will see how Lester Thurow uses the process of elimination method in his article at the end of this chapter (pp. 238–40).

EXERCISE: Understanding Causal Patterns

From the following events or situations, select the one you know best and list as many conditions, influences, and causes—remote, proximate, precipitating—as you can think of. You may want to do this exercise with your class partner or in small groups. Be prepared to explain your causal pattern to the class.

1. Teen suicide
2. Global warming
3. Increase in the numbers of women elected to public office
4. High salaries of professional athletes
5. Increased interest in soccer in the United States
6. Comparatively low scores by U.S. students on international tests in math and science
7. Majority of undergraduates now women

GUIDELINES for Analyzing Causal Arguments

When analyzing causal arguments, what should you look for? The basics of good argument apply to all arguments: a clear statement of claim, qualified if appropriate, a clear explanation of reasons and evidence, and enough relevant evidence to support the claim. How do we recognize these qualities in a causal argument? Use the following points as guides to analyzing:

- **Does the writer carefully distinguish among types of causes?** Word choice is crucial. Is the argument that A and A alone caused B or that A was one of several contributing causes?

- **Does the writer recognize the complexity of causation and not rush to assert only one cause for a complex event or situation?** The credibility of an argument about cause is quickly lost if readers find the argument oversimplified.

- **Is the argument's claim clearly stated, with qualifications as appropriate?** If the writer wants to argue for one cause, not the only cause, of an event or situation, then the claim's wording must make this limited goal clear to readers. For example, one can perhaps build the case for heavy television viewing as *one* cause of stereotyping, loss of sensitivity to violence, and increased fearfulness. But we know that the home environment and neighborhood and school environments also do much to shape attitudes.

- **What reasons and evidence are given to support the argument?** Can you see the writer's pattern of development? Does the reasoning seem logical? Are the data relevant? This kind of analysis of the argument will help you evaluate it.

- **Does the argument demonstrate causality, not just a time relationship or correlation?** A causal argument needs to prove *agency*: A is the cause of B, not just something that happened before B or something that is present when B is present. March precedes April, but March does not cause April to arrive.

- **Does the writer present believable causal agents, agents consistent with our knowledge of human behavior and scientific laws?** Most educated people do not believe that personalities are shaped by astrological signs or that scientific laws are suspended in the Bermuda Triangle, allowing planes and ships to vanish or enter a fourth dimension.

- **What are the implications for accepting the causal argument?** If A and B clearly are the causes of C, and we don't want C to occur, then we presumably must do something about A and B—or at least we must do something about either A or B and see if reducing or eliminating one of the causes significantly reduces the incidence of C.

- **Is the argument convincing?** After analyzing the argument and answering the questions given in the previous points, you need to decide if, finally, the argument works.

PREPARING A CAUSAL ARGUMENT

In addition to the guidelines for writing arguments presented in Chapter 4, you can use the following advice specific to writing causal arguments.

Planning

1. **Think:** What are the focus and limits of your causal argument? Do you want to argue for one cause of an event or situation? Do you want to argue for several causes leading to an event or situation? Do you want to argue for a cause that others have overlooked? Do you want to show how one cause is common to several situations or events? Diagramming the relationship of cause to effect may help you see what you want to focus on.

2. **Think:** What reasons and evidence do you have to support your tentative claim? Consider what you already know that has led to your choice of topic. A brainstorming list may be helpful.

3. **Think:** How, then, do you want to word your claim? As we have discussed, wording is crucial in causal arguments. Review the discussion of characteristics of causal arguments if necessary.

4. **Reality check:** Do you have a claim worth defending in a paper? Will readers care?

5. **Think:** What, if any, additional evidence do you need to develop a convincing argument? You may need to do some reading or online searching to

obtain data to strengthen your argument. Readers expect relevant, reliable, current statistics in most arguments about cause. Assess what you need and then think about what sources will provide the needed information.

6. **Think:** What assumptions (warrants) are you making in your causal reasoning? Do these assumptions hold up to logical scrutiny? Will readers be likely to agree with your assumptions, or will you need to defend them as part of your argument? For example: One reason to defend the effects of heavy TV watching on viewers is the commonsense argument that what humans devote considerable time to will have a significant effect on their lives. Will your readers be prepared to accept this commonsense reasoning, or will they remain skeptical, looking for stronger evidence of a cause/effect relationship?

Drafting

1. Begin with an opening paragraph or two that introduces your topic in an interesting way. Lester Thurow in "Why Women Are Paid Less Than Men" writes:

    In the 40 years from 1939 to 1979 white women who work full time have with monotonous regularity made slightly less than 60 percent as much as white men. Why?

    This opening establishes the topic and Thurow's purpose in examining causes. The statistics get the reader's attention.

2. Do not begin by announcing your subject. Avoid openers such as: In this essay I will explain the causes of teen vandalism.

3. Decide where to place your claim statement. You can conclude your opening paragraph with it, or you can place it in your conclusion, after you have shown readers how best to understand the causes of the issue you are examining. Thurow uses the second approach effectively in his essay.

4. Present reasons and evidence in an organized way. If you are examining a series of causes, beginning with background conditions and early influences, then your basic plan will be time sequence. Readers need to see the chain of causes unfolding. Use appropriate terms and transitional words to guide readers through each stage in the causal pattern. If you are arguing for an overlooked cause, begin with the causes that have been put forward and show what is flawed in each one. Then present and defend your explanation of cause. This process of elimination structure works well when readers are likely to know what other causes have been offered in the past. You can also use one of Mill's other two approaches, if one of them is relevant to your topic. That is, you can present the points of commonality or difference that show your explanation of cause to be valid.

5. Address the issue of correlation rather than cause, if appropriate. After presenting the results of a study of marriage that reveals many benefits (emotional, physical, financial) of marriage, Linda Waite examines the question

that she knows skeptical readers may have: Does marriage actually *cause* the benefits, or is the relationship one of *correlation* only—that is, the benefits of marriage just happen to come with being married; they are not caused by being married.

6. Conclude by discussing the implications of the causal pattern you have argued for, if appropriate. Lester Thurow ends by asserting that if he is right about the cause of the gender pay gap, then there are two approaches society can take to remove the pay gap. If, in explaining the causes of teen vandalism, you see one cause as "group behavior," a gang looking for something to do, it then follows that you can advise young readers to stay out of gangs. Often with arguments about cause, there are personal or public policy implications in accepting the causal explanation.

A CHECKLIST FOR REVISION

☐ Do I have a clear statement of my claim? Is it appropriately qualified and focused? Is it about an issue that matters?

☐ Have I organized my argument so that readers can see my pattern for examining cause?

☐ Have I used the language for discussing causes correctly, distinguishing among conditions and influences and remote and proximate causes? Have I selected the correct word—either *affect* or *effect*—as needed?

☐ Have I avoided the *post hoc* fallacy and the confusing of correlation and cause?

☐ Have I carefully examined my assumptions and convinced myself that they are reasonable and can be defended? Have I defended them when necessary to clarify and thus strengthen my argument?

☐ Have I found relevant facts and examples to support and develop my argument?

☐ Have I used the basic checklist for revision in Chapter 4 (see p. 111)?

FOR ANALYSIS AND DEBATE

WHY WOMEN ARE PAID LESS THAN MEN | LESTER C. THUROW

A professor at the MIT Sloan School of Management and consultant to both government and private corporations, Lester C. Thurow has written extensively on economic and public policy issues. His books include *The Political Economy of Income Redistribution Policies* (1977) and *Dangerous Currents* (1983). "Why Women Are Paid Less Than Men," published in the *New York Times* (March 8, 1981), offers an explanation for the discrepancy between the incomes of men and women.

PREREADING QUESTIONS When he asks "why" at the end of paragraph 1, what kind of argument does Thurow signal he will develop? Were you aware that women earn less than men?

In the 40 years from 1939 to 1979 white women who work full time have 1 with monotonous regularity made slightly less than 60 percent as much as white men. Why?

Over the same time period, minorities have made substantial progress 2 in catching up with whites, with minority women making even more progress than minority men.

Black men now earn 72 percent as much as white men (up 16 percentage 3 points since the mid-1950s) but black women earn 92 percent as much as white women. Hispanic men make 71 percent of what their white counterparts do, but Hispanic women make 82 percent as much as white women. As a result of their faster progress, fully employed black women make 75 percent as much as fully employed black men while Hispanic women earn 68 percent as much as Hispanic men.

This faster progress may, however, end when minority women finally catch 4 up with white women. In the bible of the New Right, George Gilder's *Wealth and Poverty*, the 60 percent is just one of Mother Nature's constants like the speed of light or the force of gravity.

Men are programmed to provide for their families economically while 5 women are programmed to take care of their families emotionally and physically. As a result men put more effort into their jobs than women. The net result is a difference in work intensity that leads to that 40 percent gap in earnings. But there is no discrimination against women—only the biological facts of life.

The problem with this assertion is just that. It is an assertion with no evi- 6 dence for it other than the fact that white women have made 60 percent as much as men for a long period of time.

"Discrimination against women" is an easy answer but it also has its prob- 7 lems as an adequate explanation. Why is discrimination against women not declining under the same social forces that are leading to a lessening of discrimination against minorities? In recent years women have made more use of the enforcement provisions of the Equal Employment Opportunities Commission and the courts than minorities. Why do the laws that prohibit discrimination against women and minorities work for minorities but not for women?

When men discriminate against women, they run into a problem. To dis- 8 criminate against women is to discriminate against your own wife and to lower your own family income. To prevent women from working is to force men to work more.

When whites discriminate against blacks, they can at least think that they 9 are raising their own incomes. When men discriminate against women they have to know that they are lowering their own family income and increasing their own work effort.

While discrimination undoubtedly explains part of the male-female earn-10 ings differential, one has to believe that men are monumentally stupid or irrational to explain all of the earnings gap in terms of discrimination. There must be something else going on.

11   Back in 1939 it was possible to attribute the earnings gap to large differences in educational attainments. But the educational gap between men and women has been eliminated since World War II. It is no longer possible to use education as an explanation for the lower earnings of women.

12   Some observers have argued that women earn less money since they are less reliable workers who are more apt to leave the labor force. But it is difficult to maintain this position since women are less apt to quit one job to take another and as a result they tend to work as long, or longer, for any one employer. From any employer's perspective they are more reliable, not less reliable, than men.

13   Part of the answer is visible if you look at the lifetime earnings profile of men. Suppose that you are asked to predict which men in a group of 25-year-olds would become economically successful. At age 25 it is difficult to tell who will be economically successful and your predictions are apt to be highly inaccurate.

14   But suppose that you were asked to predict which men in a group of 35-year-olds would become economically successful. If you are successful at age 35 you are very likely to remain successful for the rest of your life. If you have not become economically successful by age 35, you are very unlikely to do so later.

15   The decade between 25 and 35 is when men either succeed or fail. It is the decade when lawyers become partners in the good firms, when business managers make it onto the "fast track," when academics get tenure at good universities, and when blue-collar workers find the job opportunities that will lead to training opportunities and the skills that will generate high earnings.

16   If there is any one decade when it pays to work hard and to be consistently in the labor force, it is the decade between 25 and 35. For those who succeed, earnings will rise rapidly. For those who fail, earnings will remain flat for the rest of their lives.

17   But the decade between 25 and 35 is precisely the decade when women are most apt to leave the labor force or become part-time workers to have children. When they do, the current system of promotion and skill acquisition will extract an enormous lifetime price.

18   This leaves essentially two avenues for equalizing male and female earnings.

19   Families where women who wish to have successful careers, compete with men, and achieve the same earnings should alter their family plans and have their children either before 25 or after 35. Or society can attempt to alter the existing promotion and skill acquisition system so that there is a longer time period in which both men and women can attempt to successfully enter the labor force.

20   Without some combination of these two factors, a substantial fraction of the male-female earnings differentials are apt to persist for the next 40 years, even if discrimination against women is eliminated.

QUESTIONS FOR READING

1. What situation is the subject of Thurow's argument?
2. Briefly explain why Thurow rejects each of the possible explanations that he covers.
3. What is the author's explanation for the discrepancy between the earnings of white women and white men?

QUESTIONS FOR REASONING AND ANALYSIS

1. What question should you ask about Thurow's numbers? Do you know the answer to the question?
2. What is Thurow's claim?
3. What evidence does the author provide for his claim? Is it convincing?
4. What strategy for determining cause does Thurow use?

QUESTIONS FOR REFLECTING AND WRITING

1. Do you agree that most people who are going to be successful are so by age 35? Can you think of people who did not become successful until after 35? Is this the kind of assumption that can create its own reality?
2. Evaluate the two solutions Thurow proposes. Do they follow logically from his causal analysis?
3. Thurow's figures are based on the total earnings of workers; they are not comparisons by job category. What are other facts about jobs that men and women hold that may account for some of the discrepancy in pay?

SUPREMACY CRIMES | GLORIA STEINEM

Editor, writer, and lecturer, Gloria Steinem has been cited in *World Almanac* as one of the twenty five most influential women in America. She is the cofounder of *Ms.* magazine and of the National Women's Political Caucus and is the author of a number of books and many articles. The following article appeared in *Ms.* in the August/September 1999 issue.

PREREADING QUESTIONS Who are the teens who commit most of the mass shootings at schools? Who are the adults who commit most of the hate crimes and sadistic killings? What generalizations can you make about these groups based on your knowledge from media coverage?

You've seen the ocean of television coverage, you've read the headlines: 1 "How to Spot a Troubled Kid," "Twisted Teens," "When Teens Fall Apart."

After the slaughter in Colorado that inspired those phrases, dozens of 2 copycat threats were reported in the same generalized way: "Junior high students charged with conspiracy to kill students and teachers" (in Texas); "Five honor students overheard planning a June graduation bombing" (in New York); "More than 100 minor threats reported statewide" (in Pennsylvania). In response, the White House held an emergency strategy session titled "Children, Violence, and Responsibility." Nonetheless, another attack was soon reported: "Youth With 2 Guns Shoots 6 at Georgia School."

3   I don't know about you, but I've been talking back to the television set, waiting for someone to tell us the obvious: it's not "youth," "our children," or "our teens." It's our sons—and "our" can usually be read as "white," "middle class," and "heterosexual."

4   We know that hate crimes, violent and otherwise, are overwhelmingly committed by white men who are apparently straight. The same is true for an even higher percentage of impersonal, resentment-driven, mass killings like those in Colorado; the sort committed for no economic or rational gain except the need to say, "I'm superior because I can kill." Think of Charles Starkweather, who reported feeling powerful and serene after murdering ten women and men in the 1950s; or the shooter who climbed the University of Texas Tower in 1966, raining down death to gain celebrity. Think of the engineering student at the University of Montreal who resented females' ability to study that subject, and so shot to death 14 women students in 1989, while saying, "I'm against feminism." Think of nearly all those who have killed impersonally in the workplace, the post office, McDonald's.

5   White males—usually intelligent, middle class, and heterosexual, or trying desperately to appear so—also account for virtually all the serial, sexually motivated, sadistic killings, those characterized by stalking, imprisoning, torturing, and "owning" victims in death. Think of Edmund Kemper, who began by killing animals, then murdered his grandparents, yet was released to sexually torture and dismember college students and other young women until he himself decided he "didn't want to kill all the coeds in the world." Or David Berkowitz, the Son of Sam, who murdered some women in order to feel in control of all women. Or consider Ted Bundy, the charming, snobbish young would-be lawyer who tortured and murdered as many as 40 women, usually beautiful students who were symbols of the economic class he longed to join. As for John Wayne Gacy, he was obsessed with maintaining the public mask of masculinity, and so hid his homosexuality by killing and burying men and boys with whom he had had sex.

6   These "senseless" killings begin to seem less mysterious when you consider that they were committed disproportionately by white, non-poor males, the group most likely to become hooked on the drug of superiority. It's a drug pushed by a male-dominant culture that presents dominance as a natural right; a racist hierarchy that falsely elevates whiteness; a materialist society that equates superiority with possessions; and a homophobic one that empowers only one form of sexuality.

7   As Elliott Leyton reports in *Hunting Humans: The Rise of the Modern Multiple Murderer,* these killers see their behavior as "an appropriate—even 'manly'—response to the frustrations and disappointments that are a normal part of life." In other words, it's not their life experiences that are the

problem, it's the impossible expectation of dominance to which they've become addicted.

This is not about blame. This is about causation. If anything, ending the 8 massive cultural cover-up of supremacy crimes should make heroes out of boys and men who reject violence, especially those who reject the notion of superiority altogether. Even if one believes in a biogenetic component of male aggression, the very existence of gentle men proves that socialization can override it.

Nor is this about attributing such crimes to a single cause. Addiction to the 9 drug of supremacy is not their only root, just the deepest and most ignored one. Additional reasons why this country has such a high rate of violence include the plentiful guns that make killing seem as unreal as a video game; male violence in the media that desensitized viewers in much the same way that combat killers are desensitized in training; affluence that allows maximum access to violence-as-entertainment; a national history of genocide and slavery; the romanticizing of frontier violence and organized crime; not to mention extremes of wealth and poverty and the illusion that both are deserved.

But it is truly remarkable, given the relative reasons for anger at injustice 10 in this country, that white, non-poor men have a near-monopoly on multiple killings of strangers, whether serial and sadistic or mass and random. How can we ignore this obvious fact? Others may kill to improve their own condition, in self-defense, or for money or drugs; to eliminate enemies; to declare turf in drive-by shootings; even for a jacket or a pair of sneakers—but white males addicted to supremacy kill even when it worsens their condition or ends in suicide.

Men of color and females are capable of serial and mass killing, and com- 11 mit just enough to prove it. Think of Colin Ferguson, the crazed black man on the Long Island Railroad, or Wayne Williams, the young black man in Atlanta who kidnapped and killed black boys, apparently to conceal his homosexuality. Think of Aileen Carol Wuornos, the white prostitute in Florida who killed abusive johns "in self-defense," or Waneta Hoyt, the upstate New York woman who strangled her five infant children between 1965 and 1971, disguising their cause of death as sudden infant death syndrome. Such crimes are rare enough to leave a haunting refrain of disbelief as evoked in Pat Parker's poem "jonestown": "Black folks do not/Black folks do not/Black folks do not commit suicide." And yet they did.

Nonetheless, the proportion of serial killings that are not committed by 12 white males is about the same as the proportion of anorexics who are not female. Yet we discuss the gender, race, and class components of anorexia, but not the role of the same factors in producing epidemics among the powerful.

The reasons are buried deep in the culture, so invisible that only by revers- 13 ing our assumptions can we reveal them.

Suppose, for instance, that young black males—or any other men of 14 color—had carried out the slaughter in Colorado. Would the media reports be so willing to describe the murderers as "our children"? Would there be so little discussion about the boys' race? Would experts be calling the motive a mystery, or condemning the high school cliques for making those young men feel like "outsiders"? Would there be the same empathy for parents who gave the murderers luxurious homes, expensive cars, even rescued them from brushes with the law? Would there be as much attention to generalized causes, such as the dangers of violent video games and recipes for bombs on the Internet?

15   As for the victims, if racial identities had been reversed, would racism remain so little discussed? In fact, the killers themselves said they were targeting blacks and athletes. They used a racial epithet, shot a black male student in the head, and then laughed over the fact that they could see his brain. What if that had been reversed?

16   What if these two young murderers, who were called "fags" by some of the jocks at Columbine High School, actually had been gay? Would they have got the same sympathy for being gay-baited? What if they had been lovers? Would we hear as little about their sexuality as we now do, even though only their own homophobia could have given the word "fag" such power to humiliate them?

17   Take one more leap of the imagination: suppose these killings had been planned and executed by young women—of any race, sexuality, or class. Would the media still be so disinterested in the role played by gender-conditioning? Would journalists assume that female murderers had suffered from being shut out of access to power in high school, so much so that they were pushed beyond their limits? What if dozens, even hundreds of young women around the country had made imitative threats—as young men have done—expressing admiration for a well-planned massacre and promising to do the same? Would we be discussing their youth more than their gender, as is the case so far with these male killers?

18   I think we begin to see that our national self-examination is ignoring something fundamental, precisely because it's like the air we breathe: the white male factor, the middle-class and heterosexual one, and the promise of superiority it carries. Yet this denial is self-defeating—to say the least. We will never reduce the number of violent Americans, from bullies to killers, without challenging the assumptions on which masculinity is based: that males are superior to females, that they must find a place in a male hierarchy, and that the ability to dominate someone is so important that even a mere insult can justify lethal revenge. There are plenty of studies to support this view. As Dr. James Gilligan concluded in *Violence: Reflections on a National Epidemic,* "If humanity is to evolve beyond the propensity toward violence . . . then it can only do so by recognizing the extent to which the patriarchal code of honor and shame generates and obligates male violence."

19   I think the way out can only be found through a deeper reversal: just as we as a society have begun to raise our daughters more like our sons—more like whole people—we must begin to raise our sons more like our daughters—that is, to value empathy as well as hierarchy; to measure success by other people's welfare as well as their own.

20   But first, we have to admit and name the truth about supremacy crimes.

QUESTIONS FOR READING

1. What kinds of crimes is Steinem examining? What kinds of crimes is she excluding from her discussion?

2. What messages, according to Steinem, is our culture sending to white, non-poor males?

3. How does Elliott Leyton explain these killers' behavior?

4. What is the primary reason we have not examined serial and random killings correctly, in the author's view? What is keeping us from seeing what we need to see?

5. What do we need to do to reduce "the number of violent Americans, from bullies to killers"?

QUESTIONS FOR REASONING AND ANALYSIS

1. What is Steinem's claim? Where does she state it?

2. What is her primary type of evidence?

3. How does Steinem qualify her claim and thereby anticipate and answer counterarguments? In what paragraphs does she present qualifiers and counterarguments to possible rebuttals?

4. How does the author seek to get her readers to understand that we are not thinking soundly about the mass killings at Columbine High School? Is her strategy an effective one? Why or why not?

QUESTIONS FOR REFLECTING AND WRITING

1. Steinem concludes by writing that we must first "name the truth" about supremacy violence before we can begin to address the problem. Does this make sense to you? How can this be good advice for coping with most problems? Think of other kinds of problems that this approach might help solve.

2. Do you agree with Steinem's analysis of the causes of serial and random killings? If yes, how would you add to her argument? If no, how would you refute her argument?

SUGGESTIONS FOR DISCUSSION AND WRITING

1. Do you agree with the causes presented by Thurow to account for the pay gap by gender, or the causes presented by Steinem to account for violent and serial killers? If not, how would you refute Thurow's argument, or Steinem's argument? What cause or causes has either Thurow or Steinem, in your view, overlooked?

2. Think about your educational experiences as a basis for generating a topic for a causal argument. For example: What are the causes of writer's block? Why do some apparently good students (based on class work, grades, etc.) do poorly on standardized tests? How does pass/fail grading affect student performance? What are the causes of high tuition and fees? What might be some of the effects of higher college costs? What are the causes of binge drinking among college students? What are the effects of binge drinking?

3. *Star Trek*, in its many manifestations, continues to play on television—why? What makes it so popular a series? Why are horror movies popular? What are the causes for the great success of the Harry Potter books? If you are familiar with one of these works, or another work that has been amazingly popular, examine the causes for that popularity.

CHAPTER 11

Presenting Proposals: The Problem/Solution Argument

READ: What is this ad selling? Who is the target audience?

REASON: What strategies are used in the ad? (Consider the visual effect, the words presented, and the identification of the ad's sponsor.)

REFLECT/WRITE: In what way is this ad a proposal argument? Is the argumentative strategy an effective one?

You think that there are several spots on campus that need additional lighting at night. You are concerned that the lake near your hometown is green, with algae floating on it. You believe that bikers on the campus need to have paths and a bike lane on the main roads into the college. These are serious local issues; you should be concerned about them. And, perhaps it is time to act on your concerns—how can you do that? You can write a proposal, perhaps a letter to the editor of the college newspaper or your hometown newspaper.

These three issues invite a recommendation for change. And to make that recommendation is to offer a solution to what you perceive to be a problem. Public policy arguments, whether local and specific (such as lampposts or bike lanes), or more general and far-reaching (such as the federal government must provide health care to all children or stop the flow of illegal drugs into the country) can best be understood as arguments over solutions to problems. If there are only 10 students on campus who bike to class or only 200 Americans wanting to buy cocaine, then most people would not agree that we have two serious problems in need of debate over the best solutions. But, when the numbers become significant, then people begin to see a problem and may become interested in seeking solutions.

Consider some of these issues stated as policy claims:

- The college needs bike lanes on campus roads and more bike paths across the campus.
- We need to spend whatever is necessary to stop the flow of drugs into this country.
- The United States needs a health-care program that covers all children.

Each one of these claims offers a solution to a problem, as we can see:

- Bikers will be safer if there are bike lanes on main roads and more bike paths across the campus.
- The way to address the drug problem in this country is to eliminate the supply of drugs.
- Children with untreated illnesses cannot function well in school and may spread diseases to other children.

The basic idea of policy proposals looks like this:

Somebody   **should (or should not)**   **do X – because:**
(Individual, organization, government)   *(solve this problem)*

Observe that proposal arguments recommend action. They look to the future. And, they often advise the spending of someone's time and/or money.

CHARACTERISTICS OF PROBLEM/ SOLUTION ARGUMENTS

- *Proposal arguments may be about local and specific problems, or about broader, more general public policy issues.* We need to "think globally" these days, but we still often need to "act locally," to address the problems we see around us in our classrooms, offices, and communities.

- *Proposal arguments usually need to define the problem.* How we define a problem has much to do with what kinds of solutions are appropriate. For example, many are concerned about our ability to feed a growing world population. Some will argue that the problem is not an agricultural one—how much food we can produce. The problem is a political one—how we distribute the food, at what cost, and how competent or fair some governments are in handling the food. If the problem is agricultural, we need to worry about available farmland, water supply, and farming technology. If the problem is political, then we need to concern ourselves with price supports, distribution strategies, and embargoes for political leverage. To develop a problem/solution argument, you first need to define the problem.

- *How we define the problem also affects what we think are the causes of the problem.* Cause is often a part of the debate, especially with far-reaching policy issues, and may need to be addressed, particularly if solutions are tied to eliminating what we consider to be the causes. Why are illegal drugs coming into the United States? Because people want those drugs. Do you solve the problems related to drug addicts by stopping the supply? Or, do you address the demand for drugs in the first place?

- *Proposal arguments need to be developed with an understanding of the processes of government, from college administrations to city governments to the federal bureaucracy.* Is that dying lake near your town on city property or state land? Are there conservation groups in your area who can be called upon to help with the process of presenting proposals to the appropriate people?

- *Proposal arguments need to be based on the understanding that they ask for change—and many people do not like change, period.* Probably all but the wealthiest Americans recognize that our health-care system needs fixing. That doesn't change the fact that many working people struggling to pay premiums are afraid of any changes introduced by the federal government.

- *Successful problem/solution arguments offer solutions that can realistically be accomplished.* Consider Prohibition, for example. This was a solution to problem drinking—except that it did not work, could not be enforced, because the majority of Americans would not abide by the law.

GUIDELINES for Analyzing Problem/ Solution Arguments

When analyzing problem/solution arguments, what should you look for? In addition to the basics of good argument, use the following points as guides to analyzing:

- **Is the writer's claim not just clear but appropriately qualified and focused?** For example, if the school board in the writer's community is not doing a good job of communicating its goals as a basis for its funding package, the writer needs to focus just on that particular school board, not on school boards in general.

- **Does the writer show an awareness of the complexity of most public policy issues?** There are many different kinds of problems with American schools and many more causes for those problems. A simple solution—a longer school year, more money spent, vouchers—is not likely to solve the mixed bag of problems. Oversimplified arguments quickly lose credibility.

- **How does the writer define and explain the problem?** Is the way the problem is stated clear? Does it make sense to you? If the problem is being defined differently than most people have defined it, has the writer argued convincingly for looking at the problem in this new way?

- **What reasons and evidence are given to support the writer's solutions?** Can you see how the writer develops the argument? Does the reasoning seem logical? Is the data relevant? This kind of analysis will help you evaluate the proposed solutions.

- **Does the writer address the feasibility of the proposed solutions?** Does the writer make a convincing case for the realistic possibility of achieving the proposed solutions?

- **Is the argument convincing?** Will the solutions solve the problem as it has been defined? Has the problem been defined accurately? Can the solutions be achieved?

Read and study the following annotated argument. Complete your analysis by answering the questions that follow.

A NEW STRATEGY FOR THE WAR ON DRUGS | JAMES Q. WILSON

Author of *The Moral Sense,* James Q. Wilson is a professor of public policy at Pepperdine University. His solution to America's drug problem was published on April 13, 2000, in the *Wall Street Journal.*

Opening presents two solutions that Wilson will challenge.

1   The current Senate deliberation over aid to Colombia aimed at fighting narcotics reminds us that there are two debates over how the government ought to deal with dangerous drugs. The first is about their illegality and the second is about their control. People who wish to legalize drugs and those who wish to curtail their supply believe that their methods will reduce crime. Both these views are mistaken, but there is a third way.

2   Advocates of legalization think that both buyers and sellers would benefit. People who can buy drugs freely and at something like free-market prices would no longer have to steal to afford cocaine or heroin; dealers would no longer have to use violence and corruption to maintain their market share. Though drugs may harm people, reducing this harm would be a medical problem not a criminal-justice one. Crime would drop sharply.

PRICES WOULD FALL

Wilson rebuts first solution.

3   But there is an error in this calculation. Legalizing drugs means letting the price fall to its competitive rate (plus taxes and advertising costs). That market price would probably be somewhere between one-third and 1/20th of the

illegal price. And more than the market price would fall. As Harvard's Mark Moore has pointed out, the "risk price"—that is, all the hazards associated with buying drugs, from being arrested to being ripped off—would also fall, and this decline might be more important than the lower purchase price.

Under a legal regime, the consumption of low-priced, low-risk drugs 4 would increase dramatically. We do not know by how much, but the little evidence we have suggests a sharp rise. Until 1968 Britain allowed doctors to prescribe heroin. Some doctors cheated, and their medically unnecessary prescriptions helped increase the number of known heroin addicts by a factor of 40. As a result, the government abandoned the prescription policy in favor of administering heroin in clinics and later replacing heroin with methadone.

When the Netherlands ceased enforcing laws against the purchase or 5 possession of marijuana, the result was a sharp increase in its use. Cocaine and heroin create much greater dependency, and so the increase in their use would probably be even greater.

The average user would probably commit fewer crimes if these drugs 6 were sold legally. But the total number of users would increase sharply. A large fraction of these new users would be unable to keep a steady job. Unless we were prepared to support them with welfare payments, crime would be one of their main sources of income. That is, the number of drug-related crimes *per user* might fall even as the total number of drug-related crimes increased. Add to the list of harms more deaths from overdose, more babies born to addicted mothers, more accidents by drug-influenced automobile drivers and fewer people able to hold jobs or act as competent parents.

Treating such people would become far more difficult. As psychiatrist 7 Sally Satel has written on this page, many drug users will not enter and stay in treatment unless they are compelled to do so. Phoenix House, the largest national residential drug treatment program, rarely admits patients who admit they have a problem and need help. The great majority are coerced by somebody—a judge, probation officer or school official—into attending. Phoenix House CEO Mitchell Rosenthal opposes legalization, and for good reason. Legalization means less coercion, and that means more addicts and addicts who are harder to treat.

Douglas Anglin, drawing on experiences in California and elsewhere, has 8 shown that people compelled to stay in treatment do at least as well as those who volunteer for it, and they tend (of necessity) to stay in the program longer. If we legalize drugs, the chances of treatment making a difference are greatly reduced. And as for drug-use prevention, forget it. Try telling your children not to use a legal substance.

But people who want to keep drugs illegal have problems of their own. 9 The major thrust of government spending has been to reduce the supply of drugs by cutting their production overseas, intercepting their transfer into the U.S. and arresting dealers. Because of severe criminal penalties, especially on handlers of crack cocaine, our prisons have experienced a huge increase in persons sentenced on drug charges. In the early 1980s, about 1/12th of all prison inmates were in for drug convictions; now well over one-third are.

Wilson rebuts
second solution.

10   No one can be certain how imprisoning drug suppliers affects drug use, but we do know that an arrested drug dealer is easily replaced. Moreover, the government can never seize more than a small fraction of the drugs entering the country, a fraction that is easily replaced.

11   Emphasizing supply over treatment is dangerous. Not only do we spend huge sums on it; not only do we drag a reluctant U.S. military into the campaign; we also heighten corruption and violence in countries such as Colombia and Mexico. The essential fact is this: Demand will produce supply.

12   We can do much more to reduce demand. Some four million Americans are currently on probation or parole. From tests done on them when they are jailed, we know that half or more had a drug problem when arrested. Though a lot of drug users otherwise obey the law (or at least avoid getting arrested), probationers and parolees constitute the hard core of dangerous addicts. Reducing their demand for drugs ought to be our highest priority.

Wilson presents his solution.

13   Mark Kleiman of UCLA has suggested a program of "testing and control": Probationers and parolees would be required to take frequent drug tests—say, twice weekly—as a condition of remaining on the street. If you failed the test, you would spend more time in jail; if you passed it, you would remain free. This approach would be an inducement for people to enter and stay in treatment.

Challenges of implementing his solution.

14   This would require some big changes in how we handle offenders. Police, probation and parole officers would be responsible for conducting these tests, and more officers would have to be hired. Probation and parole authorities would have to be willing to sanction a test failure by immediate incarceration, initially for a short period (possibly a weekend), and then for longer periods if the initial failure were repeated. Treatment programs at little or no cost to the user would have to be available not only in every prison, but for every drug-dependent probationer and parolee.

15   These things are not easily done. Almost every state claims to have an intensive community supervision program, but few offenders are involved in them, the frequency with which they are contacted is low, and most were released from supervision without undergoing any punishment for violating its conditions.

16   But there is some hope. Our experience with drug courts suggests that the procedural problems can be overcome. In such courts, several hundred of which now exist, special judges oversee drug-dependent offenders, insisting that they work to overcome their habits. While under drug-court supervision, offenders reduce drug consumption and, at least for a while after leaving the court, offenders are less likely to be arrested.

How solution can work.

17   Our goal ought to be to extend meaningful community supervision to all probationers and parolees, especially those who have a serious drug or alcohol problem. Efforts to test Mr. Kleiman's proposals are under way in Connecticut and Maryland.

18   If this demand-reduction strategy works, it can be expanded. Drug tests can be given to people who apply for government benefits, such as welfare and public housing. Some critics will think this is an objectionable intrusion. But giving benefits without conditions weakens the character-building responsibility of society.

PREVENT HARM TO OTHERS

John Stuart Mill, the great libertarian thinker, argued that the only justifi- **19**
able reason for restricting human liberty is to prevent harm to others. Serious
drug abuse does harm others. We could, of course, limit government action to
remedying those harms without addressing their causes, but that is an uphill
struggle, especially when the harms fall on unborn children. Fetal drug syndrome imposes large costs on infants who have had no voice in choosing their
fate.

Even Mill was clear that full liberty cannot be given to children or barbar- **20**
ians. By "barbarians" he meant people who are incapable of being improved
by free and equal discussion. The life of a serious drug addict—the life of
someone driven by drug dependency to prostitution and crime—is the life of
a barbarian.

Defense of his solution based on practicality and values.

QUESTIONS FOR READING

1. What are the two solutions to the drug problem presented by others?
2. Why, according to Wilson, will legalizing drugs not be a good solution? What are the specific negative consequences of legalization?
3. Government strategies for controlling illegal drugs have included what activities?
4. What percentage of prisoners are now in prison on drug charges?
5. What problems do we face trying to reduce the supply of drugs? What, according to Wilson, drives supply?
6. What is Wilson's proposed solution? Explain the details of his solution.
7. What are some of the difficulties with the author's solution? What does he gain by bringing up possible difficulties?

QUESTIONS FOR REASONING AND ANALYSIS

1. What does Wilson seek to accomplish in his concluding two paragraphs? What potential counterargument does he seek to rebut in his conclusion?
2. For what reasons might one agree that Wilson's solution is workable and still object to it? (Think about his concluding comments.)

QUESTIONS FOR REFLECTING AND WRITING

1. Has Wilson convinced you that legalizing drugs will not reduce crime? Why or why not?
2. Is his argument against the supply-reduction approach convincing? Why or why not?
3. Has Wilson's defense of his solution convinced you that it is workable?
4. Do you have a solution to the drug problem?

PREPARING A PROBLEM/SOLUTION ARGUMENT

In addition to the guidelines for writing arguments presented in Chapter 4, you can use the following advice specific to defending a proposal:

Planning

1. **Think:** What should be the focus and limits of your argument? There's a big difference between presenting solutions to the problem of physical abuse of women by men and presenting solutions to the problem of date rape on your college campus. Select a topic that you know something about, one that you can realistically handle.

2. **Think:** What reasons and evidence do you have to support your tentative claim? Think through what you already know that has led you to select your particular topic. Suppose you want to write on the issue of campus rapes. Is this choice due to a recent event on the campus? Was this event the first in many years, or the last in a trend? Where and when are they occurring? A brainstorming list may be helpful.

3. **Reality check:** Do you have a claim worth defending? Will readers care? Binge drinking and the polluting of the lake near your hometown are serious problems. Problems with your class schedule may not be—unless your experience reveals a college-wide problem.

4. **Think:** Is there additional evidence that you need to obtain to develop your argument? If so, where can you look for that evidence? Are there past issues of the campus paper in your library? Will the campus police grant you an interview?

5. **Think:** What about the feasibility of each solution you plan to present? Are you thinking in terms of essentially one solution with several parts to it or several separate solutions, perhaps to be implemented by different people? Will coordination be necessary to achieve success? How will this be accomplished? For the problem of campus rape, you may want to consider several solutions as a package to be coordinated by the counseling service or an administrative vice president.

Drafting

1. Begin by either reminding readers of the existing problem you will address or arguing that a current situation should be recognized as a problem. In many cases, you can count on an audience who sees the world as you do and recognizes the problem you will address. But in some cases, your first task will be to convince readers that a problem exists that should worry them. If they are not concerned, they won't be interested in your solutions.

2. Early in your essay define the problem—as you see it—for readers. Do not assume that they will necessarily accept your way of seeing the issue. You may need to defend your assessment of the nature of the problem before moving on to solutions.

3. If appropriate, explain the cause or causes of the problem. If your proposed solution is tied to removing the cause or causes of the problem, then you need to establish cause and prove it early in your argument. If cause is important, argue for it; if it is irrelevant, move to your solution.

4. Explain your solution. If you have several solutions, think about how best to order them. If several need to be developed in a sequence, then present them in that necessary sequence. If you are presenting a package of diverse actions that together will solve the problem, then consider presenting them from the simplest to the more complex. With a problem of campus rape, for example, you may want to suggest better lighting on campus paths at night plus an escort service for women who are afraid to walk home alone plus sensitivity training for male students. Adding more lampposts is much easier than getting students to take sensitivity classes.

5. Explain the process for achieving your solution. If you have not thought through the political or legal steps necessary to implement your solution, then this step cannot be part of your purpose in writing. However, anticipating a skeptical audience that says "How are we going to do that?" you would be wise to have precise steps to offer your reader. You may have obtained an estimate of costs for new lighting on your campus and want to suggest specific paths that need the lights. You may have investigated escort services at other colleges and can spell out how such a service can be implemented on your campus. Showing readers that you have thought ahead to the next steps in the process can be an effective method of persuasion.

6. Support the feasibility of your solution. Be able to estimate costs. Show that you know who would be responsible for implementation. Explain how your solutions can be sold to people who may be unwilling to accommodate your proposals. All of this information will strengthen your argument.

7. Show how your solution is better than others. Anticipate challenges by including in your paper reasons for adopting your program rather than another program. Explain how your solution will be more easily adopted or more effective when implemented than other possibilities. Of course, a less practical but still viable defense is that your solution is the right thing to do. Values also belong in public policy debates, not just issues of cost and acceptability.

A CHECKLIST FOR REVISION ■·■

☐ Do I have a clear statement of my policy claim? Is it appropriately qualified and focused?

☐ Have I clearly explained how I see the problem to be solved? If necessary, have I argued for seeing the problem that way?

☐ Have I presented my solutions—and argued for them—in a clear and logical structure? Have I explained how these solutions can be implemented and why they are better than other solutions that have been suggested?

☐ Have I used data that are relevant and current?

☐ Have I used the basic checklist for revision in Chapter 4? (See p. 111.)

FOR ANALYSIS AND DEBATE

WHEN DENIAL CAN KILL | IRSHAD MANJI

Irshad Manji is a Canadian journalist, a Shia Muslim, and an outspoken feminist and lesbian. She has an active Web site, appears on Canadian television, and is a contributing blogger at *The Huffington Post*. Not surprisingly she has received death threats, especially since the publication of her book *The Trouble with Islam Today* (2002), now in paperback and translated into a dozen languages. The following essay was published in *Time* magazine on July 25, 2005.

PREREADING QUESTIONS Given the essay's title and the author's bio, what do you expect her essay to be about? Are you willing to read her essay with an open mind, the mind of a critical thinker? Why or why not?

1   I was surprised last week to learn how easily some Westerners believe terrorism can be explained. The realization unfolded as I looked into the sad face of a student at Oxford University. After giving a speech about Islam, I met this young magazine editor to talk about Islam's lost tradition of critical thinking and reasoned debate. But we never got to that topic. Instead, we got stuck on the July 7 bombings in London and what might have compelled four young, British-raised, observant Muslim men to blow themselves up while taking innocent others with them.

2   She emphasized their "relative economic deprivation." I answered that the lads had immigrant parents who had worked hard to make something of themselves. I reminded her that several of the 9/11 hijackers came from wealthy families, and it's not as if they left the boys out of the will. Finally, I told her about my conversation three years ago with the political leader of Islamic Jihad in Gaza. "What's the difference between suicide, which the Koran condemns, and martyrdom?" I asked. "Suicide," he replied, "is done out of despair. But remember: most of our martyrs today were very successful in their earthly lives." In short, there was a future to live for—and they detonated it anyway.

3   By this time, the Oxford student had grown somber. It was clear I had let her down. I had failed to appreciate that the London bombers were victims of British society. To be fair to her, she is right that marginalization, real or perceived, diminishes self-esteem. Which, in turn, can make young people vulnerable to those peddling a radical message of instant belonging. But suppose the messages being peddled are marinated in religious rhetoric. Then wouldn't you say religion plays some role in motivating these atrocities?

4   The student shifted uncomfortably. She just couldn't bring herself to examine my suggestion seriously. And I suppose I couldn't expect her to. Not when Muslim leaders themselves won't go there. Iqbal Sacranie, secretary-general for the Muslim Council of Britain, is an example. In the midst of a debate with me, he listed potential incentives to bomb, including

"alienation" and "segregation." But Islam? God forbid that the possibility even be entertained.

That is the dangerous denial from which mainstream Muslims need to 5 emerge. While our spokesmen assure us that Islam is an innocent bystander in today's terrorism, those who commit terrorist acts often tell us otherwise. Mohammed Atta, ringleader of the Sept. 11 hijackers, left behind a note asserting that "it is enough for us to know that the Koran's verses are the words of the Creator of the Earth and all the planets." Atta highlighted the Koran's description of heaven. In 2004 the executioners of Nick Berg, an American contractor in Iraq, alluded on tape to a different Koranic passage: "Whoever kills a human being, except as punishment for murder or other villainy in the land, shall be regarded as having killed all mankind." The spirit of that verse forbids aggressive warfare, but the clause beginning with *except* is readily deployed by militant Muslims as a loophole. If you want murder and villainy in the land, they say, look no further than U.S. bootprints in Arab soil.

For too long, we Muslims have been sticking fingers in our ears and 6 chanting "Islam means Peace" to drown out the negative noise from our holy book. Far better to own up to it. Not erase or revise, just recognize it and thereby join moderate Jews and Christians in confessing "sins of Scripture," as an American bishop says about the Bible. In doing so, Muslims would show a thoughtful side that builds trust with the wider communities of the West.

We could then cultivate the support to inspire cross-cultural understand- 7 ing. For instance, schools throughout the West should teach how Islamic civilization helped give birth to the European Renaissance. Some of the first universities in recorded history sprang up in 3rd century Iran, 9th century Baghdad and 10th century Cairo. The Muslim world gave us mocha coffee, the guitar and even the Spanish expression *olé!* (which has its root in the Arabic word Allah). Muslim students would learn there is no shame in defending the values of pluralism. Non-Muslim students would learn that those values took great inspiration from Islamic culture. All would learn that Islam and the West are more interdependent than divided.

Still, as long as Muslims live in pretense, we will be affirming that we have 8 something to hide. It's not enough for us to protest that radicals are exploiting Islam as a sword. Of course they are. Now, moderate Muslims must stop exploiting Islam as a shield—one that protects us from authentic introspection and our neighbors from genuine understanding.

QUESTIONS FOR READING

1. What is Manji's subject? Be precise.
2. What has been the economic condition of many terrorists?
3. What role can poverty and discrimination play in terrorism? What role can religion play?

4.   What incentive to terrorism are Muslim leaders ignoring, in the author's view?

5.   What reasons do terrorists often give for their actions?

6.   What must moderate Muslims do? What will they then accomplish?

QUESTIONS FOR REASONING AND ANALYSIS

1.   What is Manji's claim—What problem is she exploring?

2.   What evidence does she provide? What is her solution to the problem?

3.   What does the author gain by using the context of her Oxford speech as an opening?

QUESTIONS FOR REFLECTING AND WRITING

1.   Do you agree that the terrorists have given evidence of religious motivation? Why or why not?

2.   Do you agree that moderate Muslims can change the world's view of Islam's beliefs, culture, and history? Why or why not?

3.   Do you know moderate Muslims who actively speak out against terrorism? Are you a Muslim who speaks out against terrorism? How important is speaking out? Explain your views.

A MODEST PROPOSAL | JONATHAN SWIFT

For Preventing the Children of Poor People in Ireland from Being a Burden to Their Parents or Country, and for Making Them Beneficial to the Public

Born in Dublin, Jonathan Swift (1667–1745) was ordained in the Anglican Church and spent many years as dean of St. Patrick's in Dublin. Swift was also involved in the political and social life of London for some years, and throughout his life he kept busy writing. His most famous imaginative work is *Gulliver's Travels* (1726). Almost as well known is the essay that follows, published in 1729. Here you will find Swift's usual biting satire but also his concern to improve humanity.

PREREADING QUESTIONS Swift was a minister, but he writes this essay as if he were in a different job. What "voice" or persona do you hear? Does Swift agree with the views of this persona?

1   It is a melancholy object to those who walk through this great town[1] or travel in the country, where they see the streets, the roads, and cabin doors crowded with beggars of the female sex, followed by three, four, or six children, all in rags, and importuning every passenger for an alms. These mothers, instead of being able to work for their honest livelihood, are forced to employ all their time in strolling to beg sustenance for their helpless infants, who, as they grow up, either turn thieves for want of work, or leave their dear

---

[1] Dublin.—Ed.

native country to fight for the pretender[2] in Spain or sell themselves to the Barbados.

I think it is agreed by all parties that this prodigious number of children in the arms, or on the backs, or at the heels of their mothers, and frequently of their fathers, is in the present deplorable state of the kingdom a very great additional grievance; and therefore, whoever could find out a fair, cheap, and easy method of making these children sound and useful members of the commonwealth would deserve so well of the public as to have his statue set up for a preserver of the nation.

But my intention is very far from being confined to provide only for the children of professed beggars; it is of a much greater extent, and shall take in the whole number of infants at a certain age who are born of parents in effect as little able to support them as those who demand our charity in the streets.

As to my own part, having turned my thoughts for many years upon this important subject, and maturely weighed the several schemes of other projectors,[3] I have always found them grossly mistaken in the computation. It is true a child just dropped from its dam may be supported by her milk for a solar year with little other nourishment; at most not above the value of two shillings, which the mother may certainly get, or the value in scraps, by her lawful occupation of begging; and, it is exactly at one year that I propose to provide for them in such a manner as instead of being a charge upon their parents or the parish, or wanting food and raiment for the rest of their lives, they shall on the contrary contribute to the feeding, and partly to the clothing, of many thousands.

There is likewise another great advantage in my scheme, that it will prevent those voluntary abortions, and that horrid practice of women murdering their bastard children, alas, too frequent among us, sacrificing the poor innocent babes, I doubt, more to avoid the expense than the shame, which would move tears and pity in the most savage and inhuman breast.

The number of souls in this kingdom being usually reckoned one million and a half, of these I calculate there may be about two hundred thousand couples whose wives are breeders; from which number I subtract thirty thousand couples who are able to maintain their own children, although I apprehend there cannot be so many, under the present distress of the kingdom; but this being granted, there will remain a hundred and seventy thousand breeders. I again subtract fifty thousand for those women who miscarry, or whose children die by accident or disease within the year. There only remain a hundred and twenty thousand children of poor parents annually born. The question therefore is, how this number shall be reared and provided for, which, as I have already said, under the present situation of affairs, is utterly impossible by all the methods hereto proposed. For we can neither employ them in handicraft or agriculture; we neither build houses (I mean in the country) nor cultivate land. They can very seldom pick up a livelihood by stealing until they arrive

---

[2] James Stuart, claimant to the British throne lost by his father, James II, in 1688.—Ed.

[3] Planners.—Ed.

at six years old, except where they are of towardly parts[4]; although I confess they learn the rudiments much earlier, during which time they can, however, be properly looked upon only as probationers, as I have been informed by a principal gentleman in the country of Cavan, who protested to me that he never knew above one or two instances under the age of six, even in the part of the kingdom renowned for the quickest proficiency in that art.

7   I am assured by our merchants that a boy or girl before twelve years old is no saleable commodity; and even when they come to this age they will not yield above three pounds, or three pounds and a half a crown at most, on the exchange; which cannot turn to account either to the parents or the kingdom, the charge of nutriment and rags having been at least four times that value.

8   I shall now therefore humbly propose my own thoughts, which I hope will not be liable to the least objection.

9   I have been assured by a very knowing American of my acquaintance in London that a young healthy child well nursed is at a year old a most delicious, nourishing, and wholesome food, whether stewed, roasted, baked, or boiled; and I make no doubt that it will equally serve in a fricassee or ragout.

10   I do therefore humbly offer it to public consideration that of the hundred and twenty-thousand children, already computed, twenty thousand may be reserved for breed, whereof only one fourth part to be males, which is more than we allow to sheep, black cattle, or swine; and my reason is that these children are seldom the fruits of marriage, a circumstance not much regarded by our savages, therefore one male will be sufficient to serve four females. That the remaining hundred thousand may at a year old be offered in sale to the persons of quality and fortune, through the kingdom, always advising the mother to let them suck plentifully in the last month, so as to render them plump and fat for the table. A child will make two dishes at an entertainment for friends; and when the family dines alone, the fore or hind quarter will make a reasonable dish, and seasoned with a little pepper or salt will be very good boiled on the fourth day, especially in winter.

11   I have reckoned upon a medium that a child just born will weigh twelve pounds, and in a solar year if tolerably nursed increaseth to twenty-eight pounds.

12   I grant this food will be somewhat dear, and therefore very proper for landlords, who, as they have already devoured most of the parents, seem to have the best title to the children.

13   Infant's flesh will be in season throughout the year, but more plentiful in March, and a little before and after. For we are told by a grave author, an eminent French physician,[5] that fish being a prolific diet, there are more children born in Roman Catholic countries about nine months after Lent than at any other season; therefore reckoning a year after Lent, the markets will be more gutted than usual, because the number of popish infants is at least three to

---

[4] Innate abilities.—Ed.

[5] François Rabelais.—Ed.

one in this kingdom; and therefore it will have one other collateral advantage, by lessening the number of Papists among us.

I have already computed the charge of nursing a beggar's child (in which **14** list I reckon all cottagers, laborers, and four-fifths of the farmers) to be about two shillings per annum, rags included; and I believe no gentleman would repine to give ten shillings for the carcass of a good fat child, which, as I have said, will make four dishes of excellent nutritive meat, when he hath only some particular friend or his own family to dine with him. Thus the squire will learn to be a good landlord, and grow popular among his tenants; the mother will have eight shillings net profit, and be fit for work until she produces another child.

Those who are more thrifty (as I must confess the times require) may flay **15** the carcass; the skin of which artificially dressed will make admirable gloves for ladies and summer boots for fine gentlemen.

As to our city of Dublin, shambles[6] may be appointed for this purpose, in **16** the most convenient parts of it, and butchers we may be assured will not be wanting; although I rather recommend buying the children alive, and dressing them hot from the knife as we do roasting pigs.

A very worthy person, a true lover of his country, and whose virtues I highly **17** esteem, was lately pleased in discoursing on this matter to offer a refinement upon my scheme. He said that many gentlemen of this kingdom, having of late destroyed their deer, he conceived that the want of venison might be well supplied by the bodies of young lads and maidens, not exceeding fourteen years of age nor under twelve, so great a number of both sexes in every county being now ready to starve for want of work and service; and these to be disposed of by their parents, if alive, or otherwise by their nearest relations. But with due deference to so excellent a friend and so deserving a patriot, I cannot be altogether in his sentiments. For as to the males, my American acquaintance assured me from frequent experience that their flesh was generally tough and lean, like that of our school-boys, by continual exercise, and their taste disagreeable; and to fatten them would not answer the charge. Then as to the females, it would, I think with humble submission, be a loss to the public, because they soon would become breeders themselves; and besides, it is not probable that some scrupulous people might be apt to censure such a practice (although indeed very unjustly) as a little bordering upon cruelty; which, I confess, hath always been with me the strongest objection against any project, how wellsoever intended.

But in order to justify my friend, he confessed that this expedient was put **18** into his head by the famous Psalmanazar,[7] a native of the island Formosa who came from thence to London above twenty years ago, and in conversation told my friend that in his country when any young person happened to be put to death, the executioner sold the carcass to persons of quality as a prime dainty; and that in his time the body of a plump girl of fifteen, who was crucified for

---

[6] Butcher shops.—Ed.

[7] A known imposter who was French, not Formosan as he claimed.—Ed.

an attempt to poison the emperor, was sold to his Imperial Majesty's prime minister of state, and other great mandarins of the court, in joints from the gibbet, at four hundred crowns. Neither indeed can I deny that if the same use were made of several plump young girls in this town, who without one single groat to their fortunes cannot stir abroad without a chair, and appear at the playhouse and assemblies in foreign fineries which they never will pay for, the kingdom would not be the worse.

19   Some persons of a desponding spirit are in great concern about that vast number of poor people who are aged, diseased, or maimed, and I have been desired to employ my thoughts what course may be taken to ease the nation of so grievous an incumbrance. But I am not in the least pain upon that matter, because it is very well known that they are every day dying and rotting by cold and famine, and filth and vermin, as fast as can be reasonably expected. And as to the younger laborers, they are now in almost as hopeful a condition. They cannot get work, and consequently pine away for want of nourishment to a degree that if at any time they are accidentally hired to common labor, they have not strength to perform it; and thus the country and themselves are in a fair way of being soon delivered from the evils to come.

20   I have too long digressed, and therefore shall return to my subject. I think the advantages by the proposal which I have made are obvious and many, as well as of the highest importance.

21   For, first, as I have already observed, it would greatly lessen the number of Papists, with whom we are yearly overrun, being the principal breeders of the nation as well as our most dangerous enemies; and who stay at home on purpose with a design to deliver the kingdom to the pretender, hoping to take their advantage by the absence of so many good Protestants, who have chosen rather to leave their country than stay at home and pay tithes against their conscience to an idolatrous Episcopal curate.

22   Secondly, the poorer tenants will have something valuable of their own, which by law may be made liable to distress,[8] and help their landlord's rent; their corn and cattle being already seized, and money a thing unknown.

23   Thirdly, whereas the maintenance of a hundred thousand children, from two years old upwards, cannot be computed at less than ten shillings a piece per annum, the nation's stock will be thereby increased fifty thousand pounds per annum, besides the profit of a new dish introduced to the tables of all gentlemen of fortune in the kingdom who have any refinement in taste. And the money will circulate among ourselves, the goods being entirely of our own growth and manufacture.

24   Fourthly, the constant breeders, besides the gain of eight shillings sterling per annum by the sale of their children, will be rid of the charge of maintaining them after the first year.

25   Fifthly, this food would likewise bring great custom to taverns, where the vintners will certainly be so prudent as to procure the best receipts for dressing it to perfection, and consequently have their houses frequented by all the

---

[8] Can be seized by lenders.—Ed.

fine gentlemen, who justly value themselves upon their knowledge in good eating; and a skillful cook, who understands how to oblige his guests, will contrive to make it as expensive as they please.

Sixthly, this would be a great inducement to marriage, which all wise[26] nations have either encouraged by rewards or enforced by laws and penalties. It would increase the care and tenderness of mothers towards their children, when they were sure of a settlement for life to the poor babes, provided in some sort by the public; to their annual profit instead of expense. We should soon see an honest emulation among the married women, which of them could bring the fattest child to the market. Men would become as fond of their wives during the time of their pregnancy as they are now of their mares in foal, their cows in calf, or sows when they are ready to farrow; nor offer to beat or kick them (as it is too frequent a practice) for fear of a miscarriage.

Many other advantages might be enumerated. For instance, the addition[27] of some thousand carcasses in our exportation of barrelled beef, the propagation of swine's flesh, and improvement in the art of making good bacon, so much wanted among us by the great destruction of pigs, too frequent at our tables, which are no way comparable in taste or magnificence to a well-grown fat, yearling child, which roasted whole will make a considerable figure at a lord mayor's feast or any other public entertainment. But this and many others I omit, being studious of brevity.

Supposing that one thousand families in this city would be constant cus-[28] tomers for infants' flesh, besides others who might have it at merry meetings, particularly weddings and christenings, I compute that Dublin would take off annually about twenty thousand carcasses, and the rest of the kingdom (where probably they will be sold somewhat cheaper) the remaining eighty thousand.

I can think of no one objection that will possibly be raised against this[29] proposal, unless it should be urged that the number of people will be thereby much lessened in the kingdom. This I freely own, and it was indeed one principal design in offering it to the world. I desire the reader will observe that I calculate my remedy for this one individual kingdom of Ireland and for no other that ever was, is, or I think ever can be upon earth. Therefore let no man talk to me of other expedients: of taxing our absentees at five shillings a pound: of using neither clothes nor household furniture except what is of our own growth and manufacture: of utterly rejecting the materials and instruments that promote foreign luxury: of curing the expensiveness or pride, vanity, idleness, and gaming in our women: of introducing a vein of parsimony, prudence and temperance: of learning to love our country, wherein we differ even from Laplanders and the inhabitants of Topinamboo[9]: of quitting our animosities and factions, nor act any longer like the Jews, who were murdering one another at the very moment their city was taken[10]: of being a little cautious

---

[9] An area in Brazil.—Ed.

[10] Some Jews were accused of helping the Romans and were executed during the Roman siege of Jerusalem in 70 A.D.—Ed.

not to sell our country and consciences for nothing: of teaching landlords to have at least one degree of mercy towards their tenants. Lastly, of putting a spirit of honesty, industry, and skill into our shopkeepers; who, if a resolution could now be taken to buy only our native goods, would immediately unite to cheat and exact upon us in the price, the measure, and the goodness, nor could ever yet be brought to make one fair proposal of just dealing, though often and earnestly invited to it.

30   Therefore I repeat, let no man talk to me of these and the like expedients, till he hath at least a glimpse of hope that there will ever be some hearty and sincere attempt to put them in practice.

31   But as to myself, having been wearied out for many years with offering vain, idle, visionary thoughts, and at length utterly despairing of success, I fortunately fell upon this proposal, which, as it is wholly new, so it hath something solid and real, of no expense and little trouble, full in our own power, and whereby we can incur no danger in disobliging England. For this kind of commodity will not bear exportation, the flesh being of too tender a consistence to admit a long continuance in salt, although perhaps I could name a country which would be glad to eat up our whole nation without it.

32   After all, I am not so violently bent upon my own opinion as to reject any offer proposed by wise men, which shall be found equally innocent, cheap, easy, and effectual. But before something of that kind shall be advanced in contradiction to my scheme, and offering a better, I desire the author, or authors, will be pleased maturely to consider two points. First, as things now stand, how they will be able to find food and raiment for a hundred thousand useless mouths and backs. And secondly, there being a round million of crea- tures in human figure throughout this kingdom, whose whole subsistence put into a common stock would leave them in debt two million of pounds sterling, adding those who are beggars by profession to the bulk of farmers, cottagers, and laborers, with their wives and children who are beggars, in effect; I desire those politicians who dislike my overture, and may perhaps be so bold to attempt an answer, that they will first ask the parents of these mortals whether they would not at this day think it a great happiness to have been sold for food at a year old in the manner I prescribe, and thereby have avoided such a per- petual scene of misfortunes as they have since gone through by the oppres- sion of landlords, the impossibility of paying rent without money or trade, the want of common sustenance, with neither house nor clothes to cover them from the inclemencies of weather, and the most inevitable prospect of entail- ing the like or greater miseries upon their breed forever.

33   I profess, in the sincerity of my heart, that I have not the least personal interest in endeavoring to promote this necessary work, having no other motive than the public good of my country, by advancing our trade, providing for infants, relieving the poor, and giving some pleasure to the rich. I have no children by which I can propose to get a single penny, the youngest being nine years old, and my wife past childbearing.

QUESTIONS FOR READING

1. How is the argument organized? What is accomplished in paragraphs 1–7? In paragraphs 8–16? In paragraphs 17–19? In paragraphs 20–28? In paragraphs 29–33?
2. What specific advantages does the writer offer in defense of his proposal?

QUESTIONS FOR REASONING AND ANALYSIS

1. What specific passages and connotative words make us aware that this is a satirical piece using irony as its chief device?
2. After noting Swift's use of irony, what do you conclude to be his purpose in writing?
3. What can you conclude to be some of the problems in eighteenth-century Ireland? Where does Swift offer direct condemnation of existing conditions in Ireland and attitudes of the English toward the Irish?
4. What actual reforms would Swift like to see?

QUESTIONS FOR REFLECTING AND WRITING

1. What are some of the advantages of using irony? What does Swift gain by this approach? What are possible disadvantages in using irony? Reflect on irony as a persuasive strategy.
2. What are some current problems that might be addressed by the use of irony? Make a list. Then select one and think about what "voice" or persona you might use to bring attention to that problem. Plan your argument with irony as a strategy.

1. Think of a problem on your campus or in your community for which you have a workable solution. Organize your argument to include all relevant steps as described in this chapter. Although your primary concern will be to present your solution, depending on your topic you may need to begin by convincing readers of the seriousness of the problem or the causes of the problem—if your solutions involve removing those causes.

2. Think of a problem in education—K–12 or at the college level—that you have a solution for and that you are interested in. You may want to begin by brainstorming to develop a list of possible problems in education about which you could write—or look through Chapter 18 for ideas. Be sure to qualify your claim and limit your focus as necessary to work with a problem that is not so broad and general that your "solutions" become general and vague comments about "getting better teachers." (If one problem is a lack of qualified teachers, then what specific proposals do you have for solving that particular problem?) Include as many steps as are appropriate to develop and support your argument.

3. Think of a situation that you consider serious but that apparently many people do not take seriously enough. Write an argument in which you emphasize, by providing evidence, that the situation is a serious problem. You may conclude by suggesting a solution, but your chief purpose in writing will be to alert readers to a problem.

The Researched
and Formally
Documented Argument

CHAPTER 12

Locating, Evaluating, and Preparing to Use Sources

We do research all the time. You would not select a college or buy a car without doing research: gathering relevant information, analyzing that information, and drawing conclusions from your study. You may already have done some research in this course, using sources in this text or finding data online to strengthen an argument. Then you acknowledged your sources either informally in your essay or formally, following the documentation guidelines in this section. So, when you are assigned a more formal research essay, remember that you are not facing a brand new assignment. You are just doing a longer paper with more sources, and you have this section to guide you to success.

SELECTING A GOOD TOPIC

To get started you need to select and limit a topic. One key to success is finding a workable topic. No matter how interesting or clever the topic, it is not workable if it does not meet the guidelines of your assignment. Included in those guidelines may be a required length, a required number of sources, and a due date. Understand and accept all of these guidelines as part of your writing context.

What Type of Paper Am I Preparing?

Study your assignment to understand the type of project. Is your purpose expository, analytic, or argumentative? How would you classify each of the following topics?

1. Explain the chief solutions proposed for increasing the Southwest's water supply.
2. Compare the Freudian and behavioral models of mental illness.
3. Find the best solutions to a current environmental problem.
4. Consider: What twentieth-century invention has most dramatically changed our personal lives?

Did you recognize that the first topic calls for a report? The second topic requires an analysis of two schools of psychology, so you cannot report on only one, but you also cannot argue that one model is better than the other. Both topics 3 and 4 require an argumentative paper: You must select and defend a claim.

Who Is My Audience?

If you are writing in a specific discipline, imagine your instructor as a representative of that field, a reader with knowledge of the subject area. If you are in a composition course, your instructor may advise you to write to a general reader, someone who reads newspapers but may not have the exact information and perspective you have. For a general reader, specialized terms and concepts need definition.

> **NOTE:** Consider the expectations of readers of research papers. A research essay is not like a personal essay. A research essay is not about you; it is about a subject, so keep yourself more in the background than you might in a more informal piece of writing.

How Can I Select a Good Topic?

Choosing from assigned topics. At times students are unhappy with topic restriction. Looked at another way, your instructor has eliminated a difficult step in the research process and has helped you avoid the problem of selecting an unworkable topic. If topics are assigned, you will still have to choose from the list and develop your own claim and approach.

Finding a course-related topic. This guideline gives you many options and requires more thought about your choice. Working within the guidelines, try to write about what interests you. Here are examples of assignments turned into topics of interest to the student:

ASSIGNMENT	INTEREST	TOPIC
1. Trace the influence of any twentieth-century event, development, invention.	Music	The influence of the Jazz Age on modern music
2. Support an argument on some issue of pornography and censorship.	Computers	Censorship of pornography on the Internet
3. Demonstrate the popularity of a current myth and then discredit it.	Science fiction	The lack of evidence for the existence of UFOs

Selecting a topic without any guidelines. When you are free to write on any topic, you may need to use some strategies for topic selection.

- Look through your text's table of contents or index for subject areas that can be narrowed or focused.
- Look over your class notes and think about subjects covered that have interested you.
- Consider college-based or local issues.
- Do a subject search in an electronic database to see how a large topic can be narrowed—for example, type in "dinosaur" and observe such subheadings as *dinosaur behavior* and *dinosaur extinction.*
- Use one or more invention strategies to narrow and focus a topic:
  - Freewriting
  - Brainstorming

– Asking questions about a broad subject, using the reporter's *who, what, where, when*, and *why.*

What Kinds of Topics Should I Avoid?

Here are several kinds of topics that are best avoided because they usually produce disasters, no matter how well the student handles the rest of the research process:

1. *Topics that are irrelevant* to your interests or the course. If you are not interested in your topic, you will not produce a lively, informative paper. If you select a topic far removed from the course content, you may create some hostility in your instructor, who will wonder why you are unwilling to become engaged in the course.
2. *Topics that are broad subject areas.* These result in general surveys that lack appropriate detail and support.
3. *Topics that can be fully researched with only one source.* You will produce a summary, not a research paper.
4. *Biographical studies.* Short undergraduate papers on a person's life usually turn out to be summaries of one or two major biographies.
5. *Topics that produce a strong emotional response in you.* If there is only one "right" answer to the abortion issue and you cannot imagine counterarguments, don't choose to write on abortion. Probably most religious topics are best avoided.
6. *Topics that are too technical for you* at this point in your college work. If you do not understand the complexities of the federal tax code, then arguing for a reduction in the capital gains tax may be an unwise topic choice.

WRITING A TENTATIVE CLAIM OR RESEARCH PROPOSAL

Once you have selected and focused a topic, you need to write a tentative claim, research question, or research proposal. Some instructors will ask to see a statement—from a sentence to a paragraph long—to be approved before you proceed. Others may require as much as a one-page proposal that includes a tentative claim, a basic organizational plan, and a description of types of sources to be used. Even if your instructor does not require anything in writing, you need to write something for your benefit—to direct your reading and thinking. Here are two possibilities.

1. **SUBJECT:**   Computers

    TOPIC: The impact of computers on the twentieth century

    CLAIM: Computers had the greatest impact of any technological development in the twentieth century.

RESEARCH PROPOSAL:	I propose to show that computers had the greatest impact of any technological development in the twentieth century. I will show the influence of computers at work, in daily living, and in play to emphasize the breadth of influence. I will argue that other possibilities (such as cars) did not have the same impact as computers. I will check the library's book catalog and databases for sources on technological developments and on computers specifically. I will also interview a family friend who works with computers at the Pentagon.

This example illustrates several key ideas. First, the initial subject is both too broad and unfocused (What about computers?). Second, the claim is more focused than the topic statement because it asserts a position, a claim the student must support. Third, the research proposal is more helpful than the claim only because it includes some thoughts on developing the thesis and finding sources.

2. Less sure of your topic? Then write a research question or a more open-ended research proposal. Take, for example, a history student studying the effects of Prohibition. She is not ready to write a thesis, but she can write a research proposal that suggests some possible approaches to the topic:

TOPIC:	The effect of Prohibition
RESEARCH QUESTION:	What were the effects of Prohibition on the United States?
RESEARCH PROPOSAL:	I will examine the effects of Prohibition on the United States in the 1920s (and possibly consider some long-term effects, depending on the amount of material on the topic). Specifically, I will look at the varying effects on urban and rural areas and on different classes in society.

PREPARING A WORKING BIBLIOGRAPHY

To begin this next stage of your research, you need to know three things:

- *Your search strategy.* If you are writing on a course-related topic, your starting place may be your textbook for relevant sections and possible sources (if the text contains a bibliography). For this course, you may find some potential sources among the readings in this text. Think about what you already know or have in hand as you plan your search strategy.
- *A method for recording bibliographic information.* You have two choices: the always reliable 3×5 index cards or a bibliography file in your personal computer.

- *The documentation format you will be using.* You may be assigned the Modern Language Association (MLA) format, or perhaps given a choice between MLA and the American Psychological Association (APA) documentation styles. Once you select the documentation style, skim the appropriate pages in Chapter 14 to get an overview of both content and style.

A list of possible sources is only a *working* bibliography because you do not yet know which sources you will use. (Your final bibliography will include only those sources you cite—actually refer to—in your paper.) A working bibliography will help you see what is available on your topic, note how to locate each source, and contain the information needed to document. Whether you are using cards or computer files, follow these guidelines:

1. Check all reasonable catalogs and indexes for possible sources. (Use more than one reference source even if you locate enough sources there; you are looking for the best sources, not the first ones you find.)

2. Complete a card or prepare an entry for every potentially useful source. You won't know what to reject until you start a close reading of sources.

3. Copy (or download from an online catalog) all information needed to complete a citation and to locate the source. (When using an index that does not give all needed information, leave a space to be filled in when you actually read the source.)

4. Put bibliographic information in the correct format for every possible source; you will save time and make fewer errors. Do not mix or blend styles. When searching for sources, have your text handy and use the appropriate models as your guide.

The following brief guide to correct form will get you started. Illustrations are for cards, but the information and order will be the same in your PC file. (Guidelines are for MLA style.)

Basic Form for Books

As Figure 12.1 shows, the basic MLA form for books includes the following information in this pattern:

1. The author's full name, last name first.

2. The title (and subtitle if there is one) of the book, in italics (underlined in handwriting).

3. The facts of publication: the city of publication (followed by a colon), the publisher (followed by a comma), and the date of publication.

4. The publication medium—Print.

Note that periods are placed after the author's name, after the title, and at the end of the citation. Other information, when appropriate (e.g., the number of volumes), is added to this basic pattern. (See pp. 317–20) for many sample citations.) Include, in your working bibliography, the book's classification number so that you can find it in the library.

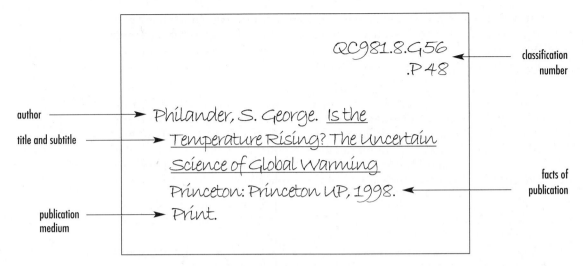

FIGURE 12.1 Bibliography Card for a Book

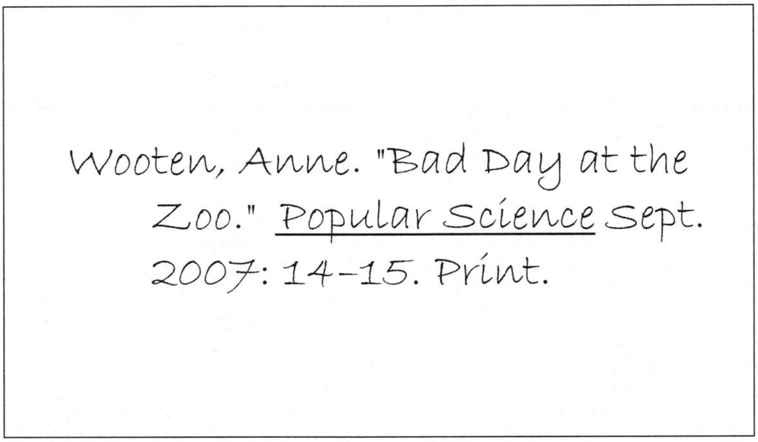

FIGURE 12.2 Bibliography Card for a Magazine Article

Basic Form for Articles

Figure 12.2 shows the simplest form for magazine articles. Include the following information, in this pattern:

1. The author's full name, last name first.
2. The title of the article, in quotation marks.
3. The facts of publication: the title of the periodical in italics (underlined in handwriting), the volume number (if the article is from a scholarly journal), the date (followed by a colon), and inclusive page numbers.
4. The publication medium—Print.

You will discover that indexes rarely present information in MLA format. Here, for example, is a source on problems with zoos, found in an electronic database:

BAD DAY AT THE ZOO.

Wooten, Anne. Popular Science, Sep2007, Vol. 271 Issue 3, p. 14–15, 2p.

If you read the article in the magazine itself, then the correct citation, for MLA, will look like that in the sample bibliography card in Figure 12.2. (Because *Popular Science* is a magazine, not a scholarly journal, you provide month and year but not volume and issue numbers.) However, if you obtain a copy of the article from one of your library's electronic databases, then your citation will need additional information to identify your actual source of the article:

Wooten, Anne. "Bad Day at the Zoo." *Popular Science* Sept. 2007: 14–15. *Academic Search Complete.* Web. 8 Sept. 2008.

Note that the medium of publication is now "Web," not "Print," and the name of the database is italicized as if it were a book containing the article.

> **NOTE:** A collection of printouts, slips of paper, and backs of envelopes is not a working bibliography! You may have to return to the library for missing information, and you risk making serious errors in documentation. Know the basics of your documentation format and follow it faithfully when collecting possible sources.

One of the famous lions sitting in front of the New York Public Library.

LOCATING SOURCES

All libraries contain books and periodicals and a system for accessing them. A library's *book collection* includes the general collection, the reference collection, and the reserve book collection. Electronic materials such as tapes and CDs will also be included in the general "book" collection. The *periodicals collection* consists of popular magazines, scholarly journals, and newspapers. Electronic databases with texts of articles provide alternatives to the print periodicals collection.

> **REMEMBER:** All works, regardless of their source or the format in which you obtain them—and this includes online sources—must be fully documented in your paper.

The Book Catalog

Your chief guide to books and audiovisual materials is the library catalog, usually an electronic database accessed from computer stations in the library or, with an appropriate password, from your personal computer.

In the catalog there will be at least four ways to access a specific book: the author entry, the title entry, one or more subject entries, and a keyword option. When you pull up the search screen, you will probably see that the keyword option is the default. If you know the exact title of the work you want, switch to the title option, type it in, and hit submit. If you want a list of all of the library's books on Hemingway, though, click on author and type in "Hemingway." Keep these points in mind:

- With a title search, do not type any initial article (a, an, the). To locate *The Great Gatsby,* type in "Great Gatsby."
- Use correct spelling. If you are unsure of spelling, use a keyword instead of an author or title search.
- If you are looking for a list of books on your subject, do a keyword or subject search.
- When screens for specific books are shown, either print screens of potential sources or copy all information needed for documentation—plus the call number for each book.

The Reference Collection

The research process often begins with the reference collection. You will find atlases, dictionaries, encyclopedias, general histories, critical studies, and biographies. In addition, various reference tools such as bibliographies and indexes are part of the reference collection.

Many tools in the reference collection once only in print form are now also online. Some are now only online. Yet online is not always the way to go. Let's consider some of the advantages of each of the formats:

Advantages of the Print Reference Collection

1. The reference tool may be only in print—use it.
2. The print form covers the period you are studying. (Most online indexes and abstracts cover only from 1980 to the present.)
3. In a book, with a little scanning of pages, you can often find what you need without getting spelling or commands exactly right.
4. If you know the best reference source to use and are looking for only a few items, the print source can be faster than the online source.

Advantages of Online Reference Materials

1. Online databases are likely to provide the most up-to-date information.
2. You can usually search all years covered at one time.
3. Full texts (with graphics) are sometimes available, as well as indexes with detailed summaries of articles. Both can be printed or e-mailed to your PC.
4. Through links to the Internet, you have access to an amazing amount of material. (Unless you focus your keyword search, however, you may be overwhelmed.)

Before using any reference work, take a few minutes to check its date, purpose, and organization. If you are new to online searching, take a few minutes to learn about each reference tool by working through the online tutorial. (Go to the Help screen.) If you get stuck, ask the reference librarian for help.

A Word About Wikipedia

Many researchers go first to a general encyclopedia, in the past in print in the reference collection, today more typically online. This is not always the best strategy. Often you can learn more about your topic from a current book or a more specialized reference source—which your reference librarian can help you find. Both may give you additional sources of use to your project. If—or when—you turn to a general encyclopedia, make it a good one that is available online through your library. Some colleges have told their students that *Wikipedia* is not an acceptable source for college research projects.

Electronic Databases

You will probably access electronic databases by going to your library's home page and then clicking on the appropriate term or icon. (You may have found the book catalog by clicking on "library catalog"; you may find the databases by clicking on "library resources" or some other descriptive label.) You will need to choose a particular database and then type in your keyword for a basic

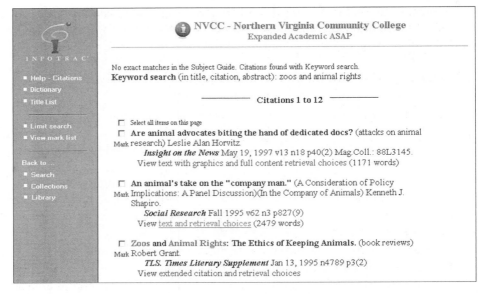

FIGURE 12.3 Partial List of Articles Found on Search Topic

search or select "advanced search" to limit that search by date or periodical or in some other way. Each library will create somewhat different screens, but the basic process of selecting among choices provided and then typing in your search commands remains the same. Figure 12.3 shows a partial list of articles that resulted from a keyword search for "zoos and animal rights."

GUIDELINES for Using Online Databases

Keep these points in mind as you use online databases.

- **Although some online databases provide full texts of all articles, others provide full texts of only some of the articles indexed.** The articles not in full text will have to be located in a print collection of periodicals.

- **Articles indexed but not available in full text often come with a brief summary or abstract.** This allows you to decide whether the article looks useful for your project. *Do not treat the abstract as the article. Do not use material from it and cite the author. If you want to use the article, find it in your library's print collection or obtain it from another library.*

- **The information you need for documenting material used from an article is not in correct format for any of the standard documentation styles.** You will have to reorder the information and use the correct style for writing titles. If your instructor wants to see a list of possible sources in MLA format, do not hand in a printout of articles from an online database.

- **Because no single database covers all magazines, you may want to search several databases that seem relevant to your project.** Ask your reference librarian for suggestions of various databases in the sciences, social sciences, public affairs, and education.

THE INTERNET

In addition to using electronic databases to find sources, you can search the Internet directly.

Keep in mind these facts about the Internet:

- The Internet is both disorganized and huge, so you can waste time trying to find information that is easily obtained in a reference book in your library.
- The Internet is best at providing current information, such as news and movie reviews. It is also a great source of government information.
- Because anyone can create a Web site and put anything on it, you will have to be especially careful in evaluating Internet sources. Remember that articles in magazines and journals have been selected by editors and are often peer reviewed as well, but no editor selects or rejects material on a personal Web site.

Access to the Internet provides information in a variety of ways, including:

- *E-mail.* E-mail can be used instead of a printed letter to request information from a government agency or company.
- *Mailing Lists (Listservs).* You can sign up to receive, via your e-mail, continually updated bulletins on a particular subject. Listservs are essentially organized mailing lists. If you find one relevant to your project, you can subscribe for a while and unsubscribe when you are no longer interested.
- *Newsgroups.* Newsgroups differ from listservs in that the discussions and exchanges are collected for you to retrieve; they are not sent to your e-mail address. Otherwise they are much the same: Both are a type of discussion group. To find newsgroups on a specific subject, go to **http://groups.google. com**, a research tool sponsored by the search engine Google that surveys all Usenet newsgroups.
- *World Wide Web.* To access the Web from a library terminal, you will probably first select "search the Internet." This will take you to a menu of various search engines and subject directories. Not all search engines are the same, and people differ on which are the best. Check out these sites for help in selecting an appropriate search engine:
  - *Librarians' Index to the Internet:* **http://lii.org**
  - *Greg R. Notess's search engine comparison pages:* **www.notess.com/search**
  - *Search Engine Watch:* **www.searchenginewatch.com**

GUIDELINES for Searching the Web

How much information you may find searching for a specific topic, and how useful it is, will vary from one research project to another. Here are some general guidelines to aid your research on the Internet:

1. **Bookmark sites you expect to use often so that you do not have to remember complicated Web addresses (URLs).**

2. **Make your search as precise as possible to avoid getting overwhelmed with hits.**

3. **If you are searching for a specific phrase, put quotation marks around the words.** This will reduce the number of hits and lead to sites more useful to your research. Examples: "Environmental Protection Agency" or "civil disobedience."

4. **Use Boolean connectors to make your search more precise.**

   - AND: This connector limits results to those sites that contain both terms, for example, "zoos AND animal rights."

   - OR: This connector extends the hits to include all sites that contain one or the other search term. So, "zoos OR animal rights" will generate a list of sites containing either term.

   - NOT: This connector limits the search to only the first term, not the second. Thus, "zoos NOT animal rights" will give you sites only about zoo issues not involving animal rights.

5. **If you are not successful with one search engine, try a different one.** Remember that each search engine searches only a part of the Internet.

6. **If you are not successful with a second search engine, check your spelling.** Search engines cannot always guess what you mean.

7. **To get the best sites for most college research projects, try a directory of evaluated sites or subject guides rather than, say, Yahoo!** (Yahoo! is better for news, people searches, and commercial sites.) Some of the best academic subject guides include:

   - The Argus Clearinghouse (**www.clearinghouse.net**)

   - The University of California's Infomine (**http://infomine.ucr.edu**)

   - Internet Scout Project (**http://scout.cs.wisc.edu**)

8. **Be certain to complete a bibliography card—including the date you accessed the material—for each separate site from which you take information.** (See pp. 319–30 for documentation guidelines.)

FIELD RESEARCH

Field research can enrich many projects. The following sections give some suggestions.

Federal, State, and Local Government Documents

In addition to federal documents you may obtain through *PAIS* or *GPO Access*, department and agency Web sites, or the Library of Congress's good legislative site, *Thomas* (**http://thomas.loc.gov**), consider state and county archives, maps, and other published materials. Instead of selecting a national or global topic, consider examining the debate over a controversial bill introduced in your state legislature. Use online databases to locate articles on the bill and the debate and interview legislators and journalists who participated in or covered the debates or served on committees that worked with the bill.

You can also request specific documents on a topic from appropriate state or county agencies and nonprofit organizations. One student, given the assignment of examining solutions to an ecological problem, decided to study the local problem of preserving the Chesapeake Bay. She obtained issues of the Chesapeake Bay Foundation newsletter and brochures prepared by them advising homeowners about hazardous household waste materials that end up in the bay. Added to her sources were bulletins on soil conservation and landscaping tips for improving the area's water quality. Local problems can lead to interesting research topics because they are current and relevant to you and because they involve uncovering different kinds of source materials.

Correspondence

Business and government officials are usually willing to respond to written requests for information. Make your letter brief and well written. Either include a self-addressed, stamped envelope for the person's convenience or e-mail your request. If you are not e-mailing, write as soon as you discover the need for information and be prepared to wait several weeks for a reply. It is appropriate to indicate your deadline and ask for a timely response. Three guidelines for either letters or e-mails to keep in mind are:

1. Explain precisely what information you need.
2. Do not request information that can be found in your library's reference collection.
3. Explain how you plan to use the information. Businesses especially are understandably concerned with their public image and will be disinclined to provide information that you intend to use as a means of attacking them.

Use reference guides to companies and government agencies or their Web sites to obtain addresses and the person to whom your letter or e-mail should be addressed.

Interviews

Some experts are available for personal interviews. Call or write for an appointment as soon as you recognize the value of an interview. Remember that interviews are more likely to be scheduled with state and local officials than with the president of General Motors. If you are studying a local problem, also consider leaders of the civic association with an interest in the issue. In many communities, the local historian or a librarian will be a storehouse of information about the community. Former teachers can be interviewed for papers on education. Interviews with doctors or nurses can add a special dimension to papers on medical issues.

If an interview is appropriate for your topic, follow these guidelines:

1. Prepare specific questions in advance.
2. Arrive on time, properly dressed, and behave in a polite, professional manner.
3. Take notes, asking the interviewee to repeat key statements so that your notes are accurate.
4. Take a tape recorder with you but ask permission to use it before taping.
5. If you quote any statements in your paper, quote accurately, eliminating only such minor speech habits as "you know's" and "uhm's." (See Chapter 14 for proper documentation of interviews.)
6. Direct the interview with your prepared questions, but also give the interviewee the chance to approach the topic in his or her own way. You may obtain information or views that had not occurred to you.
7. Do not get into a debate with the interviewee. You are there to learn.

Lectures

Check the appropriate information sources at your school to keep informed of visiting speakers. If you are fortunate enough to attend a lecture relevant to a current project, take careful, detailed notes. Because a lecture is a source, use of information or ideas from it must be presented accurately and then documented. (See Chapter 14 for documentation format.)

Films, Tapes, Television

Your library will have audiovisual materials that provide good sources for some kinds of topics. For example, if you are studying *Death of a Salesman,* view a videotaped version of the play. Also pay attention to documentaries on public television and to the many news and political talk shows on both public and commercial channels. In many cases transcripts of shows can be obtained from the TV station. Alternatively, tape the program while watching it so that you can view it several times. The documentation format for such nonprint sources is illustrated in Chapter 14.

Surveys, Questionnaires, and Original Research

Depending on your paper, you may want to conduct a simple survey or write and administer a questionnaire. Surveys can be used for many campus and local issues, for topics on behavior and attitudes of college students and/or faculty, and for topics on consumer habits. Prepare a brief list of questions with space for answers. Poll faculty through their mailboxes or e-mail and students individually on campus or in your classes. When writing questions, keep these guidelines in mind:

- Use simple, clear language.
- Devise a series of short questions rather than only a few that have several parts to them. (You want to separate information for better analysis.)
- Phrase questions to avoid wording that seeks to control the answer. For example, do *not* ask: Did you perform your civic duty by voting in the last election? This is a loaded question.

In addition to surveys and questionnaires, you can incorporate some original research. As you read sources on your topic, be alert to reports of studies that you could redo and update in part or on a smaller scale. Many topics on advertising and television give opportunities for your own analysis. Local-issue topics may offer good opportunities for gathering information on your own, not just from your reading. One student, examining the controversy over a proposed new shopping mall on part of the Manassas Civil War Battlefield in Virginia, made the argument that the mall served no practical need in the community. He supported his position by describing existing malls, including the number and types of stores each contained and the number of miles each was from the proposed new mall. How did he obtain this information? He drove around the area, counting miles and stores. Sometimes a seemingly unglamorous approach to a topic turns out to be an imaginative one.

EVALUATING SOURCES, MAINTAINING CREDIBILITY

As you study your sources, keep rethinking your purpose and approach. Test your research proposal or tentative claim against what you are learning. Remember: You can always change the direction and focus of your paper as new approaches occur to you, and you can even change your position as you reflect on what you are learning.

You will work with sources more effectively if you keep in mind why you are using them. What you are looking for will vary somewhat, depending on your topic and purpose, but there are several basic approaches:

1. *Acquiring information and viewpoints firsthand.* Suppose that you are concerned about the mistreatment of animals kept in zoos. You do not want to just read what others have to say on this issue. First, visit a zoo, taking notes on what you see. Second, before you go, plan to interview at least one person on the zoo staff, preferably a veterinarian who can explain the zoo's guidelines for animal care. Only after gathering and thinking about these *primary sources* do you want to add to your knowledge by reading articles

and books—*secondary sources.* Many kinds of topics require the use of both primary and secondary sources. If you want to study violence in children's TV shows, for example, you should first spend some time watching specific shows and taking notes.

2. *Acquiring new knowledge.* Suppose you are interested in breast cancer research and treatment, but you do not know much about the choices of treatment and, in general, where we are with this medical problem. You will need to turn to sources first to learn about the topic. You should begin with sources that will give you an overview, perhaps a historical perspective of how knowledge and treatment have progressed in the last thirty years. Similarly, if your topic is the effects of Prohibition in the 1920s, you will need to read first for knowledge but also with an eye to ways to focus the topic and organize your paper.

3. *Understanding the issues.* Suppose you think that you know your views on illegal immigration, so you intend to read only to obtain some useful statistical information to support your argument. Should you scan sources quickly, looking for facts you can use? This approach may be too hasty. As explained in Chapter 3, good arguments are built on a knowledge of counterarguments. You are wise to study sources presenting a variety of attitudes on your issue so that you understand—and can refute—the arguments of others. *Remember, too, that with controversial issues often the best argument is a conciliatory one that presents a middle ground and seeks to bring people together.*

When you use facts and opinions from sources, you are saying to readers that the facts are accurate and the ideas credible. If you do not evaluate your sources before using them, you risk losing your credibility as a writer. (Remember Aristotle's idea of *ethos,* how your character is judged.) Just because they are in print does not mean that a writer's "facts" are reliable or ideas worthwhile. Judging the usefulness and reliability of potential sources is an essential part of the research process.

GUIDELINES for Evaluating Sources

Today, with access to so much material on the Internet, the need to evaluate is even more crucial. Here are some strategies for evaluating sources, with special attention to Internet sources:

- **Locate the author's credentials.** Periodicals often list their writers' degrees, current position, and other publications; books, similarly, contain an "about the author" section. If you do not see this information, check various biographical dictionaries (*Biography Index, Contemporary Authors*) for information about the author. For articles on the Web, look for the author's e-mail address or a link to a home page. *Never use a Web source that does not identify the author or the organization responsible* *for the material. Critical question:* Is this author qualified to write on this topic? How do I know?

- **Judge the credibility of the work.** For books, read how reviewers evaluated the book when it was first published. For articles, judge the respectability of the magazine or journal. Study the author's use of documentation as one measure of credibility. Scholarly works cite sources. Well-researched and reliable pieces in quality popular magazines will also make clear the sources of any statistics used or the credentials of any authority who is quoted. One good rule: Never use undocumented statistical information. Another judge of credibility is the quality of writing. Do not use sources filled with grammatical and mechanical errors. For Web sources, find out what institution hosts the site. If you have not heard of the company or organization, find out more about it. *Critical question:* Why should I believe information/ideas from this source?

- **Select only those sources that are at an appropriate level for your research.** Avoid works that are either too specialized or too elementary for college research. You may not understand the former (and thus could misrepresent them in your paper), and you gain nothing from the latter. *Critical question:* Will this source provide a sophisticated discussion for educated adults?

- **Understand the writer's purpose.** Consider the writer's intended audience. Be cautious using works designed to reinforce biases already shared by the intended audience. Is the work written to persuade rather than to inform and analyze? Examine the writing for emotionally charged language. For Internet sources, ask yourself why this person or institution decided to have a Web site or contribute to a newsgroup. *Critical question:* Can I trust the information from this source, given the apparent purpose of the work?

- **In general, choose current sources.** Some studies published years ago remain classics, but many older works have become outdated. In scientific and technical fields, the "information revolution" has outdated some works published only five years ago. So look at publication dates (When was the Web site page last updated?) and pass over outdated sources in favor of current studies. *Critical question:* Is this information still accurate?

CHAPTER 13

Writing the Researched Essay

To continue your study and preparation for drafting a paper, you need to read and learn from your sources in an organized way. Some instructors require students to practice taking notes on their sources, either on cards or on their computer. Others recognize the ease, today, of photocopying and then annotating sources as they are read. Here are some general guidelines for studying sources.

GUIDELINES for Studying Sources

1. **Read first; take notes later.** First, do background reading, selecting the most general sources that provide an overview of the topic.

2. **Skim what appear to be your chief sources.** Learn what other writers on the topic consider the important facts, issues, and points of debate.

3. **Annotate photocopies**—do not highlight endlessly. Instead, carefully bracket material you want to use. Then write a note in the margin indicating how and where you might use that material.

4. **Either download Internet sources or take careful notes on the material.** Before preparing a note on content, be sure to copy all necessary information for documenting the material—including the date you accessed the Web site.

5. **Initially mark key passages in books with Post-Its.** Write on the Post-It how and where you might use the material. Alternatively, photocopy book pages and then annotate them. Be sure to record for yourself the source of all copied pages.

6. **As you study and annotate, create labels for source materials that will help you organize your essay.** For example, if you are writing about the problem of campus rape, you might label passages as: "facts showing there is a problem," "causes of the problem," and "possible solutions to the problem."

7. **Recognize that when you are working with many sources, note taking rather than annotating copies of sources is more helpful.** Notes, whether on cards or typed on separate sheets, provide an efficient method for collecting and organizing lots of information.

AVOIDING PLAGIARISM

Documenting sources accurately and fully is required of all researchers. Proper documentation distinguishes between the work of others and your ideas, shows readers the breadth of your research, and strengthens your credibility. In Western culture, copyright laws support the ethic that ideas, new information, and wording belong to their author. To borrow these without acknowledgment is against the law and has led to many celebrated lawsuits. For students who plagiarize, the consequences range from an F on the paper to suspension from college. Be certain, then, that you know what the requirements for correct documentation are; accidental plagiarism is still plagiarism and will be punished.

> **NOTE:** MLA documentation requires precise page references for all ideas, opinions, and information taken from sources—except for common knowledge. Author and page references provided in the text are supported by complete bibliographic citations on the Works Cited page.

In sum, you are required to document the following:

- Direct quotations from sources
- Paraphrased ideas and opinions from sources
- Summaries of ideas from sources
- Factual information, except common knowledge, from sources

Understand that putting an author's ideas in your own words in a paraphrase or summary does not eliminate the requirement of documentation. To illustrate, consider the following excerpt from Thomas R. Schueler's report *Controlling Urban Runoff* (Washington Metropolitan Water Resources Planning Board, 1987: 3–4) and a student paragraph based on the report.

SOURCE

The aquatic ecosystems in urban headwater streams are particularly susceptible to the impacts of urbanization . . . Dietemann (1975), Ragan and Dietemann (1976), Klein (1979) and WMCOG (1982) have all tracked trends in fish diversity and abundance over time in local urbanizing streams. Each of the studies has shown that fish communities become less diverse and are composed of more tolerant species after the surrounding watershed is developed. Sensitive fish species either disappear or occur very rarely. In most cases, the total number of fish in urbanizing streams may also decline.

Similar trends have been noted among aquatic insects which are the major food resource for fish . . . Higher post-development sediment and trace metals can interfere in their efforts to gather food. Changes in water temperature, oxygen levels, and substrate composition can further reduce the species diversity and abundance of the aquatic insect community.

PLAGARIZED STUDENT PARAGRAPH

Studies have shown that fish communities become less diverse as the amount of runoff increases. Sensitive fish species either disappear or occur very rarely, and, in most cases, the total number of fish declines. Aquatic insects, a major source of food for fish, also decline because sediment and trace metals interfere with their food-gathering efforts. Increased water temperature and lower oxygen levels can further reduce the species diversity and abundance of the aquatic insect community.

The student's opening words establish a reader's expectation that the student has taken information from a source, as indeed the student has. But where is the documentation? The student's paraphrase is a good example of plagiarism: an unacknowledged paraphrase of borrowed information that even collapses into copying the source's exact wording in two places. For MLA style, the author's name and the precise page numbers are needed throughout the paragraph. Additionally, most of the first sentence and the final phrase must be put into the student's own words or be placed within quotation marks. The following revised paragraph shows an appropriate acknowledgment of the source used.

REVISED STUDENT PARAGRAPH TO REMOVE PLAGIARISM

In *Controlling Urban Runoff,* Thomas Schueler explains that studies have shown "that fish communities become less diverse as the amount of runoff increases" (3). Sensitive fish species either disappear or occur very rarely and, in most cases, the total number of fish declines. Aquatic insects, a major source of food for fish, also decline because sediment and trace metals interfere with their food-gathering efforts. Increased water temperature and lower oxygen levels, Schueler concludes, "can further reduce the species diversity and abundance of the aquatic insect community" (4).

What Is Common Knowledge?

In general, common knowledge includes:

- Undisputed dates
- Well-known facts
- Generally known facts, terms, and concepts in a field of study when you are writing in that field

So, do not cite a source for the dates of the American Revolution. If you are writing a paper for a psychology class, do not cite your text when using terms such as *ego* or *sublimation.* However, you must cite a historian who analyzes the causes of England's loss to the Colonies or a psychologist who disputes Freud's ideas. *Opinions* about well-known facts must be documented. *Discussions* of debatable dates, terms, or concepts must be documented. When in doubt, defend your integrity and document.

USING SIGNAL PHRASES TO AVOID MISLEADING READERS

If you are an honest student, you do not want to submit a paper that is plagiarized, even though that plagiarism was unintentional on your part. What leads to unintentional plagiarism?

- A researcher takes careless notes, neglecting to include precise page numbers on the notes, but uses the information anyway, without documentation.

- A researcher works in material from sources in such a way that, even with page references, readers cannot tell what has been taken from the sources.

Good note-taking strategies will keep you from the first pitfall. Avoiding the second problem means becoming skilled in ways to include source material in your writing while still making your indebtedness to sources absolutely clear to readers. The way to do this: Give the author's name in the essay. You can also include, when appropriate, the author's credentials ("According to Dr. Hays, a geologist with the Department of Interior, . . ."). These *introductory tags* or *signal phrases* give readers a context for the borrowed material, as well as serving as part of the required documentation of sources. *Make sure that each signal phrase clarifies rather than distorts an author's relationship to his or her ideas and your relationship to the source.*

GUIDELINES for Appropriately Using Sources

Here are three guidelines to follow to avoid misrepresenting borrowed material:

- **Pay attention to verb choice in signal phrases.** When you vary such standard wording as "Smith says" or "Jones states," be careful that you do not select verbs that misrepresent "Smith's" or "Jones's" attitude toward his or her own work. Do not write "Jones wonders" when in fact Jones has strongly asserted her views. (See p. 300 for a discussion of varying word choice in signal phrases.)
- **Pay attention to the location of signal phrases.** If you mention Jones after you have presented her views, be sure that your reader can tell precisely which ideas in the passage belong to Jones. If your entire paragraph is a paraphrase of Jones's work, you are plagiarizing to conclude with "This idea is presented by Jones." Which of the several ideas in your paragraph comes from Jones? Your reader will assume that only the last idea comes from Jones.
- **Paraphrase properly.** Be sure that paraphrases are truly *in your own words*. To use Smith's words and sentence style in your writing is to plagiarize.

> **NOTE:** Putting a parenthetical page reference at the end of a paragraph is not sufficient if you have used the source throughout the paragraph. Use introductory tags or signal phrases to guide the reader through the material.

EXERCISES: Acknowledging Sources to Avoid Plagiarism

1. The following paragraph (from Franklin E. Zimring's "Firearms, Violence and Public Policy" [*Scientific American,* Nov. 1991]) provides material for the examples that follow of adequate and inadequate acknowledgment of sources. After reading Zimring's paragraph, study the three examples with these questions in mind: (1) Which example represents adequate acknowledgment? (2) Which

examples do not represent adequate acknowledgment? (3) In exactly what ways is each plagiarized paragraph flawed?

SOURCE

Although most citizens support such measures as owner screening, public opinion is sharply divided on laws that would restrict the ownership of handguns to persons with special needs. If the U.S. does not reduce handguns and current trends continue, it faces the prospect that the number of handguns in circulation will grow from 35 million to more than 50 million within 50 years. A national program limiting the availability of handguns would cost many billions of dollars and meet much resistance from citizens. These costs would likely be greatest in the early years of the program. The benefits of supply reduction would emerge slowly because efforts to diminish the availability of handguns would probably have a cumulative impact over time. (page 54)

STUDENT PARAGRAPH 1

One approach to the problem of handgun violence in America is to severely limit handgun ownership. If we don't restrict ownership and start the costly task of removing handguns from our society, we may end up with around 50 million handguns in the country by 2040. The benefits will not be apparent right away but will eventually appear. This idea is emphasized by Franklin Zimring (54).

STUDENT PARAGRAPH 2

One approach to the problem of handgun violence in America is to restrict the ownership of handguns except in special circumstances. If we do not begin to reduce the number of handguns in this country, the number will grow from 35 million to more than 50 million within 50 years. We can agree with Franklin Zimring that a program limiting handguns will cost billions and meet resistance from citizens (54).

STUDENT PARAGRAPH 3

According to law professor Franklin Zimring, the United States needs to severely limit handgun ownership or face the possibility of seeing handgun ownership increase "from 35 million to more than 50 million within 50 years" (54). Zimring points out that Americans disagree significantly on restricting handguns and that enforcing such laws would be very expensive. He concludes that the benefits would not be seen immediately but that the restrictions "would probably have a cumulative impact over time" (54). Although Zimring

paints a gloomy picture of high costs and little immediate relief from gun violence, he also presents the shocking possibility of 50 million guns by the year
2040. Can our society survive so much fire power?

Clearly, only the third student paragraph demonstrates adequate acknowledgment of the writer's indebtedness to Zimring. Notice that the placement of the last
parenthetical page reference acts as a visual closure to the student's borrowing; then
she turns to her response to Zimring and her own views on the problem of handguns.

2. Read the following passage and then the three plagiarized uses of the passage.
   Explain why each one is plagiarized and how it can be corrected.

   Original Text: Stanley Karnow, *Vietnam, A History. The First Complete Account of
   Vietnam at War.* New York: Viking, 1983, 319.
   Lyndon Baines Johnson, a consummate politician, was a kaleidoscopic
   personality, forever changing as he sought to dominate or persuade or placate
   or frighten his friends and foes. A gigantic figure whose extravagant moods
   matched his size, he could be cruel and kind, violent and gentle, petty, generous, cunning, naïve, crude, candid, and frankly dishonest. He commanded the
   blind loyalty of his aides, some of whom worshipped him, and he sparked bitter derision or fierce hatred that he never quite fathomed.

   a. LBJ's vibrant and changing personality filled some people with adoration and
      others with bitter derision that he never quite fathomed (Karnow 319).
   b. LBJ, a supreme politician, had a personality like a kaleidoscope, continually
      changing as he tried to control, sway, appease, or intimidate his enemies and
      supporters (Karnow 319).
   c. Often, figures who have had great impact on America's history have been
      dynamic people with powerful personalities and vibrant physical presence.
      LBJ, for example, was a huge figure who polarized those who worked for and
      with him. "He commanded the blind loyalty of his aides, some of whom wor-
      shipped him, and he sparked bitter derision or fierce hatred" from many oth-
      ers (Karnow 319).

3. Read the following passage and then the four sample uses of the passage. Judge
   each of the uses for how well it avoids plagiarism and if it is documented correctly. Make corrections as needed.

   Original Text: Stanley Karnow, *Vietnam, A History. The First Complete Account of
   Vietnam at War.* New York: Viking, 1983, 327.
   On July 27, 1965, in a last-ditch attempt to change Johnson's mind,
   Mansfield and Russell were to press him again to "concentrate on finding a
   way out" of Vietnam—"a place where we ought not be," and where "the situation is rapidly going out of control." But the next day, Johnson announced his
   decision to add forty-four American combat battalions to the relatively small
   U.S. contingents already there. He had not been deaf to Mansfield's pleas, nor
   had he simply swallowed the Pentagon's plans. He had waffled and agonized
   during his nineteen months in the White House, but eventually this was his
   final judgment. As he would later explain: "There are many, many people who
   can recommend and advise, and a few of them consent. But there is only one
   who has been chosen by the American people to decide."

a. Karnow writes that Senators Mansfield and Russell continued to try to convince President Johnson to avoid further involvement in Vietnam, "a place
where we ought not to be" they felt. (327).

b. Though Johnson received advice from many, in particular Senators Mansfield
and Russell, he believed the weight of the decision to become further engaged
in Vietnam was solely his as the one "'chosen by the American people to
decide' "(Karnow 327).

c. On July 28, 1965, Johnson announced his decision to add forty-four battalions
to the troops already in Vietnam, ending his waffling and agonizing of the past
nineteen months of his presidency. (Karnow 357).

d. Karnow explains that LBJ took his responsibility to make decisions about
Vietnam seriously (327). Although Johnson knew that many would offer
suggestions, only he had " 'been chosen by the American people to decide' "
(Karnow 327).

ORGANIZING THE PAPER

Armed with an understanding of writing strategies to avoid plagiarism, you
are now almost ready to draft your essay. Follow these steps to get organized
to write.

1. *Arrange notes (or your annotated sources) by the labels you have used and read
them through.* You may discover that some notes or marked sections of
sources now seem irrelevant. Set them aside, but do not throw them away
yet. Some further reading and note taking may also be necessary to fill in
gaps that have become apparent.

2. *Reexamine your tentative claim or research proposal.* As a result of reading and
reflection, do you need to alter or modify your claim in any way? Or, if you
began with a research question, what now is your answer to the question?
Is, for example, TV violence harmful to children?

3. *Decide on the claim that will direct your writing.* To write a unified essay with
a "reason for being," you need a claim that meets the following criteria:

- It is a complete sentence, not a topic or statement of purpose.

  TOPIC: Rape on college campuses.

  CLAIM: There are steps that both students and administrators can
  take to reduce incidents of campus rape.

- It is limited and focused.

  UNFOCUSED: Prohibition affected the 1920s in many ways.

  FOCUSED: Prohibition was more acceptable to rural than urban areas
  because of differences in values, social patterns, cultural
  backgrounds, and the economic result of prohibiting liquor
  sales.

- It establishes a new or interesting approach to the topic that makes your
  research meaningful.

NOT INVENTIVE: A regional shopping mall should not be built next to the Manassas Battlefield.

INVENTIVE: Putting aside an appeal to our national heritage, one can say, simply, that there is no economic justification for the building of a shopping mall next to the Manassas Battlefield.

4. *Write down the organization that emerges from your labels and grouping of sources and compare this with your preliminary plan.* If there are differences, justify those changes to yourself. Consider: Does the new, fuller plan provide a complete and logical development of your claim?

DRAFTING THE ESSAY

Plan Your Time

How much time will you need to draft your essay? Working with sources and taking care with documentation make research paper writing more time-consuming than writing an undocumented essay. You also need to allow time between completing the draft and revising. Do not try to draft, revise, and proof an essay all in one day.

Handle Documentation as You Draft

The Modern Language Association (MLA) recommends that writers prepare their Works Cited page(s) *before* drafting their essay. With this important information prepared correctly and next to you as you draft, you will be less likely to make errors in documentation that will result in a plagiarized essay. Although you may believe that stopping to include parenthetical documentation as you write will cramp your writing, you really cannot try to insert the documentation after completing the writing. The risk of failing to document accurately is too great to chance. Parenthetical documentation is brief; listen to the experts and take the time to include it as you compose.

You saw some models of documentation in Chapter 12. In Chapter 14, you have complete guidelines and models for in-text (parenthetical) documentation and then many models for the complete citations of sources. Study the information in Chapter 14 and then draft your Works Cited page(s) as part of your preparation for writing.

Choose an Appropriate Writing Style

Specific suggestions for composing the parts of your paper follow, but first here are some general guidelines for research essay style.

Use the Proper Person

Research papers are written primarily in the third person (*she, he, it, they*) to create objectivity and to direct attention to the content of the paper. The question is over the appropriateness of the first person (*I, we*). Although you want to avoid writing "as *you* can see," do not try to skirt around the use of *I* if you need to distinguish your position from the views of others. It is better to write "I" than "it is the opinion of this writer" or "the researcher learned" or "this project analyzed." On the other hand, avoid qualifiers such as "I think." Just state your ideas.

Use the Proper Tense

When you are writing about people, ideas, or events of the past, the appropriate tense is the past tense. When writing about current times, the appropriate tense is the present. Both may occur in the same paragraph, as the following paragraph illustrates:

> Fifteen years ago "personal" computers were all but unheard of. Computers were regarded as unknowable, building-sized mechanized monsters that required a precise 68 degree air-conditioned environment and eggheaded technicians with thick glasses and white lab coats scurrying about to keep the temperamental and fragile egos of the electronic brains mollified. Today's generation of computers is accessible, affordable, commonplace, and much less mysterious. The astonishing progress made in computer technology in the last few years has made computers practical, attainable, and indispensable. Personal computers are here to stay.

In the above example when the student moves from computers in the past to computers in the present, he shifts tenses accurately.

When writing about sources, the convention is to use the present tense *even* for works or authors from the past. The idea is that the source, or the author, *continues* to make the point or use the technique into the present—that is, every time there is a reader. So, write "Lincoln selects the biblical expression 'Fourscore and seven years ago' " and "King echoes Lincoln when he writes 'five score years ago.' "

Avoid Excessive Quoting

Many students use too many direct quotations. Plan to use your own words most of the time for these good reasons:

- Constantly shifting between your words and the language of your sources (not to mention all those quotation marks) makes reading your essay difficult.
- This is your paper and should sound like you.
- When you take a passage out of its larger context, you face the danger of misrepresenting the writer's views.
- When you quote endlessly, readers may begin to think either that you are lazy or that you don't really understand the issues well enough to put them in your own words. You don't want to present either image to your readers.

- You do not prove any point by quoting another person's opinion. All you indicate is that there is someone else who shares your views. Even if that person is an expert on the topic, your quoted material still represents the view of only one person. You support a claim with reasons and evidence, both of which can usually be presented in your own words.

When you must quote, keep the quotations brief, weave them carefully into your own sentences, and be sure to identify the author in a signal phrase. Study the guidelines for handling quotations on pages 22–25 for models of correct form and style.

Write Effective Beginnings

The best introduction is one that presents your subject in an interesting way to gain the reader's attention, states your claim, and gives the reader an indication of the scope and limits of your paper. In a short research essay, you may be able to combine an attention-getter, a statement of subject, and a claim in one paragraph. More typically, especially in longer papers, the introduction will expand to two or three paragraphs. In the physical and social sciences, the claim may be withheld until the conclusion, but the opening introduces the subject and presents the researcher's hypothesis, often posed as a question. Since students sometimes have trouble with research paper introductions in spite of knowing these general guidelines, several specific approaches are illustrated here:

1. In the opening to her study of car advertisements, a student, relating her topic to what readers know, reminds readers of the culture's concern with image:

   Many Americans are highly image conscious. Because the "right" look is essen-

   tial to a prosperous life, no detail is too small to overlook. Clichés about first

   impressions remind us that "you never get a second chance to make a first

   impression," so we obsessively watch our weight, firm our muscles, sculpt

   our hair, select our friends, find the perfect houses, and buy our automobiles.

   Realizing the importance of image, companies compete to make the "right"

   products, that is, those that will complete the "right" image. Then advertisers

   direct specific products to targeted groups of consumers. Although targeting

   may be labeled as stereotyping, it has been an effective strategy in advertising.

2. Terms and concepts central to your project need defining early in your paper, especially if they are challenged or qualified in some way by your study. The following opening paragraph demonstrates an effective use of definition:

   William Faulkner braids a universal theme, the theme of initiation, into the

   fiber of his novel *Intruder in the Dust*. From ancient times to the present, a prominent focus of literature, of life, has been rites of passage, particularly those of childhood to adulthood. Joseph Campbell defines rites of passage as "distinguished by formal, and usually very severe, exercises of severance." A "candidate" for initiation into adult society, Campbell explains, experiences a shearing away of the "attitudes, attachments and life patterns" of childhood (9). This severe, painful stripping away of the child and installation of the adult is presented somewhat differently in several works by American writers.

3. Begin with a thought-provoking question. A student, arguing that the media both reflect and shape reality, started with these questions:

> Do the media just reflect reality, or do they also shape our perceptions of reality? The answer to this seemingly "chicken-and-egg" question is: They do both.

4. Beginning with important, perhaps startling, facts, evidence, or statistics is an effective way to introduce a topic, provided the details are relevant to the topic. Observe the following example:

> Teenagers are working again, but not on their homework. Over 40 percent of teenagers have jobs by the time they are juniors (Samuelson A22). And their jobs do not support academic learning since almost two-thirds of teenagers are employed in sales and service jobs that entail mostly carrying, cleaning, and wrapping (Greenberger and Steinberg 62–67), not reading, writing, and computing. Unfortunately, the negative effect on learning is not offset by improved opportunities for future careers.

Avoid Ineffective Openings

Follow these rules for avoiding openings that most readers find ineffective or annoying.

1. *Do not restate the title* or write as if the title were the first sentence in paragraph 1. It is a convention of writing to have the first paragraph stand independent of the title.
2. *Do not begin with "clever" visuals* such as artwork or fancy lettering.
3. *Do not begin with humor* unless it is part of your topic.
4. *Do not begin with a question that is just a gimmick, or one that a reader may answer in a way you do not intend.* Asking "What are the advantages of solar energy?" may lead a reader to answer "None that I can think of." A

straightforward research question ("Is *Death of a Salesman* a tragedy?") is appropriate.

5. *Do not open with an unnecessary definition quoted from a dictionary.* "According to Webster, solar energy means . . . " is a tired, overworked beginning that does not engage readers.

6. *Do not start with a purpose statement:* "This paper will examine . . . " Although a statement of purpose is a necessary part of a report of empirical research, a report still needs an interesting introduction.

Compose Solid, Unified Paragraphs

As you compose the body of your paper, keep in mind that you want to (1) maintain unity and coherence, (2) guide readers clearly through source material, and (3) synthesize source material and your own ideas. Do not settle for paragraphs in which facts from notes are just loosely run together. Review the following discussion and study the examples to see how to craft effective body paragraphs.

Provide Unity and Coherence

You achieve paragraph unity when every sentence in a paragraph relates to and develops the paragraph's main idea. Unity, however, does not automatically produce coherence; that takes attention to wording. Coherence is achieved when readers can follow the connection between one sentence and another and between each sentence and the main idea. Strategies for achieving coherence include repetition of key words, the use of pronouns that clearly refer to those key words, and the use of transition and connecting words. Observe these strategies at work in the following paragraph:

> Perhaps the most important differences between the initiations of Robin
> and Biff and that experienced by Chick are the facts that Chick's epiphany
> does not come all at once and it does not devastate him. Chick learns about
> adulthood—and enters adulthood—piecemeal and with support. His first eye-
> opening experience occurs as he tries to pay Lucas for dinner and is rebuffed
> (15–16). Chick learns, after trying again to buy a clear conscience, the impro-
> priety and affront of his actions (24). Lucas teaches Chick how he should
> resolve his dilemma by setting him "free" (26–27). Later, Chick feels outrage
> at the adults crowding into the town, presumably to see a lynching, then dis-
> grace and shame as they eventually flee (196–97, 210).

Coherence is needed not only within paragraphs but between paragraphs. You need to guide readers through your paper, connecting paragraphs and showing relationships by the use of transitions. The following opening sentences of four paragraphs from a paper on solutions to rape on the college campus illustrate smooth transitions:

¶ 3 Specialists have provided a number of reasons why men rape.

¶ 4 Some of the causes of rape on the college campus originate with the col-

   leges themselves and with how they handle the problem.

¶ 5 Just as there are a number of causes for campus rapes, there are a num-

   ber of ways to help solve the problem of these rapes.

¶ 6 If these seem like common-sense solutions, why, then, is it so difficult to

   significantly reduce the number of campus rapes?

Without awkwardly writing "Here are some of the causes" and "Here are some of the solutions," the student guides her readers through a discussion of causes for and solutions to the problem of campus rape.

Guide Readers Through Source Material

To understand the importance of guiding readers through source material, consider first the following paragraph from a paper on the British coal strike in the 1970s:

> The social status of the coal miners was far from good. The country blamed
>
> them for the dimmed lights and the three-day work week. They had been
>
> placed in the position of social outcasts and were beginning to "consider
>
> themselves another country." Some businesses and shops had even gone so far
>
> as to refuse service to coal miners (Jones 32).

Who has learned that the coal miners felt ostracized or that the country blamed them? As readers we cannot begin to judge the validity of these assertions without some context provided by the writer. Most readers are put off by an unattached direct quotation or some startling observation that is documented correctly but given no context within the paper. Using introductory tags that identify the author of the source and, when useful, the author's credentials helps guide readers through the source material. The following revision of the paragraph above provides not only context but also sentence variety:

> The social acceptance of coal miners, according to Peter Jones, British cor-
>
> respondent for *Newsweek*, was far from good. From interviews both in London
>
> shops and in pubs near Birmingham, Jones concluded that Britishers blamed
>
> the miners for the dimmed lights and three-day work week. Several striking
>
> miners, in a pub on the outskirts of Birmingham, asserted that some of their

friends had been denied service by shopkeepers and that they "consider[ed] themselves another country" (32).

Select Appropriate Signal Phrases

When you use signal phrases, try to vary both the words you use and their place in the sentence. Look, for example, at the first sentence in the sample paragraph above. The tag is placed in the middle of the sentence and is set off by commas. The sentence could have been written two other ways:

> The social acceptance of coal miners was far from good, according to Peter Jones, British correspondent for *Newsweek*.

> OR

> According to Peter Jones, British correspondent for *Newsweek*, the social acceptance of coal miners was far from good.

Whenever you provide a name and perhaps credentials for your source, you have these three sentence patterns to choose from. Make a point to use all three options in your paper. Word choice can be varied as well. Instead of writing "Peter Jones says" throughout your paper, consider some of these verb choices:

Jones *asserts*	Jones *contends*	Jones *attests to*
Jones *states*	Jones *thinks*	Jones *points out*
Jones *concludes*	Jones *stresses*	Jones *believes*
Jones *presents*	Jones *emphasizes*	Jones *agrees with*
Jones *argues*	Jones *confirms*	Jones *speculates*

NOTE: Not all the words in this list are synonyms; you cannot substitute *confirms* for *believes*. First, select the verb that most accurately conveys the writer's relationship to his or her material. Then, when appropriate, vary word choice as well as sentence structure.

Readers need to be told how to respond to the sources used. They need to know which sources you accept as reliable and which you disagree with, and they need you to distinguish clearly between fact and opinion. Ideas and opinions from sources need introductory tags and then some discussion from you.

Synthesize Source Material and Your Own Ideas

A smooth synthesis of source material is aided by signal phrases and parenthetical documentation because they mark the beginning and ending of material taken from a source. But a complete synthesis requires something more: your ideas about the source and the topic. To illustrate, consider the problems in another paragraph from the British coal strike paper:

> Some critics believed that there was enough coal in Britain to maintain enough
>
> power to keep industry at a near-normal level for thirty-five weeks (Jones 30).
>
> Prime Minister Heath, on the other hand, had placed the country's usable coal
>
> supply at 15.5 million tons (Jones 30). He stated that this would have fallen to
>
> a critical 7 million tons within a month had he not declared a three-day work
>
> week (Jones 31).

This paragraph is a good example of random details strung together for no apparent purpose. How much coal did exist? Whose figures were right? And what purpose do these figures serve in the paper's development? Note that the entire paragraph is developed with material from one source. Do sources other than Jones offer a different perspective? This paragraph is weak for several reasons: (1) It lacks a controlling idea (topic sentence) to give it purpose and direction; (2) it relies for development entirely on one source; (3) it lacks any discussion or analysis by the writer.

By contrast, the following paragraph demonstrates a successful synthesis:

> Of course, the iridium could have come from other extraterrestrial sources
>
> besides an asteroid. One theory, put forward by Dale Russell, is that the irid-
>
> ium was produced outside the solar system by an exploding star (500).
>
> Such an explosion, Russell states, could have blown the iridium either off the
>
> surface of the moon or directly from the star itself (500–01), while also pro-
>
> ducing a deadly blast of heat and gamma rays (Krishtalka 19). This theory
>
> seems to explain the traces of iridium in the mass extinction, but it does not
>
> explain why smaller mammals, crocodiles, and birds survived (Wilford 220).
>
> So the supernova theory took a backseat to the other extraterrestrial theories:
>
> those of asteroids and comets colliding with the earth. The authors of the
>
> book *The Great Extinction,* Michael Allaby and James Lovelock, subtitled their
>
> work *The Solution to . . . the Disappearance of the Dinosaurs.* Their theory: an
>
> asteroid or comet collided with earth around sixty-five million years ago, killing
>
> billions of organisms, and thus altering the course of evolution (157). The fact
>
> that the theory of collision with a cosmic body warrants a book calls for some
>
> thought: is the asteroid or comet theory merely sensationalism, or is it rooted
>
> in fact? Paleontologist Leonard Krishtalka declares that few paleontologists

have accepted the asteroid theory, himself calling "some catastrophic theories . . . small ideas injected with growth hormone" (22). However, other scientists, such as Allaby and Lovelock, see the cosmic catastrophic theory as a solid one based on more than guesswork (10–11).

This paragraph's synthesis is accomplished by several strategies: (1) The paragraph has a controlling idea; (2) the paragraph combines information from several sources; (3) the information is presented in a blend of paraphrase and short quotations; (4) information from the different sources is clearly indicated to readers; and (5) the student explains and discusses the information.

You might also observe the different lengths of the two sample paragraphs just presented. Although the second paragraph is long, it is not unwieldy because it achieves unity and coherence. By contrast, body paragraphs of only three sentences are probably in trouble.

Write Effective Conclusions

Sometimes ending a paper seems even more difficult than beginning one. You know you are not supposed to just stop, but every ending that comes to mind sounds more corny than clever. If you have trouble, try one of the following types of endings.

1.   Do not just repeat your claim exactly as it was stated in paragraph 1, but expand on the original wording and emphasize the claim's significance. Here is the conclusion of the solar energy paper:

The idea of using solar energy is not as far-fetched as it seemed years ago. With the continued support of government plus the enthusiasm of research groups, environmentalists, and private industry, solar energy may become a household word quite soon. With the increasing cost of fossil fuel, the time could not be better for exploring this use of the sun.

2.   End with a quotation that effectively summarizes and drives home the point of your paper. Researchers are not always lucky enough to find the ideal quotation for ending a paper. If you find a good one, use it. Better yet, present the quotation and then add your comment in a sentence or two. The conclusion to a paper on the dilemma of defective newborns is a good example:

Dr. Joseph Fletcher is correct when he says that "every advance in medical capabilities is an increase in our moral responsibility" (48). In a world of many gray areas, one point is clear. From an ethical point of view, medicine is a victim of its own success.

3. If you have researched an issue or problem, emphasize your proposed solutions in the concluding paragraph. The student opposing a mall adjacent to the Manassas Battlefield concluded with several solutions:

Whether the proposed mall will be built is clearly in doubt at the moment.

What are the solutions to this controversy? One approach is, of course, not to

build the mall at all. To accomplish this solution, now, with the rezoning hav-

ing been approved, probably requires an act of Congress to buy the land and

make it part of the National Park. Another solution, one that would please the

County and the developer and satisfy citizens objecting to traffic problems, is

to build the needed roads before the mall is completed. A third approach is

to allow the office park of the original plan to be built, but not the mall. The

local preservationists had agreed to this original development proposal, but

now that the issue has received national attention, they may no longer be will-

ing to compromise. Whatever the future of the William Center, the present

plan for a new regional mall is not acceptable.

Avoid Ineffective Conclusions

Follow these rules to avoid conclusions that most readers consider ineffective and annoying.

1. *Do not introduce a new idea.* If the point belongs in your paper, you should have introduced it earlier.
2. *Do not just stop or trail off,* even if you feel as though you have run out of steam. A simple, clear restatement of the claim is better than no conclusion.
3. *Do not tell your reader what you have accomplished:* "In this paper I have explained the advantages of solar energy by examining the costs . . ." If you have written well, your reader knows what you have accomplished.
4. *Do not offer apologies or expressions of hope.* "Although I wasn't able to find as much on this topic as I wanted, I have tried to explain the advantages of solar energy, and I hope that you will now understand why we need to use it more" is a disastrous ending.

Choose an Effective Title

Give some thought to your paper's title since that is what your reader sees first and what your work will be known by. A good title provides information and creates interest. Make your title informative by making it specific. If you can create interest through clever wording, so much the better. But do not confuse "cutesiness" with clever wording. Review the following examples of acceptable and unacceptable titles:

VAGUE:	A Perennial Issue Unsolved (There are many; which one is this paper about?)
BETTER:	The Perennial Issue of Press Freedom Versus Press Responsibility
TOO BROAD:	Earthquakes (What about earthquakes? This title is not informative.)
BETTER:	The Need for Earthquake Prediction
TOO BROAD:	*The Scarlet Letter* (Never use just the title of the work under discussion; you can use the work's title as a part of a longer title of your own.)
BETTER:	Color Symbolism in *The Scarlet Letter*
CUTESY:	Babes in Trouble (The slang "Babes" makes this title seem insensitive rather than clever.)
BETTER:	The Dilemma of Defective Newborns

REVISING THE PAPER: A CHECKLIST

After completing a first draft, catch your breath and then gear up for the next step in the writing process: revision. Revision actually involves three separate steps: *rewriting*—adding or deleting text, or moving parts of the draft around, *editing*—a rereading to correct errors from misspellings to incorrect documentation format, and then *proofreading* the typed copy. If you treat these as separate steps, you will do a more complete job of revision—and get a better grade on your paper!

Rewriting

Read your draft through and make changes as a result of answering the following questions:

Purpose and Audience

☐ Is my draft long enough to meet assignment requirements and my purpose?

☐ Are terms defined and concepts explained appropriately for my audience?

Content

☐ Do I have a clearly stated thesis—the claim of my argument?

☐ Have I presented sufficient evidence to support my claim?

☐ Are there any irrelevant sections that should be deleted?

Structure

☐ Are paragraphs ordered to develop my topic logically?

☐ Does the content of each paragraph help develop my claim?

☐ Is everything in each paragraph on the same subtopic to create paragraph unity?

☐ Do body paragraphs have a balance of information and analysis, of source material and my own ideas?

☐ Are there any paragraphs that should be combined? Are there any very long paragraphs that should be divided? (Check for unity.)

Editing

Make revisions guided by your responses to the questions, make a clean copy, and read again. This time, pay close attention to sentences, words, and documentation format. Use the following questions to guide editing.

Coherence

☐ Have connecting words been used and key terms repeated to produce paragraph coherence?

☐ Have transitions been used to show connections between paragraphs?

Sources

☐ Have I paraphrased instead of quoted whenever possible?

☐ Have I used signal phrases to create a context for source material?

☐ Have I documented all borrowed material, whether quoted or paraphrased?

☐ Are parenthetical references properly placed after borrowed material?

Style

☐ Have I varied sentence length and structure?

☐ Have I avoided long quotations?

☐ Do I have correct form for quotations? For titles?

☐ Is my language specific and descriptive?

☐ Have I avoided inappropriate shifts in tense or person?

☐ Have I removed any wordiness, deadwood, trite expressions, or clichés?

☐ Have I used specialized terms correctly?

☐ Have I avoided contractions as too informal for most research papers?

☐ Have I maintained an appropriate style and tone for academic work?

Proofreading

When your editing is finished, prepare a completed draft of your paper according to the format described and illustrated below. Then proofread the completed copy, making any corrections neatly in ink. If a page has several errors, print a corrected copy. Be sure to make a copy of the paper for yourself before submitting the original to your instructor.

THE COMPLETED PAPER

Your research paper should be double-spaced throughout (including the Works Cited page) with 1-inch margins on all sides. Your project will contain the following parts, in this order:

1. *A title page,* with your title, your name, your instructor's name, the course name or number, and the date, neatly centered, if an outline follows. If there is no outline, place this information at the top left of the first page.
2. *An outline,* or statement of purpose, if required.
3. *The body or text of your paper.* Number all pages consecutively, including pages of works cited, using arabic numerals. Place numbers in the upper right-hand corner of each page. Include your last name before each page number.
4. *A list of works cited,* placed on a separate page(s) after the text. Title the first page "Works Cited." (Do not use the title "Bibliography.")

SAMPLE STUDENT ESSAY IN MLA STYLE

The following paper illustrates MLA style and an argumentative essay using sources.

Appropriate heading when separate title page is not used.

Lauren George   George 1

Dr. Dorothy U. Seyler

English Composition 2

4 August 2008

Center the title.   The Effects of Gangsta Rap on African-American Adolescent Females

Ice Cube decreed: "Do like Ice Cube, slam her ass in a ditch" (N.W.A.).

While N.W.A., one of the first rap groups to popularize gangsta rap, is no

longer creating music, its influence on mainstream rap is evident. Today,

rappers like 50 Cent, Ludacris, and Lil' Wayne, among others, perpetuate this

misogynistic theme in gansta rap and their music videos. Bob Dole, former

senator and presidential candidate, claimed that "we have reached the point

George 2

where" gansta rap and its images threaten "to undermine our character as a nation" (qtd. in Baldwin 159). But does gangsta rap negatively impact adolescent African-American females? African-American teenaged girls are in the most vulnerable periods of their lives and, by virtue of being black and female, are the direct subjects of contempt and disdain in gangsta rap. Gangsta rap may be seen as a contagiously diseased person: he may not be the cause of the disease, but he does spread it to others. Surely this music has a negative effect on the way adolescent black girls develop their sexual identities and body image.

> Double space throughout.

In a 2003 interview on "The O'Reilly Factor," Cam'ron defended his choice to rap about "pimping and bitches" by saying, "I'm just an author. So what I do is I write what goes on in the ghetto. I'm not a liar. So what I tell you goes on in my album, that's what does on the streets of Harlem." He isn't alone; many male and female rappers share Cam'ron's point of view. They believe that they are telling their story and the stories of the 'hood. Murray Forman writes that gangsta rap discusses "generally common phenomena" to further the "black struggles for empowerment"(211). Ice-T explains in his song, "O.G. Original Gangster":

> Student presents the rappers' argument.

> Indent display quotation 10 spaces.

      When I wrote about parties

      Someone always died

      When I tried to write happy

      Yo, I knew I lied, I lived a life of crime

      Why play ya blind?

Gangsta rappers clearly place more importance on the truth of their portrayals of the ghetto than on the influence they may have on young people. In doing so, they seek to show themselves as authentic "author[s]" or "keeping-it-real" (qtd. in Baldwin 160). Some analysts of rap argue that these lyrics help to build self-confidence and esteem in young people who often do not feel in control or important (qtd. in Gallo 52). Some female rappers are

George 3

no exception. Notably Lil' Kim and Foxy Brown both advocate many of the same behaviors for which male gangsta rappers are rebuked. Lil' Kim raps: "I treat y'all n*****s like y'all treat us" and Foxy Brown agrees with her, saying that she "pimp[s] hard . . . / [and] maybe a little conceited but that's always needed."

Despite the valid arguments that these artists make in favor of their rap, the good that rap can do for the black community in America is heavily outweighed by its more destructive effect on its listeners. Many—both blacks and whites—have argued that gangsta rap is filled with harmful messages are a special problem because, as Stephens and Phillips explain, young people develop their sexual selves from the messages they get about sexual roles and

behaviour (3). African-American adolescent girls and stereotypical images and ideals presented in gangsta rap. Stephens and Phillips describe the stereotype of the "the good, innocent, virginal girl [who] continues to be an idealized image of womanhood associated with white females, but unattainable for African-American females" (4). Tricia Rose argues that when faced with an ideal that society declares unattainable, black teenaged girls are likely to see their bodies as indicators of "sexual perversity and inferiority" (167). Internalizing the inferiority creates the standard of limited expectations, as Vanessa McGann and Janice Steil explain (177).

In Susanne Gallo's empirical study of the effects of gangsta rap on the adolescent female identity, she discovered that the girls who preferred gangsta rap were more likely to have been physically and sexually abused during their childhoods. Gallo also discovered that the girls who listened to gangsta rap watched roughly one hour more of corresponding music videos, on average, than girls who listened to underground rap. In addition, the grade point average of the gangsta rap listeners averaged .45 points less than the underground rap listeners (295). Although her study did not focus exclusively on African-American adolescent girls, 47 percent of her group was African-American. Her

George 4

study does reveal a negative impact on teenaged girls, and that includes black teenaged girls.

In another empirical study conducted by Shani Peterson et al., African-American adolescents, between 14 and 18, were more likely to engage in "binge drinking . . . test positive for marijuana . . . have multiple sexual partners . . . and have a negative body image" (1157). Peterson cites these outcomes as the result of being exposed to "sexual stereotypes" in rap music videos. Black Entertainment Television's target demographic is young African-Americans. Jane Brown and Carol Pardun write that "even young children prefer characters who are similar to themselves in gender, age, or race" and that, over time, "'wishful identification' with characters . . . increases" (268). Unfortunately, the medium used most by BET happens to be music videos. According to a review of 203 BET music videos, "42% . . . depicted fondling and 58% of videos featured women dancing sexually" and black American adolescents are watching more than 3 hours of music videos a day (Peterson 1158).

> Signal phrase introduces quotation.

A third study, by Gina Wingood, found that African-American girls were more likely to "fear abandonment as a result of negotiating condom use, . . . to perceive that they had fewer options for sexual partners, . . . to perceive themselves as having limited control in their sexual relationships, . . . and [to] worry about acquiring HIV" (433). This was true for African-American girls who were more dissatisfied with their body image than girls who had the same levels of self-esteem, body mass index, and depression. Wingood learned that as a result of poor body image, adolescent black girls will be more likely to "never [use] condoms during sexual intercourse in the past 30 days and . . . engage in unprotected vaginal sex in the prior 6 months" (433).

> Good use of ellipses to shorten quotation to key details.

Gallo's study created a framework upon which the findings of Peterson and Wingood can rest. Girls who listen to gangsta rap watch more music videos for that type of music. These videos objectify the black female body and depict sexual dominance over black women by means of fondling and dehumanization

> Student summarizes 3 studies to create a transition paragraph.

George 5

by men. Adolescent black girls construct their body image and sexual identities based upon the representation of the average "video ho." Due to a negative body image, black teen girls engage in risky behavior that leaves them vulnerable to more physical and sexual abuse.

Further evidence is presented.

The Centers for Disease Control's national "Youth Risk Behavior Survey: 2007" supports the findings of these researchers. CDC reports that 10% fewer Hispanic students and 16% fewer white students have engaged in sexual intercourse with four or more partners than black students. Also, black students(14%) engaged in violent relations with the romantic partner more than white (8%) or Hispanic (11%) students. Lastly, twice as many black students (63%) watch three hours or more of television than white students (27%) and one and a half times more than Hispanic students (43%). All of these studies reveal that African-American teens are taking in more of gangsta rap's images than any other group.

Conclusion connects evidence to a restated claim.

Three separate studies have shown negative effects of gangsta rap and none have shown positive results. Although themes of misogyny and violence do not inhabit gangsta rap only, these themes are repeatedly and powerfully presented in this music, music that teens, most particularly black teenaged girls, are absorbing and being shaped by. Unless or until there is change in the rap genre, black women will continue to struggle with gangsta rap's images and attitudes toward them that lead to low self-esteem and greater indulgence in risky behavior.

Works Cited   George 6

Baldwin, Davarian L. "Black Empire, White Desires: The Spatial Politics of

Identity in the Age of Hip-Hop." *That's the Joint!: The Hip-Hop Studies Reader.*

Ed. Mark Anthony Neal and Murray Forman. New York: Routledge, 2004.

159–76. Print.

Brown, Foxy. "Candy." *Broken Silence.* Def Jam Records, 2001. Recording.

Brown, Jane D., and Carol J. Pardun. "Little in Common: Racial and Gender

Differences in Adolescents' Television Diets." *Journal of Broadcasting &*

Electronic Media 48.2 (2004): 266–78. *Communication & Mass Media*

Complete. EBSCO. Web. 10 Aug. 2008.

Cam'ron and Damon Dash. "Is Gangsta Rap Hurting America's Children?"

Interview. *The O'Reilly Factor.* Host Bill O'Reilly. Fox News. 14 Nov. 2003.

Web. 10 Aug. 2008.

Centers for Disease Control and Prevention. "The National Youth Risk Behavior

Survey: 2007." Centers for Disease Control and Prevention. 2007. Web. 1

Aug. 2008.

Forman, Murray. "'Represent': Race, Space, and Place in Rap Music." *That's*

the Joint!: The Hip-Hop Studies Reader. Ed. Mark Anthony Neal and Murray

Forman. New York: Routledge, 2004. 201–22. Print.

Gallo, Susanne. "Music Preference with an Emphasis on Gangsta Rap:

Female Adolescent Identity, Beliefs, and Behavior." Diss. California

Ice-T. "O.G. Original Gangster." *O.G. Original Gangster.* Sire/Warner Bros, 1991.

Recording.

Institute of Integral Studies, 2003. *PsychINFO.* EBSCOhost. Web. 1 Aug.

2008.

Lil' Kim. "Suck My Dick." *Notorious K. I. M.* Atlantic Records, 2000.

Recording.

McGann, Vanessa L., and Janice M. Steil. "The Sense of Entitlement:

Implications for Gender Equality and Psychological Well-Being." *The*

Handbook of Girls' and Women's Psychological Health. Ed. Judith Worell and

Carol D. Goodheart. New York: Oxford UP, 2006. Print.

Start a new page for
Works Cited.

Double space
throughout.
Alphabetize
and use hanging
indentation.

N.W.A. "A Bitch Iz a Bitch." *N. W. A and the Posse.* Priority Records. 1989.
Recording.

Peterson, Shani H., et al. "Images of Sexual Stereotypes in Rap Videos and the
Health of African American Female Adolescents." *Journal of Women's Health*
16.8 (2007): 1157–64. *Women's Studies International.* EBSCOhost. Web.
20 July 2008.

Rose, Tricia. *Black Noise: Rap Music and Black Culture in Contemporary America.*
Hanover: UP of New England, 1994. Print.

Stephens, Dionne P., and Layli D. Phillips. "Freaks, Gold Diggers, Divas, and
Dykes: The Sociohistorical Development of Adolescent African American
Women's Sexual Scripts." *Sexuality and Culture* 7.1 (2003): 3–49. *Women's
Studies International.* EBSCOhost. Web. 1 Aug. 2008.

Wingood, Gina M., et al. "Body Image and African American Females' Sexual
Health." *Journal of Women's Health and Gender-Based Medicine* 11.5 (2002)
433–39. *Women's Studies International.* EBSCOhost. Web. 20 July 2008.

CHAPTER 14

Formal Documentation: MLA Style, APA Style

In Chapter 12 you were shown, in sample bibliography cards, what information about a source you would need in order to prepare the documentation for a researched essay. In Chapter 13 you were shown in-text documentation patterns as part of the discussion of avoiding plagiarism and writing effective paragraphs. The format shown is for MLA (Modern Language Association) style, the documentation style used in the humanities. APA (American Psychological Association) style is used in the social sciences. The sciences and other disciplines also have style sheets, but the most common documentation patterns used by undergraduates are MLA and APA, the two patterns explained in this chapter.

Remember that MLA recommends that writers prepare their Works Cited list—a list of all sources they have used—before drafting the essay. This list can then be used as an accurate guide to the in-text/parenthetical documentation that MLA requires along with the Works Cited list at the end of the essay. Heed this good advice. This chapter begins with guidelines for in-text documentation and then provides many models of full documentation for a Works Cited list.

REMEMBER: Never guess at documentation! Always consult this chapter to make each in-text citation and your Works Cited page(s) absolutely correct.

As you now know, MLA documentation style has two parts: in-text references to author and page number and then complete information about each source in a Works Cited list. Because parenthetical references to author and page are incomplete—readers could not find the source with such limited information—all sources referred to by author and page number in the essay require the full details of publication in a Works Cited list that concludes the essay. General guidelines for in-text citations are given below.

NOTE: You need a 100 percent correspondence between the sources listed in your Works Cited and the sources you actually cite (refer to) in your essay. Do not omit from your Works Cited any sources you refer to in your essay. Do not include in your Works Cited any sources not referred to in your paper.

GUIDELINES for Using Parenthetical Documentation

- **The purpose of documentation is to make clear exactly what material in a passage has been borrowed and from what source the borrowed material has come.**

- **Parenthetical in-text documentation requires specific page references for borrowed material—unless the source is not a print one.**
- **Parenthetical documentation is required for both quoted and para-phrased material and for both print and non-print sources.**
- **Parenthetical documentation provides as brief a citation as possible consistent with accuracy and clarity.**

THE SIMPLEST PATTERNS OF PARENTHETICAL DOCUMENTATION

The simplest in-text citation can be prepared in one of three ways:

1. Give the author's last name (full name in your first reference to the writer) in the text of your essay and put the appropriate page number(s) in parentheses following the borrowed material.

    Frederick Lewis Allen observes that, during the 1920s, urban tastes spread to the

    country (146).

2. Place the author's last name and the appropriate page number(s) in parentheses immediately following the borrowed material.

    During the 1920s, "not only the drinks were mixed, but the company as well"

    (Allen 82).

3. On the rare occasion that you cite an entire work rather than borrowing from a specific passage, give the author's name in the text and omit any page numbers.

    Leonard Sax explains, to both parents and teachers, the specific ways in which

    gender matters.

Each one of these in-text references is complete *only* when the full citation is placed in the Works Cited section of your paper:

Allen, Frederick Lewis. *Only Yesterday: An Informal History of the Nineteen-*

   Twenties. New York: Harper, 1931. Print.

Sax, Leonard. *Why Gender Matters.* New York: Random, 2005. Print.

The three patterns just illustrated should be used in each of the following situations:

1. The source referred to is not anonymous—the author is known.
2. The source referred to is by one author.
3. The source cited is the only work used by that author.
4. No other author in your list of sources has the same last name.

PLACEMENT OF PARENTHETICAL DOCUMENTATION

The simplest placing of an in-text reference is at the end of the sentence *before* the period. When you are quoting, place the parentheses *after* the final quotation mark but still before the period that ends the sentence.

> During the 1920s, "not only the drinks were mixed, but the company as well"
>
> (Allen 82).

 NOTE: Do not put any punctuation between the author's name and the page number.

If the borrowed material forms only a part of your sentence, place the parenthetical reference *after* the borrowed material and *before* any subsequent punctuation. This placement more accurately shows readers what is borrowed and what are your own words.

> Sport, Allen observes about the 1920s, had developed into an obsession (66),
>
> another similarity between the 1920s and the 1980s.

If a quoted passage is long enough to require setting off in display form (block quotation), then place the parenthetical reference at the end of the passage, *after* the final period. Remember: Long quotations in display form *do not* have quotation marks.

> It is hard to believe that when he writes about the influence of science Allen is
>
> describing the 1920s, not the 1980s:
>
> > The prestige of science was colossal. The man in the street and the woman
> >
> > in the kitchen, confronted on every hand with new machines and devices
> >
> > which they owed to the laboratory, were ready to believe that science could
> >
> > accomplish almost anything. (164)

And to complete the documentation for all three examples:

Works Cited

> Allen, Frederick Lewis. *Only Yesterday: An Informal History of the Nineteen-*
>
> *Twenties.* New York: Harper, 1931. Print.

PARENTHETICAL CITATIONS OF COMPLEX SOURCES

Not all sources can be cited in one of the three patterns illustrated above, for not all meet the four criteria listed on page 315. Works by two or more authors, for example, will need somewhat fuller references. Each sample form of in-text documentation given below must be completed with a full Works Cited reference, as shown above.

Two Authors, Mentioned in the Text

Richard Hernstein and Charles Murray contend that it is "consistently . . .

advantageous to be smart" (25).

Two Authors, Not Mentioned in the Text

The advantaged smart group forms a "cognitive elite" in our society

(Hernstein and Murray 26–27).

A Book in Two or More Volumes

Sewall analyzes the role of Judge Lord in Dickinson's life (2: 642–47).

OR

Judge Lord was also one of Dickinson's preceptors (Sewall 2: 642–47).

 NOTE: The number before the colon always signifies the volume number. The number(s) after the colon represents the page number(s).

A Book Listed by Title—Author Unknown

According to *The Concise Dictionary of American Biography,* William Jennings Bryan's

1896 campaign stressed social and sectional conflicts (117).

The New York Times' editors were not pleased with some of the changes in welfare

programs ("Where Welfare Stands" 4:16)

Always cite the title of the article, not the title of the journal, if the author is unknown. In the second example, the number before the page number is the newspaper's section number.

A Work by a Corporate Author

A report by the Institute of Ecology's Global Ecological Problems Workshop argues

that the civilization of the city can lull us into forgetting our relationship to the

total ecological system on which we depend (13).

Although corporate authors may be cited with the page number within the parentheses, your writing will be more graceful if corporate authors are introduced in the sentence. Then only page numbers go in parentheses.

Two or More Works by the Same Author

> During the 1920s, "not only the drinks were mixed, but the company as well"
>
> (Allen, *Only Yesterday* 82).

> Frederick Lewis Allen contends that the early 1900s were a period of complacency
>
> in America (*The Big Change* 4–5).

> In *The Big Change*, Allen asserts that the early 1900s were a period of complacency
>
> (4–5).

If your list of sources contains two or more works by the same author, the fullest parenthetical citation includes the author's last name, followed by a comma, the work's title, shortened if possible, and the page number. If the author's name appears in the text—or the author and title both as in the third example above—omit these items from the parenthetical citation. When you have to include the title to distinguish among sources, it is best to put the author's name in the text.

Two or More Works in One Parenthetical Reference

> Several writers about the future agree that big changes will take place in work
>
> patterns (Toffler 384–87; Naisbitt 35–36).

Separate each author with a semicolon. But, if the parenthetical reference becomes disruptively long, cite the works in a "See also" note rather than in the text.

A Source Without Page Numbers

It is usually a good idea to name the non-print source within your sentence so that readers will not expect to see page numbers.

> Although some still disagree, the *Oxford English Dictionary Online* defines global
>
> warming as "thought to be caused by various side-effects of modern energy
>
> consumption."

Complete Publication Information in Parenthetical Reference

At times you may want to give complete information about a source within parentheses in the text of your essay. Then a Works Cited list is not used. Use square brackets for parenthetical information within parentheses. This approach may be a good choice when you use only one source that you refer to several times. Literary analyses are one type of essay for which this approach to citation may be a good choice. For example:

> Edith Wharton establishes the bleakness of her setting, Starkfield, not just through
>
> description of place but also through her main character, Ethan, who is described
>
> as "bleak and unapproachable" (*Ethan Frome* [New York: Scribner's, 1911, Print]

3. All subsequent references are to this edition). Later Wharton describes winter as

"shut[ting] down on Starkfield" and negating life there (7).

Additional Information Footnotes or Endnotes

At times you may need to provide additional information that is not central to your argument. These additions belong in a content note. However, use these sparingly and never as a way of advancing your thesis. Many instructors object to content notes and prefer only parenthetical citations.

"See Also" Footnotes or Endnotes

More acceptable is the note that refers to other sources of evidence for or against the point to be established. These notes are usually introduced with "See also" or "Compare," followed by the citation. For example:

Chekhov's debt to Ibsen should be recognized, as should his debt to other

playwrights of the 1890s who were concerned with the inner life of their characters.[1]

---

[1] See also Eric Bentley, *In Search of Theater* (New York: Vintage, 1959) 330; Walter Bruford, *Anton Chekhov* (New Haven: Yale UP, 1957) 45.

PREPARING MLA CITATIONS FOR A "WORKS CITED" LIST

The partial in-text citations described and illustrated above must be completed by a full reference in a list given at the end of the essay. To prepare your Works Cited list, alphabetize, by author last name, the sources you have actually referred to and complete each citation according to the forms explained and illustrated in the following pages. The key is to find the appropriate model for each of your sources and then follow the model exactly. (Guidelines for formatting a finished Works Cited page are found pp.) But, you will make fewer errors if you also understand the basic pieces of information needed in citations and the order of that information.

Books require the following information, in the order given, with periods after each of the four major elements:

- Author, last name first.
- Title—and subtitle if there is one—in italics.
- Facts of publication: city of publication, followed by a colon, shortened publisher's name (Norton for W. W. Norton, for example), followed by a comma, and the year of publication, followed by a period.
- Medium of publication: Print.

Author	Title	Facts of Publication	Medium of Publication
Bellow, Saul.	*A Thief.*	New York: Viking Penguin, 1989.	Print.

Forms for Books: Citing the Complete Book

A Book by a Single Author

Silver, Lee M. *Remaking Eden: Cloning and Beyond in a Brave New World*. New

York: Avon, 1997. Print.

The subtitle is included, preceded by a colon, even if there is no colon on the book's title page.

A Book by Two or Three Authors

Adkins, Lesley, and Ray Adkins. *The Keys of Egypt: The Race to Crack the*

Hieroglyph Code. New York: HarperCollins, 2000. Print.

Second (and third) authors' names appear in normal signature order.

A Book with More Than Three Authors

Baker, Susan P., et al. *The Injury Fact Book*. Oxford: Oxford UP, 1992. Print.

Use the name of the first person listed on the title page. The English "and others" may be used instead of "et al." Shorten "University Press" to "UP."

Two or More Works by the Same Author

Goodall, Jane. *In the Shadow of Man*. Boston: Houghton, 1971. Print.

---. *Through a Window: My Thirty Years with the Chimpanzees of Gombe*. Boston:

Houghton, 1990. Print.

Give the author's full name with the first entry. For the second (and additional works), begin the citation with three hyphens followed by a period. Alphabetize the entries by the books' titles.

A Book Written Under a Pseudonym with Name Supplied

Wrighter, Carl P. [Paul Stevens]. *I Can Sell You Anything*. New York: Ballantine,

1972. Print.

An Anonymous Book

Beowulf: A New Verse Translation. Trans. Seamus Heaney. New York: Farrar,

2000. Print.

An Edited Book

Hamilton, Alexander, James Madison, and John Jay. *The Federalist Papers*. Ed.

Isaac Kramnick. New York: Viking-Penguin, 1987. Print.

Lynn, Kenneth S., ed. *Huckleberry Finn: Text, Sources, and Critics*. New York:

Harcourt, 1961. Print.

If you cite the author's work, put the author's name first and the editor's name after the title, preceded by "Ed." If you cite the editor's work (an introduction or notes), then place the editor's name first, followed by a comma and "ed."

A Translation

> Schulze, Hagen. *Germany: A New History.* Trans. Deborah Lucas Schneider.
>> Cambridge: Harvard UP, 1998. Print.

> Cornford, Francis MacDonald, trans. *The Republic of Plato.* New York: Oxford
>> UP, 1945. Print.

If the author's work is being cited, place the author's name first and the translator's name after the title, preceded by "Trans." If the translator's work is the important element, place the translator's name first, as in the second example above. If the author's name does not appear in the title, give it after the title. For example: By Plato.

A Book in Two or More Volumes

> Spielvogel, Jackson J. *Western Civilization.* 2 vols. Minneapolis: West, 1991. Print.

A Book in Its Second or Subsequent Edition

> O'Brien, David M. *Storm Center: The Supreme Court and American Politics.* 2nd
>> ed. New York: Norton, 1990. Print.

A Book in a Series

> Parkinson, Richard. *The Rosetta Stone.* British Museum Objects in Focus.
>> London: British Museum Press, 2005. Print.

The series title—and number, if there is one—follows the book's title but is not put in italics.

A Reprint of an Earlier Work

> Twain, Mark. *Adventures of Huckleberry Finn.* 1885. Centennial Facsimile
>> Edition. Introd. Hamlin Hill. New York: Harper, 1962. Print.

> Faulkner, William. *As I Lay Dying.* 1930. New York: Vintage-Random, 1964. Print.

Provide the original date of publication as well as the facts of publication for the reprinted version. Indicate any new material, as in the first example. The second example illustrates citing a reprinted book, by the same publisher, in a paperback version. (Vintage is a paperback imprint of the publisher Random House.)

A Book with Two or More Publishers

> Green, Mark J., James M. Fallows, and David R. Zwick. *Who Runs Congress?* Ralph
>> Nader Congress Project. New York: Bantam; New York: Grossman, 1972. Print.

Separate the publishers with a semicolon.

A Corporate or Governmental Author

California State Department of Education. *American Indian Education Handbook.*

Sacramento: California Department of Education, Indian Education Unit,

1991. Print.

The Bible

The Bible [Always refers to the King James Version.] Print.

The Reader's Bible: A Narrative. Ed. with introd. Roland Mushat Frye. Princeton:

Princeton UP, 1965. Print.

Do not underline the title. Indicate the version if it is not the King James Version. Provide facts of publication for versions not well known.

Forms for Books: Citing Part of a Book

A Preface, Introduction, Foreword, or Afterword

Sagan, Carl. Introduction. *A Brief History of Time: From the Big Bang to Black*

Holes. By Stephen Hawking. New York: Bantam, 1988, ix–x. Print.

Use this form if you are citing the author of the Preface, Introduction, Forward, or the like. Use an identifying word after the author's name and given inclusive page numbers for the part of the book by the author you are citing.

An Encyclopedia Article

Ostrom, John H. "Dinosaurs." *McGraw-Hill Encyclopedia of Science and*

Technology. 1957 ed. Print.

"Benjamin Franklin." *Concise Dictionary of American Biography.* Ed. Joseph

E. G. Hopkins. New York: Scribner's, 1964. Print.

Give complete publication facts for less well-known works or first editions.

One or More Volumes in a Multivolume Work

James, Henry. *The Portrait of a Lady.* Vols. 3 and 4 of *The Novels and Tales of*

Henry James. New York: Scribner's, 1908. Print.

A Work in an Anthology or Collection

Hurston, Zora Neale. *The First One. Black Female Playwrights: An Anthology of*

Plays Before 1950. Ed. Kathy A. Perkins. Bloomington: Indiana UP, 1989.

80–88. Print.

Comstock, George. "The Medium and the Society: The Role of Television

in American Life." *Children and Television: Images in a Changing Sociocultural*

World. Ed. Gordon L. Berry and Joy Keiko Asamen. Newbury Park, CA:

Sage, 1993. 117–31. Print.

Give inclusive page numbers for the particular work you have used.

An Article in a Collection, Casebook, or Sourcebook

MacKenzie, James J. "The Decline of Nuclear Power." *engage/social* April 1986.

Rpt. as "America Does Not Need More Nuclear Power" in *The Environmental*

Crisis: Opposing Viewpoints. Ed. Julie S. Bach and Lynn Hall. Opposing

Viewpoints Series. St. Paul: Greenhaven, 1986. 136–41. Print.

Many articles in collections have been previously published, so a complete citation needs to include the original facts of publication (excluding page numbers if they are not readily available) as well as the facts of publication for the collection. Include inclusive page numbers for the article used.

Cross-References

If you are citing several articles from one collection, you can cite the collection and then provide only the author and title of specific articles used, with a cross-reference to the editor(s) of the collection.

Head, Suzanne, and Robert Heinzman, eds. *Lessons of the Rainforest.* San

Francisco: Sierra Club, 1990. Print.

Bandyopadhyay, J., and Vandana Shiva. "Asia's Forest, Asia's Cultures." Head

and Heinzman 66–77. Print.

Forms for Periodicals: Articles in Journals and Magazines Accessed in Print

Articles from the various forms of periodicals, when read in their print format, require the following information, in the order given, with periods after each of the four major elements:

- Author, last name first.
- Title of the article, in quotation marks.
- Facts of publication: title of the journal (magazine or newspaper) in italics, volume and issue number *for scholarly journals only*, date followed by a colon and inclusive page numbers, and then a period.
- Medium of publication: Print.

The following models show the variations in the details of publication, depending on the type of publication.

Article in a Journal Paged by Year

> Brown, Jane D., and Carol J. Pardun. "Little in Common: Racial and Gender
>
>   Differences in Adolescents' Television Diets." *Journal of Broadcasting and*
>
>   *Electronic Media* 48.2 (2004): 266–78. Print.

Note that there is *no* punctuation between the title of the periodical and the volume number and date.

Article in a Journal Paged by Issue

> Lewis, Kevin. "Superstardom and Transcendence." *Arete: The Journal of Sport*
>
>   *Literature* 2.2 (1985): 47–54. Print.

Provide both volume and issue number regardless of the journal's choice of paging.

Article in a Monthly Magazine

> Tyldesley, Joyce. "I, Cleopatra: This Was My Life." *Natural History* Oct. 2008:
>
>   42–47. Print.

Do not use volume or issue number. Cite the month(s) and year followed by a colon and inclusive page numbers. Abbreviate all months except May, June, and July.

Article in a Weekly Magazine

> Stein, Joel. "Eat This, Low Carbers." *Time* 15 Aug. 2005: 78. Print.

Provide the complete date, using the order of day, month, year.

An Anonymous Article

> "Death of Perestroika." *Economist* 2 Feb. 1991: 12–13. Print.

The missing name indicates that the article is anonymous. Alphabetize under D.

A Published Interview

> Angier, Natalie. "Ernst Mayr at 93." Interview. *Natural History* May 1997: 8–11.
>
>   Print.

Follow the pattern for a published article, but add the descriptive label "Interview" (followed by a period) after the article's title.

A Review

> Bardsley, Tim. "Eliciting Science's Best." Rev. of *Frontiers of Illusion: Science,*
>
> *Technology, and the Politics of Progress,* by Daniel Sarewitz. *Scientific American*
>
> June 1997: 142. Print.

If the review is signed, begin with the author's name and then the title of the review article. Also provide the title of the work being reviewed and its author, preceded by "Rev. of." For reviews of art shows, videos, or computer software, provide place and date or descriptive label to make the citation clear.

Forms for Periodicals: Articles in Newspapers Accessed in Print

An Article from a Newspaper

> Arguila, John. "What Deep Blue Taught Kasparov—and Us." *Christian Science*
>
> *Monitor* 16 May 1997: 18. Print.

A newspaper's title should be cited as it appears on the masthead, excluding any initial article, thus *New York Times,* not *The New York Times.*

An Article from a Newspaper with Lettered Sections

> Ferguson, Niall. "Rough Week, but America's Era Goes On." *Washington Post*
>
> 21 Sept. 2008: B1+. Print.

Place the section letter immediately before the page number without any spacing. If the paging is not consecutive, give the first page and the plus sign.

An Article from a Newspaper with a Designated Edition

> Pereria, Joseph. "Women Allege Sexist Atmosphere in Offices Constitutes
>
> Harassment." *Wall Street Journal* 10 Feb. 1988, eastern ed.: 23. Print.

Cite the edition used after the date and before the page number.

An Editorial

> "Japan's Two Nationalisms." Editorial. *Washington Post* 4 June 2000: B6.

Add the descriptive label "Editorial" after the article title.

A Letter to the Editor

> Wiles, Yoko A. "Thoughts of a New Citizen." Letter. *Washington Post* 27 Dec.
>
> 1995: A22.

Forms for Web Sources

Remember that the purpose of a citation is to allow readers to obtain the source you have used. To locate online sources, more information is usually needed than for printed sources. Include as many of the items listed below, in the order given here, as are relevant—and available—for each source. Take time to search a Web site's home page to locate as much of the information as possible. AND: Always include the date you accessed the source, as the Web remains ever fluid and changing.

- Author (or editor, compiler, translator), last name first.
- Title of the work, in quotation marks if it is part of a site, in italics if it is a complete and separate work, such as an online novel.
- Facts of publication of the print version if the item was originally published in print.
- Title of the Web site, in italics—unless it is the same as item 2 above.
- Publisher or sponsor of the site (possibly a university, company, or organization).
- Date of publication. (If none if available, use n.d.)
- Medium of publication: Web.
- Your date of access: day, month, and year.

Study this annotated citation as a general model.

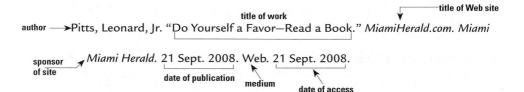

A Published Article from an Online Database

Shin, Michael S. "Redressing Wounds: Finding a Legal Framework to Remedy

Racial Disparities in Medical Care." *California Law Review* 90.6 (2002):

2047–2100. *JSTOR.* Web. 10 Sept. 2008.

Kumar, Sanjay. "Scientists Accuse Animal Rights Activists of Stifling Research."

British Medical Journal 23 Nov. 2002: 1192. *EBSCOhost.* Web. 12 Sept. 2008.

Note that no posting date is used with databases of printed articles. Postings are ongoing.

An Article from a Reference Source

"Prohibition." *Encyclopaedia Britannica Online.* Encyclopaedia Britannica, 2007.

Web. 16 July 2008.

An Online News Source

Associated Press. "Parents: Work Hinders Quality Time with Kids." *CNN.com*.

Cable News Network. 31 July 2003. Web. 31 July 2003.

An Article in an Online Magazine

Kinsley, Michael. "Politicians Lie. Numbers Don't." *Slate.com*. Washington Post

Company. 16 Sept. 2008. Web. 21 Sept. 2008.

A Poem from a Scholarly Project

Keats, John. "Ode to a Nightingale." *Poetical Works*. 1884. *Bartleby.com: Great*

Books. Ed. Steven van Leeuwen. Web. 2 Oct. 2008.

Information from a Government Site

United States Department of Health and Human Services. "The 2008 HHS

Poverty Guidelines." 23 Jan. 2008. Web. 23 Sept. 2008.

Information from a Professional Site

"Music Instruction Aids Verbal Memory." APA Press Release. Reporter: Agnes

S. Chan. *APA Online*. American Psychological Association. 27 July 2003.

Web. 16 Sept. 2008.

Information from a Professional Home Page or Blog

Sullivan, Andrew. "America: The Global Pioneer of Torture." *The Daily Dish*.

The Atlantic Monthly Group. 14 Sept. 2008. Web. 23 Sept. 2008.

For information from an untitled personal home page, use the label "Home page" (but not in italics or quotation marks).

Forms for Other Print and Non-print Sources

The materials in this section, although often important to research projects, do not always lend themselves to documentation by the forms illustrated above. Follow the basic order of author, title, facts of publication, and medium of publication as much as possible and add additional information as needed to make the citation clear and useful to a reader.

An Article Published in Print and on CD-ROM (or Diskette)

Detweiler, Richard A. "Democracy and Decency on the Internet." *Chronicle of*

Higher Education 28 June 1996: A40. CD-ROM. *General Periodicals Ondisc*.

UMI-Proquest. Apr. 1997.

A Work or Part of a Work on CD-ROM, Diskette, Etc.

Eseiolonis, Karyn. "Georgio de Chirico's *Mysterious Bathers.*" *A Passion for Art: Renoir, Cezanne, Matisse and Dr. Barnes.* CD-ROM. Corbis Productions, 1995.

Barclay, Donald. *Teaching Electronic Information Literacy.* Diskette. New York: Neal-Schuman, 1995.

An Audio (or Video) from a Web Site

Vachss, Andrew. "Dead and Gone." Interview by Bill Thompson. Aired on *Eye on Books,* 24 Oct. 2000. *The Zero.* Home page. Web. 25 Sept. 2008.

A Recording

Stein, Joseph. *Fiddler on the Roof.* Jerry Bock, composer. Original-Cast Recording with Zero Mostel. RCA, LSO-1093. 1964. LP.

The conductor and/or performers help identify a specific recording.

Plays or Concerts

Mourning Becomes Electra. By Eugene O'Neill. Shakespeare Theater. Washington, DC. 16 May 1997. Performance.

Principal actors, singers, musicians, and/or the director can be added as appropriate.

A Television or Radio Program

"Breakthrough: Television's Journal of Science and Medicine." PBS series hosted by Ron Hendren. 10 June 1997. Television.

An Interview

Plum, Kenneth. Personal Interview. 5 Mar. 1995.

A Lecture

Bateson, Mary Catherine. "Crazy Mixed-Up Families." Northern Virginia Community College, 26 Apr. 1997. Lecture.

An Unpublished Letter or E-mail

Usick, Patricia. Message to the author. 26 June 2005. E-mail.

Maps and Charts

Hampshire and Dorset. Map. Kent, UK: Geographers' A–Z, n.d. Print.

Cartoons and Advertisements

Halleyscope. "Halleyscopes Are for Night Owls." Advertisement. *Natural History* Dec. 1985: 15. Print.

United Airlines Advertisement. ESPN. 8 Aug. 2008. Television.

A Published Dissertation

Brotton, Joyce D. *Illuminating the Present Through Literary Dialogism: From the Reformation Through Postmodernism.* Diss. George Mason U, 2002. Ann Arbor: UMI, 2002. Print.

Government Documents

United States. Senate. Committee on Energy and Natural Resources. Subcommittee on Energy Research and Development. *Advanced Reactor Development Program: Hearing.* Washington: GPP, 24 May 1988. Print.

---. Environmental Protection Agency. *The Challenge of the Environment: A Primer on EPA's Statutory Authority.* Washington: GPO, 1972. Print.

If the author is not given, cite the name of the government first followed by the name of the department or agency. If you cite more than one document published by the same government, use the standard three hyphens followed by a period. If you cite a second document prepared by the EPA, use another three hyphens and period. Abbreviate the U.S. Government Printing Office: GPO.

If the author is known, follow this pattern:

Geller, William. *Deadly Force.* U.S. Dept. of Justice National Institute of Justice Crime File Study Guide. Washington: Dept. of Justice, n.d. Print.

Legal Documents

U.S. Const. Art. 1, sec. 3. Print.

The Constitution is referred to by article and section. Abbreviations are used. Do not use italics.

When citing a court case, give the name of the case, the volume, name, and page of the report cited, and the date. Italicize the name of the case in your text but not in the Works Cited.

Turner v. Arkansas. 407 U.S. 366. 1972. Print.

AUTHOR/YEAR OR APA STYLE

The *author/year system* identifies a source by placing the author's last name and the publication year of the source within parentheses at the point in the text where the source is cited. The in-text citations are supported by complete citations in a list of sources at the end of the paper. Most disciplines in the social sciences, biological sciences, and earth sciences use some version of the author/year style. The guidelines given here follow the style of the *Publication Manual of the American Psychological Association* (5th ed., 2002).

APA Style: In-Text Citations

The simplest parenthetical reference can be presented in one of three ways:

1. Place the year of publication within parentheses immediately following the author's name in the text.

    In a typical study of preference for motherese, Fernald (1985) used an

    operant auditory preference procedure.

    Within the same paragraph, additional references to the source do not need to repeat the year, if the researcher clearly establishes that the same source is being cited.

> Because the speakers were unfamiliar subjects Fernald's work eliminates the
>
> possibility that it is the mother's voice per se that accounts for the preference.

2. If the author is not mentioned in the text, place the author's last name followed by a comma and the year of publication within parentheses after the borrowed information.

    > The majority of working women are employed in jobs that are at least 75
    >
    > percent female (Lawrence & Matsuda, 1997).

3. Cite a specific passage by providing the page, chapter, or figure number following the borrowed material. *Always* give specific page references for quoted material.

- A brief quotation:

  > Deuzen-Smith (1988) believes that counselors must be involved with clients
  >
  > and "deeply interested in piecing the puzzle of life together" (p. 29).

- A quotation in display form:

  > Bartlett (1932) explains the cyclic process of perception:
  >
  > > Suppose I am making a stroke in a quick game, such as tennis or cricket.
  > >
  > > How I make the stroke depends on the relating of certain new experiences,
  > >
  > > most of them visual, to other immediately preceding visual experiences,
  > >
  > > and to my posture, or balance of posture, at the moment. (p. 201)

Indent a block quotation five spaces from the left margin, do not use quotation marks, and double-space throughout. To show a new paragraph within the block quotation, indent the first line of the new paragraph an additional five spaces. Note the placing of the year after the author's name, and the page number at the end of the direct quotation.

More complicated in-text citations should be handled as follows.

Two Authors, Mentioned in the Text

> Kuhl and Meltzoff (1984) tested 4- to 5-month-olds in an experiment . . .

Two Authors, Not Mentioned in the Text

> . . . but are unable to show preference in the presence of two mismatched
>
> modalities (e.g., a face and a voice; see Kuhl & Meltzoff, 1984).

Give both authors' last names each time you refer to the source. Connect their names with "and" in the text. Use an ampersand (&) in the parenthetical citation.

More Than Two Authors

For works coauthored by three, four, or five people, provide all last names in the first reference to the source. Thereafter, cite only the first author's name followed by "et al."

> As Price-Williams, Gordon, and Ramirez have shown (1969), . . .

> *OR*

> Studies of these children have shown (Price-Williams, Gordon, & Ramirez,
>
> 1969) . . .

> *THEN*

> Price-Williams et al. (1969) also found that . . .

If a source has six or more authors, use only the first author's last name followed by "et al." every time the source is cited.

Corporate Authors

In general, spell out the name of a corporate author each time it is used. If a corporate author has well-known initials, the name can be abbreviated after the first citation.

FIRST IN-TEXT CITATION:	(National Institutes of Health [NIH], 1989)
SUBSEQUENT CITATIONS:	(NIH, 1989)

Two or More Works Within the Same Parentheses

When citing more than one work by the same author in a parenthetical reference, use the author's name only once and arrange the years mentioned in order, thus:

> Several studies of ego identity formation (Marcia, 1966, 1983) . . .

When an author, or the same group of coauthors, has more than one work published in the same year, distinguish the works by adding the letters *a, b, c,* and so on, as needed, to the year. Give the last name only once, but repeat the year, each one with its identifying letter; thus:

> Several studies (Smith, 1990a, 1990b, 1990c) . . .

When citing several works by different authors within the same parentheses, list the authors alphabetically; alphabetize by the first author when citing coauthored works. Separate authors or groups of coauthors with semicolons; thus:

> Although many researchers (Archer & Waterman, 1983; Grotevant, 1983;
>
> Grotevant & Cooper, 1986; Sabatelli & Mazor, 1985) study identity
>
> formation . . .

APA STYLE: PREPARING A LIST OF REFERENCES

Every source cited parenthetically in your paper needs a complete bibliographic citation. These complete citations are placed on a separate page (or pages) after the text of the paper and before any appendices included in the paper. Sources are arranged alphabetically, and the first page is titled "References." Begin each source flush with the left margin and indent second and subsequent lines five spaces. Double-space throughout the list of references. Follow these rules for alphabetizing:

1. Organize two or more works by the same author, or the same group of coauthors, chronologically.

   Beck, A. T. (1991).

   Beck, A. T. (1993).

2. Place single-author entries before multiple-author entries when the first of the multiple authors is the same as the single author.

   Grotevant, H. D. (1983).

   Grotevant, H. D., & Cooper, C. R. (1986).

3. Organize multiple-author entries that have the same first author but different second or third authors alphabetically by the name of the second author or third and so on.

   Gerbner, G., & Gross, L.

   Gerbner, G., Gross, L., Jackson-Beeck, M., Jeffries-Fox, S., & Signorielli, N.

   Gerbner G., Gross, L., Morgan, M., & Signorielli, N.

4. Organize two or more works by the same author(s) published in the same year alphabetically by title.

Form for Books

A book citation contains these elements in this form:

   Seligman, M. E. P. (1991). *Learned optimism.* New York: Knopf.

   Weiner, B. (Ed.). (1974). *Achievement motivation and attribution theory.*

   Morristown, NJ: General Learning Press.

Authors

Give all authors' names, last name first, and initials. Separate authors with commas, use the ampersand (&) before the last author's name, and end with a period. For edited books, place the abbreviation "Ed." or "Eds." in parentheses following the last editor's name.

Date of Publication

Place the year of publication in parentheses followed by a period.

Title

Capitalize only the first word of the title and of the subtitle, if there is one, and any proper nouns. Italicize the title and end with a period. Place additional information such as number of volumes or an edition in parentheses after the title, before the period.

> Butler, R., & Lewis, M. (1982). *Aging and mental health* (3rd ed.).

Publication Information

Cite the city of publication; add the state (using the Postal Service abbreviation) or country if necessary to avoid confusion; then give the publisher's name, after a colon, eliminating unnecessary terms such as *Publisher, Co.,* and *Inc.* End the citation with a period.

> Mitchell, J. V. (Ed.). (1985). *The ninth mental measurements yearbook.* Lincoln:
>
> University of Nebraska Press.
>
> National Institute of Drug Abuse. (1993, April 13). *Annual national high school*
>
> *senior survey.* Rockville, MD: Author.
>
> Newton, D. E. (1996). *Violence and the media.* Santa Barbara: ABC-Clio.

Give a corporate author's name in full. When the organization is both author and publisher, place the word *Author* after the place of publication.

Form for Articles

An article citation contains these elements in this form:

> Changeaux, J-P. (1993). Chemical signaling in the brain. *Scientific American,*
>
> *269,* 58–62.

Date of Publication

Place the year of publication for articles in scholarly journals in parentheses, followed by a period. For articles in newspapers and popular magazines, give the year followed by month and day (if appropriate).

> (1997, March).

Title of Article

Capitalize only the title's first word, the first word of any subtitle, and any proper nouns. Place any necessary descriptive information in square brackets immediately after the title.

> Scott, S. S. (1984, December 12). Smokers get a raw deal [Letter to the Editor].

Publication Information

Cite the title of the journal in full, capitalizing according to conventions for titles. Italicize the title and follow it with a comma. Give the volume number, italicized, followed by a comma, and then inclusive page numbers followed by a period. *If* a journal begins each issue with a new page 1, then also cite the issue number in parentheses immediately following the volume number. Do not use "p." or "pp." before page numbers when citing articles from scholarly journals; do use "p." or "pp." in citations to newspaper and magazine articles.

> Martin, C. L., Wood, C. H., & Little, J. K. (1990). The development of gender
>
> stereotype components. *Child Development, 61,* 1891–1904.
>
> Leakey, R. (2000, April–May). Extinctions past and present. *Time,* p. 35.

Form for an Article or Chapter in an Edited Book

> Goodall, J. (1993). Chimpanzees—bridging the gap. In P. Cavalieri & P. Singer
>
> (Eds.), *The great ape project: Equality beyond humanity* (pp. 10–18). New
>
> York: St. Martin's.

Cite the author(s), date, and title of the article or chapter. Then cite the name(s) of the editor(s) in signature order after "In," followed by "Ed." or "Eds." in parentheses; the title of the book; the inclusive page numbers of the article or chapter, in parentheses, followed by a period. End with the city of publication and the publisher of the book.

A Report

> U.S. Merit Systems Protection Board. (1988). *Sexual harassment in the federal*
>
> *workplace: An update.* Washington, DC: U.S. Government Printing
>
> Office.

Electronic Sources

At a minimum, an APA reference for any type of Internet source should include the following information: a document title or description; dates—the date of publication or latest update and the date of retrieval—use (n.d.) for "no date" when a publication date is not available; an Internet address (the URL) that works; and, whenever possible, an author name.

Do not place URLs within angle brackets (< >). Also do not place a period at the end of a reference when a URL concludes it. If you need to break an Internet address across lines, you should break the URL only after a slash. Here are some examples:

Electronic Daily Newspaper Article Available by Search

> Schwartz, J. (2002, September 13). Air pollution con game. *Washington Times.*
>
> Retrieved from http://www.washtimes.com

Journal Article Available from a Periodical Database

Note that no URL is necessary; just provide the name of the database.

> Dixon, B. (2001, December). Animal emotions. *Ethics & the Environment, 6*(2),
>
> 22. Retrieved from Academic Search Premier database/EBSCO Host
>
> Research Databases.

U.S. Government Report on a Government Web Site

> U.S. General Accounting Office. (2002, March). *Identity theft: Prevalence and*
>
> *cost appear to be growing.* Retrieved from http://www.consumer.gov/
>
> idtheft/reports/gao-d02363.pdf

Cite a message posted to a newsgroup or electronic mailing list in the references list. Cite an e-mail from one person to another *only* in the essay, not in the list of references.

SAMPLE STUDENT ESSAY IN APA STYLE

The following pages illustrate APA style. Use 1-inch margins and double-space throughout, including any block quotations. Block quotations should be indented *five* spaces from the left margin (in contrast to the ten spaces required by MLA style). Observe the following elements: title page, running head, abstract, author/year in-text citations, subheadings within the text, and a list of references.

Sample title page
for a paper in
APA style.

Adoption: An Issue of Love, Not Race

Connie Childress

Northern Virginia Community College

Observe placement of running head and page number.

Papers in APA style usually begin with an abstract of the paper.

Abstract

Over 400,000 children are in foster care in the United States. The majority of these children are non-white. However, the majority of couples wanting to adopt children are white. While matching race or ethnic background when arranging adoptions may be the ideal, the mixing of race or ethnic background should not be avoided, or delayed, when the matching of race is not possible. Children need homes, and studies of racial adoptees show that they are as adjusted as adoptees with new parents of their own race or ethnicity. Legislation should support speedier adoptions of children, regardless of race or ethnic background.

. . .

Transracial Adoptions 4

Adoption Issues and Problems

Although interracial adoptions are "statistically rare in the United States," according to Robert S. Bausch and Richard T. Serpe (1997), who cite a 1990 study by Bachrach et al., the issue continues to receive attention from both social workers and the public (p. 137). A *New Republic* editorial (1994) lists several articles, including a cover story in *The Atlantic* in 1992, to illustrate the attention given to transracial adoptions. All of the popular-press articles as well as those in scholarly journals, the editors explain, describe the country's adoption and foster-care problems. While the great majority of families wanting to adopt are white, about half of the children in foster care waiting to be adopted are black. Robert Jackson (1995) estimates that, in 1995, about 440,000 children are being cared for in foster families. The *New Republic* editorial reports on a 1993 study revealing that "a black child in California's foster care system is three times less likely to be adopted than a white child" (p. 6). In some cases minority children have been in a single foster home with parents of a different race their entire life. They have bonded as a family. Yet, often when the foster parents apply to adopt these children, their petitions are denied and the children are removed from their care. For example, Beverly and David Cox, a white couple in Wisconsin, were asked to be foster parents to two young sisters, both African American. The Coxes provided love and nurturing for five years, but when they petitioned to adopt the two girls, not only was their request denied, but the girls were removed from their home. Can removing the children from the only home they have ever known just because of their skin color really be in the best interest of the children? Cole, Drummond, and Epperson (1995) quote Hillary Clinton as saying that "skin color [should] not outweigh the more important gift of love that adoptive parents want to offer" (p. 50).

The argument against transracial adoption has rested on the concern that children adopted by parents of a different race or ethnic background will lose

. . .

Subheadings are often used in papers in the social sciences.

Page numbers must be given for direct quotations.

Words added to a quotation for clarity are placed in square brackets.

Transracial Adoptions 9

References

All in the family [Editorial]. (1994, Jan. 24). *New Republic,* pp. 6–7.

Bausch, R. S., & Serpe, R. T. (1997). Negative outcomes of interethnic adoption

of Mexican American children. *Social Work, 42.2,* 136–43.

Blackman, A., et al. (1994, Aug. 22). Babies for export. *Time, Time On-disc*

[CD-ROM], pp. 64–65.

Bolles, E. B. (1984). *The Penguin adoption handbook: A guide to creating your new*

family. New York: Viking.

Cole, W., Drummond, T., & Epperson, S. E. (1995, Aug. 14). Adoption in black

and white. *Time,* pp. 50–51.

Davis, R. (1995, Apr. 13). Suits back interracial adoptions. *USA Today,* p. A3.

Harnack, A. (Ed.). (1995). *Adoption: Opposing viewpoints* (p. 188). San Diego:

Greenhaven.

Haun, S. (1997, Sept. 30). Personal interview.

Jackson, R. L. (1995, Apr. 25). U.S. stresses no race bias in adoptions. *Los*

Angeles Times, p. A26.

Kennedy, R., & Moseley-Braun, C. (1995). At issue: interracial adoption—is the

multiethnic placement act flawed? *ABA Journal 81, ABA Journal On-Disc*

[CD-ROM], pp. 44–45.

Kuebelbeck, A. (1996, Dec. 31). Interracial adoption debated. *AP US and World.*

Retrieved from http://www.donet.com/~brandyjc/p6at111.htm

Losing Isaiah (1995) [film].

Russell, A. T. (1995). Transracial adoptions should be forbidden. In A. Harnack,

Ed., *Adoption: Opposing viewpoints* (pp. 189–96). San Diego: Greenhaven.

Simon, R. J., Alstein, H., & Melli, M. S. (1995). Transracial adoptions should

be encouraged. In A. Harnack (Ed.), *Adoption: Opposing viewpoints*

(pp. 198–204). San Diego: Greenhaven.

Title the page
"References."

Double-space
throughout. In each
citation indent all
lines, after the first,
five spaces. Note
APA style placement
of date and format
for titles.

A Collection of Readings

This section is divided into nine chapters, each on a current topic or set of interrelated issues open to debate. The chapters contain six or seven articles, or a combination of articles and visuals, to remind us that complex issues cannot be divided into simple "for" or "against" positions. This point remains true even for the chapters on a rather specific topic. It is not sound critical thinking to be simply for or against any complicated public policy issue. No one is "for" or "against" protecting our environment, for example. The debate begins with restrictions on factories (raising costs), restrictions on car manufacturers, restrictions on energy use. It is when we get into these sorts of policy decisions, and ways of funding those decisions, that people have opposing viewpoints.

Questions follow each article to aid reading, analysis, and critical responses. In addition, each chapter opens with a visual to enjoy and then reflect on and with a set of questions to focus your thinking as you read.

The Media: Image and Reality

READ: What is the situation? Who speaks the lines?

REASON: Who, presumably, are the guys in suits sitting in front of the desk? Who, according to Wiley, must be controlling TV scheduling?

REFLECT/WRITE: What is Wiley's view of reality shows? Do you agree? Why or why not?

Although we may not agree with Marshall McLuhan that the medium itself IS the message, we still recognize the ways that the various media influence us, touching our emotions, shaping our vision of the world, altering our lives. The essays in this chapter explore and debate the effects of film and television, music and advertising, video games and the press on the ways we imagine the world and then construct our lives from those images. Surely we are influenced by media images, by the "reality" they reveal to us. The questions become how extensive is the influence, given the other influences in our lives, and what, if anything, can or should we do about it?

The chapter opens with a popular medium: the cartoon. Cartoons are not just a laugh; they present a view of life and seek to shape our thinking. Powerful messages also come to us in the print media—newspapers and magazines—in the form of photographs and advertisements. You have studied visuals in Chapter 5. In this chapter you can apply your knowledge to another color insert containing three ads and three photographs. Follow the guidelines in Chapter 5 for analyzing these visuals.

PREREADING QUESTIONS

1. How "real" are "reality" shows? Does it matter if they are scripted?
2. How accurate is our press coverage? Do media outlets around the world "see" and show the same worldview to their viewers? Do bloggers offer another useful way of seeing our world?
3. How do films reflect our world and also shape our image of that world?
4. What do the various forms of music (jazz, rock, gangsta rap) tell us about ourselves and our world? What does your music preference tell us about you?
5. How does advertising shape our images of the world? How realistic are those images? Do we want ads to be "realistic"?
6. What standards of reliability, objectivity, and fairness should be set for the media? What, if any, distortions are acceptable because they make the journalist's story more compelling?

OF LOSERS AND MOLES: YOU THINK REALITY TV JUST WRITES ITSELF? | DERRICK SPEIGHT

Derrick Speight is, as he tells us in his essay, a reality TV writer based in Los Angeles, with a dozen TV series to his credit, as story writer or supervising story producer. His scoop on the reality of reality TV shows was published in the *Washington Post*, July 24, 2005.

PREREADING QUESTIONS Do you enjoy watching reality TV shows—or know people who do? Why do you—or they—like these shows? What are the reasons usually given for enjoying these types of TV shows?

1   A couple of summers ago, I found myself living out a high school fantasy. I was running across the hot white sands of a Mexican beach in Playa

del Carmen, chasing after stunning Playboy playmate Angie Everhart. As her bright orange bikini disappeared into the Caribbean surf, I closed my eyes and smiled—then quickly snapped back to reality. I was there as a writer for ABC's "Celebrity Mole: Yucatan," and my job was to find out what Everhart was saying about the show's other beauty, former MTV VJ Ananda Lewis. Would they be dueling divas, headed for a catfight by day's end? I needed to find out. So I sighed, put on the earpiece that picked up the two women's microphones, and began taking notes.

Reality TV writers like me are at the heart of a lawsuit filed by the Writers 2 Guild of America, West about two weeks ago. On behalf of 12 such scribes, the union is charging four reality production companies and four networks with unfair labor practices, including providing pay and benefits far below those earned by writers of traditional drama and sitcoms. The suit says a lot about the rise of reality TV, a formerly disreputable format that last year contributed half of the 20 top-rated shows on TV. But in hearing about it, I imagine that people across America were asking the same question members of my own family have voiced ever since I started down this career path: "How exactly do you *write* reality? Isn't it already real?"

Yes, Grandma, it is—in all its undigested, contextless, boring glory. What 3 I do is shape that mass into something that'll make viewers want to tune in week after week. Like a journalist, I sniff out what I *think* the story will be, then craft the interviews or situations that'll draw it out. Like a paperback writer, I'm all about highlighting character and plot. Simply put, drama is the pursuit of a goal, with obstacles. Both by developing promising story lines and by pulling out the zingy moments burned in hours upon hours of ho-hum footage, reality TV writers like me—who go under various titles, including story editor and story producer—create it. As I tell my family, having a reality TV show without writers would be like having a countertop of cake ingredients but no idea how to put them together. So, yes, I consider myself a writer.

My voyage into reality TV began by accident. Seven years ago, I was new 4 to Hollywood, and sure that I was destined to direct the next film version of *Superman*. But by the time I finished my first fresh-out-of-film-school internship with DreamWorks' Mark Gordon Productions, I was both slightly peeved about not meeting Steven Spielberg and badly in need of a paying job. Luckily, a friend of a friend was looking for production assistants to work on "World's Most Amazing Videos." Hired for roughly $400 a week (and on top of the world about it), I was quickly promoted to logger—basically the guy who looks through all the footage and makes notes on what happens and when. That led to a job at a new company, Actual Reality Pictures, which would end up completely redirecting my career.

Actual Reality is the production company of Academy Award nominee 5 R.J. Cutler, whose documentary *The War Room* followed Bill Clinton's 1992 presidential campaign. The building was an intellectual hothouse, packed with scores of Ivy League grads who loved nothing more than to ruminate over the most minuscule story points. As we worked on Cutler's latest project, a docudrama about suburban Chicago teens called *American High*, staff meetings were virtual master classes in narrative structure. Whole walls of multicolored index cards were dedicated to the deconstruction of an episode, inviting constant rearranging until the optimal narrative was found. And through it all, Cutler, the faintly aloof, greatly admired genius among us, wandered the office hallways yelling, "What's the story?!" My job was to rummage through film footage looking to answer that question. Apparently, our process worked: *American High* went on to win an Emmy.

6   After I left Actual Reality, I would never again encounter that type of intense, academic scrutiny of story structure. I had risen through the ranks, though, from logger to story assistant to story producer, overseeing other writers. So I ended up going to work on a whole slew of reality TV shows, both Nielsen-topping and not, including "The Bachelor," "The Mole," "The Surreal Life," "The Benefactor" and "The Biggest Loser." On every one of them, whether I was dealing with desperately weeping single gals or former parachute pant wearer MC Hammer, the main question was always the same: "What is the story?"

7   Some of the crafting of these shows took place on set, as on "Celebrity Mole: Yucatan." While filming is taking place, writers keep track of all the issues that may arise and anticipate which will yield the strongest narrative. Teams of us are on location, assigned to different characters. The uniform: a good pen, steno notepads, an audio monitoring device (to overhear comments and conversations), a digital watch, walkie-talkies and a comfortable pair of shoes—in case anyone takes off running. We typically stand within earshot of what's being filmed, noting mumbled quips, telling looks and memorable exchanges. At the end of the day, we all regroup, compare notes and decide which stories have evolved, or are evolving. These are the situations to which we'll pay particular attention, and in the days following, we'll make sure the right interview questions are asked to round out what appear to be the prominent stories. Like nonfiction writers, we do not script lines—but if we have a hunch, we ask the right questions to follow it up.

8   Preparation of this kind is, of course, half the battle, but the magic really happens after the filming is done, in post-production. In its one- to four-week scripting phase, the story producers pinpoint scenes, moments and interviews from a mountain of VHS tapes, then structure them to tell the strongest story. After it's approved by the executive producer, this script is given to an editor, who cuts it together. Six-day workweeks and long hours are expected—and get longer midway through editing, when a decision is invariably made to change the direction of the show. As story producers, the responsibility for that reshaping falls to us. Sometimes it's for the better, but sometimes it's for worse. "The Benefactor," for example, began as an exciting, conceptually strong show led by billionaire Mark Cuban and dubbed the "Anti-Apprentice," to contrast with the Donald Trump hit. It was quickly mired by second guessing on all our parts, and we ended up giving in to some Trumpian gimmicks. In the end, the show floundered, suffering dismal ratings and was widely perceived as the very thing it was striving not to be . . . another "Apprentice."

The current lawsuit isn't the Writer's Guild's first attempt to reach out to **9** reality TV crew members. Since this spring, they've been on a major campaign to unionize, gathering up union authorization cards from over 1,000 writers, editors and producers. Despite the many logistics associated with unionizing, at the core, I believe the WGA's gesture to be quite complimentary: By their actions, they are recognizing us as legitimate creative contributors, I like that. It's also a sign that they expect reality TV to be more than just a passing fad. Reality is evolving, and I look forward to its next chapter.

QUESTIONS FOR READING

1. Who has recently filed a lawsuit? What is their issue?
2. What do reality TV writers "do" for reality TV shows? What do they try to find?
3. What strategies do these writers use during the filming? After the filming?
4. What do the lawsuit and unionizing attempts suggest about the future of reality TV?

QUESTIONS FOR REASONING AND ANALYSIS

1. The author gives much information about his job. Is providing information his primary purpose—or not? If not, why does he give us all of the details?
2. If this is not primarily or exclusively informative, then what is Speight's claim?
3. What is effective about Speight's opening paragraph?
4. Why does he include the information in the second half of paragraph 8?

QUESTIONS FOR REFLECTING AND WRITING

1. Are you surprised to learn about reality TV writers—and their complex jobs? Why or why not?
2. Are you shocked or disappointed in reading this essay? Why might some be disappointed?
3. Although some never watch them, many people are "hooked" on reality TV. Why? What is the appeal? Would the appeal be less if viewers understood how these shows are constructed?

NOTES FROM THE HIP-HOP UNDERGROUND | SHELBY STEELE

With a Ph.D. from the University of Utah, Shelby Steele is a research fellow at Stanford University's Hoover Institution. He has written many essays on race, some of which have been collected into his book *The Content of Our Character* (1990). His latest book is *A Dream Deferred: The Second Betrayal of Black Freedom in America* (1998). His essay on hip-hop music was published March 30, 2001, in the *Wall Street Journal*.

PREREADING QUESTIONS What are the traits of the mythic BN? Are you drawn to rap music? If so, why? If not, why not?

1   Think about it. If you were a slave, what sort of legend or myth would most warm your soul? One of the great legends in black American culture has always been that of the Bad Nigger. This figure flaunts the constraints, laws and taboos that bind a person in slavery. The BN is unbound and contemptuous, and takes his vengeance on the master's women simply to assert the broadest possible freedom. His very indifference to human feeling makes him a revolution incarnate. Nat Turner, a slave who in 1831 led an insurrection in which some 60 whites were massacred, was the BN come to life.

2   But for the most part, the BN is the imagination's compensation for the all-too-real impotence and confinement that slaves and segregated blacks actually endured. He lives out a compensatory grandiosity—a self-preening superiority combined with a trickster's cunning and a hyperbolic masculinity in which sexual potency is a vengeful and revolutionary force.

3   This cultural archetype, I believe, is at the center of rap or hip-hop culture. From "cop killer" Ice T, Tupac Shakur and, today most noticeably, Sean "Puffy" Combs and Eminem (who is white), we get versions of the BN in all his sneering and inflated masculinity.

4   Having beaten gun and bribery charges in a high-profile New York trial, Mr. Combs—who has just announced that he wishes to be known, henceforth, as "P. Diddy"—is the baddest BN for the moment. A man with both the entrepreneurial genius and the fortune (estimated to be in the hundreds of millions of dollars) to live far above the fray, he has nevertheless tried to live out the BN archetype in a series of ego feuds, thuggish assaults, and late-night escapades that ought to bore a man of his talent and wealth.

5   But Mr. Combs is caught in a contradiction. At the very least, he must posture, if not act out, BN themes, even as the actual condition of his life becomes conspicuously bourgeois. Rap culture essentially markets BN themes to American youth as an ideal form of adolescent rebellion. And this meeting of a black cultural archetype with the universal impulse of youth to find themselves by thumbing their nose at adults is extremely profitable. But the rappers and promoters themselves are pressured toward a thug life, simply to stay credible, by the very BN themes they sell. A rap promoter without an arrest record can start to look a lot like Dick Clark.

6   But the Puffys of the world cannot market to an indifferent youth. The important question is how the BN archetype—the slave's projection of lawless power and revenge—has become the MTV generation's metaphor for rebellion. And are conservatives right to see all this as yet more evidence of America's decline?

7   I think the answer to these questions begins in one fact: that what many of today's youth ironically share with yesterday's slave is a need for myths and images that compensate for a sense of alienation and ineffectuality.

8   Of course, today's youth do not remotely live the lives of slaves and know nothing of the alienation and impotence out of which slaves conjured the BN myth. Still, the injury to family life in America over the past 30 years (from

high divorce and illegitimacy rates, a sweeping sexual revolution, dual-career households, etc.) may well have given us the most interpersonally alienated generation in our history.

Too many of today's youth experienced a faithlessness and tenuousness 9 even in that all-important relationship with their parents. And outside the home, institutions rarely offer the constancy, structure, high expectations, and personal values they once did. So here is another kind of alienation that also diminishes and generates a sense of helplessness, that sets up the need for compensation—for an imagined self that is bigger than life, unbound, and powerful. Here the suburban white kid, gawky and materially privileged, is oddly simpatico with the black American experience.

The success of people like Mr. Combs is built on this sense of the sim- 10 patico. By some estimates, 80% of rap music is bought by white youth. And this makes for another irony. The blooming of white alienation has brought us the first generation of black entrepreneurs with wide-open access to the American mainstream. Russell Simmons, known as the "Godfather" of rap entrepreneurs, as well as Mr. Combs, Master P and others, have launched clothing lines, restaurant chains, record labels, and production companies—possibilities seeded, in a sense, by this strong new sympathy between black and white alienation.

Rap's adaptation, or update, of the BN archetype began in the post-'60s 11 black underclass. As is now well established, this was essentially a matriarchal world in which welfare-supported women became the center of households and men became satellite fathers only sporadically supporting or visiting their children by different women. The children of this world were not primed to support a music of teen romance—of "Stop in the Name of Love." The alienation was too withering. Not even the blues would do.

I think the appeal of the BN, on the deepest level, was his existential indif- 12 ference to feeling—what might be called his immunity to feeling. The slave wanted not to feel the loves and fears that bound him to other people and thus weakened him into an accommodation with slavery. Better not to love at all if it meant such an accommodation. So the BN felt nothing for anyone and had no fear even of death. He could slap a white man around with no regard for the consequences.

Rappers, too, gain freedom through immunity to feeling. Women are 13 "bitches" and "hos," objects of lust, but not of feeling. In many inner cities, where the illegitimacy rate is over 80%, where welfare has outbid the male as head of the household, where marriage is all but nonexistent, and where the decimation of drugs is everywhere—in such places, a young person of tender feelings is certain to be devastated. Everything about rap—the misogynistic lyrics, the heaving swagger, the violent sexuality, the cynical hipness—screams "I'm bad because I don't feel." Nonfeeling is freedom. And it is important to note that this has nothing to do with race. In rap, the BN nurtures indifference toward those he is most likely to love.

Conservatives have rightly attacked rap for its misogyny, violence and 14 over-the-top vulgarity. But it is important to remember that this music is a fairly accurate message from a part of society where human connections are fractured and impossible, so fraught with disappointments and pain that only an assault on human feeling itself can assuage. Rap makes the conservative argument about what happens when family life is eroded either by welfare and drugs, or by the stresses and indulgences of middle-class life.

15   I listened carefully to Eminem's recent Grammy performance expecting, I guess, to be disgusted. Instead I was drawn into a compelling rap about a boy who becomes a figure of terrible pathos. He is a male groupie who selfishly longs for the autograph of a rap star while he has his girlfriend tied up in the trunk of his car. Easy to be aghast at this until I remembered that Dostoyevsky's *Notes from the Underground*—the first modern novel written more than 150 years ago—was also about a pathetic antihero whose alienation from modernity made him spiteful and finally cruel toward an innocent female.

16   Both works protest what we all protest—societies that lose people to alienation. This does not excuse the vulgarity of rap. But the real problem is not as much rap's cartoonish bravado as what it compensates for.

QUESTIONS FOR READING

1. What, in Steele's view, does the BN compensate for?
2. Where do we find this mythic figure today?
3. How must rappers live—or appear to live—to be consistent with the BN image? What makes this a contradiction?
4. Even though today's young people have no concept of a slave life, they are still drawn to hip-hop. Why?

QUESTIONS FOR REASONING AND ANALYSIS

1. Steele writes that conservatives are correct when they complain about the language and attitudes of rap music. Why does he include this statement?
2. Examine the author's handling of rap language and his key term. How does he write concretely while showing concern for his readers?
3. Steele writes that "the appeal of the BN . . . was his existential indifference to feeling." What does he mean by this statement?
4. What are some of the causes, today, for feelings of alienation?
5. What is Steele's claim?

QUESTIONS FOR REFLECTION AND WRITING

1. Is Steele's concept of the mythic BN, as it relates to modern rap music, a new idea for you? Does it make sense? Why or why not?
2. Do you agree with the author's analysis of the causes of white youth's alienation? If not, how do you account for the appeal of rap for white, suburban youth?

THE BLOGS MUST BE CRAZY | PEGGY NOONAN

A contributing editor of the *Wall Street Journal* and weekly columnist for the *Journal's* editorial page Web site, Peggy Noonan is the author of seven books, including *The Case Against Hillary Clinton* (2000) and *A Heart, a Cross, and a Flag* (2003). The following column appeared February 17, 2005.

PREREADING QUESTIONS Do you regularly read a newspaper? If not, why not? And, how do you obtain news?

1 "Salivating morons." "Scalp hunters." "Moon howlers." "Trophy hunters." "Sons of Sen. McCarthy." "Rabid." "Blogswarm." "These pseudo-journalist lynch mob people."

2 This is excellent invective. It must come from bloggers. But wait, it was the mainstream media and their maidservants in the elite journalism reviews, and they were talking about bloggers!

3 Those MSMers have gone wild, I tell you! The tendentious language, the low insults. It's the Wild Wild West out there. We may have to consider legislation.

4 When you hear name-calling like what we've been hearing from the elite media this week, you know someone must be doing something right. The hysterical edge makes you wonder if writers for newspapers and magazines and professors in J-schools don't have a serious case of freedom envy.

5 The bloggers have that freedom. They have the still pent-up energy of a liberated citizenry, too. The MSM doesn't. It has lost its old monopoly on information. It is angry.

6 But MSM criticism of the blogosphere misses the point, or rather points.

7 Blogging changes how business is done in American journalism. The MSM isn't over. It just can no longer pose as if it is The Guardian of Established Truth. The MSM is just another player now. A big one, but a player.

8 The blogosphere isn't some mindless eruption of wild opinion. That isn't their power. This is their power:

9 1. They use the tools of journalists (computer, keyboard, a spirit of inquiry, a willingness to ask the question) and of the Internet (Google, LexisNexis) to look for and find facts that have been overlooked, ignored or hidden. They look for the telling quote, the ignored statistic, the data that have been submerged. What they are looking for is information that is true. When they get it they post it and include it in the debate. This is a public service.

10 2. Bloggers, unlike reporters at elite newspapers and magazines, are independent operators. They are not, and do not have to be, governed by mainstream thinking. Nor do they have to accept the directives of an editor pushing an ideology or a publisher protecting his friends. Bloggers have the freedom to decide on their own when a story stops being a story. They get to decide when the search for facts is over. They also decide on their own when the search for facts begins. It was a blogger at the World Economic Forum, as we all know, who first reported the Eason Jordan story. It was bloggers, as we all know, who pursued it. Matt Drudge runs a news site and is not a

blogger, but what was true of him at his beginning (the Monica Lewinsky story, he decided, is a story) is true of bloggers: It's a story if they say it is. This is a public service.

11   3. Bloggers have an institutional advantage in terms of technology and form. They can post immediately. The items they post can be as long or short as they judge to be necessary. Breaking news can be one sentence long: "Malkin gets Barney Frank earwitness report." In newspapers you have to go to the editor, explain to him why the paper should have another piece on the Eason Jordan affair, spend a day reporting it, only to find that all that's new today is that reporter Michelle Malkin got an interview with Barney Frank. That's not enough to merit 10 inches of newspaper space, so the *Times* doesn't carry what the blogosphere had 24 hours ago. In the old days a lot of interesting information fell off the editing desk in this way. Now it doesn't. This is a public service.

12   4. Bloggers are also selling the smartest take on a story. They're selling an original insight, a new area of inquiry. Mickey Kaus of Kausfiles has his bright take, Andrew Sullivan had his, InstaPundit has his. They're all selling their shrewdness, experience, depth. This too is a public service.

13   5. And they're doing it free. That is, the *Times* costs me a dollar and so does the *Journal,* but Kausfiles doesn't cost a dime. This too is a public service. Some blogs get their money from yearly fund-raising, some from advertisers, some from a combination, some from a salary provided by *Slate* or *National Review.* Most are labors of love. Some bloggers—a lot, I think—are addicted to digging, posting, coming up with the bright phrase. OK with me. Some get burned out. But new ones are always coming up, so many that I can't keep track of them and neither can anyone else.

14   But when I read blogs, when I wake up in the morning and go to About Last Night and Lucianne and Lileks, I remember what the late great Christopher Reeve said on "The Tonight Show" 20 years ago. He was the second guest, after Rodney Dangerfield. Dangerfield did his act and he was hot as a pistol. Then after Reeve sat down Dangerfield continued to be riotous. Reeve looked at him, gestured toward him, looked at the audience and said with grace and delight, "Do you believe this is free?" The audience cheered. That's how I feel on their best days when I read blogs.

15   That you get it free doesn't mean commerce isn't involved, for it is. It is intellectual commerce. Bloggers give you information and point of view. In return you give them your attention and intellectual energy. They gain influence by drawing your eyes; you gain information by lending your eyes. They become well-known and influential; you become entertained or informed. They get something from it and so do you.

16   6. It is not true that there are no controls. It is not true that the blogosphere is the Wild West. What governs members of the blogospheres is what governs to some degree members of the MSM, and that is the desire for status and respect. In the blogosphere you lose both if you put forward as fact information that is incorrect, specious or cooked. You lose status and respect if your take on a story is patently stupid. You lose status and respect if you are

unprofessional or deliberately misleading. And once you've lost a sufficient amount of status and respect, none of the other bloggers link to you anymore or raise your name in their arguments. And you're over. The great correcting mechanism for people on the Web is people on the Web.

There are blogs that carry political and ideological agendas. But everyone 17 is on to them and it's mostly not obnoxious because their agendas are mostly declared.

7. I don't know if the blogosphere is rougher in the ferocity of its per- 18 sonal attacks than, say, Drew Pearson. Or the rough boys and girls of the great American editorial pages of the 1930s and '40s. Bloggers are certainly not as rough as the splenetic pamphleteers of the 18th and 19th centuries, who amused themselves accusing Thomas Jefferson of sexual perfidy and Andrew Jackson of having married a whore. I don't know how Walter Lippmann or Scotty Reston would have seen the blogosphere; it might have frightened them if they'd lived to see it. They might have been impressed by the sheer digging that goes on there. I have seen friends savaged by blogs and winced for them—but, well, too bad. I've been attacked. Too bad. If you can't take it, you shouldn't be thinking aloud for a living. The blogosphere is tough. But are personal attacks worth it if what we get in return is a whole new media form that can add to the true-information flow while correcting the biases and lapses of the mainstream media? Yes. Of course.

I conclude with a few predictions. 19

Some brilliant rising young reporter with a growing reputation at the 20 *Times* or *Newsweek* or *Post* is going to quit, go into the blogging business, start *The Daily Joe,* get someone to give him a guaranteed ad for two years, and become a journalistic force. His motive will be influence, and the use of his gifts along the lines of excellence. His blog will further legitimize blogging.

Most of the blogstorms of the past few years have resulted in outcomes 21 that left and right admit or bray were legitimate. Dan Rather fell because his big story was based on a fabrication, Trent Lott said things that it could be proved he said. But coming down the pike is a blogstorm in which the bloggers turn out to be wrong. Good news: They'll probably be caught and exposed by bloggers. Bad news: It will show that blogging isn't nirvana, and its stars aren't foolproof. But then we already know that, don't we?

Some publisher is going to decide that if you can't fight blogs, you can 22 join them. He'll think like this: *We're already on the Internet. That's how blog- gers get and review our reporting. Why don't we get our own bloggers to challenge our work? Why don't we invite bloggers who already exist into the tent? Why not take the best things said on blogs each day and print them on a Daily Blog page? We'd be enhancing our rep as an honest news organization, and it will further our branding!*

Someone is going to address the "bloggers are untrained journalists" 23 question by looking at exactly what "training," what education in the art/ science/craft/profession of journalism, the reporters and editors of the MSM have had in the past 60 years or so. It has seemed to me the best of them never went to J-school but bumped into journalism along the way—walked into a radio station or newspaper one day and found their calling. Bloggers signify a welcome return to that old style. In journalism you learn by doing, which is what a lot of bloggers are doing.

24   Finally, someday in America the next big bad thing is going to happen, and lines are going to go down, and darkness is going to descend, and the instant communication we now enjoy is going to be compromised. People in one part of the country are going to wonder how people in another part are doing. Little by little lines are going to come up, and people are going to log on, and they're going to get the best, most comprehensive, and ultimately, just because it's there, most heartening information from . . . some lone blogger out there. And then another. They're going to do some big work down the road.

QUESTIONS FOR READING

1.   Why are mainstream journalists so upset? About whom are they complaining?

2.   What are the specific sources of power for bloggers? State Noonan's seven points in your own words.

3.   What predictions does the author make about the future of bloggers? State her five predictions in your own words.

QUESTIONS FOR REASONING AND ANALYSIS

1.   What is Noonan's claim? State it so as to include both the idea of bloggers' strengths and their predicted future.

2.   What makes Noonan's opening effective? What organizational and other rhetorical strategies are used to good effect?

3.   How would you describe the author's tone? How does her tone support her purpose?

QUESTIONS FOR REFLECTING AND WRITING

1.   Do you read bloggers? If so, how often? If not, has Noonan sparked your interest in checking them out? Explain.

2.   Should mainstream journalists feel threatened by bloggers—or inspired to work harder? Or, should they ignore them as a curiosity that will not last? Defend your position.

LEADING MEN: LOOKING AT PRESIDENTIAL CONTENDERS THROUGH A HOLLYWOOD LENS | STEPHEN HUNTER

A film critic for more than twenty years, first for the *Baltimore Sun* and then the *Washington Post*, Stephen Hunter has won a Pulitzer Prize for Criticism. He is also the author of many complex thriller novels, most recently *Night of Thunder* (2008). The following essay appeared in the *Post* on July 6, 2008, early in the presidential campaign.

PREREADING QUESTIONS To what movie stars would you compare Senator McCain? And to what movie stars would you compare Senator Obama?

Wonderful moment in John Ford's *The Searchers,* from way back in 1956:   1
John Wayne, as the surly, violent Ethan Edwards, signals to his young compadre that it's time to move on in their pursuit of Scar, the Comanche chief who's murdered their family and kidnapped the youngest daughter, Debbie.

"Let's go, blankethead," he scowls to the young Martin Pawley.   2

I love the Duke's pronunciation of the word "blankethead"; it *radiates* con-   3
tempt for the young and the untested. Ethan is using the blast of scorn to tell the young man not only to get going to his horse but to get going in growing up, to acquire sand, grit, salt and all the other granular metaphors for old-guy toughness and savvy. Blankethead: It's a three-syllable telegram on the theme of the fecklessness of youth, and nobody but Wayne could turn it into poetry.

But in the same instant, I remember Will Smith in the original *Men in Black.*   4
The hotshot young cop has been recruited to an alien-hunting team secretly HQ'd in a New York bridge, and now he's working for Tommy Lee Jones and Rip Torn. Torn and Jones are babbling about something and not paying attention to Smith. There's a moment of frustration on the young face, and he interrupts with his own blast of scorn: "Hey, *old guys!*"

It's a voice full of impatience, annoyance, even contempt, suggesting they   5
haven't the energy, the quickness or the attention span to take care of business. It's on him, now, the new guy, the kid: He's got to keep them from wandering off, losing track, drifting as the old are wont to do.

Both those moments come to mind when contemplating the politics of   6
the day. That's because, while the next few months can be dissected from many angles, the template that the Obama-McCain race seems to demand is familiar to anyone who has paid the slightest attention to popular culture over the years: old star/young star.

We seem to be at the classic moment when one generation of stars, with   7
their traditions of heroism, beauty, grace, sexiness, their connection to old values, directly confronts the next generation, which, of course, also has traditions of heroism, beauty, grace, sexiness and connection to values, except they're entirely different. It's not hard to see Sen. John McCain calling the young, fresh-faced Sen. Barack Obama a "blankethead," just as it's easy to imagine Obama interrupting his opponent in a debate with a hectoring, "Hey, *old guy.*"

You might consider it a lobbying effort not to win an election but to get   8
a starring role in "The Next Four Years." And the star thing that you will contemplate is contrived of two elements: *image,* as polished and packaged by PR and advertising professionals, but also a kind of *truth* the camera yields not because of the advisers, but in spite of them, sometimes in counterpoint to the official image. Trying to keep track of what the camera reveals—both on purpose and by accident—is like looking at audition clips back in the old days with a bunch of studio scouts, like the one who (possibly apocryphally) concluded about Fred Astaire, "Can't sing. Can't act. Balding. Can dance a little."

9   So put your feet up, light a cigar, nurse a Scotch and consider in the flicker of the images: Do you want the old guy with his known values, strengths and weaknesses? Many producers have trod that path, and the best thing that can be said is that sometimes it works and sometimes it doesn't. Or do you want the new guy, the fresh face, with the excitement and the sense of possibilities? It works, too. It also fails, too.

10   His image engineers want you to see a twinkly fellow, quick-moving given his age, his scars worn proudly, speaking quietly of experience. It almost works. When you look at McCain's battered face and his movie-star-stunning wife (blond, blue-eyed beauty) it's hard not to see a Duke Wayne, a Robert Mitchum, even a Harrison Ford. He seems, at times, put together from parts of various stars or their roles. He has the star's masculine charm. As a young aviator, he was studly enough to date a stripper. And as an older guy, he was cool enough to marry a woman who was probably the most beautiful rich one or the richest beautiful one in the world. Nobody will write this anywhere except me here, but we guys, you know what: We admire another guy for making a great catch.

11   He's still attractive and, old-star vanity, especially if the camera hides his shortness (he's 5-foot-9), as it did for the 5-foot-6 Alan Ladd, among others. His private mien is that of any of the macho '30s type: a jokester who on his "Straight Talk Express" was famous for the high level of hilarity he produced among reporters with an endless torrent of dirty stories.

He has, of course, Wayne's rage (the famous temper) and impatience. He 12 was formed by an extremely hard-knock system, first at Annapolis, then at flight school, then in battle, then in prison camp and torture, and finally, for 23 years, in politics. He seems like one of those alpha dogs that others kind of fear because he actually likes to fight. He doesn't fear confrontation or force like most of us; he considers their application *fun.* That makes him cool; that also makes him scary. He's like a gun in the house: unnerving, but when you need it, baby, does it feel good.

But behind it all, even the image experts can't banish the maybe too- 13 intense gleam in his eyes, and when he slides into his occasional slow, quiet cadences—remonstrating against Wesley Clark's comments on his "limited" qualifications last week—perhaps it's because he's strangling the fury that's within him. Did all those hard knocks unhinge him? What about his small-man's bellicosity? Will he crack under pressure like Bogart's Queeg, or will he hang tough forever, just like the Duke's Sgt. Stryker, even when his men hate his guts? Is violence—having dropped bombs and having been tortured—too easy a solution for him?

He'd be the only president in years and years who has actually killed peo- 14 ple, for when he flipped the toggle on his Skyhawk and dropped a couple of 500-pounders down toward some ridge or factory or SAM installation, and when they detonated, you know that people died by his direct agency, though the names are lost forever. That's a movie-star thing, isn't it: the willingness to kill? Look how much good it did the Duke or Clint Eastwood. They shot their way to the top. But while we admire that as an expression of machismo in a tight little world of fabricated melodrama, do we want it in a president today?

McCain's warriorhood, once a key star attribute, now comes freighted with 15 ambiguity. He lived up to the faith of his father and never questioned it, but today a lot of people can't endorse it without caveat and context; there's less enthusiasm for killing and killers these days, and McCain acknowledges this by stressing his suffering in wartime captivity, not his killing in wartime missions.

Yet that, too, is an issue that cuts a certain way with Obama, both as poli- 16 tician and star, and it has to be one of the issues the camera shows even as his advisers would prefer not to deal with it. Can he deploy force? He seems to hate it. Smooth, unflappable, rational, he's not quite the hopeless dork Dukakis became in that tank with the I'd-rather-be-anywhere-else expression, but still he lacks the physicality of gravitas, the imprimatur of hard-earned wisdom, and much in the way of physical commanding presence. He'd never call anyone a blankethead; he's too rational for that. He's so thin, almost spidery, he doesn't seem to cast much of a shadow. He slides, he doesn't stride. Has he ever been in a fight? Can he take a punch? Does he get nervous when people are yelling at him? Hard to say.

In movie terms, he's the new thing, the star who doesn't do his own 17 killing (see, for example, Denzel Washington in *Devil in a Blue Dress,* in which Don Cheadle comes along to take care of the dirty business). And when we look at Obama, what we see is a kind of pre-muscled-up Will Smith, the Will Smith of easy charm and suave conviction, a canoodler, a persuader. But a star needs to be able to clean up Dodge, no? Remember, John Travolta saved his career by going to the guns in Quentin Tarantino's *Pulp Fiction.*

18   It's his very newness that seems to make him a star and attract all that love and all that money. He's not from the old war-and-politics mill, and he represents himself as someone forged in a new crucible, a multiracial, internationalist upbringing, which gives him a unique, almost mystical insight and which he uses to underpin his claims of being different, not just a business-as-usual pol. It'll be fascinating to see if the performance that played so well in the Democratic primaries will galvanize a nation composed of many people not self-selected to respond to that message. And if he begins to fade, will he himself lose faith and become just another pol?

19   In Hollywood terms, he recalls the early '70s, when the old, handsome, conservative stars gave way to young actors with names like Pacino, Hoffman and De Niro, who were far from classically symmetrical with shiny meadows of Brylcreemed hair, but instead shaggy, ethnic, full of unusual rhythms and vulnerabilities and with no interest in killing Indians or blowing up Nazi dams. But then they became a new Establishment on their own, as did their directors; and now they too are being replaced.

20   It's certainly true that Obama has movie virtues that poor McCain lacks: great teeth, for example, and a big-featured, extremely expressive face. He looks sensitive; you'll never see contempt or implicit supremacy on that smooth, adorable mug. He has an orator's voice, a command of mellifluous rhythms, where poor McCain's voice and laugh are nasal, and feel crimped and nerdy. But alas, there's nothing granular about him, no grit, no salt, no sand. The ears, comic fodder for some, actually help him by giving his looks uniqueness. He's also exceedingly graceful, which the camera picks up. The footage of him driving to the hoop after a juke, controlling his body through traffic as he rises to the rim and lays off an easy two, is priceless and probably worth a million votes, as any ballplayer will recognize the assurance of natural hand-eye.

21   He's likable, but is that enough? Americans can like a star—look how far Tom Hanks has gotten—but it's an exception, a special case. Obama will last longer if he's respected. Running for office is incredibly demanding, true; Obama's a real smart guy and he'll quickly acquire the discipline that prevents him from saying "I've visited all 57 states."

22   Obama's at the clutch of a star's career crisis. He's had his breakthrough. He needs another starring movie to consolidate. Yet the scrutiny will be upgraded, the audience is larger, and rumors are starting to dog him as they do all stars. So it remains to be seen who will get the big role in "The Next Four Years"—and maybe the sequel "The Next Next Four Years."

23   You casting agents out there have to make a decision.

QUESTIONS FOR READING

1. To what stars does Hunter compare Senator McCain? Why? What does he have in common with them—or what does he want us to see in him?
2. What does McCain also have that Wayne had? What experience has he had that no recent president has had? Why does Hunter see this as "freighted with ambiguity"?
3. To whom does Hunter compare Obama? What movie star qualities does Obama have? What physical traits does Hunter emphasize?
4. What, according to Hunter, does Obama need besides being likable?

QUESTIONS FOR REASONING AND ANALYSIS

1. Hunter opens with two moments in a movie, one that seems to sum up McCain, another that captures Obama. What is clever about this opening?
2. Hunter uses many rhetorical questions. Are they effective? How can they be justified?
3. What is the author's claim? Where does he state it?

QUESTIONS FOR REFLECTION AND WRITING

1. Hunter turns over the "casting" to his readers. Does this ending work? Is it consistent with Hunter's purpose? Explain.
2. We know that movies reflect our times; how do they also shape our times? What recent movies have been the most influential, in your view? How have they contributed to modern culture?

WHAT'S UP DOC? A BLOODY OUTRAGE, THAT'S WHAT | KATHERINE ELLISON

A Pulitzer Prize–winning former foreign correspondent for Knight-Ridder Newspapers, Katherine Ellison is the author of three nonfiction books. Her latest is *The Mommy Brain: How Motherhood Makes Us Smarter* (2005). Her reaction to violent Internet cartoons appeared on October 23, 2005, in the *Washington Post*.

PREREADING QUESTIONS Do you use the Internet for "fun": games, porn, violent cartoons? Do you see any problems with such Internet sites?

The other day I found my 6-year-old son watching an Internet cartoon 1 called "Happy Tree Friends."

Purple daisies danced, high-pitched voices sang and animals with heart- 2 shaped noses waved cheerily. But then the music changed, and a previously merry green bear, wearing dog tags and camouflage, suffered an apparent psychotic breakdown.

Crrrrrack!! went the neck of a purple badger, as the bear snapped off its 3 head. Blood splashed and continued flowing as the bear gleefully garroted a

hedgehog, then finished off a whimpering squirrel already impaled on metal spikes by placing a hand grenade in its paw.

4   Joshua turned to me with a sheepish grin. He clearly had a sense that I wasn't happy about his new friends, but he couldn't have known what I was really thinking. Which was this: I'm a longtime journalist who reveres the First Amendment, and I live in California's liberal bastion of Marin County. Yet I would readily skip my next yoga class to march with right-wing fundamentalists in a cultural war against "Happy Tree Friends."

5   Just when parents thought we knew who our electronic enemies were—the shoot-'em-up video games, the TVs hawking trans fats, the pedophile e-mail stalkers and teenage-boobs Web sites—here comes this new swamp-thing mass entertainment: the Internet "Flash cartoon," pared down to pure shock value. Its music and animation are tuned to the Teletubbies set—that's its "joke." Its faux warning, "Cartoon Violence: Not for Small Children or Big Babies" is pure come-on—for those who can read. And it's easy to watch over and over again, reinforcing its empathy-dulling impact. That makes it particularly harmful to young psyches, UCLA neuroscientist Marco Iacoboni told me, because children are prompted to copy what they see—especially what they see over and over again. "Not only do you get exposed and desensitized; you're primed, facilitated, almost invited to act that way," maintains Iacoboni, whose expertise in the brain dynamics of imitation makes him an outspoken critic of media mayhem.

6   "Happy Tree Friends" appears tailor-made to sneak under the radar of blocking software (which can't filter images), unless parents are somehow Internet-savvy enough to know about the site and specifically ban it in advance.

And it's certainly suited for the kind of viral contagion that caught up with my 6-year-old, who learned of the site from his 9-year-old brother, who first saw it over the shoulder of a teenage summer camp counselor.

But the bottom line is, well, the bottom line. In its web-cartoon class, 7 "Happy Tree Friends" is a humongous moneymaker, as irresistible to big advertisers as it is to 6-year-olds. At last count, the site was drawing 15 million unique viewers a month, reaping $300,000 or more in ads for each new episode. It recently snagged a place on cable TV, while spawning DVDs, trademark mints, T-shirts and, inevitably, a planned video game.

Internet cartoons had their defining moment with the hilarious "This 8 Land Is Your Land" 2004 election-year parody, featuring George W. Bush calling John Kerry a "liberal wiener" and Kerry calling Bush a "right-wing nut job" to the famous Woody Guthrie tune. By then, the beaten-down Web ad industry was already starting to ride a dramatic recovery, thanks to burgeoning new content and the increasing prevalence of high-quality, high-speed connections. The trend has brought some truly interesting material—and also such savage fare as the graphic cartoon "Gonads & Strife" and another inviting you to repeatedly electrocute a gerbil in a light socket. The Bush-Kerry feature by some reports was the most popular cartoon ever."Happy Tree Friends," now in its fifth, most successful, year may well be the most lucrative.

Its narrative is as primitive as its business plan. In every episode, the cute 9 creatures are introduced, after which something awful happens to them, either by gruesome accident, or at the paws of the psychopathic bear. The wordless content appeals to a global audience, enhancing an already remarkably efficient delivery system for advertising. There's a running ad before each episode, while banners flash below and beside the cartoons.

The show itself reportedly began as a potential ad—ironically, *against* 10 media violence according to Kenn Navarro, its co-creator. Navarro came up with the idea while designing an eight-second spot for an educational company, to illustrate what kids *shouldn't* be watching. Indeed, 30 years of extensive research underscores the link between TV violence and increased violent behavior among viewers. One study equates the impact as larger than that of asbestos exposure to cancer—a health risk that certainly moved our society to act. But try telling that to "Happy Tree Friends" Executive Producer John Evershed, CEO of Mondo Media in San Francisco.

Evershed, the father of three children, the youngest aged 2, told me 11 during a phone conversation that he wouldn't let them watch "Happy Tree Friends." But then he argued that the cartoon wasn't really harmful. "It's like 'Tom & Jerry,'" he said. "I grew up on 'Tom & Jerry,' and I don't think I'm particularly aggressive."

Aggressive? AGGRESSIVE? Much as I'd like to, I can't fairly speak for Ever- 12 shed on this point, but I certainly do worry about the impact on my children. As for "Tom & Jerry," I know "Tom & Jerry," and this is no "Tom & Jerry." "Tom & Jerry" never pulled knives or tore heads off or used someone's intestines to strangle a third party, just for starters.

13   "Tom & Jerry" also had creativity, with surprising plot twists and a richly emotive score. Most importantly, "Tom & Jerry" had a conscience. Routinely, Tom attacks Jerry and is punished for his aggression. In terms of human evolution, the 1940s classic is light-years ahead of "Happy Tree Friends," whose authors, Navarro and Rhode Montijo, have been quoted as saying, "If we are in a room brainstorming episodes and end up laughing at the death scene, then it's all good!"

14   Mad as I am, I'm actually not suggesting that the feds step in and ban this cartoon. The basic freedom of the Internet is too precious, and government censorship too risky and probably not even feasible. The current rules—restrictions on the major airwaves, but anything goes on the Web—will have to do.

15   But what about the big mainstream advertisers who've made "Happy Tree Friends" such a wild success? I was startled, while watching the cartoon, to see banner ads for companies including Toyota and Kaiser Permanente (which has a new campaign they call "Thrive." Thrive, indeed!). Consumers ought to be able to raise a stink, threaten a reputation, even wage boycotts in the face of such irresponsibility. But many Internet ads enjoy the escape clause of being random and ephemeral, as I found out when I called Hilary Weber, Kaiser's San Francisco-based head of Internet marketing. Weber said she couldn't even confirm that her company's ad had appeared.

16   "I can't replicate it," she said, adding that it would "take a lot of research" to establish whether Kaiser indeed had purchased such an ad. That, she explained, is because Kaiser, like many other big corporations, buys bulk ads through third parties—saving money, yet relinquishing control over where the ads end up.

17   Weber said she was concerned about Kaiser's reputation and planned to investigate further, yet declined to tell me the names of the third-party companies placing the firm's ads. So I then turned to Mika Salmi, CEO of Atom Shockwave, which manages the ads on "Happy Tree Friends." Salmi, on his cell phone, said he couldn't, with confidence, name the third-party companies with whom he contracts, though he thought one "might" be Advertising.com. But when I contacted Lisa Jacobson, Advertising.com's spokeswoman, she declined to name advertisers not already listed on her firm's Web page. "We actually don't think we're the best fit for this piece," Jacobson wrote me by e-mail. "You'll probably need to speak with companies like Kaiser and Toyota directly. But thanks for thinking of us . . ."

18   In our brief telephone conversation, Evershed told me he thinks parents have the ultimate responsibility to shield their kids from media violence. In the abstract, I certainly agree with that, but I admit I sometimes wonder if I'm actually doing my kids a disservice by spending so much time and energy chasing them off the Internet, while coaching them in empathy, manners and the Golden Rule. Because if most of their peers, who lack the luxury of moms with time to meddle, are gorging on "Happy Tree Friends," it would probably serve them better to be trained to defend themselves with firearms and karate.

19   Still, for now at least, I refuse to be overwhelmed by the sheer magnitude of what society expects from parents, with so little support in return.

So I'd like to offer just two public suggestions. Why can't summer camps 20 and afterschool programs more closely supervise Internet use? And why can't Kaiser and other big companies start crafting contracts that specifically stipulate that their ads never, ever end up on sites like "Happy Tree Friends"?

Meanwhile, I'm talking to other parents because the first step in this peace- 21 ful war is to realize we're not alone. Together, we may even manage to subvert our culture's embrace of shock for shock's sake, one gory excess at a time.

QUESTIONS FOR READING

1. "Happy Tree Friends" is Ellison's primary example; what is her subject?
2. What is the problem with "Happy Tree Friends"? How does it differ from "Tom & Jerry"?
3. How did the author's 6-year-old discover the cartoon?
4. What did the author's research reveal about the Web site's advertisers?
5. What suggestions for change does Ellison propose?

QUESTIONS FOR REASONING AND ANALYSIS

1. What does Ellison *not* want to happen to the Internet? Why?
2. What is her claim?
3. In paragraph 18, Ellison writes that her sons might be better off with "firearms and karate" than encouragement in empathy and the Golden Rule. Does she really mean this? Why does she write it?

QUESTIONS FOR REFLECTING AND WRITING

1. Do you think that Ellison's suggestions will be helpful? Why or why not?
2. Should there be federal controls on Internet content? Why or why not?
3. If there are no controls, how will we protect youngsters from unhealthy sites? Or, should we not worry about protecting them? Explain and defend your position.

IN YOUR FACE . . . ALL OVER THE PLACE! | JEAN KILBOURNE

Writer and speaker Jean Kilbourne has been a visiting scholar at Wellesley College and an adviser on alcohol and tobacco advertising to two surgeons general. She is the author of *Can't Buy My Love* (2000) and editor of *Media Sharp* (2000). The following excerpt is from her book, *Deadly Persuasion*, published in 1999.

PREREADING QUESTIONS We know that TV shows are filled with stereotypes; what about advertising? Think about print or TV ads; what kinds of stereotypes come to mind?

In spite of the fact that we are surrounded by more advertising than ever 1 before, most of us still ridicule the idea that we might be personally influenced by it. The ridicule is often extremely simplistic. The argument essentially is,

"I'm no robot marching down to the store to do advertising's bidding and therefore advertising doesn't affect me at all." This argument was made by Jacob Sullum, a senior editor at *Reason* magazine, in an editorial in the *New York Times.* Writing about "heroin chic," the advertising fad in the mid-1990s of using models who looked like heroin addicts, Sullum says, "Like you, I've seen . . . ads featuring sallow, sullen, scrawny youths. Not once have I had an overwhelming urge to rush out and buy some heroin." He concludes from this in-depth research that all critics of advertising are portraying "people not as independent moral agents but as mindless automatons," as if there were no middle ground between rushing out to buy heroin and being completely uninfluenced by the media images that surround us—or no possibility that disaffected teens are more vulnerable than middle-aged executives. After all, Sullum is *not* the target audience for heroin chic ads.

2   Of course, most of us feel far superior to the kind of person who would be affected by advertising. *We* are not influenced, after all. We are skeptical, even cynical . . . but ignorant (certainly not stupid, just uninformed). Advertising is familiar, but not known. The fact that we are surrounded by it, that we can sing the jingles and identify the models and recognize the logos, doesn't mean that we are educated about it, that we understand it. As Sut Jhally says, "To not be influenced by advertising would be to live outside of culture. No human being lives outside of culture."

3   Advertisers want us to believe that we are not influenced by ads. As Joseph Goebbels said, "This is the secret of propaganda: Those who are to be persuaded by it should be completely immersed in the ideas of the propaganda, without ever noticing that they are being immersed in it." So the advertisers sometimes play upon our cynicism. In fact, they co-opt our cynicism and our irony just as they have co-opted our rock music, our revolutions and movements for liberation, and our concern for the environment. In a current trend that I call "anti-advertising," the advertisers flatter us by insinuating that we are far too smart to be taken in by advertising. Many of these ads spoof the whole notion of image advertising. A scotch ad tells the reader "This is a glass of Cutty Sark. If you need to see a picture of a guy in an Armani suit sitting between two fashion models drinking it before you know it's right for you, it probably isn't."

4   And an ad for shoes says, "If you feel the need to be smarter and more articulate, read the complete works of Shakespeare. If you like who you are, here are your shoes." Another shoe ad, this one for sneakers, says, "Shoe buying rule number one: The image wears off after the first six miles." What a concept. By buying heavily advertised products, we can demonstrate that we are not influenced by advertising. Of course, this is not entirely new. Volkswagens were introduced in the 1960s with an anti-advertising campaign, such as the ad that pictured the car and the headline "Lemon." But such ads go a lot further these days, especially the foreign ones. A British ad for Easy jeans says, "We don't use sex to sell our jeans. We don't even screw you when you buy them." And French Connection UK gets away with a double-page spread that says "fcuk advertising."

Cynicism is one of the worst effects of advertising. Cynicism learned from 5 years of being exposed to marketing hype and products that never deliver the promised goods often carries over to other aspects of life. This starts early: A study of children done by researchers at Columbia University in 1975 found that heavy viewing of advertising led to cynicism, not only about advertising, but about life in general. The researchers found that "in most cultures, adolescents have had to deal with social hypocrisy and even with institutionalized lying. But today, TV advertising is stimulating *preadolescent* children to think about socially accepted hypocrisy. They may be too young to cope with such thoughts without permanently distorting their views of morality, society, and business." They concluded that "7- to 10-year-olds are strained by the very existence of advertising directed to them." These jaded children become the young people whose mantra is "whatever," who admire people like David Letterman (who has made a career out of taking nothing seriously), whose response to almost every experience is "been there, done that," "duh," and "do ya think?" Cynicism is not criticism. It is a lot easier than criticism. In fact, easy cynicism is a kind of naivete. We need to be more critical as a culture and less cynical.

Cynicism deeply affects how we define our problems and envision their 6 solutions. Many people exposed to massive doses of advertising both distrust every possible solution *and* expect a quick fix. There are no quick fixes to the problems our society faces today, but there are solutions to many of them. The first step, as always, is breaking through denial and facing the problems squarely. I believe it was James Baldwin who said, "Not everything that is faced can be changed, but nothing can be changed until it is faced." One of the things we need to face is that we and our children are indeed influenced by advertising.

Although some people, especially advertisers, continue to argue that 7 advertising simply reflects the society, advertising does a great deal more than simply reflect cultural attitudes and values. Even some advertisers admit to this: Rance Crain of *Advertising Age* said great advertising "plays the tune rather than just dancing to the tune." Far from being a passive mirror of society, advertising is an effective and pervasive medium of influence and persuasion, and its influence is cumulative, often subtle, and primarily unconscious. Advertising performs much the same function in industrial society as myth performed in ancient and primitive societies. It is both a creator and perpetuator of the dominant attitudes, values and ideology of the culture, the social norms and myths by which most people govern their behavior. At the very least, advertising helps to create a climate in which certain attitudes and values flourish and others are not reflected at all.

Advertising is not only our physical environment, it is increasingly our spiri- 8 tual environment as well. By definition, however, it is only interested in materialistic values. When spiritual values or religious images show up in ads, it is only to appropriate them in order to sell us something. Sometimes this is very obvious. Eternity is a perfume by Calvin Klein. Infiniti is an automobile and Hydra Zen a moisturizer. Jesus is a brand of jeans. "See the light," says an ad for wool, while a face powder ad promises "an enlightening experience" and absolute heaven." One car is "born again" and another promises to "energize your soul." In a full-page ad in *Advertising Age,* the online service Yahoo! proclaims, "We've got 60 million followers. That's more than some religions," but goes on to assure readers, "Don't worry. We're *not* a religion." When Pope John Paul II visited Mexico City in the winter of 1999, he could have seen a smiling image of himself on bags of Sabritas, a popular brand of potato chips, or a giant street sign showing him bowing piously next to a Pepsi logo with a phrase in Spanish that reads, "Mexico Always Faithful." In the United States, he could have treated himself to pope-on-a-rope soap.

9   But advertising's co-optation of spirituality goes much deeper than this. It is commonplace these days to observe that consumerism has become the religion of our time (with advertising its holy text), but the criticism usually stops short of what is most important, what is at the heart of the comparison. Advertising and religion share a belief in transformation and transcendence, but most religions believe that this requires work and sacrifice. In the world of advertising, enlightenment is achieved instantly by purchasing material goods. As James Twitchell, author of *Adcult USA,* says, "The Jolly Green Giant, the Michelin Man, the Man from Glad, Mother Nature, Aunt Jemima, Speedy AlkaSeltzer, the White Knight, and all their otherworldly kin are descendants of the earlier gods. What separates them is that they now reside in manufactured products and that, although earlier gods were invoked by fasting, prayer, rituals, and penance, the promise of purchase calls forth their modern ilk."

10   Advertising constantly promotes the core belief of American culture: that we *can* re-create ourselves, transform ourselves, transcend our circumstances—but with a twist. For generations Americans believed this could be achieved if we worked hard enough, like Horatio Alger. Today the promise is that we can change our lives instantly, effortlessly—by winning the lottery, selecting the right mutual fund, having a fashion makeover, losing weight, having tighter abs, buying the right car or soft drink. It is this belief that such transformation is possible that drives us to keep dieting, to buy more stuff, to read fashion magazines that give us the same information over and over again. Cindy Crawford's makeup is carefully described as if it could transform us into her. On one level, we know it won't—after all, most of us have tried this approach many times before. But on another level, we continue to try, continue to believe that this time it will be different. This American belief that we can transform ourselves makes advertising images much more powerful than they otherwise would be.

11   The focus of the transformation has shifted from the soul to the body. Of course, this trivializes and cheapens authentic spirituality and transcendence. But, more important, this junk food for the soul leaves us hungry, empty, malnourished. The emphasis on instant salvation is parodied in an ad from *Adbusters* for a product called Mammon, in which a man says, "I need a belief system that serves my needs right away." The copy continues, "Dean Sachs has a mortgage, a family and an extremely demanding job. What he doesn't need is a religion that complicates his life with unreasonable ethical

**Your business side. Your creative side.
Inspire both. Introducing Avid's new editing lineup.**

Quality, performance and value. A new way of thinking. A new way of doing business.
Take a closer look at **Avid.com/NewThinkingScript.**

FOR STRONGER TEETH CHEW ORBIT
Orbit is now accepted by the American Dental Association

ADA
Accepted
American
Dental
Association

Orbit
SPEARMINT

The ADA Council on Scientific Affairs' Acceptance of Orbit is based on its finding that the physical action of chewing Orbit sugar-free gum for 20 minutes after eating, stimulates saliva flow, which helps to prevent cavities by reducing plaque acids and strengthening teeth.

GROCERY DELIVERY
ONE OF MANY FEATURES DESIGNED TO KEEP YOU BALANCED
MASTER THE LONG TRIP℠

RESIDENCEINN.COM

Residence Inn ®
Marriott

demands." The ad ends with the words, "Mammon: Because you deserve to enjoy life—guilt free."

As advertising becomes more and more absurd, however, it becomes 12 increasingly difficult to parody ads. There's not much of a difference between the ad for Mammon and the real ad for cruises that says "It can take several lifetimes to reach a state of inner peace and tranquillity. Or, it can take a couple of weeks." Of course, we know that a couple of weeks on a cruise won't solve our problems, won't bring us to a state of peace and enlightenment, but it is so tempting to believe that there is some easy way to get there, some ticket we can buy.

To be one of the "elect" in today's society is to have enough money to buy 13 luxury goods. Of course, when salvation comes via the sale, it becomes important to display these goods. Owning a Rolex would not impress anyone who didn't know how expensive it is. A Rolex ad itself says the watch was voted "most likely to be coveted." Indeed, one of advertising's purposes is to create an aura for a product, so that other people will be impressed. As one marketer said recently in *Advertising Age,* "It's no fun to spend $100 on athletic shoes to wear to high school if your friends don't know how cool your shoes are."

Thus the influence of advertising goes way beyond the target audience 14 and includes those who could never afford the product, who will simply be envious and impressed—perhaps to the point of killing someone for his sneakers or jacket, as has sometimes happened in our poverty-stricken neighborhoods. In the early 1990s the city health commissioner in Philadelphia issued a public health warning cautioning youths against wearing expensive leather jackets and jewelry, while in Milwaukee billboards depicted a chalk outline of a body and the warning, "Dress Smart and Stay Alive." Poor children in many countries knot the laces of their Nikes around their ankles to avoid having them stolen while they sleep.

Many teens fantasize that objects will somehow transform their lives, give 15 them social standing and respect. When they wear a certain brand of sneaker or jacket, they feel, "This is important, therefore I am important." The brand gives instant status. No wonder they are willing, even eager, to spend money for clothes that advertise the brands. A *USA Today*–CNN–Gallup Poll found that 61 percent of boys and 44 percent of girls considered brand names on clothes "very important" or "somewhat important." As ten-year-old Darion Sawyer from Baltimore said, "People will tease you and talk about you, say you got on no-name shoes or say you shop at Kmart." Leydiana Reyes, an eighth-grader in Brooklyn, said, "My father always tells me I could buy two pairs of jeans for what you pay for Calvin Klein. I know that. But I still want Calvin Klein." And Danny Shirley, a fourteen-year-old in Santa Fe decked out in Tommy Hilfiger regalia, said, "Kids who wear Levi's don't really care about what they wear, I guess."

In the beginning, these labels were somewhat discreet. Today we see 16 sweatshirts with fifteen-inch "Polo" logos stamped across the chest, jeans with four-inch "Calvin Klein" labels stitched on them, and a jacket with "Tommy Hilfiger" in five-inch letters across the back. Some of these outfits are so close to sandwich boards that I'm surprised people aren't paid to wear them. Before too long, the logo-free product probably will be the expensive rarity.

17   What people who wear these clothes are really buying isn't a garment, of course, but an *image*. And increasingly, an image is all that advertising has to sell. Advertising began centuries ago with signs in medieval villages. In the nineteenth century, it became more common but was still essentially designed to give people information about manufactured goods and services. Since the 1920s, advertising has provided less information about the product and focused more on the lives, especially the emotional lives, of the prospective consumers. This shift coincided, of course, with the increasing knowledge and acceptability of psychology, as well as the success of propaganda used to convince the population to support World War I.

18   Industrialization gave rise to the burgeoning ability of businesses to mass-produce goods. Since it was no longer certain there would be a market for the goods, it became necessary not just to mass-produce the goods but to mass-produce markets hungry for the goods. The problem became not too little candy produced but not enough candy consumed, so it became the job of the advertisers to *produce consumers*. This led to an increased use of psychological research and emotional ploys to sell products. Consumer behavior became recognized as a science in the late 1940s.

19   As luxury goods, prepared foods, and nonessential items have proliferated, it has become crucial to create artificial needs in order to sell unnecessary products. Was there such a thing as static cling before there were fabric softeners and sprays? An ad for a "lip renewal cream" says, "I never thought of my lips as a problem area until Andrea came up with the solution."

20   Most brands in a given category are essentially the same. Most shampoos are made by two or three manufacturers. Blindfolded smokers or beer-drinkers can rarely identify what brand they are smoking or drinking, including their own. Whether we know it or not, we select products primarily because of the image reflected in their advertising. Very few ads give us any real information at all. Sometimes it is impossible to tell what is being advertised. "This is an ad for the hair dryer," says one ad, featuring a woman lounging on a sofa. If we weren't told, we would never know. A joke made the rounds a while ago about a little boy who wanted a box of tampons so that he could effortlessly ride bicycles and horses, ski, and swim.

21   Almost all tobacco and alcohol ads are entirely image-based. Of course, when you're selling a product that kills people, it's difficult to give honest information about it. Think of all the cigarette ads that never show cigarettes or even a wisp of smoke. One of the most striking examples of image advertising is the very successful and long-running campaign for Absolut vodka. This campaign focuses on the shape of the bottle and the word "Absolut," as in "Absolut Perfection," which features the bottle with a halo. This campaign has been so successful that a coffee-table book collection of the ads published just in time for Christmas, the perfect gift for the alcoholic in your family, sold over 150,000 copies. Collecting Absolut ads is now a common pastime for elementary-school children, who swap them like baseball cards.

How does all this affect us? It is very difficult to do objective research about **22** advertising's influence because there are no comparison groups, almost no people who have not been exposed to massive doses of advertising. In addition, research that measures only one point in time does not adequately capture advertising's real effects. We need longitudinal studies, such as George Gerbner's twenty-five-year study of violence on television.

The advertising industry itself can't prove that advertising works. While **23** claiming to its clients that it does, it simultaneously denies it to the Federal Trade Commission whenever the subject of alcohol and tobacco advertising comes up. As an editorial in *Advertising Age* once said, "A strange world it is, in which people spending millions on advertising must do their best to prove that advertising doesn't do very much!" According to Bob Wehling, senior vice-president of marketing at Procter & Gamble, "We don't have a lot of scientific studies to support our belief that advertising works. But we have seen that the power of advertising makes a significant difference."

What research can most easily prove is usually what is least important, **24** such as advertising's influence on our choice of brands. This is the most obvious, but least significant, way that advertising affects us. There are countless examples of successful advertising campaigns, such as the Absolut campaign, that have sent sales soaring. A commercial for I Can't Believe It's Not Butter featuring a sculptress whose work comes alive in the form of romance-novel hunk Fabio boosted sales about 17 percent. Tamagotchis—virtual pets in an egg—were introduced in the United States with a massive advertising campaign and earned $150 million in seven months. And Gardenburger, a veggie patty, ran a thirty-second spot during the final episode of *Seinfeld* and, within a week, sold over $2 million worth, a market share jump of 50 percent and more than the entire category sold in the same week the previous year. But advertising is more of an art than a science, and campaigns often fail. In 1998 a Miller beer campaign bombed, costing the company millions of dollars and offending a large segment of their customers. The 1989 Nissan Infiniti campaign, known as the "Rocks and Trees" campaign, was the first ever to introduce a car without showing it and immediately became a target for Jay Leno's monologues. And, of course, the Edsel, a car introduced by Ford with great fanfare in 1957, remains a universal symbol of failure.

The unintended effects of advertising are far more important and far more **25** difficult to measure than those effects that are intended. The important question is not "Does this ad sell the product?" but rather "What else does this ad sell?" An ad for Gap khakis featuring a group of acrobatic swing dancers probably sold a lot of pants, which, of course, was the intention of the advertisers. But it also contributed to a rage for swing dancing. This is an innocuous example of advertising's powerful unintended effects. Swing dancing is not binge drinking, after all.

Advertising often sells a great deal more than products. It sells values, **26** images, and concepts of love and sexuality, romance, success, and, perhaps most important, normalcy. To a great extent, it tells us who we are and who we should be. We are increasingly using brand names to create our identities.

James Twitchell argues that the label of our shirt, the make of our car, and our favorite laundry detergent are filling the vacuum once occupied by religion, education, and our family name.

27   Even more important, advertising corrupts our language and thus influences our ability to think clearly. Critic and novelist George Steiner once talked with an interviewer about what he called "anti-language, that which is transcendentally annihilating of truth and meaning." Novelist Jonathan Dee, applying this concept to advertising, writes that "the harm lies not in the ad itself; the harm is in the exchange, in the collision of ad language, ad imagery, with other sorts of language that contend with it in the public realm. When Apple reprints an old photo of Gandhi, or Heineken ends its ads with the words 'Seek the Truth,' or Winston suggests that we buy cigarettes by proposing (just under the surgeon general's warning) that 'You have to appreciate authenticity in all its forms,' or Kellogg's identifies itself with the message 'Simple is Good,' these occasions color our contact with those words and images in their other, possibly less promotional applications." The real violence of advertising, Dee concludes, is that "words can be made to mean anything, which is hard to distinguish from the idea that words mean nothing." We see the consequences of this in much of our culture, from "art" to politics, that has no content, no connection between language and conviction. Just as it is often difficult to tell what product an ad is selling, so is it difficult to determine what a politician's beliefs are (the "vision thing," as George Bush so aptly called it, albeit unintentionally) or what the subject is of a film or song or work of art. As Dee says, "The men and women who make ads are not hucksters; they are artists with nothing to say, and they have found their form." Unfortunately, their form deeply influences all the other forms of the culture. We end up expecting nothing more.

28   This has terrible consequences for our culture. As Richard Pollay says, "Without a reliance on words and a faith in truth, we lack the mortar for social cohesion. Without trustworthy communication, there is no communion, no community, only an aggregation of increasingly isolated individuals, alone in the mass."

29   Advertising creates a worldview that is based upon cynicism, dissatisfaction, and craving. The advertisers aren't evil. They are just doing their job, which is to sell a product, but the consequences, usually unintended, are often destructive to individuals, to cultures, and to the planet. In the history of the world, there has never been a propaganda effort to match that of advertising in the twentieth century. More thought, more effort, and more money go into advertising than has gone into any other campaign to change social consciousness. The story that advertising tells is that the way to be happy, to find satisfaction—and the path to political freedom, as well—is through the consumption of material objects. And the major motivating force for social change throughout the world today is this belief that happiness comes from the market.

30   So, advertising has a greater impact on all of us than we generally realize. The primary purpose of the mass media is to deliver us to advertisers. Much

of the information that we need from the media in order to make informed choices in our lives is distorted or deleted on behalf of corporate sponsors. Advertising is an increasingly ubiquitous presence in our lives, and it sells much more than products. We delude ourselves when we say we are not influenced by advertising. And we trivialize and ignore its growing significance at our peril.

NOTES

1. "This argument was made by Jacob Sullum": Sullum, 1997, A31.
2. "As Sut Jhally says": Jhally, 1998.
3. "As Joseph Goebbels": Goebbels, 1933, March 28. Quoted in Jacobson and Mazur, 1995, 15.
4. "A study of children done by researchers at Columbia University": Bever, Smith, Bengen, and Johnson, 1975, 119.
5. " '7- to 10-year-olds are strained' ": Bever, Smith, Bengen, and Johnson, 1975, 120.
6. "Rance Crain of *Advertising Age*": Crain, 1999, 23.
7. "When Pope John Paul II": Chacon and Ribadeneria, 1999. A8.
8. " 'The Jolly Green Giant' ": Twitchell, 1996, 30.
9. " 'It's no fun to spend $100 on athletic shoes' ": Peppers and Rogers, 1997, 32.
10. "the city health commissioner in Philadelphia": Worthington, 1992, 15.
11. "A *USA Today*–CNN–Gallup Poll": Jacobson and Mazur, 1995, 26.
12. "Leydiana Reyes": Leonhardt, 1997, 65.
13. "Danny Shirley": Espen, 1999, 59.
14. "sweatshirts with fifteen-inch 'Polo' logos": Ryan, 1996, D1.
15. "Consumer behavior": Woods, 1995.
16. "Most shampoos": Twitchell, 1996, 252.
17. "Blindfolded smokers": Twitchell, 1996, 125.
18. " 'A strange world it is' ": Bernstein, 1978, August 7.
19. "According to Bob Wehling": Crain, 1998, 24.
20. "A commercial for I Can't Believe It's Not Butter": Haran, 1996, 12.
21. "Tamagotchis": Goldner, 1998, S43.
22. "And Gardenburger": Gardenburger hits the spot, 1998, 17.
23. "In 1998 a Miller beer campaign": Crain, 1998, 24.
24. "The 1989 Nissan Infiniti": Horton, 1996, S28.
25. "the Edsel": Horton, 1996, S30.
26. "An ad for Gap khakis": Cortissoz, 1998, A10.

27. "James Twitchell argues": University of Florida news release, quoted by Orlando, 1999, *http://www.sciencedaily.com/releases/1999/05/9905181 14815. htm.*

28. "Critic and novelist George Steiner": Dee, 1999, 65–66.

29. "As Richard Pollay": Pollay, 1986.

30. "there has never been a propaganda effort": Jhally, 1998.

QUESTIONS FOR READING

1. What is Kilbourne's subject? (Be more precise than just "advertising.")

2. How is advertising like propaganda?

3. What is the nature of the "anti-advertising" ad? What is one of the consequences of anti-advertising?

4. What role does advertising play in our society? How does it promote "the core belief of American culture"? How is its message different from what that core belief used to emphasize?

5. How does advertising go beyond the target audience? How do we want others to react to what we have purchased? What are we purchasing with designer-labeled clothing?

6. In the second half of the twentieth century, what became advertising's purpose or task? How did this purpose change ads?

7. How does advertising affect language?

QUESTIONS FOR REASONING AND ANALYSIS

1. What is Kilbourne's claim? What *type* of argument is this—that is, what does it seek to accomplish?

2. Kilbourne provides a brief history of advertising. What does she accomplish by including this in her discussion?

3. List the effects of advertising discussed by Kilbourne. How does her discussion of effects support her claim? What evidence does the author provide throughout her analysis?

4. The author points out that it is difficult to study the effects of ads. Why is it difficult? Why does she include these comments in her argument?

QUESTIONS FOR REFLECTING AND WRITING

1. Evaluate Kilbourne's argument. Does she convince you? If not, what would you need to be convinced?

2. Do you find considerable cynicism today? If so, have you ever connected it to the endless distortions created by ads? If not, does this seem like a reasonable causal connection to you now?

3. Should advertising be banned from children's TV programs? Why or why not?

TURNING GOYS INTO GIRLS | MICHELLE COTTLE

A graduate of Vanderbilt University, Michelle Cottle was an editor for two years at the *Washington Monthly* prior to becoming a senior editor, in 1999, at *The New Republic*. She is also a panelist on the PBS political talk show "Tucker Carlson Unfiltered." Her essay on men's magazines was published in the May 1998 issue of the *Washington Monthly*.

PREREADING QUESTIONS **What does the word *goys* mean? If you do not know, look it up before reading further.**

I love *Men's Health* magazine. There, I'm out of the closet, and I'm not **1** ashamed. Sure, I know what some of you are thinking: What self-respecting '90s women could embrace a publication that runs such enlightened articles as "Turn Your Good Girl Bad" and "How to Wake Up Next to a One-Night Stand"? Or maybe you'll smile and wink knowingly: What red-blooded hetero chick wouldn't love all those glossy photo spreads of buff young beefcake in various states of undress, ripped abs and glutes flexed so tightly you could bounce a check on them? Either way you've got the wrong idea. My affection for *Men's Health* is driven by pure gender politics—by the realization that this magazine, and a handful of others like it, are leveling the playing field in a way that *Ms.* can only dream of. With page after page of bulging biceps and Gillette jaws, robust hairlines and silken skin, *Men's Health* is peddling a standard of male beauty as unforgiving and unrealistic as the female version sold by those dewy-eyed pre-teen waifs draped across the covers of *Glamour* and *Elle*. And with a variety of helpful features on "Foods That Fight Fat," "Banish Your Potbelly," and "Save Your Hair (Before It's Too Late)," *Men's Health* is well on its way to making the male species as insane, insecure, and irrational about physical appearance as any *Cosmo* girl.

Don't you see, ladies? We've been going about this equality business all **2** wrong. Instead of battling to get society fixated on something besides our breast size, we should have been fighting spandex with spandex. Bra burning was a nice gesture, but the greater justice is in convincing our male counterparts that the key to their happiness lies in a pair of made-for-him Super Shaper Briefs with the optional "fly front endowment pad" (as advertised in *Men's Journal*, $29.95 plus shipping and handling). Make the men as neurotic about the circumference of their waists and the whiteness of their smiles as the women, and at least the burden of vanity and self-loathing will be shared by all.

This is precisely what lads' mags like *Men's Health* are accomplishing. The **3** rugged John-Wayne days when men scrubbed their faces with deodorant soap and viewed gray hair and wrinkles as a badge of honor are fading. Last year, international market analyst Euromonitor placed the U.S. men's toiletries market—hair color, skin moisturizer, tooth whiteners, etc.—at $3.5 billion. According to a survey conducted by DYG researchers for *Men's Health* in November 1996, approximately 20 percent of American men get manicures or pedicures, 18 percent use skin treatments such as masks or mud packs, and 10 percent enjoy professional facials. That same month, *Psychology Today* reported that a poll by Roper Starch Worldwide showed that "6 percent of men nationwide actually use such traditionally female products as bronzers and foundation to create the illusion of a youthful appearance."

4   What men are putting on their bodies, however, is nothing compared to what they're doing to their bodies: While in the 1980s only an estimated one in 10 plastic surgery patients were men, as of 1996, that ratio had shrunk to one in five. The American Academy of Cosmetic Surgery estimates that nationwide more than 690,000 men had cosmetic procedures performed in '96, the most recent year for which figures are available. And we're not just talking "hair restoration" here, though such procedures do command the lion's share of the male market. We're also seeing an increasing number of men shelling out mucho dinero for face peels, liposuction, collagen injections, eyelid lifts, chin tucks, and of course, the real man's answer to breast implants: penile enlargements (now available to increase both length and diameter).

5   Granted, *Men's Health* and its journalistic cousins (*Men's Journal, Details, GQ,* etc.) cannot take all the credit for this breakthrough in gender parity. The fashion and glamour industries have perfected the art of creating consumer "needs," and with the women's market pretty much saturated, men have become the obvious target for the purveyors of everything from lip balm to Lycra. Meanwhile, advances in medical science have made cosmetic surgery a quicker, cleaner option for busy executives (just as the tight fiscal leash of managed care is driving more and more doctors toward this cash-based specialty). Don't have several weeks to recover from a full-blown facelift? No problem. For a few hundred bucks you can get a microdermabrasion face peel on your lunch hour.

6   Then there are the underlying social factors. With women growing ever more financially independent, aspiring suitors are discovering that they must bring more to the table than a well-endowed wallet if they expect to win (and keep) the fair maiden. Nor should we overlook the increased market power of the gay population—in general a more image-conscious lot than straight guys. But perhaps most significant is the ongoing, ungraceful descent into middle age by legions of narcissistic baby boomers. Gone are the days when the elder statesmen of this demographic bulge could see themselves in the relatively youthful faces of those insipid yuppies on "Thirtysomething." Increasingly, boomers are finding they have more in common with the parents of today's TV, movie, and sports stars. Everywhere they turn some upstart Gen Xer is flaunting his youthful vitality, threatening boomer dominance on both the social and professional fronts. (Don't think even Hollywood didn't shudder when the Oscar for best original screenplay this year went to a couple of guys barely old enough to shave.) With whippersnappers looking to steal everything from their jobs to their women, post-pubescent men have at long last discovered the terror of losing their springtime radiance.

7   Whatever combo of factors is feeding the frenzy of male vanity, magazines such as *Men's Health* provide the ideal meeting place for men's insecurities and marketers' greed. Like its more established female counterparts, *Men's Health* is an affordable, efficient delivery vehicle for the message that physical imperfection, age, and an underdeveloped fashion sense are potentially crippling disabilities. And as with women's mags, this cycle of insanity is

self-perpetuating: The more men obsess about growing old or unattractive, the more marketers will exploit and expand that fear; the more marketers bombard men with messages about the need to be beautiful, the more they will obsess. Younger and younger men will be sucked into the vortex of self-doubt. Since 1990, *Men's Health* has seen its paid circulation rise from 250,000 to more than 1.5 million; the magazine estimates that half of its 5.3 million readers are under age 35 and 46 percent are married. And while most major magazines have suffered sluggish growth or even a decline in circulation in recent years, during the first half of 1997, *Men's Health* saw its paid circulation increase 14 percent over its '96 figures. (Likewise, its smaller, more outdoorsy relative, Wenner Media's *Men's Journal,* enjoyed an even bigger jump of 26.5 percent.) At this rate, one day soon, that farcical TV commercial featuring men hanging out in bars, whining about having inherited their mothers' thighs will be a reality. Now that's progress.

VANITY, THY NAME IS MAN

Everyone wants to be considered attractive and desirable. And most of 8 us are aware that, no matter how guilty and shallow we feel about it, there are certain broad cultural norms that define attractive. Not surprisingly, both men's and women's magazines have argued that, far from playing on human insecurities, they are merely helping readers be all that they can be—a kind of training camp for the image impaired. In recent years, such publications have embraced the tenets of "evolutionary biology," which argue that, no matter how often we're told that beauty is only skin deep, men and women are hardwired to prefer the Jack Kennedys and Sharon Stones to the Rodney Dangerfields and Janet Renos. Continuation of the species demands that specimens with shiny coats, bright eyes, even features, and other visible signs of ruddy good health and fertility automatically kick-start our most basic instinct. Of course, the glamour mags' editors have yet to explain why, in evolutionary terms, we would ever desire adult women to stand 5'10" and weigh 100 pounds. Stories abound of women starving themselves to the point that their bodies shut down and they stop menstruating—hardly conducive to reproduction—yet Kate Moss remains the dish du jour and millions of Moss wannabes still struggle to subsist on a diet of Dexatrim and Perrier.

Similarly, despite its title, *Men's Health* is hawking far more than general 9 fitness or a healthful lifestyle. For every half page of advice on how to cut your stress level, there are a dozen pages on how to build your biceps. For every update on the dangers of cholesterol, there are multiple warnings on the horrors of flabby abs. Now, without question, gorging on Cheetos and Budweiser while your rump takes root on the sofa is no way to treat your body if you plan on living past 50. But chugging protein drinks, agonizing over fat grams, and counting the minutes until your next Stairmaster session is equally unbalanced. The line between taking pride in one's physical appearance and being obsessed by it is a fine one—and one that disappeared for many women long ago.

Now with the lads' mags taking men in that direction as well, in many 10 cases it's almost impossible to tell whether you're reading a copy of *Men's Health* or of *Mademoiselle:* "April 8. To commemorate Buddha's birthday, hit a Japanese restaurant. Stick to low-fat selections. Choose foods described as yakimono, which means grilled," advised the monthly "to do list" in the April *Men's Health*. (Why readers should go Japanese in honor of the most famous religious leader in India's history remains unclear.) The January/February list was equally thought provoking: "January 28. It's Chinese New Year, so make a resolution to custom-order your next takeout. Ask that they substitute wonton soup broth for oil. Try the soba noodles instead of plain noodles. They're richer in nutrients and contain much less fat." The issue also featured a "Total Body Workout Poster" and one of those handy little "substitution" charts (loathed by women everywhere), showing men how to slash their calorie intake by making a few minor dietary substitutions: mustard for mayo, popcorn for peanuts, seltzer water for soda, pretzels for potato chips. . . .

11   As in women's magazines, fast results with minimum inconvenience is a central theme. Among *Men's Health*'s March highlights were a guide to "Bigger Biceps in 2 Weeks," and "20 Fast Fixes" for a bad diet; April offered "A Better Body in Half the Time," along with a colorful four-page spread on "50 Snacks That Won't Make You Fat." And you can forget carrot sticks—this think-thin eating guide celebrated the wonders of Reduced Fat Cheez-its, Munch 'Ems, Fiddle Faddle, Oreos, Teddy Grahams, Milky Ways, Bugles, Starburst Fruit Twists, and Klondike's Fat Free Big Bear Ice Cream Sandwiches. Better nutrition is not the primary issue. A better butt is. To this end, also found in the pages of *Men's Health,* is the occasional, tasteful ad for liposuction—just in case nature doesn't cooperate.

12   But a blueprint to rock-hard buns is only part of what makes *Men's Health* the preeminent "men's lifestyle" magazine. Nice teeth, nice skin, nice hair, and a red-hot wardrobe are now required to round out the ultimate alpha male package, and *Men's Health* is there to help on all fronts. In recent months it has run articles on how to select, among other items, the perfect necktie and belt, the hippest wallet, the chicest running gear, the best "hair-thickening" shampoo, and the cutest golfing apparel. It has also offered advice on how to retard baldness, how to keep your footwear looking sharp, how to achieve different "looks" with a patterned blazer, even how to keep your lips from chapping at the dentist's office: "[B]efore you start all that 'rinse and spit' business, apply some moisturizer to your face and some lip balm to your lips. Your face and lips won't have that stretched-out dry feeling. . . . Plus, you'll look positively radiant!"

13   While a desire to look good for their hygienists may be enough to spur some men to heed the magazine's advice (and keep 'em coming back for more), fear and insecurity about the alternatives are generally more effective motivators. For those who don't get with the *Men's Health* program, there must be the threat of ridicule. By far the least subtle example of this is the free subscriptions for "guys who need our help" periodically announced in the front section of the magazine. April's dubious honoree was actor Christopher Walken:

> Chris, we love the way you've perfected that psycho persona. But now you're taking your role in "Things to Do in Denver When You're Dead" way too seriously with that ghostly pale face, the "where's the funeral?" black clothes, and a haircut

that looks like the work of a hasty undertaker. . . . Dab on a little Murad Murasun Self-Tanner ($21). . . . For those creases in your face, try Ortho Dermatologicals' Renova, a prescription antiwrinkle cream that contains tretinoin, a form of vitamin A. Then, find a barber.

Or how the March "winner," basketball coach Bobby Knight: "Bob, your **14** trademark red sweater is just a billboard for your potbelly. A darker solid color would make you look slimmer. Also, see 'The Tale of Two Bellies' in our February 1998 issue, and try to drop a few pounds. Then the next time you throw a sideline tantrum, at least people won't say, 'look at the crazy fat man.' "

Just as intense as the obsession with appearance that men's (and wom- **15** en's) magazines breed are the sexual neuroses they feed. And if one of the ostensible goals of women's mags is to help women drive men wild, what is the obvious corollary objective for men's magazines? To get guys laid—well and often. As if men needed any encouragement to fixate on the subject, *Men's Health* is chock full of helpful "how-tos" such as, "Have Great Sex Every Day Until You Die" and "What I Learned From My Sex Coach," as well as more cursory explorations of why men with larger testicles have more sex ("Why Big Boys Don't Cry"), how to maintain orgasm intensity as you age ("Be one of the geysers"), and how to achieve stronger erections by eating certain foods ("Bean counters make better lovers"). And for those having trouble even getting to the starting line, last month's issue offered readers a chance to "Win free love lessons."

THE HIGH PRICE OF PERFECTION

Having elevated men's physical and sexual insecurities to the level of **16** grand paranoia, lads' mags can then get down to what really matters: moving merchandise. On the cover of *Men's Health* each month, in small type just above the magazine's title, appears the phrase "Tons of useful stuff." Thumbing through an issue or two, however, one quickly realizes that a more accurate description would read: "Tons of expensive stuff." They're all there: Ralph Lauren, Tommy Hilfiger, Paul Mitchell, Calvin Klein, Clinique, Armani, Versace, Burberrys, Nautica, Nike, Omega, Rogaine, The Better Sex Video Series. . . . The magazine even has those annoying little perfume strips guaranteed to make your nose run and to alienate everyone within a five-mile radius of you.

Masters of psychology, marketers wheel out their sexiest pitches and hot- **17** test male models to tempt/intimidate the readership of *Men's Health*. Not since the last casting call for *Baywatch* has a more impressive display of firm, tanned, young flesh appeared in one spot. And just like in women's magazines, the articles themselves are designed to sell stuff. All those helpful tips on choosing blazers, ties, and belts come complete with info on the who, where, and how much. The strategy is brilliant: Make men understand exactly how far short of the ideal they fall, and they too become vulnerable to the lure of high-priced underwear, cologne, running shoes, workout gear, hair dye, hair straightener, skin softener, body-fat monitors, suits, boots, energy bars, and sex aids. As Mark Jannot, the grooming and health editor for *Men's Journal*, told *Today* show host Matt Lauer in January, "This is a huge, booming market.

I mean, the marketers have found a group of people that are ripe for the picking. Men are finally learning that aging is a disease." Considering how effectively *Men's Health* fosters this belief, it's hardly surprising that the magazine has seen its ad pages grow 510 percent since 1991 and has made it onto *Adweek*'s 10 Hottest Magazines list three of the last five years.

18   To make all this "girly" image obsession palatable to their audience, lads' mags employ all their creative energies to transform appearance issues into "a guy thing." *Men's Health* tries to cultivate a joking, macho tone throughout ("Eat Like Brando and Look Like Rambo" or "Is my tallywhacker shrinking?") and tosses in a handful of Y-chromosome teasers such as "How to Stay Out of Jail," "How to Clean Your Whole Apartment in One Hour or Less," and my personal favorite, "Let's Play Squash," an illustrated guide to identifying the bug-splat patterns on your windshield. Instead of a regular advice columnist, which would smack too much of chicks' magazines, *Men's Health* recently introduced "Jimmy the Bartender," a monthly column on "women, sex, and other stuff that screws up men's lives."

19   It appears that, no matter how much clarifying lotion and hair gel you're trying to sell them, men must never suspect that you think they share women's insecurities. If you want a man to buy wrinkle cream, marketers have learned, you better pitch it as part of a comfortingly macho shaving regime. Aramis, for example, assures men that its popular Lift Off! Moisture Formula with alpha hydroxy will help cut their shave time by one-third. "The biggest challenge for products started for women is how to transfer them to men," explained George Schaeffer, the president of OPI cosmetics, in the November issue of SoapCosmetics-Chemical Specialties. Schaeffer's Los Angeles based company is the maker of Matte Nail Envy, an unobtrusive nail polish that's proved a hit with men. And for the more adventuresome shopper, last year Hard Candy cosmetics introduced a line of men's nail enamel, called Candy Man, that targets guys with such studly colors as Gigolo (metallic black) and Testosterone (gun-metal silver).

20   On a larger scale, positioning a makeover or trip to the liposuction clinic as a smart career move seems to help men rationalize their image obsession. "Whatever a man's cosmetic shortcoming, it's apt to be a career liability," noted Alan Farnham in a September 1996 issue of *Fortune*. "The business world is prejudiced against the ugly." Or how about *Forbes*' sad attempt to differentiate between male and female vanity in its Dec. 1 piece on cosmetic surgery: "Plastic surgery is more of a cosmetic thing for women. They have a thing about aging. For men's it's an investment that pays a pretty good dividend." Whatever you say, guys.

21   The irony is rich and bittersweet. Gender equity is at last headed our way—not in the form of women being less obsessed with looking like Calvin Klein models, but of men becoming hysterical over the first signs of crows-feet. Gradually, guys are no longer pumping up and primping simply to get babes, but because they feel it's something everyone expects them to do. Women, after all, do not spend $400 on Dolce & Gabbana sandals to impress their boyfriends, most of whom don't know Dolce & Gabbana from Beavis & Butthead (yet). They buy them to impress other women—and because that's what society says they

should want to do. Most guys haven't yet achieved this level of insanity, but with grown men catcalling the skin tone and wardrobe of other grown men (Christopher Walken, Bobby Knight) for a readership of still more grown men, can the gender's complete surrender to the vanity industry be far behind?

The ad for *Men's Health*'s web site says it all: "Don't click here unless 22 you want to look a decade younger . . . lose that beer belly . . . be a better lover . . . and more! *Men's Health* Online: The Internet Site For Regular Guys." Of course, between the magazine's covers there's not a "regular guy" to be found, save for the occasional snapshot of one of the publication's writers or editors—usually taken from a respectable distance. The moist young bucks in the Gap jeans ads and the electric-eyed Armani models have exactly as much in common with the average American man as Tyra Banks does with the average American woman. Which would be fine, if everyone seemed to understand this distinction. Until they do, however, I guess my consolation will have to be the image of thousands of once-proud men, having long scorned women's insecurities, lining up for their laser peels and trying to squeeze their middle-aged asses into a snug set of Super Shaper Briefs—with the optional fly front endowment pad, naturally.

QUESTIONS FOR READING

1. What is Cottle's subject?
2. What are men's magazines doing to men?
3. How are women achieving "gender equity," according to Cottle?
4. What anxieties do the men's magazines feed?
5. What is it the magazines are ultimately seeking to accomplish?

QUESTIONS FOR REASONING AND ANALYSIS

1. What is the author's claim?
2. What *kind* of evidence does Cottle provide? Is it convincing?
3. Examine the author's word choice. What "voice" does she create? What is the essay's tone?

QUESTIONS FOR REFLECTING AND WRITING

1. Does Cottle's analysis of men's magazines surprise you with new information and ideas? If so, what is most surprising to you? If you are not surprised, why not?
2. Has the author convinced you with her details and analysis of strategies in the men's magazines? Why or why not?
3. Does Cottle actually believe that women have achieved gender equity? Is she pleased with what the men's magazines are doing? Support your answer.
4. How do we resist the anxieties created by advertising—or the unnecessary purchases? What advice do you have?

The Environment: How Green Do We Go?

READ: What is the situation? Who speaks the words?

REASON: What did the original Paul Revere do? Do you think that Toles's Paul Revere will be successful? What are the reasons to worry?

REFLECT/WRITE: What is Toles's attitude toward our handling of global warming?

In 2005 psychology professor Glenn Shean published a book titled *Psychology and the Environment*. Dr. Shean argued that we are behaving as if we have no environmental problems to face, and that therefore the biggest first step to solving problems related to environmental degradation is to make people aware of and concerned about the interconnected issues of climate change, the heavy use of fossil fuels, and species extinction. Because we are programmed to make quick decisions based on immediate dangers, we find it difficult to become engaged with dangers that stretch out into an indeterminate future. There is always tomorrow to worry about the polar bears or the increasing levels of CO_2 in the atmosphere, or the rapidly melting ice caps. And besides, who wants to give up a comfortable lifestyle because it might affect future life on this planet?

By 2008 even the Bush administration began to give voice to the concerns of environmentalists such as Dr. Shean. After much resistance, there seems to be a more widespread acceptance of climate change and the problems that it can cause, but even among those grudgingly on board there is still a debate as to the degree to which human actions are a major cause of the problems—as opposed to a recognition of periods of temperature increases and decreases that have been a part of the history of the planet. Why do we resist accepting responsibility for adding to the problem? Because to admit to being a cause means that we have to accept being part of the solution—we have to agree to change some of the things we are doing that are heating up the atmosphere. And here is where sacrifice and cost enter the picture. Do we expect factories to shut down? No, but regulations governing pollutants from their smokestacks will help the atmosphere—at a cost to doing business. Do we expect people to stop enjoying the beach? No, but we could have restrictions on building that destroys the barrier islands and marshlands protecting shorelines from erosion and destruction from storms. Do we expect people to stop driving cars? No, but the government could require manufacturers to build more fuel-efficient cars—at a cost to doing business.

And so, even though the conversation has changed somewhat since 2005, the debate continues over the extent to which human actions make a difference and then what should be done, at what cost, and at whose expense. In a series of short articles and three visuals—including the one that opens this chapter—a variety of voices are heard on this debate. Dr. Shean believes that those who feel a close connection with nature, who understand that it is the natural—not the human-constructed—world that is our home, will respond to the dangers faced by our ecological home. How green is your lifestyle? Does it matter?

PREREADING QUESTIONS

1. To whom do you listen primarily when you explore scientific questions? Scientists? Politicians? Religious leaders? What is the reasoning behind your choice?

2. Does Dr. Shean describe you when he writes of those who are complacent about environment problems because there does not seem to be an immediate danger? If so, do you think you should reconsider your position? Why or why not?

3. If you accept that we have a problem, what solutions would you support? Reject? Why?

THE SIXTH EXTINCTION: IT HAPPENED TO HIM. IT'S HAPPENING TO YOU.

MICHAEL NOVACEK

Paleontologist Michael Novacek is senior vice president and provost of the American Museum of Natural History in New York City. Author of more than 200 articles and books, Novacek's most recent book is *Terra: Our 100-Million-Old Ecosystem—and the Threats That Now Put It at Risk* (2008). "The Sixth Extinction" was published on January 13, 2008, in the *Washington Post*.

PREREADING QUESTIONS Who is the "Him" in Novacek's title? Is it ridiculous to suggest that *we could be like him?*

1   The news of environmental traumas assails us from every side—unseasonal storms, floods, fires, drought, melting ice caps, lost species of river dolphins and giant turtles, rising sea levels potentially displacing inhabitants of Arctic and Pacific islands and hundreds of thousands of people dying every year from air pollution. Last week brought more—new reports that Greenland's glaciers may be melting away at an alarming rate.

2   What's going on? Are we experiencing one of those major shocks to life on Earth that rocked the planet in the past?

3   That's just doomsaying, say those who insist that economic growth and human technological ingenuity will eventually solve our problems. But in fact, the scientific take on our current environmental mess is hardly so upbeat.

4   More than a decade ago, many scientists claimed that humans were demonstrating a capacity to force a major global catastrophe that would lead to

a traumatic shift in climate, an intolerable level of destruction of natural habitats, and an extinction event that could eliminate 30 to 50 percent of all living species by the middle of the 21st century. Now those predictions are coming true. The evidence shows that species loss today is accelerating. We find ourselves uncomfortably privileged to be witnessing a mass extinction event as it's taking place, in real time.

The fossil record reveals some extraordinarily destructive events in the 5 past, when species losses were huge, synchronous and global in scale. Paleontologists recognize at least five of these mass extinction events, the last of which occurred about 65 million years ago and wiped out all those big, charismatic dinosaurs (except their bird descendants) and at least 70 percent of all other species. The primary suspect for this catastrophe is a six-mile-wide asteroid (a mile higher than Mount Everest) whose rear end was still sticking out of the atmosphere as its nose augered into the crust a number of miles off the shore of the present-day Yucatan Peninsula in Mexico. Earth's atmosphere became a hell furnace, with super-broiler temperatures sufficient not only to kill exposed organisms, but also to incinerate virtually every forest on the planet.

For several million years, a period 100 times greater than the entire known 6 history of Homo sapiens, the planet's destroyed ecosystems underwent a slow, laborious recovery. The earliest colonizers after the catastrophe were populous species that quickly adapted to degraded environments, the ancient analogues of rats, cockroaches and weeds. But many of the original species that occupied these ecosystems were gone and did not come back. They'll never come back. The extinction of a species, whether in an incinerated 65-million-year-old reef or in a bleached modern-day reef of the Caribbean, is forever.

Now we face the possibility of mass extinction event No. 6. No big killer 7 asteroid is in sight. Volcanic eruptions and earthquakes are not of the scale to cause mass extinction. Yet recent studies show that troubling earlier projections about rampant extinction aren't exaggerated.

In 2007, of 41,415 species assessed for the International Union for the Con- 8 servation of Nature (IUCN) Red List of Threatened Species, 16,306 (39 percent) were categorized as threatened with extinction: one in three amphibians, one quarter of the world's pines and other coniferous trees, one in eight birds and one in four mammals. Another study identified 595 "centers of imminent extinction" in tropical forests, on islands and in mountainous areas. Disturbingly, only one-third of the sites surveyed were legally protected, and most were surrounded by areas densely populated by humans. We may not be able to determine the cause of past extinction events, but this time we have, indisputably: We are our own asteroids.

Still, the primary concern here is the future welfare of us and our children. 9 Assuming that we survive the current mass extinction event, won't we do okay? The disappearance of more than a few species is regrettable, but we can't compromise an ever-expanding population and a global economy whose collapse would leave billions to starve. This dismissal, however, ignores an essential fact about all those species: They live together in tightly networked ecosystems responsible for providing the habitats in which even we humans thrive. Pollination of flowers by diverse species of wild bees, wasps, butterflies and other insects, not just managed honeybees, accounts for more than 30 percent of all food production that humans depend upon.

10   What will the quality of life be like in this transformed new world? Science doesn't paint a pretty picture. The tropics and coral reefs, major sources of the planet's biological diversity, will be hugely debilitated. The 21st century may mark the end of the line for the evolution of large mammals and other animals that are now either on the verge of extinction, such as the Yangtze River dolphin, or, like the African black rhinoceros, confined to small, inadequately supportive habitats. And devastated ecosystems will provide warm welcome to all those opportunistic invader species that have already demonstrated their capacity to wipe out native plants and animals. We, and certainly our children, will find ourselves largely embraced by a pest and weed ecology ideal for the flourishing of invasive species and new, potentially dangerous microbes to which we haven't built up a biological resistance.

11   Of course people care about this. Recent surveys show a sharp increase in concern over the environmental changes taking place. But much of this spike in interest is due to the marked shift in attention to climate change and global warming away from other environmental problems such as deforestation, water pollution, overpopulation and biodiversity loss. Global warming is of course a hugely important issue. But it is the double whammy of climate change combined with fragmented, degraded natural habitats—not climate change alone—that is the real threat to many populations, species and ecosystems, including human populations marginalized and displaced by those combined forces.

12   Still, human ingenuity, commitment and shared responsibility have great potential to do good. The IUCN Red List now includes a handful of species that have been revived through conservation efforts, including the European white-tailed eagle and the Mekong catfish. Narrow corridors of protected habitat now connect nature preserves in South Africa, and similar corridors link up the coral reefs of the Bahamas, allowing species in the protected areas to move back and forth, exchange genes and sustain their populations. Coffee farms planted near protected forests and benefiting from wild pollinators have increased coffee yields. New York's $1 billion purchase of watersheds in the Catskill Mountains that purify water naturally secured precious natural habitat while eliminating the need for a filtration plant that would have cost $6 to $8 billion, plus annual operating costs of $300 million. Emissions of polluting gases such as dangerous nitrogen oxides have leveled off in North America and even declined in Europe (unfortunately emissions of the same are steeply rising in China). Plans for reflective roofing, green space and increased shade to cool urban "heat islands" are at least under consideration in many cities.

13   These actions may seem puny in light of the enormous problem we face, but their cumulative effect can bring surprising improvements. Yet our recent efforts, however praiseworthy, must become more intensive and global. Any

measure of success depends not only on international cooperation but also on the leadership of the most powerful nations and economies.

The first step in dealing with the problem is recognizing it for what it is. **14** Ecologists point out that the image of Earth still harboring unspoiled, pristine wild places is a myth. We live in a human-dominated world, they say, and virtually no habitat is untouched by our presence. Yet we are hardly the infallible masters of that universe. Instead, we are rather uneasy regents, a fragile and dysfunctional royal family holding back a revolution.

The sixth extinction event is under way. Can humanity muster the leader- **15** ship and international collaboration necessary to stop eating itself from the inside?

QUESTIONS FOR READING

1. What events suggest to scientists that we may be heading for another mass extinction?
2. What is the response of many to this "doomsaying" discussion?
3. How many mass extinctions has the Earth experienced? When was the last one and what happened then?
4. How do scientists describe the consequences of extinction No. 6?
5. What are the specific problems that combine to threaten a disastrous change in our environment?

QUESTIONS FOR REASONING AND ANALYSIS

1. What is the primary cause of a potential extinction No. 6? What, then, needs to be the primary source of the solutions? What, in the author's view, is the necessary first step?
2. In paragraph 12, Novacek describes some actions we have taken to address problems. What does he seek to accomplish by including this paragraph?
3. What is Novacek's claim? State it to reveal a causal argument.
4. Of the various consequences of extinction No. 6, listed in paragraph 10, what seems most frightening or devastating to you? Why?

QUESTIONS FOR REFLECTION AND WRITING

1. Novacek lists numbers and types of endangered species. Do these figures surprise you? Concern you? Why or why not?
2. In your experience, how widespread is the concern for environmental degradation? Do your friends and family discuss this issue? Do most dismiss the seriousness of the issue, as Novacek suggests?
3. Have you made changes to be kinder to the environment? If so, what have you done and what would you recommend that others do?

4. Do you agree with Novacek—or does he overstate the problem? If you agree, how would you contribute to his argument? If you disagree, how would you refute him?

WAKE UP AMERICA. WE'RE DRIVING TOWARD DISASTER. | JAMES HOWARD KUNSTLER

Beginning his career in journalism, James Howard Kunstler turned in 1975 to the writing of novels and nonfiction books. Although he continues to contribute to newspapers and magazines (as in the article here, published in the *Washington Post*, May 25, 2008), he is best known for his nine novels and for his focus on urban design and environmental problems. In his latest book, *The Long Emergency* (2005), Kunstler examines the oil crisis and climate change problems.

PREREADING QUESTION Given the title and the context of appearing in this chapter, what do you expect this argument to be about?

1   Everywhere I go these days, talking about the global energy predicament on the college lecture circuit or at environmental conferences, I hear an increasingly shrill cry for "solutions." This is just another symptom of the delusional thinking that now grips the nation, especially among the educated and well-intentioned.

2   I say this because I detect in this strident plea the desperate wish to keep our "Happy Motoring" utopia running by means other than oil and its byproducts. But the truth is that no combination of solar, wind and nuclear power, ethanol, biodiesel, tar sands and used French-fry oil will allow us to power Wal-Mart, Disney World and the interstate highway system—or even a fraction of these things—in the future. We have to make other arrangements.

3   The public, and especially the mainstream media, misunderstands the "peak oil" story. It's not about running out of oil. It's about the instabilities that will shake the complex systems of daily life as soon as the global demand for oil exceeds the global supply. These systems can be listed concisely:

- The way we produce food
- The way we conduct commerce and trade
- The way we travel
- The way we occupy the land
- The way we acquire and spend capital

4   And there are others: governance, health care, education and more.

5   As the world passes the all-time oil production high and watches as the price of a barrel of oil busts another record, as it did last week, these systems will run into trouble. Instability in one sector will bleed into another. Shocks to the oil markets will hurt trucking, which will slow commerce and food distribution, manufacturing and the tourist industry in a chain of cascading effects.

Problems in finance will squeeze any enterprise that requires capital, including oil exploration and production, as well as government spending. These systems are all interrelated. They all face a crisis. What's more, the stress induced by the failure of these systems will only increase the wishful thinking across our nation.

And that's the worst part of our quandary: the American public's narrow 6 focus on keeping all our cars running at any cost. Even the environmental community is hung up on this. The Rocky Mountain Institute has been pushing for the development of a "Hypercar" for years—inadvertently promoting the idea that we really don't need to change.

Years ago, U.S. negotiators at a U.N. environmental conference told their 7 interlocutors that the American lifestyle is "not up for negotiation." This stance is, unfortunately, related to two pernicious beliefs that have become common in the United States in recent decades. The first is the idea that when you wish upon a star, your dreams come true. (Oprah Winfrey advanced this notion last year with her promotion of a pop book called *The Secret,* which said, in effect, that if you wish hard enough for something, it will come to you.) One of the basic differences between a child and an adult is the ability to know the difference between wishing for things and actually making them happen through earnest effort.

The companion belief to "wishing upon a star" is the idea that one can get 8 something for nothing. This derives from America's new favorite religion: not evangelical Christianity but the worship of unearned riches. (The holy shrine to this tragic belief is Las Vegas.) When you combine these two beliefs, the result is the notion that when you wish upon a star, you'll get something for nothing. This is what underlies our current fantasy, as well as our inability to respond intelligently to the energy crisis.

These beliefs also explain why the presidential campaign is devoid of 9 meaningful discussion about our energy predicament and its implications. The idea that we can become "energy independent" *and* maintain our current lifestyle is absurd. So is the gas-tax holiday. (Which politician wants to tell voters on Labor Day that the holiday is over?) The pie-in-the-sky plan to turn grain into fuel came to grief, too, when we saw its disruptive effect on global grain prices and the food shortages around the world, even in the United States. In recent weeks, the rice and cooking-oil shelves in my upstate New York supermarket have been stripped clean.

So what are intelligent responses to our predicament? First, we'll have to 10 dramatically reorganize the everyday activities of American life. We'll have to grow our food closer to home, in a manner that will require more human attention. In fact, agriculture needs to return to the center of economic life. We'll have to restore local economic networks—the very networks that the big-box stores systematically destroyed—made of fine-grained layers of wholesalers, middlemen and retailers.

We'll also have to occupy the landscape differently, in traditional towns, 11 villages and small cities. Our giant metroplexes are not going to make it, and the successful places will be ones that encourage local farming.

12   Fixing the U.S. passenger railroad system is probably the one project we could undertake right away that would have the greatest impact on the country's oil consumption. The fact that we're not talking about it—especially in the presidential campaign—shows how confused we are. The airline industry is disintegrating under the enormous pressure of fuel costs. Airlines cannot fire any more employees and have already offloaded their pension obligations and outsourced their repairs. At least five small airlines have filed for bankruptcy protection in the past two months. If we don't get the passenger trains running again, Americans will be going nowhere five years from now.

13   We don't have time to be crybabies about this. The talk on the presidential campaign trail about "hope" has its purpose. We cannot afford to remain befuddled and demoralized. But we must understand that hope is not something applied externally. Real hope resides within us. We generate it—by proving that we are competent, earnest individuals who can discern between wishing and doing, who don't figure on getting something for nothing and who can be honest about the way the universe really works.

QUESTIONS FOR READING

1. What problem does Kunstler explore?
2. Why is the problem not about finding more oil—or alternatives to oil?
3. What systems are interconnected? How will the crisis spread?
4. What two beliefs do Americans embrace? How do these beliefs feed our current energy problems?
5. What does the author recommend?

QUESTIONS FOR REASONING AND ANALYSIS

1. What is Kunstler's claim? Where does he state it?
2. The author stresses the interrelatedness of systems such as oil supply, commerce, finance, and food production. Writing in May, 2008, how is he prophetic? What crises does he anticipate?
3. Kunstler asserts that the worst part of our problem is that we insist on continuing to drive cars as usual. How much a part of our "idea" of American life includes driving a car? How difficult is it to change an idea, an image of ourselves?

QUESTIONS FOR REFLECTION AND WRITING

1. Kunstler and Novacek are examining different environment issues, but both agree that the biggest problem is our denial that there are problems. Do you accept their judgment? Are most Americans too complacent? Why or why not?
2. Do you agree with Kunstler that the car plays a leading role in our environmental problems? If you agree, what do you recommend as a solution? If you disagree, how would you refute Kunstler?
3. Kunstler recommends growing food nearer to consumers. Is this a logical solution? Is it a practical one? Defend or rebut the author.

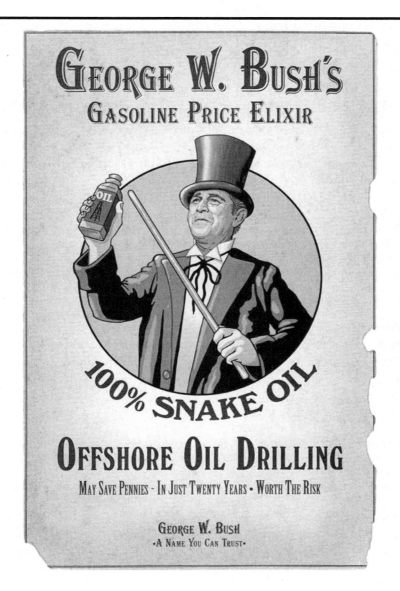

GEORGE W. BUSH'S
GASOLINE PRICE ELIXIR

100% SNAKE OIL

OFFSHORE OIL DRILLING
MAY SAVE PENNIES · IN JUST TWENTY YEARS · WORTH THE RISK

GEORGE W. BUSH
·A NAME YOU CAN TRUST·

With our economy sinking and oil prices soaring, George Bush is offering snake oil: a plan to sacrifice more of our coasts to oil drilling on the chance it will produce a few weeks' worth of oil and reduce gas prices by a few pennies a gallon…in 2028. Imagine America forever tethered to Bush's failed energy policy. It's like giving him five more terms.

It's a cruel Shell game. And BP game. And ExxonMobil game. Over the past five years, the number of domestic drilling permits has nearly doubled. But because of rising worldwide demand, oil prices have skyrocketed. More drilling off our coasts is not the answer. Once destroyed they can never be replaced. The only winners will be the oil companies.

Want gas at $1 a gallon? America needs a bold new approach to energy, from more fuel-efficient vehicles to plug-in hybrids and electric cars. A cleaner electric grid powered by renewables. Existing technologies could have us driving at the equivalent of a buck a gallon for gas!

Tell your Representative and Senators to stop the giveaway of our coasts. Tell them you won't stand for billions more for oil companies—and snake oil for the rest of us.

NRDC
ACTION FUND

MOBILIZING AMERICA
FOR OUR ENVIRONMENT

NRDCActionFund.org

Paid for by supporters of the Natural Resources Defense Council Action Fund.

QUESTIONS FOR READING

1. What is the central visual of this ad reminiscent of?
2. What is the ad's subject?

QUESTIONS FOR REASONING AND ANALYSIS

1. What is the ad's claim? What argument strategies are used—both in the visual and in the copy below?
2. What is clever about the visual? What two attacks does it achieve? How are they connected?

QUESTIONS FOR REFLECTION AND ANALYSIS

1. Is this ad entirely fair to President Bush? Why or why not?
2. Do you agree with the ad's position on offshore drilling? If so, how would you add to the discussion? If not, how would you rebut the ad's argument?

CARBON CHASTITY | CHARLES KRAUTHAMMER

A graduate of Harvard Medical School and board certified in psychiatry, Charles Krauthammer is a syndicated columnist and a regular on the political talk show *Inside Washington*. He has won a Pulitzer Prize for political commentary. The following column was published on May 30, 2008.

PREREADING QUESTIONS What do you take the title of this column to mean? What do you anticipate Krauthammer's view of environmental problems to be?

1   I'm not a global warming believer. I'm not a global warming denier. I'm a global warming agnostic who believes instinctively that it can't be very good to pump lots of CO_2 into the atmosphere but is equally convinced that those who presume to know exactly where that leads are talking through their hats.

2   Predictions of catastrophe depend on models. Models depend on assumptions about complex planetary systems—from ocean currents to cloud formation—that no one fully understands. Which is why the models are inherently flawed and forever changing. The doomsday scenarios posit a cascade of events, each with a certain probability. The multiple improbability of their simultaneous occurrence renders all such predictions entirely speculative.

3   Yet on the basis of this speculation, environmental activists, attended by compliant scientists and opportunistic politicians, are advocating radical economic and social regulation. "The largest threat to freedom, democracy, the market economy and prosperity," warns Czech President Vaclav Klaus, "is no longer socialism. It is, instead, the ambitious, arrogant, unscrupulous ideology of environmentalism."

If you doubt the arrogance, you haven't seen that *Newsweek* cover story **4** that declared the global warming debate over. Consider: If Newton's laws of motion could, after 200 years of unfailing experimental and experiential confirmation, be overthrown, it requires religious fervor to believe that global warming—infinitely more untested, complex and speculative—is a closed issue.

But declaring it closed has its rewards. It not only dismisses skeptics as the **5** running dogs of reaction, i.e., of Exxon, Cheney and now Klaus. By fiat, it also hugely re-empowers the intellectual left.

For a century, an ambitious, arrogant, unscrupulous knowledge class— **6** social planners, scientists, intellectuals, experts and their left-wing political allies—arrogated to themselves the right to rule either in the name of the oppressed working class (communism) or, in its more benign form, by virtue of their superior expertise in achieving the highest social progress by means of state planning (socialism).

Two decades ago, however, socialism and communism died rudely, then **7** were buried forever by the empirical demonstration of the superiority of market capitalism everywhere from Thatcher's England to Deng's China, where just the partial abolition of socialism lifted more people out of poverty more rapidly than ever in human history.

Just as the ash heap of history beckoned, the intellectual left was handed **8** the ultimate salvation: environmentalism. Now the experts will regulate your life not in the name of the proletariat or Fabian socialism but—even better—in the name of Earth itself.

Environmentalists are Gaia's priests, instructing us in her proper service **9** and casting out those who refuse to genuflect. (See *Newsweek* above.) And having proclaimed the ultimate commandment—carbon chastity—they are preparing the supporting canonical legislation that will tell you how much you can travel, what kind of light you will read by, and at what temperature you may set your bedroom thermostat.

Only Monday, a British parliamentary committee proposed that every citi- **10** zen be required to carry a carbon card that must be presented, under penalty of law, when buying gasoline, taking an airplane or using electricity. The card contains your yearly carbon ration to be drawn down with every purchase, every trip, every swipe.

There's no greater social power than the power to ration. And, other than **11** rationing food, there is no greater instrument of social control than rationing energy, the currency of just about everything one does and uses in an advanced society.

So what does the global warming agnostic propose as an alternative? First, **12** more research—untainted and reliable—to determine (a) whether the carbon footprint of man is or is not lost among the massive natural forces (from sunspot activity to ocean currents) that affect climate, and (b) if the human effect is indeed significant, whether the planetary climate system has the homeostatic mechanisms (like the feedback loops in the human body, for example) with which to compensate.

13   Second, reduce our carbon footprint in the interim by doing the doable, rather than the economically ruinous and socially destructive. The most obvious step is a major move to nuclear power, which to the atmosphere is the cleanest of the clean.

14   But your would-be masters have foreseen this contingency. The Church of the Environment promulgates secondary dogmas as well. One of these is a strict nuclear taboo.

15   Rather convenient, is it not? Take this major coal-substituting fix off the table, and we will be rationing all the more. Guess who does the rationing.

QUESTIONS FOR READING

1. What is Krauthammer's response to those who are concerned about the threats of global warming?

2. On what are predictions about global warming and its dangers based? What, in the author's view, is the problem with this basis?

3. What do environmentalists gain by declaring the debate over? What will they be able to do?

4. Who are these environmentalists, according to Krauthammer?

5. What immediate solutions does the author recommend?

QUESTIONS FOR REASONING AND ANALYSIS

1. What is Krauthammer's claim? (Do not state it as a personal belief. State it as a position on environmental problems.)

2. Beginning with his title, Krauthammer develops a metaphor to characterize the views and behavior of environmentalists. What is the metaphor? List specific sentences that develop the metaphor. What is the impact of the metaphor—what attitude does it convey?

3. The author discusses the demise of communism and socialism. Why? How does he connect that discussion to environmentalists? What does he want to accomplish with this discussion?

QUESTIONS FOR REFLECTION AND WRITING

1. Krauthammer asserts that environmentalists oppose nuclear power as an alternative energy source. Do you accept this assertion? Why or why not?

2. He also describes them as arrogant. Is this legitimate? Or name calling? Explain.

3. Do you agree with Krauthammer's position? If so, why? If not, why not? Either add to his argument or rebut his position.

INCONVENIENT TRUTHS: GET READY TO RETHINK WHAT IT MEANS TO BE GREEN

EDITORS, *WIRED* MAGAZINE

Wired magazine presented this brief but important statement on environmental problems and then followed this introduction with short essays on each of the "10 Green Heresies." After these ten short essays, the magazine included a counterpoint, the argument by Alex Steffen that follows this one. These arguments appeared in the magazine on May 19, 2008.

PREREADING QUESTIONS Why "inconvenient" truths in the title? What do you expect these truths to include?

The environmental movement has never been short on noble goals. Preserving wild spaces, cleaning up the oceans, protecting watersheds, neutralizing acid rain, saving endangered species—all laudable. But today, one ecological problem outweighs all others: global warming. Restoring the Everglades, protecting the Headwaters redwoods, or saving the Illinois mud turtle won't matter if climate change plunges the planet into chaos. It's high time for greens to unite around the urgent need to reduce emissions of greenhouse gases. 1

Just one problem. Winning the war on global warming requires slaughtering some of environmentalism's sacred cows. We can afford to ignore neither the carbon-free electricity supplied by nuclear energy nor the transformational potential of genetic engineering. We need to take advantage of the energy efficiencies offered by urban density. We must accept that the world's fastest-growing economies won't forgo a higher standard of living in the name of climate science—and that, on the way up, countries like India and China might actually help devise the solutions the planet so desperately needs. 2

Some will reject this approach as dangerously single-minded: The environment is threatened on many fronts, and all of them need attention. So argues Alex Steffen. That may be true, but global warming threatens to overwhelm any progress made on other issues. The planet is already heating up, and the point of no return may be only decades away. So combating greenhouse gases must be our top priority, even if that means embracing the unthinkable. Here, then, are 10 tenets of the new environmental apostasy. 3

10 GREEN HERESIES   4

- **Live in cities:** Urban living is kinder to the planet than the suburban lifestyle.
- **A/C is ok:** Air-conditioning actually emits *less* CO_2 than heating.
- **Organics are not the answer:** Surprise! Conventional agriculture can be easier on the planet.
- **Farm the forests:** Old-growth forests can actually *contribute* to global warming.

- **China is the solution:** The People's Republic leads the way in alternative-energy hardware.
- **Accept genetic engineering:** Superefficient Frankencrops could put a real dent in greenhouse gas emissions.
- **Carbon trading doesn't work:** Carbon credits were a great idea, but the benefits are illusory.
- **Embrace nuclear power:** Face it. Nukes are the most climate-friendly industrial-scale form of energy.
- **Used cars—not hybrids:** Don't buy that new Prius! Test-drive a used car instead.
- **Prepare for the worst:** Climate change is Inevitable. Get used to it.

QUESTIONS FOR READING

1. According to the editors, what is the most serious environmental problem we face?
2. To address this most serious of the problems, what must we be prepared to accept?
3. What are the 10 heresies that "greens" must accept? State them in your own words.

QUESTIONS FOR REASONING AND ANALYSIS

1. What is the editors' claim? Where do they state it?
2. Who is the primary audience for this argument? Whose views are the editors seeking to change?
3. The editors write: "Here, then, are 10 tenets of the new environmental apostasy." What does *apostasy* mean? What metaphor is used here? (Compare this essay to Charles Krauthammer's.) From this metaphor, what can we conclude to be some of the strong beliefs of those active in environmental issues?

QUESTIONS FOR REFLECTION AND WRITING

1. Do you agree with the authors that the threat of greenhouse gases is so great that it must be treated first and with most of the attention? Why or why not?
2. Are you "green"? If so, do you oppose the use of nuclear energy? Why or why not? If you are not an environmentalist, what is your reaction to using more nuclear energy?
3. Do you agree that Western countries will not be able to deny to India and China their plans to grow their economies—adding to the world's greenhouse gases? Do the editors have a useful approach to this problem in suggesting that these countries may be the ones to come up with the solutions to global warming that we all need? Either add to the editors' discussion or refute their argument.

COUNTERPOINT: DANGERS OF FOCUSING SOLELY ON CLIMATE CHANGE | ALEX STEFFEN

Alex Steffen has been the Executive Editor of WorldChanging.com since he joined in creating this Web site in 2003. Prior to WorldChanging, Steffen was an environmental journalist and active in various urban design groups. As a result of the enormous success of WorldChanging, Steffen speaks at many conferences and to many businesses worldwide. The goal of WorldChanging is to help create "a future which is sustainable, dynamic, prosperous, and fair"—and of course green. His counter to the editors of *Wired* was published, with the previous article, on May 19, 2008.

PREREADING QUESTION Based on the title, your knowledge of the author, and the previous article, what do you expect Steffen's subject and perspective to be?

> **INCONVENIENT TRUTHS:** Get Ready to Rethink What It Means to Be Green
> **1:** Live in Cities
> **2:** A/C is OK
> **3:** Organics Are Not the Answer
> **4:** Farm the Forests
> **5:** China Is the Solution
> **6:** Accept Genetic Engineering
> **7:** Carbon Trading Doesn't Work
> **8:** Embrace Nuclear Power
> **9:** Used Cars Not Hybrids
> **10:** Prepare for the Worst

1 No one with any scientific sense now disagrees about the severity of the climate crisis. But some people—and some magazines—believe that climate change trumps every other problem. If we take this argument to its extreme, we should ignore any environmental concern that gets in the way of reducing emissions. And that's just plain wrong.

2 Make no mistake: Tackling climate change is vital. But to see everything through the lens of short-term CO_2 reductions, letting our obsession with carbon blind us to the bigger picture, is to court catastrophe.

3 Climate change is not a discrete issue; it's a symptom of larger problems. Fundamentally, our society as currently designed has no future. We're chewing up the planet so fast, in so many different ways, that we could solve the climate problem tomorrow and still find that environmental collapse is imminent. Myopic responses will only hasten its arrival.

4 Take the proposal that we cut down old trees in favor of new ones. First, I don't buy the carbon accounting presented to advance this procrustean plan: Older trees can absorb CO_2 for centuries after reaching maturity, while replanted forests can emit more CO_2 than they sequester until the new trees are as much as 20 years old.

5 But even if *Wired's* math were correct, this would still be a crap fix for climate change. Chopping down forests causes massive soil erosion and leads to desertification, making repeated tree plantings a dodgy prospect. As monocultures, tree farms are far more vulnerable to pest infestations. And batches of trees planted at the same time are more susceptible to wildfires, causing the carbon they're supposed to be sequestering to go up in smoke.

6   Old-growth forests, coupled with a broad program of woodlands resto-ration and sustainable forestry, can provide not only climate relief and eco-logically responsible wood and biomass harvests but a slew of other essential ecological services, from salmon habitats to flood prevention. It's a heck of a lot more costly—in both money and emissions—to build massive dams and fish farms than to simply protect the forests we already have.

7   Another example of how carbon blindness leads to counterproductive poli-cies: embracing nuclear power as a clean energy source. This argument assumes that other clean alternatives will not improve in efficiency or affordability dur-ing the 10 years it would take to implement a nuclear program. That's short-term thinking. If we invested the money that we would spend on new nuclear facilities more wisely (and eliminated subsidies on fossil fuels), alternatives like wind, solar, hydroelectric, and wave power could deliver a clean-energy future more cheaply and probably sooner, without any of the security or health risks of nuclear plants. Nuclear power may have a role to play, but it would be far better to create a flexible energy system that draws on many clean sources, instead of on a single panacea. Again, a cut-carbon-at-all-costs approach blinds us to more-sustainable, and ultimately more-promising, solutions.

8   To have any hope of staving off collapse, we need to move forward with measures that address many interrelated problems at once. We're not going to persuade people in the developing world to go without, but neither can we afford a planet on which everyone lives like an American. Billions more people living in suburbs and driving SUVs to shopping malls is a recipe for planetary suicide. We can't even afford to continue that way of life ourselves.

9   We don't need a War on Carbon. We need a new prosperity that can be shared by all while still respecting a multitude of real ecological limits—not just atmospheric gas concentrations, but topsoil depth, water supplies, toxic chemical concentrations, and the health of ecosystems, including the diversity of life they depend upon.

10   We can build a future in which technology, design, smart incentives, and wise policies make it possible to deliver a high quality of life at lower ecologi-cal cost. But that brighter, greener future is attainable only if we embrace the problems we face in all their complexity. To do otherwise is tantamount to clear-cutting the very future we're trying to secure.

QUESTIONS FOR READING

1.   What is Steffen's subject?
2.   How does he challenge the idea of cutting down mature trees and replacing them? What are the problems with massive farming of forests?
3.   What is his response to "embracing nuclear power"?

QUESTIONS FOR REASONING AND ANALYSIS

1.   What is Steffen's claim? Where does he state it?
2.   How does paragraph 3 expand and support his claim and serve as a lead-in to the specifics that follow?

3. Is this author an environmentalist who opposes a nuclear power solution? What can you infer from his discussion?

QUESTIONS FOR REFLECTION AND WRITING

1. Has Steffen convinced you that cutting mature forests is not a solution to climate change? Why or why not?
2. Who has the more convincing argument: the *Wired* editors or Steffen? Why? Defend your choice.

You can't solve the climate crisis alone.
But if we all work together, we can.

Join we today.   wecansolveit.org

QUESTIONS FOR READING

1. What does the visual on page 397 represent?
2. What do the words in the visual communicate?

QUESTIONS FOR REASONING AND ANALYSIS

1. What is the ad's claim?
2. This ad differs significantly from the "Snake Oil" ad (see p. 391). What are these differences? Do a comparative analysis of the ads.
3. Does this ad's visual effectively support the claim? Why or why not?

QUESTIONS FOR REFLECTION AND WRITING

1. Who has to work together to solve the climate crisis? (Think about this and also draw from your reading in this chapter.) Are all of the significant players likely to work together? Why or why not?
2. Does this ad catch your attention sufficiently for you to check out their Web site? For you to think about ways that you can help solve the climate problem? Why or why not?

DON'T MESS WITH MOTHER | ANNA QUINDLEN

A syndicated columnist, Anna Quindlen has won the Pulitzer Prize for commentary and has published several volumes of her columns. She has also written novels, including *Black and Blue* (1998) and *Blessings* (2002). Her following "Last Word" *Newsweek* column was published September 19, 2005.

PREREADING QUESTIONS Based on the title alone, what would you guess this essay to be about? Adding the context of its place in this chapter, does that change your anticipation of the essay's subject?

1   The dark aftermath of the frontier, of the vast promise of possibility this country first offered, is an inflated sense of American entitlement today. We want what we want, and we want it now. Easy credit. Fast food. A straight shot down the interstate from point A to point B. The endless highway is crowded with the kinds of cars large enough to take a mountain pass in high snow. Instead they are used to take children from soccer practice to Pizza Hut. In the process they burn fuel like there's no tomorrow.

2   Tomorrow's coming.

3   The cataclysm named Katrina has inspired a Hummer-load of rumination, about class, about race, about the pathetic failure of the Feds after four long years of much-vaunted homeland-security plans. The president made himself foolish, calling for an investigation into who fouled up, perhaps ignorant of Harry Truman's desk plaque reading THE BUCK STOPS HERE. The press rose to

the occasion, awakened out of its recent somnambulant state, galvanized into empathy and rage. The public was remarkable, opening their homes and their wallets.

But the failure by government, in the midst of a hurricane season forecast 4 early on to be a monstrous one, illustrates once again the lack of a long view. The long view at the moment is not about patching levees, or building houses, or getting oil rigs back up and running, or assigning blame. It's about changing the way we all live now.

Both the left, with its endless talk of rights, and the right, with its disdain 5 for government oversight, suggest that you can do what you please. Americans have taken the message to heart, and nowhere is that clearer than in the mess we've made of the natural environment. How many times do we have to watch homes cantilevered over canyons surrender to a river of mud or beach houses on stilts slide into the surf to know that when we do high-stakes battle with Mother Nature, Mother takes all? Once I heard a businessman at a zoning-board meeting say, "Well, a person can do what he wants with his land." Actually, that's not true; that's why zoning exists. Is any city, town or state brave enough to just say no to waterfront development that destroys dunes, despoils water and creates the conditions that will, when a storm strikes, create destruction?

New Orleans lived for 80 years with the granddaddy of all environmen- 6 tally misguided plans, the project that straightened out the mighty Mississippi so its banks would be more hospitable to homes and businesses. Little by little the seductive city at the river's mouth became like one of those denuded developments built after clear-cutting. It was left with no natural protection, girded with a jerry-built belt of walled-off water, its marshland and barrier islands gone, a sitting duck for a big storm.

But it was not alone. Everywhere in the country, wetlands disappeared 7 and parking lots bloomed during the past half century of mindless growth, in which bigger was always assumed to be better. While the streets of European cities were filled with tiny compact cars, the SUV took over American roads. Show houses sprang up that will soon present an interesting lesson in what happens when cathedral ceilings meet sky-high fuel prices. In the aftermath of Katrina, one displaced person after another told TV reporters that at least they were alive, their family was safe, the stuff didn't matter. If only that were the ethic for the long haul. Consumption used to be the name for a mortal wasting disease. It still is.

This administration of big-oil guys is the last place to look for leadership on 8 conservation. Many Bush supporters scoff at global warming as a lefty myth, and early on the president made his position clear when he made the United States one of two industrialized nations to reject the Kyoto Protocol, the plan to curtail climate change by cutting down emission levels. But there has been no powerful national leadership from either party on this front in recent memory. Political officials have bowed to the public's thirst for more, more, more.

The effects of disaster fall disproportionately on those who have less, as 9 they did during Hurricane Katrina, when poor families had no cars to flee in, when there were no immediately available means for a second act in another

town and another home. But between the blackouts, the fuel costs, the erod-
ing coastlines, the disappearing open spaces, it is going to become harder and
harder to overcome the effects of blind overgrowth even for those of means.
Get ready for the $100 tank of gas, and an Armageddon of our own making.

10   New Orleans will be rebuilt, but rebuilt how? In the heedless, grasping
fashion in which so much of this country has been built over the past 50 years,
which has led to a continuous loop of floods, fires and filth in the air and
water? Or could the new New Orleans be the first city of a new era, in which
the demands of development and commerce are carefully balanced against
the good of the land and, in the long run, the good of its people? We have
been crummy stewards of the Earth, with a sense of knee-jerk entitlement that
tells us there is always more where this came from.

11   There isn't.

QUESTIONS FOR READING

1. What problems were exposed, what issues raised, as a result of Katrina?
2. What is the long-range issue made clear by Katrina, in the author's view?
3. What groups, for different reasons, contribute to Americans' sense of entitlement?
4. What was done in New Orleans that increased its danger in the face of a big storm?
5. In what other ways, across the United States, have we made bad choices "for the long haul," in the author's words?

QUESTIONS FOR REASONING AND ANALYSIS

1. What is Quindlen's claim? Where does she state it?
2. Analyze the author's style and tone.
3. Find one or two passages that use rhetorical techniques in especially effective ways. What makes these passages clever?

QUESTIONS FOR REFLECTING AND WRITING

1. Both Quindlen and Steffen argue that we are destroying our environment, but their writing is quite different. Which argument do you find more convincing? Why? Are there some readers for whom one approach might be better than the other? Explain.
2. Quindlen does not spell out solutions, but in her warnings of the trouble to come she points to problem areas. What, by implication, must we do to stop messing with Mother? How can we bring about change in these areas?

CHAPTER 17

Sports Talk—Sports Battles

Aerial performers were part of a dazzling show to close out the Games. China itself performed acrobatic feats to make the Olympics a success.

What is the purpose of the university? What is the role of sports at the university? And, what is the purpose of organized sports for youngsters? To turn out Division I stars? To win Olympic medals? Or, to be healthy and fit and have fun? These are tough questions, and they are only some of the questions the writers in this chapter raise. These and other issues lead to debate and conflict in today's sports arenas, including the debate over physical enhancement. What improvements to the body are legal, perhaps admirable, and what changes cross a line and ought to be banned? Or, should any improvements be banned? Three authors debate this current sports battle. The chapter concludes with a Canadian Olympian who speaks out on a political issue, reminding us that many athletes give much back to their communities and to the world.

After enjoying the stunning photo from the 2008 Olympics on the preceding page, consider the following questions as you prepare to study this chapter's arguments.

PREREADING QUESTIONS

1. Should the NCAA demand higher academic credentials for would-be college athletes and expect college players to carry typical course loads leading to graduation?
2. How important are the Olympics? Are they worth the money spent every four years? What do we gain from them?
3. How much "enhancement" of athletes is fair? Should steroids be allowed?

WHO'S KILLING KIDS' SPORTS? | DAVID OLIVER RELIN

An award-winning journalist, David Relin is a contributing editor to both *Parade* and *Skiing* magazines. He collaborated with Greg Mortenson in the writing of *Three Cups of Tea* (2006), the story of Mortenson's struggles in Pakistan to build schools. The following article was published in *Parade* on August 7, 2005.

PREREADING QUESTIONS Did you participate in sports as a youngster? If so, was it fun or highly competitive? Are youth sports too competitive today?

1   Two years ago, when he was still in high school, pro basketball prospect LeBron James inked an endorsement contract with Nike worth between $90 million and $100 million. Five days later, the $1 million contract Nike offered to Maryland soccer prodigy Freddy Adu seemed almost ordinary, except for one detail—Freddy was just 13 years old.

2   In the summer of 2003, Jeret Adair, a 15-year-old pitcher from Atlanta, started 64 games with his elite traveling baseball team—more than most pro players pitch in an entire season. After the ligament in his elbow snapped, he had to undergo reconstructive surgery, a process once reserved for aging professional pitchers. In 2004, his doctor, James Andrews, performed similar surgery on 50 other high school pitchers.

Last March, Valerie Yianacopolus of Wakefield, Mass., was sentenced to ₃ one year of probation, including 50 hours of community service, and ordered to watch a sportsmanship video after she was found guilty of assaulting an 11-year-old boy who was cheering for the opposing team at her son's Little League game.

And in June, according to state police, Mark Downs, the coach of a youth ₄ T-ball team near Uniontown, Pa., allegedly offered one of his players $25 to throw a baseball at the head of a 9-year-old disabled teammate so the injured boy wouldn't be able to play in an upcoming game. League rules mandate that every healthy child play at least three innings. "The coach was very competitive," said State Trooper Thomas B. Broadwater. "He wanted to win."

A SPORTS CULTURE RUN AMOK

Across the country, millions of children are being chewed up and spit ₅ out by a sports culture run amok. With pro scouts haunting the nation's playgrounds in search of the next LeBron or Freddy, parents and coaches are conspiring to run youth-sports leagues like incubators for future professional athletes. Prepubescent athletes are experimenting with performance-enhancing drugs. Doctors are reporting sharp spikes in injuries caused by year-round specialization in a single sport at an early age. And all too often, the simple pleasure of playing sports is being buried beneath cutthroat competition.

"If I had to sum up the crisis in kids' sports," says J. Duke Albanese, Maine's ₆ former commissioner of education, "I'd do it in one word—adults."

Some adults, Albanese says, are pushing children toward unrealistic goals ₇ like college sports scholarships and pro contracts. According to National Collegiate Athletic Association (NCAA) statistics, fewer than 2% of high school athletes will ever receive a college athletic scholarship. Only one in 13,000 high school athletes will ever receive a paycheck from a professional team.

"There is a terrible imbalance between the needs kids have and the needs ₈ of the adults running their sports programs," says Dr. Bruce Svare, director of the National Institute for Sports Reform. "Above all, kids need to have fun. Instead, adults are providing unrealistic expectations and crushing pressure."

As a result, Svare says, at a time when an epidemic of obesity is plagu- ₉ ing the nation's youth, 70% of America's children are abandoning organized sports by age 13. "The only way to reverse this crisis," Svare argues, "is to fundamentally rethink the way America's kids play organized sports."

IS CHANGE POSSIBLE?

Many communities *are* trying to change the way they approach children's ₁₀ sports. Florida's Jupiter-Tequesta Athletic Association, facing a rash of violent behavior by sports parents, now requires them to take an online course on how to behave at their children's athletic events. School officials in Connecticut, concerned about the toll of too much focus on a single sport, instituted a statewide ban on students playing on a private travel team during the same season they play their sport in high school.

11   But no reform effort is more aggressive than that of the state of Maine, where educators, student athletes and others have teamed up to launch a counterrevolution called Sports Done Right. Led by J. Duke Albanese and Robert Cobb, dean of the University of Maine's College of Education, and funded by a federal grant secured by U.S. Sen. Susan M. Collins, the project aims to radically remake Maine's youth-sports culture and provide a model that the rest of America might emulate.

THE MAINE CHALLENGE

12   Their first step is a sweeping campaign to dial down the kind of competition that leads many kids to drop out of sports at an early age. "I was a high school football coach—I know how badly communities want their teams to win," Albanese says. "We're not saying there's anything wrong with competition. We're saying what's appropriate at the varsity level is out of bounds in grade school and middle school. That's a time to encourage as many children as possible to play. Period."

13   To do that, the Sports Done Right team held statewide summit meetings before producing an action plan. It chose 12 school districts as the program's pilot sites, but so many other districts clamored to participate that it is now under way in dozens more.

14   The program has identified core principles that it insists must be present in a healthy sports environment for kids, including good sportsmanship, discouragement of early specialization and the assurance that teams below the varsity level make it their mission to develop the skills of every child on every team, to promote a lifelong involvement with sports.

15   Sports Done Right's second task is to attack the two problems it says are most responsible for the crisis in kids' sports—the behavior of parents and coaches.

PROBLEM #1: OUT-OF-CONTROL ADULTS

16   The behavior of adults has been at the center of the debate about reforming kids' sports ever since 2002, when Thomas Junta of Reading, Mass., was convicted of beating Michael Costin to death during an argument at their sons' youth hockey practice. "I've watched adult civility in youth sports spiral downward since the early 1990s," says Doug Abrams, a law professor at the University of Missouri, who has tracked media reports of out-of-control sports parents for more than a decade. "At one time, adults who acted like lunatics were shunned as outcasts. But today, they are too often tolerated."

17   The nearly 100 Maine students *Parade* interviewed recited a litany of incidents involving adults behaving badly, including examples of their own parents being removed from sporting events by police. Nate Chantrill, 17—a shot-putter and discus thrower at Edward Little High School in Auburn and a varsity football player—volunteers to coach a coed fifth-grade football team. "One game, a parent flipped out that we didn't start his daughter," Chantrill recalls. "He was screaming, using bad language and saying she's the best player out there. Parents take this stuff way too seriously. Fifth-grade football

is not the Super Bowl. It's a place for your kid to learn some skills and have fun. One parent can ruin it for all the kids."

That's why each Sports Done Right district is holding training sessions to **18** define out-of-bounds behavior at sporting events and requiring the parents of every student who plays to sign a compact promising to abide by higher standards of sportsmanship.

PROBLEM #2: POOR COACHING

Dan Campbell, who has coached Edward Little's track team to two state **19** championships, says he sees too many of his peers pressing to win at all costs and neglecting their primary responsibility—to educate and inspire children. "One coach can destroy a kid for a lifetime," he says. "I've seen it over and over."

"I was at an AAU basketball game where the ref gave the coach a techni- **20** cal and threw him out of the game," says Doug Joerss, who was the starting center on Cony High School's basketball team. "Then the coach swung at the ref. The kids ended up on the floor, getting into a huge brawl. You look up to coaches. Kids think, 'If it's OK for them to do it, it's OK for me to do it.' "

A campaign to improve the quality of coaching is at the center of Sports Done **21** Right. "The most powerful mentors kids have are coaches," J. Duke Albanese says. "Coaches don't even realize the extent of their influence." He disparages the national trend to offer coaches salary incentives based on their won-lost records. Instead, Sports Done Right recommends compensation based on their level of training. And each pilot school district is encouraged to send coaches to continuing-education classes in subjects like leadership and child psychology.

EXPORTING GOOD SENSE

Educators in 30 states have requested more information from Sports Done **22** Right. "We think a small place like Maine is a perfect place to get kids' sports culture under control," said Albanese. "And if we can do that, maybe we can export the good sense Maine is famous for to the rest of the country."

An example of that good sense recently occurred at a Sports Done Right **23** pilot site. "An influential parent, a guy who volunteers to coach sixth-grade basketball, wanted the kids divided into an A and a B team so he could coach just the elite kids," says Stephen Rogers, the principal of Lyman Moore Middle School. "I said we weren't going to separate the kids and discourage half of them. We were going to encourage all of our interested kids to play."

"But we won't win the championship," the parent complained.   **24**

"I don't really care," Rogers said. "We're not talking about the Celtics. **25** We're talking about sixth-graders."

QUESTIONS FOR READING

1.   What is Relin's subject? State it as a problem.
2.   What seems to be the major cause of the problem?

3. How many high school athletes go on to pro careers?

4. How many youngsters are playing sports after age 13?

5. What are the steps in Maine's Sports Done Right program?

QUESTIONS FOR REASONING AND ANALYSIS

1. What is the author's claim? Where does he state it?

2. What type of argument is this?

3. What strategy does Relin use in his opening four paragraphs? What makes this an effective opening?

QUESTIONS FOR REFLECTING AND WRITING

1. Do you agree with Relin that we have a serious problem in youth sports? If not, why not?

2. Do you agree that the behavior of many parents is unacceptable? If so, what must be done to give the game back to kids?

3. Why do parents and coaches and kids get so competitive? What sources in our culture may be influencing the situation?

MY PLAN TO PUT THE COLLEGE BACK IN COLLEGE SPORTS | GORDON GEE

With degrees in both law and education from Columbia University, Gordon Gee is currently president of Vanderbilt University. Active on many commissions and boards, Gee is also the former president of Brown University, Ohio State University, the University of Colorado, and West Virginia University. His views on college football were published in the *Washington Post* on September 21, 2003.

PREREADING QUESTIONS How important is college football to you? Why is it important to many students and alums? Is it *too* important—especially at Division I colleges?

1   I like to win. I also like to sleep at night. But after 23 years leading universities, I find it increasingly hard to do both.

2   This has been the most ignominious year in recent memory for college sports. We've seen coaches behaving badly, academic fraud, graft, possibly even murder. Clearly, the system is broken, and fixing it will require more than sideline cheering.

3   That's why, last week, we at Vanderbilt announced that we would replace our traditional athletic department with a new body that is more connected to the mission of the university and more accountable to the institution's academic leadership. We'll no longer need an athletic director. We're not eliminating varsity sports, mind you, or relinquishing our membership in the highly competitive Southeastern Conference. Rather, we're making a clear statement that the "student-athlete"—a term invented decades ago when college sports

was faced with another seemingly endless parade of scandals—belongs back in the university.

Many athletic departments exist as separate, almost semi-autonomous fief- 4
doms within universities and there is the feeling that the name on the football jersey is little more than a "franchise" for sports fans. As Bill Bowen and Sarah Levin point out in their new book, *Reclaiming the Game: College Sports and Educational Values,* student-athletes are increasingly isolated, even at the best schools in the country. They do not participate in the extracurricular activities that are so important for personal growth. They miss out on opportunities to study abroad or have internships. They spend too much time in special athletic facilities that are off-limits to the rest of the student body. And their world can too often be defined by coaches' insatiable demands for practice and workout sessions.

True, this is the cost of staying competitive in college sports, where tens of 5
millions of dollars are at stake. But should it be? Over the years I have gotten to know thousands of student-athletes. They are as different as any group of individuals could be. What they have in common, though, is a sense that they missed out on an important part of the college experience by focusing only on sports. They also lose out by being stripped of their responsibilities as citizens of the university when we say that "all will be forgiven" as long as their perfor-mance on the field is up to snuff.

This must change. At Vanderbilt, that means ensuring that every student, 6
every athlete, is part of a vibrant academic and social community.

Shifting Vanderbilt's athletics program to our division of student life and 7
university affairs is merely a step—perhaps bold, perhaps quixotic—in the much-needed reform of intercollegiate athletics. We took this step mindful that Vanderbilt is in an unusual position. It is a highly selective private university with an athletics program untarnished by scandal; our student-athletes gradu-ate at rates that are among the best in the country; and we have loyal, gener-ous supporters who have blessed us with excellent facilities. We can do things here that other universities can't or won't.

I will say this: After our announcement, I received many phone calls from 8
college presidents who said, "You go, Gordon. Walk off the cliff, and if you succeed, we will be right behind."

In recent years, there have been a number of well-meaning and forceful 9
efforts to reform college athletics, but they have not gone far enough. It is time for all those who are concerned about the future of our enterprise to get serious about addressing the crisis of credibility we now face. College presi-dents, working together, should commit themselves to the following reforms:

First, all students who participate in intercollegiate sports should be 10
required to meet the requirements of a core curriculum. The "permanent jockocracy" has for too long made a mockery of academic standards when it comes to athletes. We need to end sham courses, manufactured majors, degree programs that would embarrass a mail-order diploma mill, and the relentless pressure on faculty members to ease student-athletes through their classes.

11   Second, colleges should make a binding four-year commitment to students on athletic scholarships. One of the dirty secrets of intercollegiate athletics is that such scholarships are renewed year-to-year. A bad season? Injury? Poor relationship with a coach? Your scholarship can be yanked with very little notice. Rather than cynically offering the promise of academic enrichment, colleges should back up the promise so long as a student remains in good academic standing.

12   Third, the number of athletic scholarships a school can award should be tied to the graduation rates of its athletes in legitimate academic programs. If a school falls below a threshold graduation rate, it should be penalized by having to relinquish a certain number of scholarships for the next year's entering class. A version of this proposal is part of a reform package now snaking its way through the NCAA.

13   Fourth, graduation rates should be tied to television and conference revenues. If money is the mother's milk of college athletics, then access to it should be contingent on fulfilling the most basic mission of a university—educating students.

14   Finally, college presidents and others need to take a good look at the system we have created for ourselves, in which the professional sports leagues have enjoyed a free feeder system that exploits young people and corrupts otherwise noble institutions. We have maintained the fantasy for far too long that a big-time athletics program is for the students, the alumni, and, at public universities, even for the legislators. It is time for us to call it what it has sadly become: a prep league for the pros, who have taken far more than they have given back. We should demand nothing less than a system in which student-athletes are an integral part of the academic institutions whose names and colors they so proudly wear on game day.

QUESTIONS FOR READING

1.   What is Gee's subject? (State it as a problem.)
2.   Why, according to Gee, are there problems in college athletics? What, specifically, are the problems for the athletes themselves?
3.   What is Gee changing at Vanderbilt?
4.   What are the five reforms he recommends for all colleges?

QUESTIONS FOR REASONING AND ANALYSIS

1.   What is Gee's claim? (State it as a problem/solution assertion.)
2.   In paragraph 7, Gee explains the first move toward reform that he has made at Vanderbilt. He then describes his university. Why? How are his remarks conciliatory? What does he seek to accomplish?
3.   Examine Gee's grounds. He does not provide statistics and refers to current problems in only a general way. Why? What does he expect his readers to know?

4. What is Gee's reasoning in support of his claim? What values have been lost in the development of college athletics? Why must they be reinstated?

QUESTIONS FOR REFLECTING AND WRITING

1. Do you agree with the author that many college athletes are shortchanged in their college experience and education? Do you agree that this is a problem? Why or why not?

2. If you agree with President Gee that there are problems, do you agree with his reform proposals? Study them both individually and as a package. Do you accept them all? If so, why? If not, how would you challenge his proposed solution? Do you think that some of the package is useful and workable, but not the whole package? If so, why? What would you support? What reject? Think of yourself as in a debate with Gee, discussing each item of his reform package, one at a time.

3. What is the role or purpose of the university? What is the role or purpose of sports as a part of the university?

EDUCATION, ATHLETICS: THE ODD COUPLE | SALLY JENKINS

A sportswriter for the *Washington Post* for a number of years, Sally Jenkins left in 1990 to work at *Sports Illustrated* and write a number of books, mostly about sports figures. She has a book written with Dean Smith about his years in college basketball. In 2000 she published, with Lance Armstrong, *It's Not about the Bike: My Journey Back to Life*. She has also written *Men Will Be Boys: The Modern Woman Explains Football and Other Amusing Male Rituals* (1996). In 2000 Jenkins returned to the *Post*. The following column appeared there on September 13, 2002.

PREREADING QUESTIONS Explain Jenkins's title; what does it suggest her attitude will be toward college and athletics? How big are the problems with college athletics?

It's knee-jerk time in college athletics again. Ohio State and Maurice   1 Clarett are examples of everything wrong, while Vanderbilt has preserved the sanctity of the academic temple. For days now, we've enjoyed black and white thinking, moral certainty, and stern reform-mindedness. But the last thing we can apply to college sports any more is absolutism. Nothing is as good or bad as it seems—nor is the Ivy League, as it turns out.

Whatever you're sure of on the subject of college sports, you will certainly   2 question it after the publication of a book called *Reclaiming the Game*, by William G. Bowen and Sarah A. Levin. The book, which will appear next week from Princeton University Press, takes a hard-eyed look at the Ivies and other so-called "elite" colleges and reaches some startling conclusions: Recruited athletes are four times more likely to be admitted to the Ivies than other students, they have lower SAT scores than their peers by 119–165 points, and they chronically under-perform academically. Seem familiar? It sounds like Division I-A.

3   In other words, even the Ivies are getting it wrong?

4   It depends on your view. Every scandal, controversy and ill in the NCAA always boils down to the same question: What are college athletics really for? What are they supposed to be, and what values should they represent? This is where the real trouble begins, because college athletics have increasingly become a matter of competing moralities. And they have always been extremely human, corrupt, and mistaken-prone endeavors, too.

5   People who want to apply pat reforms or even a consistent philosophy to college athletics are simply barking up the wrong tree—and perhaps the worst tree we can bark up these days is to assume that some schools have found the higher moral ground.

6   One of the more interesting conclusions reached by Bowen, a former president of Princeton who is now head of the Andrew W. Mellon Foundation, and co-author Levin, is that academic hypocrisy is rampant.

7   "Truth-telling is important, especially for institutions that pride themselves, as colleges and universities should, on inculcating respect for evidence and for their own unequivocal commitments to honest rendering of facts and to faithful reporting," they write. "But there is something unsettling about reading stories describing the 'purity' of athletics at the non-scholarship schools when so many of their leaders are well aware of the compromises that are being made in fielding teams. There is enough cynicism today about the capacity of institutions (whether they be corporations, churches, colleges and universities, governmental entities, or foundations) to be what they claim to be . . . ."

8   It's difficult to read that passage and not think about Vanderbilt, which has presented itself as a paragon of academic virtue this week, while Ohio State, a very good school, is having a difficult time fighting off the taint of academic scandal. Ohio State Athletic Director Andy Geiger suspended Clarett for accepting money against NCAA rules. Meantime, Vanderbilt Chancellor Gordon Gee announced he was doing away with his athletic department.

9   But it turns out Gee's great reform basically amounts to a symbolic name change—he's not cutting any sports, or scholarships. He accompanied it with a speech that smacked of grandstanding. "For too long, college athletics has been segregated from the core mission of the university," Gee intoned.

10   Gee sounds like a personable, well-intentioned guy. But he doesn't sound any more personable or well-intentioned than Geiger, who insists Ohio State is basically clean and the Clarett affair was isolated.

11   "I hope we get investigated up the yin-yang," Geiger said. "I'd submit we don't have a systemic issue, we have a maverick deal, and it's been more than difficult. But it's not because we're corrupt."

12   The funny thing is, Gee wasn't always so reform-minded and he's no stranger to big athletic programs. He once was president of Ohio State, where he actually hired Geiger, and he also presided over West Virginia, and Colorado, when the Buffaloes enjoyed both national championship and scandal under Bill McCartney. You have to wonder if, now that he's at Vandy, he's simply playing to a new crowd.

13   Geiger has a varied resume too; he's been all over Division I-A, and his record for integrity is pretty good. He was the former athletic director at

Stanford University, until he got tired of what he calls "Stanford-speak" and decided he wanted to work for public universities. He went to Maryland, and then Ohio State.

Here is the central problem with any reform of college athletes: The proper **14** role of college sports on a campus depends entirely on what group is evaluating the question. Is the athletic scholarship a scam, or a tool of affirmative action? Some say Ohio State was wrong to give a scholarship to Clarett, a guy who didn't even want to be there. Others such as Geiger argue that to do away with scholarships and academic exceptions would be to kill opportunity. He also maintains that "athletics have some intellectual content unto themselves."

There are differences even within the same programs. Ohio State, for **15** instance, will have 105,000 people at the football stadium on Saturday, and about 200 at a women's soccer game. Yet both sports are supposed to be part of the same school, program, values, effort, and management.

Any truly intelligent discussion of college athletics may require what **16** Germaine Greer once called, in a discussion completely unrelated to football, "myriad-mindedness." Increasingly, if we're going to solve the "problem" of athletics we have to accept differing value systems and accept the tension between competing moralities. The NCAA is comprised of public schools, and private, of large corporatized universities and small precious intellectual havens, of Northeastern industrials and Midwestern agriculturals—and it's the clash between them that makes their games so interesting.

What are college sports for? Maybe we should first ask what a college is **17** for. The chief event that occurs in college is the emancipation of your head. The main undertaking of a student is understanding, and this is why no one expects him or her to come up with anything resembling consistency; they're too busy questioning and rejecting. College is also where scruple and low-level crime duel. Youth carouses un-enforced by parents or much else in the way of authority. Hopefully, the outcome of this formative emancipation is the development of one's own interior hall monitor. But sometimes it produces a communist, or a car wreck.

This is the risk we take by having colleges at all. The same principle could **18** be applied to games that undergraduates play.

QUESTIONS FOR READING

1. What is Jenkins's subject? (Be more precise than "college sports.")

2. What does the book *Reclaiming the Game* reveal? From the title, what do you think is the authors' view regarding college sports?

3. What, according to Jenkins, is at the core of all debates over college athletics?

4. Who are Andy Geiger and Maurice Clarett? What happened at Ohio State?

5. What is the connection between Geiger at Ohio State and Chancellor Gee at Vanderbilt? What seems to be the author's attitude toward Gee?

6. Why is discussion of reforming college athletics difficult, in Jenkins's view?

7. What, in her view, are colleges for?

QUESTIONS FOR REASONING AND ANALYSIS

1.   What is Jenkins's claim? What are the main points in her argument?

2.   Why does Jenkins present information about Gee's past positions and appointments? How does this serve as evidence in support of her thesis?

3.   Explain the concept of "myriad-mindedness" as it applies to solving problems of college sports.

4.   Examine Jenkins's images in paragraph 17. What makes them effective in support of her concept of college?

QUESTIONS FOR REFLECTING AND WRITING

1.   Evaluate Jenkins's argument. Do you agree with her approach to problems in college athletics? If yes, why? If no, how would you rebut her argument?

2.   The sports pages offer an almost continual flow of rule breaking and scandals (including, in 2003, murder and attempted cover-up at Baylor University) in college athletics, yet Jenkins argues that it is not as bad as it seems. How might you defend her assessment? If you disagree, how would you respond to her?

3.   What is the role or purpose of the university? What is the role or purpose of sports as part of the university? Do we have to "accept the tension between competing moralities," or can (should?) we agree on the basic values and goals of college and college sports?

THE BEAM IN YOUR EYE: IF STEROIDS ARE CHEATING, WHY ISN'T LASIK? | WILLIAM SALETAN

Slate's national correspondent, William Saletan writes about science and politics and society. He has published several books, including *Bearing Right: How Conservatives Won the Abortion War* (2004).

PREREADING QUESTIONS Why does Saletan begin with a quotation from the Bible? How does the quoted verse relate to his apparent topic?

> And why beholdest thou the mote that is in thy brother's eye, but considerest not the beam that is in thine own eye?
> —Matthew 7:3

1   A month ago, Mark McGwire was hauled before a congressional hearing and lambasted as a cheater for using a legal, performance-enhancing steroid precursor when he broke baseball's single-season home run record.

2   A week ago, Tiger Woods was celebrated for winning golf's biggest tournament, the Masters, with the help of superior vision he acquired through laser surgery.

3   What's the difference?

4   At the steroid hearing on March 17, numerous members of the House Committee on Government Reform, led by Chairman Tom Davis, R-Va., denounced performance-enhancing drugs. They offered three arguments: The drugs are

illegal, they're harmful, and they're cheating. But illegality doesn't explain why a drug should be illegal, and the steroid precursor McGwire took, andro, was legal at the time. The director of the National Institute on Drug Abuse conceded at the hearing that steroid precursors weren't banned until last year, that steroids "do, in fact, enhance certain types of physical performance," that some are "prescribed to treat body wasting in patients with AIDS and other diseases that result in loss of lean muscle mass," and that "not all anabolic steroid abusers experience the same deleterious outcomes."

Don't get me wrong. If you buy a steroid off the street or the Internet today just to bulk up, you're taking a stupid risk. But much of that risk comes from your ignorance and the dubious grade of steroid you're getting. A star player with access to the best stuff and the best medical supervision isn't taking the same degree of risk. Furthermore, steroids are a crude, early phase of enhancement technology. Chemists are trying every day to refine compounds and doses that might help proathletes without bad side effects. 5

Already the medical objection to doping has holes. At the hearing, lawmakers displayed a supposedly damning list of "Performance Enhancing Substances Not Covered by Baseball's New Testing Program." The first item on the list was human growth hormone. But the Food and Drug Administration has approved human growth hormone for use in short, healthy children based on studies showing its safety and efficacy. The National Institutes of Health says it's "generally considered to be safe, with rare side effects" in children, and the American Association of Clinical Endocrinologists has found the same pattern in adults. 6

That leaves one comprehensive complaint: cheating. At the hearing, I heard six lawmakers apply this term to performance-enhancing drugs. They compared the drugs to corking bats, deadening baseballs, and sharpening spikes. "When I played with Hank Aaron and Willie Mays and Ted Williams, they didn't put on 40 pounds of bulk in their careers, and they didn't hit more homers in their late thirties than they did in their late twenties," said Sen. Jim Bunning, R-Ky. "What's happening now in baseball isn't natural, and it isn't right." Rep. Mark Souder, R-Ind., chairman of the House subcommittee on drug policy, recalled that baseball had harshly punished players who threw games. He asked why such punishment didn't apply to "players today who systematically cheat through steroids and performance-enhancing drugs to alter the games." Davis, who presided at the hearing, announced that he would co-chair "Zero Tolerance: The Advisory Committee on Ending the Use of Performance-Enhancing Drugs in Sports." 7

Zero tolerance? Wait a minute. If the andro that helped McGwire hit 70 home runs in 1998 was an unnatural, game-altering enhancement, what about his high-powered contact lenses? "Natural" vision is 20/20. McGwire's custom-designed lenses improved his vision to 20/10, which means he could see at a distance of 20 feet what a person with normal, healthy vision could see at 10 feet. Think what a difference that makes in hitting a fastball. Imagine how many games those lenses altered. 8

9   You could confiscate McGwire's lenses, but good luck confiscating Woods' lenses. They've been burned into his head. In the late 1990s, both guys wanted stronger muscles and better eyesight. Woods chose weight training and laser surgery on his eyes. McGwire decided eye surgery was too risky and went for andro instead. McGwire ended up with 70 homers and a rebuke from Congress for promoting risky behavior. Woods, who had lost 16 straight tournaments before his surgery, ended up with 20/15 vision and won seven of his next 10 events.

Tiger Woods, after winning the U.S. Open on June 16.

10   Since then, scores of pro athletes have had laser eye surgery, known as LASIK (Laser-Assisted *In Situ* Keratomileusis). Many, like Woods, have upgraded their vision to 20/15 or better. Golfers Scott Hoch, Hale Irwin, Tom Kite, and Mike Weir have hit the 20/15 mark. So have baseball players Jeff Bagwell, Jeff Cirillo, Jeff Conine, Jose Cruz Jr., Wally Joyner, Greg Maddux, Mark Redman, and Larry Walker. Amare Stoudemire and Rip Hamilton of the NBA have done it, along with NFL players Troy Aikman, Ray Buchanan, Tiki Barber, Wayne Chrebet, and Danny Kanell. These are just some of the athletes who have disclosed their results in the last five years. Nobody knows how many others have gotten the same result.

11   Does the upgrade help? Looks that way. Maddux, a pitcher for the Atlanta Braves, was 0–3 in six starts before his surgery. He won nine of his next 10 games. Kite had LASIK in 1998 and won six events on the Champions Tour over the next five years. Three months after his surgery, Irwin captured the Senior PGA Tour Nationwide Championship.

According to *Golf Digest*, Woods aimed for 20/15 when he signed up 12 for LASIK. This probably didn't strike Woods as enhancement, since he was already using contacts that put him at 20/15. Now ads and quotes offering 20/15 are everywhere. One LASIK practice takes credit for giving Irwin 20/15 vision. Another boasts of raising Barber to 20/15 and calls the result "better than perfect." Other sellers promise the same thing and offer evidence to back it up. Last year, they report, 69 percent of traditional LASIK patients in a study had 20/16 vision six months after their surgery, and new "wavefront" technology raised the percentage to 85. Odds are, if you're getting LASIK, you're getting enhanced.

The medical spin for LASIK, as opposed to the entrepreneurial spin, is that 13 it's corrective. Your eyesight sucks, you go in for surgery, you hope for 20/20. Maybe you get it, maybe you don't, and that's that. But it isn't that simple. If you don't like the results, your doctor might fire up the laser for a second pass. In the business, this is literally called an "enhancement." Hoch, the golfer, got four enhancements in 2002 and 2003. He ended up 20/15 in one eye, 20/10 in the other.

Nor do you need poor vision to find a willing doctor. Most states think you're 14 fine to drive a car without corrective lenses as long as your eyesight is better than 20/40. Cirillo, then a third baseman for the Seattle Mariners, was 20/35 in one eye and 20/30 in the other when he went in for LASIK two years ago. He came out 20/20 and 20/12. Cruz, an outfielder for the Toronto Blue Jays, was 20/30 when he went for an eye exam. Five days later, he was under the beam. "The doctor kind of talked me into it," Cruz told the *Toronto Star*. He came out 20/15. According to the *Orange County Register*, Gary Sheffield, then an outfielder for the Los Angeles Dodgers, had eyesight *better* than 20/20 when he asked for laser surgery to raise his batting average. His doctor talked him out of it.

Why risk surgery for such small increments? "Every little half-centimeter 15 counts," Cruz told the *Star*. Last year, the *Seattle Times* reported that Troy Glaus, a power hitter for the Anaheim Angels, had gotten LASIK because he "felt his contacts were sufficient, just not always ideal. A windy day or a wave of dust could tip the advantage back to the pitcher." Often, coaches play a role. The Minnesota Twins training staff successfully encouraged several players to get LASIK. Maddux told the *Atlanta Journal and Constitution* that the Braves gave him "a little push" to get LASIK in 2000. Meanwhile, the Braves' manager, having talked to the same doctor about getting LASIK, in his own words "chickened out."

This is the difference between therapy and enhancement. You don't need 16 bad vision to get the surgery. Wavefront, if you've got the bucks for it, reliably gives you 20/16 or better. If your vision ends up corrected but not enhanced, you can go back for a second pass. Players calculate every increment. Pro golfers seek "to optimize any competitive advantage," a LASIK surgeon told the *Los Angeles Times*. "They're already tuned in to the best clubs, the best putter, the best ball. . . . Clearly having great vision is one of the best competitive advantages you can have." Eyes are just another piece of equipment. If you don't like 'em, change 'em.

17   The sports establishment is obtuse to this revolution. Leagues worry about how you might doctor bats, balls, or clubs. They don't focus on how you might doctor yourself. Look at the official rules of Major League Baseball: A pitcher can't put rosin on his glove, but he can put it on his hand. A batter can't alter the bat "to improve the distance factor," but the rules don't bar him from altering his body to get the same result. Baseball now has a dope-testing policy, but it isn't in the rules; the players negotiate it. That's why it's weak.

18   At last month's hearing, baseball commissioner Bud Selig testified that in 1998 and 1999 he sent his executive vice president to Costa Rica to check out reports that juiced-up baseballs were causing an epidemic of home runs. Selig was looking for the wrong kind of juice. The U.S. Golf Association's Rules of Golf share the same blind spot: You can't use a device to warm the ball, but you can use it to warm your hands. You can't use a device to measure distance or "gauge the slope of the green," but you can get the same powers through LASIK. In the age of biotechnology, you *are* the device.

19   Read the testimonials. At 20/15, Kanell can read the eyes of defensive backs. Tom Lehman, who will lead the U.S. golf team in next year's Ryder Cup, says LASIK improved his ability to "judge distances"—a common benefit, according to the technology's purveyors. Woods says he's "able to see slopes in greens a lot clearer." Woods' eye surgeon told the *Los Angeles Times*, "Golfers get a different three-dimensional view of the green after LASIK." They "can see the grain" and "small indentations. It's different. LASIK actually produces, instead of a spherical cornea, an aspherical cornea. It may be better than normal vision."

20   Just ask Tom Davis. "I was in and out in less than one hour," the congress-man reports in a testimonial for the Eye Center, a Northern Virginia LASIK practice. "I was reading and watching television that evening. My reading was not impaired and my distance vision was excellent."

21   Good for you, Tom. Now, about that committee you've established for zero tolerance of performance enhancement. Are you sure you're the right guy to chair it?

QUESTIONS FOR READING

1.   What is Saletan's subject?
2.   What were the three arguments used by the Congressional committee denouncing McGuire?
3.   What is wrong with the illegal argument, in the author's view?
4.   What is wrong with the harmful argument?
5.   Today, how are many professional athletes enhancing their performance?

QUESTIONS FOR REASONING AND ANALYSIS

1.   What kinds of evidence does the author present for athletes' use of enhancement techniques?

2. Saletan calls eye enhancement among athletes a "revolution." Based on his evidence, does that seem an appropriate label?

3. What are the rule-makers missing in today's professional sports arena?

4. What is Saletan's claim? Does he state one? Does he imply a position? Defend your answer.

QUESTIONS FOR REFLECTION AND WRITING

1. Saletan begins and ends with Congressman Tom Davis. How does this aid his argument?

2. Is the use of performance-enhancing drugs cheating? Why or why not?

3. Is the use of LASIK or weight training cheating? Why or why not?

4. Can you make a case for allowing one kind of enhancement but not another? Defend your position.

TO THE VICTOR, THE DRUG TEST | MICHAEL SOKOLOVE

A contributing writer to the *New York Times Magazine* and popular guest on radio and TV talk shows, Michael Sokolove is best known for his writing on the culture of sports. He is the author of several books on sports, including *Warrior Girls: Protecting Our Daughters Against the Injury Epidemic in Women's Sports* (2008). The following *New York Times* article appeared in August 2008.

PREREADING QUESTIONS When you think of the Olympic games, what do you focus on? Given his title, what do you expect Sokolove to focus on?

On an overcast afternoon in Mexico City in October 1968, a skinny American long jumper named Bob Beamon took 19 strides down a runway, hit the takeoff board perfectly and lifted off at what seemed like an impossible trajectory. He flew so far that he exceeded the range of the optical sighting system that measured the jumps, so officials in sport jackets and ties had to scurry into the sand pit with a tape measure. 1

Beamon, who was 22, thought at first that he might have broken the world record by a couple of inches. The length of his jump, when first announced in meters, did not fully register with him. But when it was translated to him as 29 feet 2½ inches—nearly two feet farther than anyone had ever jumped— he crumpled to the ground in shock. Fellow jumpers helped him up, and he began high-stepping around the pit as the crowd roared. A competitor, the defending gold medalist Lynn Davies of Great Britain, congratulated Beamon and told him, with a sense of awe, "You have destroyed this event."

Now, for a moment, imagine some equivalent of Beamon's "leap of the century" this month in Beijing. Let's say that the world record in the men's 100 meters—recently lowered two-hundredths of a second, to 9.72 seconds, by Usain Bolt of Jamaica—is smashed by a full tenth of a second. Or that the Australian swimmer Libby Trickett's new world record of 52.88 seconds in the women's 100-meter freestyle falls to 51 seconds flat. Or that Beamon's 2 old record, finally broken 23 years later by Michael Powell—by two inches—is exceeded by a full foot.

3   What would be our reaction? Skepticism, disbelief, perhaps disgust. To break any record in such a Beamonesque manner would seem like an act of self-incrimination, and any rival who spoke of an event being "destroyed" would certainly mean it as an accusation. Such is the legacy of decades of documented doping in Olympic sport and of a particularly downbeat four years since the previous Summer Games. From Marion Jones, Floyd Landis, Barry Bonds, Balco and Roger Clemens to spying in the N.F.L. and charges of game fixing in the N.B.A. and Italian soccer, elite sport has been awash in accusations of cheating and lying.

4   Even the site of this year's Games contributes to a feeling of impending taint. Factories in China have long been the source of much of the raw material for steroids. China's food industry is so poorly regulated that a food contractor for the United States Olympic Committee speculated (without evidence) that athletes eating local chicken pumped with high doses of drugs could test positive for banned performance enhancers. Beijing is one of the most polluted cities on the planet, and some athletes will wear respiration masks when not competing. None of this exactly evokes "Chariots of Fire."

5   Sports and cynicism do not go well together. We watch to be uplifted, to witness some transcendent moment that we can believe and fully embrace. The Olympic Games are especially poisoned by doubts over the integrity of the competition because their whole point is upward progression, the breaking of barriers. *Citius, altius, fortius.* Swifter, higher, stronger. If everyone is playing by an agreed-upon set of rules, that is. Certain assumptions can safely be made about the drug scene in Beijing: some dopers will be unmasked, shamed and sent home. Some will go undetected. And some "clean" athletes will fall short of their goals and believe they've been cheated.

6   All of them will compete in their own specialties and also, mostly invisibly, in a game within a game—the cat-and-mouse contest between the drug detectors and the chemist-coach-athlete cartel that seeks to get away with using banned substances. The Beijing Olympic organizing committee has announced that it will administer a record 4,500 tests (urine and blood samples), up from 3,700 in Athens. In scary-sounding language—intentionally so, no doubt—a Chinese sports official said that vehicles transporting samples through Beijing's streets would be accompanied by armed guards before making deliveries at a new $10 million laboratory, also heavily guarded.

7   Certain national sports federations have tended to breed doping offenders, indicating that they are either the most determined dopers or the least clever in their methods. The entire Bulgarian weight-lifting team of eight men and three women tested positive in June for a banned steroid and was disqualified from the Beijing Games. Bulgarian lifters also tested positive in the run-up to the 2004 Games in Athens, and several had to return medals after testing positive at the 1988 and 2000 Games. The Chinese swim association announced in late June that one of its top competitors had failed a drug test and would be banned for life from the sport—adding to an extensive recent history of doping by Chinese swimmers.

The outspoken former head of the World Anti-Doping Agency (WADA), 8
Dick Pound, once told me that even when Olympic athletes tested positive,
it "added luster to the Olympic brand" because it proved the International
Olympic Committee is serious about policing the use of banned drugs. He
had a point. Compared with just about any other sporting body worldwide,
including the major United States professional and college sports, the I.O.C. is
more rigorous. But that does not mean it's winning the game within the game.
In fact, it may be falling farther behind.

I asked Anthony Butch, the director at the Olympic Analytical Labora- 9
tory at the University of California at Los Angeles, who he thinks is winning.
"It's impossible to answer," said Butch, whose lab is one of two accredited
by WADA in the United States. "The reason we know we are making strides
is we are catching more people, but to catch them, you have to know what
they're abusing. It's possible there is something out there that everyone is taking that's not on the radar screens of the doping labs. We are always behind. It
is easier to take these things and get away with it than it is to figure out ways
to catch them."

The "designer steroid" that was peddled out of the Bay Area Laboratory 10
Cooperative—a previously unknown compound—was discovered only after an
informant gave a syringe full of it to authorities. That the informant, the track
coach Trevor Graham, has since been convicted for making false statements
to drug investigators pretty much sums up the *Maltese Falcon* atmosphere of
top-level sprinting.

Even tests for some of the most commonly used enhancers may be less 11
effective than authorities would like athletes to believe. Synthetic erythropoi-
etin, known as EPO, which artificially boosts red-blood-cell production, is the
drug of choice for marathoners, cyclists and other endurance athletes. A study
published in June by a respected laboratory in Denmark indicated that it can
probably be used with impunity, because the methods to detect it are woe-
fully inadequate. And while WADA has a new, better, more standardized test
for human-growth hormone that allows it to screen many more athletes at the
Olympics, the test is still not thought to be able to detect use much beyond
the previous 24 to 48 hours.

As a sports fan, I'd like to think we're at a moment of transition, moving 12
toward clarity. But we're not. A purely libertarian approach toward drugs and
sport that some advocate—let athletes dope at their own risk—is unlikely to
take hold any time soon. And I would not want it to. The medal winners might
well be those who take the highest doses and the most on-the-edge, experimental treatments—in other words, those most willing to put their health at
risk. If limits were imposed to try to keep athletes safe, some would try to
exceed them to gain an edge. That's a competition, of sorts, but not one
worth watching.

NBC and its various outlets will broadcast 3,600 hours of competition 13
from Beijing, more than anyone can consume. I suspect I won't be the only
viewer who makes choices influenced by calculations about the integrity
of the contests. I'll watch some of the so-called minor sports—kayaking,
fencing, team handball—because they seem closer to some ideal of pure

competition. I don't naively assume they're clean, but I don't know for sure they're not. I'm looking forward to seeing Sheila Taormina, a remarkable 39-year-old American who won a gold medal as a swimmer in 1996, competed as a triathlete in 2000 and 2004 and now will take part in the modern pentathlon—the very cool combo of shooting, swimming, fencing, riding and running.

14   I'm curious if the United States men's basketball team, led by Kobe Bryant, can break its international losing streak and beat the likes of Italy and Argentina. In the current climate, this competition involving N.B.A. multimillionaires seems oddly straightforward and respectable.

15   I won't go out of my way to watch much track and field—even the signature 100-meter races. It's not a moral judgment; I'm just not interested in what I think may be a contest among chemists. Two men who set world records since 2002 have had their times expunged after positive drug tests—and numerous other top male sprinters have also been implicated. The world-record holder in the women's 100 meters is the late Florence Griffith-Joyner, whose sudden changes in physique and out-of-nowhere, near-half-second improvement at the 1988 Games in Seoul remain sources of suspicion.

16   What's lost when drugs permeate sport is quite simple: authenticity and believability. For the price of a ticket, or even the investment of our time in front of the television, we don't want to have to wonder what has taken place in the shadows to influence the competition—or which athlete whose remarkable human achievement we have rejoiced in might soon be stripped of his gold and marched before a grand jury.

17   It sort of ruins the whole thing.

QUESTIONS FOR READING

1. How does Sokolove think we would react today to any huge record-breaking event at the 2008 Olympics?

2. What were the added concerns about the 2008 games in China? (Did the advance concerns prove right?)

3. What is the "game within the game"? Are authorities catching more athletes?

4. What sports will the author watch during the Olympics? What will he pass on? Why?

5. What is lost, in the author's view, with the use of enhancement drugs in sports?

QUESTIONS FOR REASONING AND ANALYSIS

1. Sokolove begins by recounting a record-breaking long jump in 1968. Why? What is effective about this opening?

2. What is the context in which the author writes? How does his specific context extend to current discussions of sport?

3. What is Sokolove's claim?

QUESTIONS FOR REFLECTION AND WRITING

1. Sokolove does not expect sport to stop banning enhancement drugs. Do you agree with his prediction? Why or why not?

2. Did you watch the 2008 Olympics? If so, did you think about doping issues in some of the competitions? Is this an issue that concerns you? Why or why not?

3. Do you agree with Sokolove that sports played "by chemists" "ruins the whole thing"? If you agree, how would you add to his argument? If you disagree, how would you refute his argument?

A SPORTING CHANCE | THE EDITORS, *NATURE*

Nature is a leading source of the most current research findings in the sciences. It is interesting, therefore, to find that the editors of this renowned journal decided to ring in on the issue of enhancement doping in sports. Their editorial appeared in the August 2007 issue.

PREREADING QUESTION Based on their title, what position on this issue do you expect the editors to take?

1 Whether you have been following the just-finished Tour de France or waiting for Barry Bonds to break the all-time record for major-league home runs in baseball, the topic of drugs in sport has been hard to avoid of late.

2 To cheat in a sporting event is a loathsome thing. For as long as the rules of the Tour de France or any sporting event ban the use of performance-enhancing drugs, those who break the rules must be punished whenever possible. But this does not preclude the idea that it may, in time, be necessary to readdress the rules themselves.

3 As more is learned about how our bodies work, more options become available for altering those workings. To date, most of this alteration has sought to restore function to some sort of baseline. But it is also possible to enhance various functions into the supernormal realm, and the options for this are set to grow ever greater.

4 The fact that such endeavours will carry risks should not be trivialized. But adults should be allowed to take risks, and experience suggests that they will do so when the benefits on offer are enticing enough. By the end of this century the unenhanced body or mind may well be vanishingly rare.

5 As this change takes place, we will have to re-examine what we expect of athletes. If spectators are seeking to reset their body mass index through pharmacology, or taking pills that enhance their memory, is it really reasonable that athletes should make do with bodies that have not seen such benefits? The more the public comes to live with the mixed and risk-related benefits of enhancement, the more it will appreciate that allowing such changes need not rob sport of its drama, nor athletes of their need for skill, training, character and dedication.

6 To change the rules on pharmacological enhancement would not be without precedent. It was once thought that a woman could not epitomize the

athletic ideal as a man could, and so should be stopped from trying. Similarly, it was thought proper to keep all payments from some athletes, thus privileging the already wealthy. These prejudices have been left behind, and the rules have changed. As pharmacological enhancement becomes everyday, views of bodily enhancement may evolve sufficiently for sporting rules to change on that, too.

7   This transition will not be painless. Some people will undoubtedly harm themselves through the use of enhancements, and there would need to be special protection for children. That said, athletes harm themselves in other forms of training, too. They may harm themselves less with drugs when doctors can be openly involved and masking agents dispensed with.

8   There is also the problem of who goes first. The first sport to change its rules to allow players to use performance-enhancing drugs will be attacked as a freak show or worse. The same may be true of the second. This may well have the effect—may already be having the effect—of delaying the inevitable.

9   Perhaps the Tour de France could show the way ahead here. In terms of public respect, endurance cycling has the least to lose and perhaps the most to gain. To be sure, a change in the rules would lead to the claim that 'the cheats have won.' But as no one can convincingly claim that cheats are not winning now, or have not been winning in the past, that claim is not quite the showstopper it might seem to be.

10   A leadership ready to ride out the outrage might be better for the sport in the long run. If some viewers and advertisers were lost along the way, the Tour could console itself with the thought that it got by with far less commercial interest in days gone by—and that it is more likely to re-establish itself through excellence and honesty than in the penumbra of doubt and cynicism that surrounds it now.

QUESTIONS FOR READING

1. What is the editors' position on athletes using banned substances?
2. What is now happening in the general population with regard to our bodies?
3. Which sport might be a good one to start the process of no longer banning enhancement drugs? Why do the editors pick this sport?

QUESTIONS FOR REASONING AND ANALYSIS

1. What is the claim of this argument?
2. What evidence do the editors present in support?
3. What rebuttal do they offer to possible counterarguments? Are their responses effective? Why or why not?
4. What style and tone do the editors use? How does their choice aid their argument?

QUESTIONS FOR REFLECTION AND WRITING

1. List for yourself and study each of the reasons given in support of the claim. Then answer: Which reason do you think has the greatest merit? Why?

2. Do you accept the observation that body enhancements by non-athletes are increasing—and that by the end of this century the un-enhanced body will be rare? Are these developments good for all of us? Why or why not?

3. Would enhancements "rob sport of its drama" or make us value an athlete's dedication or skill less? Why or why not?

BRIDGING THE HUMAN DIVIDE | ROSANNA TOMIUK

Rosanna Tomiuk is a Canadian water polo athlete who plays at Loyola Marymount University and on the Canadian national team. She is a member of Team Darfur, a group of Olympic athletes who are seeking to increase aid to Darfur. (You can find her on Facebook.) Prior to the 2008 Olympic games, Tomiuk posted the following essay on the online journal for young people, **www.voicesoftomorrow.org.**

PREREADING QUESTIONS What has been happening in Darfur—what are the problems there? Do you think that you should be involved in this or some other problem somewhere in the world?

Rosanna Tomiuk, Canadian Water Polo Olympian

When I imagine the chasm 1 that separates me from another girl my same age who struggles every day to survive what many are calling genocide, I am left wondering how I lucked out.

And when I think about 2 the pressing decisions in my life—like whether to pursue a professional water polo career in Europe or finish up my last year of eligibility as an NCAA athlete—and her life, my concerns suddenly gain a different perspective.

I was born into Canadian 3 freedom that provides endless opportunity, and she was born and raised in the Darfur region of Sudan with a freedom that exists only as a hopeful idea. Her worries? Where is my family? Will I make it to safety? I'm hungry, and I don't want to be alone.

Whenever I think about the very grave circumstances in Darfur, I challenge 4 myself to humanize the issue rather than consider it some overwhelming tragedy. In so doing, I realize I have a choice—I can either allow my feelings of helplessness to move me to indifference, or I can find a way to reach out to my peers and their families in Darfur and help make their lives better.

5   So, I joined Team Darfur, an international coalition of athletes who have come together to raise awareness and bring an end to the crisis in Darfur. As a full-time athlete with a heart to change the world, this seemed like a good fit.

6   As members of Team Darfur, we will not boycott the games. We do, however, want to challenge China to hold true to the goals of the Olympics—one being to place "sport at the service of the harmonious development of man, with a view to encouraging the establishment of a peaceful society concerned with the preservation of human dignity."

7   The reality that China, the 2008 Olympic host, buys oil from and sells weapons to Sudan, a country with a government that has backed the killing of hundreds of thousands of farmers in the Darfur region, is far too disturbing to ignore. Thus, as a part of a vibrant community of Canadian athletes, I expect us all—whether we'll be in Beijing in August or not—to encourage each other to do what's right—to correct an injustice against other innocent people.

8   In addition to Team Darfur, other activists, celebrities and politicians are calling on China to do more to honor the ideals of the Olympics. A good first step would be to have the international community, and China in particular, help secure the UNAMID peacekeeping force on the ground in Darfur by the start of the Olympic Games.

9   However, in the end, as the national sports columnist for the Associated Press, Tim Dalhberg, points out, "it may be the athletes themselves who decide how far this goes. If they begin speaking out in greater numbers, they might have a better chance of getting China to change some of its policies."

QUESTIONS FOR READING

1. What is Tomiuk's topic?
2. Why did she join Team Darfur? Who are the members of Team Darfur?
3. What is her challenge to China during the Games and after?

QUESTIONS FOR REASONING AND WRITING

1. Tomiuk's is one of the few arguments in this text that is written as a personal essay. What are the characteristics of a personal essay? How effective is her approach, given who she is and her topic?
2. Tomiuk argues that we have to humanize the killing in Darfur so that people will want to get involved. Is she right? What is gained if we can imagine people just like ourselves struggling for their very lives in some place where there is war or famine?

QUESTIONS FOR REFLECTION AND WRITING

1. Has Tomiuk moved you to learn more about the struggles in Darfur? To become involved? Why or why not?

2. If you were going to post an argument on Voices of Tomorrow, what problem would you choose to address? Why? (You might want to check out this Web site and see if there is a place there for your writing.)

3. Should athletes have boycotted the Games in China because of China's role in the killings in Darfur? Why or why not?

Education: What's Happening on Campus?

READ: What is the situation? Who is writing the words below the graph?

REASON: What does the graph show? What does the answer to the test imply about the United States?

REFLECT/WRITE: What is Toles's point about American education—and our perception of American education?

To say that the issues in education are both numerous and serious is certainly an understatement. Clinton wanted to be the "education president." Bush has his No Child Left Behind initiative. And yet criticism continues amid only a few voices defending U.S. schools. America's best schools and colleges attract students from around the world. But the variations in funding, facilities, teachers, and test scores from one school to another are often unacceptable to politicians and parents alike.

To move to the college level: Up to one-third of the freshman class at many colleges is taking at least one remedial course, and fewer than half of those who start college actually graduate. The number of college graduates in this country still remains under 30 percent. Are we failing at the goal of universal education? Is this goal unrealistic? Can we make the changes needed to be competitive in a global economy? (If our students cannot read graphs, can they participate in the global economy?)

The authors in this chapter examine various issues and realities of college campuses today, from the preparation of today's students to file-sharing issues to what is "politically correct" versus reasonable college policy. The chapter concludes with what Facebook, that Web site so dear to the college student, tells us about our culture today.

PREREADING QUESTION

Two of the following seven authors present opposing views on a campus issue. The other five explore various issues that together create a mosaic of college life and learning. Reflect on each author's particular argument but also consider what each one contributes to a snapshot of today's college culture.

SO MUCH FOR THE INFORMATION AGE | TED GUP

Professor of journalism at Case Western Reserve University until Fall 2009, when he will become chair of the journalism department at Emerson College, Ted Gup is a former staff writer for the *Washington Post* and *Time*. Gup is the author of two books on the U.S. intelligence community, the latest *Nation of Secrets: The Threat to Democracy and the American Way of Life* (2007). His article on education was published in the *Chronicle of Higher Education* on April 11, 2008.

PREREADING QUESTIONS Considering just Gup's title, what do you think his topic will be? If you add the context of this chapter, does that alter your expectation?

Today's college students have tuned out the world, and it's partly our fault. 1 I teach a seminar called "Secrecy: Forbidden Knowledge." I recently asked my class of 16 freshmen and sophomores, many of whom had graduated in the top 10 percent of their high-school classes and had dazzling SAT scores, how many had heard the word "rendition."

Not one hand went up. 2

This is after four years of the word appearing on the front pages of the 3 nation's newspapers, on network and cable news, and online. This is after years of highly publicized lawsuits, Congressional inquiries, and international controversy and condemnation. This is after the release of a Hollywood film of that title, starring Jake Gyllenhaal, Meryl Streep, and Reese Witherspoon.

4   I was dumbstruck. Finally one hand went up, and the student sheepishly asked if rendition had anything to do with a version of a movie or a play.

5   I nodded charitably, then attempted to define the word in its more public context. I described specific accounts of U.S. abductions of foreign citizens, of the likely treatment accorded such prisoners when placed in the hands of countries like Syria and Egypt, of the months and years of detention. I spoke of the lack of formal charges, of some prisoners' eventual release and how their subsequent lawsuits against the U.S. government were stymied in the name of national security and secrecy.

6   The students were visibly disturbed. They expressed astonishment, then revulsion. They asked how such practices could go on.

7   I told them to look around the room at one another's faces; they were seated next to the answer. I suggested that they were, in part, the reason that rendition, waterboarding, Guantánamo detention, warrantless searches and intercepts, and a host of other such practices have not been more roundly discredited. I admit it was harsh.

8   That instance was no aberration. In recent years I have administered a dumbed-down quiz on current events and history early in each semester to get a sense of what my students know and don't know. Initially I worried that its simplicity would insult them, but my fears were unfounded. The results have been, well, horrifying.

9   Nearly half of a recent class could not name a single country that bordered Israel. In an introductory journalism class, 11 of 18 students could not name what country Kabul was in, although we have been at war there for half a decade. Last fall only one in 21 students could name the U.S. secretary of defense. Given a list of four countries—China, Cuba, India, and Japan—not one of those same 21 students could identify India and Japan as democracies. Their grasp of history was little better. The question of when the Civil War was fought invited an array of responses—half a dozen were off by a decade or more. Some students thought that Islam was the principal religion of South America, that Roe v. Wade was about slavery, that 50 justices sit on the U.S. Supreme Court, that the atom bomb was dropped on Hiroshima in 1975. You get the picture, and it isn't pretty.

10   As a journalist, professor, and citizen, I find it profoundly discouraging to encounter such ignorance of critical issues. But it would be both unfair and inaccurate to hold those young people accountable for the moral and legal morass we now find ourselves in as a nation. They are earnest, readily educable, and, when informed, impassioned.

11   I make it clear to my students that it is not only their right but their duty to arrive at their own conclusions. They are free to defend rendition, waterboarding, or any other aspect of America's post-9/11 armamentarium. But I challenge their right to tune out the world, and I question any system or society that can produce such students and call them educated. I am concerned

for the nation when a cohort of students so talented and bright is oblivious to all such matters. If they are failing us, it is because we have failed them.

Still, it is hard to reconcile the students' lack of knowledge with the notion 12 that they are a part of the celebrated information age, creatures of the Internet who arguably have at their disposal more information than all the preceding generations combined. Despite their BlackBerrys, cellphones, and Wi-Fi, they are, in their own way, as isolated as the remote tribes of New Guinea. They disprove the notion that technology fosters engagement, that connectivity and community are synonymous. I despair to think that this is the generation brought up under the banner of "No Child Left Behind." What I see is the specter of an entire generation left behind and left out.

It is not easy to explain how we got into this sad state, or to separate 13 symptoms from causes. Newspaper readership is in steep decline. My students simply do not read newspapers, online or otherwise, and many grew up in households that did not subscribe to a paper. Those who tune in to television "news" are subjected to a barrage of opinions from talking heads like CNN's demagogic Lou Dobbs and MSNBC's Chris Matthews and Fox's Bill O'Reilly and his dizzying "No Spin Zone." In today's journalistic world, opinion trumps fact (the former being cheaper to produce), and rank partisanship and virulent culture wars make the middle ground uninhabitable. Small wonder, then, that my students shrink from it.

Then, too, there is the explosion of citizen journalism. An army of aver- 14 age Joes, equipped with cellphones, laptops, and video cameras, has commandeered our news media. The mantra of "We want to hear from you!" is all the rage, from CNN to NPR; but, although invigorating and democratizing, it has failed to supplant the provision of essential facts, generating more heat than light. Many of my students can report on the latest travails of celebrities or the sexual follies of politicos, and can be forgiven for thinking that such matters dominate the news—they do. Even those students whose home pages open onto news sites have tailored them to parochial interests—sports, entertainment, weather—that are a pale substitute for the scope and sweep of a good front page or the PBS *NewsHour with Jim Lehrer* (which many students seem ready to pickle in formaldehyde).

Civics is decidedly out of fashion in the high-school classroom, a quaint 15 throwback superseded by courses in technology. As teachers scramble to "teach to the test," civics is increasingly relegated to after-school clubs and geeky graduation prizes. Somehow my students sailed through high-school courses in government and social studies without acquiring the habit of keeping abreast of national and international events. What little they know of such matters they have absorbed through popular culture—song lyrics, parody, and comedy. *The Daily Show with Jon Stewart* is as close as many dare get to actual news.

Yes, the post-9/11 world is a scary place, and plenty of diversions can 16 absorb young people's attention and energies, as well as distract them from the anxieties of preparing for a career in an increasingly uncertain economy. But that respite comes at a cost.

17   As a journalist, I have spent my career promoting transparency and accountability. But my experiences in the classroom humble and chasten me. They remind me that challenges to secrecy and opacity are moot if society does not avail itself of information that is readily accessible. Indeed, our very failure to digest the accessible helps to create an environment in which secrecy can run rampant.

18   It is time to once again make current events an essential part of the curriculum. Families and schools must instill in students the habit of following what is happening in the world. A global economy will have little use for a country whose people are so self-absorbed that they know nothing of their own nation's present or past, much less the world's. There is a fundamental difference between shouldering the rights and responsibilities that come with citizenship—engagement, participation, debate—and merely inhabiting the land.

19   As a nation, we spend an inordinate amount of time fretting about illegal immigration and painfully little on what it means to be a citizen, beyond the legal status conferred by accident of birth or public processing. We are too busy building a wall around us to notice that we are shutting ourselves in. Intent on exporting democracy—spending blood and billions in pursuit of it abroad—we have shown a decided lack of interest in exercising or promoting democracy at home.

20   The noted American scholar Robert M. Hutchins said, decades ago: "The object of the educational system, taken as a whole, is not to produce hands for industry or to teach the young how to make a living. It is to produce responsible citizens." He warned that "the death of a democracy is not likely to be an assassination from ambush. It will be a slow extinction from apathy, indifference, and undernourishment." I fear he was right.

21   I tell the students in my secrecy class that they are required to attend. After all, we count on one another; without student participation, it just doesn't work. The same might be said of democracy. Attendance is mandatory.

QUESTIONS FOR READING

1. What does the word *rendition* mean—in its public context?
2. How knowledgeable were Gup's students?
3. What may explain the lack of knowledge of history and current events among today's college students?
4. What can happen in a society when citizens are uninformed?
5. What does democracy require?

QUESTIONS FOR REASONING AND ANALYSIS

1. Gup spends nine paragraphs demonstrating his students' lack of knowledge. That is a long introduction. Why does he do it? What is his purpose?

2. What is the author's claim? Where does he state it? Put his claim in your own words as a claim for a problem/solution argument.

3. What solution does Gup propose?

4. What makes his concluding paragraph effective?

QUESTIONS FOR REFLECTION AND WRITING

1. Do you agree that today's college students lack knowledge of history and current events? Why or why not?

2. Do you accept Gup's explanation of causes? If you disagree, what do you think are the causes?

3. Do you agree that citizens have a duty to participate in a democracy? Can you participate meaningfully when you don't understand your country's history or know current events? Explain and defend your views.

GUYS JUST WANT TO HAVE FUN | BARBARA EHRENREICH

A journalist and social critic, Barbara Ehrenreich has now written 15 books. Her best-selling *Nickel and Dimed*, a study of working-class poverty, sold over a million copies and is required reading at many colleges. Her most recent book is *This Land Is* Their *Land: Reports from a Divided Nation* (2008). The following article, a *Time* magazine column, appeared July 31, 2006.

PREREADING QUESTIONS Why are you in college? To learn? To meet people? To have fun?

When I was in college, I followed a simple strategy. Go where the boys 1 are. Sure, that led me into many settings where inebriants flowed, but my reasoning was strictly practical. Men ruled the world, as anyone could see, so the trick was to do as they did. No girlie major like art history or French lit for me. I started in chemistry and then proceeded up the gender gradient to physics, finally achieving in Classical Mechanics the exalted status of only girl in the class.

But that was an era when the cool kids smoked Gauloises and argued 2 about Kierkegaard and Trotsky. Today, as two recent reports have revealed, it's the girls who achieve and the boys who coast along on gut courses congenial to hangovers. Boys are less likely to go to college in the first place (only 45% of college students under 25 are male) and are less likely to graduate as well. If I tried to follow my original strategy now, I would probably end up with an M.A. in *Madden*, the football video game, and a postgraduate stay in rehab.

The trend has occasioned some predictions of a coming matriarchy in 3 which high-achieving women will rule over a nation of slacker guys. We've all seen the movie, an endless loop culminating most recently in *You, Me and Dupree*. That little girls' T shirt slogan—GIRLS RULE, BOYS DROOL—is beginning to look less like a slur and more like an empirical observation.

4   But it may be that the boys still know what they're doing. Among other things that have changed since the '60s is the corporate culture, which once valued literacy, numeracy, high GPAS and the ability to construct a simple sentence. No doubt there are still workplaces where such achievements are valued, but when I set out as an undercover journalist seeking a white-collar corporate job for my book *Bait and Switch*, I was shocked to find the emphasis entirely on such elusive qualities as "personality," "attitude" and "likability." Play down the smarts, the career coaches and self-help books advised, cull the experience and exude a "positive attitude."

5   In a June article on corporate personality testing, the Washington *Post* reported on a woman who passed the skills test for a customer-care job but wasn't hired because she failed the personality test. Those tests, including the ubiquitous Myers-Briggs test, have no scientific credibility or predictive value, as Annie Murphy Paul showed in her 2004 book, *Cult of Personality*. You can have one Myers-Briggs personality on Tuesday and another when you retake the test on Thursday. Their chief function, as far as I could tell when I took them, was to weed out the introverts. When asked whether you'd rather be the life of the party or curl up with a book, the correct answer is always "Party!"

6   So the best preparation for that all-important personality test may well be a college career spent playing poker and doing tequila shots. An Atlanta woman I interviewed, a skilled website writer, was fired without explanation after a few weeks at a job. "I tried to fit in," she told me. "I went to lunch with the guys, but all they talked about was sports, which I know nothing about and they all seemed to know each other from college." Poor thing, she had probably wasted her college years in the library.

7   The business world isn't totally hostile to higher education—an M.B.A. still counts for something. But as G.J. Meyer wrote in his classic 1995 book, *Executive Blues: Down and Out in Corporate America*, a higher degree in something other than business or law—or, worse, a stint of college teaching—can impart a deadly "academic stench" to one's résumé. And what are we to make of the growing corporate defiance of elementary grammar? At a job fair I attended, AT&T Wireless solicited sales reps with the question, if it was a question, "Are you ready to put your skills to work. Like the way you're a quick study. How you're good at finding solutions." Take that, you irritating, irrelevant English 101 professors!

8   Maybe we need a return to gender-segregated higher education, with the academic equivalent of Pinocchio's Pleasure Island for boys, where they can hone their "people skills" at keg parties. But we will need those high-achieving girls more than ever. Someone, after all, is going to have to figure out how to make an economy run by superannuated slacker boys competitive again in a world filled with Chinese and Indian brainiacs. I'd still major in physics if I were doing it again, just because there ought to be at least a few Americans, of whatever gender, who know something beyond the technology of beer bongs.

QUESTIONS FOR READING

1. What percentage of college students are guys? Who is more likely to graduate: guys or gals?
2. What skills are now the qualities wanted in the corporate workplace? What kind of test is often administered to those seeking jobs?
3. What are the guys, as a group, doing in college? Will their approach help or hurt them in the business world?
4. Against whom do we need to compete in the global economy?

QUESTIONS FOR REASONING AND ANALYSIS

1. Based on Ehrenreich's article, what image emerges of today's corporate world? Who dominates? What is valued? What is not valued?
2. Ehrenreich writes of a world "filled with Chinese and Indian brainiacs." What is she implying about today's college students?
3. What stylistic strategies does the author use? How would you describe the essay's tone? Is her approach to her topic effective? Why or why not?
4. What is Ehrenreich's claim?

QUESTIONS FOR REFLECTION AND WRITING

1. After allowing for the author's exaggeration for effect, do you essentially agree with her analysis of who is working harder in college? Why or why not?
2. Ehrenreich's figures are for undergraduates. Which gender dominates the grad schools? Which gender gets most of the MBAs? Do some research if necessary and then reflect on what you learn.
3. Is the author primarily concerned about gender differences in education—or what is happening in the business world? Explain and defend your answer.

LAPTOPS VS. LEARNING | DAVID COLE

A professor at Georgetown University's Law Center, David Cole is also legal affairs correspondent to *The Nation* and the author of several books, including *No Equal Justice: Race and Class in the Criminal Justice System* (1999). The following op-ed piece on his students' use of laptops appeared in the *Washington Post* on April 7, 2007.

PREREADING QUESTIONS Do you take a laptop to class? If so, why? How often do you shift attention from class to e-mail or the Internet?

"Could you repeat the question?"   1

In recent years, that has become the most common response to questions   2
I pose to my law students at Georgetown University. It is usually asked while
the student glances up from the laptop screen that otherwise occupies his or
her field of vision. After I repeat the question, the student's gaze as often as

not returns to the computer screen, as if the answer might magically appear there. Who knows, with instant messaging, maybe it will.

3   Some years back, our law school, like many around the country, wired its classrooms with Internet hookups. It's the way of the future, I was told. Now we are a wireless campus, and incoming students are required to have laptops. So my first-year students were a bit surprised when I announced at the first class this year that laptops were banned from my classroom.

4   I did this for two reasons, I explained. Note-taking on a laptop encourages verbatim transcription. The note-taker tends to go into stenographic mode and no longer processes information in a way that is conductive to the give and take of classroom discussion. Because taking notes the old-fashioned way, by hand, is so much slower, one actually has to listen, think and prioritize the most important themes.

5   In addition, laptops create temptation to surf the Web, check e-mail, shop for shoes or instant-message friends. That's not only distracting to the student who is checking Red Sox statistics but for all those who see him, and many others, doing something besides being involved in class. Together, the stenographic mode and Web surfing make for a much less engaged classroom, and that affects all students (not to mention me).

6   I agreed to permit two volunteers to use laptops to take notes that would be made available to all students. And that first day I allowed everyone to use the laptops they had with them. I posed a question, and a student volunteered an answer. I answered her with a follow-up question. As if on cue, as soon as I started to respond, the student went back to typing—and then asked, "Could you repeat the question?"

7   When I have raised with my colleagues the idea of cutting off laptop access, some accuse me of being paternalistic, authoritarian or worse. We daydreamed and did crosswords when we were students, they argue, so how can we prohibit our students, who are adults after all, from using their time in class as they deem fit?

8   A crossword hidden under a book is one thing. With the aid of Microsoft and Google, we have effectively put at every seat a library of magazines, a television and the opportunity for real-time side conversations and invited our students to check out whenever they find their attention wandering.

9   I feel especially strongly about this issue because I'm addicted to the Internet myself. I checked my e-mail at least a dozen times while writing this op-ed. I've often resolved, after a rare and liberating weekend away from e-mail, that I will wait till the end of the day to read e-mail at the office. Yet, almost as if it is beyond my control, e-mail is the first thing I check when I log on each morning. As for multitasking, I don't buy it. Attention diverted is attention diverted.

10   But this is all theory. How does banning laptops work in practice? My own sense has been that my class is much more engaged than recent past classes. I'm biased, I know. So I conducted an anonymous survey of my students after about six weeks—by computer, of course.

11   The results were striking. About 80 percent reported that they are more engaged in class discussion when they are laptop-free. Seventy percent said

that, on balance, they liked the no-laptop policy. And perhaps most surprising, 95 percent admitted that they use their laptops in class for "purposes other than taking notes, such as surfing the Web, checking e-mail, instant messaging and the like." Ninety-eight percent reported seeing fellow students do the same.

I am sure that the Internet can be a useful pedagogical tool in some set- 12 tings and for some subjects. But for most classes, it is little more than an attractive nuisance. Technology has outstripped us on this one, and we need to reassess its appropriate and inappropriate role in teaching. The personal computer has revolutionized our lives, in many ways for the better. But it also threatens to take over our lives. At least for some purposes, unplugging may still be the best response.

QUESTIONS FOR READING

1. Why did the author ban laptops from his law classes?
2. What student behavior the first day of class seemed to support Cole's argument?
3. How did some of his colleagues react?
4. What did his student survey reveal?

QUESTIONS FOR REASONING AND ANALYSIS

1. What is Cole's claim? Where does he state it most emphatically?
2. How does Cole rebut his colleagues' argument in support of laptops in the classroom?
3. What does the author gain in paragraph 9 when he describes himself as "addicted to the Internet"?

QUESTIONS FOR REFLECTION AND WRITING

1. Cole observes that the results of his survey were "striking." Are you surprised by the students' responses? Would you have agreed with the great majority of students on the questions? Why or why not?
2. Cole asserts that the Internet can be a teaching tool for some classes. In what kinds of courses or for what types of class environments might having a laptop be an aid to learning? Explain and defend your answer.

COPYRIGHT SILLINESS ON CAMPUS | FRED VON LOHMANN

A graduate of Stanford University and Stanford Law School, Fred von Lohmann is a senior staff attorney with the Electronic Frontier Foundation. Widely recognized as one of the leading intellectual property lawyers, von Lohmann has published opinion pieces in many periodicals and has frequently appeared on television to explain or debate legal issues related to intellectual property. In his essay in the *Washington Post* (June 6, 2007), he addresses issues of student file-sharing.

PREREADING QUESTIONS Have you participated in music or film file-sharing? If so, did you pay for a service such as Napster?

1   What do Columbia, Vanderbilt, Duke, Howard and UCLA have in common? Apparently, leaders in Congress think that they aren't expelling enough students for illegally swapping music and movies.

2   The House committees responsible for copyright and education wrote a joint letter May 1 scolding the presidents of 19 major American universities, demanding that each school respond to a six-page questionnaire detailing steps it has taken to curtail illegal music and movie file-sharing on campus. One of the questions—"Does your institution expel violating students?"—shows just how out-of-control the futile battle against campus downloading has become.

3   As universities are pressured to punish students and install expensive "filtering" technologies to monitor their computer networks, the entertainment industry has ramped up its student shakedown campaign. The Recording Industry Association of America has targeted more than 1,600 individual students in the past four months, demanding that each pay $3,000 for file-sharing transgressions or face a federal lawsuit. In total, the music and movie industries have brought more than 20,000 federal lawsuits against individual Americans in the past three years.

4   History is sure to judge harshly everyone responsible for this absurd state of affairs. Our universities have far better things to spend money on than bullying students. Artists deserve to be fairly compensated, but are we really prepared to sue and expel every college student who has made an illegal copy? No one who takes privacy and civil liberties seriously can believe that the installation of surveillance technologies on university computer networks is a sensible solution.

5   It's not an effective solution, either. Short of appointing a copyright hall monitor for every dorm room, there is no way digital copying will be meaningfully reduced. Technical efforts to block file-sharing will be met with clever counter measures from sharp computer science majors. Even if students were completely cut off from the Internet, they would continue to copy CDs, swap hard drives and pool their laptops.

6   Already, a hard drive capable of storing more than 80,000 songs can be had for $100. Blank DVDs, each capable of holding more than a first-generation iPod, now sell for a quarter apiece. Students are going to copy what they want, when they want, from whom they want.

7   So universities can't stop file-sharing. But they can still help artists get paid for it. How? By putting some cash on the bar.

8   Universities already pay blanket fees so that student a cappella groups can perform on campus, and they also pay for cable TV subscriptions and site licenses for software. By the same token, they could collect a reasonable amount from their students for "all you can eat" downloading.

9   The recording industry is already willing to offer unlimited downloads with subscription plans for $10 to $15 per month through services such as Napster and Rhapsody. But these services have been a failure on campuses,

for a number of reasons, including these: They don't work with the iPod, they cause downloaded music to "expire" after students leave the school, and they don't include all the music students want.

The only solution is a blanket license that permits students to get unre- 10 stricted music and movies from sources of their choosing.

At its heart, this is a fight about money, not about morality. We should have 11 the universities collect the cash, pay it to the entertainment industry and let the students do what they are going to do anyway. In exchange, the entertainment industry should call off the lawyers and lobbyists, leaving our nation's universities to focus on the real challenges facing America's next generation of leaders.

QUESTIONS FOR READING

1. What do some members of Congress want universities to do to control file-sharing among students?
2. What organization is bringing lawsuits against students for illegal file-sharing of music?
3. On what basis does the author reject the expelling of students?
4. What solution does von Lohmann recommend?

QUESTIONS FOR REASONING AND ANALYSIS

1. What is the author's claim? State it as a claim for a problem/solution argument.
2. List the specific grounds in defense of his claim. What assumption, stated by von Lohmann, underpins the solutions presented by each side in this quarrel? What does he gain by spelling out the "heart" of the conflict between the artists and the file-sharers?
3. Examine von Lohmann's style. How effective are his title and opening paragraph in getting reader interest? Why?

QUESTIONS FOR REFLECTION AND WRITING

1. Do you agree with the author that stopping file-sharing among students is futile? Is this issue like Prohibition—a law that cannot be enforced? Explain.
2. Students who break the law are expelled from universities. Why shouldn't they be expelled for breaking the law against stealing an artist's intellectual property?
3. Should part of the student activities fee go to pay for unlimited file-sharing so that recording artists are paid for their work? Why or why not?

SWEATIN' TO THE KORAN? | KATHA POLLITT

A contributor to *The Nation* since 1980, Katha Pollitt's column of politics and culture appears every other week. Many of her columns have been published in three book collections. *Learning to Drive and Other Life Stories*, a collection of personal essays, was published in 2008, and a second collection of her poetry, *The Mind-Body*

Problem: Poems, will appear in 2009. In "Sweatin' to the Koran?" Pollitt addresses Harvard's decision to have some gym hours only for women.

PREREADING QUESTIONS Should all college dorms be coed, or should some be single sex? Should colleges provide choices of this sort for students?

1   I was all geared up to write a column fulminating against Harvard for setting up women-only hours in one of its gyms because apparently some Muslim women students felt more comfortable exercising away from the eyes of men. Kowtowing to religion! Validating Islam's obsession with female—and only female—modesty! Denial of equal gym time to men! When I was an undergraduate, Harvard kept women out of all sorts of good stuff, like convenient places to eat on campus. Until a year before I got there, women were banned from centrally located Lamont Library, supposedly to discourage canoodling in the stacks. All the gyms on campus were single-sex back then, not that I knew where they were. In short, I'm very conscious of the ways single-sex arrangements have historically given men the lion's share of whatever is being divvied up.

2   Unfortunately for my life as a casuist, I made the mistake of asking my ever-sensible daughter and her friend Lindsey, both college juniors, what they thought. They thought women-only gym time was fine. "It's only six hours a week, Mom," said Sophie. "And the gym is the least used one on campus." What about the principle? "I think it's hard to be a Muslim girl in a co-ed school," Sophie answered. "If this makes it easier, they should have it." "Well, I don't know that it's especially hard for them," Lindsey put in—here followed a lengthy discussion of the social lives of Muslim and Orthodox Jewish girls. But say you were a male student, I asked, and you showed up to work out at girls-only time? "Well, I would just come back later," said Sophie, or go to another gym. Honestly, Mom, what's the big deal?" So it doesn't bother you that Harvard is making a special arrangement because of religion? "Well, it isn't really doing that," Lindsey said, "because any woman student can use the women-only hours, and Muslim women don't have to use them if they don't want to."

3   Right. Why hadn't I thought of that? The Harvard gym controversy looks like it's about religion, but really it's about whether women (or men) should have a little bit of separate space in a co-ed university.

4   But that's not so exciting. Few would be writing about this handful of single-sex gym hours if the request had come from, say, overweight women or shy women or the club of virgins recently written about in *The New York Times Magazine.* Some co-ed campuses have single-sex dorms—Cornell has one for women—to say nothing of sororities, fraternities and single-sex societies like Harvard's ghastly final clubs. None of this has aroused a lot of interest from the national opinion industry. Maybe the women writers are too busy exercising at Curves, the ubiquitous women-only chain, while the men writers are off at their Elks lodge.

5   But this situation is different: it involves *Islam* (violent, oppressive, sexist) and *Harvard* (multicultural twits). When I put "Harvard Muslim girls gym" into Google I got 151,000 hits, including articles from as far away as Japan, and bloodcurdling references to Sharia and honor killings, horrified descriptions of women using treadmills in veils and chadors ("a black, woolen blob, an

anachronism of the first degree"), calls for lawsuits and physical invasions of Muslim-girl gym time. Martin Luther King was invoked, as were Title IX, feminism, slippery slopes, appeasement, Nazis and did I mention Sharia?

Well, I shouldn't be so superior, because some of those thoughts went through my mind, too. That is what living in our time does to you: intelligent people go in a flash from "Art history major wants to work out in peace" to "What about those gays they executed in Iran?" One minute Martin Amis is turning out a stream of smart, ambitious novels; the next he's writing about Muslims taking over because Europeans don't have enough babies. I get e-mails every day from people who have been driven round the bend by fear and contempt and self-righteousness. To them, a housewife in a head scarf might as well be a suicide bomber; a taxi driver listening to an Arabic station is probably getting tips on how to murder his sister. It's as if all their lives they've been waiting for a socially acceptable hate-object to come along so they could enjoy the psychological satisfactions of racism without technically being racist.

Yes, terrible crimes against women, gays and secularists are committed in the name of Islam; yes, many Muslim countries have poor human rights records; yes, Muslim fundamentalists say, and sometimes do, horrible things. I've never favored the kind of multiculturalism that looks impassively on the abuse of women because "it's their culture." I was appalled by Archbishop of Canterbury Rowan Williams's proposal for separate Sharia courts for British Muslims and by Noah Feldman's support for that idea in *The New York Times Magazine:* that seems like a recipe for denying Muslim women equal treatment in divorce and other family matters. But what does any of this have to do with Muslim women at Harvard? They weren't taken out of school at puberty to cook and clean, like the home-schooled Pakistani girls in California featured in a recent news story; they aren't being shipped off to the old country to marry their cousins; I doubt very much if their college plan is to have ten children and bring the caliphate to Martin Amis's neighborhood. You might as well say that Harvard's Catholic students have all been molested by priests and will go on to abuse children too. Except nobody does say that.

I'm not totally sold on single-sex gyms. To be fair, there should be equal single-sex time for men as well. Maybe that's a good idea—not only women are shy about their bodies—although it might mean, in practice, that men get the better hours and facilities, because separate usually doesn't mean equal. But let's get a grip. Osama bin Laden and burqas and fascism have nothing to do with six hours a week of man-free exercise time for any female student, regardless of race, creed or national origin.

QUESTIONS FOR READING

1. What is Pollitt's subject?
2. What is her initial reaction to this issue, based on past experience?
3. What is her daughter's reaction to the women-only hours?
4. How big an issue has Harvard's decision been? How much attention has it received?

QUESTIONS FOR REASONING AND ANALYSIS

1. Pollitt is known for her witty, incisive style of writing. Find examples of clever expressions and approaches to the topic.
2. What, finally, is Pollitt's position on gym hours for women at Harvard? What is her support?
3. What analysis does she provide in paragraph 6? How does this paragraph extend her discussion?
4. What is the purpose of paragraph 7?

QUESTIONS FOR REFLECTION AND WRITING

1. Do you side with Pollitt's initial reaction to Harvard's decision? Or, with her daughter's view? Explain and defend your position.
2. Are young people too complacent today—it's not a big deal; it's only 6 hours a week; get over it? Explain and defend your response.
3. Should multiculturalism include accepting abuses of women because "it's their culture"? Does political correctness mean that we never make moral judgments or seek change in countries that oppress one group or another? Be prepared to debate these questions.

A SEPARATE AND UNEQUAL EXERCISE | HARRY LEWIS

Former dean of Harvard College, Harry Lewis is a professor of computer science at Harvard, and the author of several texts on computer science. He is also the author of *Excellence Without a Soul: Does Liberal Education Have a Future?* (2006) and, with Hal Abelson and Ken Ledeen, *Blown to Bits: Your Life, Liberty, and Happiness After the Digital Explosion* (2008). His response to Harvard's decision to provide women-only time in one of their gyms was published in the Boston *Globe* on March 25, 2008.

PREREADING QUESTIONS Based on his title, what do you expect Lewis's position on Harvard's decision to be? Why?

1   Perhaps it is simple politeness for Harvard University to close its secondary gym to men for six hours a week so conservative Muslim women can exercise without men seeing their skin.

2   Religious accommodations are usually uncontroversial, but this is different. Everyone can enjoy Harvard's kosher food; half the students are excluded from the gym, however briefly.

3   Surely only those with the most mean-spirited interpretation of gender equality could object—yet complain they did.

4   "Today I was forced to wait outside in the cold until 5," wrote one man. "The policy seems sexist and discriminatory."

5   "These hours have been put in place for equality reasons," read Harvard's announcement. The decision apparently resulted from a paradoxical collaboration between the Women's Center, which greets visitors with a sign reading

"All Genders Welcome," and adherents to a religion that imposes unequal social strictures on men and women.

Harvard didn't explain its thinking, but it seems to have adopted a post- 6 modern version of equality: Equality might be achieved only by imposing unequal access, if those seeking equality do not share the consensus view. Freedom is useless without comfort, so liberation of some might require exclusion of others.

Whatever the logic, the university failed in its educational responsibility. It 7 missed an opportunity to model for its students the kind of moral reasoning it expects of them. The resulting standards are inconsistent, and the muddle has a history.

This conflict is rooted in Harvard's uncompromising interpretation of 8 equality since 1977, which was a response to its decidedly unequal treatment of women for most of its past. When Harvard assumed full responsibility for women's education from Radcliffe, it adopted an absolute nondiscrimination standard. Everything is open to men and women on an equal basis—nothing is "separate but equal" except some athletic teams and choral singing groups. Most student organizations desegregated voluntarily. The venerable all-male Final Clubs, which the dean's office used to coordinate, refused to admit women and were severed from the university.

Harvard's nondiscrimination policies now cover "race, color, sex, sexual 9 orientation, gender identity, religion, age," and a few other things, and the same absolutism applies to all categories. Harvard has no ethnic or single-sex housing. Women's groups have to allow male members. The Black Students' Association can't close white students out of its meetings.

And, until now, the athletic department didn't bar the doors of the gym 10 against male students.

Absolutism is not the only ethical approach to discrimination issues. 11 Fraternities and sororities fall afoul of Harvard's equal-access policy, but most colleges find them unproblematic in principle. Perhaps Harvard has just been out of step with that "real world" in which constructive segregation and special interests sometimes trump integrationist principles.

The new stance seems generous and tolerant: Be nice to people, even if 12 it means excluding others, as long as the benefit is significant and the injury is minor.

Which brings us to ROTC. Harvard bans ROTC because the military vio- 13 lates the "sexual orientation" part of Harvard's nondiscrimination policy. Harvard students can participate in ROTC at MIT, but Harvard will not provide them meeting space or any other support—even bus fare down Massachusetts Avenue.

If there were ever a special case, this is it. ROTC's discriminatory policy is US 14 law. Until Congress repeals that law, Harvard should accommodate ROTC anyway, in the interests of the nation and of Harvard students wishing to serve it.

The counterargument goes, however, that if ROTC were accommodated, 15 the benefit to cadets would be far less significant than the injury to gays and lesbians. Indeed, some claim that no price would be too high for Harvard to pay for uncompromising adherence to its nondiscrimination policy, even the loss of all government funding, if it came to that.

16   Is the gym exception merely a reasonable kindness to conservative Muslim women? Then Harvard's failure of courtesy to its cadets suggests that politics determine what forms of discrimination are inoffensive.

17   That is not what Harvard should be teaching. Tolerance is good, but absolute nondiscrimination is preferable to such politicized tolerance.

QUESTIONS FOR READING

1. What decision did Harvard make?
2. How does Lewis "explain" Harvard's apparent version of "equality"?
3. What is the history—what position did Harvard take in 1977 when it became completely coed?
4. What were the consequences for housing and groups and clubs? How does their stance affect ROTC?

QUESTIONS FOR REASONING AND ANALYSIS

1. What is Lewis's claim? Where does he state it?
2. Explain Lewis's objection to Harvard's decision. What is his reasoning?
3. How does Lewis use his discussion of ROTC at Harvard to show that Harvard is now inconsistent in its policies?
4. What is clever about the essay's title?
5. Is Lewis in favor of absolutism in nondiscrimination? What evidence can you cite to support your answer?

QUESTIONS FOR REFLECTION AND WRITING

1. Has reading Lewis's argument altered your thinking based only on reading Pollitt's column on this subject? If so, how? If not, why not?
2. Lewis concludes with the assertion that "absolute nondiscrimination is preferable to such politicized tolerance." Why does he think that Harvard made its decision to close one gym to men for six hours?
3. Should nondiscrimination be absolute? (According to this article, even Harvard's absolutist position is not absolute, as some teams and singing groups are limited to one sex.) Explain and defend your position.

I'M SO TOTALLY, DIGITALLY CLOSE TO YOU | CLIVE THOMPSON

Clive Thompson writes about science, technology, and culture. He is a contributing editor to the *New York Times Magazine* and a columnist for *Wired* magazine. He maintains an interesting blog, *collision detection,* on which he posts really cool photos related to science research and musings on various research projects that interest him. What follows is a slightly shortened version of Thompson's article on the impact of Facebook among college students (*New York Times Magazine* on September 7, 2008).

PREREADING QUESTIONS Do you have a Facebook page? If so, what do you use that site for? If not, why have you stayed away from this astoundingly popular site?

On Sept. 5, 2006, Mark Zuckerberg changed the way that Facebook 1 worked, and in the process he inspired a revolt.

Zuckerberg, a doe-eyed 24-year-old C.E.O., founded Facebook in his 2 dorm room at Harvard two years earlier, and the site quickly amassed nine million users. By 2006, students were posting heaps of personal details onto their Facebook pages, including lists of their favorite TV shows, whether they were dating (and whom), what music they had in rotation and the various ad hoc "groups" they had joined (like *Sex and the City* Lovers). All day long, they'd post "status" notes explaining their moods—"hating Monday," "skipping class b/c i'm hung over." After each party, they'd stagger home to the dorm and upload pictures of the soused revelry, and spend the morning after commenting on how wasted everybody looked. Facebook became the de facto public commons—the way students found out what everyone around them was like and what he or she was doing.

But Zuckerberg knew Facebook had one major problem: It required a lot 3 of active surfing on the part of its users. Sure, every day your Facebook friends would update their profiles with some new tidbits; it might even be something particularly juicy, like changing their relationship status to "single" when they got dumped. But unless you visited each friend's page every day, it might be days or weeks before you noticed the news, or you might miss it entirely. Browsing Facebook was like constantly poking your head into someone's room to see how she was doing. It took work and forethought. In a sense, this gave Facebook an inherent, built-in level of privacy, simply because if you had 200 friends on the site—a fairly typical number—there weren't enough hours in the day to keep tabs on every friend all the time.

"It was very primitive," Zuckerberg told me when I asked him about it last 4 month. And so he decided to modernize. He developed something he called News Feed, a built-in service that would actively broadcast changes in a user's page to every one of his or her friends. Students would no longer need to spend their time zipping around to examine each friend's page, checking to see if there was any new information. Instead, they would just log into Facebook, and News Feed would appear: a single page that—like a social gazette from the 18th century—delivered a long list of up-to-the-minute gossip about their friends, around the clock, all in one place. "A stream of everything that's going on in their lives," as Zuckerberg put it.

When students woke up that September morning and saw News Feed, 5 the first reaction, generally, was one of panic. Just about every little thing you changed on your page was now instantly blasted out to hundreds of friends, including potentially mortifying bits of news—*Tim and Lisa broke up; Persaud is no longer friends with Matthew*—and drunken photos someone snapped, then uploaded and tagged with names. Facebook had lost its vestigial bit of privacy. For students, it was now like being at a giant, open party filled with everyone you know, able to eavesdrop on what everyone else was saying, all the time.

6   "Everyone was freaking out," Ben Parr, then a junior at Northwestern University, told me recently. What particularly enraged Parr was that there wasn't any way to opt out of News Feed, to "go private" and have all your information kept quiet. He created a Facebook group demanding Zuckerberg either scrap News Feed or provide privacy options. "Facebook users really think Facebook is becoming the Big Brother of the Internet, recording every single move," a California student told *The Star-Ledger* of Newark. Another chimed in, "Frankly, I don't need to know or care that Billy broke up with Sally, and Ted has become friends with Steve." By lunchtime of the first day, 10,000 people had joined Parr's group, and by the next day it had 284,000.

7   Zuckerberg, surprised by the outcry, quickly made two decisions. The first was to add a privacy feature to News Feed, letting users decide what kind of information went out. But the second decision was to leave News Feed otherwise intact. He suspected that once people tried it and got over their shock, they'd like it.

8   He was right. Within days, the tide reversed. Students began e-mailing Zuckerberg to say that via News Feed they'd learned things they would never have otherwise discovered through random surfing around Facebook. The bits of trivia that News Feed delivered gave them more things to talk about—*Why do you hate Kiefer Sutherland?*—when they met friends face to face in class or at a party. Trends spread more quickly. When one student joined a group—proclaiming her love of Coldplay or a desire to volunteer for Greenpeace—all her friends instantly knew, and many would sign up themselves. Users' worries about their privacy seemed to vanish within days, boiled away by their excitement at being so much more connected to their friends. (Very few people stopped using Facebook, and most people kept on publishing most of their information through News Feed.) Pundits predicted that News Feed would kill Facebook, but the opposite happened. It catalyzed a massive boom in the site's growth. A few weeks after the News Feed imbroglio, Zuckerberg opened the site to the general public (previously, only students could join), and it grew quickly; today, it has 100 million users.

9   When I spoke to him, Zuckerberg argued that News Feed is central to Facebook's success. "Facebook has always tried to push the envelope," he said. "And at times that means stretching people and getting them to be comfortable with things they aren't yet comfortable with. A lot of this is just social norms catching up with what technology is capable of."

10   In essence, Facebook users didn't *think* they wanted constant, up-to-the-minute updates on what other people are doing. Yet when they experienced this sort of omnipresent knowledge, they found it intriguing and addictive. Why?

11   Social scientists have a name for this sort of incessant online contact. They call it "ambient awareness." It is, they say, very much like being physically near

someone and picking up on his mood through the little things he does—body language, sighs, stray comments—out of the corner of your eye. Facebook is no longer alone in offering this sort of interaction online. In the last year, there has been a boom in tools for "microblogging": posting frequent tiny updates on what you're doing. The phenomenon is quite different from what we normally think of as blogging, because a blog post is usually a written piece, sometimes quite long: a statement of opinion, a story, an analysis. But these new updates are something different. They're far shorter, far more frequent and less carefully considered. One of the most popular new tools is Twitter, a Web site and messaging service that allows its two-million-plus users to broadcast to their friends haiku-length updates—limited to 140 characters, as brief as a mobile-phone text message—on what they're doing. There are other services for reporting where you're traveling (Dopplr) or for quickly tossing online a stream of the pictures, videos or Web sites you're looking at (Tumblr). And there are even tools that give your location. When the new iPhone, with built-in tracking, was introduced in July, one million people began using Loopt, a piece of software that automatically tells all your friends exactly where you are.

For many people—particularly anyone over the age of 30—the idea of 12 describing your blow-by-blow activities in such detail is absurd. Why would you subject your friends to your daily minutiae? And conversely, how much of their trivia can you absorb? The growth of ambient intimacy can seem like modern narcissism taken to a new, supermetabolic extreme—the ultimate expression of a generation of celebrity-addled youths who believe their every utterance is fascinating and ought to be shared with the world. Twitter, in particular, has been the subject of nearly relentless scorn since it went online. "Who really cares what I am doing, every hour of the day?" wondered Alex Beam, a Boston *Globe* columnist, in an essay about Twitter last month. "Even I don't care."

Indeed, many of the people I interviewed, who are among the most avid 13 users of these "awareness" tools, admit that at first they couldn't figure out why anybody would want to do this. Ben Haley, a 39-year-old documentation specialist for a software firm who lives in Seattle, told me that when he first heard about Twitter last year from an early-adopter friend who used it, his first reaction was that it seemed silly. But a few of his friends decided to give it a try, and they urged him to sign up too.

Each day, Haley logged on to his account, and his friends' updates would 14 appear as a long page of one- or two-line notes. He would check and recheck the account several times a day, or even several times an hour. The updates were indeed pretty banal. One friend would post about starting to feel sick; one posted random thoughts like "I really hate it when people clip their nails on the bus"; another Twittered whenever she made a sandwich—and she made a sandwich every day. Each so-called tweet was so brief as to be virtually meaningless.

But as the days went by, something changed. Haley discovered that he 15 was beginning to sense the rhythms of his friends' lives in a way he never had before. When one friend got sick with a virulent fever, he could tell by her Twitter updates when she was getting worse and the instant she finally turned the corner. He could see when friends were heading into hellish days at work or when they'd scored a big success. Even the daily catalog of sandwiches became oddly mesmerizing, a sort of metronomic *click* that he grew accustomed to seeing pop up in the middle of each day.

16   This is the paradox of ambient awareness. Each little update—each individual bit of social information—is insignificant on its own, even supremely mundane. But taken together, over time, the little snippets coalesce into a surprisingly sophisticated portrait of your friends' and family members' lives, like thousands of dots making a pointillist painting. This was never before possible, because in the real world, no friend would *bother* to call you up and detail the sandwiches she was eating. The ambient information becomes like "a type of E.S.P.," as Haley described it to me, an invisible dimension floating over everyday life.

· · ·

17   You could also regard the growing popularity of online awareness as a reaction to social isolation, the modern American disconnectedness that Robert Putnam explored in his book *Bowling Alone.* The mobile workforce requires people to travel more frequently for work, leaving friends and family behind, and members of the growing army of the self-employed often spend their days in solitude. Ambient intimacy becomes a way to "feel less alone," as more than one Facebook and Twitter user told me.

· · ·

18   In 1998, the anthropologist Robin Dunbar argued that each human has a hard-wired upper limit on the number of people he or she can personally know at one time. Dunbar noticed that humans and apes both develop social bonds by engaging in some sort of grooming; apes do it by picking at and smoothing one another's fur, and humans do it with conversation. He theorized that ape and human brains could manage only a finite number of grooming relationships: unless we spend enough time doing social grooming—chitchatting, trading gossip or, for apes, picking lice—we won't really feel that we "know" someone well enough to call him a friend. Dunbar noticed that ape groups tended to top out at 55 members. Since human brains were proportionally bigger, Dunbar figured that our maximum number of social connections would be similarly larger: about 150 on average. Sure enough, psychological studies have confirmed that human groupings naturally tail off at around 150 people: the "Dunbar number," as it is known. Are people who use Facebook and Twitter increasing their Dunbar number, because they can so easily keep track of so many more people?

19   As I interviewed some of the most aggressively social people online— people who follow hundreds or even thousands of others—it became clear that the picture was a little more complex than this question would suggest. Many maintained that their circle of true intimates, their very close friends

and family, had not become bigger. Constant online contact had made those ties immeasurably richer, but it hadn't actually increased the number of them; deep relationships are still predicated on face time, and there are only so many hours in the day for that.

But where their sociality had truly exploded was in their "weak ties"— 20 loose acquaintances, people they knew less well. It might be someone they met at a conference, or someone from high school who recently "friended" them on Facebook, or somebody from last year's holiday party. In their pre-Internet lives, these sorts of acquaintances would have quickly faded from their attention. But when one of these far-flung people suddenly posts a personal note to your feed, it is essentially a reminder that they exist. I have noticed this effect myself. In the last few months, dozens of old work colleagues I knew from 10 years ago in Toronto have friended me on Facebook, such that I'm now suddenly reading their stray comments and updates and falling into oblique, funny conversation with them. My overall Dunbar number is thus 301: Facebook (254) + Twitter (47), double what it would be without technology. Yet only 20 are family or people I'd consider close friends. The rest are weak ties—maintained via technology.

This rapid growth of weak ties can be a very good thing. Sociologists have 21 long found that "weak ties" greatly expand your ability to solve problems. For example, if you're looking for a job and ask your friends, they won't be much help; they're too similar to you, and thus probably won't have any leads that you don't already have yourself. Remote acquaintances will be much more useful, because they're farther afield, yet still socially intimate enough to want to help you out. Many avid Twitter users—the ones who fire off witty posts hourly and wind up with thousands of intrigued followers—explicitly milk this dynamic for all it's worth, using their large online followings as a way to quickly answer almost any question. Laura Fitton, a social-media consultant who has become a minor celebrity on Twitter—she has more than 5,300 followers—recently discovered to her horror that her accountant had made an error in filing last year's taxes. She went to Twitter, wrote a tiny note explaining her problem, and within 10 minutes her online audience had provided leads to lawyers and better accountants. Fitton joked to me that she no longer buys anything worth more than $50 without quickly checking it with her Twitter network.

"I outsource my entire life," she said. "I can solve any problem on Twitter 22 in six minutes." (She also keeps a secondary Twitter account that is private and only for a much smaller circle of close friends and family—"My little secret," she said. It is a strategy many people told me they used: one account for their weak ties, one for their deeper relationships.)

It is also possible, though, that this profusion of weak ties can become 23 a problem. If you're reading daily updates from hundreds of people about whom they're dating and whether they're happy, it might, some critics worry, spread your emotional energy too thin, leaving less for true intimate relation-ships. Psychologists have long known that people can engage in "parasocial" relationships with fictional characters, like those on TV shows or in books, or with remote celebrities we read about in magazines. Parasocial relationships can use up some of the emotional space in our Dunbar number, crowding out real-life people. Danah Boyd, a fellow at Harvard's Berkman Center for Internet and Society who has studied social media for 10 years, published a paper this spring arguing that awareness tools like News Feed might be creating a whole new class of relationships that are nearly parasocial—peripheral people in our network whose intimate details we follow closely online, even while they, like Angelina Jolie, are basically unaware we exist.

24   "The information we subscribe to on a feed is not the same as in a deep social relationship," Boyd told me. She has seen this herself; she has many virtual admirers that have, in essence, a parasocial relationship with her. "I've been very, very sick, lately and I write about it on Twitter and my blog, and I get all these people who are writing to me telling me ways to work around the health-care system, or they're writing saying, 'Hey, I broke my neck!' And I'm like, 'You're being very nice and trying to help me, but though you feel like you know me, you don't,'" Boyd sighed. "They can *observe* you, but it's not the same as *knowing* you."

. . .

25   This is the ultimate effect of the new awareness: It brings back the dynamics of small-town life, where everybody knows your business. Young people at college are the ones to experience this most viscerally, because, with more than 90 percent of their peers using Facebook, it is especially difficult for them to opt out. Zeynep Tufekci, a sociologist at the University of Maryland, Baltimore County, who has closely studied how college-age users are reacting to the world of awareness, told me that athletes used to sneak off to parties illicitly, breaking the no-drinking rule for team members. But then camera phones and Facebook came along, with students posting photos of the drunken carousing during the party; savvy coaches could see which athletes were breaking the rules. First the athletes tried to fight back by waking up early the morning after the party in a hungover daze to detag photos of themselves so they wouldn't be searchable. But that didn't work, because the coaches sometimes viewed the pictures live, as they went online at 2 a.m. So parties simply began banning all camera phones in a last-ditch attempt to preserve privacy.

26   "It's just like living in a village, where it's actually hard to lie because everybody knows the truth already," Tufekci said. "The current generation is never unconnected. They're never losing touch with their friends. So we're going back to a more normal place, historically. If you look at human history, the idea that you would drift through life, going from new relation to new relation, that's very new. It's just the 20th century."

27   Psychologists and sociologists spent years wondering how humanity would adjust to the anonymity of life in the city, the wrenching upheavals of mobile immigrant labor—a world of lonely people ripped from their social ties. We now have precisely the opposite problem. Indeed, our modern awareness tools reverse the original conceit of the Internet. When cyberspace came

along in the early '90s, it was celebrated as a place where you could reinvent your identity—become someone new.

"If anything, it's identity-constraining now," Tufekci told me. "You can't 28 play with your identity if your audience is always checking up on you. I had a student who posted that she was downloading some Pearl Jam, and someone wrote on her wall, 'Oh, *right,* ha-ha—I know you, and you're not into *that.*'" She laughed. "You know that old cartoon? 'On the Internet, nobody knows you're a dog'? On the Internet today, *everybody* knows you're a dog! If you don't want people to know you're a dog, you'd better stay away from a keyboard."

Or, as Leisa Reichelt, a consultant in London who writes regularly about 29 ambient tools, put it to me: "Can you imagine a Facebook for children in kindergarten, and they never lose touch with those kids for the rest of their lives? What's that going to do to them?" Young people today are already developing an attitude toward their privacy that is simultaneously vigilant and laissez-faire. They curate their online personas as carefully as possible, knowing that everyone is watching—but they have also learned to shrug and accept the limits of what they can control.

It is easy to become unsettled by privacy-eroding aspects of aware- 30 ness tools. But there is another—quite different—result of all this incessant updating: a culture of people who know much more about themselves. Many of the avid Twitterers, Flickrers and Facebook users I interviewed described an unexpected side-effect of constant self-disclosure. The act of stopping several times a day to observe what you're feeling or thinking can become, after weeks and weeks, a sort of philosophical act. It's like the Greek dictum to "know thyself," or the therapeutic concept of mindfulness. (Indeed, the question that floats eternally at the top of Twitter's Web site—"What are you doing?"—can come to seem existentially freighted. What *are* you doing?) Having an audience can make the self-reflection even more acute, since, as my interviewees noted, they're trying to describe their activities in a way that is not only accurate but also interesting to others: the status update as a literary form.

Laura Fitton, the social-media consultant, argues that her constant sta- 31 tus updating has made her "a happier person, a calmer person" because the process of, say, describing a horrid morning at work forces her to look at it objectively. "It drags you out of your own head," she added. In an age of awareness, perhaps the person you see most clearly is yourself.

QUESTIONS FOR READING

1. What was the problem with the original format of Facebook?
2. What did Zuckerberg do to eliminate that problem? How did the change alter Facebook?
3. What was the initial reaction of many Facebook users? What was Zuckerberg's compromise?

4. How successful was the change Zuckerberg made to Facebook? What did he do shortly thereafter? How many users does the site have today?

5. What is "ambient awareness"?

6. What are Dopplr, Tumblr, Twitter, and Loopt? What seems to be the impact, over time, for users of these sites?

7. What is the "Dunbar number"? Have the constant-contact online sites changed this number for humans? What has changed?

8. What is meant by "parasocial" relationships?

QUESTIONS FOR REASONING AND ANALYSIS

1. Thompson provides much information about the uses of Facebook and other similar sites. He also raises a number of questions about the effects of these sites. What seems to be his primary purpose in writing? What is the claim of his argument?

2. Analyze Thompson's organization: what does he do first? Second? Third? How does this analysis help you to understand his purpose?

3. What seem to be the potential problems with the constant exposure on Facebook? Do the comments by some users dispel those problems?

4. What seem to be the advantages of the constant connecting and updating with so many people? If one goal is to have more friends, to be less isolated, is this goal actually met by Facebook and Twitter and other similar sites?

QUESTIONS FOR REFLECTION AND WRITING

1. How many of these sites do you use? How often do you search them? Would you say that you spend a lot of time on these sites? Too much time? If you are spending much time online, and you have course work to do (and you may also have a part-time job), what is it that you are not doing in your life? Do you feel as though you are missing other activities? Do the advantages outweigh the losses? Reflect on these questions.

2. Thompson suggests that one result of constantly posting about yourself is that you must pause and reflect on what you are doing and how you feel about it. Thus, you actually know more about yourself as a result. Would you agree with this observation? Do you stop and think and plan your postings as a well-written statement about who you are and what you feel? Explain and defend your response.

3. Facebook and other similar sites are probably here to stay. Is this, on balance, a good use of the Internet—and of our time? Why or why not?

CHAPTER 19

Censorship and Free Speech Debates

READ: What does this visual show?

REASON: Where do we find a provision for basic freedoms of speech? What is the exact wording? (If you don't know, look it up.)

REFLECT/WRITE: Why are protections of speech essential to a democracy?

If we have freedom of speech, why do people keep debating it? Why an entire chapter on the topic? As you explore the specific issues debated in this chapter, keep in mind that the Supreme Court continues to hand down rulings that shape our understanding of First Amendment rights. What is protected speech under the First Amendment is never absolute—it continues to evolve or be reinterpreted, depending on your point of view. We may also need to consider that there is no such thing as absolute freedom in any society and that the First Amendment does not pretend to offer absolute freedoms. For example, you cannot go into a crowded theater and yell "Fire!" when there is no fire. You will be arrested for this behavior that puts others at risk. And so the debates continue, as we consider how to rate movies in which characters smoke or what the rules are for exposing someone else's activities on your personal Web site or what we think about (and should do about) American companies that sell computer systems to other countries, knowing that those countries will place all kinds of controls on access to the Internet for their citizens. Parents place controls on their TVs and computers to restrict their children's access to some shows and sites. What restrictions, if any, are appropriate for governments to establish? For colleges?

PREREADING QUESTIONS

1. What, if any, restrictions should be placed on the publication of obscene, pornographic, or treasonable works? Are there some restrictions that most people can agree to?

2. What, if any, restrictions should be placed on hate speech? Are there restrictions that colleges, in particular, should establish? Or not?

3. What are some ways to control what is published (in any medium) without always resorting to legal restrictions? Are there feasible alternatives to legal battles?

PHILIP MORRIS: NO SMOKING IN MOVIES | RICH THOMASELLI and T. L. STANLEY

A graduate of Fordham University, Rich Thomaselli has been a journalist and writer for a number of magazines and now online sites, including Grandparents.com and College and Pro Football Newsweekly. His range of interests that include advertising and sports can be seen at his blog: Hodgepodgeblog. T. L. Stanley, a newspaper and magazine journalist who focuses on marketing, advertising, and branded entertainment, contributed to the following article that was published November 20, 2006, in *Advertising Age*.

PREREADING QUESTIONS How often have you seen characters in films smoking? Has the smoking seemed essential to the character and situation?

1 **Print ad campaign from tobacco giant urges film industry to drop the prop**
Call it anti-product placement: Philip Morris USA is running ads in *Variety, The Hollywood Reporter* and other trade publications asking filmmakers not to put its products in films.

2   But suspicions are rising within the Hollywood community that the ads, far from being altruistic, amount to another big smokescreen from Big Tobacco.

The cigarette giant last week began a print push with headlines such as 3 "Please don't give our cigarette brands a part in any movie" with text reading: "We appeal to, and encourage, those in the entertainment industry to eliminate depictions of our brands and brand imagery in their work." The ads encourage the entertainment industry to reduce or eliminate smoking scenes directed at youth.

"Movies have the power to amuse, delight, teach and inspire. However, 4 some studies suggest they may also influence a child's decision to smoke," said Jennifer Hunter, VP, Youth Smoking Prevention and Cessation Support for Philip Morris USA, which was created in 1998 after the tobacco industry's Master Settlement Agreement with the states.

Industry experts, however, said Hollywood doesn't need Philip Morris' 5 blessing to use such leading brands as Marlboro, Virginia Slims and Benson & Hedges in films, and without a more substantial effort—such as a legal threat—the campaign is useless.

"My initial thought is, it's an excellent campaign," said Linda Swick, 6 president of International Promotions, a North Hollywood product placement specialist. "But then it becomes a question of whether Philip Morris is going to hold anybody liable for using their brand. If they really wanted to get aggressive, they certainly could make a huge impact with Hollywood so that [the industry] would not use their brands. But they're not saying, 'Do not use cigarettes at all,' they're just saying, 'Don't use our brand.'"

There is one ad in the campaign, however, that is more generic, urging the 7 industry not to depict smoking of any brand in film. "You have the power to help prevent youth smoking—just by losing one little prop," it says. The effort was created by WPP Group's Y&R Advertising, New York.

Philip Morris policy since 1990 has been to deny all requests for permis- 8 sion to use its brands in movies and TV shows intended for general audiences, making the timing of this campaign a bit curious. So why did the company decide to make such a push 16 years later?

A Philip Morris spokesman said that after the company spoke with "rele- 9 vant stakeholders," including trade associations and public-health advocates, it decided an effective way to raise awareness of the 1990 policy of denying all requests for brand use was to "do a focused print campaign."

Due to the Master Settlement Agreement in 1998 that severely limited 10 tobacco advertising, the idea of branded entertainment or product placement remains one of the few venues where cigarette makers can see their brands on display. The company acknowledges as much by saying it "can't stop all displays of our brands because federal and state trademark laws, as well as the U.S. Constitution, protect freedom of expression and the 'fair use' of trademarks in works such as movies and television shows."

That's another reason why some critics have charged PM's campaign is 11 actually grandstanding. "Philip Morris' move doesn't make any difference unless Hollywood significantly scales back smoking in the movies or agrees to rate movies based on smoking," said Matt Myers, president of the Washington-based Campaign for Tobacco-Free Kids. "The problem isn't which brand is shown, it's that Hollywood portrays smoking by kids who emulate those on the screen. Hollywood can't continue to act as if the problem doesn't exist or it has no responsibility."

12   Several groups have led past efforts to have Hollywood eliminate smoking in feature films. In four of the last five years, the Centers for Disease Control has cited tobacco in movies as a major factor in teen smoking.

13   Though Hollywood has made an effort to curtail lighting up in films— most of the mainstream movies have cut back on the practice, and smoking is mostly now seen in R-rated and independent productions—cigarettes are nonetheless a cheap prop, and they are an everyday product still used by 44% of Americans. The realism lends itself to films, can be easily explained as part of a story of character, and producers aren't as beholden to a company to provide that particular product, such as a car manufacturer.

QUESTIONS FOR READING

1. What kinds of ads did Philip Morris run? What were they designed to accomplish?
2. What has been the policy of this company since 1990?
3. What question is raised by the authors regarding Philip Morris's ad campaign?

QUESTIONS FOR REASONING AND ANALYSIS

1. This brief article appeared in a trade magazine. How would you describe its style and tone? Does the writing appear to be what you would expect, given the audience and purpose?
2. Will the Philip Morris campaign have any effect on Hollywood movies? What is the view of the authors? Explain.
3. If Philip Morris wanted to keep their brands out of movies, what other steps could they take?

QUESTIONS FOR REFLECTION AND WRITING

1. Are you bothered by smoking in the movies? Why or why not?
2. Would you argue that the presentation of smoking in films is realistic? (Only about 20 percent of Americans smoke, and the percentage of smokers is much higher among the poor than the rich.) How might these facts affect your response to the question?
3. Should the Motion Picture Association of America be lobbied to give an R rating to all films with smoking to reduce youth exposure to onscreen smoking? Explain and defend your position.

QUESTIONS FOR READING

1. Who is the sponsor of this ad? What is this an ad for?
2. What will be included in DVDs with smoking? Why is this not sufficient in the view of SmokeFreeMovies.ucsf.edu? (You might want to visit their Web site to see their response to the Philip Morris ad campaign.)

[One in a Series]

Necessary, yes.   Sufficient, no.

Does a polluter become "green" by handing out free gas masks?

Adding anti-tobacco spots to DVDs with smoking is necessary. DVDs with smoking harm children and teens every time they're watched. Proven spots from experienced health organizations can reduce the impact of films with smoking. They need to be in all distribution channels, not just DVDs.

But spots don't keep kids from being exposed in the first place.

Movies rated G, PG and (mainly) PG-13 deliver at least half of young people's exposure. The least intrusive, most effective way to keep smoking out of future youth-rated movies is to rate smoking "R."

Of course, teens will still see some R-rated movies. That's why leading health authorities endorse the R-rating for smoking *and* proven anti-tobacco spots before any film with smoking.

Spots are intended as a backstop to the "R," not a substitute for it.

Given that tobacco is the leading cause of preventable death and that films with smoking are the single biggest recruiter of new young smokers, anti-tobacco spots are the very least that media companies can do.

Spots are a start. Now, minimize the need for them.

SMOKE FREE MOVIES

SmokeFreeMovies.ucsf.edu

SMOKING IN MOVIES KILLS IN REAL LIFE. Smoke Free Movie policies—the R-rating, certification of no payoffs, anti-tobacco spots, and an end to brand display—are endorsed by the World Health Organization, American Medical Association, AMA Alliance, American Academy of Pediatrics, American Heart Association, American Legacy Foundation, American Lung Association, American Public Health Association, Campaign for Tobacco-Free Kids, L.A. County Dept. of Health Services, New York State Dept. of Health, New York State PTA, and others. To explore this critical health issue, visit our web site or write: Smoke Free Movies, UCSF School of Medicine, San Francisco, CA 94143-1390.

QUESTIONS FOR REASONING AND ANALYSIS

1. Why is the visual in this ad a gas mask? What is its connection to the ad's purpose?

2. Explain the slogan: "Necessary, yes. Sufficient, no."

3.   What is "the least" that the ad endorses? What is its larger goal?

4.   What evidence does the ad provide in support of its goals?

QUESTIONS FOR REFLECTION AND WRITING

1.   Will spots reduce the impact of seeing smoking in a movie? Why or why not?

2.   Should films with smoking automatically be given an R rating by the Motion Picture Association? Why or why not?

3.   One can argue that some characters would, realistically, smoke. If this is true, then would the R rating for films with smoking become a form of industry-imposed "censorship" (even though the rating is voluntary)? Should industry ratings be considered a form of censorship? (Consider other ways that we restrict or control access to potentially harmful substances and activities.) Explain and defend your position on what should be done about smoking in films.

SMOKING IN THE MOVIES | EVAN R. GOLDSTEIN

Based in Washington, DC, Evan Goldstein is a contributing editor to *Moment* magazine and a staff editor at *The Chronicle Review*. Goldstein's examination of smoking in movies was published July 13, 2007, in the *Chronicle of Higher Education*.

PREREADING QUESTIONS Do you smoke? If so, why, given that you know it is the single worst decision you can make for your health? What are the appeals—despite all the health warnings?

1   Has there been a worse time to be a smoker? In an ever-expanding swath of the West, cigarettes are denounced as evil, and smokers are being shamed—and legislated—to the margins of society. Even China, where around two-thirds of men smoke, is reportedly taking steps to curb smoking in some public places. And now this: The Motion Picture Association of America recently announced that "depictions that glamorize smoking or movies that feature pervasive smoking outside of a historic or other mitigating context" will be taken into account by the organization's rating board—joining the ranks of other film taboos such as profanity, nudity, drug use, and violence.

2   In all of this, Richard Klein sees a rising tide of American prudery and censorship. "Why not ban overeating on film, or overdrinking on film?" he asks. "If you can ban the representation of one reality—which is that a lot of cool people smoke—then why not just keep going?" Klein is the author of *Cigarettes Are Sublime* (Duke University Press, 1993), which he describes as "a piece of literary criticism, an analysis of popular culture, a political harangue, a theoretical exercise, and an ode to cigarettes." In a recent interview, Klein spoke about what our culture stands to lose if (when?) the last smoldering butt is stamped out.

3   Richard Klein, professor of French literature, Cornell University: Despite the fact that for 40 years all the principal institutions in our society have been telling people from a very early age about the dangers of smoking, cigarettes are as alluring and as evocative as they have ever been before. They continue to be immensely attractive to at least 20 percent of the adult population. Every day billions of people around the world are lighting up. Why?

Cigarettes would not be so popular if they did not provide a great many 4 pleasures and a great many benefits. After all, cigarettes taste bad. But it is the bad taste that you quickly learn to love. How is that possible? In *The Critique of Judgment,* Kant distinguished sublime aesthetic pleasure from ordinary aesthetic pleasure, like that we might take from a beautiful form. A sublime aesthetic pleasure is one that we take in the presence of awe or fear. These moments are ecstatic precisely because they contain a warning, a reminder of our own mortality. In other words, the pleasure is found in the poison. It is not in spite of its harmfulness, but rather because it is a harmful substance that people derive so much pleasure from smoking. That is what Kant very technically and specifically calls sublime aesthetic pleasure.

Many of the sublime pleasures of smoking can be seen in the movies. For 5 instance, in *My Best Friend's Wedding* when Julia Roberts hunkers down in moments of the greatest loss and desperation, she is smoking furiously. The cigarette is a friend and a form of consolation. Smoking is a remarkable tool for mitigating anxiety. And it also happens to be beautiful. Movies attest wonderfully to the Promethean beauty of fire, smoke, and ash that cigarettes evoke.

The MPAA decision to take into account depictions of smoking when rating 6 films is a form of censorship. It is a discouraging but unsurprising development. America has always been a Puritan country that harbors a deep resentment against pleasure. But this puritanical opposition to beauty impoverishes our culture. There is a long paragraph at the end of *Being and Nothingness* in which Jean-Paul Sartre explains how cigarettes allowed him to appropriate the world. And by that he meant that every time he found himself in a new situation—before a beautiful landscape or in the theater or reading a book— whenever he had a momentous moment to celebrate or consecrate, he would light a cigarette. And in so doing, it somehow turns the moment into an idea. Cigarettes allowed him to experience life. And he even says that life without cigarettes is not worth living.

If advocates of this new ratings system think that adolescents are going 7 to be deceived because the motion-picture industry censors the seductive charms of smoking, I think they are disastrously mistaken. Censorship inevitably incites the very practice it wishes to inhibit. The more disreputable cigarettes become, the more the taboo provokes interest, arouses fascination, and becomes dangerously compulsive.

In a certain sense, those who continue to light up are offering a brazen 8 protest on behalf of freedom for all of us. Public health used to be about typhoid and drinking water. Now the role of public health has become to warn us against our own bad habits, and to more and more inhibit our pleasures: how we eat, smoke, drink, and all the rest. It is a very intimate, very menacing form of social control.

QUESTIONS FOR READING

1. What is Richard Klein's response to the Motion Picture Association's decision to take smoking into account in its rating of films?

2.   Why, apparently, do people continue to smoke, knowing the health hazard?

3.   How do movies often depict smoking?

4.   Why does the author think that the new ratings system will not deter adolescents from smoking?

QUESTIONS FOR REASONING AND ANALYSIS

1.   What is Goldstein's claim? Where does he state it?

2.   How does the author use Kant's philosophy and Sartre's experiences to support his claim? How effective are these references as support? (The author assumes readers who will know both writers; if you do not, look them up before evaluating their use in the argument.)

3.   The author implies that "censorship" of smoking in films could lead to inhibiting our eating and drinking, and other pleasures. Is this an effective support of his claim?

4.   Goldstein ends with a strongly written statement. Has he made his case? Evaluate his argument.

QUESTIONS FOR REFLECTION AND WRITING

1.   Do you agree with Goldstein that adding smoking to the way movies are rated is a form of censorship? Why or why not? (Remember that the rating system is voluntary and self-imposed within the U.S. film industry, and smoking would not be restricted in R-rated films.)

2.   Do you agree with Goldstein that pressure to get an R rating on films with smoking should be opposed? Why or why not?

3.   We saw that Prohibition did not work; people drank even though it was illegal. Will restricting films with smoking to R ratings "incite the very practice it wishes to inhibit," as Goldstein asserts? Is an analogy to Prohibition valid—or not?

4.   Do you agree with the charge that our country has, as a result of our Puritan heritage, harbored "a deep resentment against pleasure"? Explain and defend your position.

IF YOU ASSIGN MY BOOK, DON'T CENSOR IT | MARK MATHABANE

A former White House Fellow at the Department of Education, Mark Mathabane is best known for his widely read—and at times controversial—novel *Kaffir Boy*. Mathabane lives and writes in North Carolina; his most recent novel is *Ubuntu*. The following article appeared in the *Washington Post* on November 28, 1999.

PREREADING QUESTIONS Should cutting out parts of or changing parts of a book be seen as censorship? Should publishers—or teachers—change texts in these ways?

1   A few weeks ago, school officials at Kearsley High School in Flint, Mich., decided to censor *Kaffir Boy*, my story of growing up in a South African

ghetto during apartheid. On the recommendation of a special committee of administrators, teachers and staff, the school has begun taping over several sentences and parts of sentences in its copies of the book after a half-dozen parents objected to my graphic description of one of the most harrowing experiences of my life: When I was 7 years old and trapped in the poverty-stricken ghetto of the Alexandra township, 10 miles north of Johannesburg, hunger drove me to tag along with a ring of boys who prostituted themselves for food. One parent called my description "pornography," according to the *Flint Journal*, adding that *Kaffir Boy* belonged in an adult bookstore rather than in a 10th-grade English class.

I wasn't altogether surprised by the parents' objections. The raw emotions 2 and experiences in *Kaffir Boy*, which constitute the core of its power and appeal, have made the book controversial ever since its publication in the United States in 1986. When it became required reading for thousands of high school students nationwide several years ago, it was challenged by parents in school districts in a dozen states and, in some cases, withdrawn. No, what surprises—and disturbs—me is the decision at Kearsley to censor the text, altering a passage that marks a crucial turning point in the book—and in my life.

As a parent of three public school students, ages 6, 8 and 10, I pay atten- 3 tion to what they are assigned to read. I've read them portions of *Kaffir Boy* and my other books, which deal with issues of hunger, child abuse, poverty, violence, the oppression of women and racism. I'm always careful to provide context, to talk to them in a language they can understand.

Every year I also talk to thousands of students about my work and my life in 4 South Africa. I tell them how fortunate they are to live in America, how important it is not to take this nation's freedoms for granted. I recall for them how my peers and I were forbidden by the government in Pretoria to read the U.S. Constitution and the Bill of Rights. I recall how empowered I felt after I clandestinely secured a copy of the Declaration of Independence. And I recall how, during the Soweto uprising of 1976, hundreds of students died fighting for recognition of their unalienable rights to "life, liberty and the pursuit of happiness."

When I came to America in 1978, I was stunned—and exhilarated—to find 5 out that I could walk into any library and check out books that were uncensored and read them without fear of being harassed, thrown in jail or killed.

I have that experience in mind when I think about my own children's read- 6 ing lists. In large part, I trust their teachers to have the judgment to assign books that are not only consistent with educational goals, but also with my children's maturity level. Should my children bring home a book I find objectionable, the responsible thing for me to do would be to request that my child be assigned a different one.

That's why I have no problem with parents who make such a request about 7 *Kaffir Boy.* The parents of a sophomore at West Mecklenburg High School in Charlotte, N.C., where the book has also been challenged, did just that. They were not only uncomfortable with the prostitution scene, but also with my use of racially graphic language such as the word "kaffir" (a pejorative term for "black").

8   But I strongly disagree with censoring portions of the book. They have no right to decide the issue for other students. Should those students be deprived of what I believe is a key scene in order to make a few parents comfortable?

9   I don't think so. Books aren't written with the comfort of readers in mind. I know I didn't write *Kaffir Boy* that way. I wrote it to reflect reality, to show the world the inhumanity of the apartheid system. It wasn't an easy book for me to write. The memories gave me nightmares. What's more, after the book was published in the United States, members of my family in South Africa were persecuted by the Pretoria regime, which subsequently banned the book there.

10   *Kaffir Boy* is disturbing, but it isn't pornographic. As Kari Molter, chairwoman of the English department at Kearsley High, said, the prostitution scene, which makes up three pages, is "frightening," but it is "an important scene." I included it in the book not to titillate readers, but to reveal a disturbing truth about life under apartheid.

11   That disturbing truth included the terror and helplessness I felt as a child during brutal midnight police raids; the grinding, stunting poverty in which I, my family and millions of other blacks were steeped; the emasculation of my father by a system that denied him the right to earn a living in a way that gave him dignity; the hopelessness and psychic pain that led me to contemplate suicide at age 10; the sacrifices and faith of my long-suffering mother as she battled to save me from the dead-end life of the street and its gangs.

12   Not the least disturbing of those truths is the passage about prostitution. My father, the only breadwinner in a family of nine, had been arrested for the crime of being unemployed. There was no food in our shack, and my mother couldn't even get the usual cattle blood from the slaughterhouse to boil as soup. Desperate for food, one afternoon I linked up with a group of 5-, 6- and 7-year-old boys on the way to the nearby men's hostel. Their pimp, a 13-year-old boy named Mphandlani, promised that at the hostel we would get money and "all the food we could eat" in exchange for playing "a little game" with the migrant workers who lived there.

13   Once inside the hostel, I stood by in confusion and fear as the men and boys began undressing. In the book, I give some physical descriptions of what happened. When Mphandlani told me to undress, too, I refused. One of the men came after me, and I bolted out of the hostel. I fled because I knew that what the men were doing to the boys was wrong, and recalled my parents telling me never to do wrong things. I was called a fool—and shunned—by those boys afterward.

14   Resisting peer pressure is one of the toughest things for young people to do. That is the lesson of the prostitution scene. It's a lesson that seems to be lost on the people who want to censor my book. Teenagers understand what peer pressure is. They confront tough choices every day, particularly if they happen to live in environments where child abuse, poverty, violence and death are commonplace, where innocence dies young, and where children can't afford to be children.

15   Many students have connected powerfully with the story of *Kaffir Boy*. The book, they've told me in letters and e-mail, teaches them to never give up in the

face of adversity, not to take freedom—or food—for granted, to regard education as a powerful weapon of hope, and always to strive to do the right thing.

Could *Kaffir Boy* have had this impact without the prostitution scene? I 16
doubt it. It was an event that changed me forever. Could I have made that point
using less graphic language? Perhaps. But language is a very sacred thing for
a writer. When I write, I strive for clarity and directness, so the reader understands precisely what I mean. To fudge language in order to avoid offending
the sensibilities of one group or another leads to doublespeak, which is the
death of honesty.

That very honesty is what prompted a senior from Sentinel High School in 17
Missoula, Mont., to send me a letter a few days ago. In it she wrote that *Kaffir
Boy* made her realize "that no matter what, there is always hope." It is this
hope that I'm seeking to keep alive with my books.

I owe my life to books. While I was in the ghetto, groaning under the yoke 18
of apartheid, wallowing in self-pity, believing that I was doomed to die from
the sheer agony of frustrated hopes and strangled dreams, books became my
best friends and my salvation. Reading broadened my horizons, deepened my
sensibilities and, most importantly, made me think. Books liberated me from
mental slavery and opened doors of opportunity where none seemed to exist.

Censorship is not the solution to the legitimate concern some parents 19
have about what is appropriate for their children to read. I wish child abuse
and racism weren't facts of life, but they are. Only by knowing about them can
we combat them effectively.

What's more, there are alternatives to censorship. One possible solution 20
lies in schools developing reading-list guidelines, such as those being drawn up
by the Charlotte-Mecklenburg school system in the wake of objections to *Kaffir
Boy*. Under the guidelines, teachers will still choose their own books, but they
will be required to give students and parents a summary of the contents and
potential concerns, such as profanity or sexually explicit scenes. I don't mind if
my book doesn't make the list, or if some parents choose another title for their
offspring, but if students do read it, let them read it the way I wrote it.

QUESTIONS FOR READING

1. What is the author's occasion for writing? What is the specific issue with regard
   to *Kaffir Boy?*

2. What does Mathabane approve of parents doing? What does he object to?

3. Why is the prostitution scene disturbing? Why is it not, in the author's view,
   pornographic? What definition of pornography emerges from Mathabane's
   discussion?

4. How does the author defend his choice of language in *Kaffir Boy?*

5. What did books do for the author?

6. What can schools do, instead of censoring, to help parents guide their children's
   reading?

QUESTIONS FOR REASONING AND ANALYSIS

1. What does the author seek to accomplish in paragraphs 3–7 when he writes of his children and U.S. freedoms that he admired from South Africa?

2. What is Mathabane's claim?

3. Mathabane would rather students not read his book than read it with parts removed. Can you understand his position? Why does he think it inappropriate to change someone's words?

4. Has the author presented an effective argument against altering books? Against censorship? Explain.

QUESTIONS FOR REFLECTION AND WRITING

1. Have you read *Kaffir Boy*? If so, did you find it disturbing? Did you find it moving and encouraging, as the author suggests?

2. Are there other assigned readings that bothered you—or that your parents did not want you to read? If so, how did you handle the situation?

3. Do you agree with Mathabane's definition of pornography? If not, why not?

WHY THE FIRST AMENDMENT (AND JOURNALISM) MIGHT BE IN TROUBLE | KEN DAUTRICH and JOHN BARE

Ken Dautrich, chair of the department of public policy at the University of Connecticut, directed the study, "The Future of the First Amendment," with colleague David Yalof. They are coauthors of the book *The First Amendment and the Media in the Court of Public Opinion* (2002). John Bare, Dautrich's coauthor for this article, is vice president for strategic planning and evaluation at the Arthur M. Blank Family Foundation in Atlanta. Their article appeared in the Summer 2005 issue of *Nieman Reports*, published by Harvard University.

PREREADING QUESTIONS Should the government control content on the Internet? Does the First Amendment protect flag burning?

1   Our first-of-its-kind exploration of the future of the First Amendment among American high school students—a highly visible study of 112,000 students and 8,000 teachers in over 300 high schools—suggests a fragile future for key constitutional freedoms while also pointing us to potential remedies. This study, "The Future of the First Amendment," which was released earlier this year, arrived at a timely moment in American history, on the heels of a national election and amid a war the President is using, by his account, to spread democratic freedoms. The results drew remarkable media attention, which tended to focus on one of the more fearful statistics to emerge from the study: Only 51 percent of 9th to 12th graders agree that newspapers should be allowed to publish freely without government approval of stories—in other words, nearly half entertain the idea of newspaper censorship.

Beyond that flashpoint finding, the study allows for a more thorough 2 understanding of today's high school students and can point us to potential remedies. The research also suggests ways to improve support for the First Amendment. While many of the findings raise concern, some are not so bad. Some are even encouraging. Most of all, the results should be viewed within the context of the history of the First Amendment, which faced challenges—some would say it was compromised—as soon as it was adopted.

FIRST AMENDMENT CHALLENGES

One of the first acts of the first Congress in 1789 was to append a Bill of 3 Rights to the U.S. Constitution, which, among other things, explicitly denied Congress the ability to tamper with Americans' rights of free expression. Indeed, through the course of our history, Americans and their leaders have proclaimed a commitment to freedom and liberty. Most recently, President Bush, in his second inaugural address, justified the Iraqi and Afghani military operations as a vehicle to spread freedom and liberty throughout the world.

Despite a long history of veneration to these values, freedom of expres- 4 sion has met with a number of challenges. Not long after adoption of the First Amendment, President John Adams and the Federalist Congress passed the Alien and Sedition Acts, severely thwarting the freedom to speak out against government. Abraham Lincoln's suspension of habeas corpus, the internment of Japanese Americans during Franklin Roosevelt's administration after Pearl Harbor, Senator Joseph McCarthy's "red scare," and Attorney General John Ashcroft's aggressive implementation of the USA Patriot Act represent just a few of the more notable breaches to liberty in America.

Like any value in our society, the health and vitality of freedom and lib- 5 erty are largely dependent upon the public's attention to, appreciation for, and support of them. When Americans are willing to compromise freedom of expression in return for a sense of being more secure, then government officials can more readily take action to curtail freedom. Public fear of Communism allowed McCarthy to tread on people's liberty, just as fear of terrorism allowed Ashcroft to curb freedoms.

The real protection of free expression rights lies not in the words of the 6 First Amendment. Rather, it lies in the people's willingness to appreciate and support those rights. That idea led the Freedom Forum's First Amendment Center to commission an annual survey on public knowledge, appreciation and support for free expression rights since 1997 to gauge the health and well-being of the First Amendment.

If public opinion is a good measure of the First Amendment's well-being, 7 then its annual checkup has been fraught with health problems.

- While more than 9-in-10 agree that "people should be allowed to express unpopular opinions," a paltry 4-in-10 believe that high school students should be able to report on controversial issues in school newspapers without the consent of school officials.

- More than one-third say the press has too much freedom.

- Fewer than 6-in-10 say that musicians should be able to sing songs with lyrics that may be offensive to some.

8   These annual checkups have shown over time that half of adults think that flag burning as a method of protest should not be tolerated. In general, the surveys have revealed that the public holds low support for, a lack of appreciation for, and dangerously low levels of knowledge of free expression rights. Is it no wonder, then, that the suspension of liberty in this land of freedom has been so readily accomplished by its leaders from time to time?

9   It was these rather anemic annual checkups that convinced the John S. and James L. Knight Foundation to commission this unique survey of American high school students and to begin a wider discussion about how to strengthen the polity's commitment to the democratic ideal of freedom and liberty.

10   What follows are some findings from the Knight Foundation survey of high school students that explain, in part, why Americans should be concerned about the First Amendment's future.

- Thirty-six percent of high school students openly admit that they take their First Amendment rights for granted and another 37 percent say they never thought enough about this to have an opinion.

- Seventy-five percent incorrectly believe that it is illegal to burn the flag as a means of political protest, and 49 percent wrongly think that government has the right to restrict indecent material on the Internet.

- A source of the lack of support for free press rights might be due to the fact that only four percent of students trust journalists to tell the truth all of the time.

- Thirty-five percent say the First Amendment goes too far in the rights it guarantees, and 32 percent think the press has too much freedom to do what it wants.

PROPOSING SOME REMEDIES

11   This is a bleak picture of what may be in store for the First Amendment as this group matures into adulthood. More importantly, however, a number of findings from the study suggest policies or actions that might better prepare students to value and use their constitutional freedoms. While the suggestions below grow out of findings that are based on correlations, not causation, the logic of the policy ideas holds up against both our experience and our understanding of the data.

12   1. Instruction on the First Amendment matters. Education works! Students who have taken classes that deal with journalism, the role of the media in society, and the First Amendment exhibit higher levels of knowledge and support for free expression rights than those who haven't. The problem, of course, is that the strong trend toward math and science and "teaching to the standardized test" has crowded out instruction that could help students develop good citizenship skills. The less the schools focus on developing strong citizens, the weaker our democracy becomes. The positive lesson to learn from this is that through enhancements to the high school curriculum. students can become better prepared to value and use their freedoms.

13   2. Use leads to greater appreciation. When students are given an opportunity to use their freedoms, they develop a better appreciation for them.

The Knight project found that students who are engaged in extracurricular student media (such as school newspaper, Internet sites, etc.) are more aware and much more supportive of free expression rights.

3. School leaders need lessons, too. Most high school principals need 14 to be reminded of the value of experiential learning and its implications for the future of the First Amendment. While 80 percent of principals agree that "newspapers should be allowed to publish freely without government approval of a story," only 39 percent say their students should be afforded the same rights for publishing in the school newspaper. Granted, principals have many issues to deal with (like parents and school board members calling and asking how they could have ever allowed a story to be printed in a school paper). But if we are to expect students to mature into responsible democratic citizens, they should be given the freedom to express themselves and act responsibly while in school.

4. Place the issues in the context of their daily lives. The project suggests 15 that, as with most people, when issues affecting one's freedom are brought close to home, students are best able to discern the true meaning and value of freedom. When asked if they agreed or disagreed with this statement— "Musicians should be allowed to sing songs with lyrics that might be offensive to others"—70 percent agreed (only 43 percent of principals and 57 percent of adults agree with this). Music matters to many young people. When this form of free expression is challenged, most students come to its defense. The lesson, of course, is that in teaching students about the virtues of free expression, showing how it relates to things important to them will best instill in students why it is so important to the life of a democracy.

The future of the First Amendment is, at best, tenuous. As the current 16 group of high school students takes on their important role as citizens in our democracy, their lack of appreciation and support for free expression rights will provide a ripe atmosphere for government to further intrude on these freedoms. Many institutions in society should shoulder part of the responsibility to ensure good citizenship skills for our youth. Parents, religious institutions, the media, as well as leadership from public officials, just to name a few. But the public schools play an especially important role in socializing youngsters in how to be responsible citizens, and through the schools the future health and vitality of the First Amendment might be restored.

QUESTIONS FOR READING

1. What is the occasion for the authors' article? What was the purpose of the study?

2. What is the primary source of protection for free expression? For what reason do Americans allow free expression to be restricted?

3. What views revealed in the nation's "annual checkup" put First Amendment rights at risk, according to the authors? What did the study reveal about high school students' views?

4. State the four remedies proposed by the authors in your own words.

QUESTIONS FOR REASONING AND ANALYSIS

1. What, specifically, is the essay's topic? What is the authors' claim?

2. What assumption about freedom is part of this argument?

3. Analyze the four proposals. Do they seem logical remedies to you? Do some seem more likely to produce change than others?

QUESTIONS FOR REFLECTION AND WRITING

1. What statistic is most surprising to you? Why?

2. Do you share the authors' concerns for the tenuous state of free speech in the United States? If you disagree, how would you rebut them?

3. Can democracy survive without First Amendment rights? Be prepared to debate this issue.

ONLINE LESSONS ON UNPROTECTED SEX | ANDREW J. McCLURG

A graduate of the University of Florida, Andrew McClurg is a law professor at Florida International University and author of many law review articles and two legal humor books. He has frequently been recognized as an outstanding teacher. He maintains a Web site: lawhaha.com. His essay published August 15, 2005, in the Washington Post.

PREREADING QUESTIONS Have you posted personal information online? If so, why? Should you post personal details that expose the private lives of others?

1   Kiss-and-tell is as old as love itself. Fortunately, most indiscreet paramours limit their blabbing to a few confidants. Not Jessica Cutler. In May 2004, she spilled out the graphic details of her sexual exploits on Capitol Hill on a blog accessible to hundreds of millions of Internet users.

2   Now a federal lawsuit by one of her past lovers has set up a potentially high-stakes battle between privacy and speech rights and could give new meaning to the idea of safe sex in a wired world.

3   Cutler's blog, written under the pseudonym Washingtonienne, was a daily diary of her sex life while working as a staffer for Sen. Mike DeWine (R-Ohio). It recounted, entertainingly and in considerable—sometimes embarrassing—detail, her ongoing relationships with six men, including plaintiff Robert Steinbuch, a lawyer who also worked for DeWine. Although Cutler never used his full name, and usually referred to the plaintiff by his initials, Steinbuch alleges the blog revealed sufficient information, including his first name, physical description and where he worked, to identify him.

4   The Internet gossip site Wonkette published excerpts from Cutler's blog, touching off a media "feeding frenzy" in which Steinbuch was repeatedly identified by his full name. Cutler capitalized on the publicity. She gave print, broadcast and online interviews, posed nude for *Playboy* and reportedly received a $300,000 advance for her just-published book, a veiled fictional account of a Senate staffer's sexual adventures on Capitol Hill.

Steinbuch's argument is compelling. By any normative standard, he 5 suffered a genuine wrong. As he asserts in his complaint, "It is one thing to be manipulated and used by a lover, it is another thing to be cruelly exposed to the world."

The law, however, appears to be against him. This is because Steinbuch 6 does not allege that any of the statements about him are untrue. False statements that damage one's reputation can be actionable as defamation. The essence of Steinbuch's claim is: You humiliated me by publicizing these true details about my private life.

His case hinges on a century-old privacy tort claim known as "public dis- 7 closure of private facts." In theory, the tort provides a remedy when one publicizes private, embarrassing, non-newsworthy facts about a person in a manner that reasonable people would find highly offensive. But while Cutler's actions may meet this standard, courts have long been hostile to such lawsuits because of a fear of inhibiting free speech. The Supreme Court has never upheld punishment, based on a privacy theory, for the publication of true information.

In 1989 the court tossed out a lawsuit against a newspaper for publishing a 8 rape victim's name in violation of Florida law. While it stopped short of ruling that a state may never punish true speech, the test it adopted for when that can be done without violating the First Amendment is so stringent Justice Byron White lamented in dissent that the court had "obliterate[d]" the public disclosure tort.

One might think the non-newsworthiness of Steinbuch's sex life would 9 save his privacy claim from a free-speech defense. It could, but newsworthiness has proved to be a broad and elusive legal test in privacy lawsuits. The rape victim's name in the 1989 Florida case, for example, was deemed to be sufficiently related to the public's interest in crime to doom her claim.

Steinbuch's case spotlights the inadequacy of privacy law—developed 10 back when gossip mostly traveled across backyard fences—for responding to the challenges of the Internet age. Today's technology grants any person—no matter how selfish, irresponsible or malicious—the power to invade privacy globally, at almost no cost. All it takes is a computer and Internet access. Some blogging companies offer free services.

And blogs are just the tip of the iceberg. In May an Oregon woman sued 11 Yahoo after her ex-boyfriend posted nude pictures of her on the site and Yahoo failed to remove them. Expect more litigation.

While we wait to see if old law can adapt to new realities, don't forget the 12 C-word when making safe-sex inquiries. No, not condoms or contraceptives. Ask potential partners if they own a computer.

QUESTIONS FOR READING

1. Who is Jessica Cutler? What did she do?
2. Who is Robert Steinbuch? What was his response to Cutler's disclosures?
3. What laws protect Cutler? What legal precedent is Steinbuch using? What two issues will affect the outcome of his case?

QUESTIONS FOR REASONING AND ANALYSIS

1. McClurg can be expected to be interested in this situation as a technical legal debate. What else about this modern example of gossip interests the author?
2. Is the author just reporting on a current legal debate—or does he have a position? What, if any, is his claim?
3. What is clever about McClurg's opening and closing paragraphs?

QUESTIONS FOR REFLECTION AND WRITING

1. The Internet poses interesting questions regarding free speech. If you were the judge, how would you rule on Steinbuch's suit? Why?
2. Even if the law supports Cutler, does that make her "wired gossip" right? Defend your position.

LET A THOUSAND FILTERS BLOOM | ANNE APPLEBAUM

Currently a columnist and editorial board member of the *Washington Post,* Anne Applebaum was a journalist and writer in Poland and London for 20 years before returning to the United States. She is the author of *Gulag: A History* (2003). The following *Post* column appeared July 20, 2005.

PREREADING QUESTION What controls, if any, should governments have over the Internet?

1   In 1949, when George Orwell wrote his dystopian novel *1984,* he gave its hero, Winston, a job at the Ministry of Truth. All day long, Winston clips politically unacceptable facts, stuffs them into little pneumatic tubes, and then pushes the tubes down a chute. Beside him sits a woman in charge of finding and erasing the names of people who have been "vaporized." And their office, Orwell wrote, "with its fifty workers or thereabouts, was only one sub-section, a single cell, as it were, in the huge complexity of the Records Department."

2   It's odd to read *1984* in 2005, because the politics of Orwell's vision aren't outdated. There are still plenty of governments in the world that go to extraordinary lengths to shape what their citizens read, think and say, just like Orwell's Big Brother. But the technology envisioned in *1984* is so—well, 1980s. Paper? Pneumatic tubes? Workers in cubicles? Nowadays, none of that is necessary: It can all be done electronically, especially if, like the Chinese government, you seek the cooperation of large American companies.

3   Without question, China's Internet filtering regime is "the most sophisticated effort of its kind in the world," in the words of a recent report by Harvard Law School's Berkman Center for Internet and Society. The system involves the censorship of Web logs, search engines, chat rooms and e-mail by "thousands of public and private personnel." It also involves Microsoft Inc., as Chinese bloggers discovered last month. Since early June, Chinese bloggers who post messages containing a forbidden word—"Dalai Lama,"

for example, or "democracy"—receive a warning: "This message contains a banned expression, please delete." It seems Microsoft has altered the Chinese version of its blog tool, MSN Spaces, at the behest of Chinese government. Bill Gates, so eloquent on the subject of African poverty, is less worried about Chinese free speech.

But he isn't alone: Because Yahoo Inc. is one of several companies that have ⁴ signed a "public pledge on self-discipline," a Yahoo search in China doesn't turn up all of the (politically sensitive) results. Cisco Systems Inc., another U.S. company, has also sold hundreds of millions of dollars of equipment to China, including technology that blocks traffic not only to banned Web sites, but even to particular pages within an otherwise accessible site.

Until now, most of these companies have defended themselves on ⁵ the grounds that there are side benefits—a Microsoft spokesman has said that "we're helping millions of people communicate, share stories, share photographs and build relationships"—or on the grounds that they can't control technology anyway. A Cisco spokesman told me that this is the "same equipment technology that your local library uses to block pornography," and besides, "we're not doing anything illegal."

But as U.S. companies become more deeply involved in China, and as ⁶ technology itself progresses, those lines may begin to sound weaker. Over the past couple of years, Harry Wu, a Chinese human rights activist and former political prisoner, has carefully tracked Western corporate cooperation with Chinese police and internal security, and in particular with a Chinese project called "Golden Shield," a high-tech surveillance system that has been under construction for the past five years. Although the company won't confirm it, Wu says, Cisco representatives in China have told him that the company has contracts to provide technology to the police departments of at least 31 provinces. Some of that technology may be similar to what the writer and former businessman Ethan Gutmann describes in his recent book, *Losing the New China: A Story of American Commerce, Desire and Betrayal*. Gutmann—whose account is also bitterly disputed by Cisco ("He's getting a lot of press out of this," complained the spokesman)—claims to have visited a Shanghai trade fair where Cisco was advertising its ability to "integrate judicial networks, border security, and vertical police networks" and more generally its willingness to build Golden Shield.

If this isn't illegal, maybe it should be. After the Tiananmen Square massa- ⁷ cre in 1989, the United States passed a law prohibiting U.S. firms from selling "crime control and detection" equipment to the Chinese. But in 1989, the definition of police equipment ran to truncheons, handcuffs and riot gear. Has it been updated? We may soon find out: A few days ago, Rep. Dan Burton of the House Foreign Relations Committee wrote a letter to the Commerce Department asking exactly that. In any case, it's time to have this debate again. There could be other solutions—such as flooding the Chinese Internet with filter-breaking technology.

Beyond legality, of course, there's morality. And here the judgment of his- ⁸ tory will prove more important than whatever Congress does or does not do today. Sixty years after the end of World War II, IBM is still battling lawsuits from plaintiffs who accuse the company of providing the "enabling technologies" that facilitated the Holocaust. Sixty years from now, will Microsoft, Cisco and Yahoo be doing the same?

QUESTIONS FOR READING

1. What is this column about? Be precise.
2. What U.S. companies are involved? What are they doing?
3. How do the U.S. companies defend their business in China?

QUESTIONS FOR REASONING AND ANALYSIS

1. What does Applebaum seek to accomplish in her opening paragraphs? How is *1984* still relevant? How is it outdated?
2. What is Applebaum's attitude toward the sales of censorship technology to the Chinese government? How do you know?
3. Explain the meaning of the title.

QUESTIONS FOR REFLECTION AND WRITING

1. Do you think sales of censorship technology to China should be illegal? Why or why not?
2. Should these sales by U.S. companies be viewed as immoral and judged in the court of public opinion? Why or why not?

BUSINESS IS BUSINESS | DAVID McHARDY REID

A professor at the Rochester Institute of Technology, David Reid is director of the Center of International Business. He regularly consults on strategy with companies all over the world and is the author of numerous articles and books on business management and international strategy. Reid's argument was published June 20, 2005, in *USA Today*.

PREREADING QUESTION The United States does restrict the sales of some products to some nations. Should it control the sale of electronic products that restrict freedom on the Internet?

1   Readers shouldn't be surprised by Microsoft's recent agreement to ban words such as "democracy" and "freedom" from use by bloggers on its China Web portal.

2   It is not the role of major corporations to police the behavior of other cultures. Companies of all hues regularly adjust their positions to meet the acceptable standards of the countries in which they operate. Adaptation is intrinsic to the reality of doing business around the globe. Brands and products must be adapted and trade-offs made.

3   For example, a tire manufacturer has to choose whether a particular tire will deliver road-holding performance or longevity. The two are in

counterpoint. Similarly, the whitening ingredients in toothpaste may deliver a brighter smile but serve to weaken teeth. When information is available, consumers and manufacturers have to choose what to consume and what properties to deliver.

U.S.-based consumer products companies operating in Bangkok, for 4 instance, fill the trucks of cash-paying customers arriving at their distribution facilities. They neither ask the source of their customers' funds nor the destination of the merchandise; nor should they. These companies are not government agents. They have a fiduciary duty to their stockholders to focus on their businesses. Yet the funds may stem from narcotics trafficking through the Golden Triangle, and the goods may be destined for Burma, also known as Myanmar. In this way, critics might argue these companies are subsidizing the corrupt anti-democratic Myanmar regime.

As for Microsoft, its primary role is to sell software and other products 5 in the context of the political environments in which it operates. It is preferable that it concentrates on selling its products. In so doing, it makes the trade-off between accepting potential damage to its brand, in the longer term, by being perceived as kowtowing to a nondemocratic regime, but benefiting by satisfying the needs of Chinese consumers.

Good works are on a different agenda. The Bill and Melinda Gates Foun- 6 dation, created on the vast wealth of Microsoft, is able to support much noble work, including promising to wipe out malaria. That's appropriate. Let's not confuse necessary business practices with charity or political objectives.

QUESTIONS FOR READING

1. What is Reid's subject?
2. What do businesses do to sell products in different countries? What choices do consumers as well as companies make all of the time?
3. What is the point of the example of selling in Bangkok?

QUESTIONS FOR REASONING AND ANALYSIS

1. What is Reid's claim? What are the specific points of support for his claim?
2. Analyze his argument. Would you challenge any of his points? If so, how?
3. Some might rebut by asserting that Reid uses a false analogy. What point of his might be viewed as a false analogy?
4. What does the author want to accomplish in his concluding paragraph?

QUESTIONS FOR REFLECTION AND WRITING

1. Compare Reid's and Applebaum's arguments. Who has the more compelling argument, in your view? Why?
2. Is business always business only? Are there no ethical restrictions in business? If there are some, then how do we decide what they are? When they apply? Be prepared to debate these issues.

CHAPTER 20

Ethics and the Law—Current and Enduring Debates

READ: Do you recognize this building? What might the sculptured figure be holding?

REASON: What *kind* of building would be an appropriate choice for this chapter? Why?

REFLECT/WRITE: Which branch of government has the greatest impact on our daily lives? Why? Defend your choice.

The visuals, letters, and articles in this chapter explore and debate three current criminal justice issues: the Supreme Court handgun decision, trying juveniles as adults, and the sanctioning of torture. In the spring of 2008, the Supreme Court, in a close decision, struck down the District of Columbia's ban on handguns. The decision is seen as affirming the Second Amendment's guarantee to individuals. But, not everyone thinks that this debate is over. One response to teens committing murder has been to try them as adults so that adult sentencing, rather than juvenile detention, can be applied. We need to think, as individuals and as a society, about our handling of juvenile offenders. Finally, do we want our nation using torture, even in the interest of national security? And, is waterboarding torture? Tough questions. Consider these and the following questions as you study this chapter.

PREREADING QUESTIONS

1. What kinds of restrictions—if any—on guns will be consistent with the Supreme Court ruling?
2. Why did we separate juveniles from the adult penal system? Why have some changed their views on trying juveniles as adults?
3. Under what circumstances—if any—is torture justified?
4. If you wanted to change any of the current laws on these issues to make them reflect your views, how would you go about trying to get the laws changed?

Jim Morin for the Miami Herald, Cartoon Arts International. Reprinted with permission.

QUESTIONS FOR READING

1. Who are the five figures?
2. What words have they painted over? (If you don't know the exact wording, look it up.)
3. Who speaks the words to the right of the group?

QUESTIONS FOR REASONING AND ANALYSIS

1. This cartoon was created as a comment on what Supreme Court decision? What in the cartoon lets you know the answer?
2. What is Morin's view of the court's decision? What point does he make?
3. What elements make the cartoon clever?

QUESTIONS FOR REFLECTION AND WRITING

1. Do you agree with Morin's view that the Court has misread the Second Amendment? Why or why not?
2. Does the Constitution need to be reinterpreted for current times? If so, how should the Second Amendment be reinterpreted? If not, why not?

LETTERS TO THE EDITOR: THE COURT'S HANDGUN COMMON SENSE | MICHAEL HOXIE

The Washington Post, June 28, 2008

1 In *District of Columbia v. Heller*, the U.S. Supreme Court struck down the city's ban on handguns [front page, June 27]. The court found that the Second Amendment to the U.S. Constitution guarantees an individual's right to bear arms.

2 Aside from the constitutional debate over the language of the Second Amendment, the decision to strike down the law was correct. The law banning the ownership of handguns was a ridiculous attempt to curb gun violence in the District. The fact that it was unconstitutional was just one of its flaws. The law reminded me of attempts by anti-smoking fanatics to ban smoking in private homes—or anywhere for that matter.

3 The correct way to regulate dangerous or potentially dangerous instruments is to make them illegal, not to make their ownership illegal. If gun control advocates

really want to ban handguns, they should make manufacturing and selling them illegal. The same goes for tobacco products.

MICHAEL HOXIE
Kensington

QUESTIONS FOR READING

1.   What position did the Court take?
2.   What does Hoxie think the gun ban was originally designed to accomplish in Washington, DC?

QUESTIONS FOR REASONING AND ANALYSIS

1.   What is Hoxie's claim?
2.   What are his grounds? What comparisons are used? Are they effective? Why or why not?
3.   Hoxie uses some strong language. Is it appropriate? Is it effective? Why or why not?

QUESTIONS FOR REFLECTION AND WRITING

1.   Do you agree with Hoxie's idea that the way to ban handguns is to make their manufacturing and selling illegal, not their ownership? Is this a new idea for you? Does it make sense? Explain and defend your response.
2.   If you were going to write a short Letter to the Editor on this topic, what would you include?

GUNS FOR SAFETY? DREAM ON, SCALIA | ARTHUR KELLERMAN

Arthur Kellerman is professor and founding chair of the department of Emergency Medicine at Emory University. He has published widely on emergency cardiac care, health care for the poor, and firearms as a public health hazard. Kellerman has served on many boards and committees exploring these issues and has received recognition for his leadership in the fields of emergency care and prevention. His response to the Supreme Court's decision on handguns appeared in the *Washington Post* on June 28, 2008.

PREREADING QUESTIONS Given his title, what position on the ruling do you expect from Arthur Kellerman? Who is Scalia? (If you do not know, look it up.)

The Supreme Court has spoken: Thanks to the court's blockbuster 5 to 4   1 decision Thursday, Washingtonians now have the right to own a gun for self-defense. I leave the law to lawyers, but the public health lesson is crystal clear: The legal ruling that the District's citizens *can* keep loaded handguns in their homes doesn't mean that they *should*.

2   In his majority opinion, Justice Antonin Scalia explicitly endorsed the wisdom of keeping a handgun in the home for self-defense. Such a weapon, he wrote, "is easier to store in a location that is readily accessible in an emergency; it cannot easily be redirected or wrestled away by an attacker; it is easier to use for those without the upper-body strength to lift and aim a long rifle; it can be pointed at a burglar with one hand while the other hand dials the police." But Scalia ignored a substantial body of public health research that contradicts his assertions. A number of scientific studies, published in the world's most rigorous, peer-reviewed journals, show that the risks of keeping a loaded gun in the home strongly outweigh the potential benefits.

3   In the real world, Scalia's scenario—an armed assailant breaks into your home, and you shoot or scare away the bad guy with your handy handgun—happens pretty infrequently. Statistically speaking, these rare success stories are dwarfed by tragedies. The reason is simple: A gun kept loaded and readily available for protection may also be reached by a curious child, an angry spouse or a depressed teen.

4   More than 20 years ago, I conducted a study of firearm-related deaths in homes in Seattle and surrounding King County, Washington. Over the study's seven-year interval, more than half of all fatal shootings in the county took place in the home where the firearm involved was kept. Just nine of those shootings were legally justifiable homicides or acts of self-defense; guns kept in homes were also involved in 12 accidental deaths, 41 criminal homicides and a shocking 333 suicides. A subsequent study conducted in three U.S. cities found that guns kept in the home were 12 times more likely to be involved in the death or injury of a member of the household than in the killing or wounding of a bad guy in self-defense.

5   Oh, one more thing: Scalia's ludicrous vision of a little old lady clutching a handgun in one hand while dialing 911 with the other (try it sometime) doesn't fit the facts. According to the Justice Department, far more guns are lost each year to burglary or theft than are used to defend people or property. In Atlanta, a city where approximately a third of households contain guns, a study of 197 home-invasion crimes revealed only three instances (1.5 percent) in which the inhabitants resisted with a gun. Intruders got to the homeowner's gun twice as often as the homeowner did.

6   The court has spoken, but citizens and lawmakers should base future gun-control decisions—both personal and political—on something more substantive than Scalia's glib opinion.

QUESTIONS FOR READING

1.   What is Kellerman's subject?

2.   Why are loaded guns in the house a risk?

3.   Statistically, who is more likely to use a homeowner's gun, the homeowner or the intruder?

QUESTIONS FOR REASONING AND ANALYSIS

1.   What is Kellerman's claim? Where does he state it?
2.   What is the author's response to Scalia's majority opinion defense? What attitude does he express?
3.   How effective are the author's statistics in support of his position?

QUESTIONS FOR REFLECTION AND WRITING

1.   Have you been aware of the information provided by Kellerman, or are you surprised by the statistics? Does his evidence affect your thinking on this issue in any way? Explain.
2.   Should handguns be restricted? If so, in what ways? If not, why not?

ADULT CRIME, ADULT TIME | LINDA J. COLLIER

An attorney, Linda J. Collier is currently dean of public services and social sciences at Delaware County Community College in Pennsylvania. She has been the director of student legal services at Pennsylvania State University and special assistant for legal affairs to two college presidents, in addition to teaching courses in sociology and criminal justice. The following essay, published in the *Washington Post* in 1998, is written in response to the case of a 12-year-old and a 14-year-old shooting four students and a teacher at their school in Jonesboro, Arkansas, that same year.

PREREADING QUESTIONS Why do some think that the juvenile justice system is inadequate? What kinds of cases was it originally designed to handle?

When prosecutor Brent Davis said he wasn't sure if he could charge 1 11-year-old Andrew Golden and 13-year-old Mitchell Johnson as adults after Tuesday afternoon's slaughter in Jonesboro, Ark., I cringed. But not for the reasons you might think.

I knew he was formulating a judgment based on laws that have not had 2 a major overhaul for more than 100 years. I knew his hands were tied by the longstanding creed that juvenile offenders, generally defined as those under the age of 18, are to be treated rather than punished. I knew he would have to do legal cartwheels to get the case out of the juvenile system. But most of all, I cringed because today's juvenile suspects—even those who are accused of committing the most violent crimes—are still regarded by the law as children first and criminals second.

As astonishing as the Jonesboro events were, this is hardly the first time 3 that children with access to guns and other weapons have brought tragedy to a school. Only weeks before the Jonesboro shootings, three girls in Paducah, Ky., were killed in their school lobby when a 14-year-old classmate allegedly opened fire on them. Authorities said he had several guns with him, and the alleged murder weapon was one of seven stolen from a neighbor's garage. And the day after the Jonesboro shootings, a 14-year-old in Daly City, Calif., was charged as a juvenile after he allegedly fired at his middle-school principal with a semiautomatic handgun.

4   It's not a new or unusual phenomenon for children to commit violent crimes at younger and younger ages, but it often takes a shocking incident to draw our attention to a trend already in progress. According to the U.S. Department of Justice, crimes committed by juveniles have increased by 60 percent since 1984. Where juvenile delinquency was once limited to truancy or vandalism, juveniles now are more likely to be the perpetrators of serious and deadly crimes such as arson, aggravated assault, rape and murder. And these violent offenders increasingly include those as young as the Jonesboro suspects. Since 1965, the number of 12-year-olds arrested for violent crimes has doubled and the number of 13- and 14-year-olds has tripled, according to government statistics.

5   Those statistics are a major reason why we need to revamp our antiquated juvenile justice system. Nearly every state, including Arkansas, has laws that send most youthful violent offenders to the juvenile courts, where they can only be found "delinquent" and confined in a juvenile facility (typically not past age 21). In recent years, many states have enacted changes in their juvenile crime laws, and some have lowered the age at which a juvenile can be tried as an adult for certain violent crimes. Virginia, for example, has reduced its minimum age to 14, and suspects accused of murder and aggravated malicious wounding are automatically waived to adult court. Illinois is now sending some 13-year-olds to adult court after a hearing in juvenile court. In Kansas, a 1996 law allows juveniles as young as 10 to be prosecuted as adults in some cases. These are steps in the right direction, but too many states still treat violent offenders under 16 as juveniles who belong in the juvenile system.

6   My views are not those of a frustrated prosecutor. I have represented children as a court-appointed guardian *ad litem,* or temporary guardian, in the Philadelphia juvenile justice system. Loosely defined, a guardian *ad litem* is responsible for looking after the best interest of a neglected or rebellious child who has come into the juvenile courts. It is often a humbling experience as I try to help children whose lives have gone awry, sometimes because of circumstances beyond their control.

7   My experience has made me believe that the system is doing a poor job at treatment as well as punishment. One of my "girls," a chronic truant, was a foster child who longed to be adopted. She often talked of how she wanted a pink room, a frilly bunk bed and sisters with whom she could share her dreams. She languished in foster care from ages 2 to 13 because her drug-ravaged mother would not relinquish her parental rights. Initially, the girl refused to tolerate the half-life that the state had maintained was in her best interest. But as it became clear that we would never convince her mother to give up her rights, the girl became a frequent runaway. Eventually she ended up pregnant, wandering from place to place and committing adult crimes to survive. No longer a child, not quite a woman, she is the kind of teenage offender for whom the juvenile system has little or nothing to offer.

8   A brief history: Proceedings in juvenile justice began in 1890 in Chicago, where the original mandate was to save wayward children and protect them

from the ravages of society. The system called for children to be processed through an appendage of the family court. By design, juveniles were to be kept away from the court's criminal side, the district attorney and adult correctional institutions.

Typically, initial procedures are informal, non-threatening and not open to **9** public scrutiny. A juvenile suspect is interviewed by an "intake" officer who determines the child's fate. The intake officer may issue a warning, lecture and release; he may detain the suspect; or, he may decide to file a petition, subjecting the child to juvenile "adjudication" proceedings. If the law allows, the intake officer may make a recommendation that the juvenile be transferred to adult criminal court.

An adjudication is similar to a hearing, rather than a trial, although **10** the juvenile may be represented by counsel and a juvenile prosecutor will represent the interests of the community. It is important to note that throughout the proceedings, no matter which side of the fence the parties are on, the operating principle is that everyone is working in the best interests of the child. Juvenile court judges do not issue findings of guilt, but decide whether a child is delinquent. If delinquency is found, the judge must decide the child's fate. Should the child be sent back to the family—assuming there is one? Declare him or her "in need of supervision," which brings in the intense help of social services? Remove the child from the family and place him or her in foster care? Confine the child to a state institution for juvenile offenders?

This system was developed with truants, vandals and petty thieves in mind. **11** But this model is not appropriate for the violent juvenile offender of today. Detaining a rapist or murderer in a juvenile facility until the age of 18 or 21 isn't even a slap on the hand. If a juvenile is accused of murdering, raping or assaulting someone with a deadly weapon, the suspect should automatically be sent to adult criminal court. What's to ponder?

With violent crime becoming more prevalent among the junior set, it's a **12** mystery why there hasn't been a major overhaul of juvenile justice laws long before now. Will the Jonesboro shootings be the incident that makes us take a hard look at the current system? When it became evident that the early release of Jesse Timmendequas—whose murder of 7-year-old Megan Kanka in New Jersey sparked national outrage—had caused unwarranted tragedy, legislative action was swift. Now New Jersey has Megan's law, which requires the advance notification of a sexual predator's release into a neighborhood. Other states have followed suit.

It is unequivocally clear that the same type of mandate is needed to estab- **13** lish a uniform minimum age for trying juveniles as adults. As it stands now, there is no consistency in state laws governing waivers to adult court. One reason for this lack of uniformity is the absence of direction from the federal government or Congress. The Bureau of Justice Statistics reports that adjacent states such as New York and Pennsylvania respond differently to 16-year-old criminals, with New York tending to treat offenders of that age as adults and Pennsylvania handling them in the juvenile justice system.

14   Federal prosecution of juveniles is not totally unheard of, but it is uncommon. The Bureau of Justice Statistics estimates that during 1994, at least 65 juveniles were referred to the attorney general for transfer to adult status. In such cases, the U.S. attorney's office must certify a substantial federal interest in the case and show that one of the following is true: The state does not have jurisdiction; the state refuses to assume jurisdiction or the state does not have adequate services for juvenile offenders; the offense is a violent felony, drug trafficking or firearm offense as defined by the U.S. Code.

15   Exacting hurdles, but not insurmountable. In the Jonesboro case, prosecutor Davis has been exploring ways to enlist the federal court's jurisdiction. Whatever happens, federal prosecutions of young offenders are clearly not the long-term answer. The states must act. So as far as I can see, the next step is clear: Children who knowingly engage in adult conduct and adult crimes should automatically be subject to adult rules and adult prison time.

QUESTIONS FOR READING

1.   What are some of the problems with current state laws governing juvenile crimes?

2.   Briefly summarize the author's history of the juvenile justice system.

3.   In addition to failing to punish properly, in the author's view, what else do juvenile court systems fail to do?

4.   Where does Collier look for help in correcting the juvenile justice system?

QUESTIONS FOR REASONING AND ANALYSIS

1.   What is Collier's claim? Where does she state it?

2.   In paragraph 11, when she writes "What's to ponder?" what response does she want from readers?

3.   Although Collier is writing in response to the Jonesboro murders, she refers to other juvenile murders in paragraph 3. What does she seek to gain by this?

4.   The author asserts that she is not writing as a "frustrated prosecutor" and describes her experience as a court-appointed guardian. What does she gain by this discussion in paragraphs 6 and 7?

QUESTIONS FOR REFLECTION AND WRITING

1.   Could the example of one of Collier's court-appointed "girls" be used to argue for, rather than against, the juvenile justice system? Explain your answer.

2.   Do you think that juveniles should be tried as adults? If so, in what situations? If not, why not?

KIDS WHO KILL ARE STILL KIDS | RICHARD COHEN

Richard Cohen is a journalist with a syndicated column. The following column appeared in newspapers on August 3, 2001.

PREREADING QUESTIONS Should we, as a country, have a cutoff age for capital sentencing? If so, what should the cutoff age be?

1   When I was about 12, I heaved a cinder block over my neighbor's fence and nearly killed her. I didn't know she was there. When I was about the same age, I started a small fire in a nearby field that spread until it threatened some nearby houses. I didn't mean to do it. When I was even younger, I climbed on top of a toolshed, threw a brick in the general direction of my sister and sent her, bleeding profusely and crying so that I can still hear her, to the hospital. I didn't mean to do that, either.

2   I tell these stories to remind us all that kids are kids and to suggest that even the worst of them—even the ones who commit murder—are still kids. I would be lying if I said that I knew what to do with them—how long they should be jailed and where—but I do know that something awful has come over this country. It seems the more incomprehensible the crime, the more likely it is that a child will be treated as an adult.

3   This is what happened to Nathanial Brazill, 14, who was recently sentenced to 28 years in prison for the murder of a teacher, Barry Grunow. Brazill was only 13 when he shot the teacher on the final day of school. Grunow, a much-beloved teacher, had stopped Brazill from talking to two girls and disrupting the class. Earlier in the day, the boy had been suspended for throwing water balloons. He had gone home, gotten a gun and returned to school. Grunow was Brazill's favorite teacher.

4   I always feel in columns of this sort the necessity to say something about the victim and how his life was taken from him. I feel a particular need to do so in this case because Grunow seemed to be an exceptional teacher, a good person. Anyway—and this is only me talking—I feel a certain awe, a humility, toward people who dedicate their lives to teaching kids instead of, say, peddling tech stocks or mouthing off on television about Gary Condit.[1]

5   But Grunow is gone and nothing can be done to bring him back. That is not merely a cliché but also an important point. Because always in these cases when it comes time to justify why a minor was treated as an adult, someone says something about sending a message to other kids. This is absurd.

6   Consider what Brazill did. He shot his teacher before oodles of witnesses. He shot a man he liked. He shot someone without any chance of his getting away. He shot someone for almost no reason at all. He shot someone not in the course of a robbery or a sex crime or because he put a move on his girlfriend but because he is a screwed-up kid, damaged, full of anger and with not much self-control. He shot someone without fully comprehending the

---

[1] Former member of Congress from California.—Ed.

consequences. He shot someone, because, among other things, he was just 13 years old.

7   And yet, he was prosecuted—and sentenced to three years more than the mandatory minimum—as an adult. If there is one thing he is not, it is an adult. But Brazill and, earlier, 13-year-old Lionel Tate were sentenced as if they were button men for some crime family. Tate was given life without parole for the killing of a 6-year-old girl he maintained died in a wrestling accident. These boys were tried as adults but, I'd guess, their ability to participate in their own defense would be labeled juvenile.

8   Amnesty International says about 200,000 children have been tried as adults by American courts. Florida alone reports that 3,300 kids were prosecuted as adults in fiscal 1999–2000. This sends a message—but it's to the adult community: We're getting tough. Kids, however, are unlikely to get the message. I mean, you know how kids are.

9   Where is the deterrence in this policy? Will other 13-year-olds now hesitate before killing their teacher? Hardly. Who is being punished? The child at first, but later the adult he becomes.

10   Brazill will be over 40 when he gets out of jail. When he's, say, 35, will he have anything in common with the child who pulled the trigger? No more, I'd say, than I do with the jerk who nearly killed Richie Miller's mother with a cinder block. I didn't set out to hurt anyone, it's true. But neither did Brazill, he says. He just pulled the trigger and the man, somehow, died. It is, when you think about it, a childish explanation.

QUESTIONS FOR READING

1. How many years was Brazill sentenced to? What was his crime?
2. What is Cohen's explanation of Brazill's behavior?
3. What message is supposed to be sent by trying children as adults? What is Cohen's assessment of the success of this strategy?

QUESTIONS FOR REASONING AND ANALYSIS

1. Cohen tells readers that 200,000 children have been tried as adults. Why does he include this statistic?
2. The author begins by reporting some of his actions as a youngster. What does he seek to gain from this beginning?
3. What is Cohen's claim? Evaluate his argument: Is his evidence convincing? Why or why not?

QUESTIONS FOR REFLECTION AND WRITING

1. The United States and Iran are the only two countries that allow for the execution of juveniles. Forty percent of the U.S. states allow the execution of people as young as 16. What should be the cutoff age for capital punishment regardless of the crime? Be prepared to support your position.

2. When you were young, did you do anything that hurt another person, either accidentally—or not so accidentally? If so, what were the consequences? How do you feel now about the incident?

3. How should the two boys Cohen uses as examples have been tried and sentenced, in your view? Be prepared to support your position.

TYING OUR HANDS | MICHAEL LOUD

A member of the United States Marine Corps, Michael Loud published his views on the debate about military interrogation strategies in the *Marine Corps Gazette* in their February 2007 issue.

PREREADING QUESTIONS How would you define *torture*? In the debate over interrogation strategies, does it matter if we agree on this term or not?

The current situation in Iraq demands that U.S. commanders receive the   1 best intelligence available, in the most expedient manner, to protect Americans and defeat the insurgency. One of the most reliable methods by which the military has been gathering information regarding upcoming attacks, individual insurgent personalities, and the enemy's organizational structure has been through intelligence interrogations of captured insurgents. However, the politically charged debate over U.S. interrogation practices and the amount of related information made available in public venues is crippling the ability of U.S. intelligence officers to gather this vital information.

The U.S. military is conducting a counterinsurgency campaign in Iraq   2 against zealots who use religion as a rallying cry, who possess no apparent fear of death, and who can readily hide amid a largely apathetic Sunni population. Fighting an insurgency as determined and capable as this one requires an array of intelligence collection and analysis skills. Our interrogators have these skills and have been trained extensively to use them with prudence and judgment.

SETTING THE STAGE

Much of the public debate over interrogation practices surrounds the pro-   3 cedures used to question the foreign detainees held in Iraq, Afghanistan, and Guantanamo Bay, Cuba, as well as those reportedly held at Central Intelligence Agency "secret prisons" around the world. Nearly all of the debates stem from political rhetoric and partisan attacks, complaints from biased human rights groups, or complaints from the detainees themselves. These same detainees have a vested interest in the delay and subversion of the detainee handling system. They want to delay interrogations as long as possible to make the information they possess irrelevant and outdated, or so they can attempt to gain freedom by manipulating the U.S. legal system.

Many human rights groups' experts, media personalities, and politicians   4 focus on the reported use of "torture" by U.S. interrogators. First, many of the supposed incidents of torture by U.S. forces occurred not at the hands of professionally trained military interrogators but by improperly trained and led military policemen and infantrymen, such as the Abu Ghraib and Guantanamo prison guards. In the Abu Ghraib incident, the soldiers involved were from a National Guard unit, with no detainee handling training, who put on a "show" for a fellow soldier's birthday. This kind of immature, improper behavior is already banned under the Uniform Code of Military Justice, the Geneva Conventions Relating to the Treatment of Prisoners of War (including detained persons), and the law of land warfare. Those soldiers involved in the Abu Ghraib atrocities were punished for their actions through the military justice system. One of the basic principles of military leadership is that a leader is responsible for the actions or inactions of his subordinates. As such, the officers in charge of those guards were responsible for everything that happened in that facility, whether other government agencies were present or not, and those officers were held accountable by the military justice system. Adding more laws and restrictions will not prevent another Abu Ghraib, only training and supervision will accomplish that.

5   Cases are rare in which military interrogators have been found responsible for substantiated prisoner abuse. An investigation by the Department of Defense's Inspector General found that some interrogators at Guantanamo Bay had indeed conducted improper interrogations, using methods such as "gender coercion," "short shackling," and dogs that "growled at the detainees." While some of the physical techniques used (such as binding to cause physical pain and smearing fake menstrual fluid on a detainee's face) may have been improper, the manipulation of the detainee's cultural fear of dogs and perceptions toward women were calculated to reduce the will of the detainee to resist questioning. Interrogators often rely on their knowledge of the detainees' cultural biases to manipulate detainees into providing truthful information. Uncooperative prisoners, likely encouraged and educated by the international news media, will continue to claim they are victims of torture and abuse at the hands of American interrogators. They do so primarily because the prisoners understand that this behavior is an effective counterinterrogation technique; interrogations have to stop until an investigation of the incident is conducted. A military as justly and legally regulated as that of the United States will not tolerate violations of law by its personnel. The detainees understand this fact and use it to manipulate the American sense of morality and the U.S. legal system to their advantage.

6   Additionally, the term torture is poorly defined by both the media and the politicians involved in the debate. The *Oxford English Dictionary* defines torture as "the infliction of severe bodily pain, especially as a punishment or a means of persuasion" or "severe mental or physical suffering." Politicians, bureaucrats, and human rights advocates expanded that definition to include shouting at prisoners, placing them in solitary confinement, disrupting their sleep patterns, altering their diets, and exposing them to loud noises and music. While these practices are not enjoyable for the prisoner, defining them as severe mental or physical pain is specious. All of these methods are frequently used in U.S. prisons and, more commonly, in military basic training. If the new recruits to America's military can endure the rigors of basic training,

can those same rigors be considered torture when used against people who are trying to destroy the American way of life?

Those combatants who deliberately violate the rules about maintaining a clear separation between combatant and non-combatant groups—and thus endanger the civilian population—should not enjoy the protection of the Geneva Conventions. The insurgents operating in Iraq relinquished their right to be considered legitimate combatants and can be compelled to provide information beyond the standard "name, rank, serial number, and date of birth" that legitimate prisoners of war must provide. **7**

INTERROGATION OF PRISONERS

Intelligence interrogations, while different in scope, are not very different from the interrogations U.S. law enforcement officers routinely conduct on criminal suspects. Police officers use trickery, deceit, lies, fabrications, and psychological ploys to convince guilty suspects to confess and cooperate with the investigation. Intelligence interrogators use these same mental games to play on the detainees' weaknesses and manipulate their emotions. Fear is one of the most powerful emotions. Causing and exploiting a detainee's fear frequently provides valuable information. At the same time, trained interrogators know when to escalate fear and when to downplay fear and console the detainee. Every detainee requires a different approach. Restricting the use of interrogation approaches effectively hamstrings interrogators. Instead of artfully manipulating the detainee into confessing that he is an improvised explosive device maker, for example, the interrogator is limited to asking direct questions that are easily resisted or result in short, useless responses. The skilled interrogators of the military and intelligence communities are trained professionals who understand that an interrogation is a mental battle of wills between the detainee and the interrogator. Successful interrogators need not abuse captives but instead will focus on outwitting the suspect and convincing him that it is in his best interest to cooperate with U.S. forces. Perseverance and time are on the side of the interrogator during an interrogation, until politically spirited deadlines are imposed for the processing of detainees. The 72-hour rule now used in Iraq significantly hamstrings U.S. interrogators since the detainees know exactly how long they need to remain quiet before they will be released. The objective of an interrogation is to gain the cooperation of the detainee and get the detainee to willingly provide information on his fellow insurgents and future attacks. The best way to make this happen is not through physical or mental abuse but through calculated verbal attacks, praise, and rapport building, each applied specifically to garner the greatest result possible with the least resistance by the captive. But, while the application of actual physical force is unwarranted, often the detainee's preconceived notions of the force to come or harm that will befall him can be effectively used by an interrogator. **8**

The public debate and openly available information on U.S. interrogation policy has removed all fear of the unknown for the detainee, thus making the interrogator's job more difficult, if not impossible. By repeatedly discussing **9** the limits of U.S. interrogation tactics and techniques, the U.S. media makes it more difficult for U.S. interrogators to gather information that can protect American lives. Al-Qaeda suspects and Iraqi insurgents in custody repeatedly exhibit evidence of counterinterrogation training that reveals a familiarity with U.S. interrogation methods. One tool in the interrogators' arsenal is the ability to keep the detainee confused and disoriented by prolonging the shock of capture, which is—by design—an unnerving and uncomfortable experience. A detainee experiencing the shock of capture has more difficulty following a cover story or supplying false information to the interrogator.

10   Interrogations provide a wealth of information, both at the tactical and the national policymaking level. However, politically motivated measures are being taken in response to an outcry from an often misinformed public, and these measures hinder interrogation methods, endanger military personnel, and can prevent the intelligence services from gathering vital information that could prevent future attacks on Americans overseas and in the United States.

QUESTIONS FOR READING

1. What is Loud's subject?
2. What, in his view, are the sources of the complaints about interrogation procedures?
3. What is the author's explanation for the Abu Ghraib incident?
4. Why do prisoners complain that they are being tortured?
5. What strategies of interrogation are used by trained personnel? How does the media debate over torture interfere with this process, in the view of the author?

QUESTIONS FOR REASONING AND ANALYSIS

1. What is Loud's claim? Where does he state it? Where does he restate it? What does he gain by this writing choice?
2. What are his grounds? List his reasons and evidence.
3. What assumptions play a role in Loud's argument? Are they assumptions you are willing to accept? Why or why not?
4. Loud asserts, in paragraph 6, that politicians and others have expanded the *OED*'s definition of torture in specific ways that he lists. Is there anything in that list that expands the definition, in your view? If so, what?
5. How effective is Loud's argument? Evaluate it.

QUESTIONS FOR REFLECTION AND WRITING

1. Do you agree with Loud that the interrogation strategies listed are not torture and should be allowed? Why or why not?
2. Do you agree that the media debate has interfered with the work of the military intelligence personnel? Why or why not?

WHY IT WAS CALLED "WATER TORTURE" | RICHARD E. MEZO

A veteran of thirteen years of military service, in both the Air Force and the Navy, Richard Mezo holds a Ph.D. from the University of North Dakota and now teaches in the English department at the Fredericksburg Campus of Germanna Community College. He has published books and articles on literature and a book of poetry. His response to the debate on interrogation strategies appeared in the *Washington Post* on February 10, 2008.

PREREADING QUESTION What does Mezo's title suggest that his position on this issue will be?

Last week, much to my dismay, government officials testified before Congress that the United States has used the interrogation technique known as waterboarding and would like to hold out the option of using it in the future. As someone who has experienced waterboarding, albeit in a controlled setting, I know that the act is indeed torture. I was waterboarded during my training to become a Navy flight crew member. As has been noted in *The Post* and other media outlets, waterboarding is "real drowning that simulates death." It's an experience our country should not subject people to. 1

In February 1963, I was ordered from the Naval Air Station in Alameda, Calif., to Whidbey Island, Wash., for survival training. Part of the week-long program was a brief incarceration in a simulated prisoner-of-war camp; at that time, the program was modeled on events that had occurred during the Korean War. First we were to be "held" in a mock North Korean camp and later transferred to a Chinese camp. 2

The enlisted men who supervised the training worked to make the situation realistic, and they succeeded in convincing me that I never wanted to become a prisoner of war. I recall that after our "capture," the sailors—wearing Red Army uniforms—marched the dozen or so of us along the ocean without our boots. It was very cold, and all our resolve and determination could not prevent our courage from eventually draining out through our wet feet. They took us to a compound of small huts with dirt floors. The camp was surrounded by barbed wire, and the entrance was guarded by armed soldiers. 3

Several times that night I was on the verge of speaking out, of trying to call the whole thing off, and I suspect that I was not the only one. We held on because none of us trainees wanted to be the person to quit. The camp had an array of torture devices, including the infamous "black box" (which I actually liked because it was the only time I was off the ground and not miserably cold), and our captors also threatened executions, though we had the comfort of knowing that they would not carry through on such threats. 4

We were all interrogated a few times, some of us more than others. During one interrogation, I was led blindfolded into a room. Suddenly one of the "enemy" hit me hard in the stomach—a sucker punch that left me doubled over, out of breath. I think three other people were present, but I was never sure. Two men grabbed me at my sides. They put a pole of some kind under my knees and bent me over backward. My head went down lower than the rest of my body. 5

6   The questions (What is your unit? Where are you from?) were asked by one man. But we were not supposed to talk. I remember that the blindfold was heavy and completely covered my face. As the two men held me down, one on each side, someone began pouring water onto the blindfold, and suddenly I was drowning. The water streamed into my nose and then into my mouth when I gasped for breath. I couldn't stop it. All I could breathe was water, and it was terrifying. I think I began to lose consciousness. I felt my lungs begin to fill with burning liquid.

7   Pulling out my fingernails or even cutting off a finger would have been preferable. At least if someone had attacked my hands, I would have had to simply tolerate pain. But drowning is another matter.

8   Even though I knew that I was in a military facility and that my "captors" would not kill me, no matter what they threatened, my body sensed and reacted to the danger it was in. Adrenaline helped me to fight out of the position the men were holding me in. I can't really explain how I managed to stand up, still with one man clinging to each arm. I only know how horrible it was. The experience was probably only a few minutes, but to me it seemed much longer.

9   Waterboarding has, unfortunately, become a household word. Back then, we didn't call it waterboarding—we called it "water torture." We recognized it as something the United States would never do, whatever the provocation. As a nation, we must ask our leaders, elected and appointed, to be aware of such horrors; we must ask them to stop the narrow and superficial thinking that hinges upon "legal" definitions and to use common sense. Waterboarding is torture, and torture is clearly a crime against humanity.

QUESTIONS FOR READING

1. Why was Mezo dismayed?
2. What did he experience during his Navy training?
3. How did he feel during waterboarding?

QUESTIONS FOR REASONING AND ANALYSIS

1. What is Mezo's claim?
2. What is his basic reasoning?
3. What *kind* of evidence does he present primarily? Is that an effective strategy? Why or why not?

QUESTIONS FOR REFLECTION AND WRITING

1. Mezo's strategy of argument is quite different from Loud's. Which strategy usually works best for you? Which works best on this issue? Explain.
2. Have you ever struggled in water, perhaps swimming out too far from shore or getting caught in a strong current? Can you imagine what it would be like to experience waterboarding? How do you think you would react?

FIVE MYTHS ABOUT TORTURE AND TRUTH | DARIUS REJALI

A professor of political science at Reed College, Iranian-born Darius Rejali is a recognized expert on the causes and meaning of violence, especially on torture, in our world. His book *Torture and Democracy* (2007) has won acclaim and resulted in frequent interview sessions for Rejali. *Approaches to Violence* is due out in 2008. The following essay appeared on December 16, 2007, in the *Washington Post*.

PREREADING QUESTIONS Can you think of five myths about torture? What do you expect Rejali to cover in this essay?

So the CIA did indeed torture Abu Zubaida, the first al-Qaeda terrorist 1 *suspect to have been waterboarded. So says John Kiriakou, the first former CIA employee directly involved in the questioning of "high-value" al-Qaeda detainees to speak out publicly. He minced no words last week in calling the CIA's "enhanced interrogation techniques" what they are.*

But did they work? Torture's defenders, including the wannabe tough 2 *guys who write Fox's "24," insist that the rough stuff gets results. "It was like flipping a switch," said Kiriakou about Abu Zubaida's response to being water-boarded. But the al-Qaeda operative's confessions—descriptions of fantastic plots from a man who intelligence analysts were convinced was mentally ill—probably didn't give the CIA any actionable intelligence. Of course, we may never know the whole truth, since the CIA destroyed the videotapes of Abu Zubaida's interrogation. But here are some other myths that are bound to come up as the debate over torture rages on.*

1. Torture worked for the Gestapo. Actually, no. Even Hitler's notorious 3 secret police got most of their information from public tips, informers and interagency cooperation. That was still more than enough to let the Gestapo decimate anti-Nazi resistance in Austria, Czechoslovakia, Poland, Denmark, Norway, France, Russia and the concentration camps.

Yes, the Gestapo did torture people for intelligence, especially in later 4 years. But this reflected not torture's efficacy but the loss of many sea-soned professionals to World War II, increasingly desperate competition for intelligence among Gestapo units and an influx of less disciplined younger members. (Why do serious, tedious police work when you have a uniform and a whip?) It's surprising how unsuccessful the Gestapo's brutal efforts were. They failed to break senior leaders of the French, Danish, Polish and German resistance. I've spent more than a decade collecting all the cases of Gestapo torture "successes" in multiple languages; the number is small and the results pathetic, especially compared with the devastating effects of public coopera-tion and informers.

2. Everyone talks sooner or later under torture. Truth is, it's surpris- 5 ingly hard to get anything under torture, true or false. For example, between 1500 and 1750, French prosecutors tried to torture confessions out of 785 individuals. Torture was legal back then, and the records document such prac-tices as the bone-crushing use of splints, pumping stomachs with water until they swelled and pouring boiling oil on the feet. But the number of prisoners who said anything was low, from 3 percent in Paris to 14 percent in Toulouse (an exceptional high). Most of the time, the torturers were unable to get any statement whatsoever.

6   And such examples could be multiplied. The Japanese fascists, no strangers to torture, said it best in their field manual, which was found in Burma during World War II: They described torture as the clumsiest possible method of gathering intelligence. Like most sensible torturers, they preferred to use torture for intimidation, not information.

7   **3. People will say anything under torture.** Well, no, although this is a favorite chestnut of torture's foes. Think about it: Sure, someone would lie under torture, but wouldn't they also lie if they were being interrogated without coercion?

8   In fact, the problem of torture does not stem from the prisoner who *has* information; it stems from the prisoner who doesn't. Such a person is also likely to lie, to say anything, often convincingly. The torture of the informed may generate no more lies than normal interrogation, but the torture of the ignorant and innocent overwhelms investigators with misleading information. In these cases, nothing is indeed preferable to anything. Anything needs to be verified, and the CIA's own 1963 interrogation manual explains that "a time-consuming delay results"—hardly useful when every moment matters.

9   Intelligence gathering is especially vulnerable to this problem. When police officers torture, they know what the crime is, and all they want is the confession. When intelligence officers torture, they must gather information about what they don't know.

10   **4. Most people can tell when someone is lying under torture.** Not so—and we know quite a bit about this. For about 40 years, psychologists have been testing police officers as well as normal people to see whether they can spot lies, and the results aren't encouraging. Ordinary folk have an accuracy rate of about 57 percent, which is pretty poor considering that 50 percent is the flip of a coin. Likewise, the cops' accuracy rates fall between 45 percent and 65 percent—that is, sometimes less accurate than a coin toss.

11   Why does this matter? Because even if torturers break a person, they have to recognize it, and most of the time they can't. Torturers assume too much and reject what doesn't fit their assumptions. For instance, Sheila Cassidy, a British physician, cracked under electric-shock torture by the Chilean secret service in the 1970s and identified priests who had helped the country's socialist opposition. But her devout interrogators couldn't believe that priests would ever help the socialists, so they tortured her for another week until they finally became convinced. By that time, she was so damaged that she couldn't remember the location of the safe house.

12   In fact, most torturers are nowhere near as well trained for interrogation as police are. Torturers are usually chosen because they've endured hardship and pain, fought with courage, kept secrets, held the right beliefs and earned a reputation as trustworthy and loyal. They often rely on folklore about what lying behavior looks like—shifty eyes, sweaty palms and so on. And, not surprisingly, they make a lot of mistakes.

5. You can train people to resist torture. Supposedly, this is why we   13
can't know what the CIA's "enhanced interrogation techniques" are: If
Washington admits that it waterboards suspected terrorists, al-Qaeda will set
up "waterboarding-resistance camps" across the world. Be that as it may, the
truth is that no training will help the bad guys.

Simply put, nothing predicts the outcome of one's resistance to pain bet-   14
ter than one's own personality. Against some personalities, nothing works;
against others, practically anything does. Studies of hundreds of detainees
who broke under Soviet and Chinese torture, including Army-funded studies
of U.S. prisoners of war, conclude that during, before and after torture, each
prisoner displayed strengths and weaknesses dependent on his or her own
character. The CIA's own "Human Resources Exploitation Manual" from 1983
and its so-called Kubark manual from 1963 agree. In all matters relating to
pain, says Kubark, the "individual remains the determinant."

The thing that's most clear from torture-victim studies is that you can't   15
train for the ordeal. There is no secret knowledge out there about how to
resist torture. Yes, there are manuals, such as the IRA's "Green Book," the
anti-Soviet "Manual for Psychiatry for Dissidents" and "Torture and the Interrogation Experience," an Iranian guerrilla manual from the 1970s. But none of
these volumes contains specific techniques of resistance, just general encouragement to hang tough. Even al-Qaeda's vaunted terrorist-training manual
offers no tips on how to resist torture, and al-Qaeda was no stranger to the
brutal methods of the Saudi police.

And yet these myths persist. "The larger problem here, I think," one active   16
CIA officer observed in 2005, "is that this kind of stuff just makes people feel
better, even if it doesn't work."

QUESTIONS FOR READING

1. What context for his discussion does the author provide in the opening two
   paragraphs?
2. What worked better than torture for the Gestapo? What led to an increase in
   torture in the Gestapo?
3. What does the data show about getting people to speak by torturing them?
4. Who are the people most likely to lie under torture?
5. How good are we in recognizing when someone is lying under torture?
6. Is it possible to train people to resist torture?

QUESTIONS FOR REASONING AND ANALYSIS

1. Rejali explains that most of what the Gestapo learned it learned from public
   tips and informers. He describes this as having "devastating effects." How can
   we explain why so many cooperated with the Gestapo?
2. Why is the torturing of innocent people likely to do more harm than good?

3. Why are torturers not very good at recognizing when the tortured are lying?

4. Is Rejali reporting on this topic only, or does he have a position? What do you think is his view of torture?

QUESTIONS FOR REFLECTION AND WRITING

1. Which of the five discussions has surprised you the most? Why?

2. Has the author convinced you that all five myths lack substance? Why or why not?

3. Why do intelligence and military personnel continue to use harsh interrogation strategies even though the evidence suggests that what, if anything, they learn not be useful? Ponder this question.

CHAPTER 21

Marriage and Gender Issues: The Debates Continue

READ: What happens in the cartoon? How does Marvin characterize the dog's attitude?

REASON: What attitude is reflected in the way the dog is drawn in frame 4? What attitude is reflected in the way the cat is drawn in frame 5?

REFLECT/WRITE: What makes the cartoon a clever way of expressing the artist's opposition to stereotyping?

Seven writers provide much for readers to reflect on and debate in this chapter of controversial marriage and gender issues. These writers examine the incredible changes that the twentieth century brought to the institution of marriage—and, by extension, to the family. Some approach these changes—and their effects on our politics, our culture, and our personal lives—from the social science perspective; others take a more jocular or satiric approach. Some write from the perspective of research data; others develop their arguments from emotion or from a legal perspective. Some express strongly held views; others seek common ground. Some focus specifically on marriage—how it affects lives and who should be allowed to participate. Others focus on gender issues—and on the stereotyping that continues to affect women and gays. However, whatever their specific topic, the source of their arguments, or the basis of their values, all of these writers would certainly agree that the changes of the past thirty years, with regard to how we live and work together as men and women, straight and gay, have had a profound effect on our culture and our personal lives.

PREREADING QUESTIONS

1. Do you expect to have a career? To have a spouse and children? Should society support both men and women having these choices? If so, how?
2. What role, if any, should the government and the courts have in defining marriage?
3. What has been meant by the "traditional family"?
4. Do you have a position on gay marriage? On partnership recognition and rights? If you have a position, what is it—and what is its source?
5. Is there anything you can learn from arguments seeking to alter stereotypic views of women? Why or why not?

SOCIAL SCIENCE FINDS: "MARRIAGE MATTERS" | LINDA J. WAITE

A former senior sociologist at the Rand Corporation, Linda Waite is currently a professor at the University of Chicago. She has coauthored several books, including *Teenage Motherhood* (1979) and *New Families, No Families?* (1991). In this article, published in *The Responsive Community* in 1996, Waite pulls together various studies to explore the effects that marriage has on married people.

PREREADING QUESTIONS Although marriage has declined, what has taken its place? How important is marriage to you? Why?

1   As we are all too aware, the last few decades have witnessed a decline in the popularity of marriage. This trend has not escaped the notice of politicians and pundits. But when critics point to the high social costs and taxpayer burden imposed by disintegrating "family values," they overlook the fact that individuals do not simply make the decisions that lead to unwed parenthood,

marriage, or divorce on the basis of what is good for society. Individuals weigh the costs and benefits of each of these choices to themselves—and sometimes their children. But how much is truly known about these costs and benefits, either by the individuals making the choices or demographers like myself who study them? Put differently, what are the implications, for individuals, of the current increases in nonmarriage? If we think of marriage as an insurance policy—which it is, in some respects—does it matter if more people are uninsured, or are insured with a term rather than a whole-life policy? I shall argue that it does matter, because marriage typically provides important and substantial benefits, benefits not enjoyed by those who live alone or cohabit.

A quick look at marriage patterns today compared to, say, 1950 shows the 2 extent of recent changes. Figures from the Census Bureau show that in 1950, at the height of the baby boom, about a third of white men and women were not married. Some were waiting to marry for the first time, some were divorced or widowed and not remarried. But virtually everyone married at least once at some point in their lives, generally in their early twenties.

In 1950 the proportion of black men and women not married was approxi- 3 mately equal to the proportion unmarried among whites, but since that time the marriage behavior of blacks and whites has diverged dramatically. By 1993, 61 percent of black women and 58 percent of black men were not married, compared to 38 percent of white men and 41 percent of white women. So, in contrast to 1950 when only a little over one black adult in three was not married, now a majority of black adults are unmarried. Insofar as marriage "matters," black men and women are much less likely than whites to share in the benefits, and much less likely today than they were a generation ago.

The decline in marriage is directly connected to the rise in cohabitation— 4 living with someone in a sexual relationship without being married. Although Americans are less likely to be married today than they were several decades ago, if we count both marriage and cohabitation, they are about as likely to be "coupled." If cohabitation provides the same benefits to individuals as marriage does, then we do not need to be concerned about this shift. But we may be replacing a valuable social institution with one that demands and offers less.

Perhaps the most disturbing change in marriage appears in its relation- 5 ship to parenthood. Today a third of all births occur to women who are not married, with huge but shrinking differences between blacks and whites in this behavior. One in five births to white mothers and two-thirds of births to black mothers currently take place outside marriage. Although about a quarter of the white unmarried mothers are living with someone when they give birth, so that their children are born into two-parent—if unmarried—families, very few black children born to unmarried mothers live with fathers too.

I believe that these changes in marriage behavior are a cause for concern, 6 because in a number of important ways married men and women do better than those who are unmarried. And I believe that the evidence suggests that they do better because they are married.

MARRIAGE AND HEALTH

7   The case for marriage is quite strong. Consider the issues of longevity and health. With economist Lee Lillard, I used a large national survey to follow men and women over a 20-year period. We watched them get married, get divorced, and remarry. We observed the death of spouses and of the individuals themselves. And we compared deaths of married men and women to those who were not married. We found that once we took other factors into account, married men and women faced lower risks of dying at any point than those who have never married or whose previous marriage has ended. Widowed women were much better off than divorced women or those who had never married, although they were still disadvantaged when compared with married women. But all men who were not currently married faced significantly higher risks of dying than married men, regardless of their marital history. Other scholars have found disadvantages in death rates for unmarried adults in a number of countries besides the United States.

8   How does marriage lengthen life? First, marriage appears to reduce risky and unhealthy behaviors. For example, according to University of Texas sociologist Debra Umberson, married men show much lower rates of problem drinking than unmarried men. Umberson also found that both married men and women are less likely to take risks that could lead to injury than are the unmarried. Second, as we will see below, marriage increases material well-being—income, assets, and wealth. These can be used to purchase better medical care, better diet, and safer surroundings, which lengthen life. This material improvement seems to be especially important for women.

Third, marriage provides individuals—especially men—with someone who 9 monitors their health and health-related behaviors and who encourages them to drink and smoke less, to eat a healthier diet, to get enough sleep and to generally take care of their health. In addition, husbands and wives offer each other moral support that helps in dealing with stressful situations. Married men especially seem to be motivated to avoid risky behaviors and to take care of their health by the sense of meaning that marriage gives to their lives and the sense of obligation to others that it brings.

MORE WEALTH, BETTER WAGES—FOR MOST

Married individuals also seem to fare better when it comes to wealth. One 10 comprehensive measure to financial well-being—household wealth—includes pension and Social Security wealth, real and financial assets, and the value of the primary residence. According to economist James Smith, in 1992 married men and women ages 51–60 had median wealth of about $66,000 per spouse, compared to $42,000 for the widowed, $35,000 for those who had never married, $34,000 among those who were divorced, and only $7,600 for those who were separated. Although married couples have higher incomes than others, this fact accounts for only about a quarter of their greater wealth.

How does marriage increase wealth? Married couples can share many 11 household goods and services, such as a TV and heat, so the cost to each individual is lower than if each one purchased and used the same items individually. So the married spend less than the same individuals would for the same style of life if they lived separately. Second, married people produce more than the same individuals would if single. Each spouse can develop some skills and neglect others, because each can count on the other to take responsibility for some of the household work. The resulting specialization increases efficiency. We see below that this specialization leads to higher wages for men. Married couples also seem to save more at the same level of income than do single people.

The impact of marriage is again beneficial—although in this case not for 12 all involved—when one looks at labor market outcomes. According to recent research by economist Kermit Daniel, both black and white men receive a wage premium if they are married: 4.5 percent for black men and 6.3 percent for white men. Black women receive a marriage premium of almost 3 percent. White women, however, pay a marriage *penalty*, in hourly wages, of over 4 percent. In addition, men appear to receive some of the benefit of marriage if they cohabit, but women do not.

Why should marriage increase men's wages? Some researchers think that 13 marriage makes men more productive at work, leading to higher wages. Wives may assist husbands directly with their work, offer advice or support, or take over household tasks, freeing husbands' time and energy for work. Also, as I mentioned earlier, being married reduces drinking, substance abuse, and other unhealthy behaviors that may affect men's job performance. Finally, marriage increases men's incentives to perform well at work, in order to meet obligations to family members.

14   For women, Daniel finds that marriage and presence of children together seem to affect wages, and the effects depend on the woman's race. Childless black women earn substantially more money if they are married but the "marriage premium" drops with each child they have. Among white women only the childless receive a marriage premium. Once white women become mothers, marriage decreases their earnings compared to remaining single (with children), with very large negative effects of marriage on women's earnings for those with two children or more. White married women often choose to reduce hours of work when they have children. They also make less per hour than either unmarried mothers or childless wives.

15   Up to this point, all the consequences of marriage for the individuals involved have been unambiguously positive—better health, longer life, more wealth, and higher earnings. But the effects of marriage and children on white women's wages are mixed, at best. Marriage and cohabitation increase women's time spent on housework; married motherhood reduces their time in the labor force and lowers their wages. Although the family as a whole might be better off with this allocation of women's time, women generally share their husbands' market earnings only when they are married. Financial well-being declines dramatically for women and their children after divorce and widowhood; women whose marriages have ended are often quite disadvantaged financially by their investment in their husbands and children rather than in their own earning power. Recent changes in divorce law—the rise in no-fault divorce and the move away from alimony—seem to have exacerbated this situation, even while increases in women's education and work experience have moderated it.

IMPROVED INTIMACY

16   Another benefit of married life is an improved sex life. Married men and women report very active sex lives—as do those who are cohabiting. But the married appear to be more satisfied with sex than others. More married men say that they find sex with their wives to be extremely physically pleasurable than do cohabiting men or single men say the same about sex with their partners. The high levels of married men's physical satisfaction with their sex lives contradicts the popular view that sexual novelty or variety improves sex for men. Physical satisfaction with sex is about the same for married women, cohabiting women, and single women with sex partners.

17   In addition to reporting more active and more physically fulfilling sex lives than the unmarried, married men and women say that they are more emotionally satisfied with their sex lives than do those who are single or cohabiting. Although cohabitants report levels of sexual activity as high as the married, both cohabiting men and women report lower levels of emotional satisfaction with their sex lives. And those who are sexually active but single report the lowest emotional satisfaction with it.

18   How does marriage improve one's sex life? Marriage and cohabitation provide individuals with a readily available sexual partner with whom they

have an established, ongoing sexual relationship. This reduces the costs—in some sense—of any particular sexual contact, and leads to higher levels of sexual activity. Since married couples expect to carry on their sex lives for many years, and since the vast majority of married couples are monogamous, husbands and wives have strong incentives to learn what pleases their partner in bed and to become good at it. But I would argue that more than "skills" are at issue here. The long-term contract implicit in marriage—which is not implicit in cohabitation—facilitates emotional investment in the relationship, which should affect both frequency of and satisfaction with sex. So the wife or husband who knows what the spouse wants is also highly motivated to provide it, both because sexual satisfaction in one's partner brings similar rewards to oneself and because the emotional commitment to the partner makes satisfying him or her important in itself.

To this point we have focused on the consequences of marriage for adults— [19] the men and women who choose to marry (and stay married) or not. But such choices have consequences for the children born to these adults. Sociologists Sarah McLanahan and Gary Sandefur compare children raised in intact, two-parent families with those raised in one-parent families, which could result either from disruption of a marriage or from unmarried childbearing. They find that approximately twice as many children raised in one-parent families than children from two-parent families drop out of high school without finishing. Children raised in one-parent families are also more likely to have a birth themselves while teenagers, and to be "idle"—both out of school and out of the labor force—as young adults.

Not surprisingly, children living outside an intact marriage are also more [20] likely to be poor. McLanahan and Sandefur calculated poverty rates for children in two-parent families—including stepfamilies—and for single-parent families. They found very high rates of poverty for single-parent families, especially among blacks. Donald Hernandez, chief of marriage and family statistics at the Census Bureau, claims that the rise in mother-only families since 1959 is an important cause of increases in poverty among children.

Clearly poverty, in and of itself, is a bad outcome for children. In addi- [21] tion, however, McLanahan and Sandefur estimate that the lower incomes of single-parent families account for only half of the negative impact for children in these families. The other half comes from children's access— or lack of access—to the time and attention of two adults in two-parent families. Children in one-parent families spend less time with their fathers (this is not surprising given that they do not live with them), but they also spend less time with their mothers than children in two-parent families. Single-parent families and stepfamilies also move much more frequently than two-parent families, disrupting children's social and academic environments. Finally, children who spend part of their childhood in a single-parent family report substantially lower quality relationships with their parents as adults and have less frequent contact with them, according to demographer Diane Lye.

CORRELATION VERSUS CAUSALITY

22   The obvious question, when one looks at all these "benefits" of marriage, is whether marriage is responsible for these differences. If all, or almost all, of the benefits of marriage arise because those who enjoy better health, live longer lives, or earn higher wages anyway are more likely to marry, then marriage is not "causing" any changes in these outcomes. In such a case, we as a society and we as individuals could remain neutral about each person's decision to marry or not, to divorce or remain married. But scholars from many fields who have examined the issues have come to the opposite conclusion. Daniel found that only half of the higher wages that married men enjoy could be explained by selectivity; he thus concluded that the other half is causal. In the area of mental health, social psychologist Catherine Ross—summarizing her own research and that of other social scientists—wrote, "The positive effect of marriage on well-being is strong and consistent, and the selection of the psychologically healthy into marriage or the psychologically unhealthy out of marriage cannot explain the effect." Thus marriage itself can be assumed to have independent positive effects on its participants.

23   So, we must ask, what is it about marriage that causes these benefits? I think that four factors are key. First, the institution of marriage involves a long-term contract—"'til death do us part." This contract allows the partners to make choices that carry immediate costs but eventually bring benefits. The time horizon implied by marriage makes it sensible—a rational choice is at work here—for individuals to develop some skills and to neglect others because they count on their spouse to fill in where they are weak. The institution of marriage helps individuals honor this long-term contract by providing social support for the couple as a couple and by imposing social and economic costs on those who dissolve their union.

24   Second, marriage assumes a sharing of economic and social resources and what we can think of as co-insurance. Spouses act as a sort of small insurance pool against life's uncertainties, reducing their need to protect themselves—by themselves—from unexpected events.

25   Third, married couples benefit—as do cohabiting couples—from economies of scale.

26   Fourth, marriage connects people to other individuals, to their social groups (such as in-laws), and to other social institutions (such as churches and synagogues) which are themselves a source of benefits. These connections provide individuals with a sense of obligation to others, which gives life meaning beyond oneself.

27   Cohabitation has some but not all of the characteristics of marriage and so carries some but not all of the benefits. Cohabitation does not generally imply a lifetime commitment to stay together; a significant number of cohabiting couples disagree on the future of their relationship. Frances Goldscheider and Gail Kaufman believe that the shift to cohabitation from marriage signals "declining commitment within unions, of men and women to each other and to their relationship as an enduring unit, in exchange for more freedom,

primarily for men." Perhaps as a result, many view cohabitation as an especially poor bargain for women.

The uncertainty that accompanies cohabitation makes both investment **28** in the relationship and specialization with this partner much riskier than in marriage and so reduces them. Cohabitants are much less likely than married couples to pool financial resources and more likely to assume that each partner is responsible for supporting himself or herself financially. And whereas marriage connects individuals to other important social institutions, cohabitation seems to distance them from these institutions.

Of course, all observations concern only the average benefits of marriage. **29** Clearly, some marriages produce substantially higher benefits for those involved. Some marriages produce no benefits and even cause harm to the men, women, and children involved. That fact needs to be recognized.

REVERSING THE TREND

Having stated this qualification, we must still ask, if the average marriage **30** produces all of these benefits for individuals, why has it declined? Although this issue remains a subject of much research and speculation, a number of factors have been mentioned as contributing. For one, because of increases in women's employment, there is less specialization by spouses now than in the past; this reduces the benefits of marriage. Clearly, employed wives have less time and energy to focus on their husbands, and are less financially and emotionally dependent on marriage than wives who work only in the home. In addition, high divorce rates decrease people's certainty about the long-run stability of their marriage, and this may reduce their willingness to invest in it, which in turn increases the chance they divorce—a sort of self-fulfilling prophecy. Also, changes in divorce laws have shifted much of the financial burden for the breakup of the marriage to women, making investment within the marriage (such as supporting a husband in medical school) a riskier proposition for them.

Men, in turn, may find marriage and parenthood a less attractive option **31** when they know that divorce is common, because they may face the loss of contact with their children if their marriage dissolves. Further, women's increased earnings and young men's declining financial well-being may have made women less dependent on men's financial support and made young men less able to provide it. Finally, public policies that support single mothers and changing attitudes toward sex outside of marriage, toward unmarried childbearing, and toward divorce have all been implicated in the decline in marriage. This brief list does not exhaust the possibilities, but merely mentions some of them.

So how can this trend be reversed? First, as evidence accumulates and **32** is communicated to individuals, some people will change their behavior as a result. Some will do so simply because of their new understanding of the costs and benefits, to them, of the choices involved. In addition, we have seen that attitudes frequently change toward behaviors that have been shown to have negative consequences. The attitude change then raises the social cost of the newly stigmatized behavior.

33   In addition, though, we as a society can pull some policy levers to encourage or discourage behaviors. Public policies that include asset tests (Medicaid is a good example) act to exclude the married, as do AFDC programs in most states. The "marriage penalty" in the tax code is another example. These and other policies reinforce or undermine the institution of marriage. If, as I have argued, marriage produces individuals who drink less, smoke less, abuse substances less, live longer, earn more, are wealthier, and have children who do better, we need to give more thought and effort to supporting this valuable social institution.

QUESTIONS FOR READING

1. What is Waite's subject?
2. What groups are healthiest and live the longest? What three reasons does Waite list to explain these health facts?
3. In what ways can marriage increase wealth? Who, when married, loses in hourly wages?
4. What may be the causes of increased productivity for married men?
5. What are some effects of single-parent families on children?
6. If marriage has such benefits, why are fewer people getting married and more getting divorced?

QUESTIONS FOR REASONING AND ANALYSIS

1. What is Waite's claim? Where does she state it?
2. How does the author help readers move through and see the parts of her argument?
3. How does the author defend her causal argument—that marriage itself is a cause of the financial, health, and contentment effects found in married people? Do you find her argument convincing? Why or why not?
4. What kind of evidence, primarily, does Waite provide? Is this evidence persuasive? Why or why not?

QUESTIONS FOR REFLECTION AND WRITING

1. Which statistic most surprises you? Why?
2. What can be done to increase marriage benefits for women, the ones who have least benefited?
3. Should the evidence Waite provides encourage people to choose marriage over divorce, cohabitation, or the single life? If so, why? If no, why not? (Do you have a sense that most adults know—or do not know—the data that Waite provides?)
4. What can be done to change the movement away from marriage? What are Waite's suggestions? What are yours?

GAY MARRIAGE BY JUDICIAL DECREE | STUART TAYLOR, JR.

A nonresident senior fellow at the Brookings Institute, Stuart Taylor is also a contributing editor to *Newsweek* and a columnist for the *National Journal*. His specialty is constitutional law, as is evident in the following article, published May 24, 2008, in the *National Journal*.

PREREADING QUESTION How should issues such as legalizing gay marriage be resolved?

I wholeheartedly support gay marriage. And I am happy for the many gays 1 who rejoiced at the California Supreme Court's 4–3 decision on May 15 ordering the state to stop calling committed gay couples "domestic partners" and start calling them "married."

So why do I see the decision as an unfortunate exercise in judicial imperi- 2 alism? Let me count the ways. Then I'll touch on how it could be a harbinger of the constitutional innovating that we might see if the next president engineers a strong liberal majority—a likelier prospect than a strong conservative majority—on the U.S. Supreme Court.

First, the California court's 121-page opinion was dishonest. This was most 3 evident in its ritual denial of the fact that it was usurping legislative power: "Our task . . . is not to decide whether we believe, as a matter of policy, that the officially recognized relationship of a same-sex couple should be designated a marriage rather than a domestic partnership . . . but instead only to determine whether the difference in the official names of the relationships violates the California Constitution."

This was a deeply disingenuous dodge, if not a bald-faced lie, to conceal 4 from gullible voters the fact that the decision was a raw exercise in judicial policy-making with no connection to the words or intent of the state constitution. It is inconceivable that anyone but a supporter of gay marriage "as a matter of policy" could have found in vague constitutional phrases such as "equal protection" a right to judicial invalidation of the marriage laws of every state and nation in the history of civilization.

To be sure, this was not exactly a bolt from the blue. The steady accretion of 5 both state and federal judicial power since the 1950s has left a malleable mass of hundreds of precedents straying ever-further from the original understanding of the constitutions and laws they purport to be "interpreting." This made it easy for the California court to take the leap—as the Massachusetts Supreme Judicial Court had done in 2004—to overriding the state's voters on gay marriage in the guise of enforcing "the ultimate expression of the people's will."

But President Franklin Roosevelt's indictment of the conservative U.S. 6 Supreme Court of the 1930s, which struck down much of the New Deal, fits here as well: "The Court . . . has improperly set itself up as . . . a superlegislature . . . reading into the Constitution words and implications which are not there, and which were never intended to be there."

The California court's majority descended into especially slick sophistry 7 when it suggested that the many gay-rights reforms that the state's elected branches had already adopted were not a reason to let the democratic process work but rather a mandate for judicial imposition of gay marriage. The message to voters in other states may be: If you give the judges an inch on gay rights, they will take a mile.

8   Also disingenuous was the majority's vague dismissal of the powerful argument by opponents of judicially imposed gay marriage that the made-up constitutional principle underlying the decision would also—if seriously applied—require the state to recognize polygamous and incestuous marriages among adults.

9   Chief Justice Ronald George's majority opinion exuded impatience bordering on contempt for the government by the people that is the foundation of our democratic system. California's voters and elected branches had already made great progress toward full legal equality for gay couples. They enjoyed all of the state-law rights and privileges of marriage except the name, which 61.4 percent of the voters had reserved for heterosexual couples in a 2000 ballot initiative. California's domestic-partnership laws were more generous to gays than the laws of almost all other states and almost all nations.

10   But to the majority, this domestic-partnership-but-not-gay-marriage compromise—also advocated by Barack Obama, Hillary Rodham Clinton, and John McCain—was "a mark of second-class citizenship." George analogized domestic partnerships to the "separate but equal" laws of the segregated South, including laws making interracial marriage a crime in some states until they were struck down by the U.S. Supreme Court in 1967. (The California court, admirably, had voided that state's ban on interracial marriage in 1948.) The chief justice thus insulted the voters—not to mention all three presidential candidates—and treated California's denial of official benediction as the legal equivalent of the Jim Crow South's system of grinding oppression.

11   This is not to deny the importance to many gay couples and their children of being officially recognized as "married." They should be treated as married. But to decree this by judicial fiat has large costs to democratic governance. Judicial power to override the deeply felt values of popular majorities should be used sparingly, to enforce clear constitutional commands or redress great injustices, not deployed whenever the judges think they can improve on the work of the elected branches or accelerate progressive reforms already under way.

12   Also troubling is the majority's eagerness to move beyond enforcing substantive rights into dictating what words the government must and must not use: Same-sex couples, the majority ruled, have a "fundamental right . . . to have their official family relationship accorded the same dignity, respect, and stature as that accorded to all other officially recognized family relationships."

13   This urge to regulate government speech resonates with the logic of those federal judges who have sought to strip "under God" out of the Pledge of Allegiance. Can court-ordered erasure of "In God We Trust" from U.S. currency, and perhaps a judicial rewrite of the National Anthem, be far behind?

14   It's true, as defenders of the California decision stress, that the justices there and elsewhere are politically astute enough to avoid flying too boldly into the teeth of public opinion; that Gov. Arnold Schwarzenegger has accepted the decision; and that California's voters will have a chance to override it, if they choose, through the state's ballot initiative process. All of this mitigates the affront to democracy. But it is still an affront, no less for the fact that three of the four majority justices are Republican appointees.

And while conservative judges are not above displacing democratic choices 15 with made-up constitutional law . . . that urge seems stronger on the Left.

Looking to the future of the U.S. Supreme Court, a sharp lurch to the 16 right seems unlikely. Even if McCain wins the presidency and ends up replacing liberals John Paul Stevens and Ruth Bader Ginsburg—who at 88 and 75, respectively, are the oldest justices—an enhanced Democratic majority in the Senate would no doubt block any strong conservative nominees to replace them.

A Democratic president, on the other hand, would probably have a free 17 hand to appoint the sort of justices envisioned by Obama, who opposed the nominations of Chief Justice John Roberts and Justice Samuel Alito. Obama has suggested that his criteria would not be fidelity to constitutional text or modesty in the use of judicial power, but rather "what is in the judge's heart" and "one's deepest values, one's core concerns, one's broader perspectives on how the world works, and the depth and breadth of one's empathy."

Based on the wish lists published by liberal judges and law professors, 18 justices who fit Obama's description might well invent federal constitutional rights not only to gay marriage but also to Medicaid abortions, physician-assisted suicide, human cloning, and perhaps free medical care, food, and housing for poor people; strike down the death penalty (as Stevens recently advocated) and laws making English the official language; ban publicly funded vouchers for poor kids to attend parochial schools; bless ever-more-aggressive use of racial and gender preferences; and more.

As a policy matter, this prospect worries me less than it does my con- 19 servative friends. I support legislative adoption not only of gay marriage but also of Medicaid abortions and some other policies on the liberal wish list. And I would not much miss the death penalty, "under God," or "In God We Trust."

But I am concerned about the gradual, relentless strangulation of Abraham 20 Lincoln's vision of ours as "government of the people, by the people, for the people," by judges who see constitutions not as binding law but as invitations for judicial rule.

I am also struck by the official list of "Attorneys for Respondent" join- 21 ing amicus briefs supporting gay marriage in the California case. It included more than 700 lawyers, law firms, and legal groups. Justice Antonin Scalia had a point in complaining 12 years ago, when his colleagues struck down a Colorado ballot initiative in the name of gay rights, that they were enforcing not the Constitution but rather "the views and values of the lawyer class from which the Court's members are drawn."

QUESTIONS FOR READING

1. What is the occasion for Taylor's article?
2. What is Taylor's response to the California Supreme Court's assertion that it was only testing language against the California Constitution?
3. What trend is the California Court a part of?

4. To what past laws did California's Chief Justice compare the California law denying the label of marriage to gay partners?

5. What changes does Taylor anticipate from a new Supreme Court with Obama as president? What is his objection to these changes if they are brought about by the judiciary?

QUESTIONS FOR REASONING AND ANALYSIS

1. What is Taylor's claim? What is his position on the California court decision?

2. Taylor also uses this decision as representative of a trend that includes the Supreme Court. What is his objection to the trend?

3. The author presents a list of changes that he predicts coming from a new Supreme Court altered by Obama's appointments. Does he present any evidence for his predictions? Is it appropriate for him to expect readers to agree with his speculations?

QUESTIONS FOR REFLECTION AND WRITING

1. What important decisions did the Supreme Court make in the twentieth century? Does this history suggest that some civil rights changes will need to come from the courts? Why or why not?

2. How should gay rights issues be resolved, if not in the courts?

3. Should gays be allowed to marry? Why or why not?

JUSTICE DELIVERED | RICHARD JUST

Richard Just is the Managing Editor of *The New Republic*. His response to the California Supreme Court's decision appeared in *The New Republic* on June 11, 2008.

PREREADING QUESTION What does Just's title suggest to you about his position?

WHY CALIFORNIA GOT IT RIGHT

1   It wasn't exactly a shock when conservatives greeted last week's decision by the California Supreme Court legalizing gay marriage with their usual denunciations of "activist judges" and the "imperial judiciary." And it's easy to understand why conservatives dislike court-imposed progress on gay rights, since most would prefer that progress on gay rights didn't happen at all. More interesting has been the reaction of liberals who do support gay rights but who have nevertheless sharply criticized

the decision. The *Washington Post* editorial page, for instance, called the rul-
ling "an unnecessary bout of judicial micromanagement," while, in this issue
of *The New Republic,* my colleague Jeffrey Rosen questions "the wisdom of
imposing gay marriage by judicial fiat." According to this view, progress on
gay rights should take place through state legislatures and governors, not
through the courts.

Liberals who advance this argument are essentially making two points—   2
one strategic, the other normative. First, they worry that securing gay marriage
via judicial intervention will lead to a public backlash. Second, they contend
that there is something undemocratic about judges reinterpreting state constitutions to arrive at conclusive judgments on hot-button social issues. Both
arguments carry a certain logical appeal. But neither, upon closer examination,
is particularly persuasive.

Take the strategic argument first. Four years ago, when Massachusetts   3
began marrying gay couples after a ruling by its state supreme court, there
was plenty of similar hand-wringing about the alleged backlash to come. But,
in a piece she wrote for *TNR* at the time, journalist E. J. Graff predicted that
the decision was unlikely to spark a backlash. In fact, she wrote that it was likely
to solidify an emerging consensus in favor of gay marriage. That's because gay
marriage is much more threatening in theory than in practice. Conservative
arguments against gay marriage rest on dire predictions about how it will tear
apart the country's social fabric. Once gay marriage is a reality and those predictions don't come true, the arguments against it start to look silly at best,
cruel at worst. E. J.'s argument was vindicated in Massachusetts. In February
2004, according to *The Boston Globe,* a majority of residents (53 percent)
opposed gay marriage; by March 2005, just ten months after gay marriages
began taking place, a majority (56 percent) supported them. Why did so many
people change their minds? I'm guessing many went through the same evolution as the Massachusetts legislator who explained why he switched sides on
same-sex marriage in the years after the court made it legal: "I couldn't take
away the happiness those people have been able to enjoy."

What about the backlash outside of Massachusetts? What about all those   4
state constitutional amendments that passed in 2004 banning gay marriage?
There's no doubt that the Massachusetts decision helped to motivate anti-
gay marriage activists in the rest of the country. But the idea that gay marriage opponents were angered primarily by the way that decision was reached
rather than the substance of the outcome is absurd. If gay marriage had arrived
in Massachusetts at the behest of state legislators rather than judges, would
gay marriage opponents in the rest of the country really have been any less
annoyed? Of course not. No matter how gay marriage comes about, it's going
to anger and discomfit some people. The idea that such people would be mol-
lified by a different process seems more than a little unrealistic.

But it's the normative objections to the California decision that bother me   5
most—the idea put forward by some commentators that winning gay marriage through the courts rather than through the legislative process is somehow a form of cheating. Is progress in a democracy somehow purer or more
legitimate if it does not involve the judiciary? I can understand the appeal

of this idea: Let the voters arrive at a consensus themselves; let the politicians do the voters' bidding; this is how democracy is supposed to work—end of story. But this is not how democracy works, at least not our democracy. Progress does not always happen perfectly in our country, and, if we demand that progress only happen in certain ways, we set ourselves up for a situation in which progress cannot happen at all. Most dramatic leaps forward in our country's history—and the gay rights revolution is one such leap—have happened through a combination of forces. They have neither been imposed solely from above nor driven solely from below. They have generally involved the work of courts, of legislators, of governors, and of faceless bureaucrats. Because their jobs carry different responsibilities, these actors rarely pull in precisely the same direction, and, on certain questions, some may rightly prove more influential than others. But to argue that judges have no role to play in one of the key issues of our time—to pretend that state constitutions, not to mention centuries of accumulated legal precedent, have nothing to say on the question of whether it is permissible for government to treat gays and lesbians as second-class citizens—defies any rational understanding of the way a constitutional democracy is supposed to work.

6   The California Supreme Court did not rule in a vacuum. For one thing, its decision comes in the midst of a generation-long shift in the way Americans view homosexuality. What was once viewed as a mental disorder is today widely recognized as a normal human attribute. More concretely, the court did not act in a political vacuum. The legislature has twice passed bills to legalize gay marriage, and one of the state's largest cities had been performing gay marriages before the courts ordered it to stop. What the California Supreme Court was doing last week was not judicial imperialism. It was simply taking a moral consensus that is clearly emerging, and applying it to the state's constitution.

7   Indeed, if you read the 120-page-plus decision itself, you can see the powerful and rather simple thinking behind what the court did. Critics have suggested that the decision is overly expansive or poorly reasoned. In fact, its logic is relatively straightforward. First, the court established that an implicit right to marry has long been recognized in California law. Then it established that inherent in this right to marry is a right to the dignity and respect that comes with marriage—a right that California's "domestic partnership" law could not fully afford. The court then distinguished between two standards of judicial review: a "rational basis" standard, which allows the court to strike down a measure only if it serves no legitimate purpose; and a "strict scrutiny" standard, which the court applies to laws concerning "suspect classifications," such as race and gender, and which allows the court to strike down a measure if the state cannot show that it is needed to achieve a compelling interest. Does sexual orientation constitute a suspect classification? It is not exactly analogous to race or gender, but it is comparable in two key respects: First, people do not choose to be gay, just as people do not choose to be black or female. And second, discrimination against gays and lesbians has been both widespread and institutional throughout American history. None of this

should be controversial, and it is exactly what the court concluded. Having established that sexual orientation constitutes a suspect classification and is therefore subject to strict scrutiny, it was relatively easy for the court to conclude that the state had no compelling interest in excluding gays and lesbians from marriage. After all, the supposition that denying marriage rights to gays will somehow preserve the institution's dignity for everyone else is hardly a persuasive argument.

Anyone who has ever looked at a poll on gay issues that disaggregates   8 the responses by age knows how the story of gay marriage is going to end. What no one knows is when it is going to end. Had the California Supreme Court let the state's political process grind forward—its obligation to interpret the state's constitution be damned—how long would it have taken for the state's gays and lesbians to win their marriage rights? Perhaps it would have taken only a year. But what if it had taken ten years? Or even a generation? Meanwhile, stuck waiting patiently would have been the million-plus gay and lesbian Californians who want to live as first-class citizens, not in some theoretical, distant day to come, when the maddeningly slow work of legislators and governors finally delivers the outcome via means that we might regard as ever so slightly more democratic—but now, right now.

If courts, by interpreting state or federal constitutions in light of the coun-   9 try's changing mores on homosexuality, can hasten the day when gays and lesbians throughout the country fully enjoy the fundamental rights they are owed, then I, for one, am not going to quibble. Yes, if I were drawing things up from scratch, I might marginally prefer to have gay marriage enacted by legislatures, not by courts. But history is not drawn up from scratch. And, sometimes, waiting for the perfect process means waiting much too long.

QUESTIONS FOR READING

1. For what two reasons do those who support gay marriage object to California's Supreme Court decision?

2. How does Just respond to the first type of objection?

3. What is his challenge to the second type of objection?

4. How has the thinking changed on gays? What, according to polls broken down by age, will be the final decision on gay marriage?

5. What is meant, legally, by a "suspect classification"? Why does this allow for "strict scrutiny"?

6. In the author's view, how do the courts' decisions contribute to, rather than work against, democracy?

QUESTIONS FOR REASONING AND ANALYSIS

1. Just offers two responses to the strategic objection: People adjust to the ruling when they see that it really does not harm them, and those who oppose gay marriage will do so regardless of the process by which it comes about. That is,

anti-gay activists are not responding to the process but to an objection to the outcome. Do you agree with Just on these two points? Does the evidence, and his reasoning from it, seem reasonable to you? Why or why not?

2. Just rebuts the normative argument in two ways. He points out that progress does not always "happen perfectly"; to demand this is to ignore reality. Secondly, he provides information about the activity relevant to gay rights in California to argue that the court did not act in a vacuum. Is this part of his argument convincing? Why or why not?

3. Who has the more convincing argument, Taylor or Just, regardless of your position on gay marriage? Can you evaluate the logic and evidence of each argument without your views interfering? (Why is this so difficult to do?)

ABOLISH MARRIAGE | MICHAEL KINSLEY

A member of the bar with a law degree from Harvard, Michael Kinsley is a former editor of both *Harper's* and *The New Republic*. He is the founding editor (1996) of *Slate*, the online magazine, has been a cohost of CNN's *Crossfire*, and currently writes a weekly column for the *Washington Post*. The following column appeared in the *Post*, July 3, 2003.

PREREADING QUESTIONS What are the key issues in the debate over gay marriage? What are gay marriage proponents seeking? What are social conservatives seeking?

1   Critics and enthusiasts of *Lawrence* v. *Texas*, last week's Supreme Court decision invalidating state anti-sodomy laws, agree on one thing: The next argument is going to be about gay marriage. As Justice Antonin Scalia noted in his tart dissent, it follows from the logic of *Lawrence*. Mutually consenting sex with the person of your choice in the privacy of your own home is now a basic right of American citizenship under the Constitution. This does not mean that the government must supply it or guarantee it. But the government cannot forbid it, and the government also should not discriminate against you for choosing to exercise a basic right of citizenship. Offering an institution as important as marriage to male-female couples only is exactly this kind of discrimination. Or so the gay rights movement will now argue. Persuasively, I think.

2   Opponents of gay rights will resist mightily, although they have been in retreat for a couple of decades. General anti-gay sentiments are now considered a serious breach of civic etiquette, even in anti-gay circles. The current line of defense, which probably won't hold either, is between social toleration of homosexuals and social approval of homosexuality. Or between accepting the reality that people are gay, even accepting that gays are people, and endorsing something called "the gay agenda." Gay marriage, the opponents will argue, would cross this line. It would make homosexuality respectable and, worse, normal. Gays are welcome to exist all they want, and to do their inexplicable thing if they must, but they shouldn't expect a government stamp of approval.

It's going to get ugly. And then it's going to get boring. So we have two 3 options here. We can add gay marriage to the short list of controversies— abortion, affirmative action, the death penalty—that are so frozen and ritu- alistic that debates about them are more like kabuki performances than intellectual exercises. Or we can think outside the box. There is a solution that ought to satisfy both camps, and may not be a bad idea even apart from the gay marriage controversy.

That solution is to end the institution of marriage. Or rather (he hastens to 4 clarify, dear) the solution is to end the institution of government-sanctioned marriage. Or, framed to appeal to conservatives: End the government monop- oly on marriage. Wait, I've got it: Privatize marriage. These slogans all mean the same thing. Let churches and other religious institutions continue to offer marriage ceremonies. Let department stores and casinos get into the act if they want. Let each organization decide for itself what kinds of couples it wants to offer marriage to. Let couples celebrate their union in any way they choose and consider themselves married whenever they want. Let others be free to consider them not married, under rules these others may prefer. And, yes, if three people want to get married, or one person wants to marry herself, and someone else wants to conduct a ceremony and declare them married, let 'em. If you and your government aren't implicated, what do you care?

In fact, there is nothing to stop any of this from happening now. And a lot 5 of it does happen. But only certain marriages get certified by the government. So, in the United States we are about to find ourselves in a strange situation where the principal demand of a liberation movement is to be included in the red tape of a government bureaucracy. Having just gotten state governments out of their bedrooms, gays now want these governments back in. Meanwhile, social-conservative anti-gays, many of them southerners, are calling on the government in Washington to trample states' rights and nationalize the rules of marriage, if necessary, to prevent gays from getting what they want. The Senate majority leader, Bill Frist of Tennessee, responded to the Supreme Court's *Lawrence* decision by endorsing a constitutional amendment, no less, against gay marriage.

If marriage were an entirely private affair, all the disputes over gay mar- 6 riage would become irrelevant. Gay marriage would not have the official sanc- tion of government, but neither would straight marriage. There would be official equality between the two, which is the essence of what gays want and are entitled to. And if the other side is sincere in saying that its concern is not what people do in private but government endorsement of a gay "lifestyle" or "agenda," that problem goes away too.

Yes, yes, marriage is about more than sleeping arrangements. There are 7 children, there are finances, there are spousal job benefits such as health insur- ance and pensions. In all of these areas, marriage is used as a substitute for other factors that are harder to measure, such as financial dependence or devo- tion to offspring. It would be possible to write rules that measure the real factors at stake and leave marriage out of the matter. Regarding children and finances, people can set their own rules, as many already do. None of this would be easy.

Marriage functions as what lawyers call a "bright line," which saves the trouble of trying to measure a lot of amorphous factors. You're either married or you're not. Once marriage itself becomes amorphous, who-gets-the-kids and who-gets-health-care become trickier questions.

8   So, sure, there are some legitimate objections to the idea of privatizing marriage. But they don't add up to a fatal objection. Especially when you consider that the alternative is arguing about gay marriage until death do us part.

QUESTIONS FOR READING

1.   What will the next argument be about? What ruling will bring on this argument? What about the ruling invites the argument?

2.   Who will win the argument, in Kinsley's view?

3.   According to the author, where are we in the "tug-of-war" over gay rights? Where would allowing gay marriage put us in the battle?

4.   What is the author's solution to end the argument?

5.   What is ironic about gays fighting for the right to marry? What is ironic about conservatives seeking a constitutional amendment against gay marriage?

6.   What problems would emerge if governments stopped sanctioning marriage altogether? Are these problems insurmountable, in the author's view?

QUESTIONS FOR REASONING AND ANALYSIS

1.   What is Kinsley's claim? Where does he state it?

2.   When Kinsley writes that the argument over gay marriage will "get boring," what does he mean? How does his comparison to kabuki performances or to debates over abortion or the death penalty illustrate his point here?

3.   How does Kinsley seek to convince both sides of the argument that his solution should please them?

4.   The author anticipates counterarguments in his last two paragraphs. How effective is his rebuttal?

5.   Analyze the essay's tone. How serious do you think Kinsley is in presenting his solution to the argument over gay marriage? If he does not think his solution is viable, then why is he proposing it? What is his purpose in writing?

QUESTIONS FOR REFLECTION AND WRITING

1.   What is your reaction to Kinsley's proposal? Is the best solution to get government out of certifying marriage? If we wanted to "think outside the box," could we solve the other problems—of finances, child custody, and so forth—if we wanted to? How would you support the proposal or challenge it?

2.   Is there any hope of finding common ground on this issue, or are we doomed to live with another issue that generates only ritualistic "debates"? Do you have any new suggestions for thinking outside the box on social issues that are currently so divisive?

GAY ASIAN-AMERICAN MALE SEEKS HOME | CHONG-SUK HAN

A doctoral candidate in the social welfare program at the University of Washington, Chong-suk Han currently teaches in the sociology department at Temple University. While living in Seattle, he served on its Human Rights Commission. The following article was published in the September/October 2005 issue of the *Gay and Lesbian Review Worldwide.*

PREREADING QUESTIONS What does Han's title remind you of—where might you find such a line? What makes it a clever title?

"The West thinks of itself as masculine—big guns, big industry, big money—so the East is feminine—weak, delicate, poor . . . but good at art, and full of inscrutable wisdom—the feminine mystique . . . I am an Oriental. And being an Oriental, I could never be completely a man."

—Song Linling in *M Butterfly*

In the critically acclaimed play *M Butterfly,* by David Henry Hwang, the main 1 character, Song Linling, explains his ability to fool a French lieutenant into believing that he was a woman for nearly two decades, a feat based not on his mastery of deception but on the lieutenant's inability to see him as anything other than a woman. For decades, the mainstream media have usually portrayed Asian men as meek, asexual houseboy types or as sexual deviants of some kind. When it comes to attitudes about sex, Asian-American men have generally been portrayed as being on the "traditional" or "conservative" side of the spectrum. Recently the magazine *Details*, which caters to "hip, young, urban males," prominently featured an item entitled "Gay or Asian," and challenged its readers to ascertain whether a given man was, in fact, gay or Asian. Interestingly enough, while the broader Asian-American community mounted a protest against the presentation of Asian men as "gay," the larger gay community stood silently by.

   "The Orient was almost a European invention," observed Edward Said 2 (1978), "and had been since antiquity a place of romance, exotic beings, haunting memories and landscapes, remarkable experiences." These are all images that happen to be female evocations in the Western mind, and indeed the association between the Orient and the feminine can be traced back to ancient times. The West's view of itself as the embodiment of the male principle was further justified by—and undoubtedly served to justify—Europe's subordination of much of Asia starting in the 18th century: its "masculine thrust" upon the continent, if you will.

   This discourse of domination at the level of civilizations has played itself 3 out in countless ways over the centuries. For men of Asian descent who have resided in the United States, this has often meant their exclusion from the labor market of "masculine" jobs and the denial of leadership positions in their communities and even in their families. The cultural emasculation of Asian men in America has produced what Eng (2001) has called "racial castration." This in turn has led to the image of Asian men as largely sexless or undersexed—but this hasn't prevented another stereotype from arising, that of Asian men as sexual deviants, helplessly lusting after white women who don't want them. But more often they fade into the sexual background—even as Asian women are often portrayed as highly desirable, notably to sexually competent white men.

4   The situation for gay men of Asian descent in the U.S. has been intimately tied to the same processes that led non-gay Asian men to be racialized and marginalized by mainstream society. While straight men have been able to function within the growing Asian-American community, gay Asian men continue to be marginalized both by the dominant society and by the Asian communities. If anything, they've been rendered even more invisible by a new cultural formation that stresses "family values" while it perpetuates the image of Asians as "America's model minority"—an image that denies the very existence of gay Asian-Americans. Studies on gender and sexuality have largely ignored racial minorities in their discussions. Given this invisibility, it is not surprising that so little has been written about the process of identity formation for gay Asian men. What is known about gay Asian-American men has come from the small but growing number of literary and artistic works produced by gay Asian men, as well as the literature on HIV/AIDS in the Asian-American community.

5   In Chay Yew's acclaimed play *Porcelain*, both the Chinese and the gay communities deny "ownership" of John Lee when he's charged with murdering his white lover in a London lavatory. In a particularly trenchant scene, members of the Chinese community exclaim, "He is not one of us!"—a sentiment that's echoed in the gay community as well. Choi et al. (1998) argues that marginalization by both of these communities may lead to low self-esteem among gay Asian men and contribute to the increasing percentage of gay Asian men who engage in unsafe sex and seroconvert.

6   In his essay "China Doll," Tony Ayers (1999) discusses his sense of being outside the gay mainstream due to his Chinese ethnicity. In addition to discussing the overt forms of racism—such as gay classified ads that specifically state, "no fats, no femmes, no Asians," and being told by other gay men that they are "not into Asians"—Ayers describes some of the more subtle forms of racism, such as that of "rice queens" who desire Asian men purely for their exotic eroticism. What rice queens are often attracted to in Asian men is an idealized notion of a passive, docile, submissive—in short, a feminized—lover, eager to please his virile white man.

7   It is indeed striking how the image of gay white men has been transformed from that of "sissy nelly" to "macho stud" over the past few decades, but no such transformation has occurred where gay API (Asian and Pacific Island) men are concerned. Gay white men are often portrayed as rugged, chiseled studs. But the masculinization of gay white men has been coupled with a feminization of gay API men. When a white man and an API man are presented together in a sexual situation, the former is almost always the sexual dominator while the latter is submissive. For better or worse, many gay Asian men seem to have accepted this stereotype, often participating in their own exotification and playing up their "feminine" allure.

What's more, Asian men themselves have also bought into the gay 8 Western notion of what is desirable. Ayers explains that "The sexually marginalized Asian man who has grown up in the West or is Western in his thinking is often invisible in his own fantasies. [Their] sexual daydreams are populated by handsome Caucasian men with lean, hard Caucasian bodies." In a survey of gay Asian men in San Francisco, Choi et al. (1995) found that nearly seventy percent of gay Asian men indicate a preference for white men. More damaging to the gay Asian population is that most of these men seem to be competing for the attention of a limited number of "rice queens." This competition hinders the formation of a unified gay Asian community and further acts to splinter those who should be seen as natural allies.

Not surprisingly, many gay Asian men report feeling inadequate within 9 the larger gay community that stresses a Eurocentric image of physical beauty. Given these feelings of inadequacy, gay Asian men may suffer from low self-esteem and actively pursue the company of white men in order to feel accepted. In addition to seeking the company of white men, the obsession with white beauty leads gay Asian men to reject their cultural roots. For example, Chuang (1999) writes about how he tried desperately to avoid anything related to his Chinese heritage and his attempts to transform his "shamefully slim Oriental frame . . . into a more desirable Western body." Other manifestations of attempting to hide one's heritage may include bleaching one's hair or even the wearing of blue contact lenses.

The fear of rejection from family and friends may be more acute for 10 gay Asians than for other groups. While some have noted the cultural factors associated with Confucianism and the strong family values associated with Asian-Americans, these explanations fall short, given that many Asian-American communities (particularly Filipino and South Asian) are not rooted in a Confucian ethic. Instead, the compounded feeling of fear may have more to do with their status as racial and ethnic minorities within the U.S., which isolates these groups and increases the importance of the family as a nexus of support. By coming out to their families, Asian-American gays and lesbians risk losing the support of their family and community and facing the sometimes hostile larger society on their own. Unlike gay white men, who can find representation and support in the gay community, gay Asian men often do not have the option of finding a new community outside of the ethnic one they would be leaving behind. In fact, there is some evidence that gay Asian men who are less integrated into the Asian-American community may be at higher risk for HIV/AIDS due to a lack of available support networks. In a study with gay Asian men, Choi et al. (1998) found that gay Asian men often feel that their families would not support their sexual orientation, which leads them to remain closeted until a later age than is typical for white men.

In the absence of a vocabulary to describe their experiences, gay Asian 11 men and women have had to create new words and concepts to define their identity. Within the past few years, a number of gay Asian groups and activists have challenged the Western notions of beauty and questioned the effects of these notions on the gay Asian community. Eric Reyes (1996) asks, "which do you really want—rice queen fantasies at your bookstore or freedom rings at the checkout stand of your local Asian market?" In posing this question, Reyes asks us where we should begin to build our home in this place we call America, in the "heterosexual male-dominated America, white gay male–centered Queer America, the marginalized People of Color America, or our often-romanticized Asian America?" It is this continuing attempt to find a gay Asian space that lies at the heart of one group's quest for a place in the American sun.

REFERENCES

Ayers, T. "China Doll: The experience of being a gay Chinese Australian," in *Multicultural Queer: Australian Narratives,* by P. Jackson and G. Sullivan (eds.). Haworth Press, 1999.

Choi K. H., et al. (1998). "HIV prevention among Asian and Pacific Islander American men who have sex with men." *AIDS Education and Prevention,* 1998.

Choi K. H., et al. (1995). "High HIV risk among gay Asian and Pacific Islander men in San Francisco." *AIDS.* 9.

Chuang, K. "Using chopsticks to eat steak," in *Multicultural Queer: Australian Narratives,* by P. Jackson and G. Sullivan (eds.). Haworth Press, 1999.

Eng, D. *Racial Castration: Managing Masculinity in Asian America.* Duke University Press, 2001.

Reyes, Eric E. "Strategies for Queer Asian and Pacific Islander Spaces," in *Asian American Sexualities,* Russell Leong (ed.). Routledge, 1996.

Said, Edward. *Orientalism.* Vintage Books, 1978.

QUESTIONS FOR READING

1. What has been the Western view of the East, the Orient, for a long time?

2. What has been the result of this image of the East for Asian-American men? How have they been treated? How are they "viewed"?

3. What has contributed to the "invisibility" of gay Asian-American men?

4. What can happen to these men who are excluded by both the Asian community and the gay community? How can they be viewed by other gays—what can they be desired for? How does this affect their view of themselves?

QUESTIONS FOR REASONING AND ANALYSIS

1. Han opens his paper with a quotation from *M Butterfly* and then discusses the play in his first paragraph. What does he gain by the reference as an opening?

2. What is Han's claim? What is the central point of his study?

3. Analyze Han's style and tone. What does he gain from this approach?

4. Han's analysis of problems facing gay Asian-American men is based on sociological theories; does that come through? Does that scholarly perspective strengthen his argument? If so, how?

QUESTIONS FOR REFLECTION AND WRITING

1.   Can you relate to the sadness and emptiness experienced by anyone who feels "homeless," who cannot find a community or who lacks family support? If so, does your empathy extend to gays who are not fully accepted into that community? Why or why not?

2.   Were you aware that gay Asian-American men may feel "homeless," or quite literally be without a home? (Were you aware that there are gays among the Asian community?) If Han has given you some new knowledge, what is your reaction to it? Would you recommend this essay to others to read? Why or why not?

3.   Would you accept—or have you accepted—gay or lesbian members of your family? Why or why not?

THE OVERLOOKED VICTIMS OF AIDS | JUDITH D. AUERBACH

A sociologist and former college professor, Judith Auerbach is now vice president for public policy at the American Foundation for AIDS Research. Auerbach has published on a variety of topics, including AIDS, health research, and family policy and gender. The following column, published in the *Washington Post* October 14, 2004, deplores our lack of awareness of who is suffering from AIDS.

PREREADING QUESTIONS Who, now, is most often becoming infected with HIV/AIDS? Do you know how most women become infected with AIDS?

In last week's vice presidential debate, moderator Gwen Ifill talked about 1 the disproportionate impact of HIV-AIDS on African American women and asked what role the government should play in slowing the growth of this domestic epidemic. Both candidates displayed an alarming ignorance of the reality of the crisis in the United States, choosing instead to focus their comment on AIDS in Africa, which Ifill had explicitly asked them not to do.

What is inexcusable among the nation's top policymakers is a persistent 2 problem in the general public as well: a failure to recognize that AIDS now disproportionately affects women.

According to the Centers for Disease Control and Prevention, the propor- 3 tion of all AIDS cases reported among adolescent and adult women in the United States has more than tripled since 1986. AIDS is the fourth-leading cause of death among women in this country between the ages of 25 and 44, and is the *leading* cause of death among African American women ages 25 to 34. Black women represent about two-thirds of all new HIV infections among adult and adolescent females.

Globally, about half of the 12,000 people ages 15 to 49 infected every 4 day are women. Sixty-two percent of those ages 15 to 24 living with HIV-AIDS are girls and women. In South Africa, that figure climbs to 77 percent. Most women worldwide, including in the United States, acquire HIV infection through heterosexual intercourse.

Why is this "feminization of AIDS" occurring? The answer lies in the com- 5 plex ways that sex and gender intersect, conferring increased vulnerability to

HIV infection on women and girls. Biological, sociological and political factors interact differently for women and men, leaving women more susceptible to viral transmission, more distant from prevention and care services, farther away from accurate information, and far more vulnerable to human rights violations. Here are some of the specifics:

- Women are more vulnerable to HIV infection than men. The physiology of the female genital tract makes women twice as likely to acquire HIV from men as vice versa. Among adolescent girls, this effect is even more pronounced.

- Poverty is correlated with higher rates of HIV infection all over the world. Globally, more than half of the people living in poverty are women. In the United States, nearly 30 percent are African American women.

- Lack of education is associated with higher HIV infection rates. Girls in developing countries are less likely to complete secondary education than boys, and almost twice as likely to be illiterate.

- Early marriage is a significant risk factor for HIV among women and girls. In developing countries, a majority of sexually active girls ages 15 to 19 are married. Married adolescent girls tend to have higher HIV infection rates than their sexually active unmarried peers.

- A significant risk factor for HIV infection is violence, to which women are more susceptible in virtually all societies. In a South African study, for example, women who were beaten or dominated by their partners were 48 percent more likely to become infected than women who lived in non-violent households.

- Rape of women has been used as a tool for subjugation and so-called ethnic cleansing in war and conflict situations. Of the 250,000 women raped during the Rwandan genocide, about 70 percent of the survivors are HIV-positive.

6   The experience of women and girls in the HIV-AIDS epidemic in the United States and around the world highlights how social arrangements, cultural norms, laws, policies and institutions contribute to the unequal status of women in society and to the spread of disease. Together they undermine the capacity of women and girls to exercise power over their own lives and to control the circumstances that increase their vulnerability to HIV infection, particularly in the context of sexual relationships. For African American women, gender inequalities are exacerbated by persistent racism.

7   It is only when this unhealthy mix is acknowledged and addressed—particularly by the highest levels of government—that we will be able to stem the alarming increase of HIV-AIDS among more than half the world's population.

QUESTIONS FOR READING

1. What do politicians, and Americans generally, seem not to know about AIDS?
2. How do most women become infected?

3. For what group of Americans is AIDS the leading cause of death?

4. What are six specifics about women's experiences that make them more vulnerable to HIV infection? Explain in your own words.

QUESTIONS FOR REASONING AND ANALYSIS

1. What is Auerbach's purpose in writing? How does she want to affect readers?

2. What is the author's claim?

3. How would you describe Auerbach's style—her sentence structure and word choice?

4. What is effective about the use of bullets in this essay?

5. Is the author's style effective for her subject and purpose? Explain.

QUESTIONS FOR REFLECTION AND WRITING

1. Were you aware of the "feminization of AIDS"? Does this surprise? Shock? Make you wonder how this shift has happened? Explain.

2. Which statistic is most shocking to you? Why?

3. Which one of the six experiences correlating with increased risk for AIDS is most surprising to you? Why?

4. What should be done to address this serious world health problem? If you were the president's "AIDS czar," what specific programs would you seek to put into place in this country? Around the world? Explain your cause/effect reasoning.

WHY GENDER MATTERS | LEONARD SAX

A family physician and psychologist, Leonard Sax is the author of *Why Gender Matters* (2005) and *Boys Adrift* (2007). A strong supporter of single-sex schools, in recognition of the different ways that boys and girls learn, Sax is a frequent guest on radio and television talk shows. The following piece is a passage from *Why Gender Matters*.

PREREADING QUESTION Is it possible to embrace the concept that anatomy is not destiny and to open more doors to women to achieve alongside men and, at the same time, recognize that gender can influence the ways we grow and learn and interact with others?

For many teenage boys, sex is an impersonal urge that has its own agenda, 1 not necessarily connected to a relationship with another person. That's not news. Teenage boys have always been that way. For most teenage girls, a satisfying and fulfilling sexual experience is most likely to occur in the context of a loving and mutually caring relationship. That's not news, either. What's changed?

The fundamental change that has occurred over the past thirty years is a 2 change from the female paradigm to the male paradigm. Thirty years ago, a boy usually had at least to give lip service to the notion of being in love if he expected a young woman to be sexually intimate with him. No longer. That's the significance of the hook-up replacing the romantic relationship as the primary sexual mode in teenage culture.

3   That change has led to a fundamental transformation in the dynamics of sexual activity. In engineering terms, it's a change from linear dynamics to zero-order dynamics. The likelihood of sex is no longer related to the closeness of the relationship. It used to be the case—as recently as ten or fifteen years ago—that the more serious the relationship was between a girl and a boy, the more likely they were to have sex. That correspondence no longer holds. A recent survey by the Kaiser Family Foundation found that teenagers nationwide are now just as likely to engage in sex during a casual "hook-up" as they are in a serious, committed relationship. The major difference in sexual behavior in an ongoing relationship compared with a hook-up, in this study, is *not* in the type of sex the teenagers engage in, but only in whether or not a condom is used. Condoms are used more often in a "hook-up" than in a committed relationship. (A New York school stirred up controversy when teachers proposed passing out fruit-flavored condoms, to make the experience of fellatio more agreeable for the girls.)[1]

4   What's the result? Barbara Dafoe Whitehead concluded that the effect of today's "sex-drenched teen culture . . . is not to help young people learn how to choose a future life partner" (that's an understatement). At best, it helps them only to "manage their sex lives."[2] But what good is a sex life without any emotional connection?

5   Dr. Drew Pinsky recently made an important observation about gender differences in hooking up. Both girls and boys are usually partly or totally drunk when they hook up. . . . Dr. Pinsky has found that girls and boys give completely different reasons *why* they get drunk before they hook up. Boys like to get drunk because it slows down their sexual response, allows them to relax, and decreases the likelihood of premature ejaculation. Girls like to get drunk because it numbs the experience for them, making it less embarrassing and less emotionally painful.[3]

6   Another change: kids are having sex earlier than before. The National Longitudinal Study of Adolescent Health is the largest study ever conducted of teenage behavior in the United States. Over ten thousand teenagers—a representative sample of kids from cities, suburbs, and rural areas, rich and poor, Asian and white and black and Hispanic—were periodically interviewed about everything from cigarette smoking to sex to thoughts of suicide. In 2002 the doctors running the study reported that there has been a "dramatic trend toward early initiation of sex." In 1988, 11 percent of adolescent females fourteen years of age and younger reported having had sexual intercourse; a decade later it was 19 percent. In other words, about one girl in five age fourteen and younger has now had sexual intercourse.[4] A separate study, published in 2003 by the National Campaign to Prevent Teen Pregnancy, independently arrived at the same conclusion: among girls age fourteen or younger, one in five has had sexual intercourse.[5] This study also found that most parents of sexually active daughters are NOT aware that their daughters are having

sex. "Parents are overwhelmingly clueless about their kids' sexual experiences and knowledge," agrees journalist Hall. "Most teens [interviewed by Hall] said their parents have no idea what their real sex lives are like."[6]

CLUELESS

Pediatrician Thomas Young and psychologist Rick Zimmerman wanted to 7 find out just how much parents know about what their kids are really doing. They asked 140 middle school students and their parents about smoking cigarettes, smoking marijuana, drinking alcoholic beverages, and having sexual intercourse.

Question for parents: Does your child smoke cigarettes? 12% of parents said
  yes.
Question for the kids: Do you smoke cigarettes? 43% of students said yes.

Question for parents: Has your child smoked marijuana? 3% of parents said
  yes.
Question for the kids: Have you smoked marijuana? 34% of kids said yes.

Question for parents: Does your child drink alcoholic beverages? 5% of parents said yes.
Question for the kids: Do you drink alcoholic beverages? 49% of students said
  yes.

Question for parents: Has your child had sexual intercourse? 2% of parents
  said yes.
Question for the kids: Have you had sexual intercourse? 52% of kids said yes.

The authors titled their report "Clueless: Parental Knowledge of Risk 8 Behaviors of Middle School Students."[7] It's not hard to see why.

ARE BOYS HUMAN?

Three big changes have occurred since you and I were in middle school 9 and high school:

- Girls and boys are engaging in sexual activities earlier than they used to;
- Girls and boys who are going steady today are no more and no less likely to have sexual intercourse than are girls and boys who are just hooking up;
- Oral sex has become the most common mode of sexual interaction.

Most of the articles and books about these changes in teenage sexual 10 behavior have focused on the harm done to teenage girls. There's no question that teenage girls are the most obvious victims. A girl is more likely to feel used and abused after a typical twenty-first-century sexual encounter. In the most common type of hook-up, oral sex, the girl is far more likely to be servicing the boy than the other way around. And if the hook-up progresses to sexual intercourse, girls bear the risk of an unwanted pregnancy.

11   The impersonality of-twenty-first-century adolescent sex victimizes girls. No argument there. But to focus only on that side of the story misses the harm done to boys. What harm? you may ask. How does impersonal sex harm boys?

12   I see plenty of harm. By the time a heterosexual young man is in his early twenties, he will rely on his girlfriend or his wife to be his primary emotional caregiver.[8] And that reliance only becomes greater as he moves through adult life. For the great majority of heterosexual adult men, the wife or girlfriend is the man's most important source of emotional support. Straight men who don't have a wife or girlfriend are substantially more likely to become seriously depressed, commit suicide, or die from illness.[9] It's not unreasonable to conclude that a heterosexual man's happiness and maybe even his life expectancy depend on his ability to establish a sound relationship with a woman he loves and who loves him.

13   Women are different in that respect. Women as a rule have more diverse support systems than men do. Husbands and boyfriends matter to them, sure, but so do their girlfriends, coworkers, and (often) family, especially a sister or mom. One reason for this has to do with the difference between female-female friendship and male-male camaraderie. . . . Close friendships between girls are usually intimate and personal. Friendships between boys are usually built around shared activities. David may have a great time playing video games with Juan, but that doesn't mean that David will confide in Juan about how he feels when his parents get divorced.

14   So here's the irony. Even though many of us think of teenage romance as something that interests girls more than it interests boys, it's the boys, ultimately, who will have greater need for an intimate and durable romantic relationship in their lives.

PLAYING A ROLE

15   Here's what we know:

- Most kids don't date anymore. They hook up instead.
- Kids are just as likely to have sex if they're just hooking up as they are if they're in an ongoing relationship.

16   As a result, relationships are no longer defined by sexual intimacy. Relationships today are defined by group affiliation. What does that mean?

17   To use the jargon employed by psychologists who study teenage dating: "Romantic pairs form most often on the basis of rank order rather than personal characteristics." Here's what that means: When fourteen-year-olds form romantic relationships, they do so less on the basis of individual characteristics and more on the basis of how popular the teenager is in the teenager's group. The most popular boy in the group is "going out with" the most popular girl, the second most popular boy goes out with the second most popular girl, and on down the line, with the least popular boy paired with the least popular girl.[10] "Going out with" usually doesn't mean actually going anywhere together. It just means that in the collective consciousness in the

group, that girl is linked with that boy. Sexual relationships in this age group, far from involving intimate personal connection, usually are more of an exercise in role-playing.

Journalist Linda Perlstein spent a year living with middle schoolers, much as Dian Fosse lived with the gorillas. Perlstein described what relationships are really like at the middle school she visited. Girls choose who they will "go out with" mostly "because the guy is someone her friends would approve of. It's mostly about the superficial stuff. He's got the right look, he's got the right clothes. . . . The asking out and dumping are done through intermediaries. . . . Jackie and Anton [a girl and boy who are "going out together"] don't go anywhere together. They don't talk much, on the phone or at school. Mainly their relationship means Jackie checks herself in the bathroom every day after lunch and runs around Anton on the playground, except when she carefully ignores him." In this age group, Perlstein observes, *going out together* "doesn't have much meaning. Generally they just realize the roles they are supposed to play and pretend to do so."[11]

The average high school romantic relationship lasts about eleven weeks.[12] In middle school, not even that long. The typical high school romantic relationship—with its two weeks of infatuation, four weeks of relative happiness, and five weeks of gradual disintegration—may be the worst possible preparation for a lasting and loving relationship, for a lifetime commitment to stick together even when times are tough and when both you and your partner are less attractive than you used to be.

We all want our children to grow up to enjoy a loving, mutually supportive and *lasting* relationship. Many parents imagine, reasonably enough, that romantic relationships in adolescence provide good "practice" for more serious relationships in adulthood. You can't run before you walk. Practice makes perfect.

Psychologists who study romantic relationships in adolescence are coming to a different conclusion. Practice makes perfect only if you're practicing the right task. Most adolescents aren't. Psychologists Wyndol Furman and Elizabeth Wehner have studied adolescent romantic relationships for years. For middle school and even most high school students, they report that "adolescents are not very concerned with the fulfillment of attachment or caregiving needs. . . . Instead, their focus is on who they are, how attractive they are . . . and *how it all looks to their peer group.*" Adolescents often develop bad habits in their dating relationships. A boy may get in the habit of regarding his girlfriend as a source of sexual gratification without really connecting with her as a human being. A girl may get in the habit of seeing her romantic partner as a "trophy boyfriend" without any idea of how to integrate him into her life. And both of them may get in the habit of dumping their current partner whenever a better-looking or more popular one becomes available. Over time, Furman and Wehner have found, "these individuals may become more skillful, but more skillful in developing the relationships they have come to expect."[13] By the time they reach adulthood and it's time to build a marriage that will last a lifetime, they've accumulated all sorts of bad habits that they need to break. They might be better off had they never had those teen relationships.

21   There are other reasons to be skeptical about the value of romantic relationships in early adolescence. According to a large survey published in 2003, kids who become sexually active before fifteen years of age are three times more likely to be regular smokers, four times more likely to have tried marijuana, and six times more likely to drink alcohol once a week or more.[14] Maybe we should regard sexual relationships in the same way we regard alcoholic beverages: as an adult pleasure to be enjoyed by adults only. As with alcoholic beverages, romantic relationships can be wonderful when responsible adults are partaking. But if unprepared teens use them, they can be deadly. Drunk driving kills. So does AIDS. And the boy who gets in the habit of exploiting his girlfriend sexually while ignoring her emotional needs is setting himself up for a lifetime of frustration, loneliness, and failure.

SO WHAT CAN YOU DO ABOUT IT?

22   I hope I've persuaded you that for most teens, early sexual activity—whether in or out of a romantic relationship—does more harm than good. But so what? Your kid won't ask you for permission to hook up at a party Saturday night. What difference does it make what you think?

23   It makes a big difference. As much as your teen may mock you and claim to consider your opinions out of date and irrelevant, study after study confirms that teens almost universally regard their parents as being the most important and influential people in their lives.[15] That doesn't mean that you can change your teen's behavior just by telling her or him that you don't think hooking up is a good idea. It does mean that you can have some leverage, if you know what to do and how to do it.

24   Think about *when* and *how* your teen might engage in sexual activity. Researchers have found that teens typically engage in sex in one of two opportunistic settings. The most common venue for teens to have sex is in their own home or their partner's home, right after school, before parents come home. That leads to rule number one:

- Know *where* your teen is. Make it a habit to call your teen after school. And vary the time you call. If your teen is supposed to be at an after-school activity, verify that she or he actually went to that activity. If you're into high-tech, you can even buy one of the new GPS watches for your teen to wear. You lock the watch on your teen's wrist and then monitor your child's location in real time, online. Some brand names include the Wherify GPS Locator and Lojack for Kids.

- Second rule: Know *who* your child is with. Even when your child is at home, you need to know who she's with. Ask her: Is anyone at home with you? Will anyone be coming over? *Why* are they coming over?

- The third rule has to do with *parties*. You need to know everything about the party: where it is going to be, who your teen is going with, and so on. When your teen announces that she or he is going to a party, ask whose house it will be at. Call ahead and speak to the parents. Verify that the parents will be present and supervising, not just upstairs with the door closed. Announce that you may drop in on the party. (Your teen will be mortified if you actually show up, but the mere possibility that you *might* has some deterrent value.) And don't forget about teen party-hopping: teens often start at one party, then move on to another party later in the evening. Make it an ironclad rule that your teen *must* notify you before going to another party.

If you have a daughter, then there's a fourth rule:

- No more than *three years'* age difference between your daughter and the oldest boy in the group. Girls who go out with substantially older boys are more likely to be pressured into having sex, more likely to get a sexually transmitted disease, and more likely to experience an unwanted pregnancy.[16]

With girls, there's another way to decrease the risk of early sexual activ- 25 ity and teenage pregnancy: encouraging girls-only activities. Girls who participate in activities that are mostly or entirely girls-only—such as a girls-only soccer team, or ballet, or horseback riding—are less likely to be sexually active and much less likely to experience an unwanted pregnancy.[17] Competitive sports have been shown to be especially effective in getting girls to focus on something other than the rating and dating game. The more involved a girl is in competitive sports, the less likely she is to be sexually active and the less likely she is to get pregnant.[18]

That doesn't hold for boys. Boys who play competitive sports are actu- 26 ally somewhat *more* likely to be sexually active than nonathletes. How come? Why does participation in sports have opposite effects on girls and boys with regard to sex?

The answer has to do with self-esteem. Athletes, both girls and boys, typi- 27 cally have higher self-esteem than nonathletes.[19] Higher self-esteem increases the likelihood that a boy will have sex, while higher self-esteem *decreases* the likelihood that a teenage girl will have sex. Why the difference? Athletic boys usually rate somewhat higher in the popularity game than nonathletic boys do. So, athletic boys will have more opportunities for sex than boys who are not athletic. More opportunity for sex equals more sex—if you're a boy.

Girls choose to have sex not so much because they want to have sex but 28 for other, more complex reasons. A girl with low self-esteem may be looking for affirmation of her femininity. She may think she's not pretty. She may think she's not popular. A boy who tells her she's beautiful, a boy who listens to her with interest, may be the boy she allows into her bed.

So. Tell your daughter to play sports and everything will be fine? Maybe. 29 Encouraging your teenage daughter to sign up for sports or to continue in a sport she has been playing is not as easy as it sounds. A recent study of teenage American girls found that girls drop out of sports in droves beginning in middle school and continuing into high school.[20] Girls often perceive competitive sports as unfeminine, and girls often become more concerned with femininity as gender becomes more salient. Group membership also becomes more important as kids move through adolescence. In many middle schools and in most high schools, it's become uncool for any but the most talented jock girls to play competitive sports.

30   Another factor, often overlooked, is that most adolescent girls don't like boys staring at them. Several researchers have found that girls drop out of sports because they don't like the spooky feeling that boys—and even men—are watching their practices and their games just to stare at their bodies. "You can feel them looking at you," says one girl.[21]

31   So what can you do about that? Make sure that girls-only sports and physical education are available at your daughter's school, for one thing.[22] Psychologist Anna Engel found that girls were much more likely to participate in physical education if P.E. classes were girls-only rather than coed.[23]

32   More generally, you should encourage your daughter to participate in activities where the focus is on what she *does* rather than on how she *looks*. In cheerleading, poms, ice skating, and ballet, for example, a major focus of the activity is on how you look. Is your uniform clean? Do your socks match? And don't forget to smile! In soccer, field hockey, and basketball, on the other hand, the focus is on what you *do*. Your daughter's soccer coach doesn't (and shouldn't) care whether your daughter's socks match or whether her uniform is spotless. Nor should you.

33   The two basic rules for guiding your child's behavior are:

34   First, make clear what's forbidden, and enforce that prohibition.

35   Second, offer alternatives. . . .

36   In the case of sex, this strategy means: First, make sure your kid understands that you don't approve of sexual activity involving genital contact between young teens. No oral sex. No penile-vaginal intercourse. And you're going to do your best to enforce that prohibition.

37   Second, offer alternatives. For girls, as I've said, that means sports, ballet, jazz dance, and other all-female activities. We have good data, as you've seen, showing that girls who participate in these activities are less likely to be sexually active.

38   For guys, it's tougher. There are no alternative activities that are unequivocally proven to decrease boys' proclivity to engage in premature sexual activity. I have a theory about what might work, though: encourage *cross-generational* community activities in which boys and men work together.

39   A school near my home sponsors a summertime program called Somos Amigos, "We Are Friends." A group of sixteen teenage boys under the leadership of three or four adult men travels to the Dominican Republic for the summer. Their mission: to build three small houses for the local villagers. The boys eat what the villagers eat, mostly beans and rice. No McDonald's, no Burger King, no Pizza Hut. There's no air conditioning. The conditions are brutal: hot and humid all day and all night. The boys are doing work, real work, shoulder-to-shoulder with the adult men: hammering four-by-fours, putting up drywall, installing toilets. Despite the rugged conditions, each year between forty and fifty boys apply for the privilege of spending their summer this way. Those who've participated say it was among the most meaningful experiences of their lives.

Here's what's really interesting, though: the organizers have told me that 40 those boys *subsequently* are more respectful to women. You don't hear about those boys sleeping around with every girl who will let them. That's not scientific proof. But these boys are impressive.

My other hope is that if we can generate enough real change in teen 41 culture—if we can empower enough girls to take charge of their sexual agenda, so that girls will stop providing oral sex on demand—then such a change might offer another way to shift teenage sexuality toward a more person-centered, relationship-oriented basis and away from the impersonal, experience-oriented bias that is skewing teenage sexuality at the present time. We need more girls to say No.

NOTES

1. Anne Jarrell, "The Face of Teenage Sex Grows Younger," *New York Times,* April 2, 2000.

2. This quote comes from Whitehead's article "Forget Sex in the City, Women Want Romance in Their Lives," *Washington Post,* February 9, 2003, p. B2.

3. Dr. Pinsky made these remarks as a guest on the NPR program "Fresh Air," September 24, 2003, online at http://freshair.npr.org. See also Dr. Pinsky's book *Cracked: Putting Broken Lives Together Again* (New York: HarperCollins, 2003), especially chapter 10, pp. 111–17.

4. Renee Sieving, Jennifer Oliphant, and Robert Blum, "Adolescent Sexual Behavior and Sexual Health," *Pediatrics in Review,* 22(12):407–16, 2002.

5. National Campaign to Prevent Teen Pregnancy, *14 and Younger: The Sexual Behavior of Young Adolescents* (Washington, DC: 2003), summarized at http://www.teenpregnancy.org/resources/reading/pdf/14summary.pdf.

6. Alexandra Hall, "The Mating Habits of the Suburban High School Teenager," *Boston* magazine, May 2003.

7. Thomas Young and Rick Zimmerman, "Clueless: Parental Knowledge of Risk Behaviors of Middle School Students," *Archives of Pediatrics and Adolescent Medicine,* 152:1137–39, 1998.

8. See, for example, Wyndol Furman and Elizabeth Wehner, "Adolescent Romantic Relationships: A Developmental Perspective," in *Romantic Relationships in Adolescence: Developmental Perspectives,* ed. Shmuel Shulman and Andrew Collins (San Francisco: Wiley/Jossey-Bass, 1997), pp. 21–36. See especially the chart and discussion on page 25.

9. A large body of scholarly work over the past thirty years demonstrates this fact. See, for example, Jason Luoma and Jane Pearson, "Suicide and Marital Status in the United States, 1991–1996," *American Journal of Public Health,* 92:1518–22, 2002; and Robin Simon, "Assessing Sex

Differences in Vulnerability among Employed Parents: The Importance of Marital Status," *Journal of Health & Social Behavior,* 39:38–54, 1998; also Allan Horwitz and associates, "Becoming Married and Mental Health: A Longitudinal Study of a Cohort of Young Adults," *Journal of Marriage & the Family,* 58:895–907, 1996; and also Walter Gove, Carolyn Stile, and Michael Hughes, "The Effect of Marriage on the Well-Being of Adults," *Journal of Family Issues,* 11:4–35, 1990.

10. B. Bradford Brown, " 'You're Going Out with WHO?' Peer Group Influences on Adolescent Romantic Relationships," in Wyndol Furman, B. Bradford Brown, and Candice Feiring, eds., *The Development of Romantic Relationships in Adolescence* (New York: Cambridge University Press, 1999), pp. 291–329.

11. Linda Perlstein, *Not Much Just Chillin': The Hidden Lives of Middle Schoolers* (New York: Farrar, Straus & Giroux, 2003), pp. 84, 43.

12. Neville Bruce and Katherine Sanders, "Incidence and Duration of Romantic Attraction in Students Progressing from Secondary to Tertiary Education," *Journal of Biosocial Science,* 33:173–84, 2001.

13. Wyndol Furman and Elizabeth Wehner, "Adolescent Romantic Relationships: A Developmental Perspective," in *Romantic Relationships in Adolescence: Developmental Perspectives,* ed. Shmuel Shulman and Andrew Collins (San Francisco: Wiley/Jossey-Bass, 1997), pp. 23, 27.

14. National Campaign to Prevent Teen Pregnancy, *14 and Younger: The Sexual Behavior of Young Adolescents* (Washington, DC: 2003), summary at http://www.teenpregnancy.org/resources/reading/pdf/14summary.pdf.

15. See, for example, Bradford Brown and associates, "Parenting Practices and Peer Group Affiliation in Adolescence," *Child Development,* 64:467–82, 1993. Several reports have shown a link between the closeness of the mother-daughter relationship and the likelihood of the daughter's becoming pregnant: the closer the relationship, the lower the risk of pregnancy. See Brent Miller, "Family Influences on Adolescent Sexual and Contraceptive Behavior," *Journal of Sex Research,* 39:22–26, 2002, and "Family Relationships and Adolescent Pregnancy Risk," *Developmental Review,* 21:1–38, 2001. See also Sunita Stewart and associates, "Parent and Adolescent Contributors To Teenage Misconduct in Western and Asian High School Students in Hong Kong," *International Journal of Behavioral Development,* 22:847–69, 1998.

16. See, for example, Mike Males, "Adult Liaison in the Epidemic of Teenage Birth, Pregnancy, and Venereal Disease," *Journal of Sex Research,* 29:525–45, 1992.

17. See, for example, Les Whitbeck and associates, "Early Adolescent Sexual Activity: A Developmental Study," *Journal of Marriage and the Family,* 61:934–46, 1999.

18. Donald Sabo, Kathleen Miller, and associates, "High School Athletic Participation, Sexual Behavior and Adolescent Pregnancy: A Regional Study," *Journal of Adolescent Health,* 25(3):207–16, 1999. See also (by the same group) "Athletic Participation and Sexual Behavior in Adolescents: The Different Worlds of Boys and Girls," *Journal of Health & Social Behavior,* 39(2):108–23, 1998.

19. Wendy Delany and Christina Lee, "Self-Esteem and Sex Roles among Male and Female High School Students: Their Relationship to Physical Activity," *Australian Psychologist,* 30(2):84–87, 1995. See also Karen Stein and Kristen Hedger, "Body Weight and Shape Self-Cognitions, Emotional Distress, and Disordered Eating in Middle Adolescent Girls," *Archives of Psychiatric Nursing,* 11:264–75, 1997. See also Marika Tiggemann, "The Impact of Adolescent Girls' Life Concerns and Leisure Activities on Body Dissatisfaction, Disordered Eating, and SelfEsteem," *Journal of Genetic Psychology,* 162:133–42, June 2001. Tiggemann found that girls who participate in competitive sports have substantially higher self-esteem than girls who don't. In addition, girls who competed were less likely to have eating disorders and less likely be concerned about their weight.

20. Sue Kimm and associates, "Decline in Physical Activity in Black Girls and White Girls during Adolescence," *New England Journal of Medicine,* 347:709–15, 2002.

21. James Kandy, " 'You Can Feel Them Looking at You': The Experiences of Adolescent Girls at Swimming Pools," *Journal of Leisure Research,* 32:262–80.

22. American school administrators may claim that single-sex P.E. classes violate Title IX regulations. That was true before the regulations were changed as a result of the Hutchison-Clinton amendment. More information is available at www.SingleSexSchools.org/nprm.html.

23. Anna Engel, "Sex Roles and Gender Stereotyping in Young Women's Participation in Sport," *Feminism and Psychology,* 4:439–48, 1994.

QUESTIONS FOR READING

1. What has changed in teen sexual relationships?

2. Why do boys get drunk before sex? Why do girls?

3. How well do parents understand what their teens are doing?

4. Which gender, as an adult, relies more, emotionally, on the other gender?

5. How helpful are current teen relationships in preparing for long-term, happy adult relationships?

6. What should parents do to guide teen girls? To guide their teen sons?

QUESTIONS FOR REASONING AND ANALYSIS

1. This excerpt from Sax's book for teachers and parents examines teen sexual behavior—and the adult consequences. Within this excerpt, what is Sax's claim? (Write it as a claim for a problem/solution argument.)

2. What kind of evidence does Sax provide? Is it convincing?

3. How good is Sax's advice to parents—in theory? How hard, in your view, will executing the advice be? Why?

QUESTIONS FOR REFLECTION AND WRITING

1. How accurately do the studies in this work reflect your knowledge/experience of teens? If your young teen world was different, what might be some causes of the differences?

2. Sax asserts that hooking up actually hurts teen boys, perhaps even more than the girls. Is this a new idea for you? Does his explanation make sense? Why or why not?

3. In our sex-drenched culture, is there any hope of redirecting teen sexual experiences? Explain and defend your response.

Globalism: How Do We Fit In?

READ: What is the situation in the cartoon? Who speaks the words?

REASON: What is the point of the cartoon?

REFLECT/WRITE: How successful have we been in exporting American culture? American goods? American values? Why are we viewed negatively in many parts of the world?

New ages and eras seem to keep coming at us faster than we can adjust. One way to organize the twentieth century in our minds is to look at each war as creating an era: the two big wars followed by the Korean War and then the Vietnam "conflict" (never officially declared a war). Moving into the twenty-first century, we have the first and the second "Gulf Wars," again not officially declared as wars. After World War II, our country was defined in large part by the long Cold War, the amassing of weapons in the chill of U.S./Soviet non-relations. But then the Berlin Wall came down and the Cold War ended, and some historians declared "the end of history." Presumably we would all live together peacefully in a global community.

Well, we are certainly not living peacefully, but are there any signs of a global community nonetheless? Apparently eras are not just about wars. They are also about other ways that we structure relationships with other nations—and peoples—around the world. At least two developments have taken us past the Information Age to Globalization: the development of global companies doing business, and making products, around the world; and the creation of the Internet that brings people together instantly—to shop, to chat, to do business. We all know that technical help for our computer glitches is likely to come from India, not from the computer company's home office in the United States. Cell phones capture pictures of disasters halfway around the world and send them to viewers in real time.

Globalization is both more obvious and mundane—and more complex and scary than most people understand. The six writers in this chapter will help us to get a clearer picture of our re-shaped world and of America's place in it.

PREREADING QUESTIONS

1. How often do you buy products produced and sold by a non-American company? How often do you buy products sold by an American company but manufactured someplace else? Do you pause to think about these purchases?

2. Should we worry about manufacturing jobs that are taken out of the United States to countries providing cheaper labor? Why or why not?

3. Why do some people object to treaties such as NAFTA? How can these treaties be good for everyone?

4. Is it possible that the Internet will be able to advance democracy around the world more effectively than the American military?

5. In the midst of a worldwide economic downturn, can we find ways to work with other countries to improve the global economy, not just our own, and help to improve our image in the world?

UNDERSTANDING GLOBALIZATION | THOMAS L. FRIEDMAN

Pultizer-Prize–winning former *New York Times* reporter Thomas L. Friedman is the author of several successful books, including *The World Is Flat: A Brief History of the Twenty-First Century* (2005) and *The Lexus and the Olive Tree* (1999), from which the following excerpt is taken.

PREREADING QUESTION If you were asked to explain globalization to the class, what would be your explanation?

When I say that globalization has replaced the Cold War as the defining 1 international system, what exactly do I mean?

I mean that, as an international system, the Cold War had its own structure 2 of power: the balance between the United States and the U.S.S.R. The Cold War had its own rules: in foreign affairs, neither superpower would encroach on the other's sphere of influence; in economics, less developed countries would focus on nurturing their own national industries, developing countries on export-led growth, communist countries on autarky and Western economies on regulated trade. The Cold War had its own dominant ideas: the clash between communism and capitalism, as well as detente, nonalignment and perestroika. The Cold War had its own demographic trends: the movement of people from east to west was largely frozen by the Iron Curtain, but the movement from south to north was a more steady flow. The Cold War had its own perspective on the globe: the world was a space divided into the communist camp, the Western camp, and the neutral camp, and everyone's country was in one of them. The Cold War had its own defining technologies: nuclear weapons and the second Industrial Revolution were dominant, but for many people in developing countries the hammer and sickle were still relevant tools. The Cold War had its own defining measurement: the throw weight of nuclear missiles. And lastly, the Cold War had its own defining anxiety: nuclear annihilation. When taken all together the elements of this Cold War system influenced the domestic politics, commerce and foreign relations of virtually every country in the world. The Cold War system didn't shape everything, but it shaped many things.

Today's era of globalization is a similar international system, with its own 3 unique attributes, which contrast sharply with those of the Cold War. To begin with the Cold War system was characterized by one over-arching feature— division. The world was a divided-up, chopped-up place and both your threats and opportunities in the Cold War system tended to grow out of who you were divided from. Appropriately, this Cold War system was symbolized by a single word: the *wall*—the Berlin Wall. One of my favorite descriptions of that world was provided by Jack Nicholson in the movie *A Few Good Men*. Nicholson plays a Marine colonel who is the commander of the U.S. base in Cuba, at Guantánamo Bay. In the climactic scene of the movie, Nicholson is pressed by

Tom Cruise to explain how a certain weak soldier under Nicholson's command, Santiago, was beaten to death by his own fellow Marines: "You want answers?" shouts Nicholson. "You want answers?" I want the truth, retorts Cruise. "You can't handle the truth," says Nicholson. "Son, we live in a world that has walls and those walls have to be guarded by men with guns. Who's gonna do it? You? You, Lieutenant Weinberg? I have a greater responsibility than you can possibly fathom. You weep for Santiago and you curse the Marines. You have that luxury. You have the luxury of not knowing what I know—that Santiago's death, while tragic, probably saved lives. And my existence, while grotesque and incomprehensible to you, saves lives. You don't want the truth because deep down in places you don't talk about at parties, you want me on that wall. You need me on that wall."

4   The globalization system is a bit different. It also has one overarching feature—integration. The world has become an increasingly interwoven place, and today, whether you are a company or a country, your threats and opportunities increasingly derive from who you are connected to. This globalization system is also characterized by a single word: the *Web*. So in the broadest sense we have gone from a system built around division and walls to a system increasingly built around integration and webs. In the Cold War we reached for the "hotline," which was a symbol that we were all divided but at least two people were in charge—the United States and the Soviet Union—and in the globalization system we reach for the Internet, which is a symbol that we are all increasingly connected and nobody is quite in charge.

5   This leads to many other differences between the globalization system and the Cold War system. The globalization system, unlike the Cold War system, is not frozen, but a dynamic ongoing process. That's why I define globalization this way: it is the inexorable integration of markets, nation-states and technologies to a degree never witnessed before—in a way that is enabling individuals, corporations and nation-states to reach around the world farther, faster, deeper and cheaper than ever before, and in a way that is enabling the world to reach into individuals, corporations and nation-states farther, faster, deeper, cheaper than ever before. This process of globalization is also producing a powerful backlash from those brutalized or left behind by this new system.

6   The driving idea behind globalization is free-market capitalism—the more you let market forces rule and the more you open your economy to free trade and competition, the more efficient and flourishing your economy will be. Globalization means the spread of free-market capitalism to virtually every country in the world. Therefore, globalization also has its own set of economic rules—rules that revolve around opening, deregulating and privatizing your economy, in order to make it more competitive and attractive to foreign investment. In 1975, at the height of the Cold War, only 8 percent of countries worldwide had liberal, free-market capital regimes, and foreign direct investment at the time totaled only $23 billion, according to the World Bank. By 1997, the number of countries with liberal economic regimes constituted 28 percent, and foreign investment totaled $644 billion.

Unlike the Cold War system, globalization has its own dominant culture, 7 which is why it tends to be homogenizing to a certain degree. In previous eras this sort of cultural homogenization happened on a regional scale—the Romanization of Western Europe and the Mediterranean world, the Islamification of Central Asia, North Africa, Europe and the Middle East by the Arabs and later the Ottomans, or the Russification of Eastern and Central Europe and parts of Eurasia under the Soviets. Culturally speaking, globalization has tended to involve the spread (for better and for worse) of Americanization—from Big Macs to iMacs to Mickey Mouse.

Globalization has its own defining technologies: computerization, minia- 8 turization, digitization, satellite communications, fiber optics and the Internet, which reinforce its defining perspective of integration. Once a country makes the leap into the system of globalization, its elites begin to internalize this perspective of integration, and always try to locate themselves in a global context. I was visiting Amman, Jordan, in the summer of 1998 and having coffee at the Inter-Continental Hotel with my friend Rami Khouri, the leading political columnist in Jordan. We sat down and I asked him what was new. The first thing he said to me was: "Jordan was just added to CNN's worldwide weather highlights." What Rami was saying was that it is important for Jordan to know that those institutions which think globally believe it is now worth knowing what the weather is like in Amman. It makes Jordanians feel more important and holds out the hope that they will be enriched by having more tourists or global investors visiting. The day after seeing Rami I happened to go to Israel and meet with Jacob Frenkel, governor of Israel's Central Bank and a University of Chicago–trained economist. Frenkel remarked that he too was going through a perspective change: "Before, when we talked about macroeconomics, we started by looking at the local markets, local financial systems and the interrelationship between them, and then, as an afterthought, we looked at the international economy. There was a feeling that what we do is primarily our own business and then there are some outlets where we will sell abroad. Now we reverse the perspective. Let's not ask what markets we should export to, after having decided what to produce; rather let's first study the global framework within which we operate and then decide what to produce. It changes your whole perspective."

While the defining measurement of the Cold War was weight—particularly 9 the throw weight of missiles—the defining measurement of the globalization system is speed—speed of commerce, travel; communication and innovation. The Cold War was about Einstein's mass-energy equation, $e = mc^2$. Globalization tends to revolve around Moore's Law, which states that the computing power of silicon chips will double every eighteen to twenty-four months, while the price will halve. In the Cold War, the most frequently asked question was: "Whose side are you on?" In globalization, the most frequently asked question is: "To what extent are you connected to everyone?" In the Cold War, the second most frequently asked question was: "How big is your missile?" In globalization, the second most frequently asked question is: "How fast is your modem?" The defining document of the Cold War system was "The Treaty."

The defining document of globalization is "The Deal." The Cold War system even had its own style. In 1961, according to *Foreign Policy* magazine, Cuban President Fidel Castro, wearing his usual olive drab military uniform, made his famous declaration "I shall be a Marxist-Leninist for the rest of my life." In January 1999, Castro put on a business suit for a conference on globalization in Havana, to which financier George Soros and free-market economist Milton Friedman were both invited.

10   If the defining economists of the Cold War system were Karl Marx and John Maynard Keynes, who each in his own way wanted to tame capitalism, the defining economists of the globalization system are Joseph Schumpeter and Intel chairman Andy Grove, who prefer to unleash capitalism. Schumpeter, a former Austrian Minister of Finance and Harvard Business School professor, expressed the view in his classic work *Capitalism, Socialism and Democracy* that the essence of capitalism is the process of "creative destruction"—the perpetual cycle of destroying the old and less efficient product or service and replacing it with new, more efficient ones. Andy Grove took Schumpeter's insight that "only the paranoid survive" for the title of his book on life in Silicon Valley, and made it in many ways the business model of globalization capitalism. Grove helped to popularize the view that dramatic, industry-transforming innovations are taking place today faster and faster. Thanks to these technological breakthroughs, the speed by which your latest invention can be made obsolete or turned into a commodity is now lightning quick. Therefore, only the paranoid, only those who are constantly looking over their shoulders to see who is creating something new that will destroy them and then staying just one step ahead of them, will survive. Those countries that are most willing to let capitalism quickly destroy inefficient companies, so that money can be freed up and directed to more innovative ones, will thrive in the era of globalization. Those which rely on their governments to protect them from such creative destruction will fall behind in this era.

11   James. Surowiecki, the business columnist for *Slate* magazine, reviewing Grove's book, neatly summarized what Schumpeter and Grove have in common, which is the essence of globalization economics. It is the notion that: "Innovation replaces tradition. The present—or perhaps the future—replaces the past. Nothing matters so much as what will come next, and what will come next can only arrive if what is here now gets overturned. While this makes the system a terrific place for innovation, it makes it a difficult place to live, since most people prefer some measure of security about the future to a life lived in almost constant uncertainty . . . We are not forced to re-create our relationships with those closest to us on a regular basis. And yet that's precisely what Schumpeter, and Grove after him, suggest is necessary to prosper [today]."

12   Indeed, if the Cold War were a sport, it would be sumo wrestling, says Johns Hopkins University foreign affairs professor Michael Mandelbaum. "It would be two big fat guys in a ring, with all sorts of posturing and rituals and stomping of feet, but actually very little contact, until the end of the match, when there is a brief moment of shoving and the loser gets pushed out of the ring, but nobody gets killed."

By contrast, if globalization were a sport, it would be the 100-meter dash, 13 over and over and over. And no matter how many times you win, you have to race again the next day. And if you lose by just one-hundredth of a second it can be as if you lost by an hour. (Just ask French multinationals. In 1999, French labor laws were changed, requiring—*requiring*—every employer to implement a four-hour reduction in the legal workweek, from 39 hours to 35 hours, with no cut in pay. Many French firms were fighting the move because of the impact it would have on their productivity in a global market. Henri Thierry, human resources director for Thomson–CSF Communications, a high-tech firm in the suburbs of Paris, told *The Washington Post*: "We are in a worldwide competition. If we lose one point of productivity, we lose orders. If we're obliged to go to 35 hours it would be like requiring French athletes to run the 100 meters wearing flippers. They wouldn't have much of a chance winning a medal.")

To paraphrase German political theorist Carl Schmitt, the Cold War was a 14 world of "friends" and "enemies." The globalization world, by contrast, tends to turn all friends and enemies into "competitors."

If the defining anxiety of the Cold War was fear of annihilation from an 15 enemy you knew all too well in a world struggle that was fixed and stable, the defining anxiety in globalization is fear of rapid change from an enemy you can't see, touch or feel—a sense that your job, community or workplace can be changed at any moment by anonymous economic and technological forces that are anything but stable. The defining defense system of the Cold War was radar—to expose the threats coming from the other side of the wall. The defining defense system of the globalization era is the X-ray machine—to expose the threats coming from within.

Globalization also has its own demographic pattern—a rapid acceleration 16 of the movement of people from rural areas and agricultural lifestyles to urban areas and urban lifestyles more intimately linked with global fashion, food, markets and entertainment trends.

Last, and most important, globalization has its own defining structure of 17 power, which is much more complex than the Cold War structure. The Cold War system was built exclusively around nation-states. You acted on the world in that system through your state. The Cold War was primarily a drama of states confronting states, balancing states and aligning with states. And, as a system, the Cold War was balanced at the center by two superstates: the United States and the Soviet Union.

The globalization system, by contrast, is built around three balances, which 18 overlap and affect one another. The first is the traditional balance between nation-states. In the globalization system, the United States is now the sole and dominant superpower and all other nations are subordinate to it to one degree or another. The balance of power between the United States and the other states, though, still matters for the stability of this system. And it can still explain a lot of the news you read on the front page of the papers, whether it is the containment of Iraq in the Middle East or the expansion of NATO against Russia in Central Europe.

19   The second balance in the globalization system is between nation-states and global markets. These global markets are made up of millions of investors moving money around the world with the click of a mouse. I call them "the Electronic Herd," and this herd gathers in key global financial centers, such as Wall Street, Hong Kong, London and Frankfurt, which I call "the Supermarkets." The attitudes and actions of the Electronic Herd and the Supermarkets can have a huge impact on nation-states today, even to the point of triggering the downfall of governments. Who ousted Suharto in Indonesia in 1998? It wasn't another state, it was the Supermarkets, by withdrawing their support for, and confidence in, the Indonesian economy. You will not understand the front page of newspapers today unless you bring the Supermarkets into your analysis. Because the United States can destroy you by dropping bombs and the Supermarkets can destroy you by downgrading your bonds. In other words, the United States is the dominant player in maintaining the globalization gameboard, but it is not alone in influencing the moves on that gameboard. This globalization gameboard today is a lot like a Ouija board—sometimes pieces are moved around by the obvious hand of the superpower, and sometimes they are moved around by hidden hands of the Supermarkets.

The third balance that you have to pay attention to in the globalization system—the one that is really the newest of all—is the balance between individuals and nation-states. Because globalization has brought down many of the walls that limited the movement and reach of people, and because it has

Twenty-Nation Summit on the Global Economy, November, 2008

simultaneously wired the world into networks, it gives more power to individuals to influence both markets and nation-states than at any time in history. Individuals can increasingly act on the world stage directly—unmediated by a state. So you have today not only a superpower, not only Supermarkets, but, as will be demonstrated later in the book, you now have Super-empowered individuals. Some of these Super-empowered individuals are quite angry, some of them quite wonderful—but all of them are now able to act directly on the world stage.

Without the knowledge of the U.S. government, Long-Term Capital 21 Management—a few guys with a hedge fund in Greenwich, Connecticut—amassed more financial bets around the world than all the foreign reserves of China. Osama bin Laden, a Saudi millionaire with his own global network, declared war on the United States in the late 1990s, and the U.S. Air Force retaliated with a cruise missile attack on him (where he resided in Afghanistan) as though he were another nation-state. Think about that. The United States fired 75 cruise missiles; at $1 million apiece, at a person! That was a superpower against a Super-empowered angry man. Jody Williams won the Nobel Peace Prize in 1997 for her contribution to the international ban on landmines. She achieved that ban not only without much government help, but in the face of opposition from all the major powers. And what did she say was her secret weapon for organizing 1,000 different human rights and arms control groups on six continents? "E-mail."

Nation-states, and the American superpower in particular, are still hugely 22 important today, but so too now are Supermarkets and Super-empowered individuals. You will never understand the globalization system, or the front page of the morning paper, unless you see it as a complex interaction between all three of these actors: states bumping up against states, states bumping up against Supermarkets, and Supermarkets and states bumping up against Super-empowered individuals.

Unfortunately, . . . the system of globalization has come upon us far faster 23 than our ability to retrain ourselves to see and comprehend it. Think about just this one fact: Most people had never even heard of the Internet in 1990, and very few people had an E-mail address then. That was just ten years ago! But today the Internet, cell phones and E-mail have become essential tools that many people, and not only in developed countries, cannot imagine living without. It was no different, I am sure, at the start of the Cold War, with the first appearance of nuclear arsenals and deterrence theories. It took a long time for leaders and analysts of that era to fully grasp the real nature and dimensions of the Cold War system. They emerged from World War II thinking that this great war had produced a certain kind of world, but they soon discovered it had laid the foundations for a world very different from the one they anticipated. Much of what came to be seen as great Cold War architecture and strategizing were responses on the fly to changing events and evolving threats. Bit by bit, these Cold War strategists built the institutions, the perceptions and the reflexes that came to be known as the Cold War system.

24   It will be no different with the globalization system, except that it may take us even longer to get our minds around it, because it requires so much retraining just to see this new system and because it is built not just around superpowers but also around Supermarkets and Super-empowered individuals. I would say that in 2000 we understand as much about how today's system of globalization is going to work as we understood about how the Cold War system was going to work in 1946—the year Winston Churchill gave his speech warning that an "Iron Curtain" was coming down, cutting off the Soviet zone of influence from Western Europe. We barely understood how the Cold War system was going to play out thirty years after Churchill's speech! That was when Routledge published a collection of essays by some of the top Soviet-ologists, entitled *Soviet Economy Towards the Year 2000.* It was a good seller when it came out. It never occurred at that time to any of the authors that there wouldn't be a Soviet economy in the year 2000.

25   If you want to appreciate how few people understand exactly how this system works, think about one amusing fact. The two key economists who were advising Long-Term Capital Management, Robert C. Merton and Myron S. Scholes, shared the Nobel Prize for economics in 1997, roughly one year before LTCM so misunderstood the nature of risk in today's highly integrated global marketplace that it racked up the biggest losses in hedge fund history. And what did LTCM's two economists win their Nobel Prize for? For their studies on how complex financial instruments, known as derivatives, can be used by global investors to offset risk! In 1997 they won the Nobel Prize for managing risk. In 1998 they won the booby prize for creating risk. Same guys, same market—new world.

QUESTIONS FOR READING

1. How do globalization and the Cold War differ?
2. In what ways does the Internet symbolize the era of globalization?
3. What culture dominates the globalization era?
4. What is Moore's Law?
5. How does the expression "only the paranoid survive" apply to Silicon Valley?
6. Who are the "Electronic Herd" and what are the Supermarkets?
7. What are the three balances Friedman describes? Who is an example of a Super-empowered individual?

QUESTIONS FOR REASONING AND ANALYSIS

1. What is Friedman's claim? What type or genre of argument does this excerpt represent?
2. Do Friedman's contrasts between the Cold War era and our times convince you that we are living in a different era? Why or why not?
3. Do his details and examples of globalization match your sense of our times? Why or why not?

4. What are some of the elements of the author's style? What makes it effective? What makes his final paragraph an effective ending?

QUESTIONS FOR REFLECTION AND WRITING

1. What descriptions of our time surprise you the most? Why do you think you are surprised?

2. Some of the characteristics of globalization are clearly advantages, but are there any disadvantages, or potential problems? If so, what are they? If not, why not?

THE COGNITIVE AGE | DAVID BROOKS

A columnist for the *New York Times* and a commentator on *The NewsHour with Jim Lehrer*, David Brooks has appeared in many newspapers and magazines and has published two books, including *On Paradise Drive: How We Live Now (and Always Have) in the Future Tense* (2004). The following column was published May 2, 2008.

PREREADING QUESTION Brooks uses the word *paradigm* in his column. What does the word mean? If you do not know the word, look it up.

If you go into a good library, you will find thousands of books on globalization. Some will laud it. Some will warn about its dangers. But they'll agree that globalization is the chief process driving our age. Our lives are being transformed by the increasing movement of goods, people and capital across borders. 1

The globalization paradigm has led, in the political arena, to a certain historical narrative: There were once nation-states like the U.S. and the European powers, whose economies could be secured within borders. But now capital flows freely. Technology has leveled the playing field. Competition is global and fierce. 2

New dynamos like India and China threaten American dominance thanks to their cheap labor and manipulated currencies. Now, everything is made abroad. American manufacturing is in decline. The rest of the economy is threatened. 3

Hillary Clinton summarized the narrative this week: "They came for the steel companies and nobody said anything. They came for the auto companies and nobody said anything. They came for the office companies, people who did white-collar service jobs, and no one said anything. And they came for the professional jobs that could be outsourced, and nobody said anything." 4

The globalization paradigm has turned out to be very convenient for politicians. It allows them to blame foreigners for economic woes. It allows them to pretend that by rewriting trade deals, they can assuage economic anxiety. It allows them to treat economic and social change as a great mercantilist competition, with various teams competing for global supremacy, and with politicians starring as the commanding generals. 5

But there's a problem with the way the globalization paradigm has evolved. It doesn't really explain most of what is happening in the world. 6

7   Globalization is real and important. It's just not the central force driving economic change. Some Americans have seen their jobs shipped overseas, but global competition has accounted for a small share of job creation and destruction over the past few decades. Capital does indeed flow around the world. But as Pankaj Ghemawat of the Harvard Business School has observed, 90 percent of fixed investment around the world is domestic. Companies open plants overseas, but that's mainly so their production facilities can be close to local markets.

8   Nor is the globalization paradigm even accurate when applied to manufacturing. Instead of fleeing to Asia, U.S. manufacturing output is up over recent decades. As Thomas Duesterberg of Manufacturers Alliance/MAPI, a research firm, has pointed out, the U.S.'s share of global manufacturing output has actually increased slightly since 1980.

9   The chief force reshaping manufacturing is technological change (hastened by competition with other companies in Canada, Germany or down the street). Thanks to innovation, manufacturing productivity has doubled over two decades. Employers now require fewer but more highly skilled workers. Technological change affects China just as it does America. William Overholt of the RAND Corporation has noted that between 1994 and 2004 the Chinese shed 25 million manufacturing jobs, 10 times more than the U.S.

10   The central process driving this is not globalization. It's the skills revolution. We're moving into a more demanding cognitive age. In order to thrive, people are compelled to become better at absorbing, processing and combining information. This is happening in localized and globalized sectors, and it would be happening even if you tore up every free trade deal ever inked.

11   The globalization paradigm emphasizes the fact that information can now travel 15,000 miles in an instant. But the most important part of information's journey is the last few inches—the space between a person's eyes or ears and the various regions of the brain. Does the individual have the capacity to understand the information? Does he or she have the training to exploit it? Are there cultural assumptions that distort the way it is perceived?

12   The globalization paradigm leads people to see economic development as a form of foreign policy, as a grand competition between nations and civilizations. These abstractions, called "the Chinese" or "the Indians," are doing this or that. But the cognitive age paradigm emphasizes psychology, culture and pedagogy—the specific processes that foster learning. It emphasizes that different societies are being stressed in similar ways by increased demands on human capital. If you understand that you are living at the beginning of a cognitive age, you're focusing on the real source of prosperity and understand that your anxiety is not being caused by a foreigner.

13   It's not that globalization and the skills revolution are contradictory processes. But which paradigm you embrace determines which facts and remedies you emphasize. Politicians, especially Democratic ones, have fallen in love with the globalization paradigm. It's time to move beyond it.

QUESTIONS FOR READING

1. How do many Americans, including many of our politicians, see globalization? What does the standard view allow politicians to do?
2. What is Brooks's response to the common view of globalization?
3. What is the primary force reshaping manufacturing?
4. What does Brooks mean by "the cognitive age"?

QUESTIONS FOR REASONING AND ANALYSIS

1. What is the author's claim? Where does he state it?
2. What does he gain by a lengthy introduction before we come to his claim?
3. Brooks asserts that globalization and the cognitive paradigm are not contradictory. How, then, are they at odds? What happens if you embrace one instead of the other?

QUESTIONS FOR REFLECTION AND WRITING

1. Were you surprised to read that manufacturing is up in the United States—and that China has lost ten times more jobs in manufacturing than the United States? If so, why? What have you read or heard that would make these facts a surprise?
2. Has Brooks convinced you that technology is the cause of some kinds of lost jobs—not China or India—and that they are also affected? If not, why not?
3. When we embrace the cognitive paradigm, what, as a society, do we need to pay attention to? Why do critical thinking skills become so important? Explain.

THE SUPERCLASS: THEY'RE GLOBAL CITIZENS. THEY'RE HUGELY RICH. AND THEY PULL THE STRINGS. | DAVID ROTHKOPF

David Rothkopf is currently a visiting scholar at the Carnegie Endowment for International Peace. He is also president and CEO of Garten Rothkopf, an international advisory firm. In the Clinton administration he was deputy under secretary of commerce. Rothkopf is the author of several books and numerous articles, his most recent titled *Superclass: The Global Power Elite and the World They Are Making* (2008). The following article, on the subject of his new book, appeared May 4, 2008, in the *Washington Post*.

PREREADING QUESTIONS Who are some of the people you would place in a "superclass"? Why?

We didn't elect them. We can't throw them out. And they're getting more 1 powerful every day.

Call them the superclass. 2

3 At the moment, Americans are fixated on the political campaign. In the meantime, many are missing a reality of the global era that may matter much more than their presidential choice. On an ever-growing list of issues, the big decisions are being made or profoundly influenced by a little-understood international network of business, financial, government, cultural and military leaders who are beyond the reach of American voters.

4 In addition to top officials, these people include corporate executives, leading investors, top bankers, media moguls, heads of state, generals, religious leaders, heads of terrorist and criminal organizations and a handful of important cultural and scientific figures. Each of these roughly 6,000 individuals is set apart by their power and ability to regularly influence millions of lives across international borders. The group is not monolithic, but none is more globalized or has more influence over the direction in which the global era is heading.

5 Doubt it? Just look at the current financial crisis. As government regulators have sought to head off further market losses, they've found that perhaps the most effective tool at their disposal is what the president of the New York Federal Reserve Bank described to me as their "convening power"—their ability to get the big boys of Wall Street and world financial capitals into a room or on a conference call to collaborate on solving a problem. This has, in fact, become a central part of crisis management, both because national governments have limited regulatory authority over global markets and because financial flows have become so large that the real power lies with the biggest players—such as the top 50 financial institutions that control almost $50 trillion in assets, by one measure nearly a third of all assets worldwide.

6 Most major companies are both bigger and more global today, which effectively makes them able to pick and choose among various governments' regulatory regimes or investment incentive programs. They play officials in country X against those in country Y, gaining leverage that makes the old rules of trade obsolete. The world's biggest corporations, such as Exxon or Wal-Mart, have annual sales (and thus financial resources) that rival the gross domestic product of all but the 20 or so wealthiest nations. The top 250 companies in the world have sales equal to about a third of global GDP (these are very different measures, but they give a rough sense of relative size).

7 Major media organizations such as Rupert Murdoch's News Corp., which is effectively controlled by a single individual, touch far more people each day than any national government can. Just a few weeks ago, Italian media billionaire Silvio Berlusconi once again used his extraordinary resources to win election as prime minister, which will give him a seat at G-8 summits and other global conclaves. Even global terrorist organizations such as al-Qaeda or Hezbollah have both the ability, through their international networks, and the will to project force more effectively on an international level than all but a handful of governments.

8 The people who run these big international organizations can have much more power over key aspects of your daily life and over global trends than most officials in Washington are likely to have, except in the most extreme

circumstances. They can affect investments and job creation, shape culture and influence lawmakers. The Federal Reserve Bank has played a critical role in the financial crisis, but it couldn't have intervened successfully without a financial leader like Jamie Dimon, chief executive of J.P. Morgan Chase, which stepped in to purchase the failing investment bank Bear Stearns.

The rise of the global superclass signals the latest evolution in the age- **9** old tale of the few who corner the market on power. There have always been elites. But this contemporary group is very different from those that preceded it. Study these 6,000 or so individuals, and you'll find that unlike past aristocrats who inherited their wealth, many—Bill Gates, for instance, or Warren Buffett—have built their fortunes over their lifetimes. Many more come from the worlds of business, finance and media than in the past.

What's more, many acknowledge that they increasingly have more in com- **10** mon with fellow members of the global elite than they do with the people of their own nations. Russian oligarch Roman Abramovich, for instance, may be governor of a Siberian province, but he also manages to live large in London, where he owns a famous English soccer club. Even though he has donated millions to help his province, he spends considerably more time with global business partners or his posh neighbors in Britain than he does with his constituents back home.

At the same time, political and military elites are fading in relative **11** influence—the former bound by geography, the latter by the extraordinarily high cost of modern warfare. The regional composition of the group is changing as well, as transatlantic elites who today make up about 60 percent of the class gradually give way to a rising cadre of Asian leaders, such as the 100 Chinese billionaires estimated to have emerged in the last couple of years.

In a world with only two kinds of international institutions—weak and **12** dysfunctional—the members of this superclass are filling a power vacuum when it comes to influencing decisions about transnational issues such as financial-market regulation or climate change. (Many countries voted for the Kyoto accords on global warming, but it took just Exxon and a handful of other oil companies to successfully lobby the White House to opt out and undercut the entire initiative.) In so doing, they raise real questions about the future of global governance. Will the global era be more democratic or less so? Will inequality continue to grow, as it has for the past three decades of this group's rise, or recede? Will the few dominate because the government mechanisms that traditionally represent the views of the many are so underdeveloped on a global scale?

Once again, the meltdown in global financial markets brings this aspect **13** of the story into focus. For years, financial elites have argued that markets should self-regulate even as instruments grew more complex and risks more opaque. Then, when a crisis came, they used their influence to get top government officials to come in and help cauterize their self-inflicted wounds, warning of a "systemic failure." But critics are already correctly charging that new regulations to rein in global markets are largely protecting the interests of the richest.

14   One distinguishing characteristic of the superclass is the concentration of extreme wealth in the hands of so few. Inequality has always existed in the world, but the international trend toward leave-it-to-the-market policies of the past 25 years has resulted both in great growth worldwide (what superclass member Martha Stewart might call "a good thing") and in growing inequality (not so much, as superclass member Jon Stewart might say). Today, the world's more than 1,100 billionaires have a net worth that's roughly double that of the bottom 2.5 billion people on the planet. The richest 10 percent of adults worldwide own 85 percent of global wealth, while the poorest half only barely one percent. The world's almost 10 million millionaires have seen their wealth double to nearly $37 trillion over the past 10 years.

15   Growth is taking place, but it is disproportionately benefiting the few. And there's a sense that the issue of class conflict, confined not too long ago to the ash heap by our (premature) celebration of the "end of history" after communism's fall, remains with us.

16   A backlash is inevitable. Are these elites especially talented? Hard-working? Lucky? Some are all of these things. But conspiracy theories don't hold water in a group whose members are so diverse and self-interested. Still, when their self-interests align to cause them to act together they can be hard to resist. They often get their way—and thus often get much more than the rest of us. And that leads to angry reaction. "When a CEO is making more in 10 minutes than an ordinary worker's making in an entire year . . . something is wrong, something has to change," Sen. Barack Obama declares on the stump. Sen. Hillary Rodham Clinton chimes in that "it is wrong that somebody who makes $50 million a year on Wall Street pays a lower tax rate than somebody who makes $50,000 a year."

17   The next U.S. president will still be the most powerful person in the world because of his or her control of the nation's unparalleled military might and influence over our economic and political resources. But that influence is on the wane, for a number of reasons: the relative decline in the power of national governments; the relative rise in the power of others in the world's fastest-growing places; U.S. trade and fiscal deficits; and a third, geopolitical deficit arising from both damaged national prestige and what might be characterized either as Iraq fatigue or as having learned from the mistakes of the past several years.

18   None of this makes the decision that U.S. voters will make in November less important. Government still offers the average citizen the best means of counterbalancing the superclass or redressing growing inequality. And governments will have to play a key role in shaping the new regulatory frameworks and governance mechanisms that will be essential to a more balanced distribution of power in the global era. But what it does mean is that "change" isn't just a slogan in this year's campaign. It's a reality that will redefine the landscape of power worldwide for U.S. presidents of the future.

QUESTIONS FOR READING

1. What does Rothkopf mean by the "superclass"? Who are they? Why are they important?
2. Who may own nearly "a third of all assets worldwide"?
3. What gives some of the big companies their global influence?
4. How do the new aristocrats differ from those of the past?
5. In the last 25 years, how has wealth been redistributed?
6. How has the U.S. president's power changed?

QUESTIONS FOR REASONING AND ANALYSIS

1. What is Rothkopf's claim? What is his attitude toward the superclass?
2. What most bothers the author about the superclass? How do you know?
3. What kinds of evidence does Rothkopf provide in support of his claim? How effective is the evidence in supporting his claim? Evaluate his argument.

QUESTIONS FOR REFLECTION AND WRITING

1. What fact in the article most surprised you? Why? What concept most surprised you? Why?
2. Are you concerned about the power of the superclass? Why or why not?
3. Are you concerned about the decline in power of nation-states? Or, is this a good change, giving more push to the "citizen of the world" reality? Explain and defend your response.

INEQUALITY IN INDIA AND CHINA: IS GLOBALIZATION TO BLAME? | PRANAB BARDHAN

An economics professor at the University of California, Berkeley, Pranab Bardhan holds a Ph.D. from the University of Cambridge. Currently he co-chairs the Network on the Effects of Inequality on Economic Performance, funded by the MacArthur Foundation International Research Network. His research interests in globalization and poverty are reflected in the following essay, posted October 15, 2007, at *YaleGlobal*, the Web site of the Yale Center for the Study of Globalization.

PREREADING QUESTIONS Given the argument's title, what do you expect to read about? What type (genre) of argument do you anticipate?

Economic inequality is on the rise around the world, and many analysts 1 point their fingers at globalization. Are they right?

Economic inequality has even hit Asia, a region long characterized by rela- 2 tively low inequality. A report from the Asian Development Bank states that economic inequality now nears the levels of Latin America, a region long characterized by high inequality.

3　　In particular, China, which two decades back was one of the most equal countries in the world, is now among the most unequal countries. Its Gini coefficient—a standard measure of inequality, with zero indicating no inequality and one extreme inequality—for income inequality has now surpassed that of the US. If current trends continue, China may soon reach that of high-inequality countries like Brazil, Mexico and Chile. Bear in mind, such measurements are based on household survey data—therefore most surely underestimate true inequality as there is often large and increasing non-response to surveys from richer households.

4　　The standard reaction in many circles to this phenomenon is that all this must be due to globalization, as Asian countries in general and China in particular have had major global integration during the last two decades. Yes, it is true that when new opportunities open up, the already better-endowed may often be in a better position to utilize them, as well as better-equipped to cope with the cold blasts of increased market competition.

5　　But it is not always clear that globalization is the main force responsible for increased inequality. In fact, expansion of labor-intensive industrialization, as has happened in China as the economy opened up, may have helped large numbers of workers. Also, the usual process of economic development involves a major restructuring of the economy, with people moving from agriculture, a sector with low inequality, to other sectors. It is also the case that inequality increased more rapidly in the interior provinces in China than in the more globally exposed coastal provinces. In any case it is often statistically difficult to disentangle the effects of globalization from those of the ongoing forces of skill-biased technical progress, as with computers; structural and demographic changes; and macroeconomic policies.

6　　The other reaction, usually on the opposite side, puts aside the issue of inequality and points to the wonders that globalization has done to eliminate extreme poverty, once massive in the two Asian giants, China and India. With global integration of these two economies, it is pointed out that poverty has declined substantially in India and dramatically in China over the last quarter century.

7　　This reaction is also not well-founded. While expansion of exports of labor-intensive manufacturing lifted many people out of poverty in China during the last decade (but not in India, where exports are still mainly skill- and capital-intensive), the more important reason for the dramatic decline of poverty over the last three decades may actually lie elsewhere.

8　　Estimates made at the World Bank suggest that two-thirds of the total decline in the numbers of poor people—below the admittedly crude poverty line of $1 a day per capita—in China between 1981 and 2004 already happened by the mid-1980s, before the big strides in foreign trade and investment in China during the 1990s and later. Much of the extreme poverty was concentrated in rural areas, and its large decline in the first half of the 1980s is perhaps mainly a result of the spurt in agricultural growth following de-collectivization, egalitarian land reform and readjustment of farm procurement prices—mostly internal factors that had little to do with global integration.

In India the latest survey data suggest that the rate of decline in poverty somewhat slowed for 1993–2005, the period of intensive opening of the economy, compared to the 1970s and 1980s, and that some child-health indicators, already dismal, have hardly improved in recent years. For example, the percentage of underweight children in India is much larger than in sub-Saharan Africa and has not changed much in the last decade or so. The growth in the agricultural sector, where much of the poverty is concentrated, has declined somewhat in the last decade, largely on account of the decline of public investment in areas like irrigation, which has little to do with globalization. **9**

The Indian pace of poverty reduction has been slower than China's, not just because growth has been much faster in China, but also because the same 1 percent growth rate reduces poverty in India by much less, largely on account of inequalities in wealth—particularly, land and education. Contrary to common perception, these inequalities are much higher in India than in China: The Gini coefficient of land distribution in rural India was 0.74 in 2003; the corresponding figure in China was 0.49 in 2002. India's educational inequality is one of the worst in the world: According to the World Development Report 2006, published by the World Bank, the Gini coefficient of the distribution of adult schooling years in the population around 2000 was 0.56 in India, which is not just higher than 0.37 in China, but higher than that of almost all Latin American countries. **10**

Another part of the conventional wisdom in the media as well as in academia is how the rising inequality and the inequality-induced grievances, particularly in the left-behind rural areas, cloud the horizon for the future of the Chinese polity and hence economic stability. **11**

Frequently cited evidence of instability comes from Chinese police records, which suggest that incidents of social unrest have multiplied nearly nine-fold between 1994 and 2005. While the Chinese leadership is right to be concerned about the inequalities, the conventional wisdom in this matter is somewhat askew, as Harvard sociologist Martin Whyte has pointed out. Data from a 2004 national representative survey in China by his team show that the presumably disadvantaged people in the rural or remote areas are not particularly upset by the rising inequality. This may be because of the familiar "tunnel effect" in the inequality literature: Those who see other people prospering remain hopeful that their chance will come soon, much like drivers in a tunnel, whose hopes rise when blocked traffic in the next lane starts moving. This is particularly so with the relaxation of restrictions on mobility from villages and improvement in roads and transportation. **12**

More than inequality, farmers are incensed by forcible land acquisitions or toxic pollution, but these disturbances are as yet localized. The Chinese leaders have succeeded in deflecting the wrath towards corrupt local officials and in localizing and containing the rural unrest. Opinion surveys suggest that the central leadership is still quite popular, while local officials are not. **13**

14   Paradoxically, the potential for unrest may be greater in the currently-booming urban areas, where the real-estate bubble could break. Global recession could ripple through the excess-capacity industries and financially-shaky public banks. With more internet-connected and vocal middle classes, a history of massive worker layoffs and a large underclass of migrants, urban unrest may be more difficult to contain.

15   Issues like globalization, inequality, poverty and social discontent are thus much more complicated than are allowed in the standard accounts about China and India.

QUESTIONS FOR READING

1. In what countries is income inequality increasing?
2. Why is the measurement of inequality probably greater than the data suggest?
3. Why is it difficult to isolate globalization as a cause of increased inequality?
4. What changes in China have reduced poverty in rural areas?
5. What are likely reasons for the slower reduction in poverty in India?
6. What are some reasons why the Chinese are not in revolt over increased inequality? Where in China is the unrest most likely to occur?

QUESTIONS FOR REASONING AND ANALYSIS

1. What type (genre) of argument is this?
2. What is Bardhan's claim? State it to make clear the genre of the argument.
3. Where does Bardhan state his claim? What does he gain by beginning with a question and not stating his position until later in the argument?
4. Bardhan is examining issues of globalization and poverty in two countries. How does he organize his discussion? What strategies are used to make shifts in topic clear?
5. One country receives more attention than the other. What may account for this? Is this okay—in terms of evaluating the argument? (Consider his primary purpose in writing.)

QUESTIONS FOR REFLECTION AND WRITING

1. What data surprise you the most in Bardhan's essay? Why?
2. Did you think that globalization was the primary cause of increased inequality? If so, has the author changed your thinking? Why or why not?
3. Bardhan writes about China and India; why should we be concerned about globalization and poverty in these countries? Explain and defend your response.
4. The United States has also seen an increase in inequality of income in recent decades. Is globalization to blame? Are there other possible causes? Should we care? Why or why not?

Rx FOR GLOBAL POVERTY | ROBERT J. SAMUELSON

A graduate of Harvard University, Robert Samuelson began his career as a reporter and is now a columnist whose articles are syndicated in many newspapers each week and biweekly in *Newsweek* magazine. Although he usually writes about economics, Samuelson also writes about political and cultural issues, especially when they connect to the economy. You will see these connections in the following column which appeared May 28, 2008.

PREREADING QUESTION What do you think is the world's greatest moral challenge?

1   What's the world's greatest moral challenge, as judged by its capacity to inflict human tragedy? It is not, I think, global warming, whose effects—if they become as grim as predicted—will occur over many years and provide societies time to adapt. A case can be made for preventing nuclear proliferation, which threatens untold deaths and a collapse of the world economy. But the most urgent present moral challenge, I submit, is the most obvious: global poverty.

2   There are roughly 6 billion people on the planet; in 2004, perhaps 2.5 billion survived on $2 a day or less, says the World Bank. By 2050, the world may have 3 billion more people; many will be similarly impoverished. What's baffling and frustrating about extreme poverty is that much of the world has eliminated it. In 1800, almost everyone was desperately poor. But the developed world has essentially abolished starvation, homelessness and material deprivation.

3   The solution to being poor is getting rich. It's economic growth. We know this. The mystery is why all societies have not adopted the obvious remedies. Just recently, the 21-member Commission on Growth and Development—including two Nobel-prize winning economists, former prime ministers of South Korea and Peru, and a former president of Mexico—examined the puzzle.

4   Since 1950, the panel found, 13 economies have grown at an average annual rate of 7 percent for at least 25 years. These were: Botswana, Brazil, China, Hong Kong, Indonesia, Japan, South Korea, Malaysia, Malta, Oman, Singapore, Taiwan and Thailand. Some gains are astonishing. From 1960 to 2005, per capita income in South Korea rose from $1,100 to $13,200. Other societies started from such low levels that even rapid economic growth, combined with larger populations, left sizable poverty. In 2005, Indonesia's per capita income averaged just $900, up from $200 in 1966.

5   Still, all these economies had advanced substantially. The panel identified five common elements of success:

- Openness to global trade and, usually, an eagerness to attract foreign investment.

- Political stability and "capable" governments "committed" to economic growth, though not necessarily democracy (China, South Korea and Indonesia all grew with authoritarian regimes).

- High rates of saving and investment, usually at least 25 percent of national income.

- Economic stability, keeping government budgets and inflation under control and avoiding a broad collapse in production.

- A willingness to "let markets allocate resources," meaning that governments didn't try to run industry.

6   Of course, qualifications abound. Some countries succeeded with high inflation rates of 15 to 30 percent. Led by Japan, Asian countries pursued export-led growth with undervalued exchange rates that favored some industries over others. Good government is relative; some fast-growing societies tolerated much corruption. Still, broad lessons are clear.

7   One is: Globalization works. Countries don't get rich by staying isolated. Those that embrace trade and foreign investment acquire know-how and technologies, can buy advanced products abroad, and are forced to improve their competitiveness. The transmission of new ideas and products is faster than ever. After its invention, the telegram took 90 years to spread to four-fifths of developing countries; for the cellphone, the comparable diffusion was 16 years.

8   A second is: Outside benevolence can't rescue countries from poverty. There is a role for foreign aid, technical assistance and charity in relieving global poverty. But it is a small role. It can improve health, alleviate suffering from natural disasters or wars, and provide some types of skills. But it cannot single-handedly stimulate the policies and habits that foster self-sustaining growth. Japan and China (to cite easy examples) have grown rapidly not because they received foreign aid but because they pursued pro-growth policies and embraced pro-growth values.

9   The hard question (which the panel ducks) is why all societies haven't adopted them. One reason is politics; some regimes are more interested in preserving their power and privileges than in promoting growth. But the larger answer, I think, is culture, as Lawrence Harrison of Tufts University argues. Traditional values, social systems or religious views are often hostile to risk-taking, wealth accumulation and economic growth. In his latest book, *The Central Liberal Truth,* Harrison contends that politics can alter culture, but it isn't easy.

10   Globalization has moral as well as economic and political dimensions. The United States and other wealthy countries are experiencing an anti-globalization backlash. Americans and others are entitled to defend themselves from economic harm, but many of the allegations against globalization are wildly exaggerated. Today, for example, the biggest drag on the U.S. economy—the housing crisis—is mainly a domestic problem. By making globalization an all-purpose scapegoat for economic complaints, many "progressives" are actually undermining the most powerful force for eradicating global poverty.

QUESTIONS FOR READING

1.   How many people are living in poverty in the world?
2.   What is the solution to poverty?
3.   What are the five identified elements of economic growth? State them in your own words.

4. What are the two key lessons we have learned about economic growth? What does each provide?

5. Why haven't all societies adopted the strategies for growth that will reduce poverty?

QUESTIONS FOR REASONING AND ANALYSIS

1. What type (genre) of argument is this? State Samuelson's claim to make the type of argument clear.

2. Samuelson asserts that globalization has a "moral dimension." What does he mean by this?

3. The author objects to using globalization as a scapegoat for economic problems. Why?

QUESTIONS FOR REFLECTION AND WRITING

1. Samuelson asserts that one part of the solution to poverty is to let market forces work. But the United States—and many other countries—are bailing out industries and propping up banks. Are we ignoring the evidence for eliminating poverty? Can the government's intervention be justified? Ring in on this issue.

2. Think about cultures whose values may be a cause for continued poverty. What countries would you list? Why?

3. What is the most important idea in this essay for you? Why did you select that idea?

THE POST-AMERICAN WORLD | FAREED ZAKARIA

The editor of *Newsweek International,* Fareed Zakaria also writes a weekly column on international affairs and hosts a weekly talk show on CNN. He is the author of *The Future of Freedom* and the best-seller *The Post-American World* (2008), from which the following excerpt is taken.

PREREADING QUESTIONS Do you think that we live in a post-American world? In what ways might this be an accurate statement? Can the response of much of the world to the 2008 election of Barack Obama give America another chance to change its image in the world?

Let me begin with an analogy drawn from my favorite sport, tennis. 1 American tennis enthusiasts have noted a worrying recent trend: the decline of America in championship tennis. The *New York Times'* Aron Pilhofer ran the numbers. Thirty years ago, Americans made up half the draw (the 128 players selected to play) in the U.S. Open. In 1982, for example, 78 of the 128 players selected were Americans. In 2007, only 20 Americans made the draw, a figure that accurately reflects the downward trend over twenty-five years. Millions of pixels have been devoted to wondering how America could have slipped so far and fast. The answer lies in another set of numbers. In the 1970s, about twenty-five countries sent players to the U.S. Open. Today, about thirty-five countries do, a 40 percent increase. Countries like Russia, South Korea, Serbia, and Austria are now churning out world-class players, and Germany, France, and Spain are training many more players than ever before. In the 1970s, three Anglo-Saxon nations—America, Britain, and Australia—utterly dominated tennis. In 2007, the final-sixteen players came from ten different countries. In other words, it's not that the United States has been doing badly over the last two decades. It's that, all of a sudden, everyone is playing the game.

2   If tennis seems trivial, consider a higher-stakes game. In 2005, New York City got a wake-up call. Twenty-four of the world's twenty-five largest initial public offerings (IPOs) that year were held in countries other than the United States. This was stunning. America's capital markets have long been the biggest, deepest, and most liquid in the world. They financed the turnaround in manufacturing in the 1980s, the technology revolution of the 1990s, and the ongoing advances in bioscience. It was the fluidity of these markets that had kept American business nimble. If America was losing this distinctive advantage, it was very bad news. The worry was great enough that Mayor Michael Bloomberg and Senator Chuck Schumer of New York commissioned McKinsey and Company to do a report assessing the state of New York's financial competitiveness. It was released late in 2006.[1]

3   Much of the discussion around the problem focused on America's over-regulation, particularly with post-Enron laws like Sarbanes-Oxley, and the constant threat of litigation that hovers over business in the United States. These findings were true enough, but they did not really get at what had shifted business abroad. America was conducting business as usual. But others were joining in the game. Sarbanes-Oxley and other such regulatory measures would not have had nearly the impact they did had it not been for the fact that *there are now alternatives.* What's really happening here, as in other areas, is simple: the rise of the rest. America's sum total of stocks, bonds, deposits, loans, and other instruments—its financial stock, in other words—still exceeds that of any other region, but other regions are seeing their financial stock grow much more quickly. This is especially true of the rising countries of Asia—at 15.5 percent annually between 2001 and 2005—but even the Eurozone's is outpacing America's, which clips along at 6.5 percent. Europe's total banking and trading revenues, $98 billion in 2005, have nearly pulled equal to U.S. revenues of $109 billion. In 2001, 57 percent of high-value IPOs occurred on American stock exchanges; in 2005, just 16 percent did. In 2006, the United States hosted barely a third of the number of total IPOs it did in 2001, while European exchanges expanded their IPO volume by 30 percent, and in Asia (minus Japan) volume doubled. IPOs are important because they generate "substantial recurring revenues for the host market" and contribute to perceptions of market vibrancy.

---

[1] *Sustaining New York's and the U.S.'s Global Financial Services Leadership,* available at www.senate .gov/~schumer/SchumerWebsite/pressroom/special_reports/2007/NY_REPORT%20_ FINAL.pdf.

IPOs and foreign listings are only part of the story. New derivatives based 4 on underlying financial instruments like stocks or interest-rate payment are increasingly important for hedge funds, banks, insurers, and the overall liquidity of international markets. And the dominant player on the international derivatives market (estimated at a notional value of $300 trillion) is London. London exchanges account for 49 percent of the foreign-exchange derivatives market and 34 percent of the interest-rate derivatives market. (The United States accounts for 16 percent and 4 percent of these markets, respectively.) European exchanges as a whole represent greater than 60 percent of the interest rate, foreign exchange, equity, and fund-linked derivatives. McKinsey's interviews with global business leaders indicate that Europe dominates not only in existing derivatives products but also in the innovation of new ones. The only derivatives product in terms of which Europe trails the U.S. is commodities, which accounts for the lowest overall revenue among major derivatives categories.

There were some specific reasons for the fall. Many of the massive IPOs in 5 2005 and 2006 were privatizations of state-owned companies in Europe and China. The Chinese ones naturally went to Hong Kong, and the Russian and Eastern European ones to London. In 2006, the three biggest IPOs all came from emerging markets. But this is all part of a broader trend. Countries and companies now have options that they never had before. Capital markets outside America—chiefly Hong Kong and London—are well regulated and liquid, which allows companies to take other factors, such as time zones, diversification, and politics, into account.

The United States is not doing worse than usual. It functions as it always 6 has—perhaps subconsciously assuming that it is still leagues ahead of the pack. American legislators rarely think about the rest of the world when writing laws, regulations, and policies. American officials rarely refer to global standards. After all, for so long the United States *was* the global standard, and when it chose to do something different, it was important enough that the rest of the world would cater to its exceptionality. America is the only country in the world, other than Liberia and Myanmar, that is not on the metric system. Other than Somalia, it is alone in not ratifying the international Convention on the Rights of the Child. In business, America didn't need to benchmark. It was the one teaching the world how to be capitalist. But now everyone is playing America's game, and playing to win.

For the last thirty years, America had the lowest corporate tax rates of 7 the major industrialized countries. Today, it has the second highest. American rates have not gone up; others have come down. Germany, for example, long a staunch believer in its high-taxation system, cut its rates (starting in 2008) in response to moves by countries to its east, like Slovakia and Austria. This kind of competition among industrialized countries is now widespread. It is not a race to the bottom—Scandinavian countries have high taxes, good services, and strong growth—but a quest for growth. American regulations used to be more flexible and market friendly than all others. That's no longer true. London's financial system was overhauled in 2001, with a single entity replacing a confusing mishmash of regulators, one reason that London's financial sector now beats out New York's on some measures. The entire British government works aggressively to make London a global hub. Washington, by contrast, spends its time and energy thinking of ways to tax New York, so that it can send its revenues to the rest of the country. Regulators from Poland to Shanghai to Mumbai are moving every day to make their systems more attractive to investors and manufacturers all over the world. Even on immigration, the European Union is creating a new "blue card," to attract highly skilled workers from developing countries.

8   Being on top for so long has its downsides. The American market has been so large that Americans have always known that the rest of the world would take the trouble to understand it and them. We have not had to reciprocate by learning foreign languages, cultures, and markets. Now that could leave America at a competitive disadvantage. Take the spread of English worldwide as a metaphor. Americans have delighted in this process because it makes it so much easier for them to travel and do business abroad. But for the locals, it gives them an understanding of and access to two markets and cultures. They can speak English but also Mandarin or Hindi or Portuguese. They can penetrate the American market but also the internal Chinese, Indian, or Brazilian one. (And in all these countries, the non-English-speaking markets remain the largest ones.) Americans, by contrast, can swim in only one sea. They have never developed the ability to move into other peoples' worlds.

9   We have not noticed how fast the rest has risen. Most of the industrialized world—and a good part of the nonindustrialized world as well—has better cell phone service than the United States. Broadband is faster and cheaper across the industrial world, from Canada to France to Japan, and the United States now stands sixteenth in the world in broadband penetration per capita. Americans are constantly told by their politicians that the only thing we have learned from other countries' health care systems is to be thankful for ours. Most Americans ignore the fact that a third of the country's public schools are totally dysfunctional (because their children go to the other two-thirds). The American litigation system is now routinely referred to as a huge cost to doing business, but no one dares propose any reform of it. Our mortage deduction for housing costs a staggering $80 billion a year, and we are told it is crucial to support home ownership. Except that Margaret Thatcher eliminated it in Britain, and yet that country has the same rate of home ownership as the United States. We rarely look around and notice other options and alternatives, convinced that "we're number one." But learning from the rest is no longer a matter of morality or politics. Increasingly it's about competitiveness.

10   Consider the automobile industry. For a century after 1894, most of the cars manufactured in North America were made in Michigan. Since 2004, Michigan has been replaced by Ontario, Canada. The reason is simple: health care. In America, car manufacturers have to pay $6,500 in medical and insurance costs for every worker. If they move a plant to Canada, which has a government-run health care system, the cost to the manufacturer is around $800 per worker. In 2006, General Motors paid $5.2 billion in medical and insurance bills for its active and retired workers. That adds $1,500 to the cost of every GM car

sold. For Toyota, which has fewer American retirees and many more foreign workers, that cost is $186 per car. This is not necessarily an advertisement for the Canadian health care system, but it does make clear that the costs of the American health care system have risen to a point that there is a significant competitive disadvantage to hiring American workers. Jobs are going not to countries like Mexico but to places where well-trained and educated workers can be found: it's smart benefits, not low wages, that employers are looking for. Tying health care to employment has an additional negative consequence. Unlike workers anywhere else in the industrialized world, Americans lose their health care if they lose their job, which makes them far more anxious about foreign competition, trade, and globalization. The Pew survey found greater fear of these forces among Americans than among German and French workers, perhaps for this reason.

For decades, American workers, whether in car companies, steel plants, [11] or banks, had one enormous advantage over all other workers: privileged access to American capital. They could use that access to buy technology and training that no one else had—and thus produce products that no one else could, and at competitive prices. That special access is gone. The world is swimming in capital, and suddenly American workers have to ask themselves, what can we do better than others? It's the dilemma not just for workers but for companies as well. What's critical now is not how a company compares with its own past (are we doing better than we were?), but how it compares with the present elsewhere (how are we doing relative to others?). The comparison is no longer along a vertical dimension of time but along a horizontal one of space.

When American companies went abroad, they used to bring with them [12] capital and know-how. But when they go abroad now, they discover that the natives already have money and already know how. There really isn't a Third World anymore. So what do American companies bring to India or Brazil? What is America's competitive advantage? It's a question few American businessmen thought they would ever have to answer. The answer lies in something the economist Martin Wolf noted. Describing the changing world, he wrote that economists used to discuss two basic concepts, *capital* and *labor*. But these are now commodities, widely available to everyone. What distinguishes economies today are *ideas* and *energy*. A country must be a source of either ideas or energy (meaning oil, natural gas, coal, etc.). The United States has been and can be the world's most important, continuing source of new ideas, big and small, technical and creative, economic and political. But to do that, it has to make some significant changes.

A DO-NOTHING POLITICS

The United States has a history of worrying that it is losing its edge. This [13] is at least the fourth wave of such concern since 1945. The first was in the late 1950s, a result of the Soviet Union's launch of the *Sputnik* satellite. The second was in the early 1970s, when high oil prices and slow growth in the United States convinced Americans that Western Europe and Saudi Arabia

Responses Around the World to the 2008 Election

Sand Sculpture in India

were the powers of the future, and President Nixon heralded the advent of a multipolar world. The most recent one arrived in the mid-1980s, when most experts believed that Japan would be the technologically and economically dominant superpower of the future. The concern in each of these cases was well founded, the projections intelligent. But none of these scenarios came to pass. The reason is that the American system was proved to be flexible, resourceful, and resilient, able to correct its mistakes and shift its attention. A focus on American economic decline ended up preventing it. The problem today is that the American political system seems to have lost its ability to create broad coalitions that solve complex issues.

14   The economic dysfunctions in America today are real, but, by and large, they are not the product of deep inefficiencies within the American economy, nor are they reflections of cultural decay. They are the consequences of specific government policies. Different policies could quickly and relatively easily move the United States onto a far more stable footing. A set of sensible reforms could be enacted tomorrow to trim wasteful spending and subsidies, increase savings, expand training in science and technology, secure pensions, create a workable immigration process, and achieve significant efficiencies in the use of energy.* Policy experts do not have wide disagreements on most of these

---

*I would not add fixing health care to this list, because that is not an easy problem with an easy fix. Most problems in Washington have simple policy solutions but face political paralysis. Health care is an issue that is complex in both policy and political terms. That doesn't mean it doesn't need to be fixed, far from it. But solving it would have been difficult under any circumstances, as it is today.

Celebration in Kenya

issues, and none of the proposed measures would require sacrifices reminiscent of wartime hardship, only modest adjustments of existing arrangements. And yet, because of politics, they appear impossible. The American political system has lost the ability for large-scale compromise, and it has lost the ability to accept some pain now for much gain later on.

As it enters the twenty-first century, the United States is not fundamentally a weak economy, or a decadent society. But it has developed a highly dysfunctional politics. An antiquated and overly rigid political system to begin with—about 225 years old—has been captured by money, special interests, a sensationalist media, and ideological attack groups. The result is ceaseless, virulent debate about trivia—politics as theater—and very little substance, compromise, and action. A "can-do" country is now saddled with a "do-nothing" political process, designed for partisan battle rather than problem solving. By every measure—the growth of special interests, lobbies, pork-barrel spending—the political process has become far more partisan and ineffective over the last three decades. 15

It is clever contrarianism to be in favor of sharp party politics and against worthy calls for bipartisanship. Some political scientists have long wished that America's political parties were more like European ones—ideologically pure and tightly disciplined. Well, it has happened—there are fewer and fewer moderates on either side—and the result is gridlock. Europe's parliamentary systems work well with partisan parties. In them, the executive branch always controls the legislative branch, and so the party in power can implement its agenda easily. The British prime minister doesn't need any support from the 16 opposition party; he has a ruling majority by definition. The American system, by contrast, is one of shared power, overlapping functions, and checks and balances. Progress requires broad coalitions between the two parties and politicians who will cross the aisle. That's why James Madison distrusted political parties, lumping them together with all kinds of "factions" and considering them a grave danger to the young American Republic.

17   I know that these complaints all sound very high-minded and squishy. And I know there has long been nasty partisanship in America, even in Madison's own era. But there has also been a lot of bipartisanship, especially over the past century. Reacting to the political bitterness of the late nineteenth century—the last time there were two close elections in succession—many American leaders tried to create forces for good, problem-solving government. Robert Brookings established the Brookings Institution in Washington in 1916 because he wanted an organization "free from any political or pecuniary interest . . . to collect, interpret, and lay before the country in a coherent form, the fundamental economic facts." The Council on Foreign Relations, founded five years later, also consciously reached across party lines. The first editor of its magazine, *Foreign Affairs,* told his deputy that if one of them became publicly identified as a Democrat, the other should immediately start campaigning for the Republicans. Contrast that with a much more recently founded think tank, the conservative Heritage Foundation, whose former senior vice president Burton Pines has admitted, "Our role is to provide conservative policymakers with arguments to bolster our side."

18   The trouble is that progress on any major problem—health care, Social Security, tax reform—will require compromise from both sides. In foreign policy, crafting a strategic policy in Iraq, or one on Iran, North Korea, or China, will need significant support from both sides. It requires a longer-term perspective. And that's highly unlikely. Those who advocate sensible solutions and compromise legislation find themselves marginalized by the party's leadership, losing funds from special-interest groups, and being constantly attacked by their "side" on television and radio. The system provides greater incentives to stand firm and go back and tell your team that you refused to bow to the enemy. It's great for fund-raising, but it's terrible for governing.

19   The real test for the United States is, in some ways, the opposite of that faced by Britain in 1900. Britain's economic power waned while it managed to maintain immense political influence around the world. The American economy and American society, in contrast, are capable of responding to the economic pressures and competition they face. They can adjust, adapt, and persevere. The real test for the United States is political—and it rests not just with America at large but with Washington in particular. Can Washington adjust and adapt to a world in which others have moved up? Can it respond to shifts in economic and political power? This challenge is even more difficult in foreign policy than in domestic policy. Can Washington truly embrace a world with a diversity of voices and viewpoints? Can it thrive in a world it cannot dominate?

QUESTIONS FOR READING

1. What is happening to reduce America's share of economic growth? (Even if you don't understand IPOs and derivatives, what can you gather from the numbers Zakaria provides in the opening five paragraphs?)

2. What are the U.S. corporate tax rates compared to other countries? How did this happen?

3. How has being on top now put Americans at a disadvantage?

4. What are some of our costs of doing business that other countries do not have, making them more competitive?

5. What is a source of anxiety and fear among American workers?

6. What did countries used to need to be competitive? What do they need now? What has America had that has, up to now, kept it competitive?

7. What is the primary cause of economic dysfunction in the United States today?

QUESTIONS FOR REASONING AND ANALYSIS

1. What is Zakaria's claim? State it as a problem/solution argument.

2. Zakaria begins with an analogy. What is its point? How does it provide a lead-in to the author's subject?

3. The author explains the problem and identifies a reason why the United States may not be able to change and remain competitive, but he does not provide specific solutions. What does this tell readers about his primary purpose in writing?

QUESTIONS FOR REFLECTION AND WRITING

1. What specifics most surprise you in Zakaria's analysis? Why?

2. Zakaria lists all kinds of problems, from the tax code to the cost of health care to dysfunctional public schools. Has he convinced you that we face serious problems? Why or why not? If you disagree, how would you refute him?

3. Should we learn to cope in a post-American world? If so, how? If not, why not?

CHAPTER 23

The American Dream:
Reality, Myth, Goal?

Reprinted with permission from *Psychology Today*. Copyright © 2008 by Sussex Publishers. Distributed by Tribune Media Services.

READ: What is the situation? Who speaks the words?

REASON: How have the words been changed from the original ones spoken at the event represented in the cartoon? Why?

REFLECT/WRITE: What makes this cartoon a clever comment on the 2008 primary campaign?

In the fall of 2008, eight years of Republican leadership ended with the convincing election of the Democratic candidate. Perhaps more significantly, Americans for the first time elected a president who is the son of a white American woman and an African national. Barack Obama proclaimed, in his election night speech before more than 100,000 in Chicago's Grant Park, that his election demonstrated the possibility of achieving the American Dream. Many signs and posters throughout the campaign also proclaimed HOPE.

Prior to this momentous election, many had written America off, asserting, as Fareed Zakaria shows in the previous chapter, that we are now in a post-American world, our status lost, our competitiveness overtaken by both Europe and Asia. Can one election, one new president, change America's sense of itself and its possibilities? Perhaps. Can it alter the economic downturn, end wars in Iraq and Afghanistan, fix the health-care system, improve public schools, and address issues of global warming and immigration—just to name a few of our problems? Not likely, at least in the short term.

And so, where are we headed? A nation of immigrants, we still cannot get along, divided by race and ethnic differences, divided by poverty and affluence, by those educated to be successful in a "cognitive age" and those lacking skills to share in America's wealth. Still, young people voted in great numbers in 2008, and polls indicate that they are more accepting of diversity and more concerned about the environment than older Americans. Can they lead the country past the culture wars to a reinventing of America? Some of the writers in this chapter are more hopeful than others. Some describe the problems we face; others offer solutions.

Certainly one solution is for all to become and stay informed, to read a newspaper every day, to know the facts and not be swayed by the emotional speeches of those who would gain power for themselves by keeping Americans divided rather than bringing us together to solve the problems we face both at home and abroad. Many of the authors in this text have blogs, another source of information about current events. Others participate in television talk shows. Seek out the authors who have struck you as interesting, as exploring issues about our times that concern you, as capable of offering you new information and new ideas. Also read all of the chapter's essays

The Obama Family on Election Night

and reflect on the opening visual and the chapter's photographs. You might also ask yourself: What can I do to make a difference?

TATTERED DREAM | EUGENE ROBINSON

A graduate of the University of Michigan where he was the first black student to be co-editor-in-chief of the university's student newspaper, Eugene Robinson joined the *Washington Post* in 1980. He has served as city reporter, foreign correspondent, and managing editor in charge of the lifestyle section. He is now an associate editor and twice-weekly columnist. Robinson focuses on the mix of culture and politics, as the following column, published November 23, 2007, reveals.

PREREADING QUESTION What do Robinson's facts reveal about America, in spite of the upward mobility demonstrated in Obama's presidential election in 2008?

1   We're not who we think we are.

2   The American self-image is suffused with the golden glow of opportunity. We think of the United States as a land of unlimited possibility, not so much a classless society but as a place where class is mutable—a place where brains, energy and ambition are what counts, not the circumstances of one's birth. But three new studies suggest that Horatio Alger doesn't live here anymore.

3   The Economic Mobility Project, an ambitious research initiative led by the Pew Charitable Trusts, looked at the economic fortunes of a large group of families over time, comparing the income of parents in the late 1960s with the income of their children in the late 1990s and early 2000s. Here's the finding that jumps out at me:

4   "The 'rags to riches' story is much more common in Hollywood than on Main Street. Only 6 percent of children born to parents with family income at the very bottom move to the very top."

5   That's right, just 6 percent of children born to parents who ranked in the bottom fifth of the sample, in terms of income, were able to bootstrap their way into the top fifth. Meanwhile, an incredible 42 percent of children born into that lowest quintile are still stuck at the bottom, having been unable to climb a single rung of the income ladder.

6   The study notes that even in Britain—a nation we tend to think of as burdened with a hidebound, anachronistic class system—children who are born poor have a better chance of moving up.

7   The Economic Mobility Project can't be accused of having an ideological bias; it's a collaboration, led by Pew, involving four leading think tanks that pretty much cover the political spectrum—the American Enterprise Institute, the Brookings Institution, the Heritage Foundation and the Urban Institute.

8   "Both left and right can care about this," said John E. Morton, Pew's managing director of economic policy. "Traditionally, Americans have been ready to accept high levels of inequality because of our belief in the American dream. What happens if we can't believe in the dream any longer?"

When the three studies were released last week, most reporters focused on 9
the finding that African Americans born to middle-class or upper-middle-class
families are earning slightly less, in inflation-adjusted dollars, than did their parents. Julia B. Isaacs, the Brookings scholar who authored the reports, said the
reason for this is still unclear; overall, the data suggest that blacks are somewhat less upwardly mobile than whites, although about two-thirds of African
Americans do earn more than their parents did.

Isaacs said she was surprised at finding that the personal income of Ameri- 10
can men—including white men—has been almost perfectly flat for the past
three decades. One of Isaacs's studies indicates, in fact, that most of the financial gains white families have made in that time can be attributed to the entry
of white women into the labor force. This is not the case for African Americans; in 1968, when the group was first surveyed, black women were far more
likely to already have income-producing jobs.

The picture that emerges from all the quintiles, correlations and percent- 11
ages is of a nation in which, overall, "the current generation of adults is better
off than the previous one," as one of the studies notes. The median income
of the families studied was $55,600 in the late 1960s; their children's median
family income was $71,900. However, this rising tide has not lifted all boats
equally. The rich have seen far greater income gains than have the poor.

Even more troubling is that our notion of America as the land of oppor- 12
tunity gets little support from the data. Americans move fairly easily up and
down the middle rungs of the ladder, but there is "stickiness at the ends"—
four out of 10 children who are born poor will remain poor, and four out of 10
children who are born rich will stay rich.

Isaacs, who specializes in child and family policy at Brookings, said she 13
thought that improved early-childhood education was one way to begin making the promise of economic mobility more of a reality; one key to understanding the racial disparities found in the studies, she said, might be the vast
difference in wealth (as opposed to income) between white and black families.

The Economic Mobility Project's work should be part of the political 14
debate. Every candidate for president should read these studies and then
explain why it's acceptable that a poor kid has only a 6 percent chance of
reaching the top.

QUESTIONS FOR READING

1. What does the Economic Mobility Project reveal about upward mobility in the
   United States?

2. How does the United States compare with Britain in the opportunity to
   move up?

3. How do blacks compare with whites in terms of the chance to move up the
   economic scale? In general, are adults today better off than their parents?

4. In what income categories can Americans most easily move up and down?

QUESTIONS FOR REASONING AND ANALYSIS

1. What is Robinson's claim? Where does he first indicate his subject and his attitude?
2. How is his opening sentence an effective attention-getter?
3. Who is Horatio Alger? If you don't know, look it up, as there are frequent references to him when the American dream is discussed.
4. What is Robinson's explanation of the American dream? What does it recognize? What does it include?

QUESTIONS FOR REFLECTION AND WRITING

1. Do you agree with Robinson's definition of the American dream? Why or why not?
2. Do you agree that it is unacceptable that "a poor kid has only a 6 percent chance of reaching the top"? Consider the other statistic the author provides: "four out of 10 children who are born poor will remain poor." That means that the other six were able to move out of poverty, just not to the very top of the income scale. Explain and defend your responses to these passages.
3. Should society's (and government's) concern be to improve the road to the top for everyone? Or, should the concern be to eliminate the poverty of the bottom fifth of society? If you were an economic advisor to the president, what would you push for? And how would you advise that we achieve your goal?

THE "F WORD" | FIROOZEH DUMAS

Born in Iran, Firoozeh Dumas moved to California when she was seven, returned to Iran with her family for two years and then came back to California. She attended the University of California at Berkeley, married, and has three children. Initially she started to write stories for her children. These were developed into *Funny in Farsi: A Memoir of Growing Up Iranian in America* (2003), from which the following excerpt is taken. *Laughing Without an Accent* was published in 2008.

PREREADING QUESTIONS Based on her title, what did you first think this work would be about? How does the information above help you to adjust your thinking?

1   My cousin's name, Farbod, means "Greatness."

2   When he moved to America, all the kids called him "Farthead." My brother Farshid ("He Who Enlightens") became "Fartshit." The name of my friend Neggar means "Beloved," although it can be more accurately translated as "She Whose Name Almost Incites Riots." Her brother Arash ("Giver") initially couldn't understand why every time he'd say his name, people would laugh and ask him if it itched.

3   All of us immigrants knew that moving to America would be fraught with challenges, but none of us thought that our names would be such an obstacle.

How could our parents have ever imagined that someday we would end up in a country where monosyllabic names reign supreme, a land where "William" is shortened to "Bill," where "Susan" becomes "Sue," and "Richard" somehow evolves into "Dick"? America is a great country, but nobody without a mask and a cape has a *z* in his name. And have Americans ever realized the great scope of the guttural sounds they're missing? Okay, so it has to do with linguistic roots, but I do believe this would be a richer country if all Americans could do a little tongue aerobics and learn to pronounce "kh," a sound more commonly associated in this culture with phlegm, or "gh," the sound usually made by actors in the final moments of a choking scene. It's like adding a few new spices to the kitchen pantry. Move over, cinnamon and nutmeg, make way for cardamom and sumac.

Exotic analogies aside, having a foreign name in this land of Joes and 4
Marys is a pain in the spice cabinet. When I was twelve, I decided to simplify my life by adding an American middle name. This decision serves as proof that sometimes simplifying one's life in the short run only complicates it in the long run.

My name, Firoozeh, chosen by my mother, means "Turquoise" in Persian. 5
In America, it means "Unpronounceable" or "I'm Not Going to Talk to You Because I Cannot Possibly Learn Your Name and I Just Don't Want to Have to Ask You Again and Again Because You'll Think I'm Dumb or You Might Get Upset or Something." My father, incidentally, had wanted to name me Sara. I do wish he had won that argument.

To strengthen my decision to add an American name, I had just finished 6
fifth grade in Whittier, where all the kids incessantly called me "Ferocious." That summer, my family moved to Newport Beach, where I looked forward to starting a new life. I wanted to be a kid with a name that didn't draw so much attention, a name that didn't come with a built-in inquisition as to when and why I had moved to America and how was it that I spoke English without an accent and was I planning on going back and what did I think of America?

My last name didn't help any. I can't mention my maiden name, because: 7

"Dad, I'm writing a memoir." 8

"Great! Just don't mention our name." 9

Suffice it to say that, with eight letters, including a *z*, and four syllables, my 10
last name is as difficult and foreign as my first. My first and last name together generally served the same purpose as a high brick wall. There was one exception to this rule. In Berkeley, and only in Berkeley, my name drew people like flies to baklava. These were usually people named Amaryllis or Chrysanthemum, types who vacationed in Costa Rica and to whom lentils described a type of burger. These folks were probably not the pride of Poughkeepsie, but they were refreshingly nonjudgmental.

When I announced to my family that I wanted to add an American name, 11
they reacted with their usual laughter. Never one to let mockery or good judgment stand in my way, I proceeded to ask for suggestions. My father suggested "Fifi." Had I had a special affinity for French poodles or been considering a career in prostitution, I would've gone with that one. My mom suggested

"Farah," a name easier than "Firoozeh" yet still Iranian. Her reasoning made sense, except that Farrah Fawcett was at the height of her popularity and I didn't want to be associated with somebody whose poster hung in every post-pubescent boy's bedroom. We couldn't think of any American names beginning with *F*, so we moved on to *J*, the first letter of our last name. I don't know why we limited ourselves to names beginning with my initials, but it made sense at that moment, perhaps by the logic employed moments before bungee jumping. I finally chose the name "Julie" mainly for its simplicity. My brothers, Farid and Farshid, thought that adding an American name was totally stupid. They later became Fred and Sean.

12   That same afternoon, our doorbell rang. It was our new next-door neighbor, a friendly girl my age named Julie. She asked me my name and after a moment of hesitation, I introduced myself as Julie. "What a coincidence!" she said. I didn't mention that I had been Julie for only half an hour.

13   Thus I started sixth grade with my new, easy name and life became infinitely simpler. People actually remembered my name, which was an entirely refreshing new sensation. All was well until the Iranian Revolution, when I found myself with a new set of problems. Because I spoke English without an accent and was known as Julie, people assumed I was American. This meant that I was often privy to their real feelings about those "damn I-raynians." It was like having those X-ray glasses that let you see people naked, except that what I was seeing was far uglier than people's underwear. It dawned on me that these people would have probably never invited me to their house had they known me as Firoozeh. I felt like a fake.

14   When I went to college, I eventually went back to using my real name. All was well until I graduated and started looking for a job. Even though I had graduated with honors from UC–Berkeley, I couldn't get a single interview. I was guilty of being a humanities major, but I began to suspect that there was more to my problems. After three months of rejections, I added "Julie" to my résumé. Call it coincidence, but the job offers started coming in. Perhaps it's the same kind of coincidence that keeps African Americans from getting cabs in New York.

15   Once I got married, my name became Julie Dumas. I went from having an identifiably "ethnic" name to having ancestors who wore clogs. My family and non-American friends continued calling me Firoozeh, while my coworkers and American friends called me Julie. My life became one big knot, especially when friends who knew me as Julie met friends who knew me as Firoozeh. I felt like those characters in soap operas who have an evil twin. The two, of course, can never be in the same room, since they're played by the same person, a struggling actress who wears a wig to play one of the twins and dreams of moving on to bigger and better roles. I couldn't blame my mess on a screen writer; it was my own doing.

16   I decided to untangle the knot once and for all by going back to my real name. By then, I was a stay-at-home mom, so I really didn't care whether people remembered my name or gave me job interviews. Besides, most of the people

I dealt with were in diapers and were in no position to judge. I was also living in Silicon Valley, an area filled with people named Rajeev, Avishai, and Insook.

Every once in a while, though, somebody comes up with a new permuta- 17 tion and I am once again reminded that I am an immigrant with a foreign name. I recently went to have blood drawn for a physical exam. The waiting room for blood work at our local medical clinic is in the basement of the building, and no matter how early one arrives for an appointment, forty coughing, wheezing people have gotten there first. Apart from reading *Golf Digest* and *Popular Mechanics*, there isn't much to do except guess the number of contagious diseases represented in the windowless room. Every ten minutes, a name is called and everyone looks to see which cough matches that name. As I waited patiently, the receptionist called out, "Fritzy, Fritzy!" Everyone looked around, but no one stood up. Usually, if I'm waiting to be called by someone who doesn't know me, I will respond to just about any name starting with an *F*. Having been called Froozy, Frizzy, Fiorucci, and Frooz and just plain "Uhhhh . . .," I am highly accommodating. I did not, however, respond to "Fritzy" because there is, as far as I know, no *t* in my name. The receptionist tried again, "Fritzy, Fritzy DumbAss." As I stood up to this most linguistically original version of my name, I could feel all eyes upon me. The room was momentarily silent as all of these sick people sat united in a moment of gratitude for their own names.

Despite a few exceptions, I have found that Americans are now far more 18 willing to learn new names, just as they're far more willing to try new ethnic foods. Of course, some people just don't like to learn. One mom at my children's school adamantly refused to learn my "impossible" name and instead settled on calling me "F Word." She was recently transferred to New York where, from what I've heard, she might meet an immigrant or two and, who knows, she just might have to make some room in her spice cabinet.

QUESTIONS FOR READING

1. What happened when the author changed her name to Julie?
2. What happened when she sought a job after college, using her original name?
3. When did she decide to use only her original name?
4. When Dumas is called at the medical clinic, what does she think the other patients are feeling?

QUESTIONS FOR REASONING AND ANALYSIS

1. How does this work differ from most of the arguments in this text?
2. Still, as an argument it must make a claim. What is Dumas's claim?
3. What has changed in America since her arrival as a young girl? Is the change complete? What would she like to see Americans learn to do?
4. What writing strategies are noteworthy in creating her style? Illustrate with examples.

QUESTIONS FOR REFLECTION AND WRITING

1. How much effort do you make to pronounce names correctly? Why is it important to get a person's name right?

2. Have you had the experience of Americans impatient with the pronunciation of your name—or just refusing to get it right? If so, what has been your response?

3. What might be some of the reasons why Americans have trouble with the pronunciation of ethnic names—whether the names belong to foreign nationals or to ethnic Americans? Reflect on possible causes.

4. What are the advantages of facing the world with humor?

THE ENGAGED GENERATION | E. J. DIONNE, JR.

Holding a doctorate in philosophy from Oxford University, E. J. Dionne is a senior fellow at the Brookings Institution, an adjunct professor at Georgetown University, and a syndicated columnist. Two of his books include *Why Americans Hate Politics* (1991) and *Souled Out: Reclaiming Faith and Politics After the Religious Right* (2008). The following column appeared during the 2008 campaign (July 24, 2008) in *The New Republic*.

PREREADING QUESTIONS What might the author mean by his title? How might young people be "engaged" today?

1   WASHINGTON—The conventional wisdom on certain subjects is so deeply rooted that no amount of evidence disturbs its hold. That's how it is with those dreary predictions that young Americans just won't vote.

2   Since the late 1960s, the same chorus has been heard from election to election: The young don't care. They're disengaged. They're too wrapped up in their music, their favorite sports and their parties to care about politics. Predicting that the young will vote in large numbers is like saying the Cubs will finally win the World Series.

3   As it happens, the Cubs are doing well this season, and the evidence is overwhelming that this year, the young really will vote in large numbers—and they just might tip the election.

4   The trend started four years ago. According to the Center for Information and Research on Civic Learning and Engagement, or CIRCLE, electoral participation among 18- to 24-year-olds rose from 36 percent in 2000 to 47 percent in 2004. For the larger 18 to 29 group, participation rose from 40 percent to 49 percent.

5   The 2006 midterm election saw a larger increase in off-year voting among the under-30s than any other age group.

6   Then came this year's primaries: According to CIRCLE, the turnout rate for the under-30s nearly doubled between 2000 and 2008, from 9 percent to 17 percent.

Obama's Young Supporters

None of this means that young people will vote at the same rate as middle- 7
aged people or senior citizens. The young move around more, and voter registration laws in most states make it harder for the footloose to exercise their
rights. And it's long been the case that citizens become more involved in politics when they settle down and develop stronger community ties.

Nonetheless, on present trends, it's a near certainty that young people's 8
overall share of the electorate will rise substantially this year.

Defying stereotypes, the young are more engaged in this campaign than 9
are their elders. A Pew Research Center study released earlier this month
asked voters whether they considered this year's campaign "interesting" or
"dull." Among those 18 to 29, 67 percent called the campaign interesting, as
did 66 percent of those 30 to 49. By contrast, 58 percent of those 50 to 64 and
52 percent of those over 65 saw the campaign as interesting.

The increase in political interest among the young is staggering. Between 10
2000 and this year, the percentage of those under 30 describing the campaign
as interesting was up 36 points; the increase among those over 65 was a more
modest 18 points.

Could the young make a difference in Barack Obama's favor? Again, the 11
answer is clearly yes. Age is one of the most powerful lines of division in this
election. In Pew's survey, the under-30s gave Obama his largest lead, 56 percent to 36 percent. He also led among voters aged 30 to 49, but ran behind
among voters 65 and over.

12   This is not a one-time trend. The under-30s were by far John Kerry's best age group in 2004—he carried them over George Bush 54 percent to 45 percent—and they voted better than 3–2 for Democratic House candidates in 2006.

13   A study released last week by the Rockefeller Foundation and *Time* magazine helps explain why the under-30s are so engaged, and why their political views have more in common with those of the New Deal generation than of the Reagan generation.

14   According to the survey, nearly half of the under-30s said that America was a better place to live in the 1990s, and they think the country will continue to decline. This is a more pessimistic view than that of the older generational groups. They are also the generation most worried about their own or their family's economic security, and half of them went without health insurance at some point in the last year, more than double the percentage of any other group.

15   In light of this, it's not surprising that the Rockefeller report found that 86 percent of the under-30s—significantly more than any other generational group—said that "more government programs should help those struggling under current economic conditions."

16   Young Americans show all signs of being interested enough and upset enough to flock to the polls this year. If they do, they could be the most politically consequential generation since the cohort of the Great Depression and World War II. Think of these newcomers as the Engaged Generation.

QUESTIONS FOR READING

1. What is the conventional wisdom regarding young people?
2. What do the numbers indicate about voting trends for the under-30s?
3. For what reasons do young people vote in fewer numbers than older citizens?
4. Could the young make a difference in 2008 for Obama, in the author's view?
5. Why are young people more engaged than since World War II? What are their attitudes and concerns?

QUESTIONS FOR REASONING AND ANALYSIS

1. What is Dionne's claim? Where does he state it?
2. What does the author gain with an opening that states conventional wisdom rather than his claim?
3. What *kind* of evidence does Dionne provide? Is it effective? Evaluate the argument?

QUESTIONS FOR REFLECTION AND WRITING

1. Are you surprised by any of Dionne's data? If so, what surprises you? If not, why not?

2. What did happen in the 2008 election? Did young people vote in large numbers? Did they help to give Obama his victory? If you don't know, do some research to find the answers.

3. Is Dionne correct to call today's under-30s the Engaged Generation? Are you—and your friends—engaged? Why or why not?

NO HUMAN BEING IS ILLEGAL | MAE M. NGAI

Professor of Asian American Studies at Columbia University, Mae Ngai explores questions of immigration, citizenship, and nationalism in United States history. She has written extensively on immigration history and policy and is the author of *Impossible Subjects: Illegal Aliens and the Making of Modern America* (2004). The following article appeared in *Women's Studies Quarterly* in 2006.

PREREADING QUESTIONS What are your attitudes toward illegal immigrants? Do you think that Ngai is going to challenge the thinking of many Americans in this article?

Like abortion and guns, immigration has emerged as a hot-button issue 1 in American politics. Because immigration involves concerns in different registers, economic and cultural, it is strangely and perhaps uniquely misaligned in traditional partisan terms (Wong 2006; Zolberg 2006). President Bush cannot manage the split in his own party, between those Republicans who want to exploit immigrants and those who want to expel them. Among Democratic voters, some support cultural diversity and inclusion while others worry that cheaper immigrant labor depresses domestic wages. Political consultants, sensing a no-win situation, are advising Democrats with presidential aspirations to stay clear of the issue altogether.

The lack of partisan coherence, however, does not explain why immigration 2 evokes such heated debate. There is a dimension to the debate that seems irrational, impervious to arguments involving empirical data, historical experience, or legal precedent. This was brought home to me after I wrote an op-ed in a major newspaper about how, during the first half of the twentieth century, the U.S. government legalized tens of thousands of illegal European immigrants (Ngai 2006). I received postcards with invectives like, "stupid professor!" I faced similar hostility during a live call-in show on public radio. Confronted with ranting about how immigrants are bad for the United States, I wanted to counter that immigrants are good for the United States. At one level, negative generalizations about immigrants can be refuted point by point: they do not hurt the economy, they expand it; they are more law abiding than the native-born population; they want to learn English and their children all do (Smith and Edmonston 1997; Alba and Nee 2003).

But this approach is risky. Generalizations reproduce stereotypes and efface 3 the complexity and diversity of immigrant experience. As Bonnie Honig (2001) has argued, xenophilia is the flip side of xenophobia. In both cases citizens use "immigrants" as a screen onto which they project their own aspirations or

A march on Washington in support of immigrants

frustrations about American democracy. Casting immigrants as bearers of the work ethic, family values, and consensual citizenship renews the tired citizen's faith-liberal capitalism. But when the immigrants disappoint or when conditions change, they become easy scapegoats.

4   As Honig suggests, this kind of immigration discourse is an exercise in nationalism. In an important sense, "Are immigrants good or bad for us?" is the wrong question. It takes as its premise that immigrants are not part of "us." The idea falsely posits that non-citizens are not part of American society and leaves them out of the discussion. The mass demonstrations of Mexicans and other immigrants last spring were significant because they showed that immigrants are no longer content to be the object of discussion but have emerged as subjects with voice and agency. It was particularly noteworthy but perhaps not surprising that so many of the participants were female, from older hotel workers to high school students, giving lie to the stereotypes that the "illegal alien" is a solo male laborer or that immigrants are meek. Undocumented immigration involves men, women, and families, and they are all standing up.

5   Further, the question assumes that "we" (the United States, defined by its citizens) have a singular interest above and against the interests of "them" (all non-citizens and the foreign countries from whence they came). To be sure, while human migration is as old as human history, immigration and naturalization are modern phenomena, part of the international system based on nation-states that was consolidated in the period between the late nineteenth century and World War I. In this system, sovereign nations assert their absolute right to determine, in the first instance, who shall be admitted to territory and membership and who shall not.

In the United States, immigration was not regulated by the federal govern- 6
ment until after the civil war, and not until the late 1880s and 1890s did the
U.S. Supreme Court invoke the sovereign principle as the basis for immigration
policy. Before that, it considered immigration part of the commerce clause of
the Constitution; as laborers, immigrants were easily imagined as "articles of
commerce" (Bilder 1996).

But Chinese exclusion, first legislated in 1882, required the Court to 7
justify why some laborers were desired and others were not. Was the claim
that Chinese were racially inassimilable an acceptable reason? The Court said
yes; in fact, it said that Congress did not have to justify itself in terms of the
Constitution. In the Chinese Exclusion Case (130 U.S. 518 [1889]) the Court
recognized Congress's plenary, or absolute power to regulate immigration
as part of its authority over foreign relations, in the same realm as declaring
war and making treaties. "Aliens enter and remain in the United States only
with the license, permission, and sufferance of Congress," it opined (Fong Yue
Ting v. U.S., 149 U.S. 698 [1893]). To this day the plenary power doctrine over
immigration stands.

American political culture has thoroughly normalized the primacy of 8
national sovereignty in immigration affairs, and with important consequences.
Nationalism generates the view that immigration is a zero-sum game among
competitive nation-states. Americans like to believe that immigration to the
United States proves the superiority of liberal capitalism, that "America" is the
object of global envy; we resist examining the role that American world power
has played in global structures of migration, including the gendered dimensions of migrant exploitation. Increasing numbers of women from the global
south are leaving their families behind as they migrate to the affluent countries
to work as caretakers for other people's children, as hotel-room cleaners, or
as indentured sex-workers. We prefer to ignore these realities and to think,
instead, that our immigration policy is generous—indeed, too generous, as we
also resent the demands made upon us by others and we think we owe outsiders nothing (Ngai 2004).

The emphasis on national sovereignty is the basis for the alarm that we've 9
"lost control" of the border and for the draconian proposals against unauthorized immigration: more fencing, criminalization of the undocumented
and those who hire or assist them, mass deportations. But many liberals who
are sympathetic to Mexican immigrants also want "something done" to stop
illegal immigration, although few would actually support turning the entire
country into a police state, which is what would be necessary to truly seal the
border from unauthorized entry. The cost of viewing sovereignty as the exclusive grounds for immigration policy is that we push to the margins other considerations, such as human rights and global distributive justice. The current
debate over immigration policy reform reminds us that sovereignty is not just
a claim to national right; it is a theory of power (Carens 1998).

Just two months before September 11, 2001, it will be recalled, President 10
Bush announced his intention to legalize undocumented Mexican immigrants
and institute a guest-worker program that would offer a path to permanent

residency and citizenship. In its details it was not particularly generous and it faced a complex process of legislative negotiation, as have all efforts to reform the immigration laws. But it did not provoke the kind of emotional controversy that we hear today.

11   However, after 9/11 the immigration issue disappeared from the Washington scene. It resurfaced a couple of years ago, with Bush's proposal receiving support from then-president of Mexico, Vicente Fox. But only in the last year has it become an explosive issue in national politics, with vociferous rhetoric like "stop the invasion" and "no amnesty for lawbreakers." It seems no accident that immigration restriction has moved to the fore as public disaffection with the war in Iraq grows. According to Republican strategist Don Allen, immigration is an issue that "gets us talking about security and law and order" (Hulse 2006). House majority leader Dennis Hastert deploys flexible rhetoric of popular sovereignty most succinctly: "We're at war. Our borders are a sieve" (Swarns 2006). Whether mongering terrorism and illegal immigration will result in greater mass support for U.S. wars against both will succeed remains to be seen. But the very connections made between them suggest broad ground for oppositional action.

WORKS CITED

Alba, Richard, and Victor Nee. 2003. *Remaking the American Mainstream.* Cambridge: Harvard University Press.

Bilder, Mary Sarah. 1996. "The Struggle over Immigration: Indentured Servants, Slaves, and Articles of Commerce," *Missouri Law Review.*

Carens, Joseph. 1998. "Aliens and Citizens: The Case for Open Borders," in *The Immigration Reader: America in Multidisciplinary Perspective,* ed. David Jacobson. Malden, MA: Blackwell Publications.

Honig, Bonnie. 2001. *Democracy and the Foreigner.* Princeton: Princeton University Press.

Hulse, Carl. 2006. "In Bellweather District, GOP Runs on Immigration," *New York Times,* September 6, A1.

Ngai, Mae M. 2004. *Impossible Subjects: Illegal Aliens and the Making of Modern America.* Princeton: Princeton University Press.

_____. 2006. "How Granny Got Legal." *Los Angeles Times,* May 18.

Smith, James P., and Barry Edmonston, eds. 1997. *The New Americans: Economic, Demographic, and Fiscal Effects of Immigration.* Washington, DC: National Academy Press.

Swarns, Rachel. 2006. "Immigration Overhaul Takes a Backseat as Campaign Season Begins," *New York Times,* September 8, A1.

Wong, Carolyn. 2006. *Lobbying for Inclusion.* Stanford: Stanford University Press.

Zolberg, Aristide. 2006. *A Nation by Design.* New York: Russell Sage Foundation; Cambridge: Harvard University Press.

QUESTIONS FOR READING

1. When the author wrote about the United States' past legalization of immigrants, what response did she receive?
2. Why is the question "Are immigrants good or bad for us?" not a useful way to discuss immigration?
3. When did controlling immigration by nations become the norm?
4. When did the Supreme Court rule that Congress has power to regulate immigration, including deciding who is acceptable?
5. What attitude toward immigrants do Americans often hold? As a result, what reality of female migration gets overlooked?
6. What current concern of the United States has added heat to the immigration debate?

QUESTIONS FOR REASONING AND ANALYSIS

1. What is Ngai's approach to the issue of immigration? What gives her essay focus? With this analysis in mind, what, then, is her claim?
2. Ngai says that objections to illegals can be refuted. Based on her assertions (paragraph 2), what can you conclude to be typical objections?

QUESTIONS FOR REFLECTION AND WRITING

1. Do you find it helpful to look at immigration from the perspective of national sovereignty—so that when we feel threatened as a nation we become upset over our borders and immigrants? Does this response match your experience with this issue? Why or why not?
2. Do you think of illegal immigrants as "them"? Do you agree with Ngai that such thinking denies their partnership in our society? Is this a problem? Why or why not?
3. Do you agree with the author's position on immigrants? If so, why? If not, why not?

OUR SAD NEGLECT OF MEXICO | MARCELA SANCHEZ

Washington Post journalist Marcela Sanchez reports on events in Latin America in her weekly online column "Desede Washington." Sanchez is also Washington correspondent for several news outlets in Colombia and is a frequent commentator on *Foro Inertamericano* of Worldnet TV. The following column was published May 28, 2005.

PREREADING QUESTIONS In what ways might the United States be perceived as neglecting Mexico? What would you like to see America do to help Mexico?

1   Whether you believe Mexican immigrants help or hurt the United States, there is one truth you have to accept: Work here pays much, much better. A low-skill Mexican worker earns five to six times as much in this country as back home, assuming he or she could find a comparable job there.

2   This truth is so obvious it seems a cliché and yet it remains mostly absent from the debate on how to reform U.S. immigration. For all the talk around the country of border enforcement, guest-worker programs, employer sanctions and driver's license restrictions, the sad fact is that none of these "solutions" addresses the root of the problem: a persistent and large income disparity between the United States and Mexico.

3   Even the most comprehensive and progressive immigration reform proposal in years, introduced this month by Sens. John McCain (R-Ariz.) and Edward Kennedy (D-Mass.), is more concerned with making U.S. immigration policy more humane than dealing with this income disparity. The bill crafts a guest-worker program—creating new visa categories and quotas and a secure identification system for employers—but provides only a vague indication that income disparity might be a problem or a responsibility to take on.

4   Why such reluctance? How can a proposal that purports to reduce the flow of illegal Mexican workers to the United States not take a stab at the root cause? Won't better conditions for immigrant workers here only be an invitation for more illegal migrants from Mexico, as the argument goes, as long as wage disparity remains unaddressed?

5   To alter income disparity, it is obvious that Mexico must reduce its development gap and raise incomes. What is just as apparent is that Americans do

A civilian border watcher

not feel, at least at the moment, that they have a responsibility or even an interest in reducing that gap through investments of money and expertise. They don't feel the same obligation they once felt, say, after World War II for Europe, or that the European Union took on when it bolstered its poorest members. Mexico and the United States may share a 2,000-mile border, but their sense of a shared future runs about two inches deep.

There is a strong sense in this country that Mexico's problems are of its 6 own making, and must be solved by Mexico. That is why former Bush official Richard A. Falkenrath and others say a significant infusion of U.S. aid into Mexico is a "nonstarter." Indeed, Mexico desperately needs to collect more taxes and reform its energy sector and labor laws—healing itself by removing structural constraints that make it more a Third World nation than the economic powerhouse it could become.

The North American Free Trade Agreement, signed more than 10 years 7 ago by Canada, Mexico and the United States, was supposed to generate more jobs in Mexico, raise salaries and reduce people's incentive to emigrate. That proved to be wishful thinking. In fact, NAFTA has not generated the number of new jobs predicted, nor has it alleviated rural poverty in many areas of Mexico. That would require, according to an upcoming report on NAFTA by the Institute for International Economics, "a sustained period of strong growth and substantial income transfers to poorer states."

There are some in this country, a minority to be sure, who say Washington 8 must get involved more directly. Otherwise, they argue, Mexico won't be able to reduce disparities for at least another hundred years. Among them is Robert Pastor, a former Carter administration official who has tirelessly argued for a North American Investment Fund. Pastor cites a 2000 World Bank estimate that Mexico would need $20 billion per year for a decade in essential infrastructure and educational projects to reduce that 100 years to 10.

Pastor is under no illusions that such a fund will be created any time soon. 9 Certainly the Bush administration is not talking about any such ideas within the recently launched Security and Prosperity Partnership of North America, the latest ambitiously named project that won't even touch on immigration, although immigration is directly connected to security and prosperity.

The administration and Congress are under little pressure to deepen the 10 U.S. commitment to Mexico, not when the public is increasingly fearful of and resentful toward immigrants, particularly Mexicans. But if anything, such sentiments prolong illegal immigration in the sense that they distract citizens and leaders alike into thinking that if you put up enough barriers, Mexicans will go away.

QUESTIONS FOR READING

1. How much more can a low-skilled Mexican make working illegally in the United States than at home?

2. What seems to be the United States' response to U.S./Mexican income disparity as a part of the immigration debate?

3. What seems to be the United States' attitude toward their southern neighbor?

4. Has NAFTA worked to increase jobs in Mexico?

QUESTIONS FOR REASONING AND ANALYSIS

1. What kind (genre) of argument is this? State Sanchez's claim to make the type
   of argument clear.

2. Sanchez appears to object to the McCain/Kennedy bill that would have created
   a guest-worker program. Why? What fundamental problem would such a program fail to address?

3. Sanchez seems to have little confidence that the United States will do much to
   help Mexico. How do you know? Where in her essay does she express or imply
   this view?

QUESTIONS FOR REFLECTION AND WRITING

1. Do you agree with the author that the poverty and low wages in Mexico are a
   part of the problem of illegal immigration from that country? Does this make
   sense to you? Why or why not?

2. If Sanchez has convinced you of a major cause of the problem, has she then
   convinced you of what must be part of the solution? Do you see the logic of her
   argument? Why or why not?

3. If you agree with Sanchez's analysis of part of the problem but disagree with
   her solution, what solution would you propose? Explain and defend your
   response.

IMMIGRATE, ASSIMILATE | AMY CHUA

A professor at Yale Law School since 2001, Amy Chua specializes in international
business transactions, ethnic conflict, and globalization and the law. She is the
author of *World on Fire* (2004) and *Day of Empire: How Hyperpowers Rise to Global
Dominance—And Why They Fall* (2007). Her essay on immigration, published
February 3, 2008, was a special to the *Washington Post*.

PREREADING QUESTIONS Given the title, where do you expect to find Chua on the
immigration debate? Given her education and expertise, how do you expect her
to support her argument?

1   If you don't speak Spanish, Miami really can feel like a foreign country. In
any restaurant, the conversation at the next table is more likely to be in Spanish
than English. And Miami's population is only 65 percent Hispanic. El Paso is
76 percent Latino. Flushing, N.Y., is 60 percent immigrant, mainly Chinese.

Chinatowns and Little Italys have long been part of America's urban land- **2** scape, but would it be all right to have entire U.S. cities where most people spoke and did business in Chinese, Spanish or even Arabic? Are too many Third World, non-English-speaking immigrants destroying our national identity?

For some Americans, even asking such questions is racist. At the other end **3** of the spectrum, conservative talk-show host Bill O'Reilly fulminates against floods of immigrants who threaten to change America's "complexion" and replace what he calls the "white Christian male power structure."

But for the large majority in between, Democrats and Republicans alike, **4** these questions are painful, and there are no easy answers. At some level, most of us cherish our legacy as a nation of immigrants. But are all immigrants really equally likely to make good Americans? Are we, as Samuel Huntington warns, in danger of losing our core values and devolving "into a loose confederation of ethnic, racial, cultural and political groups, with little or nothing in common apart from their location in the territory of what had been the United States of America"?

My parents arrived in the United States in 1961, so poor that they couldn't **5** afford heat their first winter. I grew up speaking only Chinese at home (for every English word accidentally uttered, my sister and I got one whack of the chopsticks). Today, my father is a professor at Berkeley, and I'm a professor at Yale Law School. As the daughter of immigrants, a grateful beneficiary of America's tolerance and opportunity, I could not be more pro-immigrant.

Nevertheless, I think Huntington has a point.   **6**

Around the world today, nations face violence and instability as a result **7** of their increasing pluralism and diversity. Across Europe, immigration has resulted in unassimilated, largely Muslim enclaves that are hotbeds of unrest and even terrorism. The riots in France late last year were just the latest manifestation. With Muslims poised to become a majority in Amsterdam and elsewhere within a decade, major West European cities could undergo a profound transformation. Not surprisingly, virulent anti-immigration parties are on the rise.

Not long ago, Czechoslovakia, Yugoslavia and the Soviet Union disintegrated **8** when their national identities proved too weak to bind together diverse peoples. Iraq is the latest example of how crucial national identity is. So far, it has found no overarching identity strong enough to unite its Kurds, Shiites and Sunnis.

The United States is in no danger of imminent disintegration. But this is **9** because it has been so successful, at least since the Civil War, in forging a national identity strong enough to hold together its widely divergent communities. We should not take this unifying identity for granted.

The greatest empire in history, ancient Rome, collapsed when its cultural **10** and political glue dissolved, and peoples who had long thought of themselves as Romans turned against the empire. In part, this fragmentation occurred because of a massive influx of immigrants from a very different culture. The "barbarians" who sacked Rome were Germanic immigrants who never fully assimilated.

11   Does this mean that it's time for the United States to shut its borders and reassert its "white, Christian" identity and what Huntington calls its Anglo-Saxon, Protestant "core values"?

ANTI-IMMIGRANT MISTAKES

12   No. The anti-immigration camp makes at least two critical mistakes.

13   First, it neglects the indispensable role that immigrants have played in building American wealth and power. In the 19th century, the United States would never have become an industrial and agricultural powerhouse without the millions of poor Irish, Polish, Italian and other newcomers who mined coal, laid rail and milled steel. European immigrants led to the United States' winning the race for the atomic bomb.

14   Today, American leadership in the Digital Revolution—so central to our military and economic preeminence—owes an enormous debt to immigrant contributions. Andrew Grove (co-founder of Intel), Vinod Khosla (Sun Microsystems) and Sergey Brin (Google) are immigrants. Between 1995 and 2005, 52.4 percent of Silicon Valley startups had one key immigrant founder. And Vikram S. Pundit's recent appointment to the helm of Citigroup means that 14 CEOs of Fortune 100 companies are foreign-born.

15   The United States is in a fierce global competition to attract the world's best high-tech scientists and engineers—most of whom are not white Christians. Just this past summer, Microsoft opened a large new software-development center in Canada, in part because of the difficulty of obtaining U.S. visas for foreign engineers.

16   Second, anti-immigration talking heads forget that their own scapegoating vitriol will, if anything, drive immigrants further from the U.S. mainstream. One reason we don't have Europe's enclaves is our unique success in forging an ethnically and religiously neutral national identity, uniting individuals of all backgrounds. This is America's glue, and people like Huntington and O'Reilly unwittingly imperil it.

17   Nevertheless, immigration naysayers also have a point.

18   America's glue can be subverted by too much tolerance. Immigration advocates are too often guilty of an uncritical political correctness that avoids hard questions about national identity and imposes no obligations on immigrants. For these well-meaning idealists, there is no such thing as too much diversity.

MAINTAINING OUR HERITAGE

19   The right thing for the United States to do—and the best way to keep Americans in favor of immigration—is to take national identity seriously while maintaining our heritage as a land of opportunity. U.S. immigration policy should be tolerant but also tough. Here are five suggestions:

• **Overhaul Admission Priorities.**

20   Since 1965, the chief admission criterion has been family reunification. This was a welcome replacement for the ethnically discriminatory quota system that

preceded it. But once the brothers and sisters of a current U.S. resident get in, they can sponsor their own extended families. In 2006, more than 800,000 immigrants were admitted on this basis. By contrast, only about 70,000 immigrants were admitted on the basis of employment skills, with an additional 65,000 temporary visas granted to highly skilled workers.

This is backward. Apart from nuclear families (spouse, minor children, possibly parents), the special preference for family members should be drastically reduced. As soon as my father got citizenship, his relatives in the Philippines asked him to sponsor them. Soon, his mother, brother, sister and sister-in-law were also U.S. citizens or permanent residents. This was nice for my family, but frankly there is nothing especially fair about it. 21

Instead, the immigration system should reward ability and be keyed to the country's labor needs, skilled or unskilled, technological or agricultural. In particular, we should significantly increase the number of visas for highly skilled workers, putting them on a fast track for citizenship. 22

• Make English the Official National Language.

A common language is critical to cohesion and national identity in an ethnically diverse society. Americans of all backgrounds should be encouraged to speak more languages—I've forced my own daughters to learn Mandarin (minus the threat of chopsticks)—but offering Spanish-language public education to Spanish-speaking children is the wrong kind of indulgence. Native-language education should be overhauled, and more stringent English proficiency requirements for citizenship should be set up. 23

• Immigrants Must Embrace the Nation's Civic Virtues.

It took my parents years to see the importance of participating in the larger community. When I was in third grade, my mother signed me up for Girl Scouts. I think she liked the uniforms and merit badges, but when I told her that I was picking up trash and visiting soup kitchens, she was horrified. 24

For many immigrants, only family matters. Even when immigrants get involved in politics, they often focus on protecting their own and protesting discrimination. That they can do so is one of the great virtues of U.S. democracy. But a mind-set based solely on taking care of your own factionalizes our society. 25

Like all Americans, immigrants have a responsibility to contribute to the social fabric. It's up to each immigrant community to fight off an "enclave" mentality and give back to their new country. It's not healthy for Chinese to hire only Chinese, or Koreans only Koreans. By contrast, the free health clinic set up by Muslim Americans in Los Angeles—serving the entire poor community—is a model to emulate. Immigrants are integrated at the moment they realize that their success is intertwined with everyone else's. 26

• Enforce the Law.

Illegal immigration, along with terrorism, is the chief cause of today's anti-immigration backlash. It is also inconsistent with the rule of law, which, as any 27 immigrant from a developing country will tell you, is a critical aspect of U.S. identity. But if we're serious about this problem, we need to enforce the law against not only illegal aliens, but also against those who hire them.

28   It's the worst of all worlds to allow U.S. employers who hire illegal aliens—thus keeping the flow of illegal workers coming—to break the law while demonizing the aliens as lawbreakers. An Arizona law that took effect Jan. 1 tightens the screws on employers who hire undocumented workers, but this issue can't be left up to a single state.

• **Make the United States an Equal-Opportunity Immigration Magnet.**

29   That the 11 million to 20 million illegal immigrants are 80 percent Mexican and Central American is itself a problem. This is emphatically not for the reason Huntington gives—that Hispanics supposedly don't share America's core values. But if the U.S. immigration system is to reflect and further our ethnically neutral identity, it must itself be ethnically neutral, offering equal opportunity to Sudanese, Estonians, Burmese and so on. The starkly disproportionate ratio of Latinos—reflecting geographical fortuity and a large measure of lawbreaking—is inconsistent with this principle.

30   Immigrants who turn their backs on American values don't deserve to be here. But those of us who turn our backs on immigrants misunderstand the secret of America's success and what it means to be American.

QUESTIONS FOR READING

1. What is Huntington's concern for America?
2. What has happened in some European cities? To several European countries? What causes internal conflict in Iraq?
3. What are the two mistakes of those who oppose immigration, in the author's view?
4. What are the author's suggestions for a tough immigration policy? State her five proposals in your own words.

QUESTIONS FOR REASONING AND ANALYSIS

1. Why does Chua provide her immigrant experience and family success story? As a part of her argument, what purpose does it serve?
2. What is clever about her concluding paragraph? How does it mirror the approach of her argument?
3. What is Chua's claim? Express her position as a problem/solution argument.
4. Look at Chua's five proposals. What kinds of grounds does she provide in support?
5. Is the author convincing? If so, what makes her argument effective? If not, why not?

QUESTIONS FOR REFLECTION AND WRITING

1. Chua asserts that the chief cause of anti-immigration attitudes is a combination of terrorism and illegal aliens. Do you agree with this assessment? (Compare Chua and Ngai.)

2. Where do you stand on immigration? In opposition? Embracing diversity? Or somewhere in the middle? Has Chua established a good argument for the middle ground? Why or why not?

3. Is there any specific proposal with which you disagree? If so, why? How would you refute Chua's defense of that proposal?

I HAVE A DREAM | MARTIN LUTHER KING, JR.

Martin Luther King, Jr. (1929–1968), Baptist minister, civil rights leader dedicated to nonviolence, president of the Southern Christian Leadership Conference, Nobel Peace Prize winner in 1964, was assassinated in 1968. He was an important figure in the August 1963 poor people's march on Washington, where he delivered his speech from the steps of the Lincoln Memorial.

King's plea for equality, echoing the language and cadences of both the Bible and "The Gettysburg Address," has become a model of effective oratory.

PREREADING QUESTION What is the purpose or what are the purposes of King's speech?

1   Five score years ago, a great American, in whose symbolic shadow we stand, signed the Emancipation Proclamation. This momentous decree came as a great beacon light of hope to millions of Negro slaves who had been seared in the flames of withering injustice. It came as a joyous daybreak to end the long night of captivity.

2   But one hundred years later, we must face the tragic fact that the Negro is still not free. One hundred years later, the life of the Negro is still sadly crippled by the manacles of segregation and the chains of discrimination. One hundred years later, the Negro lives on a lonely island of poverty in the midst of a vast ocean of material prosperity. One hundred years later, the Negro is still languished in the corners of American society and finds himself an exile in his own land. So we have come here today to dramatize an appalling condition.

3   In a sense we have come to our nation's Capital to cash a check. When the architects of our republic wrote the magnificent words of the Constitution and the Declaration of Independence, they were signing a promissory note to which every American was to fall heir. This note was a promise that all men would be guaranteed the unalienable rights of life, liberty, and the pursuit of happiness.

4   It is obvious today that America has defaulted on this promissory note insofar as her citizens of color are concerned. Instead of honoring this sacred obligation, America has given the Negro people a bad check which has come back marked "insufficient funds." But we refuse to believe that the bank of justice is bankrupt. We refuse to believe that there are insufficient funds in

the great vaults of opportunity of this nation. So we have come to cash this check—a check that will give us upon demand the riches of freedom and the security of justice. We have also come to this hallowed spot to remind America of the fierce urgency of *now*. This is no time to engage in the luxury of cooling off or to take the tranquilizing drug of gradualism. *Now* is the time to make real the promises of Democracy. *Now* is the time to rise from the dark and desolate valley of segregation to the sunlit path of racial justice. *Now* is the time to open the doors of opportunity to all of God's children. *Now* is the time to lift our nation from the quicksands of racial injustice to the solid rock of brotherhood.

5   It would be fatal for the nation to overlook the urgency of the moment and to underestimate the determination of the Negro. This sweltering summer of the Negro's legitimate discontent will not pass until there is an invigorating autumn of freedom and equality. 1963 is not an end, but a beginning. Those who hope that the Negro needed to blow off steam and will now be content will have a rude awakening if the nation returns to business as usual. There will be neither rest nor tranquility in America until the Negro is granted his citizenship rights. The whirlwinds of revolt will continue to shake the foundations of our nation until the bright day of justice emerges.

6   But there is something that I must say to my people who stand on the warm threshold which leads into the palace of justice. In the process of gaining our right place we must not be guilty of wrongful deeds. Let us not seek to satisfy our thirst for freedom by drinking from the cup of bitterness and hatred. We must forever conduct our struggle on the high plane of dignity and discipline. We must not allow our creative protest to degenerate into physical violence. Again and again we must rise to the majestic heights of meeting physical force with soul force. The marvelous new militancy which has engulfed the Negro community must not lead us to a distrust of all white people, for many of our white brothers, as evidenced by their presence here today, have come to realize that their destiny is tied up with our destiny and their freedom is inextricably bound to our freedom. We cannot walk alone.

7   And as we walk, we must make the pledge that we shall march ahead. We cannot turn back. There are those who are asking the devotees of civil rights, "When will you be satisfied?" We can never be satisfied as long as the Negro is the victim of the unspeakable horrors of police brutality. We can never be satisfied as long as our bodies, heavy with the fatigue of travel, cannot gain lodging in the motels of the highways and the hotels of the cities. We cannot be satisfied as long as the Negro's basic mobility is from a smaller ghetto to a larger one. We can never be satisfied as long as a Negro in Mississippi cannot vote and a Negro in New York believes he has nothing for which to vote. No, no, we are not satisfied, and we will not be satisfied until justice rolls down like waters and righteousness like a mighty stream.

8   I am not unmindful that some of you have come here out of great trials and tribulations. Some of you have come fresh from narrow jail cells. Some of you have come from areas where your quest for freedom left you battered by the storms of persecution and staggered by the winds of police brutality. You

have been the veterans of creative suffering. Continue to work with the faith that unearned suffering is redemptive.

Go back to Mississippi, go back to Alabama, go back to South Carolina, 9 go back to Georgia, go back to Louisiana, go back to the slums and ghettos of our northern cities, knowing that somehow this situation can and will be changed. Let us not wallow in the valley of despair.

I say to you today, my friends, that in spite of the difficulties and frustrations 10 of the moment I still have a dream. It is a dream deeply rooted in the American dream.

I have a dream that one day this nation will rise up and live out the true 11 meaning of its creed: "We hold these truths to be self-evident; that all men are created equal."

I have a dream that one day on the red hills of Georgia the sons of former 12 slaves and the sons of former slaveowners will be able to sit down together at the table of brotherhood.

I have a dream that one day even the state of Mississippi, a desert state 13 sweltering with the heat of injustice and oppression, will be transformed into an oasis of freedom and justice.

I have a dream that my four little children will one day live in a nation 14 where they will not be judged by the color of their skin but by the content of their character.

I have a dream today. 15

I have a dream that one day the state of Alabama, whose governor's lips 16 are presently dripping with the words of interposition and nullification, will be transformed into a situation where little black boys and black girls will be able to join hands with little white boys and white girls and walk together as sisters and brothers.

I have a dream today. 17

I have a dream that one day every valley shall be exalted, every hill and 18 mountain shall be made low, the rough places will be made plain, and the crooked places will be made straight, and the glory of the Lord shall be revealed, and all flesh shall see it together.

This is our hope. This is the faith with which I return to the South. With this 19 faith we will be able to hew out of the mountain of despair a stone of hope. With this faith we will be able to transform the jangling discords of our nation into a beautiful symphony of brotherhood. With this faith we will be able to work together, to pray together, to struggle together, to go to jail together, to stand up for freedom together, knowing that we will be free one day.

This will be the day when all of God's children will be able to sing with new 20 meaning

My country, 'tis of thee,
Sweet land of liberty,
  Of thee I sing;
Land where my fathers died,
Land of the pilgrims' pride,

> From every mountain-side
> Let freedom ring.

21   And if America is to be a great nation this must become true. So let freedom ring from the prodigious hilltops of New Hampshire. Let freedom ring from the mighty mountains of New York. Let freedom ring from the heightening Alleghenies of Pennsylvania!

22   Let freedom ring from the snowcapped Rockies of Colorado!

23   Let freedom ring from the curvaceous peaks of California!

24   But not only that; let freedom ring from Stone Mountain of Georgia!

25   Let freedom ring from Lookout Mountain of Tennessee!

26   Let freedom ring from every hill and molehill of Mississippi. From every mountainside, let freedom ring.

27   When we let freedom ring, when we let it ring from every village and every hamlet, from every state and every city, we will be able to speed up that day when all of God's children, black men and white men, Jews and Gentiles, Protestants and Catholics, will be able to join hands and sing in the words of the old Negro spiritual, "Free at last! thank God almighty, we are free at last!"

QUESTIONS FOR READING

1. King is directly addressing those participants in the poor people's march who are at the Lincoln Memorial. What other audience did he have as well?

2. How does the language of the speech reflect King's vocation as a Christian minister? How does it reflect his sense of his place in history?

QUESTIONS FOR REASONING AND ANALYSIS

1. List all the elements of style discussed in Chapter 2 that King uses. What elements of style dominate?

2. What stylistic techniques do Lincoln and King share?

3. Find one sentence that you think is especially effective and explain why you picked it. Is the effect achieved in part by the way the sentence is structured?

4. Explain each metaphor in paragraph 2.

5. State the claim of King's argument.

QUESTIONS FOR REFLECTION AND WRITING

1. Which, in your view, is King's most vivid and powerful metaphor? Why do you find it effective?

2. If King were alive today, would he want to see another march on Washington? If so, what would be the theme, or purpose, of the march? If not, why not?

3. Would King have supported the Million Man March? The rally of the Promise Keepers? Why or why not? (If necessary, do some research on these two events.)

Understanding Literature

The same process of reading nonfiction can be used to understand literature—fiction, poetry, and drama. You still need to read what is on the page, looking up unfamiliar words and tracking down references you don't understand. You still need to examine the context, to think about who is writing to whom, under what circumstances, and in what literary format. And, to respond fully to the words, you need to analyze the writer's techniques for developing ideas and expressing attitudes.

Although it seems logical that the reading process should be much the same regardless of the work, not all readers of literature are willing to accept that logic. Some readers want a work of literature to mean whatever they think it means. But what happened to the writer's desire to communicate? If you decide that a Robert Frost poem, for example, should mean whatever you are feeling when you read it, you might as well skip the reading of Frost and just commune with your feelings. Presumably you read Frost to gain some new insight from him, to get beyond just your vision and see something of human experience and emotion from a new vantage point.

Other readers of literature hesitate over the concept of *literary analysis,* or at least over the word *analysis.* These readers complain that analysis will "tear the work apart" and "ruin it." If you are inclined to share this attitude, stop for a minute and think about the last sports event you watched. Perhaps a friend explained: "North Carolina is so good at stalling to use up the clock; Duke will have to foul to get the ball and have a chance to tie the game." The game is being analyzed! And that analysis makes the event more fully experienced by those who understand at least some of the elements of basketball.

The analogy is clear. You, too, can be a fan of literature. You can enjoy reading and discussing your reading once you learn to use your active reading and analytic skills to open up a poem or story, and once you sharpen your knowledge of literary terms and concepts so that you can "speak the language" of literary criticism with the same confidence with which you discuss the merits of a full court press.

GETTING THE FACTS: ACTIVE READING, SUMMARY, AND PARAPHRASE

Let's begin with the following poem by Paul Dunbar. As you read, make marginal notes, circling a phrase you fancy, putting a question mark next to a difficult line, underscoring words you need to look up. Note, too, your emotional reactions as you read.

PROMISE | PAUL LAWRENCE DUNBAR

Born of former slave parents, Dunbar (1872–1906) was educated in Dayton, Ohio. After a first booklet of poems, *Oak and Ivy*, was printed in 1893, several friends helped Dunbar get a second collection, *Majors and Minors*, published in 1895. A copy was given to author and editor William Dean Howells, who reviewed the book favorably, increasing sales and Dunbar's reputation. This led to a national publisher issuing *Lyrics of Lowly Life* in 1896, the collection that secured Dunbar's fame.

I grew a rose within a garden fair,
And, tending it with more than loving care,
I thought how, with the glory of its bloom,
I should the darkness of my life illume;
5   And, watching, ever smiled to see the lusty bud
Drink freely in the summer sun to tinct its blood.

My rose began to open, and its hue
Was sweet to me as to it sun and dew;
I watched it taking on its ruddy flame
10   Until the day of perfect blooming came,
Then hasted I with smiles to find it blushing red—
Too late! Some thoughtless child had plucked my rose and fled!

"Promise" should not have been especially difficult to read, although you may have paused a moment over "illume" before connecting it to "illuminate," and you may have to check the dictionary for a definition of "tinct." Test your knowledge of content by listing all the facts of the poem. Pay attention to the poem's basic situation. Who is speaking? What is happening, or what thoughts is the speaker sharing? In this poem, the "I" is not further identified, so you will have to refer to him or her as the "speaker." You should not call the speaker "Dunbar," however, because you do not know if Dunbar ever grew a rose.

In "Promise" the speaker is describing an event that has taken place. The speaker grew a rose, tended to it with care, and watched it begin to bloom. Then, when the rose was in full bloom, some child picked the rose and took it away. The situation is fairly simple, isn't it? Too simple, unfortunately, for some readers who decide that the speaker never grew a rose at all. But when anyone writes, "I grew a rose within a garden fair," it is wise to assume that the writer means just that. People do grow roses, most often in gardens, and then the gardens are made "fair" or beautiful by the flowers growing there. Read first for the facts; try not to jump too quickly to broad generalizations.

As with nonfiction, one of the best ways to make certain you have understood a literary work is to write a summary or paraphrase. Since a summary condenses, you are most likely to write a summary of a story, novel, or play, whereas a paraphrase is usually reserved for poems or complex short passages. When you paraphrase a difficult poem, you are likely to end up with more words than in the original because your purpose is to turn cryptic lines into more ordinary sentences. For example, Dunbar's "Then hasted I with smiles" can be paraphrased to read: "Then, full of smiles, I hurried."

When summarizing a literary work, remember to use your own words, draw no conclusions, giving only the facts, but focus your summary on the key events in the story. (Of course the selecting you do to write a summary represents preliminary analysis; you are making some choices about what is important in the work.) Read the following short story by Langston Hughes and then write your own summary. Finally, compare yours to the summary that follows the story.

EARLY AUTUMN | LANGSTON HUGHES

Like many American writers, Langston Hughes (1902–1967) moved from the Midwest to New York City, lived and worked in France, and then returned to the United States to a career in writing. He was a journalist, fiction writer, and poet, the author of more than sixty books. The success of his novel *Not Without Laughter* (1930) secured his reputation and enabled him to become the first black American to support himself as a professional writer. Known as "the bard of Harlem," Hughes was an important public figure and voice for black writers. "Early Autumn" is reprinted from the collection *Something in Common* (1963).

When Bill was very young, they had been in love. Many nights they had 1 spent walking, talking together. Then something not very important had come between them, and they didn't speak. Impulsively, she had married a man she thought she loved. Bill went away, bitter about women.

Yesterday, walking across Washington Square, she saw him for the first 2 time in years.

"Bill Walker," she said.   3

He stopped. At first he did not recognize her, to him she looked so old.   4

"Mary! Where did you come from?"   5

Unconsciously, she lifted her face as though wanting a kiss, but he held 6 out his hand. She took it.

"I live in New York now," she said.   7

"Oh"—smiling politely. Then a little frown came quickly between his eyes. 8

"Always wondered what happened to you, Bill."   9

10   "I'm a lawyer. Nice firm, way downtown."

11   "Married yet?"

12   "Sure. Two kids."

13   "Oh," she said.

14   A great many people went past them through the park. People they didn't know. It was late afternoon. Nearly sunset. Cold.

15   "And your husband?" he asked her.

16   "We have three children. I work in the bursar's office at Columbia."

17   "You're looking very . . ." (he wanted to say *old*) ". . . well," he said.

18   She understood. Under the trees in Washington Square, she found herself desperately reaching back into the past. She had been older than he then in Ohio. Now she was not young at all. Bill was still young.

19   "We live on Central Park West," she said. "Come and see us sometime."

20   "Sure," he replied. "You and your husband must have dinner with my family some night. Any night. Lucille and I'd love to have you."

21   The leaves fell slowly from the trees in the Square. Fell without wind. Autumn dusk. She felt a little sick.

22   "We'd love it," she answered.

23   "You ought to see my kids." He grinned.

24   Suddenly the lights came on up the whole length of Fifth Avenue, chains of misty brilliance in the blue air.

25   "There's my bus," she said.

26   He held out his hand. "Good-by."

27   "When . . ." she wanted to say, but the bus was ready to pull off. The lights on the avenue blurred, twinkled, blurred. And she was afraid to open her mouth as she entered the bus. Afraid it would be impossible to utter a word.

28   Suddenly she shrieked very loudly, "Good-by!" But the bus door had closed.

29   The bus started. People came between them outside, people crossing the street, people they didn't know. Space and people. She lost sight of Bill. Then she remembered she had forgotten to give him her address—or to ask him for his—or tell him that her youngest boy was named Bill, too.

Summary of "Early Autumn"

Langston Hughes's short story "Early Autumn" is about two people, Mary and Bill, who were in love once but broke up and did not speak to each other. Mary married someone else "impulsively" and does not see Bill again until one late afternoon, years later, in New York City's Washington Square. When Mary speaks, Bill does not at first recognize her. They discuss their jobs, their marriages, their children. When Mary invites Bill to visit, he says "Sure" and that she should have dinner with his family sometime. When Mary's bus arrives and she gets on, she has trouble speaking. She realizes that they have not set a date or exchanged addresses. She has also forgotten to tell him that her youngest son is named Bill.

Note that the summary is written in the present tense. Brevity is achieved by condensing several lines of dialogue into a statement such as "they discuss their jobs." Notice, too, that the summary is not the same as the original; the emotions of the characters, conveyed through what is said—and not said—are missing.

Now for a paraphrase. Read the following sonnet by Shakespeare, looking up unfamiliar words and making notes. Remember to read to the end of a unit of thought, not just to the end of a line. Some sentences continue through several lines; if you pause before you reach punctuation, you will be confused. Write your own paraphrase, not looking ahead in the text, and then compare yours with the one that follows the poem.

SONNET 116 | WILLIAM SHAKESPEARE

Surely the best-known name in literature, William Shakespeare (1564–1616) is famous as both a dramatist and a poet. Rural Warwickshire and the market town of Stratford-on-Avon, where he grew up, showed him many of the character types who were to enliven his plays, as did the bustling life of a young actor in London. Apparently his sonnets were intended to be circulated only among his friends, but they were published nonetheless in 1609. His thirty-seven plays were first published together in 1623. Shakespeare's 154 sonnets vary, some focusing on separation and world-weariness, others on the endurance of love.

> Let me not to the marriage of true minds
> Admit impediments. Love is not love
> Which alters when it alteration finds,
> Or bends with the remover to remove.
> O, no! it is an ever-fixed mark   5
> That looks on tempests and is never shaken;
> It is the star to every wand'ring bark,
> Whose worth's unknown, although his height be taken.
> Love's not Time's fool, though rosy lips and cheeks
> Within his bending sickle's compass come;   10
> Love alters not with his brief hours and weeks,
> But bears it out even to the edge of doom.
>   If this be error and upon me proved,
>   I never writ, nor no man ever loved.

Paraphrase of "Sonnet 116"

I cannot accept barriers to the union of steadfast spirits. We cannot call love love if it changes because it discovers change or if it disappears during absence. On the contrary, love is a steady guide that, in spite of difficulties, remains unwavering. Love can define the inherent value in all who lack self-knowledge, though superficially they know who they are. Love does not lessen with time, though signs of physical beauty may fade. Love endures, changeless, eternally. If anyone can show me to be wrong in this position, I am no writer and no man can be said to have loved.

We have examined the facts of a literary work, what we can call the internal situation. But, as we noted in Chapter 2, there is also the external situation or context of any piece of writing. For many literary works, the context is not as essential to understanding as it is with nonfiction. You can read "Early Autumn," for instance, without knowing much about Langston Hughes, or the circumstances in which he wrote the story, although such information would enrich your reading experience. There is a body of information, however, that is important: the external literary situation. Readers should take note of these details before they begin to read:

- First, don't make the mistake of calling every work a "story." Make clear distinctions among stories, novels, plays, and poems.
- Poems can be further divided into narrative, dramatic, and lyric poems.
- A *narrative poem,* such as Homer's *The Iliad,* tells a story in verse. A *dramatic poem* records the speech of at least one character.
- A poem in which only one figure speaks—but clearly addresses words to someone who is present in a particular situation—is called a *dramatic monologue.*
- *Lyric poems,* Dunbar's "Promise" for example, may place the speaker in a situation or may express a thought or feeling with few, if any, situational details, but lyric poems have in common the convention that we as readers are listening in on someone's thoughts, not listening to words directed to a second, created figure. These distinctions make us aware of how the words of the poem are coming to us. Are we hearing a storyteller or someone speaking? Or, are we overhearing someone's thoughts?

REMEMBER: Active reading includes looking over a work first and predicting what will come next. Do not just start reading words without first understanding what kind of work you are about to read.

Lyric poems can be further divided into many subcategories or types. Most instructors will expect you to be able to recognize some of these types. You should be able to distinguish between a poem in *free verse* (no prevailing metrical pattern) and one in *blank verse* (continuous unrhymed lines of iambic pentameter). (Note: A metrical line will contain a particular number—pentameter is five—of one kind of metrical "foot." The iambic foot consists of one unstressed syllable followed by one stressed syllable.) You should also be able to tell if a poem is written in some type of *stanza* form (repeated units with the same number of lines, same metrical pattern, and same rhyme scheme), or if it is a *sonnet* (always fourteen lines of iambic pentameter with one of two complex rhyme schemes labeled either "English" or "Italian"). You want to make it a habit to observe these external elements before you read. To sharpen your observation, complete the following exercise.

EXERCISE: Observing Literary Types and Using Literary Terms

1. After surveying this appendix, make a list of all the works of literature by primary type: short story, poem, play.
2. For each work on your list, add two additional pieces of information: whether the author is American or British, and in what century the work was written. Why should you be aware of the writer's dates and nationality as you read?
3. Further divide the poems into narrative, dramatic, or lyric.
4. List as many of the details of type or form as you can for each poem. For example, if the poem is written in stanzas, describe the stanza form used: the number of lines, the meter, the rhyme scheme. If the poem is a sonnet, determine the rhyme scheme. (Note: Rhyme scheme is indicated by using letters, assigning *a* to the first sound and using a new letter for each new sound. Thus, if two consecutive lines rhyme, the scheme is *aa, bb, cc, dd,* and so on.)

SEEING CONNECTIONS: ANALYSIS

Although we read first for the facts and an initial emotional response, we do not stop there, because as humans we seek meaning. Surely there is more to "Early Autumn" than the summary suggests; emotionally we know this to be true. As with nonfiction, one of the best places to start analysis is with a work's organization or structure. Lyric poems will be shaped by many of the same structures found in essays: chronological, spatial, general to particular, particular to general, a list of particulars with an unstated general point, and so forth. In "Promise," Dunbar gives one illustration, recounted chronologically, to make a point that is left unstated. "Sonnet 116" contains a list of characteristics of love underscored in the conclusion by the speaker's conviction that he is right.

Analysis of Narrative Structure

In stories (and plays and narrative poems) we are given a series of events, in time sequence, involving one or more characters. In some stories, episodes are only loosely connected but are unified around a central character (Mark Twain's *Adventures of Huckleberry Finn,* for example). Most stories present events that are at least to some extent related causally; that is, action A by the main character leads to event B, which requires action C by the main character. This kind of plot structure can be diagrammed, as in Figure 1 on the next page.

Figure 1 introduces some terms and concepts useful in analyzing and discussing narratives. The story's *exposition* refers to the background details needed to get the story started, including the time and place of the story and

FIGURE 1 Plot Structure

relationships of the characters. In "Early Autumn" Hughes begins by telling us that the action will take place in lower Manhattan, late in the afternoon, between a man and a woman who had once loved each other. The *complication* refers to an event; something happens to produce tension or conflict. In "Early Autumn" the meeting of Mary and Bill, after many years, could be an occasion for joy but seems to cause a complication instead. Mary expects to be kissed but Bill merely offers his hand; Bill smiles "politely" and then frowns. The meeting becomes a complication for both characters because it generates a *conflict* within each character. Bill's conflict seems the more manageable; he turns on his polite behavior to get through the unexpected encounter. Mary is more upset; seeing Bill makes her feel old, and she is hardly able to speak when she boards the bus. A key question arises: Why is Mary so upset?

Although some stories present one major complication leading to a climactic moment of decision or insight for the main character, many actually repeat the pattern, presenting several complications—each with an attempted resolution that generates yet another complication—until we reach the high point of tension, the *climax*. The climax then generates the story's *resolution* and ending. These terms are useful even though some stories end abruptly without having much resolution. An abbreviated resolution is part of the modern writer's view of reality, that life goes on, with problems remaining unresolved. The climax in "Early Autumn" comes when Mary boards her bus and then realizes that she will once again be separated from Bill. This story's climax is muted and merges quickly into the resolution of the last line. The ending offers little genuine resolution; our recognizing this fact helps us better understand the story.

Analysis of Character

An analysis of plot structure has shown that Mary is the more troubled character. You should recognize that Mary is not in conflict *with* Bill but rather is in conflict *over* him, or over her feelings for him, still strong in spite of years of a life without him. Note the close connection between complication (event) and conflict (what the characters are feeling). Fiction requires both plot and character, events and players in those events. In serious literature the greater emphasis is usually on character, on what we learn about human life through the interplay of character and incident.

As we shift attention from the plot of "Early Autumn" to the characters, it helps to consider how writers present character. Writers have several techniques for conveying character:

- Descriptive details. (Bill's polite smile followed by a frown.)
- Dramatic scenes. (Instead of telling us, they show us. Most of "Early Autumn" consists of dialogue between Mary and Bill.)
- Contrast among characters. (We have already observed that Mary and Bill react differently to their encounter.)
- Other elements in the work. (Names can be significant, or characters can become associated with objects, or details of setting can become symbolic.)

Understanding character is always a challenge because we must infer from a few words, gestures, and actions. Looking at all of a writer's options for presenting character will keep us from overlooking important details.

Analysis of Elements of Style and Tone

Important elements in "Early Autumn" include the time of day and the title. How are they connected? What do they suggest about the characters? All the elements, discussed in Chapter 2, that shape a writer's style and create tone can be found in literary works as well and need to be considered as a part of your analysis. Hughes's title is actually a metaphor and, reinforced by the late-in-the-day meeting, suggests that this meeting comes too late for Mary to regain what she has lost—her youth and her youthful love.

Shakespeare's "Sonnet 116" develops the speaker's ideas about love through a series of metaphors. The rose in Dunbar's "Promise," is not a metaphor, though, because it is not part of a comparison. Yet, as we read "Promise" we sense that the poem is about something more serious than the nurturing and stealing of one flower, no matter how beautiful. Again, this work's title gives us a clue that the rose stands for something more than itself; it is a symbol. Traditionally the red rose is a symbol of love. To tie the poem together, we will have to see how the title, the usual symbolic value of the rose, and the specifics of the poem connect.

DRAWING CONCLUSIONS: INTERPRETATION

We have studied the facts of several works and analyzed their structures and other key elements. To reach some conclusions from this information and shape it into an organized form is to offer an interpretation of the work. At this point, readers can be expected to disagree somewhat, but if we have all read carefully and applied our knowledge of literature, differences should, most of the time, be ones of focus or emphasis. Presumably no one is prepared to argue that "Promise" is about pink elephants or "Early Autumn" about the Queen of England, because neither work contains any facts to support those conclusions.

What conclusions can we reach about "Promise"? A beautiful flower has been nurtured into bloom by a speaker who expects it to brighten his or her life.

The title lets us know that the rose represents great promise. Has a rival stolen the speaker's loved one, represented symbolically by the rose? A thoughtless child would not be an appropriate rival for an adult speaker, so in the context of this poem, the rose represents, more generally, something that the speaker cherishes in anticipation of the pleasure it will bring.

In "Early Autumn" the pain that Mary feels when she meets Bill in Washington Square comes from her awareness that she still loves Bill and that he is lost to her. Bill has gone on to a happy life in which she has no part. The lights blur because Mary's eyes are filled with tears as the conversation makes her aware that Bill has given her little thought over the years, whereas Mary, to keep some part of Bill in her life, has named her youngest son Bill. The details of the story, an analysis of plot and character conflict, and the story's metaphors support these conclusions.

WRITING ABOUT LITERATURE

When you are assigned a literary essay, you will usually be asked to write either an explication or an analysis. An *explication* presents a reading of a complex poem. It will combine paraphrase and explanation to clarify the poem's meaning. A *literary analysis* can take many forms. You may be asked to analyze one element in a work: character conflict, the use of setting, the tone of a poem. Or you could be asked to contrast two works. Usually an analytic assignment requires you to connect analysis to interpretation, for we analyze the parts to better understand the whole. If you are asked to examine the metaphors in a Shakespeare sonnet, for example, you will want to show how understanding the metaphors contributes to an understanding of the entire poem. In short, literary analysis is much the same as a style analysis of an essay, and thus the guidelines for writing about style discussed in Chapter 2 apply here as well.* Successful analyses are based on accurate reading, reflection on the work's emotional impact, and the use of details from the work to support conclusions.

Literary analyses can also incorporate material beyond the particular work. We can analyze a work in the light of biographical information or from a particular political ideology. Or, we can study the social-cultural context of the work, or relate it to a literary tradition. These are only a few of the many approaches to the study of literature, and they depend on the application of knowledge outside the work itself. For undergraduates, topics based on these approaches usually require research. The student research essay at the end of the Appendix is a literary analysis. Alan examines Faulkner's *Intruder in the Dust* as an initiation novel. He connects his analysis to works by Hawthorne and Arthur Miller. What is taken from his research is documented and helps develop and support his own conclusions about the story.

To practice close reading, analysis, and interpretation of literature, read the following works. Use the questions after each work to aid your response.

---

* Remember: The guidelines for referring to authors, titles, and direct quotations—presented in Chapter 1—also apply.

TO HIS COY MISTRESS | ANDREW MARVELL

One of the last poets of the English Renaissance, Andrew Marvell (1621–1678) graduated from Cambridge University, spent much of his young life as a tutor, and was elected to Parliament in 1659. He continued in public service until his death. Most of his best-loved lyric poems come from his years as a tutor. "To His Coy Mistress" was published in 1681.

Had we but world enough, and time,
This coyness, lady, were no crime.
We would sit down, and think which way
To walk, and pass our long love's day.
Thou by the Indian Ganges' side   5
Shouldst rubies find; I by the tide
Of Humber would complain. I would
Love you ten years before the Flood,
And you should, if you please, refuse
Till the conversion of the Jews.   10
My vegetable° love should grow   *slowly vegetative*
Vaster than empires, and more slow;
An hundred years should go to praise
Thine eyes, and on thy forehead gaze;
Two hundred to adore each breast,   15
But thirty thousand to the rest;
An age at least to every part,
And the last age should show your heart.
For, lady, you deserve this state,
Nor would I love at lower rate.   20
    But at my back I always hear
Time's wingèd chariot hurrying near;
And yonder all before us lie
Deserts of vast eternity.
Thy beauty shall no more be found,   25
Nor in thy marble vault shall sound
My echoing song; then worms shall try
That long preserved virginity,
And your quaint honor turn to dust,
And into ashes all my lust.   30
The grave's a fine and private place,
But none, I think, do there embrace.
    Now therefore, while the youthful hue
Sits on thy skin like morning dew,
And while thy willing soul transpires   35
At every pore with instant fires,
Now let us sport us while we may,
And now, like amorous birds of prey,

Rather at once our time devour
40 Than languish in his slow-chapped power.
Let us roll all our strength and all
Our sweetness up into one ball,
And tear our pleasures with rough strife
45 Thorough° the iron gates of life.   *through*
Thus, though we cannot make our sun
Stand still, yet we will make him run.

QUESTIONS FOR READING, REASONING, AND REFLECTING

1. Describe the poem's external form.
2. How are the words coming to us? That is, is this a narrative, dramatic, or lyric poem?
3. Summarize the speaker's argument, using the structures *if, but,* and *therefore.*
4. What figure of speech do we find throughout the first verse paragraph? What is its effect on the speaker's tone?
5. Find examples of irony and understatement in the second verse paragraph.
6. How does the tone shift in the second section?
7. Explain the personification in line 22.
8. Explain the metaphors in lines 30 and 45.
9. What is the paradox of the last two lines? How can it be explained?
10. What is the idea of this poem? What does the writer want us to reflect on?

THE PASSIONATE SHEPHERD TO HIS LOVE | CHRISTOPHER MARLOWE

Cambridge graduate, Renaissance dramatist second only to Shakespeare, Christopher Marlowe (1564–1593) may be best known for this lyric poem. Not only is it widely anthologized, it has also spawned a number of responses by such significant writers as the seventeenth-century poet John Donne and the twentieth-century humorous poet Ogden Nash. For the Renaissance period the shepherd was a standard figure of the lover.

Come live with me and be my love,
And we will all the pleasures prove
That valleys, groves, hills, and fields,
Woods, or steepy mountain yields.

5   And we will sit upon the rocks,
Seeing the shepherds feed their flocks,
By shallow rivers to whose falls
Melodious birds sing madrigals.

And I will make thee beds of roses
And a thousand fragrant posies,   **10**
A cap of flowers, and a kirtle
Embroidered all with leaves of myrtle;

A gown made of the finest wool
Which from our pretty lambs we pull;
Fair lined slippers for the cold,   **15**
With buckles of the purest gold;

A belt of straw and ivy buds,
With coral clasps and amber studs:
And if these pleasures may thee move,
Come live with me, and be my love.   **20**

The shepherds' swains shall dance and sing
For thy delight each May morning:
If these delights thy mind may move,
Then live with me and be my love.

QUESTIONS FOR READING, REASONING, AND REFLECTING

1. Describe the poem's external structure.

2. What is the speaker's subject? What does he want to accomplish?

3. Summarize his "argument." How does he seek to convince his love?

4. What do the details of his argument have in common—that is, what kind of world or life does the speaker describe? Is there anything missing from the shepherd's world?

5. Would you like to be courted in this way? Would you say yes to the shepherd? If not, why?

THE NYMPH'S REPLY TO THE SHEPHERD | SIR WALTER RALEIGH

The renowned Elizabethan courtier, Sir Walter Raleigh (1552–1618) led a varied life as both a favorite of Queen Elizabeth and out of favor at court, as a colonizer and writer, and as one of many to be imprisoned in the Tower of London. In the following poem, Raleigh offers a response to Marlowe, using the nymph as the voice of the female lover.

If all the world and love were young,
And truth in every shepherd's tongue,
These pretty pleasures might me move
To live with thee and be thy love.

5   Time drives the flocks from field to fold
       When rivers rage and rocks grow cold,
       And Philomel becometh dumb;
       The rest complains of cares to come.

       The flowers do fade, and wanton fields
10   To wayward winter reckoning yields;
       A honey tongue, a heart of gall,
       Is fancy's spring, but sorrow's fall.

       Thy gowns, thy shoes, thy beds of roses,
       Thy cap, thy kirtle, and thy posies
15   Soon break, soon wither, soon forgotten,—
       In folly ripe, in reason rotten.

       Thy belt of straw and ivy buds,
       Thy coral clasps and amber studs,
       All these in me no means can move
20   To come to thee and be thy love.

       But could youth last and love still breed,
       Had joys no date nor age no need,
       Then these delights my mind might move
       To live with thee and be thy love.

QUESTIONS FOR READING, REASONING, AND REFLECTING

1. Describe the poem's external structure.
2. What is the context of the poem, the reason the speaker offers her words?
3. Analyze the speaker's argument, using *if* and *but* as your basic structure—and then the concluding, qualifying *but*.
4. What evidence does the speaker provide to support her argument?
5. Who has the more convincing argument: Marlowe's shepherd or Raleigh's nymph? Why?

IS MY TEAM PLOUGHING | A. E. HOUSMAN

British poet A. E. Housman (1859–1936) was a classicist, first a professor of Latin at University College, London, and then at the University of Cambridge. He spent the rest of his life at Trinity College, Cambridge. He is best known for his first volume of poetry, *A Shropshire Lad* (1896), a collection of crystal clear and deceptively simple verses that give expression to a world that has been lost—perhaps the innocence of youth.

"Is my team ploughing,
   That I was used to drive

And hear the harness jingle
   When I was man alive?"

Ay, the horses trample,   5
   The harness jingles now:
No change though you lie under
   The land you used to plough.

"Is football playing
   Along the river shore,   10
With lads to chase the leather,
   Now I stand up no more?"

Ay, the ball is flying,
   The lads play heart and soul;
The goal stands up, the keeper   15
   Stands up to keep the goal.

"Is my girl happy,
   That I thought hard to leave,
And has she tired of weeping
   As she lies down at eve?"   20

Ay, she lies down lightly,
   She lies not down to weep:
Your girl is well contented.
   Be still, my lad, and sleep.

"Is my friend hearty,   25
   Now I am thin and pine,
And has he found to sleep in
   A better bed than mine?"

Yes, lad, I lie easy,
   I lie as lads would choose;   30
I cheer a dead man's sweetheart,
   Never ask me whose.

QUESTIONS FOR READING, REASONING, AND REFLECTING

1. Classify the poem according to its external structure.
2. Is this a narrative, dramatic, or lyric poem? How are we to read the words coming to us?
3. What is the relationship between the two speakers? What has happened to the first speaker? What has changed in the life of the second speaker?
4. What ideas are suggested by the poem? What does Housman want us to take from his poem?

TAXI | AMY LOWELL

Educated at private schools and widely traveled, American Amy Lowell (1874–1925) was both a poet and a critic. Lowell frequently read her poetry and lectured on poetic techniques, defending her verse and that of other modern poets.

> When I go away from you
> The world beats dead
> Like a slackened drum.
> I call out for you against the jutted stars
> 5 And shout into the ridges of the wind.
> Streets coming fast,
> One after the other,
> Wedge you away from me,
> And the lamps of the city prick my eyes
> 10 So that I can no longer see your face.
> Why should I leave you,
> To wound myself upon the sharp edges of the night?

QUESTIONS FOR READING, REASONING, AND REFLECTING

1. Classify the poem according to its external structure.

2. Is this a narrative, dramatic, or lyric poem?

3. Explain the simile in the opening three lines and the metaphor in the last line of the poem.

4. What is the poem's subject? What seems to be the situation in which we find the speaker?

5. How would you describe the tone of the poem? How do the details and the emotional impact of the metaphors help to create tone?

6. What is the poem's meaning or theme? In other words, what does the poet want us to understand from reading her poem?

THE STORY OF AN HOUR | KATE CHOPIN

Now a highly acclaimed short-story writer, Kate Chopin (1851–1904) enjoyed a decade of publication and popularity from 1890 to 1900 and then critical condemnation followed by sixty years of neglect. Chopin began her writing career after her husband's death, having returned to her home in St. Louis with her six children. She saw two collections of her stories published—*Bayou Folk* in 1894 and *A Night in Acadie* in 1897—before losing her popularity with the publication of her short novel *The Awakening* in 1899, the story of a woman struggling to free herself from years of repression and subservience.

Knowing that Mrs. Mallard was afflicted with a heart trouble, great care was 1
taken to break to her as gently as possible the news of her husband's death.

It was her sister Josephine who told her, in broken sentences; veiled hints 2
that revealed in half concealing. Her husband's friend Richards was there, too,
near her. It was he who had been in the newspaper office when intelligence
of the railroad disaster was received, with Brently Mallard's name leading the
list of "killed." He had only taken the time to assure himself of its truth by a
second telegram, and had hastened to forestall any less careful, less tender
friend in bearing the sad message.

She did not hear the story as many women have heard the same, with a 3
paralyzed inability to accept its significance. She wept at once, with sudden,
wild abandonment, in her sister's arms. When the storm of grief had spent
itself she went away to her room alone. She would have no one follow her.

There stood, facing the open window, a comfortable, roomy armchair. Into 4
this she sank, pressed down by a physical exhaustion that haunted her body
and seemed to reach into her soul.

She could see in the open square before her house the tops of trees that 5
were all aquiver with the new spring life. The delicious breath of rain was in the
air. In the street below a peddler was crying his wares. The notes of a distant
song which some one was singing reached her faintly, and countless sparrows
were twittering in the eaves.

There were patches of blue sky showing here and there through the clouds 6
that had met and piled one above the other in the west facing her window.

She sat with her head thrown back upon the cushion of the chair, quite 7
motionless, except when a sob came up into her throat and shook her, as a
child who has cried itself to sleep continues to sob in its dreams.

She was young, with a fair, calm face, whose lines bespoke repression and 8
even a certain strength. But now there was a dull stare in her eyes, whose gaze
was fixed away off yonder on one of those patches of blue sky. It was not a
glance of reflection, but rather indicated a suspension of intelligent thought.

There was something coming to her and she was waiting for it, fearfully. 9
What was it? She did not know; it was too subtle and elusive to name. But she
felt it, creeping out of the sky, reaching toward her through the sounds, the
scents, the color that filled the air.

Now her bosom rose and fell tumultuously. She was beginning to recognize 10
this thing that was approaching to possess her, and she was striving to beat it
back with her will—as powerless as her two white slender hands would have
been.

When she abandoned herself a little whispered word escaped her slightly 11
parted lips. She said it over and over under her breath: "free, free, free!" The
vacant stare and the look of terror that had followed it went from her eyes.
They stayed keen and bright. Her pulses beat fast, and the coursing blood
warmed and relaxed every inch of her body.

She did not stop to ask if it were or were not a monstrous joy that held her. 12
A clear and exalted perception enabled her to dismiss the suggestion as trivial.

13   She knew that she would weep again when she saw the kind, tender hands folded in death; the face that had never looked save with love upon her, fixed and gray and dead. But she saw beyond that bitter moment a long procession of years to come that would belong to her absolutely. And she opened and spread her arms out to them in welcome.

14   There would be no one to live for her during those coming years; she would live for herself. There would be no powerful will bending hers in that blind persistence with which men and women believe they have a right to impose a private will upon a fellow-creature. A kind intention or a cruel intention made the act seem no less a crime as she looked upon it in that brief moment of illumination.

15   And yet she had loved him—sometimes. Often she had not. What did it matter! What could love, the unsolved mystery, count for in face of this possession of self-assertion which she suddenly recognized as the strongest impulse of her being!

16   "Free! Body and soul free!" she kept whispering.

17   Josephine was kneeling before the closed door with her lips to the key-hole, imploring for admission. "Louise, open the door! I beg; open the door—you will make yourself ill. What are you doing, Louise? For heaven's sake open the door."

18   "Go away. I am not making myself ill." No; she was drinking in a very elixir of life through that open window.

19   Her fancy was running riot along those days ahead of her. Spring days, and summer days, and all sorts of days that would be her own. She breathed a quick prayer that life might be long. It was only yesterday she had thought with a shudder that life might be long.

20   She arose at length and opened the door to her sister's importunities. There was a feverish triumph in her eyes, and she carried herself unwittingly like a goddess of Victory. She clasped her sister's waist, and together they descended the stairs. Richards stood waiting for them at the bottom.

21   Someone was opening the front door with a latchkey. It was Brently Mallard who entered, a little travel-stained, composedly carrying his grip-sack and umbrella. He had been far from the scene of accident, and did not even know there had been one. He stood amazed at Josephine's piercing cry; at Richards' quick motion to screen him from the view of his wife.

22   But Richards was too late.

23   When the doctors came they said she had died of heart disease—of joy that kills.

QUESTIONS FOR READING, REASONING, AND REFLECTING

1. Analyze the story's plot structure, using the terms presented in Figure 1 (p. 596).
2. What is Mrs. Mallard's conflict? Explain the opposing elements of her conflict as precisely as you can.

3. When Mrs. Mallard goes to her room, she gazes out the window. Consider the details of the scene; what do these details have in common? How do the details help us understand what Mrs. Mallard experiences?

4. Why is it inaccurate to say that Mrs. Mallard does not love her husband? Cite evidence from the story.

5. The author James Joyce has described a character's moment of insight or intuition as an "epiphany." What is Mrs. Mallard's epiphany?

6. Are we to agree with the doctor's explanation for Mrs. Mallard's death? What term is appropriate to describe the story's conclusion?

THE ONES WHO WALK AWAY FROM OMELAS | URSULA K. LE GUIN

A graduate of Radcliffe College and Columbia University, Ursula K. Le Guin is the author of more than twenty novels and juvenile books, several volumes of poetry, and numerous stories and essays published in science fiction, scholarly, and popular journals. Her fiction stretches the categories of science fiction or fantasy and challenges a reader's moral understanding. First published in 1973, the following story, according to Le Guin, was inspired by a passage in William James's "The Moral Philosopher and the Moral Life" in which he asserts that we could not tolerate a situation in which the happiness of many people was purchased by the "lonely torment" of one "lost soul."

With a clamor of bells that set the swallows soaring, the Festival of Summer came to the city Omelas, bright-towered by the sea. The rigging of the boats in harbor sparkled with flags. In the streets between houses with red roofs and painted walls, between the old moss-grown gardens and under avenues of trees, past great parks and public buildings, processions moved. Some were decorous: old people in long stiff robes of mauve and gray, grave master workmen, quiet, merry women carrying their babies and chatting as they walked. In other streets the music beat faster, a shimmering of gong and tambourine, and the people went dancing, the procession was a dance. Children dodged in and out, their high calls rising like the swallows' crossing flights over the music and the singing. All the processions wound towards the north side of the city, where on the great water-meadow called the Green Fields boys and girls, naked in the bright air, with mudstained feet and ankles and long, lithe arms, exercised their restive horses before the race. The horses wore no gear at all but a halter without bit. Their manes were braided with streamers of silver, gold, and green. They flared their nostrils and pranced and boasted to one another; they were vastly excited, the horse being the only animal who has adopted our ceremonies as his own. Far off to the north and west the mountains stood up half circling Omelas on her bay. The air of morning was so clear that the snow still crowning the Eighteen Peaks burned with white-gold fire across the miles of sunlit air, under the dark blue of the sky. There was just enough wind to make the banners that marked the racecourse snap and flutter now and then. In the silence of the broad green meadows one 1 could hear the music winding through the city streets, farther and nearer and ever approaching, a cheerful faint sweetness of the air that from time to time trembled and gathered together and broke out into the great joyous clanging of the bells.

2   Joyous! How is one to tell about joy? How describe the citizens of Omelas?

3   They were not simple folk, you see, though they were happy. But we do not say the words of cheer much any more. All smiles have become archaic. Given a description such as this one tends to make certain assumptions. Given a description such as this one tends to look next for the King, mounted on a splendid stallion and surrounded by his noble knights, or perhaps in a golden litter borne by great-muscled slaves. But there was no king. They did not use swords, or keep slaves. They were not barbarians. I do not know the rules and laws of their society, but I suspect that they were singularly few. As they did without monarchy and slavery, so they also got on without the stock exchange, the advertisement, the secret police, and the bomb. Yet I repeat that these were not simple folk, not dulcet shepherds, noble savages, bland utopians. They were not less complex than us. The trouble is that we have a bad habit, encouraged by pedants and sophisticates, of considering happiness as something rather stupid. Only pain is intellectual, only evil interesting. This is the treason of the artist: a refusal to admit the banality of evil and the terrible boredom of pain. If you can't lick 'em, join 'em. If it hurts, repeat it. But to praise despair is to condemn delight, to embrace violence is to lose hold of everything else. We have almost lost hold, we can no longer describe a happy man, nor make any celebration of joy. How can I tell you about the people of Omelas? They were not naïve and happy children—though their children were, in fact, happy. They were mature, intelligent, passionate adults whose lives were not wretched. O miracle! But I wish I could describe it better. I wish I could convince you. Omelas sounds in my words like a city in a fairy tale, long ago and far away, once upon a time. Perhaps it would be best if you imagined it as your own fancy bids, assuming it will rise to the occasion, for certainly I cannot suit you all. For instance, how about technology? I think that there would be no cars or helicopters in and above the streets; this follows from the fact that the people of Omelas are happy people. Happiness is based on a just discrimination of what is necessary, what is neither necessary nor destructive, and what is destructive. In the middle category, however—that of the unnecessary but undestructive, that of comfort, luxury, exuberance, etc.—they could perfectly well have central heating, subway trains, washing machines, and all kinds of marvelous devises not yet invented here, floating light-sources, fuelless power, a cure for the common cold. Or they could have none of that: it doesn't matter. As you like it. I incline to think that people from towns up and down the coast have been coming in to Omelas during the last days before the Festival on very fast trains and double-decked trams, and that the train station of Omelas is actually the handsomest building in town, though plainer than the magnificent Farmers' Market. But even granted trains, I fear that Omelas so far strikes some of you as goody-goody. Smiles, bells, parades, horses, bleh. If so, please add an orgy.

If an orgy would help, don't hesitate. Let us not, however, have temples from which issue beautiful nude priests and priestesses already half in ecstasy and ready to copulate with any man or woman, lover or stranger, who desires union with the deep godhead of the blood, although that was my first idea. But really it would be better not to have any temples in Omelas—at least, not manned temples. Religion yes, clergy no. Surely the beautiful nudes can just wander about, offering themselves like divine soufflés to the hunger of the needy and the rapture of the flesh. Let them join the processions. Let tambourines be struck above the copulations, and the glory of desire be proclaimed upon the gongs, and (a not unimportant point) let the offspring of these delightful rituals be beloved and looked after by all. One thing I know there is none of in Omelas is guilt. But what else should there be? I thought that first there were no drugs, but that is puritanical. For those who like it, the faint insistent sweetness of *drooz* may perfume the ways of the city, *drooz* which first brings a great lightness and brilliance to the mind and limbs, and then after some hours a dreamy languor, and wonderful visions at last of the very arcana and inmost secrets of the Universe, as well as exciting the pleasure of sex beyond all belief; and it is not habit-forming. For more modest tastes I think there ought to be beer. What else, what else belongs in the joyous city? The sense of victory, surely, the celebration of courage. But as we did without clergy, let us do without soldiers. The joy built upon successful slaughter is not the right kind of joy; it will not do; it is fearful and it is trivial. A boundless and generous contentment, a magnanimous triumph felt not against some outer enemy but in communion with the finest and fairest in the souls of all men everywhere and the splendor of the world's summer; this is what swells the hearts of the people of Omelas, and the victory they celebrate is that of life. I really don't think many of them need to take *drooz*.

Most of the processions have reached the Green Fields by now. A marvel-   4 ous smell of cooking goes forth from the red and blue tents of the provisioners. The faces of small children are amiably sticky; in the benign grey beard of a man a couple of crumbs of rich pastry are entangled. The youths and girls have mounted their horses and are beginning to group around the starting line of the course. An old woman, small, fat, and laughing, is passing out flowers from a basket, and tall young men wear her flowers in their shining hair. A child of nine or ten sits at the edge of the crowd, alone, playing on a wooden flute. People pause to listen, and they smile, but they do not speak to him, for he never ceases playing and never sees them, his dark eyes wholly rapt in the sweet, thin magic of the tune.

He finishes, and slowly lowers his hands holding the wooden flute.   5

As if that little private silence were the signal, all at once a trumpet sounds   6 from the pavilion near the starting line: imperious, melancholy, piercing. The horses rear on their slender legs, and some of them neigh in answer. Sober-faced, the young riders stroke the horses' necks and soothe them, whispering, "Quiet, quiet, there my beauty, my hope." They begin to form in rank along the starting line. The crowds along the racecourse are like a field of grass and flowers in the wind. The Festival of Summer has begun.

7   Do you believe? Do you accept the festival, the city, the joy? No? Then let me describe this one more thing.

8   In a basement under one of the beautiful public buildings of Omelas, or perhaps in the cellar of one of its spacious private homes, there is a room. It has one locked door, and no window. A little light seeps in dustily between cracks in the boards, secondhand from the cobwebbed window somewhere across the cellar. In one corner of the little room a couple of mops, with stiff, clotted, foul-smelling heads, stand near a rusty bucket. The floor is dirt, a little damp to the touch, as cellar dirt usually is. The room is about three paces long and two wide: a mere broom closet or disused tool room. In the room a child is sitting. It could be a boy or a girl. It looks about six, but actually is nearly ten. It is feeble-minded. Perhaps it was born defective, or perhaps it has become imbecile through fear, malnutrition, and neglect. It picks its nose and occasionally fumbles vaguely with its toes or genitals, as it sits hunched in the corner farthest from the bucket and the two mops. It is afraid of the mops. It finds them horrible. It shuts its eyes, but it knows the mops are still standing there; and the door is locked; and nobody will come. The door is always locked; and nobody ever comes, except that sometimes—the child has no understanding of time or interval—sometimes the door rattles terribly and opens, and a person, or several people, are there. One of them may come in and kick the child to make it stand up. The others never come close, but peer in at it with frightened, disgusted eyes. The food bowl and the water jug are hastily filled, the door is locked, the eyes disappear. The people at the door never say anything, but the child, who has not always lived in the tool room, and can remember sunlight and its mother's voice, sometimes speaks. "I will be good," it says. "Please let me out. I will be good!" They never answer. The child used to scream for help at night, and cry a good deal, but now it only makes a kind of whining, "eh-haa-eh-haa," and it speaks less and less often. It is so thin there are no calves to its legs; its belly protrudes; it lives on a half-bowl of corn meal and grease a day. It is naked. Its buttocks and thighs are a mass of festered sores, as it sits in its own excrement continually.

9   They all know it is there, all the people of Omelas. Some of them have come to see it, others are content merely to know it is there. They all know that it has to be there. Some of them understand why, and some do not, but they all understand that their happiness, the beauty of their city, the tenderness of their friendships, the health of their children, the wisdom of their scholars, the skill of their makers, even the abundance of their harvest and the kindly weathers of their skies, depend wholly upon this child's abominable misery.

10   This is usually explained to children when they are between eight and twelve, whenever they seem capable of understanding; and most of those who come to see the child are young people, though often enough an adult comes, or comes back, to see the child. No matter how well the matter has been explained to them, these young spectators are always shocked and sickened at the sight. They feel disgust, which they had thought themselves superior to. They feel anger, outrage, impotence, despite all the explanations. They would like to do something for the child. But there is nothing they can do. If the child

were brought up into the sunlight out of that vile place, if it were cleaned and fed and comforted, that would be a good thing, indeed; but if it were done, in that day and hour all the prosperity and beauty and delight of Omelas would wither and be destroyed. Those are the terms. To exchange all the goodness and grace of every life in Omelas for that single, small improvement: to throw away the happiness of thousands for the chance of the happiness of one: that would be to let guilt within the walls indeed.

The terms are strict and absolute; there may not even be a kind word 11 spoken to the child.

Often the young people go home in tears, or in a tearless rage, when they 12 have seen the child and faced this terrible paradox. They may brood over it for weeks or years. But as time goes on they begin to realize that even if the child could be released, it would not get much good of its freedom: a little vague pleasure of warmth and food, no doubt, but little more. It is too degraded and imbecile to know any real joy. It has been afraid too long ever to be free of fear. Its habits are too uncouth for it to respond to humane treatment. Indeed, after so long it would probably be wretched without walls about it to protect it, and darkness for its eyes, and its own excrement to sit in. Their tears at the bitter injustice dry when they begin to perceive the terrible justice of reality, and to accept it. Yet it is their tears and anger, the trying of their generosity and the acceptance of their helplessness, which are perhaps the true source of the splendor of their lives. Theirs is no vapid, irresponsible happiness. They know that they, like the child, are not free. They know compassion. It is the existence of the child, and their knowledge of its existence, that makes possible the mobility of their architecture, the poignancy of their music, the profundity of their science. It is because of the child that they are so gentle with children. They know that if the wretched one were not there snivelling in the dark, the other one, the flute-player, could make no joyful music as the young riders line up in their beauty for the race in the sunlight of the first morning of summer.

Now do you believe in them? Are they not more credible? But there is one 13 more thing to tell, and this is quite incredible.

At times one of the adolescent girls or boys who go to see the child, does 14 not go home to weep or rage, does not, in fact, go home at all. Sometimes also a man or woman much older falls silent for a day or two, and then leaves home. These people go out into the street, and walk down the street alone. They keep walking, and walk straight out of the city of Omelas, through the beautiful gates. They keep walking across the farmlands of Omelas. Each one goes alone, youth or girl, man or woman. Night falls; the traveler must pass down village streets, between the houses with yellow-lit windows, and on out into the darkness of the fields. Each alone, they go west or north, towards the mountains. They go on. They leave Omelas, they walk ahead into the darkness, and they do not come back. The place they go towards is a place even less imaginable to most of us than the city of happiness. I cannot describe it at all. It is possible that it does not exist. But they seem to know where they are going, the ones who walk away from Omelas.

QUESTIONS FOR READING, REASONING, AND REFLECTING

1. What is the general impression you get of the city of Omelas from the opening paragraph? To what senses does the author appeal?

2. Describe the people of Omelas. Are they happy? Do they have technology? Guilt? Religion? Soldiers? Drugs?

3. What shocking detail emerges about Omelas? On what does this ideal community thrive?

4. How do the children and teens respond to the locked-up child at first? How do they reconcile themselves to the situation? What do some residents do?

5. Can you understand the reason most residents accept the situation? Can you understand those who walk away? With which group do you most identify? Why?

6. On what does Le Guin want us to reflect? How would you state the story's theme?

TRIFLES | SUSAN GLASPELL

Born in Iowa, Susan Glaspell (1882?–1948) attended Drake University and then began her writing career as a reporter with the *Des Moines Daily News*. She also started writing and selling short stories; her first collection, *Lifted Masks*, was published in 1912. She completed several novels before moving to Provincetown with her husband, who started the Provincetown Players in 1915. Glaspell wrote seven short plays and four long plays for this group, including *Trifles* (1916). The well-known "Jury of Her Peers" (1917) is a short-story version of the play *Trifles*. Glaspell must have recognized that the plot of *Trifles* was a gem worth working with in more than one literary form.

Characters
George Henderson, County Attorney
Henry Peters, Sheriff
Lewis Hale, A Neighboring Farmer
Mrs. Peters
Mrs. Hale

SCENE: *The kitchen in the now abandoned farmhouse of* JOHN WRIGHT, *a gloomy kitchen, and left without having been put in order—unwashed pans under the sink, a loaf of bread outside the bread-box, a dish-towel on the table—other signs of incompleted work. At the rear, the outer door opens and the* SHERIFF *comes in followed by the* COUNTY ATTORNEY *and* HALE. *The* SHERIFF *and* HALE *are men in middle life; the* COUNTY ATTORNEY *is a young man; all are much bundled up and go at once to the stove. They are followed by the two women—the* SHERIFF's *wife first; she is a slight wiry woman, a thin nervous face.* MRS. HALE *is larger and would ordinarily be called more comfortable looking, but she is disturbed now and looks fearfully about as she enters. The women have come in slowly, and stand close together near the door.*

COUNTY ATTORNEY

[*Rubbing his hands.*] This feels good. Come up to the fire, ladies.

MRS. PETERS

[*After taking a step forward.*] I'm not—cold.

SHERIFF

[*Unbuttoning his overcoat and stepping away from the stove as if to mark the beginning of official business.*] Now, Mr. Hale, before we move things about, you explain to Mr. Henderson just what you saw when you came here yesterday morning.

COUNTY ATTORNEY

By the way, has anything been moved? Are things just as you left them yesterday?

SHERIFF

[*Looking about.*] It's just the same. When it dropped below zero last night I thought I'd better send Frank out this morning to make a fire for us—no use getting pneumonia with a big case on, but I told him not to touch anything except the stove—and you know Frank.

COUNTY ATTORNEY

Somebody should have been left here yesterday.

SHERIFF

Oh—yesterday. When I had to send Frank to Morris Center for that man who went crazy—I want you to know I had my hands full yesterday. I knew you could get back from Omaha by today and as long as I went over everything here myself—

COUNTY ATTORNEY

Well, Mr. Hale, tell just what happened when you came here yesterday morning.

HALE

Harry and I had started to town with a load of potatoes. We came along the road from my place and as I got here I said, "I'm going to see if I can't get John Wright to go in with me on a party telephone." I spoke to Wright about it once before and he put me off, saying folks talked too much anyway, and all he asked was peace and quiet—I guess you know about how much he talked himself; but I thought maybe if I went to the house and talked about it before his wife, though I said to Harry that I didn't know as what his wife wanted made much difference to John—

COUNTY ATTORNEY

Let's talk about that later, Mr. Hale. I do want to talk about that, but tell now just what happened when you got to the house.

HALE

I didn't hear or see anything; I knocked at the door, and still it was all quiet inside. I knew they must be up, it was past eight o'clock. So I knocked again, and I thought I heard somebody say, "Come in." I wasn't sure, I'm not sure yet, but I opened the door—this door [*indicating the door by which the two women are still standing*] and there in that rocker—[*pointing to it*] sat Mrs. Wright.
[*They all look at the rocker.*]

COUNTY ATTORNEY

What—was she doing?

HALE

She was rockin' back and forth. She had her apron in her hand and was kind of—pleating it.

COUNTY ATTORNEY

And how did she—look?

HALE

Well, she looked queer.

COUNTY ATTORNEY

How do you mean—queer?

HALE

Well, as if she didn't know what she was going to do next. And kind of done up.

COUNTY ATTORNEY

How did she seem to feel about your coming?

HALE

Why, I don't think she minded—one way or other. She didn't pay much attention. I said, "How do, Mrs. Wright, it's cold, ain't it?" And she said, "Is it?"—and went on kind of pleating at her apron. Well, I was surprised; she didn't ask me to come up to the stove, or to set down, but just sat there, not even looking at me, so I said, "I want to see John." And then she—laughed. I guess you would call it a laugh. I thought of Harry and the team outside, so I said a little sharp: "Can't I see John?" "No," she says, kind o' dull like. "Ain't he home?" says I. "Yes," says she, "he's home." "Then why can't I see him?" I asked her, out of patience. " 'Cause he's dead," says she. "*Dead?*" says I.

She just nodded her head, not getting a bit excited, but rockin' back and forth. "Why—where is he?" says I, not knowing what to say. She just pointed upstairs—like that [*himself pointing to the room above*]. I got up, with the idea of going up there. I walked from there to here—then I says, "Why, what did he die of?" "He died of a rope around his neck," says she, and just went on pleatin' at her apron. Well, I went out and called Harry. I thought I might— need help. We went upstairs and there he was lyin'—

COUNTY ATTORNEY

I think I'd rather have you go into that upstairs, where you can point it all out. Just go on now with the rest of the story.

HALE

Well, my first thought was to get that rope off. It looked . . . [*Stops, his face twitches*] . . . but Harry, he went up to him, and he said, "No, he's dead all right, and we'd better not touch anything." So we went back downstairs. She was still sitting that same way. "Has anybody been notified?" said Harry. He said it business-like—and she stopped pleatin' of her apron. "I don't know," she says. "You don't *know?*" says Harry. "No," says she. "Weren't you sleepin' in the bed with him?" says Harry. "Yes," says she, "but I was on the inside." "Somebody slipped a rope round his neck and strangled him and you didn't wake up?" says Harry. "I didn't wake up," she said after him. We must'a looked as if we didn't see how that could be, for after a minute she said, "I sleep sound." Harry was going to ask her more questions but I said maybe we ought to let her tell her story first to the coroner, or the sheriff, so Harry went fast as he could to Rivers' place, where there's a telephone.

COUNTY ATTORNEY

And what did Mrs. Wright do when she knew that you had gone for the coroner?

HALE

She moved from that chair to this one over here [*Pointing to a small chair in the corner*] and just sat there with her hands held together and looking down. I got a feeling that I ought to make some conversation, so I said I had come in to see if John wanted to put in a telephone, and at that she started to laugh, and then she stopped and looked at me—scared. [*The County Attorney, who has had his notebook out, makes a note.*] I dunno, maybe it wasn't scared. I wouldn't like to say it was. Soon Harry got back, and then Dr. Lloyd came, and you, Mr. Peters, and so I guess that's all I know that you don't.

COUNTY ATTORNEY

[*Looking around.*] I guess we'll go upstairs first—and then out to the barn and around there. [*To the Sheriff.*] You're convinced that there was nothing important here—nothing that would point to any motive.

SHERIFF
Nothing here but kitchen things.
[*The County Attorney, after again looking around the kitchen, opens the door of a cupboard closet. He gets up on a chair and looks on a shelf. Pulls his hand away, sticky.*]

COUNTY ATTORNEY
Here's a nice mess.
[*The women draw nearer.*]

MRS. PETERS
[*To the other woman.*] Oh, her fruit; it did freeze. [*To the Lawyer.*] She worried about that when it turned so cold. She said the fire'd go out and her jars would break.

SHERIFF
Well, can you beat the woman! Held for murder and worryin' about her preserves.

COUNTY ATTORNEY
I guess before we're through she may have something more serious than preserves to worry about.

HALE
Well, women are used to worrying over trifles.
[*The two women move a little closer together.*]

COUNTY ATTORNEY
[*With the gallantry of a young politician.*] And yet, for all their worries, what would we do without the ladies? [*The women do not unbend. He goes to the sink, takes a dipperful of water from the pail and pouring it into a basin, washes his hands. Starts to wipe them on the roller-towel, turns it for a cleaner place.*] Dirty towels! [*Kicks his foot against the pans under the sink.*] Not much of a housekeeper, would you say, ladies?

MRS. HALE
[*Stiffly.*] There's a great deal of work to be done on a farm.

COUNTY ATTORNEY
To be sure. And yet [*with a little bow to her*] I know there are some Dickson County farmhouses which do not have such roller towels.
[*He gives it a pull to expose its full length again.*]

MRS. HALE
Those towels get dirty awful quick. Men's hands aren't always as clean as they might be.

COUNTY ATTORNEY

Ah, loyal to your sex, I see. But you and Mrs. Wright were neighbors. I suppose you were friends, too.

MRS. HALE

[*Shaking her head.*] I've not seen much of her of late years. I've not been in this house—it's more than a year.

COUNTY ATTORNEY

And why was that? You didn't like her?

MRS. HALE

I liked her all well enough. Farmers' wives have their hands full, Mr. Henderson. And then—

COUNTY ATTORNEY

Yes—?

MRS. HALE

[*Looking about.*] It never seemed a very cheerful place.

COUNTY ATTORNEY

No—it's not cheerful. I shouldn't say she had the homemaking instinct.

MRS. HALE

Well, I don't know as Wright had, either.

COUNTY ATTORNEY

You mean that they didn't get on very well?

MRS. HALE

No, I don't mean anything. But I don't think a place'd be any cheerfuller for John Wright's being in it.

COUNTY ATTORNEY

I'd like to talk more of that a little later. I want to get the lay of things upstairs now.
[*He goes to the left, where three steps lead to a stair door.*]

SHERIFF

I suppose anything Mrs. Peters does'll be all right. She was to take in some clothes for her, you know, and a few little things. We left in such a hurry yesterday.

COUNTY ATTORNEY

Yes, but I would like to see what you take, Mrs. Peters, and keep an eye out for anything that might be of use to us.

MRS. PETERS

Yes, Mr. Henderson.

[*The women listen to the men's steps on the stairs, then look about the kitchen.*]

MRS. HALE

I'd hate to have men coming into my kitchen, snooping around and criticizing.

[*She arranges the pans under the sink which the Lawyer had shoved out of place.*]

MRS. PETERS

Of course it's no more than their duty.

MRS. HALE

Duty's all right, but I guess that deputy sheriff that came out to make the fire might have got a little of this on. [*Gives the roller towel a pull.*] Wish I'd thought of that sooner. Seems mean to talk about her for not having things slicked up when she had to come away in such a hurry.

MRS. PETERS

[*Who has gone to a small table in the left corner of the room, and lifted one end of a towel that covers a pan.*] She had bread set.
[*Stands still.*]

MRS. HALE

[*Eyes fixed on a loaf of bread beside the breadbox, which is on a low shelf at the other side of the room. Moves slowly toward it.*] She was going to put this in there. [*Picks up loaf, then abruptly drops it. In a manner of returning to familiar things.*] It's a shame about her fruit. I wonder if it's all gone. [*Gets up on the chair and looks.*] I think there's some here that's all right, Mrs. Peters. Yes—here; [*holding it toward the window*] this is cherries, too. [*Looking again.*] I declare I believe that's the only one. [*Gets down, bottle in her hand. Goes to the sink and wipes it off on the outside.*] She'll feel awful bad after all her hard work in the hot weather. I remember the afternoon I put up my cherries last summer.

[*She puts the bottle on the big kitchen table, center of the room. With a sigh, is about to sit down in the rocking-chair. Before she is seated realizes what chair it is; with a slow look at it, steps back. The chair which she has touched rocks back and forth.*]

MRS. PETERS

Well, I must get those things from the front room closet. [*She goes to the door at the right, but after looking into the other room, steps back.*] You coming with me, Mrs. Hale? You could help me carry them.

[*They go in the other room; reappear, Mrs. Peters carrying a dress and skirt, Mrs. Hale following with a pair of shoes.*]

MRS. PETERS

My, it's cold in there.
[*She puts the clothes on the big table, and hurries to the stove.*]

MRS. HALE

[*Examining the skirt.*] Wright was close. I think maybe that's why she kept so much to herself. She didn't even belong to the Ladies Aid. I suppose she felt she couldn't do her part, and then you don't enjoy things when you feel shabby. She used to wear pretty clothes and be lively, when she was Minnie Foster, one of the town girls singing in the choir. But that—oh, that was thirty years ago. This all you was to take in?

MRS. PETERS

She said she wanted an apron. Funny thing to want, for there isn't much to get you dirty in jail, goodness knows. But I suppose just to make her feel more natural. She said they was in the top drawer in this cupboard. Yes, here. And then her little shawl that always hung behind the door. [*Opens stair door and looks.*] Yes, here it is.
[*Quickly shuts door leading upstairs.*]

MRS. HALE

[*Abruptly moving toward her.*] Mrs. Peters?

MRS. PETERS

Yes, Mrs. Hale?

MRS. HALE

Do you think she did it?

MRS. PETERS

[*In a frightened voice.*] Oh, I don't know.

MRS. HALE

Well, I don't think she did. Asking for an apron and her little shawl. Worrying about her fruit.

MRS. PETERS

[*Starts to speak, glances up, where footsteps are heard in the room above. In a low voice.*] Mr. Peters says it looks bad for her. Mr. Henderson is awful sarcastic in a speech and he'll make fun of her sayin' she didn't wake up.

MRS. HALE

Well, I guess John Wright didn't wake when they was slipping that rope under his neck.

MRS. PETERS

No, it's strange. It must have been done awful crafty and still. They say it was such a—funny way to kill a man, rigging it all up like that.

MRS. HALE

That's just what Mr. Hale said. There was a gun in the house. He says that's what he can't understand.

MRS. PETERS

Mr. Henderson said coming out that what was needed for the case was a motive; something to show anger, or—sudden feeling.

MRS. HALE

[*Who is standing by the table.*] Well, I don't see any signs of anger around here. [*She puts her hand on the dish towel which lies on the table, stands looking down at table, one half of which is clean, the other half messy.*] It's wiped to here. [*Makes a move as if to finish work, then turns and looks at loaf of bread outside the breadbox. Drops towel. In that voice of coming-back to familiar things.*] Wonder how they are finding things upstairs. I hope she had it a little more red-up up there. You know, it seems kind of sneaking. Locking her up in town and then coming out here and trying to get her own house to turn against her!

MRS. PETERS

But Mrs. Hale, the law is the law.

MRS. HALE

I s'pose 'tis. [*Unbuttoning her coat.*] Better loosen up your things, Mrs. Peters. You won't feel them when you go out.
[*Mrs. Peters takes off her fur tippet, goes to hang it on hook at back of room, stands looking at the under part of the small corner table.*]

MRS. PETERS

She was piecing a quilt.
[*She brings the large sewing basket and they look at the bright pieces.*]

MRS. HALE

It's log cabin pattern. Pretty, isn't it? I wonder if she was goin' to quilt it or just knot it? [*Footsteps have been heard coming down the stairs. The Sheriff enters followed by Hale and the City Attorney.*]

SHERIFF

They wonder if she was going to quilt it or just knot it!
[*The men laugh, the women look abashed.*]

COUNTY ATTORNEY

[*Rubbing his hands over the stove.*] Frank's fire didn't do much up there, did it? Well, let's go out to the barn and get that cleared up.
[*The men go outside.*]

MRS. HALE

[*Resentfully.*] I don't know as there's anything so strange, our takin' up our time with little things while we're waiting for them to get the evidence. [*She sits down at the big table smoothing out a block with decision.*] I don't see as it's anything to laugh about.

MRS. PETERS

[*Apologetically.*] Of course they've got awful important things on their minds. [*Pulls up a chair and joins Mrs. Hale at the table.*]

MRS. HALE

[*Examining another block.*] Mrs. Peters, look at this one. Here, this is the one she was working on, and look at the sewing! All the rest of it has been so nice and even. And look at this! It's all over the place! Why, it looks as if she didn't know what she was about!
[*After she has said this they look at each other, then start to glance back at the door. After an instant Mrs. Hale has pulled at a knot and ripped the sewing.*]

MRS. PETERS

Oh, what are you doing, Mrs. Hale?

MRS. HALE

[*Mildly.*] Just pulling out a stitch or two that's not sewed very good. [*Threading a needle.*] Bad sewing always made me fidgety.

MRS. PETERS

[*Nervously.*] I don't think we ought to touch things.

MRS. HALE

I'll just finish up this end. [*Suddenly stopping and leaning forward.*] Mrs. Peters?

MRS. PETERS

Yes, Mrs. Hale?

MRS. HALE

What do you suppose she was so nervous about?

MRS. PETERS

Oh—I don't know. I don't know as she was nervous. I sometimes sew awful queer when I'm just tired. [*Mrs. Hale starts to say something, looks at Mrs. Peters, then goes on sewing.*] Well I must get these things wrapped up. They may be through sooner than we think. [*Putting apron and other things together.*] I wonder where I can find a piece of paper, and string.

MRS. HALE

In that cupboard, maybe.

MRS. PETERS

[*Looking in cupboard.*] Why, here's a bird-cage. [*Holds it up.*] Did she have a bird, Mrs. Hale?

MRS. HALE

Why, I don't know whether she did or not—I've not been here for so long. There was a man around last year selling canaries cheap, but I don't know as she took one; maybe she did. She used to sing real pretty herself.

MRS. PETERS

[*Glancing around.*] Seems funny to think of a bird here. But she must have had one, or why would she have a cage? I wonder what happened to it.

MRS. HALE

I s'pose maybe the cat got it.

MRS. PETERS

No, she didn't have a cat. She's got that feeling some people have about cats—being afraid of them. My cat got in her room and she was real upset and asked me to take it out.

MRS. HALE

My sister Bessie was like that. Queer, ain't it?

MRS. PETERS

[*Examining the cage.*] Why, look at this door. It's broke. One hinge is pulled apart.

MRS. HALE

[*Looking too.*] Looks as if someone must have been rough with it.

MRS. PETERS

Why, yes.
[*She brings the cage forward and puts it on the table.*]

MRS. HALE

I wish if they're going to find any evidence they'd be about it. I don't like this place.

MRS. PETERS

But I'm awful glad you came with me, Mrs. Hale. It would be lonesome for me sitting here alone.

MRS. HALE

It would, wouldn't it? [*Dropping her sewing.*] But I tell you what I do wish, Mrs. Peters. I wish I had come over sometimes when *she* was here. I—[*looking around the room*]—wish I had.

MRS. PETERS

But of course you were awful busy, Mrs. Hale—your house and your children.

MRS. HALE

I could've come. I stayed away because it weren't cheerful—and that's why I ought to have come. I—I've never liked this place. Maybe because it's down in a hollow and you don't see the road. I dunno what it is, but it's a lonesome place and always was. I wish I had come over to see Minnie Foster sometimes. I can see now—
[*Shakes her head.*]

MRS. PETERS

Well, you mustn't reproach yourself, Mrs. Hale. Somehow we just don't see how it is with other folks until—something comes up.

MRS. HALE

Not having children makes less work—but it makes a quiet house, and Wright out to work all day, and no company when he did come in. Did you know John Wright, Mrs. Peters?

MRS. PETERS

Not to know him; I've seen him in town. They say he was a good man.

MRS. HALE

Yes—good; he didn't drink, and kept his word as well as most, I guess, and paid his debts. But he was a hard man, Mrs. Peters. Just to pass the time of day with him—[*Shivers.*] Like a raw wind that gets to the bone. [*Pauses, her eye falling on the cage.*] I should think she would'a wanted a bird. But what do you suppose went with it?

MRS. PETERS

I don't know, unless it got sick and died.

[*She reaches over and swings the broken door, swings it again, both women watch it.*]

MRS. HALE

You weren't raised round here, were you? [*Mrs. Peters shakes her head.*] You didn't know—her?

MRS. PETERS

Not till they brought her yesterday.

MRS. HALE

She—come to think of it, she was kind of like a bird herself—real sweet and pretty, but kind of timid and—fluttery. How—she—did—change. [*Silence; then as if struck by a happy thought and relieved to get back to everyday things.*] Tell you what, Mrs. Peters, why don't you take the quilt in with you? It might take up her mind.

MRS. PETERS

Why, I think that's a real nice idea, Mrs. Hale. There couldn't possibly be any objection to it, could there? Now, just what would I take? I wonder if her patches are in here—and her things.
[*They look in the sewing basket.*]

MRS. HALE

Here's some red. I expect this has got sewing things in it. [*Brings out a fancy box.*] What a pretty box. Looks like something somebody would give you. Maybe her scissors are in here. [*Opens box. Suddenly puts her hand to her nose.*] Why—[*Mrs. Peters bends nearer, then turns her face away.*] There's something wrapped up in this piece of silk.

MRS. PETERS

Why, this isn't her scissors.

MRS. HALE

[*Lifting the silk.*] Oh, Mrs. Peters—it's—
[*Mrs. Peters bends closer.*]

MRS. PETERS

It's the bird.

MRS. HALE

[*Jumping up.*] But, Mrs. Peters—look at it! Its neck! Look at its neck! It's all—other side *to*.

MRS. PETERS

Somebody—wrung—its—neck.

[*Their eyes meet. A look of growing comprehension, or horror. Steps are heard outside. Mrs. Hale slips box under quilt pieces, and sinks into her chair. Enter Sheriff and County Attorney. Mrs. Peters rises.*]

COUNTY ATTORNEY

[*As one turning from serious things to little pleasantries.*] Well ladies, have you decided whether she was going to quilt it or knot it?

MRS. PETERS

We think she was going to—knot it.

COUNTY ATTORNEY

Well, that's interesting, I'm sure. [*Seeing the bird-cage.*] Has the bird flown?

MRS. HALE

[*Putting more quilt pieces over the box.*] We think the—cat got it.

COUNTY ATTORNEY

[*Preoccupied.*] Is there a cat?
[*Mrs. Hale glances in a quick covert way at Mrs. Peters.*]

MRS. PETERS

Well, not now. They're superstitious, you know. They leave.

COUNTY ATTORNEY

[*To Sheriff Peters, continuing an interrupted conversation.*] No sign at all of anyone having come from the outside. Their own rope. Now let's go up again and go over it piece by piece. [*They start upstairs.*] It would have to have been someone who knew just the—
[*Mrs. Peters sits down. The two women sit there not looking at one another, but as if peering into something and at the same time holding back. When they talk now it is in the manner of feeling their way over strange ground, as if afraid of what they are saying, but as if they can not help saying it.*]

MRS. HALE

She liked the bird. She was going to bury it in that pretty box.

MRS. PETERS

[*In a whisper.*] When I was a girl—my kitten—there was a boy took a hatchet, and before my eyes—and before I could get there—[*Covers her face an instant.*] If they hadn't held me back I would have—[*Catches herself, looks upstairs where steps are heard, falters weakly*]—hurt him.

MRS. HALE

[*With a slow look around her.*] I wonder how it would seem never to have had any children around. [*Pause.*] No, Wright wouldn't like the bird—a thing that sang. She used to sing. He killed that, too.

MRS. PETERS

[*Moving uneasily.*] We don't know who killed the bird.

MRS. HALE

I knew John Wright.

MRS. PETERS

It was an awful thing was done in this house that night, Mrs. Hale. Killing a man while he slept, slipping a rope around his neck that choked the life out of him.

MRS. HALE

His neck. Choked the life out of him.
[*Her hand goes out and rests on the bird-cage.*]

MRS. PETERS

We don't know who killed him. We don't *know*.

MRS. HALE

[*Her own feeling not interrupted.*] If there'd been years and years of nothing, then a bird to sing to you, it would be awful—still, after the bird was still.

MRS. PETERS

[*Something within her speaking.*] I know what stillness is. When we homesteaded in Dakota, and my first baby died—after he was two years old, and me with no other then—

MRS. HALE

[*Moving.*] How soon do you suppose they'll be through, looking for the evidence?

MRS. PETERS

I know what stillness is. [*Pulling herself back.*] The law has got to punish crime, Mrs. Hale.

MRS. HALE

[*Not as if answering that.*] I wish you'd seen Minnie Foster when she wore a white dress with blue ribbons and stood up there in the choir and sang. [*A look around the room.*] Oh, I *wish* I'd come over here once in a while! That was a crime! That was a crime! Who's going to punish that?

MRS. PETERS

[*Looking upstairs.*] We mustn't—take on.

MRS. HALE

I might have known she needed help! I know how things can be—for women. I tell you, it's queer, Mrs. Peters. We live close together and we live far apart. We all go through the same things—it's all just a different kind of the same thing. [*Brushes her eyes, noticing the bottle of fruit, reaches out for it.*] If I was you I wouldn't tell her her fruit was gone. Tell her it *ain't*. Tell her it's all right. Take this in to prove it to her. She—she may never know whether it was broke or not.

MRS. PETERS

[*Takes the bottle, looks about for something to wrap it in; takes petticoat from the clothes brought from the other room, very nervously begins winding this around the bottle. In a false voice.*] My, it's a good thing the men couldn't hear us. Wouldn't they just laugh! Getting all stirred up over a little thing like a—dead canary. As if that could have anything to do with—with—wouldn't they *laugh!*

[*The men are heard coming downstairs.*]

MRS. HALE

[*Under her breath.*] Maybe they would—maybe they wouldn't.

COUNTY ATTORNEY

No, Peters, it's all perfectly clear except a reason for doing it. But you know juries when it comes to women. If there was some definite thing. Something to show—something to make a story about—a thing that would connect up with this strange way of doing it—

[*The women's eyes meet for an instant. Enter Hale from outer door.*]

HALE

Well, I've got the team around. Pretty cold out there.

COUNTY ATTORNEY

I'm going to stay here awhile by myself. [*To the Sheriff.*] You can send Frank out for me, can't you? I want to go over everything. I'm not satisfied that we can't do better.

SHERIFF

Do you want to see what Mrs. Peters is going to take in?
[*The Lawyer goes to the table, picks up the apron, laughs.*]

COUNTY ATTORNEY

Oh, I guess they're not very dangerous things the ladies have picked out.
[*Moves a few things about, disturbing the quilt pieces which cover the box.*

Steps back.] No, Mrs. Peters doesn't need supervising. For that matter, a sheriff's wife is married to the law. Ever think of it that way, Mrs. Peters?

MRS. PETERS

Not—just that way.

SHERIFF

[*Chuckling.*] Married to the law. [*Moves toward the other room.*] I just want you to come in here a minute, George. We ought to take a look at these windows.

COUNTY ATTORNEY

[*Scoffingly.*] Oh, windows!

SHERIFF

We'll be right out, Mr. Hale.

[*Hale goes outside. The Sheriff follows the County Attorney into the other room. Then Mrs. Hale rises, hands tight together, looking intensely at Mrs. Peters, whose eyes make a slow turn, finally meeting Mrs. Hale's. A moment Mrs. Hale holds her, then her own eyes point the way to where the box is concealed. Suddenly Mrs. Peters throws back quilt pieces and tries to put the box in the bag she is wearing. It is too big. She opens box, starts to take bird out, cannot touch it, goes to pieces, stands there helpless. Sound of a knob turning in the other room. Mrs. Hale snatches the box and puts it in the pocket of her big coat. Enter County Attorney and Sheriff.*]

COUNTY ATTORNEY

[*Facetiously.*] Well, Henry, at least we found out that she was not going to quilt it. She was going to—what is it you call it, ladies?

MRS. HALE

[*Her hand against her pocket.*] We call it—knot it, Mr. Henderson.

QUESTIONS FOR READING, REASONING, AND REFLECTING

1. Explain the situation as the play begins.
2. Examine the dialogue of the men. What attitudes about themselves—their work, their abilities, their importance—are revealed? What is their collective opinion of women?
3. When Mrs. Hale and Mrs. Peters discover the dead bird, what do they begin to understand?
4. What other "trifles" in the kitchen provide additional evidence as to what has happened?

5. What trifles can be seen as symbols? What do they reveal about Mrs. Wright's life and character?

6. What is the play about primarily? Is it a murder mystery? Does it speak for feminist values? Is it about not seeing—not really knowing—others? In a few sentences, state what you consider to be the play's dominant theme. Then list the evidence you would use to support your conclusion.

7. Is there any sense in which one could argue that Mrs. Wright had a right to kill her husband? If you were a lawyer, how would you plan her defense? If you were on the jury, what sentence would you recommend?

SAMPLE STUDENT LITERARY ANALYSIS

Peterson 1

Alan Peterson

American Literature 242

May 5, 2008

Faulkner's Realistic Initiation Theme

William Faulkner braids a universal theme, the theme of initiation, into

the fiber of his novel *Intruder in the Dust*. From ancient times to the present,

a prominent focus of literature, of life, has been rites of passage, particularly

those of childhood to adulthood. Joseph Campbell defines rites of passage as

"distinguished by formal, and usually very severe, exercises of severance." A

"candidate" for initiation into adult society, Campbell explains, experiences a

shearing away of the "attitudes, attachments and life patterns" of childhood

(9). This severe, painful stripping away of the child and installation of the adult

is presented somewhat differently in several works by American writers.

One technique of handling this theme of initiation is used by Nathaniel

Hawthorne in his story "My Kinsman, Major Molineaux." The story's main

character, Robin, is suddenly awakened to the real world, the adult world, when

he sees Major Molineaux "in tar-and-feathery dignity" (Hawthorne 528). A

terrified and amazed Robin gapes at his kinsman as the large and colorful crowd

laughs at and ridicules the Major; then an acquiescent Robin joins with the crowd

in the mirthful shouting (Hawthorne 529). This moment is Robin's epiphany, his

sudden realization of reality. Robin goes from unsophisticated rube to resigned

cynical adult in one quick scene. Hawthorne does hold out hope that Robin will

not let this event ruin his life, indeed that he will perhaps prosper from it.

A similar, but decidedly less optimistic, example of an epiphanic initiation

occurs in Arthur Miller's play *Death of a Salesman*. Miller develops an initiation

theme within a flashback. A teenaged Biff, shockingly confronted with Willy's

Peterson 2

infidelity and weakness, has his boyhood dreams, ambitions—his vision—

shattered, leaving his life in ruins, a truth borne out in scenes in which Biff is

an adult during the play (1083–84, 1101). Biff's discovery of the vices and

shortcomings of his father overwhelms him. His realization of adult life is a

revelation made more piercing when put into the context of his naive and overly

hopeful upbringing. A ravaged and defeated Biff has adulthood wantonly thrust

upon him. Unlike Hawthorne's Robin, Biff never recovers.

> ¶ concludes with emphasis on contrast.

    William Faulkner does not follow these examples when dealing with the

initiation of his character Chick in *Intruder in the Dust.* In Robin's and Biff's cases,

each character's passage into adulthood was brought about by realization of

and disillusionment with the failings and weaknesses of a male adult playing an

important role in his life. By contrast, Chick's male role models are vital, moral

men with integrity. Chick's awakening develops as he begins to comprehend the

mechanisms of the adult society in which he would be a member.

> Transition to Faulkner's story by contrast with Hawthorne and Miller.

    Faulkner uses several techniques for illustrating Chick's growth into a man.

Early in the novel, at the end of the scene in which Chick tries to pay for his dinner,

Lucas warns Chick to "stay out of that creek" (Faulkner 16).[1] The creek is an

effective symbol: it is both a physical creek and a metaphor for the boy's tendency

to slide into gaffes that perhaps a man could avoid. The creek's symbolic meaning

is more evident when, after receiving the molasses, Chick encounters Lucas in

town. Lucas again reminds Chick not to "fall in no more creeks this winter" (24).

At the end of the novel, Lucas meets Chick in Gavin's office and states: "you ain't

fell in no more creeks lately, have you?" (241). Although Lucas phrases this as

a question, the answer is obvious to Lucas, as well as to the reader, that indeed

Chick has not blundered into his naive boyhood quagmire lately. When Lucas asks

his question, Chick's actual falling into a creek does not occur to the reader.

> Footnote first parenthetical reference to inform readers that subsequent citations will exclude the author's name and give only the page number.

---

[1] Subsequent references to Faulkner's novel cite page numbers only.

Note transition.

Another image Faulkner employs to show Chick growing into a man is the single-file line. After Chick gets out of the creek, he follows Lucas into the house, the group walking in single file. In the face of Lucas's much stronger adult will, Chick is powerless to get out of the line, to go to Edmonds's house (7). Later in the novel, when Miss Habersham, Aleck Sander, and Chick are walking back from digging up the grave, Chick again finds himself in a single-file line with a strong-willed adult in front. Again he protests, then relents, but

Note interpolation in square brackets.

clearly he feels slighted and wonders to himself "what good that [walking single file] would do" (130). The contrast between these two scenes illustrates Chick's growth, although he is not yet a man.

Good use of brief quotations combined with analysis.

Faulkner gives the reader other hints of Chick's passage into manhood. As the novel progresses, Chick is referred to (and refers to himself) as a "boy" (24), a "child" (25), a "young man" (46), "almost a man" (190), a "man" (194), and one of two "gentlemen" (241). Other clues crop up from time to time. Chick wrestles with himself about getting on his horse and riding away, far away, until Lucas's lynching is "all over finished done" (41). But his growing sense of responsibility and outrage quell his boyish desire to escape, to bury his head in the sand. Chick looks in the mirror at himself with amazement at his deeds (125). Chick's mother serves him coffee for the first time, despite the agreement she has with his father to withhold coffee until his eighteenth birthday (127). Chick's father looks at him with pride and envy (128–29).

Characteristics of Chick's gradual and positive initiation explained. Observe coherence techniques.

Perhaps the most important differences between the epiphanic initiations of Robin and Biff and that experienced by Chick are the facts that Chick's epiphany does not come all at once and it does not devastate him. Chick learns about adulthood—and enters adulthood—piecemeal and with support. His first eye-opening experience occurs as he tries to pay Lucas for dinner and is rebuffed (15–16). Chick learns, after trying again to buy a clear conscience, the impropriety and affront of his actions (24). Lucas teaches